Understanding Child Behavior Disorders

Third Edition

Understanding Child Behavior Disorders

Third Edition

Donna M. Gelfand
William R. Jenson
Clifford J. Drew

Harcourt Brace College Publishers

**Fort Worth Philadelphia San Diego New York Orlando Austin San Antonio
Toronto Montreal London Sydney Tokyo**

Publisher	Christopher P. Klein
Senior Acquisitions Editor	Jo-Anne Weaver
Senior Product Manager	Don Grainger
Project Editor	Tamara Neff Vardy
Art Director	Bill Brammer
Production Manager	Melinda Esco

Cover image: © Joanne Leonard, *Julia and the Window of Vulnerability*, 1983. Photograph with chalk paste, 20" by 16". Collection of René di Rosa, Napa, California.

ISBN: 0-15-501701-2
Library of Congress Catalog Card Number: 96-77605

Address orders to:
Harcourt Brace & Company
6277 Sea Harbor Drive
Orlando, FL 32887-6777
1-800-782-4479

Address editorial correspondence to:
Harcourt Brace College Publishers
301 Commerce Street, Suite 3700
Fort Worth, TX 76102

Website address:
http://www.hbcollege.com

Harcourt Brace may provide complimentary instructional aids and supplements or supplement packages to those adopters qualified under our adoption policy. Please contact your sales representative for more information. If as an adopter or potential user you receive supplements you do not need, please return them to your sales representative or send them to: Attn: Returns Department, Troy Warehouse, 465 South Lincoln Drive, Troy, MO 63379.

Printed in the United States of America

7 8 9 0 1 2 3 4 5 6 039 9 8 7 6 5 4 3 2 1

Preface

Developmental psychopathology is a rapidly expanding field, and this third edition of our book contains much that is new. Since the previous edition, a revised and expanded guide to diagnosis has appeared, the *Diagnostic and Statistical Manual of Mental Disorders,* DSM-IV, 4th edition (American Psychiatric Association, 1994), as have notable innovations in research, assessment, and treatment. Also new to this edition is a chapter on child neglect, physical and sexual abuse, and children's courtroom testimony and legal rights. The increased professional attention given previously neglected conditions such as childhood obsessive-compulsive, depressive, and anxiety disorders, including posttraumatic stress disorder, also is represented here. Social concerns about juvenile criminal gangs, substance abuse, poverty, discriminatory practices, dysfunctional families, and inadequate health, legal, and social services all receive attention as contributors to children's psychological and educational problems. This is not to suggest that the only new developments are negative. In the time since this book was last revised, researchers have learned more about the effectiveness of psychosocial and psychopharmacological therapies, and have made significant advances in the prevention of mental retardation, school failure, juvenile depression, and conduct disorder. All of these advances are presented in this book.

The contents and orientation of the book represent the authors' professional training and experience. Donna Gelfand was trained in clinical psychology and specialized in the study of children's social and emotional development. Her research traces the effects of maternal depression on child development. She first worked in a community mental health agency and taught at San Jose State University. For many years, she has taught at the University of Utah, where she is currently professor of psychology and dean of the College of Social and Behavioral Science. William (Bill) Jenson has degrees in experimental and child psychology, and postdoctoral training in clinical psychology. After directing a child and family treatment unit of a community mental health service, he joined the faculty of the Department of Educational Psychology at the University of Utah. He is currently the chair of that department and the coauthor (with Ginger Rhode and H. Kenton Reavis) of the very popular *Tough Kid Book* (Sopris West, 1992–1995). Clifford Drew is professor of special education and educational psychology and coordinator of instructional technology in the Office of the Vice President for Administrative Affairs at the University of Utah. He is versed in research methodology, administration in higher education, computer use in education, and mental retardation, and he has written 21 textbooks to date. This volume represents our collective interests in teaching in education and the social sciences.

Our intended readership is broadly defined. This book is designed for use in courses in many fields, including child psychopathology, educational psychology, special education, social work, family sociology, family ecology, nursing, public health, and related fields. Advanced undergraduate and graduate students with a background in social science, social work, or the health sciences can use this book. Guideposts for student readers in each chapter include definitions of key terms, brief previews of chapter contents, and concluding summaries of the major points in the chapter. Wherever possible, we have avoided unnecessary technical terms and explanations so the content will be accessible to most readers.

Our book is based on the best, most definitive research available. While not neglecting knowledge derived from clinical and educational practice, we focus on findings of a vast number of empirical studies. This means that we give greater weight to replicated results from well-controlled research studies than on less controlled individual case studies. We deplore the "band wagon" effect that sometimes produces widespread excitement about unsubstantiated claims for the effectiveness of dramatic sounding interventions, which lack any serious research basis or evaluation. After a period of media attention to these unlikely cures, they prove ineffective and eventually vanish. To the degree possible, we have not given credence here to practices for which there is no research basis. Fads such as eye movement exercises, "primal" screams, group belittling and demeaning of targeted members, exposure of troubled or disobedient children to physically dangerous survival situations, or other such dramatic interventions nearly always betray the hopes of desperate families and create public mistrust of mental health professionals. This book focuses on carefully developed and responsibly evaluated methods for diagnosis and treatment.

We tried to make the book's organization logical, but recognize that instructors have individual preferences regarding the number and order of chapters presented in their courses. Consequently, the chapters are designed to stand alone and can be used in a variety of sequences. Cross-referencing within the text refers readers to related material in other portions of the book. Aids for instructors include a manual of new test items and useful films and videos.

Inevitably, a research orientation favors some theories and treatments over others that are less empirically based. For example, cognitive social theory (also called social learning theory) and behavioral and cognitive therapy all originated in research and have stimulated further scientific inquiry. Other perspectives are also presented, including psychoanalytic, object relations, attachment, and client-centered theories. The book also presents new developments in behavioral genetics and the biochemical basis of childhood psychosocial disorders. Each approach is evaluated for both strengths and weaknesses. We aim for informed, impartial scholarship rather than favoritism to any particular orientation. We have tried conscientiously to present all schools of thought ac-

curately and fairly, and to criticize each, using objective criteria.

We appreciate the efforts of many clinicians, educators, and researchers who produced the body of knowledge underlying this book. The final product reflects the helpful critical comments of a number of reviewers including Dr. Michael Alessandri, San Jose State University; Dr. Eric Cooley, Western Oregon State College; Dr. Hagop Pambookian, Shawnee State University; Dr. Paul Ramirez, Hunter College; Dr. Lee Rosen, Colorado State University; Dr. Susan Scharoun, LeMoyne College; Dr. Sean Ward, LeMoyne College; Dr. Kimberly Wolk-Gulletz, Oregon State University. Office staff colleagues who assisted us in many ways include Cathleen Callison and Jodi Scott, and we gratefully acknowledge our expert editor at Harcourt Brace, Jo-Anne Weaver; Editorial Assistant, Linda Blundell; Project Editor, Tamara Vardy; Production Manager, Melinda Esco; and Art Director, Bill Brammer.

Our families gave us tremendous support on this writing project. As always, we are grateful to Sid Gelfand and Linda James for doing many things that allowed us to keep working on this book. Thanks for your support and patience. We dedicate this book to Grayson Jenson, Bill's son, who lost his life in a swimming accident in June 1995. His memory will live on in the hearts of his family and many friends.

CONTENTS

C H A P T E R   I

INTRODUCTION

Continuity hypothesis. The view that unless successfully treated childhood problems will persist rather than be overcome.

Delusion. A false belief based on ideosyncratic logic such as a person believing that her thoughts are controlled by microwave transmissions or that she is a holy or famous person.

Growth hypothesis. The view that childhood psychological problems are typically outgrown or overcome without recourse to professional treatment.

Hallucination. A compelling but false perception such as a person believing that worms are crawling on his skin or that disembodied voices are belittling him.

Identity crisis. Erik Erikson's concept that in adolescence the person undergoes a stressful transition and develops an individual, adult character.

Incidence. The number of new cases of a specific disorder identified during a specified period, usually a single calendar year.

Prevalence. The total number of new and continuing cases of a specific disorder present at a given time.

Psychopathology. A general term referring to any type of emotional, social, or cognitive disturbance sufficiently severe as to require professional attention.

Psychosis. A serious psychological disorder often involving delusions, hallucinations, thought disturbances, impaired social functioning, and bizarre emotional reactions.

Syndrome. A constellation of problem behaviors that together constitute a psychological disorder, for example, the delusions, thought disturbances, social impediments, and other symptoms of psychosis.

T his chapter recounts the tremendous improvements in the social status and societal protection of children over
the past several centuries. Educational and juvenile justice systems and treatment services for children have
expanded significantly. The major nations of the world, excepting the United States, have formally agreed
upon a common, global standard of protections for children's rights and welfare. Yet the standard remains an elusive
ideal and is not reflected in many children's everyday lives.

Various criteria are discussed that are used to determine whether a child's behavior is normal or disturbed and whether
professional attention is justified. Criteria include the age- and sex-appropriateness, severity, and duration of the child's
problem behavior. The child's ability to meet teachers' expectations and standards and cultural prescriptions for children's
conduct are also considered in diagnosis. Next, the prevalence rates of various types of child adjustment problems are
presented, together with the long-term prognosis for the various disorders.

WHAT IS CHILD PSYCHOPATHOLOGY?

This book is dedicated to exploring the nature, prevention, and treatment of children's psychological disorders
of many types. This is an ambitious task because of the
diversity of opinions concerning the definition of *disorder*
and its appropriate treatment. The term *psychopathology*
literally means illness (pathology) of the mind (psyche),
but mental health authorities now recognize that there
are many different sources and types of psychological disorder. Not only can thinking and other cognitive processes be disrupted, but so can entire patterns of behavior
such as aggression and self-control. Child psychopathology encompasses problems such as mental retardation;
severe antisocial-aggressive behavior patterns technically
termed conduct disorder; profoundly incapacitating developmental disorders of early childhood such as autism
and dysfunctional moods and emotions, including depression and eating disorders such as anorexia nervosa,
and many more. In the following chapters, we will explore what factors these various disorders share as well

as how they differ. To begin, we present three brief case
histories and follow the cases through this chapter to illustrate how each child's disturbed behavior might have
been explained in different historical periods and whether
the syndrome would be considered normal or deviant
using alternative criteria of abnormality.

Three Case Descriptions

The following are descriptions of two children and an
adolescent whose behavior concerns their parents and
teachers. All of these children were referred to a child
mental health outpatient clinic for evaluation. The questions in each case were: (1) Is this child's adjustment
normal or disordered? (2) If disordered, what diagnosis
should be given? (3) Is any type of mental health treatment required? (4) If so, what is the prognosis for this
child? Will the child probably improve dramatically, stay
the same, or will the condition worsen? Readers are challenged to study these brief characterizations, try to decide
whether the child's behavior should be classified as nor-

mal or disordered, and identify the criteria used to make the decision.

CHERYL

Cheryl is a large, athletically built 9-year-old girl with curly red hair and lots of freckles. She is taller and more active than the other girls in her class, and they complain that she is bossy. She can often be heard issuing loud orders to playmates. Recently she was caught stealing another girl's lunch money from her purse at school. More than once she has taken younger children's possessions away from them and then threatened to beat them up when they walk home from school if they told on her. When confronted with evidence of the lunch money theft, Cheryl angrily denied taking anything, accused the teachers of picking on her, and blamed another girl for taking the money. Her classmates dislike and avoid her because she bullies them, picks fights, and becomes physically threatening. In one of her rages at home, she tore apart a sofa, stabbing it with scissors and a kitchen knife. Her mother is an ill-groomed and belligerent alcoholic whose boyfriend lives with them. He is unemployed because of his alcoholism, and the police have been called to their home more than once because of their noisy fights. Is Cheryl's behavior pattern understandable and normal under the circumstances or is it abnormal? Does she require professional attention? What are her chances of a normal adulthood?

BOBBY

Bobby is a cute little 5-year-old boy with blond hair and big blue eyes, but his behavior strikes people as odd. His mother says that her pregnancy and delivery were normal and that Bobby was a very good baby who hardly ever fussed or cried. Yet he seems to lag behind age norms in his language and social development, is distant and unresponsive ("spacy" some people say), and lacks the affectionate nature of a normal preschool child. He hardly speaks a word of normal conversation. He does not reach out to his parents, smile, or return their hugs when they attempt to hold or cuddle him. Earlier, a pediatrician reassured his parents that Bobby was just slow to develop, but he still hasn't learned to talk, except for repeating the commercials he sees on television over and over again.

His parents ask, how worried should they be about their son who looks so normal but acts so delayed?

STEVE

Seventeen-year-old *Steve* has led his usually mild-mannered parents to despair and uncharacteristic outbursts of rage about his behavior. Formerly an average to good student, Steve has virtually stopped studying and rarely attends school. His grades have dropped from average to failing. Once a promising guitarist, Steve doesn't touch his guitar anymore. He seems to have no interests and no hope; he only sits alone in front of the TV set for hours at a time. His two closest friends are heavy drug users, and his parents have found drugs and a handgun in his room. Family friends console them with descriptions of similar problems with their teenaged sons, but Steve's parents continue to worry and fight with him, warning him repeatedly that he will never amount to anything if he does not try. Is Steve's behavior characteristic of typical adolescent turmoil and alienation or does it represent psychopathology?

As these three cases illustrate, it is not always easy to determine whether a child or adolescent is acting in a developmentally normal fashion or is disturbed. In order to make this determination, child mental health workers use a set of criteria, which we will now examine. The more formal aspects of child assessment systems are presented in Chapter 13. General considerations discussed later in this chapter include the age- and sex-appropriateness of the child's behavior and its social and cultural acceptability. Other criteria are the behavior's frequency, intensity, and pervasiveness or generality. It also is important to consider whether the child's conduct is personally fulfilling and whether it enhances or endangers the long-term well-being of the child and those who must deal with the child. Behavior that causes the child or others great distress and interferes with functioning at home or school is likely to represent a clinical problem. In addition, we will consider the degree of resemblance between adult and child psychopathology and the predictability of future problems from childhood disturbances. But first, child psychopathology will be placed in historical context. How would our ancestors have viewed the three children's behavior, and what measures would have been used to improve their conduct?

HISTORY OF CHILD PSYCHOPATHOLOGY

Laws now recognize children's rights to proper care, but that was not always the case. For millennia, much of the world tolerated the suffering of large numbers of abused and neglected babies. People were hardened to suffering generally, whether that of children or of adults who were different in some way, such as "village fools," and who were ridiculed for having mental retardation or psychosis. Our ancestors, who were primarily concerned about children's spiritual salvation and physical survival, might not have understood present day respect for juveniles' rights to autonomy, education, and humane care.

Neglect and Abandonment. In the past, many European babies were seriously neglected or completely abandoned. In 18th-century Paris, parents deposited one-third of all babies at foundling homes. So many parents came from the countryside to leave their children that laws prohibited transporting babies into the city. Desperately poor parents tried to save their infants' lives by delivering them to charitable institutions where they might receive adequate food and shelter. Most of the babies died anyway. In Dublin between 1775 and 1800, 10,272 infants were admitted to foundling homes, but of this vast number only 45 survived (Kessen, 1965, p. 8) because of the unsanitary, crowded conditions, meager and nutritionally inadequate diet, and infectious diseases that raged throughout the institutions. The babies who remained at home also had high mortality rates. Prior to the late 1700s, less than about one-third of infants born survived the first year of life (Borstelmann, 1983).

Harsh Discipline. Responsible parents used forceful measures to ensure their children's conformity to religious and social commandments. In order to save their souls, many rebellious children like Cheryl and Steve, who were previously described, were whipped into obedience, immersed in ice water, confined in dark cupboards, and threatened with abandonment or abduction (deMause, 1974). Disobedient children were thought to be in imminent peril of hellfire and damnation, and could endanger their parents' salvation as well, so all the resources of the family, church, and community were directed to their reform. In the 16th century, babies who persistently cried and could not be soothed were thought to be possessed by demons and were sometimes put to death on the advice of Christian church leaders (deMause, 1974). Concerns about conformity and salvation were paramount, and the children's comfort and happiness were less important.

However, not all of our ancestors were insensitive to children's suffering (Gordon, 1978; Pollock, 1983). Some educated, upper-class parents showed delight in their children and intense concern for their safety. For example, Mrs. Clifford (1590–1676), wrote about her ill 2-year-old: "The Child had a bitter fit of her ague again, insomuch I was fearful of her that I could hardly sleep all night, so I beseeched GOD Allmighty to be merciful to me and spare her life" (Clifford, 1923, p. 54, cited in Pollock, 1983). Mrs. Clifford was an unusual mother of her time in being literate. Thus, she was not representative of most of the population.

Stern discipline was considered normal and proper, and so might not have represented parental rejection or indifference. In fact, today's children may be more emotionally disadvantaged because they are taught to believe that they have a right to an unrealistic level of parental love (Kagan, 1978). Because children now spend less time with their parents and more with other caretakers, many may feel rejected by their parents. Some developmental psychologists (Belsky & Cassidy, 1994) believe that spending too much time in day care rather than with parents distorts the normal socialization process, causing noncompliance, insecure attachment to parents, and aggressivity, while other researchers report no apparent ill effects of high quality day care (Andersson, 1992). With so many social changes occurring simultaneously, the exact causes of societal problems are not clear.

The Rise of Modern Attitudes Toward Children

In the 18th century, children were increasingly valued for their innocence, charm, and playfulness. The English philosopher John Locke (1632–1704) taught that children were not born perverse but mentally resembled a blank slate (*tabula rasa*) to be developed through suitable education and experience. It was not necessary to combat the child's presumed evil nature through cruel discipline since children are not innately corrupt. Later, the French philosopher Jean Jacques Rousseau (1712–1778) glorified

In the 19th century, poor children labored long hours in hazardous conditions before child labor laws were enacted. Working them hard and paying them little was viewed as "good business" and morally correct.

childhood, writing that children have a natural tendency toward healthy growth both in body and spirit. Consequently, children should require only developmentally appropriate instruction and a clean, healthful, and non-restrictive environment in order to develop optimally. Only the malevolent influences of adults' cruelty and teachers' ignorance of their pupils' learning limitations could interfere with normal development. Educated parents began to view their children as innately sweet and innocent rather than sinful and depraved. Ironically, Rousseau failed to live by his own philosophy. He fathered several illegitimate children, but forced their mother to give them away.

Industrialization and Child Welfare. The growth of industry (1750–1850), which brought prosperity to Western Europe and the United States, also threatened the health of multitudes of impoverished child workers:

"According to the 1870 [U.S.] census about one out of every eight children were employed. By 1900 approximately 1,750,000 children, or one out of six, were gainfully employed. Sixty percent were agricultural workers; of the 40 percent in industry over half were children of immigrant families." (Bremner, 1971, p. 601)

The conditions under which child workers were forced to labor were shockingly inhumane. Employers forced them to work 12- to 15-hour days, often in dangerous and unsanitary surroundings. The children were paid almost nothing, and their small stature enabled them to perform extraordinarily dangerous jobs such as cleaning and oiling machinery that remained in operation as they worked. Child labor was profitable and children's welfare was not seriously considered by most people. Almost no concern was expressed for their mental health.

Elitism and Exploitation. One force opposed to social reform was "Social Darwinism," a corruption of Darwin's theory of evolution mistakenly used to rationalize individual and group differences in prosperity. Victims of all types are often blamed for bringing on their own misfortunes, and the uneducated peasant immigrants who spoke foreign tongues and their scruffy offspring were natural targets for such prejudice. Many people of wealth and privilege drew an erroneous parallel between evolutionist Charles Darwin's principle of the survival of the fittest in the animal kingdom and their own social advantages, which they attributed to their innate genetic superiority. In contrast, they viewed the poor, uneducated, and ill as genetically unfit and unworthy of decent treatment, even if they were defenseless children. This inhumaneness was rationalized by the assertion that it was better for them to die young than to grow up to breed additional generations of the socially dangerous and unfit.

Reputable scientists no longer consider this view as defensible genetically, historically, or morally. Today, we realize that all groups of humans are genetically highly similar and that no social class or geographic, national, racial, or ethnic group is generally genetically inferior or superior to any other. There are wider genetic differences *within* racial and geographic groups than exist *across* groups. Group differences in rates of psychopathology, intellectual and social achievement, crime, and other characteristics are largely attributable to sociocultural factors, primarily wealth and access to educational and employment opportunities. Every human group contains individuals who are capable of extraordinary achievements, given favorable circumstances. This nurturing view of children paved the way for contemporary compensatory educational programs such as Head Start, community mental health and drug prevention services for children, and more enlightened child custody and child protection practices.

The Study and Assessment of Child Psychopathology

With the advent of compulsory public education in the later 1800s, it became evident that some children were not progressing normally, although the nature of their problem was not understood. In the early 1900s, the French minister of education employed Binet and Simon to develop standardized tests to identify children who

lacked the intellectual ability to cope with the regular school curriculum so they could be given special education in the schools or so the less capable could be institutionalized. Institutions for the retarded were not viewed as dead-end placements, but were expected to return the children to regular community life (Rie, 1971). The test devised by Binet and Simon was a great success, was translated into English, and later was revised by Lewis Terman of Stanford University in 1916 to become the Stanford-Binet Intelligence Test. A revision of this intelligence test remains in use today and is generally viewed as the standard against which other tests are compared (Drew, Hardman, & Logan, 1996).

The great popularity of Darwin's theory of evolution led early psychiatrists to believe that most forms of deviance could be traced to hereditary flaws. Social influences were given much less recognition. Francis Galton's discovery of disproportionately large numbers of eminent persons in certain prominent English families was widely considered to prove the hereditary basis of intellectual and personality characteristics. Heredity was assumed to be the prime determinant of character, intelligence, and social and economic success (Kessen, 1965).

Given a person's genetic predisposition to psychopathology, Victorians believed that certain types of environmental events and personal practices could bring on madness. Masturbation was considered the presumed cause of adolescent "masturbatory insanity," a mysterious malady with ill-specified characteristics. The lack of specificity was understandable since the disorder was imaginary. As a good example of faulty reasoning, mental institution staff members observed that many of the insane inmates masturbated frequently, thus "proving" that masturbation caused insanity (Rie, 1971).

The onset of children's and adolescents' psychological disorders was attributed to any form of excess, such as studying or working too hard, changes in climate, or a sudden fright or shock (Spitzka, 1890). High fever, head injuries, and intestinal parasites were believed to produce "brain irritability" and deviant behavior. Superstition and popular beliefs long formed the basis for mental health practice because there was virtually no systematic and objective research on the development of psychological disturbances.

Many 19th-century medications were more harmful than helpful. Fussy, irritable infants were sometimes soothed with laudanum, a potent and addicting mixture of opium and alcohol. Various other medicines contain-

---

BOX 1-1   NINETEENTH-CENTURY EXPLOITATION OF INSTITUTIONALIZED JUVENILE DELINQUENTS

Following is an excerpt from testimony given by William Pryor Letchworth, a commissioner of the New York State Board of Charities in 1882. Letchworth testified before the New York legislature in support of a bill that would forbid refuges and reformatories for children from contracting the children's work, for a fee, to private employers. Although the 1882 bill was vetoed, similar legislation went into effect in New York in 1884 (Bremner, 1971, p. 469).

> Children under sixteen years of age, when subjected to long hours of labor, in irksome positions, under a task contract system, are likely to be retarded in their development, and fagged out at the end of their long confinement, are too weary to derive due advantage from the teachings imparted in the evening school.
>
> While flogging has long been abolished in the Navy and the use of the "cat" in the State Prisons, it is still thought necessary, in order to realize a fair pecuniary return from the children's labor, for the contractor to inflict severe corporal punishment for deficiency in imposed tasks. One institution in the State, in order to meet the expectation of contractors, was forced in a single year to inflict on the boys employed, upon the direct complaints of contractors, their superintendent, overseer, and employees, corporal punishments two thousand two hundred and sixty-three times. This was administered with a strap or rattan on the hand, or on the posterior bare or covered, as the gravity of the case demanded. During the same period the punishments in school, in order as it was said, to "wake up" their already overtaxed attention, was so considerable as to swell up the aggregate punishments for the year to the magnitude of ten thousand.
>
> The tendency of the contract system in reformatory institutions for boys, is to retain as long as possible those who are most valuable to the contractor, and as these generally belong to the most dutiful class and consequently entitled to an early discharge, a great injustice is done, which sometimes drives boys to desperation. On the other hand, the intent of the contractor being to rid himself of the unskillful and careless workers, there is danger of a premature discharge of such before the work of reformation is completed.

SOURCE: Letchworth, W. P. (1882). *Labor of children in reform schools.* New York, pp. 3–7. Reprinted in R. H. Bremner (Ed.). (1971). *Children and youth in America: A documentary history, Vol. 2: 1866–1932* (pp. 469–471). Cambridge, MA: Harvard University Press.

---

ing generous amounts of alcohol or opiates were used to treat children's lassitude, fearfulness, and academic problems. Addictive drugs were prescribed freely and were available over the counter. Steve, in our example of a troubled teenager, would not have had to go far to buy and use addictive drugs that would be strictly outlawed today.

Improved Protection of Children

As late as the 19th century, few social institutions protected children. Many orphans were simply abandoned, and attempts to reform or protect delinquent children were primitive, as Box 1-1 describes.

However, social reform was beginning. During the early 1900s, reform schools were established to attempt to teach and rehabilitate young offenders. Poverty and starvation forced great numbers of citizens and immigrants to search for work in teeming city slums. Sympathy for their plight and fear that they might become violent and produce political unrest stimulated public interest in social reform. Clergymen and educated middle-class women reformers set up settlement houses and formed social clubs to help the poor. Ironically, institutions to protect mistreated animals predated those for protecting children. The first American branch of the Society for the Prevention of Cruelty to Children was formed in 1874 as a part of the already established Society for the Prevention of Cruelty to Animals. By 1900, 250 societies were devoted to rescuing abandoned, abused, and exploited children (Bremner, 1971). Ironically, many children were placed in large, impersonal, and inadequate institutions that stunted them emotionally and exposed them to highly contagious diseases such as tuberculosis. Only later was it recognized that children need affectionate care in a healthful, stimulating, home-like setting in order to thrive.

Treatment Services for Children

Progress is not inevitable. It is disturbing to note that some American school systems of the 1800s and early 1900s provided children and families with better mental health services than are currently available. At that time, public school systems hired visiting teachers to coordinate and deliver a wide range of services to children who had special problems that interfered with their academic achievement. Visiting teachers were forerunners of today's school social workers and home teachers.

Children's Clinics. If there is one date to remember from this chapter, it is *1896,* when Lightner Witmer established the first true psychological clinic for children at the University of Pennsylvania. Thus, children's clinics are just over a century old. Witmer's clinic specialized in the treatment of children's broadly defined educational problems. The approach used was surprisingly modern, for it emphasized the joint efforts of the clinic, the school, and the family in the solution of the child's problems (Levine & Levine, 1970).

Juvenile Justice Systems. With the emerging view that the community had some responsibility for children's welfare, concern arose for the fate of juveniles who had committed crimes. Imprisonment with adult criminals no longer seemed appropriate for children, although public sentiment now favors the return to this practice for juveniles who have committed violent crimes. Recognizing the special needs of children, the public-spirited Women's Club of Chicago helped to organize the first Juvenile Court. The court's charge included protecting children in addition to rehabilitating and punishing them for their illegal behavior.

It soon became apparent that many of the young delinquents were also seriously emotionally disturbed, so in 1909 the psychiatrist William Healy was chosen to head a new Juvenile Psychopathic Institute for the treatment of children under the jurisdiction of the Juvenile Court. Together with psychologists Grace Fernold and Augusta F. Bronner, Healy studied the origins of delinquency and attempted to rehabilitate individual juvenile offenders. Their treatment methods were flexible and included psychoanalytic techniques, residential placement, consultation with judges and police officers, advice to parents, and short-term child counseling.

Over the years, clinics came to neglect the more challenging prevention and consultation services and to concentrate on treating the many families desperately seeking services (Levine & Levine, 1970). Poor, ill-educated families do not seek and may actively avoid mental health services, so most clinics serve primarily middle-class families with mildly disturbed children. The office-based interview and play therapy methods used at the time proved ineffective with children who were brain damaged, psychotic, highly aggressive, mentally retarded, or who had severe learning disabilities. Until recent times, children with these more serious problems were kept at home or institutionalized in inadequate state hospitals or juvenile justice facilities.

Reforms of the 1960s. The growth of federally supported community mental health services in the social reforms of the 1960s offered help to more children and families than ever before. Although the need was always greater than the services available, many community mental health services were exemplary and included programs aimed at prevention as well as treatment. However in the 1970s, the economic and, more importantly, the political climate turned against the generous provision of treatment services to the poorest families. Citizens' groups intent on cutting their taxes and civil liberties groups concerned about involuntary institutionalization of mental patients joined forces to slash the number of mental hospitals and treatment services for adults, children, and families. Also, under increasingly harsh anti-drug laws, many more drug users and dealers were imprisoned for longer sentences, but funding for research, prevention, and treatment of drug abuse was cut during the Reagan administration and thereafter. Treatment and educational services for children and families were severely curtailed. Government funding has been drastically cut or eliminated for impoverished women and their infants, child welfare, family nutrition and health, and impressive federal compensatory education programs such as Head Start (described in Chapter 4). There is some evidence that such social welfare programs decrease the costs of other health, legal, and criminal justice services (Tarnowski & Rohrbeck, 1993). Ultimately, such severe reductions in educational and health services to children may well lead to increases in other social problems such as family breakup, crime, violence, riots, drug use, and outbreaks of disease, and will eventually be seen as counterproductive, leading to another era of social reform.

NORMAL AND ABNORMAL PSYCHOLOGICAL DEVELOPMENT

Nearly every child experiences adjustment problems from time to time. Professionals who work with children must determine whether their difficulties are normal and temporary or whether they represent more serious problems. The variability of children's behavior adds to the diagnostic challenge, since a child's responses may change within weeks, days, or hours, whereas adults' social behavior is usually more stable and predictable. Children experience more marked physical and social changes during their development than most adults do during a similar amount of time. A child's behavior may change dramatically when she enters school at first grade or later and when she makes friends with a different group of children. Further, most children display a mixture of desirable and undesirable behavior. The playground bully may also be kind to his friends and family, or a girl who is painfully shy at school may control her sisters. Children may show even more situational variability in their behavior than do adults, also making diagnosis difficult.

Certain problems are common at particular ages and may even constitute a normal part of growing up. Most transitory adjustment disturbances require no professional attention. As will be seen, child psychopathology consists largely of those childhood problems that are *not* simply outgrown. It is important for clinicians to be trained in developmental psychology so they are familiar with the types and timing of adjustment problems characteristic of children of different ages. Some behaviors are not truly problematic, but represent normative attempts to become independent from adults or may serve other important developmental functions. The goal, type, and intensity of a behavior pattern must be considered in characterizing it as normal or deviant.

Criteria for Normality

AGE-APPROPRIATENESS

It is not by accident that each youngster's age received prominent mention in the preceding case descriptions. A child's age and developmental status are of paramount importance in determining the normality of the child's behavior. As an example, a strong fear of dogs and of being separated from one's parents are quite acceptable in a 3-year-old, but would be suspect if the child were 13 years old. Similarly, adult-like behavior such as drinking and smoking is common among high school students, but unusual in a 9-year-old. These illustrations indicate that certain problem behaviors are more socially acceptable and much more frequent at some age periods than at others. When a high proportion of children in a particular age period engage in certain behavior patterns,

TABLE 1-1 PROBLEM BEHAVIORS CHARACTERISTIC OF CHILDREN AND YOUTH AT VARIOUS AGES

Age Period	Problem Behaviors
1½–2 years	Temper tantrums, refusal to do things when asked, demanding attention constantly, overactivity, specific fears, inattentiveness.
3–5 years	Temper tantrums, refusal to do things when asked, demanding attention constantly, overactivity, specific fears, oversensitivity, lying, negativism.
6–10 years	Temper tantrums, overactivity, specific fears, oversensitivity, lying, school achievement problems, jealousy, excessive reserve.
11–14 years	Temper tantrums, oversensitivity, jealousy, school achievement problems, excessive reserve, moodiness.
15–18 years	School achievement problems, skipping school, cheating on exams, depression, drinking, smoking, drug misuse, early sexual activity, trespassing, shoplifting and other minor law violations.

then behaving similarly is developmentally normal and does *not* indicate that a child has some form of psychopathology. That is, if nearly all high school seniors have tried alcohol, it would be unfair to say that any senior is disturbed simply because he or she has had a drink.

Clinicians must be familiar with the behavior typical of children of various ages in order to determine whether a particular youngster's reactions are normal or not. Many behaviors that concern parents and teachers actually occur in one-third to one-half or more of children at a particular age, and so might be considered statistically normal, even if undesirable. Table 1-1 summarizes the troublesome behaviors found in normal children of different ages.

Preschool Years. Children have been described as negativistic at the ages of 1½ to 3 years because of their frequent temper tantrums and contrariness (Goodenough, 1931; Macfarlane, Allen, & Honzik, 1954). Mothers report that at least half of them throw temper tantrums and often disobey. In addition, many toddlers demand constant adult attention and protest loudly when they are ignored. These observations come primarily from older reports such as the Berkeley Guidance Study (Macfarlane et al., 1954), but were confirmed in a more recent study (Crowther, Bond, & Rolf, 1981; Rolf, Hakola, Klemchuk,

---

BOX 1-2   Is Boyhood a Mental Disorder?

There are many possible reasons for the much greater prevalence of mental or adjustment disorders among boys than girls, but one is particularly striking. The ordinary signs of boyhood such as energy, curiosity, and rough-and-tumble play could be mistaken for symptoms of disorder (Angier, 1994). The DSM-IV, the official manual of mental disorders of the American Psychiatric Association (1994), contains descriptions of some disorders that sound highly similar to traditional "boy" behavior. For example, symptoms of Attention-Deficit/Hyperactivity Disorder include: "often fails to give close attention to details or makes careless mistakes in schoolwork, work, or other activities" (p. 83); "often loses things necessary for tasks or activities (e.g., toys, school assignments, pencils, books, or tools);" "often avoids, dislikes, or is reluctant to engage in tasks that require sustained mental effort (such as schoolwork or homework);" "often fidgets with hands and/or feet or squirms in seat;" "often talks excessively;" "often has difficulty awaiting turn" (p. 84). These inattentive, highly active, and impulsive behaviors are characteristic of vast numbers of boys. Other masculine behaviors such as persistent aggression and rebelliousness might earn them a diagnosis of Conduct Disorder. However, the behavior must be severe, prolonged, and must interfere with the child's social or academic functioning in order to constitute a disorder.

If there is a danger of misdiagnosing ordinary masculine rowdiness as a disorder, the cause may lie in America's concern about increasing crime and violence and the immense prison population. Also, concerned parents can count on the ready availability of Ritalin and other drugs that reduce children's inattentiveness and hyperactivity. Or perhaps worries about the national economy and the disappearance of high-paying jobs has convinced parents that their children must be as nearly perfect as possible if they are to succeed as adults. There are many possible reasons for misdiagnosing males' high activity and aggressiveness as a mental disorder.

SOURCES: American Psychiatric Association. (1994). *Diagnostic and statistical manual of mental disorders* (4th ed., DSM-IV). Washington, DC: Author; Angier, N. (1994, July 24). The debilitating malady called boyhood. *New York Times*, Section 4, pp. A11, 16.

& Hasazi, 1976). The Vermont Child Development Project studied the problems of 588 preschoolers and found that 36 percent of 2-year-old boys and 30 percent of the girls had an overabundance of energy according to their parents and teachers. In addition, 29 percent of the boys but only 18 percent of the girls had problems paying attention to an activity; other types of problems were less frequent. Problems with both aggression and shyness decreased beginning at 3 to 5 years of age.

Angry protests, tantrums, destructiveness, bullying, and lying decreased further between the ages of 5 and 9 years (Quay, 1986; Shepherd, Oppenheim, & Mitchell, 1971), much to the relief of parents. Yet, many kindergarten children, particularly boys, continue to engage in tantrums and develop some new problems. Adults complain that from one-third to one-half of 5-year-old boys lie and that they have an overabundance of energy that exhausts their parents and teachers (see Box 1-2). Some kindergarten children are oversensitive to minor slights. At this age, too, children may become very shy and withdrawn and develop specific fears of animals, electrical storms, of being in the dark, or of swimming (Macfarlane et al., 1954).

Elementary School Years. Typical problems among elementary schoolchildren include temper tantrums, lying,

and oversensitivity. About one-third of the 7- to 8-year-old boys are described by parents and teachers as overactive (Rolf et al., 1976), but this problem decreases thereafter. Jealousy of siblings and other children characterizes nearly a third of the children at this age level. During the later elementary school years, excessive reserve, oversensitivity, and temper outbursts are common, and a new problem, moodiness, emerges. Their mothers report that a third or more of preadolescents display unaccountable and troublesome mood swings. They are happy, excited, and energetic one day and sulky, irritable, and withdrawn the next, leaving their families and friends perplexed and at a loss as to how to treat them. Overactivity is considered a problem for only about one-fourth of the 10- to 12-year-old boys and becomes increasingly rare in older children (Macfarlane et al., 1954).

Many elementary schoolchildren experience at least fleeting behavior problems. In a multiyear study of over 1,500 Minnesota schoolchildren, teachers identified 58.6 percent of the children as having had at least one behavior problem. Fortunately, only 11.3 percent of the boys and just 3.5 percent of the girls were *consistently* rated as behaviorally disturbed by more than one of their teachers. Many more were considered disturbed by a single teacher. Nevertheless, these findings suggest that the ma-

"If you don't mind your teachers and do your schoolwork, you'll grow up to be a bum!" Young boys tend to perform less well in school and are more often scolded for lack of effort than girls.

jority of elementary schoolchildren suffer some social adjustment difficulty in the early to middle grades.

Academic achievement problems are common. A study of the children of the Hawaiian island of Kauai revealed that more than half of the 10-year-old boys (51 percent) and more than a third of the girls (37 percent) had serious academic achievement problems (Werner, Bierman, & French, 1971). Many received unsatisfactory or failing grades in basic skill subjects such as reading or arithmetic, or were enrolled in remedial classes. The Hawaiian children long have had academic achievement problems, perhaps because their traditional culture conflicts with the more impersonal, competitive, and directive atmosphere of standard schools (Jordan & Tharp, 1979). Hawaiian children may not be representative of schoolchildren elsewhere, but similar academic problems are common in all school systems. Large numbers of the

nation's elementary schoolchildren have both academic and social problems that warrant professional attention.

Adolescence. The adolescent years often are considered particularly stormy, emotional, and conflict-ridden. Many adults remember adolescence as the most turbulent, confusing, and troubled period of their lives (Macfarlane, 1964). This view of adolescents as conflicted is an ancient one, dating back to the Classical period of Greece and the teachings of Plato, who referred to youth as a drunkenness of the spirit. A similar opinion is found in the doctrine of the 20th-century child psychoanalysts Anna Freud and Erik Erikson. Classical psychoanalysis maintains that middle childhood is a latency period of quiet intellectual and social development, which draws to a close in emotional upsets and personality turmoil at puberty. Erikson's (1956) influential concept of the *identity crisis* portrays adolescence as a time of stress and strain during which problem behavior is common but of little permanent consequence.

Some authors have disputed this view and presented evidence of surprisingly little adolescent turmoil or personality instability among American adolescents (Douvan & Adelson, 1966; Offer & Offer, 1975). Contrary to popular belief, most adolescents report that they respect and admire their parents, want to emulate them, and get along well with them and with other adults (Meissner, 1965; Weiner, 1982). Yet, at the same time, most American teenagers also experiment with alcohol, drugs, and illicit drugs, and a great number engage in petty crimes. Many adolescents have a propensity for sensation seeking that leads them to reckless acts (Arnett, 1995). Many boys in a large group of high school sophomores studied by Bachman (1970) reported engaging in various forms of mildly aggressive and antisocial behavior. Skipping school at least once and cheating on exams were relatively common. But over one-third had also been in trouble with the police at least once, and one-half had shoplifted. However, most of their illegal behavior was of a one-time, experimental nature. Only a small fraction of the boys had shoplifted more than a single time.

Some teenage girls also engage in antisocial and rebellious behavior. In fact, a large group of Colorado youth displayed no notable sex differences in overall antisocial behavior rates (Jessor & Jessor, 1977). About two-thirds of the teenagers interviewed drank alcohol, and one-third were frequently drunk, which led to conflict with family, teachers, and law enforcement officers. Sexual activity and the use of alcohol and marijuana were so prevalent among the older adolescents that Jessor and Jessor concluded that such activities are typical of the growing-up process for many American teens. Some patterns of rebellious behavior were more problematic than others. Teenagers who drank or took drugs to excess earlier in life had a more stormy transition to adulthood. Nevertheless, one-third of the entire group continued to accept conventional parental values. A recent study of Australian 15-year-olds (Fergusson, Horwood, & Lynskey, 1994) revealed that 85 percent were relatively problem-free, while 7 percent had problems with antisocial or law-breaking activities such as trouble with the police and cannabis use, 5 percent had precocious sexual activity and substance use problems, and 3 percent ex-

perienced multiple problem behaviors. There were no sex differences in overall problem rates, but the predominant problems in females related to an accelerated transition to adulthood (early sexual activity, alcohol and drug use), while males had more problems with antisocial behavior and law breaking.

Offer and Offer (1975) found that only 23 percent of a representative group of adolescent boys entered young adulthood uneventfully and without outbursts of antisocial rebellion or backsliding into emotional dependence on their parents. The other 77 percent experienced periods of anger, anxiety, and self-doubt, as described in Box 1-3. Again, however, these troubled periods tended to be brief.

The teen years appear neither as tumultuous as commonly believed nor as smoothly adaptive as interview studies with parents and adolescents indicate. Emotional upheaval, antisocial and highly reckless behavior may occur, but are not a *necessary* part of normal adolescent development.

Reprise of the Three Case Studies. The cases of the three children described earlier can be considered using the information on age-appropriateness just presented. By the standard of behavior typical of 9-year-olds, Cheryl's stealing, lying, and fighting would be highly unusual. Very few girls her age have such serious problems with antisocial and aggressive behavior. Similarly, 5-year-old Bobby's failure to develop normal speech, strange preoccupations, and profound social unresponsivity are highly unusual and suggestive of infantile autism or pervasive developmental disorder. He may also have mental retardation. It is unclear whether 17-year-old Steve's school problems, disengagement, and alcohol and drug misuse are transitory and typical for his age group or whether they represent psychopathology. A persistent loss of motivation and ability to enjoy usual activities, school failure, and family conflict combined with drug use could indicate depression, and a ready access to a gun possibly could increase the lethality of a suicide attempt. In the best case, Steve's behavior can cause him serious trouble with his family, his school, and the law; in the worst, he could be charged with committing felonies or could become seriously depressed and suicidal. All three children require closer diagnostic scrutiny, but at first glance each appears to represent major psychopathology

---

BOX 1-3 PATTERNS OF ADOLESCENT DEVELOPMENT

Daniel Offer and Judith Baskin Offer studied a group of adolescent boys from the time the boys were 14 until their 22nd birthdays. Unlike most groups subjected to psychiatric scrutiny, these boys were chosen because of their normality. They scored normal on a personality test and were described as normal by the teachers and their parents, who had never sought psychological help for any of them.

Surprisingly, only about one-quarter of this carefully selected group of adolescents were largely trouble-free. Of the remainder, 35 percent had particular difficulty in coping with stress such as that occasioned by a death in the family, although their overall adjustment was good most of the time. However, 21 percent of the group experienced a stormy adolescence marked by increasing conflicts with their parents, social and academic problems, and recurrent periods of extreme self-doubt. Of this latter "tumultuous growth" group, 46 percent eventually received psychotherapy. (As in most classification systems, one subgroup of 21 percent was impossible to classify.)

CASE STUDY

Carl was typical of those with the tumultuous growth profile. His adoptive parents had some marital difficulties. They also disagreed on how severely to judge Carl, although both felt that he was overly sensitive to criticism, didn't study, and had difficulty controlling his temper. Carl was bright and worked only enough to get average grades, but was discontented with his failure to perform better. He was active in sports, however, and got along well with his friends.

Although Carl had originally wanted to attend law school, his poor grades prevented that and he had to settle for a job as a salesman, which was a disappointment to him. He did not date much in high school, but in college he found a steady girlfriend and moved in with her.

The investigators predicted that, following his difficult teen years, Carl would probably make a good social and vocational adjustment. They believed that he might never be very happy and contented, however.

SOURCE: D. Offer and J. B. Offer. (1975). *From teenage to young manhood: A psychological study.* New York: Basic Books.

---

requiring expert attention. Criteria of behavioral normality in addition to age norms must be considered. These include the standard of optimal adjustment marked by good functioning and freedom from emotional distress, and the severity, intensity, and number of problems the child experiences. In some cases, the sex role appropriateness of the child's behavior is considered as well.

Ideal or Optimal Adjustment. The case of Steve raises the interesting question of whether a behavior pattern can be pathological in itself regardless of how many other youngsters engage in it also. Harmful drug use, smoking, overindulgence in alcohol, and even possession of a handgun all provide a good case in point. The possession and use of illicit drugs represent criminal offenses and are considered psychiatrically diagnosable behaviors. Some activities can endanger health and personal adjustment regardless of how many other teenagers engage in the same behavior. This suggests that in addition to a *statistical* definition of abnormality based on a behavior's

prevalence, there must be an optimal adjustment or even an ideal adjustment standard. In the *optimal adjustment model,* a behavioral reaction would be considered pathological if it presented a health or adjustment hazard to the child, family, or their associates (Coleman, Butcher, & Carson, 1980). Conceivably, some behavioral patterns could be pathological even if engaged in by almost all youngsters, if the behaviors also proved demonstrably harmful. The *ideal adjustment standard* is even more demanding and includes as pathological any factors that interfere with "the actualization of potentialities" (Coleman et al., 1980, p. 14). By this ideal standard of adjustment, Steve's failure to realize his academic and musical potential, his endangering his own health, and his defiance of his parents would all be considered maladjusted behaviors; it would not matter how many other teenagers behaved similarly. Blind application of a statistical definition is inadvisable, as Steve's case demonstrates. Some very common reactions can be undesirable and psychologically crippling. Consequently, diagnosticians should consider a behavioral pattern's effect on the child's present and future functioning as well as taking note of its statistical frequency or prevalence.

Intensity. Steve's heavy use of illicit substances suggests another criterion by which to judge behavior: its intensity. A particular reaction could be relatively common but still could constitute disordered behavior because of its severity. For example, it is normal for a 5-year-old child to have temper tantrums. But if the tantrums involve destruction of valuable possessions or cruelty and physical assaults on other people, as in the case of Cheryl, then the behavior is deviant. Behavior that is so intense as to do major damage to oneself, to other people, or to property certainly qualifies as deviant.

Duration. Many childhood problems are transitory, so should not be defined as behavior disorders. A preschool child who had a temper tantrum every day for several weeks but not thereafter would not be considered deviant. Nor would the adolescent who has dramatic mood swings from day to day, but only for a few months. If these behaviors persist, however, and become more or less permanent aspects of the child's life, then a clinical problem might be indicated. The official psychiatric diagnostic system of the American Psychiatric Association, the DSM-IV (American Psychiatric Association, 1994), presents standards for judging whether a particular problem has lasted long enough to be classified as a genuine disorder. These standards are presented as each type of problem is discussed in subsequent chapters.

Additional criteria include the *number* and *diversity* of the maladaptive behaviors. Some behaviors such as fire setting or extreme cruelty to animals might be very rare, but are severe and quite pathological. Even if it has happened only a few times, an adolescent's delusion that the actors on television shows are saying evil things about him would probably represent serious adjustment difficulties, possibly of a psychotic nature. There is even more cause for concern if the delusion is combined with other indicators of serious disturbance, such as marked neglect of hygiene and physical appearance, inappropriate emotional reactions, hallucinations such as hearing imaginary voices, illogical speech, or outbursts of physical or verbal aggression. These are features characteristic of a schizophrenic disorder. In general, the more persistent the adjustment problem, the more serious it is. But even a brief problem might be highly pathological if it is highly in-

tense, bizarre, dangerous, and appears as a part of a *syndrome* in which it is accompanied by a characteristic set of other disordered behaviors. The concept of a related group of problems (psychiatric syndrome) is important in abnormal psychology. Only very rarely is a single problem behavior sufficient for a psychiatric diagnosis. As Chapter 12 reveals, diagnostic classification depends on the occurrence of a syndrome of several related problem behaviors. The co-occurrence of several associated problems is usually considered to be more serious than is the presence of a single one.

Sex-Typed Behavior. All cultures have somewhat different behavioral expectations for males and females. In our culture, boys are expected to behave more boldly and aggressively than girls, who are expected to be more nurturant and sensitive. These expectations are communicated to children directly as they are taught to act appropriately for their gender and through the actions of adult men and women who serve as models of socially approved behavior. Behavioral indicators of gender identity and gender role appear early in life, typically by ages 2 to 4 years, and become even more stable in later years (Fagot, 1985). Children who behave in a sex-appropriate fashion are better socially accepted than those whose behavior is at variance with sex stereotypes. Atypical sex-role behavior is generally more acceptable for "tomboy" girls than for boys, who are likely to be severely criticized for acting like girls (Fagot, 1977). A girl as aggressive as 9-year-old Cheryl would certainly be considered to engage in aberrant behavior, although girls who are physically strong, enjoy athletics, and prefer the company of boys would be more likely to be viewed as just somewhat unusual. In contrast, boys who have predominantly feminine interests (e.g., dolls, interior or fashion design, makeup) are often shunned by other boys, even in the preschool years (Huston, 1983; Lamb & Roopnarine, 1979). Adolescents who are gay, lesbian, or bisexual report that they typically suffer some degree of social exclusion or victimization (verbal insults or threats to safety or property). However, their psychological adjustment remains normal if victimization is mild, family support is high, and the teenager has a positive self-evaluation (Hershberger & D'Augelli, 1995). Childhood cross-sex-typed behavior reliably but not inevitably predicts adult homosexual or bisexual orientation for males (Bailey & Zucker, 1995). No matter whether the research

These little girls eagerly learn all aspects of the feminine sex role. When they act like little women, they are rewarded and feel proud of themselves.

sampled retrospective accounts of adult men or traced individuals from childhood to maturity, men's cross-sex-typed behavior predicted a greater likelihood, but *not* a certainty, of a stronger sexual attraction to males than females in adulthood.

Sex-role definitions for adults are somewhat more relaxed now than in past decades. Many more occupations and interests are considered acceptable for women than was so in any previous peacetime period, and men's involvement in typically feminine activities such as home-making and child care is increasingly acknowledged and often positively valued. Yet sex-typed behavioral prescriptions for children, and especially for boys, remain highly traditional. It is only later in life that people more freely express their individual interests and the strict sex-stereotyping of activities breaks down (Nash & Feldman, 1981).

Effects of Rater Familiarity

The observer's degree of familiarity with the child and opportunities to observe the child over an extended time period affect the likelihood that the observer will accurately identify the child's behavior as normal or deviant.

A good example of this familiarity effect is the different rates of child problems reported by school principals and teachers.

Teachers' Expectations. Teachers are often the first to notice a child's problem behavior and to label it as deviant. They do so with amazing frequency. In a study of 1,366 Minnesota schoolchildren rated by at least three different teachers in different years of elementary school, only 53 percent of the girls and 30 percent of the boys were consistently rated as having *no* behavior problems (Rubin & Balow, 1978). This finding suggests that only a very narrow band of behaviors is considered acceptable in the schools. Children who do not fit into this limited range are classified as presenting problems. The idealized expectations teachers sometimes hold regarding children's behavior may lead them to pressure children to meet unrealistic standards. Problems are the predictable result. Pressures for adequate academic achievement may cause emotional problems in large numbers of children, some of whom lack sufficient ability, have a limited command of English, or have sufficient ability but also have specific learning disabilities in basic areas such as reading or mathematics.

School and Culture Mismatches. Cultural factors may contribute to school problems. Conflict and misunderstanding may result when children from one cultural group enroll in the educational system of another, quite different culture. Teachers complain that their traditional instructional methods are ineffective with ethnic minority group children and with the children of the poor. Then, rather than developing more appropriate teaching methods and materials, educators too often abandon the effort as futile and blame the children's cultural background or low income status for their school failure. Because of the repeated frustration of school failure, culturally different children may withdraw from school or may remain enrolled but cease trying to succeed. Some become resentful and hostile toward their teachers (Rosenfeld, 1971). School becomes a misery for these children and their achievement levels are dismal. This depressing scenario is not inevitable, however. Ethnic groups such as some Asians so prize scholarship that parents demand and get extremely high levels of effort from their children. In contrast to the 6 hours of homework per week completed by black males and 8 hours per week

---

BOX 1-4 LEARNING TO TEACH NATIVE HAWAIIAN CHILDREN

For many years, native Hawaiian children had adapted poorly to schools, and their achievement had been extremely low. However, researchers at the Kamehameha Early Education Program, or KEEP, have devised new teaching methods that have transformed these children into industrious, eager, and successful learners (Jordan & Tharp, 1979). How was this possible? KEEP researchers first studied modern Hawaiian culture very closely, then attempted to incorporate Hawaiian elements into the children's school curriculum. When the children enter the KEEP kindergarten, they are welcomed by an affectionate, demonstrative teacher who hugs, praises, and smiles at them like their familiar "auntie." This behavior builds emotional ties between the children and the teacher and sets the stage for learning.

Since Hawaiian children have a strong peer and sibling orientation, instruction takes place in small groups to allow much interaction. A child moves often from place to place within the classroom working with a changing group of one to six children at each location. The atmosphere is informal, but the children are busy learning school material.

Finally, the investigators discovered a Hawaiian practice that engaged the children actively in speaking, listening, and problem solving. This is the "talk-story," in which a group of friends joins together to create or recall a story (Watson-Gegeo & Boggs, 1977). In the school setting, about five children join the teacher in reading a text silently. Then the teacher begins asking questions about the characters' motives and feelings, the outcome, other details of the story, and the children's personal experiences as related to the theme of the story. The children respond spontaneously, noisily, and enthusiastically to this familiar custom. In contrast to their listlessness and inattentiveness in the traditional classroom with large teacher-oriented classes, the children are active and happy learners. They are now achieving above national norms, an outcome that few previously thought to be possible.

SOURCES: Jordan, C., & Tharp, R. G. (1979). Culture and education. In A. Marsella, R. Tharp, & T. Ciborowski (Eds.), *Perspectives on cross-cultural psychology*. New York: Academic Press; Watson-Gegeo, K. A., & Boggs, S. T. (1977). From verbal play to talk-story: The role of routines in speech events among Hawaiian children. In S. Ervin-Tripp & C. Mitchell-Kernan (Eds.), *Child discourse*. New York: Academic Press.

---

by whites, male Asian Americans average 12 hours of homework each week (Asians in College, 1986). Their extra effort seems to compensate for cultural and linguistic differences and for any lingering social prejudices. However, when parents lack experience with formal educational systems themselves and do not know how to help their children succeed in school, parental pressure alone may only increase family conflict and not promote children's school achievement.

Culturally Appropriate Schooling. Another method for overcoming a mismatch between students' culture and the demands of schooling is to transform the nature of the school. Through generous private funding and the creative efforts of a group of educators and social scientists, an effective educational program was devised to significantly enhance the achievement of Hawaiian schoolchildren, as described in Box 1-4. White schoolteachers and Hawaiian children long had misunderstood each other. The children were acting as good members of their culture; they were not obstinate nor were they uninterested in learning. When this misunderstanding was corrected, the children's school achievement levels soared. Other educational programs for special groups

at risk for underachievement have proved successful, such as the Head Start program described in Chapter 4. Obviously, cultural factors must be considered in framing definitions of behavior disorder and developing educational systems.

Cultural and Temporal Differences in Definitions of Disorder

This question lies at the very heart of the study of human psychopathology: Are definitions of psychopathology culture- and time-bound or is deviance recognized regardless of such factors? At least some forms of self-starvation in adolescent girls, which is currently considered to be pathological and diagnosed as anorexia nervosa, once were seen as signs of extreme, highly admired spirituality and religious zeal (see Box 1-5). Recognition of some forms of abnormality appear and disappear over the centuries. There are changes in values, religious beliefs, and social practices over time, and even if we live in the same geographic region, we do not live in exactly the same culture as our own ancestors once did. There is commonality but not identity in concepts of deviance over time.

Is there a universal definition of disordered behavior shared by all cultures or do definitions of abnormality differ across the world? A common factor is that virtually all cultures recognize *some* types of behavior as abnormal, for example, behaviors generally considered deviant include ideosyncratic, or not shared, delusions, hallucinations, violence, sexual deviations, and phobias (Strauss, 1979). However, some aspects of disorder do vary across cultures, such as which types of behaviors are considered deviant and the prevalence of particular types of deviant behavior. Eskimos label as *nuthkavik*, or crazy, people who do bizarre things such as hide in strange places, talk to themselves, drink urine, refuse to eat, and scream at nonexistent listeners. However, the behaviors in themselves do not define abnormality, which is culturally determined. The highly respected Indian leader Mahatma Gandhi fasted until near death in protest over British colonial policies and drank his own urine daily as a health and religious measure (two behaviors considered deviant in other cultures). Yet Gandhi would not be considered psychologically disordered in his own culture where his behavior was recognized as principled, idealistic and highly rational rather than disordered. In another example of culturally defined psychopathology, the Yoruba people of tropical Africa recognize as insane (*were*) people who hear voices, babble incoherently or refuse to speak, set fires in inappropriate places, and tear off their clothing (Murphy, 1976). The particular behaviors recognized as insane differ somewhat in different cultures, but severe psychotic reactions are recognized by all groups, because the person becomes incapacitated. Worldwide, the *inability to function, individual oddity, and deranged quality* mark a person's behavior as deviant, regardless of the particular behavior displayed.

Certain psychiatric disorders are more prevalent in some areas of the world than in others. For example, clinical depression is much more common in Western countries than in Asia (Marsella, 1979) and is currently increasing in the United States, particularly among young people (Kessler, McGonagle, Zhao, Nelson, Hughes, Eshleman, Wittchen, & Kendler, 1994). Disorder rates could vary geographically because of genetic factors, environmental influences, or use of differing definitions of disorder. Also, official estimates of psychopathology are necessarily and artificially low in countries and regions with very few trained diagnosticians. In most instances, however, similar major categories of mental and emo-

In the native Hawaiian culture, kids often work together and teach each other, rather than learn directly from adults.

tional difficulties are recognized cross-nationally even though some regional variations are found.

Prevalence of Serious Behavior Disorders

It is almost impossible to provide a definitive answer to the question about how many children have serious mental health problems. Comparing the results of different studies is difficult because they vary in their definitions of disorder, in the training of the persons making the assessment (e.g., teachers, professionals, parents, or the children themselves), and in the sex, age, and backgrounds of the children studied. Even the manner in which disorder rates are calculated differs among studies. It is important to distinguish between two terms that are used in epidemiological research on the rates of disorders. These terms are a disorder's *incidence* and *prevalence*. This is important because some of the literature about children's adjustment disorders has either ignored the distinction or used the terms loosely and interchangeably. The terms are different because *prevalence* refers to the number of cases identified in a given sample at a particular point in time. In contrast, *incidence* refers to

---

BOX 1-5   ANOREXIA NERVOSA: A NEW DISORDER?

Imagine the most fanatic dieter possible—someone who eats almost nothing and exercises vigorously and continuously; someone who carries this regimen to life-threatening extremes while continuing to insist that she is too fat. This is a description of a young woman with *anorexia nervosa*, a condition that affects mostly females and is described more fully in Chapter 10. There are so many anorexics among high school and college students that most readers will know of at least one. Anorexia nervosa may strike as many as 1 in every 100 girls between the ages of 16 and 18 years (American Psychiatric Association, 1994). In a related eating disorder called *bulimia*, the acutely weight-conscious person will go on eating binges in which thousands of calories may be consumed. Then, to avoid the weight gain associated with the excessive eating, she will self-induce vomiting. These eating disorders are not rare, but they have not always been as common as they are now. Historical documents indicate no such disorders prior to the 19th century. Either they were not recognized as eating disorders, or they were extremely rare.

Anorexia nervosa appears to have been identified as a psychiatric condition only in the late 19th century. Earlier, extreme fasting was found among female saints who were suppose to subsist exclusively on the Eucharist (the communal wafer and wine symbolizing the body and blood of Christ) (Brumberg, 1986). In addition, a few celebrated "miraculous maids" seemingly consumed almost nothing for long periods of time. These fasting women were considered to be highly spiritual, and their survival without food was seen as a demonstration of divine providence, not as psychopathology. Brumberg (1986) has suggested that secularization may generate the view that voluntary starvation represents a psychiatric disease. In secularization, there is a decline in religious explanations of all types of events. Piety and psychopathology offer alternative explanations of severe fasting, and so the religious explanation may have been replaced by the secular and social one. Are the early "miraculous maids" and present-day anorexics sufficiently similar in their motivations for self-starvation, their behavioral patterns, and the course of their eating problems to say that they suffered from the same syndrome of psychopathology? We do not know, but dangerous and excessive fasting practices have long been known and the primary sufferers have always been young women. At present, eating disorders are relatively common. Societal interpretations of the young women's fasting have varied dramatically, however, from considering them to be miraculous instruments of the divine will to diagnosing them as psychologically disturbed and in need of mental health treatment.

SOURCES: American Psychiatric Association. (1994). *Diagnostic and statistical manual of mental disorders* (4th ed., DSM-IV). Washington, DC: Author; Bruch, H. (1982). Anorexia nervosa: Therapy and theory. *American Journal of Psychiatry, 139,* 1531–1538; Brumberg, J. J. (1986). "Fasting girls": Reflections on writing the history of anorexia nervosa. In A. B. Smuts & J. W. Hagen (Eds.), History and research in child development. *Monographs of the Society for Research in Child Development, 50* (4–5, Serial No. 211).

---

the rate of occurrence or the number of new cases identified within a specified period of time such as during one particular calendar year. If mental retardation rates were being studied, those cases counted in a study of incidence would include new births (all babies in the sample who were identified as retarded at birth) plus older individuals who are newly diagnosed as retarded, for example when they begin elementary school. Those cases counted in a prevalence study would include all of those just mentioned plus all individuals who were previously diagnosed and remain retarded at the time the study is conducted. Thus prevalence rates will always be significantly greater than incidence rates, which are based only on new cases and do not include continuing ones. Readers of the clinical literature will encounter both incidence and prevalence estimates, and it is important to keep the distinction in mind.

Because of the previously discussed factors, epidemiological studies are not comparable and are unlikely to

yield uniform results. Yet it is necessary to have some idea of the frequency of various types of disorders in order to plan for needed treatment services. Well-conducted studies of large groups of children from the same region can provide some idea of the range of problem rates. Table 1-2 provides information on U.S. estimates of child psychopathology. Problems appear to be increasing. A 13-year study of parent and teacher ratings of U.S. children showed that child problem scores increased and child competence scores decreased over this period, although the increases were small (Achenbach & Howell, 1993). Also, more untreated children need help now than in the recent past because of decreased governmental and health insurance support of mental health services.

Estimates of children's problem prevalence rates vary with the assessor's training, experience, and familiarity with the child. Those who have the least direct contact with children, such as school principals, report fairly low

TABLE 1-2 ESTIMATES OF RATES OF BEHAVIOR
PROBLEMS AMONG SCHOOL-AGE CHILDREN

Estimators	Estimated Rates (in percents)
1. School principals and U.S. Office of Education	1.5–2.0
2. National Association of Mental Health	10–11
3. Institute of Medicine, National Academy of Sciences	12
4. President's Committee on Mental Health	15
5. Psychologists, psychiatrists, and other child helping professionals	17–33
6. School teachers	20–33
7. Parents and adolescents (self-report)	15

SOURCES: American Psychiatric Association. (1994). *Diagnostic and statistical manual of mental disorders (DSM-IV).* Washington, DC: American Psychiatric Press; U.S. Office of Education, Bureau of Education for the Handicapped. (1975, May 16). *State education agency estimates unserved by type of handicap.* Washington, DC: Author; Rubin, R. A., & Balow, B. (1978). Prevalence of teacher identified behavior problems: A longitudinal study. *Exceptional Children, 45,* 102–111; Institute of Medicine, National Academy of Sciences. (1989). *Research on children and adolescents with mental, behavioral, and developmental disorders.* Washington, DC: National Academy Press; Kelly, T. J., Bullock, L. M., & Dykes, M. K. (1978). Behavioral disorders: Teachers' perceptions. *Exceptional Children, 43,* 316–318; Werner, E. E., & Smith, R. S. (1977). *Kauai's children come of age.* Honolulu: University of Hawaii Press; Werner, E. E., Bierman, J. M., & French, F. E. (1971). *The children of Kauai.* Honolulu: University of Hawaii Press; Snapper, K. J., & Ohms, J. S. (1977). *The status of children 1977.* Washington, DC: U.S. Government Printing Office; Fergusson, D., Horwood, L. J., & Lynskey, M. T. (1994). The comorbidities of adolescent problem behaviors. *Journal of Abnormal Child Psychology, 22,* 339–372.

rates of disorder, while higher rates are reported by teachers who deal with the children on a daily basis. Estimates from the U.S. Office of Education are based largely on surveys of school principals, and indicate that only 2 percent of school-age children are emotionally disturbed. The principals themselves reported behavioral problems in just 1.5 percent of the children attending their schools (U.S. Office of Education, 1975). However, principals do not know all that goes on in classrooms and playgrounds in their schools and so fail to observe a certain amount of disordered student behavior.

In marked contrast, teachers must deal with their students for extended time periods each day and see many problems they do not report to others. The demands of managing difficult children may also lead teachers to be oversensitive to deviance and to overestimate its prevalence. In one study (Rubin & Balow, 1978), teachers judged between 23 percent and 31 percent of a large group of children to have "attitude and/or behavior problems" at some time between kindergarten and third grade. In another study of kindergarten through twelfth-grade students, teachers perceived 20 percent as having behavior disorders, although only 2.2 percent of the children were considered disturbed enough to require special educational placement (Kelly, Bullock, & Dykes, 1978). Highest estimates are obtained when psychologists' judgments are combined with teachers' impressions, which yielded a 33 percent likelihood of children experiencing a problem at some point in their development (Zax & Cowen, 1967).

The exhaustive study of all children born on the Hawaiian island of Kauai in 1955 (Werner & Smith, 1977, 1992) found that by age 10 years about one-quarter had behavior problems and about 17 percent had problems severe enough to interfere with their school achievement. Ten percent of the children were judged to need short-term mental health services, mostly for excessive shyness, anxiety, and chronic nervous habits, and an additional 4 percent needed long-term mental health services largely because of their antisocial and aggressive behavior. Approximately one-third of the children (30 percent) were thought to be high-risk because they had experienced ill health or injury very early in life, their families were very poor and troubled by chronic discord, divorce, or parental illness. Two-thirds of the high risk children developed problems, but one-third were *resilient* children who developed into competent, responsible adults (Werner, 1995). The children and families were assessed by a panel composed of a pediatrician, a psychologist, and a public health nurse, who judged 14 percent of the total group to have adjustment problems serious enough to warrant professional attention and 3 percent more to require special education services because of serious reading and communication difficulties.

Official U.S. estimates of the prevalence of childhood psychological disturbance and learning problems are roughly comparable to the rate yielded by the Kauai study (U.S. Bureau of the Census, 1994). Dismissing the school principals' estimates as too low and the teachers' estimates as too high leaves a more generally agreed-on range of 11 to 17 percent. The President's Committee on Mental Health offered an estimate of 15 percent (Snapper & Ohms, 1977), while the Institute of Medicine of the National Academy of Sciences (1989) decided to use 12 percent as the most conservative estimate based on a number of reliable studies. The Institute of Medicine report also recognized that the prevalence may exceed 20 percent in some populations, such as "inner-city children, who are exposed to severe psychosocial adversity" (p. 33).

Prevalence of Academic Achievement Problems

It is easier to estimate the number of children with academic problems than adjustment disorders. Widely shared standards of academic performance and the use of standardized achievement tests make it relatively easy to identify children with school achievement problems. However, many children with academic problems have emotional ones as well, so the two groups are not mutually exclusive. For example, Werner and Smith (1977) found that children with serious academic underachievement problems had *nine times* as much contact with police, mental health, and other social service agencies as did children with no academic problems. Cultural differences, poverty, and language problems contribute to children's school difficulties, so that on the ethnically diverse and impoverished island of Kauai, 51 percent of the boys and 37 percent of the girls had serious academic difficulties. In contrast, a higher-income group of English-speaking Minnesota schoolchildren had rates of academic problems averaging 31 percent for the boys and 17.7 percent for the girls (Rubin & Balow, 1971, 1978). These two sets of estimates differ greatly. Selecting the one to use depends upon the similarity between the group used to derive the prevalence rate and the type of group to which one hopes to generalize. In considering impoverished groups composed largely of rural minority children, the Hawaiian statistics would be more useful, while the Minnesota figures more likely represent middle America.

AGE AND GENDER DIFFERENCES IN PSYCHOPATHOLOGY

During childhood many more boys than girls are identified as having psychological problems. This is especially true for antisocial aggression, with between four times and twelve times as many boys as girls having this type of problem (Gelfand & Peterson, 1985). In addition, as many as ten times more boys than girls are diagnosed as having attention-deficit disorder with hyperactivity, which often accompanies aggression (American Psychi-

atric Association, 1994). Boys also clearly outnumber girls in prevalence of mental retardation (2 to 1), and in infantile autism and childhood psychosis (3 to 1) (American Psychiatric Association, 1994). Boys also predominate in language disorders and learning disabilities (Gelfand & Peterson, 1985).

Despite the greater prevalence of psychopathology among boys, the sexes may differ more in the *type* of problem than in the number of problems they experience. Boys have more trouble in controlling their impulses and aggression—the types of problems that cannot easily be ignored, especially in structured school situations. Boys also tend to have more serious problems associated with developmental delays and disruptions which require professional attention. Girls are more likely to suffer from disorders of overcontrol (e.g., phobias, social withdrawal), whereas boys exhibit more easily detected problems with undercontrol (antisocial aggression, attention deficit, and hyperactivity) (Achenbach & Edelbrock, 1978). In adolescence, the pattern of sex differences in psychopathology changes. Girls lose their apparent adjustment superiority over boys and begin to develop the adult pattern at double the males' rates of affective or emotional disorders, especially those involving depression (Lewinsohn & Rohde, 1993). In adolescence, too, girls begin to develop high rates of eating disorders such as bulimia (alternate gorging and vomiting) and anorexia nervosa (self-imposed starvation and compulsive over-exercise). Although some males also develop these eating disorders, it is estimated that 95 percent of the victims are young women (American Psychiatric Association, 1994). The swing to increased female psychopathology during adolescence could stem from heightened cultural demands for female attractiveness and accomplishment at that age, possibly to hormonal changes associated with puberty, or to some combination of environmental and physiological factors. Certainly, the appearance of adolescent eating disorders and affective disturbances suggests that there are radical age-related changes in the nature of psychopathology (Gelfand & Peterson, 1985). Males continue to predominate in the disorders involving antisocial aggression throughout the life span (Al-Issa, 1982a).

In industrialized Western countries about twice as many women as men are treated for depression (American Psychiatric Association, 1994), especially in the higher cost private treatment services (Al-Issa, 1982a).

Considering all types of mental disorders, women and men are approximately equally likely to use community mental health centers and outpatient psychiatric services. However, proportionally more men than women are served by lower-cost facilities, such as state and county hospitals (Kramer, 1977). Overall, the sexes seem to be equivalent in number of psychological problems.

Predicting Future Development

Life would be much simpler but less interesting if we could accurately predict a child's future. Do violent temper tantrums at the age of 3 years indicate a stormy, difficult adolescence? Will a preschool girl's joy in helping her mother predict that she will be a diligent student in school? Perhaps her early curiosity about how things work will enable her to become a successful scientist, or perhaps it is just a passing phase. The research data indicate that success in long-term prediction depends largely on what one is attempting to predict. Although some aspects of future development can be anticipated, many others defy prediction. Next we will discuss three considerations in attempting to predict children's long-range adjustment outcomes: developmental status of the child, changes in the child's environment, and accuracy in measuring the child's behavioral characteristics.

DEVELOPMENTAL CHANGES IMPAIR PREDICTION

Development brings new challenges, opportunities, and hazards. Developmentally significant events include learning to speak, entering kindergarten and first grade, adapting to junior high school, graduating from high school, and other such milestones. New demands present challenges to children, and their ability to cope with one transition, such as entering kindergarten, may set the stage for their future adjustment success (Cicchetti, Toth, & Lynch, 1995). Prediction is difficult because change is the essence of development. Yet, as developmental psychopathologists have observed, some degree of prediction is possible (Cicchetti et al., 1995). On the whole, fortunate children who are cognitively and socially advanced can be expected to continue their superior adjustment in later years. The direction of development for virtually all children is from less to more advanced—physically, intellectually, socially, and emotionally—and there is relatively little backsliding in major areas of functioning.

General vs. Specific Traits. Kohlberg and his associates (1972) distinguish between *general traits* such as intellectual capacity, ego development (self-control and general psychological maturity), and moral development on the one hand and "symptoms" or *discrete problem behaviors* on the other. Discrete problem behaviors may be temporary and relatively useless for prediction. In contrast, the general characteristics of intellectual capacity, ego development, attachment to the major caretaker, and moral development are better predictors of adult adjustment. The presence or absence of specific problems may not aid prediction (Kohlberg et al., 1972), especially if the problems are minor.

ENVIRONMENTAL CHANGE DISRUPTS PREDICTION

It is more difficult to predict long-term outcomes if the environment changes drastically than if life continues as usual. Such dramatic changes might include parental divorce and the dissolution of the family, serious illness of a family member or of the child, financial emergencies, or a move to a very different social and geographical setting. Even commonplace events can prove upsetting. As an example, the birth of a sibling often produces behavioral problems, particularly among 2- to 3-year-olds (Dunn, Kendrick, & MacNamee, 1981; Gelfand & Peterson, 1985). And, as Chapter 4 indicates, parental conflict and divorce could stimulate children's aggression, school problems, and other types of adjustment difficulties. Young children in particular may be upset by changes in their routine or surroundings, and their behavior may deteriorate following major disruptions in family life.

MEASUREMENT ACCURACY AIDS PREDICTION

Prediction is impossible without accurate measures. For example, a child's relative height and weight can be predicted fairly well from accurate physical measurements taken as early as age 3, barring major physical problems such as serious malnutrition, injuries, or other conditions that could adversely affect physical development (Macfarlane, 1963).

In contrast, psychological characteristics are difficult to predict because they are difficult to measure adequately. Intelligence tests are well-constructed, but examiners who vary in experience, motivation, and skill in test administration produce varying IQ scores for the same child. Moreover, momentary factors such as fatigue, poor motivation, language problems, and illness can all distort a child's IQ test performance. Thus, there are many more sources of error in psychological tests than in measures of some physical characteristics, which may simply require reading a scale or meter. Among the psychological characteristics, personality and social attributes are perhaps the most difficult to measure accurately, but some prediction is possible.

The more precise and microscopically detailed measures are not always better than looser, more general ones. In a study of nearly 700 young people over a 14-year period, Cairns and Cairns (1994) found that more general teacher ratings and peer nominations were better predictors of later adjustment than were precise second-by-second behavioral observations at school. That is, teachers and classmates could identify a child's behavior as unusually aggressive and likely to lead to later criminal arrests, but early classroom behavioral observations could not identify later criminal offenders.

SEVERE PROBLEMS PERSIST

Prediction is easier for severely psychologically deviant children or those who are unusually healthy and well-adjusted. Adult intellectual status is highly predictable, although discouragingly so, for severely developmentally delayed and mentally retarded youngsters. With increasing age, extremely developmentally disabled children predictably continue to score much below average on intelligence and achievement tests. It is within the large normal range that prediction is difficult.

SHORT-TERM PREDICTION IS MORE ACCURATE

Short-term prediction is more accurate than longer-term forecasts, perhaps because fewer dramatic environmental changes are likely to occur during short periods. Children change so much during development that different types of tests must be used at different ages. For example, infant intelligence tests assess alertness, coordination, and instruction-following, while tests for adolescents chiefly evaluate verbal skills. Because the tests measure different skills at various ages, it is virtually impossible to predict adult intelligence level for any but the most retarded infants. Prediction improves when tests assess very similar skills. There is a high correlation between children's intelligence scores between the ages of 9 and 12 years and those obtained at 18 years since tests at those ages are highly similar. This strikingly high correlation indicates

great stability for most youngsters, although individual children may show dramatic swings in their IQ scores over time. In one study a third of the children's IQ scores changed up to 30 points between separate testing occasions when they were between the ages of 2½ and 17 years (McCall, Appelbaum, & Hogarty, 1973).

GROUP DATA DON'T PREDICT INDIVIDUAL OUTCOMES

Averages obtained from a group of children cannot be used to predict outcomes for individual children. Unfortunately, it is just such individual predictions that are most needed by parents, teachers, and clinicians. At present, data from large numbers of children can be used to provide a *probability estimate* about the development of other groups of children with similar characteristics. For example, if four of each five children from a large, representative sample have serious and persistent underachievement problems (Werner & Smith, 1977), then we could expect that about 80 percent of a similar group of children also would fail to improve. But it would still be difficult to predict the outcome for a single child, which is our eventual goal.

Continuity and Discontinuity in Disordered Behavior

The question of whether or not children "grow out of" deviant behavior is an important one for caretakers and researchers. If the answer is generally yes, then there should be less concern about a child's disordered behavior, but if spontaneous improvement is unlikely, then intervention is necessary. The child development literature presents two possibilities. One, the *continuity hypothesis*, (Lewis, 1965) is that adjustment status is relatively stable. That is, maladjusted children continue to be maladjusted as they grow older. Either their original problems persist or new ones develop, but in either case there is a poor prognosis for children with problems. The alternative and more optimistic *growth hypothesis* is that children have an extraordinary capacity to overcome their problems. With development comes increasing experience and greater intellectual and social skills, which may enable people to overcome childhood problems. If the growth hypothesis is correct, then children's problems should be transitory and would not predict adult adjustment difficulties. The following discussion suggests which viewpoint is the more accurate.

PERSISTENT CHARACTERISTICS

Problem type and severity are related to problem persistence. Specific problem behaviors tend to be less persistent than are general attributes such as social and intellectual competence. Table 1-3 shows the relative persistence of various academic and social characteristics. Research indicates that children who are socially outgoing and self-confident are likely to remain that way into adulthood. Achievers who are determined to master skills of any type, whether athletic, academic, artistic, or mechanical, typically continue to be achievement-oriented as adults. Children's sex-typed activities and sexual orientation also tend to endure.

Some clearly negative characteristics are also persistent according to retrospective studies of the past histories of disturbed adults and prospective studies that follow groups of children as they develop. Extremely anxious children who have *obsessions*, or persistent unwelcome and unavoidable ideas, thoughts, impulses, or images, or *compulsions* to engage in repetitive behaviors such as handwashing, checking on or ordering objects do not overcome these problems readily. Of a group of children and adolescents diagnosed with obsessive-compulsive disorder, only 6 percent were considered truly recovered in a 2- to 7-year follow-up (Swedo, Lenanare, Rettew, Hamburger, Bartko, & Rapoport, 1993). In adolescence, serious sexually assaultive behavior in males tends to persist into adulthood, accompanied by violent nonsexual offenses (Peters, McMahon, & Quincy, 1992).

Persistent Problems That Change Over Time. Sometimes the type of problem behaviors changes somewhat over time although adjustment difficulties continue. One study (Maziade et al., 1985) found that children who had difficult temperaments at age 7 years developed more clinical psychiatric disorders of various types when they were 12 than did children with initially easy temperaments. The children with difficult temperaments also had less well-functioning families, so it is impossible to determine whether genetic or environmental factors primarily produced their problems.

Researchers have long attempted to identify the childhood precursors of adult schizophrenia, a serious disor-

TABLE 1-3 PERSISTENCE OF CHILDHOOD CHARACTERISTICS

Persistent Characteristics

Self-confidence and sociability.
Intellectual interests, achievement motivation.
Preference for sex-typed rather than opposite-sex activities.
Clinically significant depression.
Obsessional, recurrent thoughts and compulsive rituals.
Developmental disorders such as autism, psychotic reactions.
Highly aggressive, antisocial, illegal, defiant behavior.
Academic underachievement and other school problems.
Unpopularity linked with aggression.
Negative self-image, strong inferiority feelings, tension, physical complaints.
Marked mental retardation.
Sexual assaultiveness in adolescent males.
Severe or numerous adjustment problems.

Transitory Characteristics

Nonsevere shyness and social withdrawal.
Anxiety, fears, and phobias, except for agoraphobia (terror about leaving the house), which is more persistent.
Chronic nervous habits such as nail biting.
Sleep disturbances and minor eating problems, except for obesity or anorexia (self-starvation), which persist.

der that accounts for many psychiatric hospitalizations. No childhood disorder resembles adult schizophrenia very closely, which makes early detection challenging. Schizophrenia tends to run in families, with children of schizophrenics experiencing heightened risk of later developing the disorder. Some studies found that children of schizophrenic parents have subtle problems in attention and information processing, but other research has failed to confirm these findings (Watt, 1986). Children who later develop schizophrenia have sometimes been reported to be odd, socially isolated, and oppositional, but so have many others who were not pre-schizophrenic. To date, the only variable that clearly places a child at increased risk is having a schizophrenic parent, although it is not known why this is so. Schizophrenia is a clear example of a disorder that is extremely difficult to predict from a child's adjustment status.

Highly disturbed psychotic children continue to be very deviant and developmentally delayed throughout their lives. They lag behind developmentally and fail to master normal speech, social skills, or even appropriate self-care and toileting skills in severe cases. In addition, psychotic children may exhibit uncontrolled tantrums and become physically assaultive or engage in self-injurious behavior such as persistent headbanging, scratching, hair pulling, or eye gouging. The more severely psychotic the child's behavior, the poorer the outlook, especially if the child's IQ is very low (50 or less) (Bartak & Rutter, 1975). If the developmental delay and psychotic reaction appear within the first several years of life, the child may be diagnosed as autistic, and the chances are only one in four that the child will ever improve appreciably (Bartak & Rutter, 1975). Fortunately, the self-injurious and assaultive behavior can be controlled through proper treatment (see Chapter 14).

Box 1-6 presents excerpts from the diary of a father of a severely disabled boy who suffers from a pervasive developmental disorder including features of brain damage, mental retardation, and autism. Most such children eventually must be institutionalized because their parents cannot ceaselessly provide the continuous, exhausting, and intensive care they require.

Other, less serious syndromes can also persist. Most people remember some early classmate who was the most rejected member of the class: the butt of the jokes, the one excluded from play groups, the one chosen last for every team. Unfortunately, such outcast status is sometimes not shed as the years pass. Children who are rejected by classmates and who also are highly aggressive and immature are likely to remain very unpopular over periods of at least a year or more, and often longer (Bukowski & Newcomb, 1984). By itself, being rejected by other children at one time period does not predict future social status, but being aggressive and immature adds greatly to the stability of peer rejection. Similarly, popularity with peers is more stable over time if the popular children also are seen as cooperative and as leaders than if they are popular but also disruptive and aggressive (Coie & Dodge, 1983). These research findings suggest that even relatively mild aggressive tendencies may indicate continuing adjustment problems.

"The homicide rate among teenagers has trebled in the United States since the 1960s, and homicide is the leading cause of death for young black males." (Lykken, 1993, p. 13)

The Persistence of Antisocial Behavior. Highly antisocial, aggressive tendencies can be remarkably persistent especially if they develop early in childhood. Children with diagnosable conduct disorders are in trouble constantly because they start fights, defy teachers, lie, steal, and assault people. Antisocial behavior intimidates others, bringing the youth short-term benefits, but long-term adjustment perils. Such children often continue to be antisocial as they become older. Highly aggressive behavior is especially difficult to control if it occurs frequently both at home and at school. Also, antisocial behavior tends to continue if the child displays a number of different types of aggression (e.g., fighting, stealing, lying, and cruelty) and if his problematic aggression begins before age 15 (Loeber, 1990). Boys who meet all of the preceding criteria are very likely to continue to be antisocial and aggressive. However, with increasing age the nature of their aggressive behavior changes, and public confrontations decline while covert activities that escape detection, such as stealing and vandalism, become more common (Loeber, 1990). Violent, aggressive conduct is most likely to persist in environments in which social unrest is high and violence is widely viewed as desirable and justified.

Underachievement. Children whose academic work quality is significantly below their capacity as measured by their IQ scores are likely to continue to be underachievers as they grow older. Four out of five of the Kauai study children who were underachievers in elementary school continued to show significant academic underachievement throughout secondary school (Werner & Smith, 1977). In adolescence, they displayed increasing absenteeism, sexual misconduct, and problems with the police. Nearly all of those who became deviant in adolescence had earlier academic difficulties or social adjustment problems by the age of 10 years. Other investigators (Robins, 1966) also reported that earlier poor peer relations, working below capacity in school, and conflicts with teachers predict adolescent delinquency. In general, poor adjustment to the academic and social demands of school forecasts future adjustment problems.

Mental Retardation. Mental retardation may or may not persist depending upon its severity. When they become adults, mildly retarded children may appear to improve and score within the dull normal range rather than the

---

BOX 1-6 LIVING WITH NOAH

Parents provide the best picture of life with a severely disordered child. The following passages by writer Josh Greenfeld describes the parents' dilemma as their child grows older and less manageable.

December 4, 1971

Foumi [Noah's mother] had a good day with Noah, teaching him to put out his tongue. And touch his nose. The only problem is that as he learns a new thing he proceeds to forget the last thing he learned. Leaky, freaky kid, head moving from side to side as he continually sings the gibberish song of himself.

September 13, 1974

When Noah came home from school yesterday he ran out into the middle of the street to lay down. Foumi tried to drag him back onto the sidewalk. He kicked her in the stomach so hard that she doubled over in pain. She has been in tears all evening, not only from the physical hurt but also from the spiritual one.

 Yes, the time has come to separate Noah from us. Oh that we could part from him irrevocably. . . .

September 20 , 1974

I've spent my love on Noah. I know it's an existential situation, that I should enjoy him as long as I can, but I've turned the corner. I dread the future more than any pleasures I can possibly derive from the present.

September 22, 1974

Another bloody weekend. On Saturday I tried to go shopping with Noah. He sat himself down in the middle of the street and would not move. On Sunday we took him to the cat show. Again the same thing: he would sit down and not move whenever the whim hit him. He is harder for me to handle physically, impossible for me to deal with any longer spiritually.

July 1, 1975

We never all quite had breakfast together this morning. But a moment came when Noah, draped over the golden love seat in his color-coordinating yellow Charlie Brown pajamas, listened to us sing "Happy Birthday" to him. He shyly rose when we reached "Stand up. Stand up. Stand up and show us your face," and ran into Foumi's arms. So it was tear time again at the sentimental Greenfelds'.

November 8, 1976

Noah has taken to moistening the tips of his fingers with his tongue—as if he were about to turn the page of a book—and then touching a wall, a surface, an object, or a person instead. It's a habit he picked up from one of his day-care classmates and it annoys me greatly. Yesterday he did two other things that upset and frightened me:

 I was watching television in the den. I thought Noah was in the living room. When suddenly he attacked me from behind, scratching at my face, clawing at my throat, and going off in a painful yowl himself after I beat him off.

 Later, at dinner, for no discernible reason he turned to me and pulled my hair. I can only suspect that on both occasions he suddenly had a pain—a toothache, for example—and he was reacting to it, assigning me the cause of it, and hence also the source of possible alleviation.

 Both incidents frightened me. Not physically but psychically. I do not look forward to a future in which he could overpower me.

Josh Greenfeld later published a book describing life with an older Noah. As Noah's parents feared, they were no longer able to care for their son at home. His mother developed arthritis and his father has heart disease; neither their health nor their marriage could survive Noah's continued failures in toilet training, his extreme moods, and his destructive rages. Now an adult, Noah lives in a residential group home and is visited frequently by his parents and brother. It is clear that he never will develop mentally, socially, or emotionally, despite the best psychological and medical care. His father says "with Noah, you think of the old Pearl Buck line—a continuing sadness that never ends."

SOURCE: Greenfeld, J. (1986). *A client called Noah: A family journey continued.* New York: Henry Holt.

---

retarded range on intelligence tests. Many of them hold jobs and perform better vocationally than predicted from their childhood intelligence test scores (Sparks & Younie, 1969). In contrast, children with severe retardation (IQ scores below 50) rarely improve significantly and may require continuing supervision in sheltered workshops and institutions. Many of the low-scoring group can acquire basic eating, toileting, and self-care skills and can learn simple, repetitive jobs, but few can live independently.

Summation. To conclude, future prospects are best for the fortunate children who come from harmonious families and are bright, work hard, achieve in school, and are popular and cooperative. Compensatory experiences can help children deal with some types of difficulties. Children from multiproblem families adjust better, and appear more resilient, if they have a surrogate parent, such as a grandparent, aunt, older sibling or friend, to act in place of their dysfunctional parents (Werner & Smith, 1992). The persistence of severe antisocial behavior such as cruelty and aggression is striking. Early, frequent, and varied antisocial aggression is highly predictive of continuing problems in self-control. In general, the outlook is worst for children with: (1) severe or intense psychopathology such as serious autistic or psychotic disorders, uncontrollable hostility, severe retardation, or developmental delay, and (2) a large number of different problems, especially after age 5 (Macfarlane et al., 1954).

Less Persistent Characteristics. Many childhood problems either diminish or disappear over time. For example, in most cases, children's extreme shyness and social withdrawal neither persist nor precede other types of adjustment difficulties. Approximately 70 percent of such problems disappear as the child becomes older. The same is true for chronic nervous habits such as nail biting and hair twirling, and for mild food finickiness and sleep disturbances. Strange food preferences and aversions often are overcome, but overeating and obesity are more likely to persist (Berg, 1970). In the same vein, most specific fears and simple phobias dissipate with age (King, 1993), as is described in Chapter 7.

SUMMARY

In past centuries children were accorded few rights. Many were beaten, abandoned, raised by wet nurses, and ruthlessly exploited by employers. However, their expectations for comfort, love, and self-fulfillment were not high. Only recently have children received educational and psychological treatment services. The 19th-century social reform movement established juvenile courts, special education services, and treatment programs first for delinquents and ultimately for children with a range of problems.

Several criteria are used to determine whether a child's problem is truly deviant and worthy of clinical attention: age- and sex-appropriateness, severity, persistence, discomfort to the child and others, and interference with normal functioning. A problem is clinically significant when the behavior is inappropriate for the child's age, gender, or sociocultural group, or is intense, persistent and disturbs the child's social or academic functioning. Children may be misdiagnosed as having problems when they confront unrealistically high adult standards or when they are normal but are judged by the standards of a different culture. Approximately 12 to 15 percent of schoolchildren suffer from behavior disorders serious enough to merit treatment, and as many as one-half of boys and one-third of girls experience significant academic achievement difficulties. The prevalence of childhood psychological disorders appears to be increasing slightly.

Persistent childhood problems include pervasive developmental disorders, severe mental retardation, psychosis, early onset, severe conduct disorder, and obsessive-compulsive disorder. In addition, a history of academic underachievement is difficult to remedy. The more enduring positive characteristics include sociability, self-confidence, achievement strivings, a work orientation, and general social and intellectual competence. Many mild social and emotional problems do not persist. For example, fears and phobias, shyness, social withdrawal, and nervous habits all tend to abate with time. Whether a child will outgrow a problem depends on many factors including the age of onset; and the type, severity, and persistence of the problem; comorbidity with other problems, and, as Chapter 14 describes, the availability of an effective treatment intervention.

C H A P T E R   2

EXPLANATIONS OF CHILD

BEHAVIOR DISTURBANCE

Key Terms

Cognitive development. The growth of intellectual functions such as memory, reasoning, planning, and problem-solving.

Constructivism. The philosophy that truth cannot be determined because there is no absolute truth, but only experience as affected by the beliefs of the viewer.

Diathesis-stress hypothesis (or vulnerability-stress hypothesis). The view that psychopathology arises from a combination of some pre-existing physical or psychological vulnerability and some later physical or psychological stress.

Dopamine. One of the neurotransmitter substances that transmit nerve impulses across synaptic junctions between neurons or nerve cells.

Internal working model. In attachment theory, the internalized mental representation of oneself or another formed through repeated experiences with the other person.

Logical Positivism. Philosophical position that builds theory through logical extension, producing hypotheses that can be tested scientifically through controlled observation and experimentation.

Object relations theory. Also interpersonal theory. A psychodynamic theory that views interpersonal relationships as derived from the individual's past experiences with attachment figures such as parents that become internalized and shape perceptions, thoughts, feelings, and behavior.

Operant behavior. A term from Skinner's theory indicating the type of behavior that operates on or changes the environment some way and is controlled by its consequences.

Parsimony. Simplicity. Used as a criterion for judging theoretical explanations specifying that if theories are otherwise equivalent, the simpler one is preferred.

Psychoanalytic theory. Any theory based on the assumption that psychopathology derives from unconscious psychological conflict and basic character is formed early in life.

Reinforcement. Occurrence of any stimulus that increases or maintains the rate of an immediately preceding behavior. Positive reinforcement serves as a reward and increases the behavior it follows, while negative reinforcement increases behavior that removes or avoids an aversive stimulus.

Temperament. General dispositions such as activity level, sociability, and emotionality that appear in infancy and may be heritable.

Why does one child experience adjustment problems while another, even as closely related as a twin, does not? This challenging question has no final answer at present, although there are many competing explanations of the etiology of childhood psychological disturbance. This chapter will review and evaluate some of the most influential of the explanations of abnormal behavior including the psychoanalytic approach and a contemporary variant, object relations theory; learning and cognitive theories; the humanistic model; the developmental psychopathology approach; and some biological and genetic models of psychopathology. Some of the rich diversity in explanations of children's problem behaviors is described in Box 2-1. At present, no theory is completely satisfactory, and each one has major gaps and other significant problems. Each approach best explains some portion of the psychopathology spectrum, leaving other types of disorders neglected or unconvincingly explained. After a review of the criteria for evaluating theories, we describe and compare the major theories of the development of normal and deviant behavior. Since no single account deals with all disorders equally well, we identify the particular types of disorders each theory explains best and least well.

WHAT ARE THEORIES?

In the study of abnormal behavior or psychopathology, a theory states a set of principles believed to account for disordered behavior. To qualify as a theory rather than simply a conceptual model, the principles must apply broadly to a number of types of psychopathology and must have some empirical support from research findings or clinical observations. The study of theories of human functioning traces back to the origins of European and Asian philosophy, but this chapter focuses on theories that emerged during the 20th century. In studying theories, it is helpful to know something about the people who constructed them. Theories are the result of individual human beings' attempts to understand and explain some phenomenon. The boxes in this chapter provide personal descriptions of the major theorists that reveal them as a group of very human and highly creative visionaries with a fascinating range of interests and some interesting peculiarities. The content of the theories reflects each theorist's historical era, social influences, and individual personality.

Some writers believe that there are no objective ways to assess the worth of theories, no fixed, absolute measurement that is independent of the beliefs of the person who is doing the knowing (Overton & Horowitz, 1991). If so, there is no independent, objective measure of a theory's adequacy because the theory we accept so profoundly influences how we do research and interpret research findings. This *constructivist approach to science* maintains that there is no single, most nearly accurate view of reality, but rather many alternative views that are constructed by the various observers. The philosopher Norwood R. Hanson (1958) argued that all observations are "theory laden," representing data interpreted in the context of our beliefs. At best, we can discern *patterns* in behavior but not cause-effect sequences. For example, a researcher might discern a consistent pattern between maternal mental illness and child maladjustment, but could not identify the cause-effect relationships in the pattern. Most researchers admit to limitations derived from cultural, historical, methodological, and theoretical factors, but nevertheless they try to probe the origins, course, and treatment of psychopathology.

BOX 2-1   ALTERNATIVE THEORIES OF ETIOLOGY OF A BOY'S AGGRESSION

THE PROBLEM

Mark, a 7-year-old boy, is identified by his teacher as a likely future delinquent. He keeps the class in turmoil by teasing, hitting, throwing things, complaining, and talking back to adults. At home, he lies about not having any homework, doesn't come home after school, and steals money from his parents. His dad can keep him in line with threats of a whipping, but his mother is helpless in disciplining him and he defies her constantly. Teacher-parent conferences often end in shouting matches as the father defends his son and blames the teacher and other children for his son's problems.

ALTERNATIVE THEORIES

Mark is expressing an unconscious identification with the aggressor, his intimidating father, in an unresolved Oedipal conflict. Therapy would help him gain insight into the nature of his anxious-hostile feelings, which would help him to overcome them. Then he would become less destructive and rebellious.

Mark's mother was passive, but also cold, insensitive, and unresponsive, when he was a baby, leading him to form an insecure attachment to her, together with self-hate and an expectation that others will be equally rejecting. The persisting poor self-image and negative expectations of others produce Mark's antagonistic behavior.

His experiences with his family, teachers, and others have taught Mark that aggression is rewarded. He copies his intimidating father and his favorite, aggressive TV actors, and strikes out at others. He is so unpleasant that he frequently gets his own way, which is reinforcing. At the least he attracts attention, which is also rewarding, and sometimes he is punished, which just makes him angrier and more determined to hurt someone.

Since no one knows precisely why most forms of psychopathology develop, many different explanations are possible ranging from inadequate mothering to faulty genetic structure. When fully elaborated these speculations are conceptual models or theories of psychological deviance. *A theory provides a general explanation for a variety of related events and behavioral patterns.* Based upon a set of stated of implied assumptions (e.g., that personality either is modifiable or fixed during infancy), a theoretical model attempts to fit research and clinical observations into a comprehensive and convincing account of psychological processes. In the study of child behavior disorders, for example, a theory might explain why troubled parents so frequently have disturbed children by suggesting a genetic or a learning mechanism (or both) for the transmission of problems from one generation to the next. The theory organizes what is known about some aspects of behavior, and may go beyond simple description to offer an explanation of the causes of the behavior.

Can One Judge a Theory?

Evaluating theories is not easy because each one is highly complex and has particular assumptions and implications. As we noted previously, the *rationalist* or *constructivist* approach to theories maintains that it is inherently impossible to judge theories because investigators' beliefs pervade their selection of theories to champion as well as their supposedly objective observational data (Kuhn, 1977). Thus, although new and novel theories may arise, it may be impossible to say whether they are in any sense "better" than the belief systems they replace. This constructivist view would logically lead one to the extreme position that a theory of influence by green beings from another planet could be as convincing an explanation of psychopathology as any other, if many people accepted it. This is a argumentative extreme, though, and the constructivists are obviously referring to theories found to be convincing by many knowledgeable investigators.

In contrast, the philosophy of science or *logical positivist* tradition maintains that theories *can* be judged for adequacy when tested against objective scientific observations. A number of criteria are typically used to determine whether theories meet formal standards of acceptability. Epstein (1973) has offered six criteria for the evaluation of theories of human social behavior: the theory's extensiveness, parsimony, empirical validity, internal consistency, testability, and usefulness. Scientific theories have long been judged by these criteria, which can be used as a guide for assessing the theories to follow. In this chapter, each theory is rated on Epstein's criteria, as shown in Table 2-1.

Extensiveness. The more general and inclusive a theory, the better, all other characteristics being equally good. Examples of broader theories include psychoanalytic theory and Skinner's operant approach, while narrower theories focus on a particular type of psychopathology, such as the learned helplessness model of depression (Abramson, Seligman, & Teasdale, 1978). It is much easier to construct theoretical models of limited types of psychopathology than it is to develop an all-embracing theory covering many types of disorders. A broader theory is preferred when it can explain the same phenomena nearly as well as several more limited ones.

Parsimony. If two theories explain some phenomenon about equally well, the simpler, more elegant theory is preferred to an unnecessarily complex one. Simplicity or parsimony makes the theoretical model more readily understood, less likely to add unsound assumptions, and easier to apply.

Empirical Validity. Scientific theories should be solidly based on and consistent with objectively collected data. When the empirical evidence is lacking or contradictory, a theory can be accepted only provisionally at best. The rules of scientific inquiry through research are strict and formal, and casual observations do not suffice to establish a theory's empirical validity. Folklore, biased observations, and poor science can never legitimately be used to confirm theoretical conjectures.

Flexibility. Because theories go beyond the available evidence in their explanations of behavior, subsequent research may find a theory's predictions to be incorrect or limited in some respects. Kuhn (1970) noted that theories account for data for a while, but eventually limits are reached and no new findings of consequence are reported or inexplicable results are found. When the research becomes repetitive, encounters a dead end, or results are contradictory, theories are typically modified. Alternatively, they may be replaced by a dramatically different approach in a fashion that Kuhn describes as a *scientific revolution.* For example, such a revolution occurred when Freud's psychoanalytic theory came to dominate psychi-

atry, replacing the preexisting theory that psychopathology was physically based.

Internal Consistency. A good theory is logically consistent. The conclusions drawn from one set of theoretical assumptions and propositions should not contradict the conclusions drawn from other parts of the theory. This criterion can be difficult to achieve in practice when complex human behavior is being explained. At the least, the various assumptions and predictions of a model should fit together into a coherent whole and correspond with research findings.

Testability. Some psychological theories (such as Freud's psychoanalytic theory) are not amenable to rigorous empirical testing. Nevertheless, some aspects of Freud's theory have withstood the test of time in clinical use, but in general, testable theories are preferred to ones that are not. If we cannot test predictions drawn from a theory then it cannot be scientifically verified or refuted, which ultimately brings its usefulness into question. Although children's misbehavior may be explained by appeals to superstition or demonic possession, such explanations are not scientifically useful if they are inherently untestable (see Chapter 3 for a discussion of scientific method).

Usefulness. Theories are developed in order to answer particular questions such as the origins and prediction of deviant behavior. A theory of child psychopathology should help us understand the etiology, prevention, and treatment of children's psychological problems and predict the conditions for problem occurrence. Theories that do not prove useful are ultimately replaced by those that do. In general, preferred theories stimulate the creation of new research techniques and areas of study, and they promote the discovery of new knowledge (Thomas, 1979).

In addition, theories of child psychopathology take various positions on *behavioral flexibility,* that is, whether the effects of early childhood experiences are viewed as permanent or can be overcome. Usually this refers to the importance and permanence of the mother-child bond. Theories of abnormal child behavior also differ on the *nature-nurture balance* or the relative importance of biological-genetic and social-cultural influences. Is a child difficult primarily because of his inborn negative

TABLE 2-1 EVALUATIONS OF MAJOR THEORIES OF CHILD BEHAVIOR DISTURBANCE

Theory	Criteria					
	Extensiveness	Parsimony	Empirical Validity	Internal Consistency	Testability	Usefulness
Psychoanalytic	High	Low	Debatable (see text)	Low	Low	High, as indicated by the number of clinicians using it
Skinner's learning approach	High	High	Debatable (see text)	High	Moderate to high	High, especially in clinical and educational settings
Bandura's cognitive social theory	High	High	High	High	High	High, but has been used with limited range of clinical problems thus far
Roger's theory of the person	High	High	High	High	High	High, especially in counseling and clinical psychology

temperament or because of his parents' inept discipline and hostility?

OVERVIEW OF THEORIES OF NORMAL DEVELOPMENT

It is difficult to understand pathology without some knowledge of normal development. Unfortunately, there is no single view of normal development to serve as a gauge for assessing childhood abnormalities. Rather, theories of human development vary along certain specific dimensions: (1) *Model of development.* Varying from *organismic* (in which the child is viewed as an active, highly complex, organized entity whose properties or components cannot be examined in isolation) to *mechanistic* (which systematically and painstakingly examines the effects of different stimuli and events on each type of behavior, for example, anxiety level, aggression, or perceptions of others) (Overton & Horowitz, 1991). The developmental model may be highly *genetic* and *maturational* or more *environmental*, emphasizing the role of family and other associates in the child's development. (2) *Process of development.* Is development seen as continuous, proceeding by small increments of growth, or discontinuous, as in the punctuated stages or periods of Piaget's and Freud's theories? Is change presumed to be qualitative (so the child thinks and reacts quite differently

at different points in development), as in Piaget's model, or quantitative, based more on an accumulation of experiences, as in environmental models? (3) *Influence of early experience.* Some theories view the effects of early experiences as permanent, molding one's personality from infancy or early childhood, while others allow for greater flexibility as the child grows. Do traumatic early experiences doom a child for life or can they be overcome? Psychoanalytic theories attribute great power to early experiences in determining the course of personality development, whereas Skinner's theory views behavior as powerfully controlled by present events. (4) *Child characteristics v. environmental characteristics as determiners of behavior.* Some theorists such as Freud attribute psychopathology more to the child's own nature than to external events. At the other extreme, behaviorists and learning theorists assign major importance to observable events in the child's home and school. Each of the theories reviewed here can be viewed as occupying some point on each of the preceding dimensions, as shown in Table 2-2.

Piaget's Theory of Cognitive Development

Swiss psychologist Jean Piaget's conceptualization of cognitive development is one of the most influential theories of the development of thinking, perceiving, and reasoning. After describing Piaget's theory, we will briefly

TABLE 2-2 **Comparison of Theories of Child Psychopathology**

Features	Theory				
	Freud	Erikson	Skinner	Rogers	Bandura
Studied children, not solely adults	N	Y	N	S	Y
Stages or levels	Y	Y	N	N	N
Strongly environmental	N	N	Y	S	S
Early experiences can be overcome	N	S	Y	Y	Y

N = No, S = Some or somewhat, Y = Yes.

describe its applications in education and clinical psychology. Piaget traced the transformations that take place over a lifetime, but particularly during childhood and youth, and attempted to explain how we change as we grow older, yet remain the same person.

Piaget's theory attempts to explain the general developmental sequence in thinking and problem-solving followed by all children and stimulated by children's natural curiosity about the world. In encountering a new phenomenon, children can *assimilate* the novel happening into their preexisting concepts or *schemas*, or they can adapt and *accommodate* their schemas and learn something new. Good examples of assimilation occur when children use one object in place of another in pretend play, for example, using a stick as a sword. In contrast, accommodation is most noticeable when children imitate the actions of others. Many actions contain elements of *both* assimilation (recognition) and accommodation to some new situation. New forms of thinking and behavior emerge from interactions that occur naturally within the cognitive system itself as well as from environmental stimulation (Karmiloff-Smith, 1993).

Children pass through a sequence of cognitive stages beginning in the *sensorimotor phase* when babies begin to appreciate that objects remain the same even when they are hidden briefly, change speed or direction, or undergo some other change in appearance. In the next phase of *preoperational* thought, the young child begins to use language and other symbolic processes, and then in the con-

crete operational phase, the older child begins to solve tangible or nonabstract problems such as whether a clay ball (which is shown to the child) gains or loses mass when it is reshaped to present a different visual appearance. Finally, in the mature *formal operations* phase, the young adult solves abstract problems in a systematic, logical manner.

Evaluation of Piaget's Theory. Piaget's writing is richly descriptive, containing detailed descriptions of the problem-solving behavior of individual children. At the same time, Piaget is often imprecise and difficult to understand, leading to endless debates about what he really meant (Karmiloff-Smith, 1993). Developmental stages are much less general and inclusive than Piaget originally suggested. In fact, children usually think and act in a manner representative of several different levels or stages, and not of just one (Flavell, 1963; Gelman & Baillargeon, 1983). Thus, Sally, a 5-year-old, may state rules such as that one should take turns with playthings, but be unable to recognize a "turn" when at play. Humans are capable of fine distinctions in reasoning and behavior, which brings into question the applicability of stages or well-defined periods in development.

Applications of Piaget's Work. Of all the theories described here, Piaget's has perhaps the least practical application. Piaget himself repeatedly denied any interest in educational or clinical applications of his work. Undeterred, educators applied Piaget's concepts in planning the sequence and grade placement of mathematics and science concepts in school curricula (Thomas, 1979). Child psychologists also constructed intelligence tests based on Piaget's periods or stages of development (Elkind, 1976; Phillips, 1975). In addition, Piaget's description of cognitive growth led to research showing that children with mental retardation progress through the same sequence of development, but more slowly than other children, perhaps never reaching the higher levels (Borkowski & Day, 1987).

Kohlberg's Moral Development Theory. Inspired by Piaget's work, Kohlberg (1969, 1981a) developed a detailed theory of the development of moral reasoning that has led to educational programs featuring discussions and group resolutions of moral dilemmas. Such interactions are intended to promote prosocial, mature reasoning

---

BOX 2-2 SELYE'S GENERAL ADAPTATION SYNDROME

Hans Selye led the study of stress and its effects on mind and body. In Selye's opinion, stress is produced by any severe mental or physical demand on the body, including high levels of pain, effort, concern, fatigue, concentration, or even sudden great success (Selye, 1982). Thus many different types of stressors are alike in their physiological impact. The body's initial and subsequent lines of defense against the effects of stress are termed the *general adaptation syndrome*. The first response to stress is the *alarm reaction*, a generalized mobilization of the body's defensive forces through increased activity of the cortex of the adrenal glands, decreased blood pressure, irregular heartbeat, decreased temperature, loss of weight and appetite, diminished muscular strength, and listlessness. There may be a rebound reaction featuring increased activity of the adrenal gland cortex after the initial shock. This leads to the *stage of resistance* when there is an acquired resistance to the stress and a return to normal weight. But if the extreme stress persists, adaptative resources diminish and a *stage of exhaustion* is reached as "reserves of adaptation" are exhausted.

Stress is now thought to be related to the onset and course of various physical and psychological disorders. The most common stress-related problems include some gastrointestinal illnesses, high blood pressure, cardiovascular disease, persistent anxiety, and affective (emotional) disorders such as depression. The role of stress and the general adaptation syndrome in the etiology and course of these disorders is not well understood, although it is agreed that stress alone does not account for disease. Instead problems may stem from a complex interplay of genetics, environmental factors such as infection or injury, and additional stressors at home, in school, or on the job..

SOURCES: Selye, H. (1980). The stress concept today. In I. L. Kutash, L. B. Schlesinger, & Associates (Eds.), *Handbook on stress and anxiety*. San Francisco: Jossey-Bass; Selye, H. (1982). History and present status of the stress concept. In L. Goldberger & S. Breznitz (Eds.), *Handbook of stress: Theoretical and clinical aspects*. New York: Free Press.

---

about values conflicts (Kohlberg, 1981b), although there is little research support for the effectiveness of such educational programs.

THEORIES OF CHILD PSYCHOPATHOLOGY
The Diathesis-Stress Hypothesis

Many of the theories of child psychopathology maintain that deviant behavior arises from some biological or learned predisposition that, in itself, does not produce disordered behavior. Rather, the disorder arises when the child with a predisposing condition encounters extreme or chronic stress. That is, a person may have a physical or psychological predisposition to develop a certain type of problem, but does so only under particular environmental conditions. The original vulnerability itself is insufficient to cause abnormal behavior, but the behavioral difficulties develop when the person is forced to cope with stress. This has been called the *diathesis-stress hypothesis* (or the vulnerability-stress hypothesis) because it postulates both a predisposition (diathesis) and an immediate cause (stress), which combine to produce a breakdown in psychological functioning. The diathesis could consist of some genetic disorder or maltreatment

in early childhood that makes the child particularly vulnerable to ill effects from certain stressors. The stress may be emotional (the death of a parent or rejection by a romantic partner) or physical (birth injuries, later trauma, or infections) (see Box 2-2). In either case, *both* the predisposition and the current factors combine to create psychological dysfunction.

In psychological versions of the diathesis-stress hypothesis, the predisposing factors are not physical, but result from inadequate early care and early traumatic experiences. Freud, Rogers, and many learning theorists maintain that early experiences predispose children to develop later deviant behavior. Some form of the diathesis-stress hypothesis is accepted by most authorities on psychopathology cited in this book.

Freud's Psychoanalytic Theory

Freud's is the single most influential personality theory of the 20th century, fundamentally affecting such diverse fields as psychiatry, medicine, social science, history, literature, and art. Generations of writers and practitioners have been profoundly influenced by Freud's dramatic account of human development. His work altered our views of the nature of childhood, parent-child relations, and human nature in general, introducing a model of human functioning featuring more emotional turmoil and less rational control than was previously believed. Freud's theory was predictable from his social and educational background.

Sigmund Freud (1856–1939) began his career as an obscure Viennese physician who treated people with puzzling neurological illnesses of undetermined origin including irrational fears, compulsive rituals such as repeated hand-washing, and psychologically based paralysis and numbness of the limbs. In treating these "neurotics," Freud became convinced that their symptoms derived from unconscious psychological conflicts out of their awareness and beyond their control. He concluded that human motivation is basically irrational and that people are driven by unconscious sexual and aggressive desires that are expressed indirectly and in symbolic form in dreams, speech, and play. For example, an unconscious need to punish oneself may be responsible for a person's acting so clumsily as to get caught in deceptions, having repeated accidents, or failing in school despite superior ability. In this view, nearly all behavior has a purpose and is not attributable to chance or accident.

THE STRUCTURE OF PERSONALITY

In Freud's view, personality is composed of three systems: the id, the ego, and the superego, which interact to produce normal and abnormal behavior. The first system to develop is called the *id*, a primitive component of personality. The id seeks immediate gratification of needs regardless of circumstances or of consequences to oneself or others. "It [the id] is demanding, impulsive, irrational, asocial, selfish, and pleasure-loving. It is the spoiled child of personality" (Hall, 1954, p. 21).

The immediate fulfillment of sexual and aggressive id impulses is impossible, so the *ego* develops in response to the need to operate realistically. The ego operates on the *reality principle*, taking existing constraints into account in seeking satisfaction. As the decision-making or executive branch of personality, the ego must deal with the demands of the infantile, impulsive id; it must take reality factors into account; and it must simultaneously serve a third, equally demanding system of the personality, the superego.

The *superego* represents the person's harsh, internalized moral code. It derives from the child's idea of strict, unforgiving parents and drives the person to try to meet unattainably high standards in controlling the sex and

A charming photo of Sigmund Freud and his daughter Anna in Bavarian dress. Anna applied her father's psychoanalytic concepts in her writing and clinical work, which was devoted mostly to children.

aggression instincts. Only morally perfect behavior is acceptable to the superego, which punishes the ego with guilt even for thinking about satisfying the id's demands, whether or not they are carried out.

Psychoanalysis maintains that great portions of the personality are at work outside of the individual's conscious awareness. The id, ego, and superego are all at least partly unconscious in the adult psyche, and an even larger share of the personality of the child is unconscious, and thus irrational and not under voluntary control.

ANXIETY AND THE DEFENSE MECHANISMS

Defense mechanisms represent unrealistic methods by which the ego reduces unbearable anxiety. Children tend to rely on *denial*, one of the most primitive, least realistic of the defense mechanisms, in which they simply deny the existence of unpleasant facts, such as being displaced in the parents' favor by a new sibling, and may act as though the upsetting event had never happened. Older children may use *repression*, or the forgetting or pushing from awareness, of objectionable impulses or perceptions. The impulses and thoughts still persist, but the child remains unaware of them.

Other defense mechanisms include *projection*, which is denying one's own hostile or sexual impulses but attributing them to others, and *reaction formation*, or the concealing of one type of feeling by expressing its more acceptable opposite. In reaction formation, a resentful homemaker may smotheringly overprotect her children.

In *fixation*, anxiety is relieved through the failure to progress and grow psychologically or respond flexibly. If the threat is too great, *regression* to earlier, less mature states may occur, and a child under stress might revert to a dream world with protective imaginary companions. In these and other ways (discussed by A. Freud, 1946) the child attempts to reduce the threat of utter panic stimulated by unacceptable impulses.

STAGES OF PSYCHOSEXUAL PERSONALITY DEVELOPMENT

Freud sought to explain both normal and deviant development throughout life. He believed that much of adult personality is formed during the first five years of life, when powerfully pleasant sensations are focused on different parts of the body or erogenous zones. Prior to and during weaning, the *oral* area of the mouth and lips is the major source of gratification for the infant. Either overgratification or frustration can produce a *fixation* at the oral stage that is thought to result in lifelong character traits such as dependency and could lead to later dependence on tobacco, alcohol, and other types of "oral" activity.

Next in the *anal* stage, the anal area supposedly becomes the focus of erogenous stimulation. Toilet training occurs at this time and can help determine later personality traits such as overeagerness to please others by producing products such as projects, art, or books. In contrast, frustration in the anal stage might produce a person who is compulsively neat, stingy, and unable to complete projects.

At around four or five years, the *phallic* stage begins and the child's genital area becomes the primary focus for gratification. This is the time of the crucially important *Oedipus complex* when the child is supposed to become sexually attracted to the parent of the opposite sex, much as the ancient Greek mythical hero Oedipus did to

his own mother. The little boy feels sexual rivalry toward his father and fears his father's retaliation by castration for having sexual feelings toward his mother. To relieve his anxiety, the boy is presumed to *repress* his incestuous desire for his mother and his hostility toward his father by *identifying* closely with his father and trying to be as much like him as possible. In this way, the boy reduces anxiety, possesses the mother at least vicariously through his bond with the father, and forms a masculine sexual identity. Failure to resolve the Oedipal conflict results in enduring psychological problems. Thus, even seemingly inconsequential events and minor adjustment difficulties during childhood are likely to produce lifelong problems according to Freud.

EVALUATION OF FREUD'S PSYCHOANALYTIC THEORY

Freud's theory remains perhaps the best known of all the psychological explanations of human conduct. Before Freud, most people believed that children lacked sexual interests and that adults generally behaved rationally. Moreover, as Chapter 14 describes, variants of Freud's theory guided psychiatric assessment and treatment for many decades.

Yet Freud's work has been both savagely criticized and stoutly defended. Even today, over a century after Freud's work began, debate rages over the value and validity of his contribution (examples are Crews, 1996; Grunbaum, 1984; Macmillan, 1991). Nevertheless, psychoanalytic theories are less internally consistent, more complex, and less parsimonious than competing theories. Critics complain about the lack of rigorous research testing of psychoanalytic propositions. Crews (1996) has termed Freud's theory pseudoscience, complaining that it lacks independent confirmation and instead relies on other aspects of the same theory, such as Freudian dream interpretation, for supposed verification. In addition, critics charge that the theory is too vague and inconsistent to be testable, and that proponents rely too much on Freud's personal authority and clinical experience for support of the theory itself (Crews, 1996; Macmillan, 1991). Opponents question the validity of scientifically uncontrolled and subjective investigative procedures. Other psychoanalysts, such as the ego theorists discussed next, regret the emphasis on sex and aggression in Freud's theory of personality development; they suggest devoting greater attention to the less-conflicted and more rational aspects of the psyche.

Erikson's Psychoanalytic Ego Theory

Unlike Freud, Erikson wrote about the development of the healthy personality in the broader culture. Erikson pursued the theme of *ego identity* or the individual's healthy solution of identity crises associated with each psychosocial stage of growth. The individual's interaction with the social environment results in a progression of eight major psychosocial crises, each of which must be worked through in order to achieve psychological health (ego identity). These psychosocial crises are presented in Table 2-3.

Some of Erikson's psychosocial stages resemble Freud's stages, at least in their ages of occurrence, while others do not, and Erikson's stages extend into old age. Although the stages are labeled as though the alternatives are absolute opposites (e.g., industry v. inferiority), Erikson believed that most individual's adjustment lies somewhere between the opposite poles of each scale. Thus, we all have some trust of others and some mistrust. The mother's handling of the feeding situation can determine how trusting the infant will be, and her mishandling can lead the baby to be wary permanently. Autonomy v. shame and doubt surround toilet training and the child's growing sense of independence. Good experiences lead to self-control and high self-esteem and bad ones to problems such as compulsivity, stinginess, low self-esteem, and hostility. Next comes the time of the Oedipal conflict, then the "latency" years prior to puberty, when parents can help the child realize his abilities through industry. In early adolescence, the child faces an *identity crisis* (Erikson, 1968) because physical changes and new role expectations can lead to confusion about who one is or should be. Successful resolution of this crisis produces a strong sense of one's own individuality and comfort with one's place in society.

Erikson's view is that the sequence and general timing of these psychosocial stages are genetically determined, but how a psychosocial crisis is resolved largely depends on the way the person interacts with cultural social institutions. Unfortunately, although Erikson's theory is more positive and social in orientation, it is scarcely more clearly focused and scientifically verifiable than Freud's

(Thomas, 1979). On this criterion, all psychoanalytic theories fail.

Object Relations Theory

Freud's influence on clinicians and researchers lives on, most recently in a psychoanalytic approach termed *object relations theory* (Cashdan, 1988). The term object relations actually refers to human social relations. Object relations theory stresses the lasting importance of interpersonal relationships with important others, particularly the quality of the young child's relationship with the mother. From this important early social tie, the child forms stable, internalized self-expectations and beliefs about other people. In the infant's cognitively unsophisticated world, people and experiences consist of *bipolar representations* that are either good or bad, positive or negative, (Kernberg, 1984). If the infant's mother is warm and sensitive and their relationship is satisfying, the infant forms a lasting internal working model featuring positive expectations of the self and the mother. The infant's emotional attachment to the mother is said to be secure, with the mother affording her child a safe emotional base from which to explore the world (Ainsworth et al., 1978).

Psychological problems arise if the mother is rejecting, self-preoccupied, or highly stressed and consequently insensitive to her child. Basically, the object relations view is that the child comes to imitate and *identify* with the mother, father, and other important caretakers. The child begins to view and treat herself or himself as these close people do (*introjection*). The child even adopts the conversational dialogue and assessments made by these others, calling herself or himself dumb or smart, good or bad as a parent did. The child reacts as though the attachment object was present (*internalization*), so a protected child becomes generally trusting with people, even when it is inappropriate. In this way the child develops a general sense of high or low self-esteem, which may persist and be resistant to later influences.

The person who was emotionally abandoned as a child, although physically cared for, is deprived of the means to develop a stable, healthy sense of self-identity. Other children may internalize conflict and power struggles with a hostile, dominating parent, and may adopt maladaptive expectations and modes of interacting with others throughout life (Benjamin, 1994). In Benjamin's

TABLE 2-3 Erikson's Psychosocial Stages

Stage Name	Age	Description
Autonomy versus shame and doubt	Infant	The infant learns to trust or mistrust the mother and others.
Initiative versus guilt	Years 3–5	At the time of toilet training, the child learns independence, self-control, and self-esteem or hostility, compulsivity, and low self-esteem.
Industry versus inferiority	Before puberty	At the resolution of the Oedipal conflict, the child develops initiative and competency or guilt and inability to function. The child realizes his abilities through work or sloth and inferiority.
Identity versus role diffusion	Adolescence	The adolescent's successful resolution of the identity crisis yields comfort and good adjustment or the opposite.
Intimacy versus isolation	Young adulthood	The young adult chooses between love and marriage or loneliness.
Generativity versus stagnation	Maturity	The adult chooses children and interests in others or selfish self-interest.
Integrity versus despair	Old age	The elderly person feels pride in her life or despair.

Source: E. H. Erikson. (1963). *Childhood and society* (2nd ed.). New York: Norton.

view, IPIRs, or Important People and Their Internalized Representations, affect an individual's adjustment. People tend to act toward others as their attachment objects (usually parents) acted toward them, and treat themselves similarly to the way they were treated by their parents, whether good or bad.

Benjamin's model of interpersonal functioning describes complementary roles played by parents and children or other pairs of interactants such as therapists and clients. For example, a mother who is nurturing and protecting would be likely to have a child who is trusting and relying. Or a mother who engages in much independence granting and forgetting will have a child who is assertive and separate.

Parent-child interaction patterns tend to become progressively more stable and predictable as children approach adolescence (Benjamin, 1974). The principle of *similarity* holds that children identify with their parents and eventually show the same behavior patterns as their parents. This implies that a boy with a hostile, controlling parent may develop into a man who callously aims to control others with utter disregard for their feelings or welfare. Because parent and child behaviors are so often complementary, it is often impossible to say whether the parent's behavior is influencing the child or vice versa. Rather, this object relations approach stresses that one particular type of behavior naturally stimulates certain complementary types of responses from the partner.

The interpersonal theory model, which is gaining popularity and research support, focuses on the lasting heritage of the distribution of power, autonomy, affection, and hostility in the important, intimate relationships of early childhood. This approach is new and research evaluations are just beginning. Researchers have reported that Benjamin's work is useful in understanding the dynamics of therapist-client interactions, marital relations, and mother-child interactions involving depressed and well mothers (Benjamin, 1994; Henry, Schacht, & Strupp, 1986; Teti, Heaton, Benjamin, & Gelfand, 1995).

Attachment Theory

An allied approach, *attachment theory*, stresses the importance of the security of the child's early emotional attachments to mother and other major caretakers (termed *attachment figures*) as a basis for normal psychological development (Ainsworth et al., 1978; Bowlby, 1969). Like psychodynamic theory, attachment theory is based on the belief that early life experiences strongly influence adult functioning and vulnerability to psychopathology (Paterson & Moran, 1988). The establishment of the child's trust in a warm, sensitive attachment figure (usually initially the mother) sets the stage for normal social development throughout the formative years. From experiencing many interactions with the mother, the baby forms *internal working models* of the roles played by the mother and the self. That is, the infant internalizes the mother's reactions as a prototype of the assumptions and beliefs about how others will behave, whether warm and caring or rejecting and possibly violent. The relationship to the mother becomes crucial when the baby encounters threat or danger and must command the parent's protection (*safe base behavior*). The infant's social life is marked by the search for balance between exploration and independence, and comfort and safety in the protective presence of a caretaker or attachment figure.

Beliefs about oneself also stem from early interactions with the mother, so the child may view himself as worthy or unworthy of others' affection based on his perceptions of his mother. A warm, responsive caretaker facilitates a *secure attachment* and positive internal working models, while a rejecting, ambivalent, or neglectful one produces a child who is insecurely attached and either indifferent to the mother, ambivalent, or avoidant. The quality of the developing child's attachment to major caretakers may change over time, but is more often set early in life. A child who has formed an insecure attachment may become generally distrustful of others, socially maladjusted, and unable to achieve independence, although there is still insufficient evidence regarding the link between early insecure attachment and later psychopathology (Cicchetti, Toth, & Lynch, 1995).

THE DEVELOPMENTAL PSYCHOPATHOLOGY APPROACH

In recent years, the *developmental psychopathology* movement (Cichetti, 1984; Cicchetti et al., 1995; Sroufe & Rutter, 1984) has incorporated developmental principles such as Piaget's sequences of development in reasoning and thinking into the study of child psychopathology. Developmental psychopathology aims for a comprehensive understanding of the origins, maintenance, and change of adaptational problems in individual children as they grow and develop. The approach seeks to understand the child by measuring the effects of *all* developmental influences including genetic, evolutionary, cognitive, emotional, biochemical, and social factors (Achenbach, 1991; Rolf & Read, 1984). Rather than concentrating on either environmental or biological-physiological factors in development, developmental psychopathology aims to incorporate an understanding of both sets of influences as they interact to promote or impede normal development (Sroufe & Rutter, 1984). The ultimate goal is accurate prediction of long-range outcomes from the study of early experiences and ad-

justment status. Developmental psychopathology seeks answers to questions such as: How does infant insecure attachment affect the person's adjustment at later periods such as at preschool, elementary and high school, and adult periods? and does difficult infant temperament predict later adjustment? Developmental psychopathologists have advocated a wide-ranging, interdisciplinary study of the etiology and course of individual patterns of behavior adaptation related to problems such as mental retardation, autism, externalizing or aggressive behavior, and hyperactivity (described in the series of volumes of the *Rochester Symposium on Developmental Psychopathology* and published by the University of Rochester Press). This approach incorporates the developmental theory of Piaget and contributions from ethology, developmental neurology, and physiology, emphasizing that the developing child cannot be understood or long-term predictions made without an understanding of all aspects of physical and psychosocial functioning.

Learning and Social Theories

During the 1930s and 1940s, American social scientists such as Robert Sears, John Dollard, and Neal Miller attempted to unite psychoanalytic and learning concepts into a more comprehensive account of human development. This approach was fruitfully pursued for a number of years, but psychoanalytic explanations remained extremely difficult to translate into testable propositions and the research results were often unsupportive (Chaplin & Krawiec, 1979). Predictably, a scientific revolution ensued, producing dramatically different learning and personality theories. One of these was B. F. Skinner's operant conditioning approach (see Box 2-3).

SKINNER'S OPERANT CONDITIONING

Skinner's primary goal was to understand behavior of all types and in all its richness (Holland, 1992). To do so, he insisted on the detailed, direct observation, in a controlled laboratory environment, of causal relations between the presentation of various stimuli and the occurrence of particular responses. From controlled studies of learning by laboratory animals, he derived general principles of behavior that could apply to all species. In his novel, *Walden Two*, he even envisioned a Utopian society

---

BOX 2-3   ABOUT B. F. SKINNER

As a boy, B. F. Skinner (1904–1990) was fascinated by mechanical devices. To teach himself to hang up his pajamas, Skinner constructed a string-and-pulley system extending from his pajama hook to a sign reading, "Hang up your pajamas!" When the pajamas were left off the hook, the sign was automatically lowered into the middle of his door frame as a reminder. Later his continuing interest in building things led Skinner to design a light-and-sound-controlled chamber for experiments with small animals, teaching machines for classroom use, and an improved crib (the Aircrib), which maintains a comfortable temperature for a lightly clad baby.

He had initially hoped to become a writer, but when the goal eluded him, Skinner entered Harvard's graduate school in psychology. He was later to combine his interest in literature with his scientific work in writing the novel *Walden Two* (1948), which presents Skinner's vision of an ideal society run on learning principles. Skinner's writing skills are immediately evident in his forceful and persuasive books.

Skinner published a two-volume autobiography, *Particulars of My Life* (1976) and *The Shaping of a Behaviorist* (1979), and a highly controversial book, *Beyond Freedom and Dignity* (1971), in which he argued that freedom is an illusion and human behavior is controlled by environmental factors. The achievement of humane goals, he contended, is more likely through the development of planned societies run on behavioral principles than through the absence of planning for fear of loss of freedom. There is no more controversial or better known contemporary psychologist than B. F. Skinner. He offered a complete, consistent, and unflattering view of human behavior—a view that may be rejected, but cannot be ignored.

SOURCE: B F. Skinner. (1967). In E. G Boring and G. Lindzey (Eds.), *A history of psychology in autobiography* (Vol. 5). New York: Appleton-Century-Crofts.

---

in which people's lives were completely managed by enlightened leaders according to Skinnerian principles. Skinner was as optimistic as Freud was negative about the prospects for improving human behavior:

> If we are to use the methods of science in the field of human affairs, we must assume that behavior is lawful and determined. We must expect to discover that what a man does is the result of specifiable conditions and that once these conditions have been discovered, we can anticipate and to some extent determine his actions. (Skinner, 1953, p. 6)

In pursuit of this vision, Skinner and his many followers pursued the *experimental analysis of behavior* or the discovery of the lawful effect of observable environmental events on precisely defined and measured behaviors.

His work with animals earned him the derision of many people who could not see how studies of pigeons pecking keys or rats pressing bars could possibly apply to complex human behavior. Nevertheless, from this laboratory experimentation, Skinner formulated a set of powerful behavior principles concerning the effects of various schedules of reinforcement (immediate response consequences that affect behavior rates) on the frequency of any voluntary or purposefully performed behavior. According to Skinner, simple procedures such as reinforcing

a rat's bar-pressing with food have counterparts in complex human behavior such as making a speech praising a leader or rescuing a child from a burning building. Skinner maintained that principles derived from the animal laboratory apply to behavior generally and can be used to explain human thinking, language, classroom learning, and the development of behavior disorders.

Conditioning Procedures. Skinner maintained that the two basic types of learning are operant and respondent conditioning. Skinner devoted most of his attention to operant conditioning, which involves behaviors that are called voluntary and are emitted purposefully. In contrast, *respondent conditioning* typically involves automatic physiological reflexes such as salivation, release of gastric juices, blood pressure, breathing, or heart beat.

Here we concentrate on the analysis of operant behavior. Most human social and intellectual behavior is operant (can be engaged in purposely) rather than reflexive. *Operant behavior alters or operates on the physical or social environment in some way.* Operant behavior is controlled by the events that *follow* it. Examples of operant behavior include actions such as gesturing, walking, dancing, marching, and reading, as well as speaking, singing, aiding, hitting, and a host of other purposeful behaviors.

Operant acts that produce *reinforcing consequences* become more likely to be repeated in similar circumstances in the future (*operant conditioning*). Any event that strengthens a preceding response or makes it more likely to recur is a reinforcer, no matter whether it appears unpleasant or pleasant to an observer. What is reinforcing for a person at one time may not be so at another time and what one person finds reinforcing might be ineffective or even aversive for another. The identification of reinforcers is a purely empirical, observational search to find something that is effective for a particular person at a particular time and place. Some *generalized reinforcers* such as money and praise are widely effective and are often used with groups of children in classroom and treatment settings. However, even these stimuli aren't invariably reinforcing, since praise from the wrong people or delivered at the wrong time can be repugnant. Perversely, some children find adults' scolding to have reinforcing properties, simply because it brings attention to the child. This means that scolding can and often does unintentionally increase the rate of the child's misbehavior.

Operantly conditioned deviant behavior can be eliminated through *extinction* in which customary reinforcement is systematically withheld for a prolonged period. For example, parents may completely stop responding to their 5-year-old daughter when she whines for candy and praise her warmly when she speaks in a more age-appropriate fashion. Attempts at extinction may be unsuccessful if the behavior receives even occasional or intermittent reinforcement, which is often the case. Human violent or bizarre psychotic behavior that has been maintained by very occasional intermittent reinforcement may be highly resistant to extinction.

Punishment and Negative Reinforcement.

Much human misery arises from punishment and negative reinforcement, two procedures that differ but are often confused. *Negative reinforcement* increases the rate of the behavior it follows exactly as positive reinforcement does. In negative reinforcement, the operant behavior is repeated because it *removes* an aversive stimulus. For example, when Mark turns up the volume on his stereo, the noise is an aversive stimulus for his parents. His father may get angry and begin to shout at Mark to turn it off or have it taken away. Then Mark turns down the volume. This is an example of negative reinforcement, for his turning down

the volume is negatively reinforced by his father's no longer yelling and threatening him. Similarly, the father's shouting is negatively reinforced because his shouting reduces the unpleasantly loud teenage music. In contrast, *punishment* is the delivery of an aversive stimulus following some action, which reduces the future probability of that action. If the father in our example abandons shouting and smashes his son's boom box or deprives him of the use of the car, he would be using punishment.

Skinner deplored the cruelty of punishment and noted its unpredictable effects. The punished child might obey, resist, or ignore the punishment and does not learn what to do, but only what not to do. Despite widespread criticism of his cool, scientific approach to human problems, Skinner consistently maintained that punishment is used much too freely and is often ineffective in deterring people from misbehaving. On the contrary, punishment creates resentment and invites retaliation.

Evaluation of Skinner's Psychology.

B. F. Skinner was perhaps the most controversial psychologist of our time. Revered by many as a distinguished scientist and visionary, he was reviled by others as unfeeling, mechanistic, and naive. Whatever his ultimate place in the history of psychology, Skinner has had tremendous influence in the fields of education, childrearing, rehabilitation, and the treatment of disordered behavior. Many of the behavior therapy procedures discussed in Chapter 14 and elsewhere in this book stem directly from Skinner's work. He aimed to improve human life in as many ways as possible (see Tables 2-1 and 2-2), and he has propounded one of the most focused, general, easily understood, and parsimonious explanations of behavior. Skinner proposed a limited number of well-defined, demonstrably powerful mechanisms to account for a wide range of abnormal and normal behavior across species.

The Skinnerian explanation for less easily observed and quantified human skills such as language, memory, and thinking seems labored, clumsy, and unconvincing. Critics such as linguist Noam Chomsky (1959) contend that in dealing with topics such as language, Skinner has been vague and imprecise and that one cannot meaningfully speak of simple stimuli and responses in analyzing complex grammatical structures. Other psychologists have criticized Skinner's portrayals of conditioning as being vastly oversimplified and as ignoring the innate abilities and propensities of humans and other species (e.g.,

Rescorla, 1988). Skinner's proponents have heatedly replied that Skinner's writings have been misrepresented and his approach accounts better for complex human behavior than do rival cognitive and psychodynamic models (Schlinger, 1992; Todd & Morris, 1992). Ironically, it has been in the treatment of the complex and ill-understood syndrome of infantile autism that Skinner's work has seen its most impressive application (see Chapters 11 and 14). Skinnerian psychologists, who term themselves applied behavior analysts, have made great strides in the treatment of persons with mental retardation, autistic or psychotic disorders, conduct disorders or antisocial personality disorder, and those with physical disabilities. The approach requires highly trained, closely supervised caretakers working with the more seriously disturbed children continuously for prolonged time periods. Skinner's work has been highly generative in inspiring others to extend or to attempt to discredit his efforts.

BANDURA'S SOCIAL COGNITIVE THEORY

To what extent can people control their own behavior and determine their lives? Social cognitive theory (also called social learning theory) holds that humans' impressive mental abilities allow us to exert a significant amount of control over our own conduct regardless of even powerful external influences. An individual's *interpretation* of an event is the chief determinant of that person's reaction. For example, a student can consider being called on to answer a question in class a welcome opportunity to excel, a matter of little importance, or a resented public humiliation. The social cognitive or social learning position maintains that taking such cognitive processes into account should improve prediction of people's behavior far beyond the level possible from knowledge of external events alone. This emphasis on reasoning and interpretation has led Mischel (1993) and Bandura to stress the roles of both cognitive and social influences in their conceptualizations of human behavior. The theory is considered to be social because of its focus on interpersonal influences in the development of aggressive and prosocial (helpful) behavior, sex typing, observational learning, and self-regulation. Unlike psychoanalytic approaches, cognitive social accounts avoid the use of trait concepts that imply high consistency and generality of responding (e.g., hostility, dependence, conscientiousness). Like the Skinnerians, the social cognitive

Albert Bandura. His view that people initiate actions as well as being acted upon by their environment has changed psychology in the United States. He believes that one of the strongest determinants of behavior is a person's self-perception.

theorists have emphasized the impact of *current* life events in directing behavior (Mischel, 1976). As people and circumstances change, the person's behavioral responses change. Consequently, most people alter their behavior depending upon their companions, resources, current psychological state, and the provocation present.

Mischel and colleagues (e.g., Shoda, Mischel, & Peake, 1993) studied children throughout their stay in a residential summer camp, and found that individual children responded distinctively and consistently to particular types of interpersonal situations such as being teased by peers or speaking before a group. However, the same child who usually responded to teasing by crying and withdrawing might aggressively defend a younger child who was being teased. The child interpreted the two types of teasing situations differently and behaved in very different ways in the two types of settings. A person's own *interpretations, skills,* and *competencies* importantly affect attitudes and actions, but behavior is determined by *current* factors more than by early childhood experiences as psychoanalytic theory maintains.

BOX 2-4   ABOUT ALBERT BANDURA

Albert Bandura was born in 1925 in a small town in northern Alberta. After completing his earlier education in the only school in town, and before entering college, Bandura worked on a road crew repairing the Alaska highway. As he described it in a personal communication, "Finding himself in the midst of a curious collection of characters, most of whom had fled creditors, alimony, and probation officers, [Bandura] quickly developed a keen appreciation for the psychopathy of everyday life, which seemed to blossom in the austere tundra."

After graduating from the University of British Columbia, Bandura earned his Ph.D. in clinical psychology from the University of Iowa, where the psychology program was extremely research-oriented. At that time, the Iowa psychology department was predominantly influenced by the learning theories of Hull and Spencer, which caused Bandura to become interested in the application of learning concepts to clinical problems.

Both a clinician and a researcher by training, Bandura has taught at Stanford University for many years. Now David Starr Jordan Professor of Social Science, Bandura is a major social learning theorist. He has stressed the importance of observational learning in normal and atypical human development, and has made important contributions to the study of imitation, aggression, human development, behavior problems, behavior therapy, and the application of psychological concepts to the solution of social problems. Bandura's awards and honors include election to the presidency of the American Psychological Association, and he has received that group's Distinguished Scientific Contribution Award. True to his scientific beliefs, Bandura has served as an exemplary model of ethical and scientific excellence. He has influenced contemporary psychology as much as any living person and is today's most often cited psychologist in the world.

SOURCES: A. Bandura. (1980, September 9). Personal communication. Awards for distinguished scientific contributions: 1980. (1981). *American Psychologist, 36,* 27–34.

There have been many major contributors to the social learning viewpoint (e.g., Miller & Dollard, 1941; Rotter, 1954; Mischel, 1968), but at present the best known and most comprehensive account is that of Albert Bandura. Bandura (see Box 2-4) believes that most human behavior involves thinking, interpretation, and self-regulation rather than simple conditioning. Bandura and Walters (1963) pointed out that humans are remarkably adept at *observational learning* (also called imitation, modeling, and vicarious learning). When we teach a child to speak, we do not go through a laborious shaping process of waiting until the infant happens upon each correct sound and then administering reinforcement. That would take forever. Instead the child simply listens to people speaking around her and imitates their language as best she can. Some praise may be used to inform the child that her speech is correct, but external reward is largely unnecessary. Many key skills are acquired though imitation alone.

Children imitate only some of the behavioral sequences available to them. Bandura (1977b) described the factors that determine whether observers imitate a model. These steps include:

1. Attending to the model's demonstration. Of course, inattention deprives an observer of crucial information on how to act.

2. Mentally encoding and remembering the behavior. A faulty memory of what was done would prevent its emulation, so an observer must take care to encode the action vividly and accurately.

3. Possessing the skills to perform the necessary behaviors. One must have the requisite athletic, musical, educational, or social skills in order to imitate the model.

4. Being motivated to imitate the model. That is, the observer must anticipate positive consequences for repeating the behavior if imitation is to take place.

All steps must be successfully completed or the observer will fail to imitate the model.

Causes of Deviant Behavior. Like Skinner, Bandura believes that both normal and deviant behavior develop from the same general processes. Note that social influences are not one-way, but that people continuously influence each other. There are a number of ways in which faulty social learning could result in behavior problems (Bandura, 1968, 1969):

1. *Exposure to socially deviant models* could teach the child inappropriate forms of behavior. Such deviant models could be found in homes with addicted, depressed, schizophrenic, or bizarre and fanatically religious parents or in delinquent gangs.

2. *Insufficient reinforcement* could lead to extinction of appropriate behaviors as in the case of hostile or dangerously neglectful parents failing to reinforce a child's appropriate behavior.

3. *Inappropriate reinforcement or reinforcement of undesirable behavior* can promote problem behavior. Delinquent subcultures may differentially reinforce youths' cruel and violent acts, as shown by the remarks of a juvenile gang member about a murder in which he was involved: "If I would have got the knife, I would have stabbed him. That would have gave me more of a buildup. People would have respected me for what I've done and things like that. They would say, 'there goes a cold killer'" (Yablonsky, 1962, p. 8).

This is a chilling example of the effects of social reinforcement of violence by a deviant group. Inappropriate reinforcement can also take the form of parental inconsistency. Parents can bewilder a child by violently punishing him for talking back to them on one occasion, ignoring him for the same behavior at other times, and then later praising him for sticking up for himself. The unpredictably treated child might come to behave erratically and perhaps violently because of his parents' inappropriate reinforcement and deviant modeling.

4. *Faulty learning* of negative emotional states can derive from experiencing fear and anxiety either directly or vicariously from observing another person. The child might develop a persistent fear of doctors through being hurt while at the doctor's office or might be alarmed by observing a parent terrified at the thought of going to the doctor.

5. *Fictional reinforcement contingencies* (Skinner's superstitious behavior) can exert great control over some people's behavior. Confused beliefs that household objects are dangerously contaminated by dirt can lead to compulsive cleaning and handwashing rituals, and many other irrational beliefs may be acquired through the teachings of other people or may be self-generated. These fictional reinforcement contingencies can be even more powerful than real ones.

6. *Faulty self-reinforcement* can occur when people hold themselves to overly strict or too-generous standards. Some people maintain such exalted standards for themselves that success is impossible so they eventually cease trying (Bandura, 1979). Others are content with nearly anything they do. Self-standards are learned from others through modeling and instruction from parents or teachers. Inappropriately demanding or highly permissive families and schools can instill unrealistic expectations and deviant self-reinforcement practices.

Self-Efficacy Theory. Bandura's (1981, 1995) self-efficacy theory attempts to explain the mutual interacting influences of people's self-perceptions and their behavior. *Self-efficacy* is belief in oneself, a personal conviction that one can achieve a positive outcome through effort and persistence. People high in self-efficacy are convinced of their own problem-solving effectiveness; those who are low in self-efficacy believe that their efforts are doomed to failure. Self-efficacy convictions can prove self-fulfilling. People who have failed repeatedly in certain situations begin to believe that they can never succeed at those types of tasks. Their pessimism leads them to avoid such situations and to dread them. Their fear and avoidance further handicaps these people when they are forced to act. Consider the aspiring scholar who is so terrified of failure and unconvinced of his own ability that he cannot think clearly while taking an achievement test and decides just to answer at random. Lack of self-efficacy interferes with many types of skilled performance.

Appropriate psychological treatment can break the sequence of negative emotion and inadequate performance in several ways. The client's self-evaluation could be improved through positive self-talk, so he learns and practices confident statements (I'm smart; I can do this.) in formerly avoided situations. His confidence leads to vigorous, persistent, and probably more successful attempts to cope with the problem. Success increases his perceived self-effectiveness even further, creating a positive cycle of optimistic beliefs and effective behavior, as shown in Figure 2-1.

A person's faulty self-perceptions can be improved in several different ways, each varying in probable effectiveness. These include *performance accomplishment*, or actually succeeding at some difficult task. Success heightens expectations for future victories. For example, the snake phobic person who manages to touch a snake, the shy student who asks several reasonable questions in class, the fearful toddler who manages to go to sleep without a

FIGURE 2-1 ◆Bandura's explanation of the mutual influences of self-efficacy beliefs and performance effectiveness before and after successful psychological treatment.

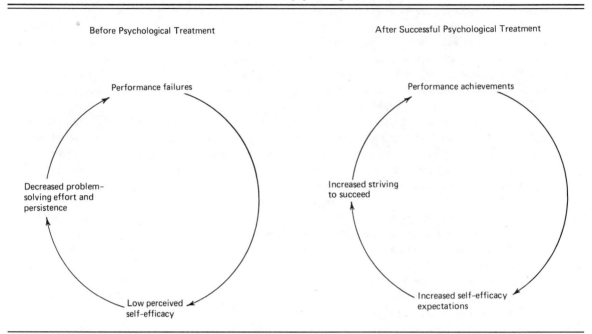

Before Psychological Treatment

Performance failures

Decreased problem-solving effort and persistence

Low perceived self-efficacy

After Successful Psychological Treatment

Performance achievements

Increased striving to succeed

Increased self-efficacy expectations

night-light all have learned that they have the resolve and competence to perform a challenging task. Such success is the most potent and convincing source of increased self-confidence.

Other sources of information also may be helpful at times. Observing others succeed (*vicarious success*) can also boost insecure observers' self-confidence, but not as much as does experiencing one's own success. The other person could be perceived as unusually brave, skillful, or lucky, none of which might apply to the hapless observer. People who have had problems tend to doubt their own skills until they have actually succeeded in performing a difficult task.

Many forms of instruction and psychotherapy rely on *verbal persuasion*, an even less-convincing source of self-efficacy expectations than the preceding ones. Readers probably have had the experience of attempting to convince a reluctant friend to engage in some feared activity or have received such advice themselves. An even more formidable challenge is to try to convince a truly depressed person to cheer up. It doesn't work very well in most cases. If only verbal persuasion and enthusiastic encouragement are used and the recipient ineffectually tries

but fails to perform the task, then the situation is worse than ever.

Finally, the person's own *emotional arousal state* can increase or undermine her expectations of success. The child who observes herself tremble at the thought of going to school may be negatively affected by her own nervousness and less able to approach the school than a less shaky student. In observing our own emotional states, we reach conclusions about our own probable effectiveness. Extreme anxiety can interfere with many types of performance, whether in the form of stage fright, social anxieties, writer's block, or inhibited athletic performance. Anxiety reduction through relaxation training, tranquilizing drugs, or social support can bolster self-confidence and increase the chances of success.

Evaluation of Cognitive Social Approaches. Cognitive social theory has practical utility, making it popular among experimentally oriented clinicians and developmentalists. The cognitive social approach offers explanations for the source and maintenance of both normal and abnormal behavior and has yielded some effective treatments (see Table 2–1 and Chapter 14). Many research studies demonstrate the usefulness of social learning formulations. In their influential textbook on theories of learning, Hilgard and Bower concluded: "In broad outline, social learning theory provides the best integrative summary of what modern learning theory has to contribute to solutions of practical problems" (1975, p. 605). But some critics have pointed out that most of the supportive evidence comes from highly controlled, artificial laboratory studies rather than from confirming observations of everyday life (Stevenson, 1983). The degree of correspondence between laboratory and naturalistic study findings may be high, but is not perfect, leaving the theory's validity in some doubt. Mischel's current attempt to study children's behavior patterns in natural settings such as a summer camp responds to the criticism of artificiality of laboratory experiments in the cognitive social tradition. Moreover, all of the theories we consider are difficult to validate. Many approaches are carefully devised and intuitively appealing, but may not be valid models of human development and psychopathology.

Social cognitive theory is adequately internally consistent and it is comprehensive. It draws together cognitive psychology, social-psychological concepts, and learning phenomena in the explanation of normal and deviant behavior. Some Skinnerians have charged that it is too broad, ambitious, vague, and loosely conceptualized (Biglan & Kass, 1977). Biglan and Kass (1977) suggested that it would be safer and more conservative to refer to the specific procedures used (e.g., expectancy ratings or experimental instructions) and to the behaviors they affect (e.g., approaching a feared object) rather than to a less precise concept such as expectancy. In defense of the social learning position, Auch (1976) asserted that it is logically consistent to maintain that both external and internal variables affect behavior. Both Skinner's and cognitive social theories are useful in predicting and controlling behavior. It is not yet clear which is superior in this respect. At this time, the Skinnerian conceptual model appears to have reached maturity and is stimulating few new, testable ideas (Stevenson, 1983). In contrast, the cognitive social approach has proved flexible in incorporating concepts from other branches of psychology and in stimulating new ideas and a healthy degree of controversy. But new approaches continue to arise. Within developmental psychology, attachment theory is attracting great interest and stimulating much research, while the object relations and interpersonal approaches are becoming increasingly popular with clinicians.

Humanistic Psychology and Rogers' Theory of the Person

Human nature is at worst morally neutral and very probably positively good. This benign tenet of humanistic psychology contrasts sharply with Freud's pessimistic view of human motivation and the behaviorists' neutrality, which stresses that a person can learn to be either good or bad.

According to the humanistic psychologists, humans have powerful *self-actualization* needs for continuing individual growth, greater ability to experience feelings, and accomplishing something in which one believes (Buhler & Allen, 1972). When these needs are blocked by circumstances, psychological growth ceases. The ultimate evil is deviance from the pursuit of one's potential and one's own nature. Carl Rogers is one of the most prominent humanistic psychologists, and this section will feature his theory of the person.

Rogers (see Box 2-5) firmly believes that people strive toward growth and self-actualization. His theory is *humanistic* since it is concerned chiefly with human experience and the fulfillment of human potential. It is *phenomenological* because it studies conscious experience including beliefs, values, feelings, and perceptions. People's perceptions of events (subjective reality) rather than the events themselves (objective reality) are the subject matter for the phenomenologist. The somewhat related *existentialist* view of philosophers such as Kierkegaard, Camus, and Sartre and psychological writers such as May and Binswanger pictures humans as capable of making choices and assuming responsibility for their own destinies, even in the most restrictive environments. These conceptual roots quite naturally lead to reliance on self-report for understanding the person. This emphasis on exploring conscious self-awareness contrasts with the psychoanalysts' focus on unconscious processes and with the behaviorists' concentration on environmental factors as determining behavior.

THE FULLY FUNCTIONING PERSON

Rogers based his person-centered theory on many years of clinical work with troubled people. As his clients improved, Rogers noted that they went from discontent

---

BOX 2-5   ABOUT CARL ROGERS

Of himself, Carl Rogers wrote:

> I am a psychologist; a clinical psychologist, I believe, a humanistically oriented psychologist certainly; a psychotherapist, deeply interested in the dynamics of personality change; a scientist, to the limit of my ability investigating such change; an educator, challenged by the possibility of facilitating learning; a philosopher in a limited way, especially in relation to the philosophy of science and the philosophy and psychology of human values. (1967, p. 343)

A recipient of the American Psychological Association's awards for distinguished scientific contribution and for distinguished clinical contribution, Rogers was one of the first psychotherapists to devise and conduct carefully controlled research investigating the process and outcomes of therapy. Rogers began his career as a graduate student at Union Theological Seminary because he was interested in going into religious work. However, religious doubts coupled with his lifelong commitment to individual freedom of thought made it impossible for him to profess a required set of beliefs in order to pursue a career in religion. Consequently, he entered the clinical and educational graduate program at Teachers College, Columbia University, where he studied methods of research and applied psychology. He earned a Ph.D. in 1931, then worked with abused and delinquent children several years before commencing his university teaching career. After many years as a professor at various universities, Rogers gave up traditional teaching because he believed that many faculty members held unduly rigid and punitive attitudes concerning graduate education. In contrast, Rogers maintained that courses should be student-centered and largely student-directed.

In recent years Rogers has continued to write his challenging and influential books and has served first as a Visiting Fellow and then as a permanent staff member at the Western Behavioral Sciences Institute, a center for interdisciplinary research in interpersonal relationships. Throughout his professional life, Carl Rogers has stressed the importance of warmth, genuineness, and concern for others, a set of values that, if adopted widely, would surely improve our lives.

SOURCE: C. R. Rogers. (1967). In E. G. Boring and G. Lindzey (Eds.), *A history of psychology in autobiography* (Vol. 5). New York: Appleton-Century-Crofts.

---

with themselves to self-satisfaction and decreased discrepancy between their self-concepts and the type of person they wished to be. They saw themselves as coming closer to their ideal selves, and in so doing they became less defensive, more accurate in their perceptions of self and others, and their relationships with other people improved. Most important, the clients became more open to their own feelings of all types. Rogers described this transformation as follows:

> "... [the client] becomes acquainted with elements of his experience which have in the past been denied to awareness as too threatening, too damaging, to the structure of the self. He finds himself experiencing these feelings fully, completely, in the relationship, so that for the moment he is his fear, or his anger, or his tenderness, or his strength. And as he lives these widely varied feelings in all their degrees of intensity, he discovers that he has experienced himself, that he is all these feelings ... He approaches the realization that he no longer needs to fear what experience may hold, but can welcome it freely as a part of his changing and developing self." (Rogers, 1961, p. 185)

The well-adjusted person accepts others as well as accepting himself, and so social adjustment improves as inner turmoil decreases.

Origin and Management of Children's Problems. From Rogers' perspective. when the child's parents find some aspects of her behavior unacceptable, then the child may come to share her parents' disapproval. To ensure her acceptance, the child may deny her own socially dangerous feelings such as hostility toward siblings. She may demand irreproachable behavior of herself as a *condition of worth*, just as her parents did. She denies her hostility and projects it onto others, treating them as though they were threatening, thus creating interpersonal problems.

To improve, the child should experience *unconditional positive regard* or whole-hearted and complete acceptance just as she is. Parents and therapists must create safe environments in which children can express themselves freely without fear of rejection. As portrayed in Chapter 14, such positive and accepting relationships free the child of the need to be shy or defiant, and behavior problems disappear or never develop in the first place.

Evaluation of Rogers' Person-Centered Theory. Rogers was one of the first counselors to encourage research scrutiny of therapy process and outcome, thus in some respects his approach rates high in testability (see Table 2–1). Research shows that counseling does lead clients to speak more positively of themselves as the theory predicts. However, it is unclear whether the improved self-description comes about through greater self-acceptance or through undetected subtle influence by the counselor as the Skinnerians suggest. Through eliciting and approving of clients' positive statements about themselves, counselors could unwittingly influence what clients say. Also undemonstrated is the positive influence of heightened self-esteem on the client's behavior. It is at least as plausible that success experiences increase a client's self-esteem as that heightened self-esteem leads to success, as Rogers would maintain. Regardless of the therapeutic change mechanisms at work, Rogers' easily taught client-centered counseling methods are extremely popular with clinicians, educators, nurses, and the clergy, so the Rogerian model receives high marks for utility.

Like other psychological theories, Rogers' explanation of human behavior is incomplete and raises as many questions as it answers. Viewing the ever-present specter of warfare in human history, is it reasonable to view human nature as basically positive and growth-oriented? Self-actualization sounds admirable, but precisely what does it mean? Perhaps different people mean different things when they use the same humanistic term, which would be a weakness of the theory (Thomas, 1979). Human conscious experience is supremely important to Rogers' model, but the phenomenon is elusive and difficult to specify, communicate, and quantify. Consequently, one cannot really determine whether tests of the theory are adequate. Like the psychoanalytic approach, the humanistic model must be evaluated largely on the basis of personal experience and conviction rather than by the tests of science.

Biological Roots of Abnormal Behavior

THE GENETIC BASIS OF HUMAN BEHAVIOR

Research on the genetics of human behavior is one of the most exciting fields of scientific study today. Unfortunately, it is also one of the most difficult for several reasons, including:

1. the expense and complexity of modern molecular genetic research,
2. the difficulty in defining psychological disorders with the precision needed to identify and study the sufferers, and
3. the preliminary and sketchy nature of our current understanding of genetic mechanisms underlying human behavior in general.

Every week seems to bring new evidence for the genetic basis of physical disorders. Researchers have sometimes made news with claims that they have found genes for behavioral or psychological conditions such as aggressive conduct disorder, schizophrenia, or manic-depressive disorder. These claims have had to be retracted because they were premature and the results could not be repeated, but the retractions receive much less news coverage than the original, incorrect announcement. As a result, many people presume that there is ample scientific evidence for the genetic basis for many mental disorders. Not so. So much about both genetic and environmental influences remains to be discovered, environment so profoundly affects biochemical and behavioral functioning, and environment and genetic factors so frequently interact that the contributions of DNA to behavioral disorders remain vitually unknown. In contrast, several types of mental retardation are now known to be hereditary or result from chromosomal anomalies.

A first requirement in behavior genetics is that the behavior investigated be well defined (Medina, 1996), as in the case of a distinct physical feature such as albinism or a particular behavior such as a tic. For example, Down syndrome and phenylketonuria (PKU) are well defined physically and behaviorally, allowing researchers to study affected individuals and discover the genetic basis of their disorders.

SINGLE GENE DISORDERS

In *autosomal* (not sex-chromosome) *dominant disorders*, the presence of a bad gene from one parent is sufficient to cause the appearance of the disorder. There is a 50 percent chance that an afflicted parent will have an afflicted child, since about half of the offspring will inherit the defective dominant gene. Each child born to the couple has a 50 percent chance of inheriting the disorder. An example of an abnormality inherited in this manner is Huntington's Chorea, a tragic progressive neurological disorder that produces irrational psychotic behavior and eventually total mental and physical disability.

In *autosomal recessive disorders,* both parents must carry a defective gene and both must transmit it to the child in order to produce the disorder. The children of such parents have a 25 percent chance of developing the condition. PKU (described in Chapter 9) is an autosomal recessive disorder resulting in failure to produce the enzyme that breaks down phenylalanine, a protein found in common foods such as milk. This enzyme deficit can result in damage to the central nervous system and severe mental retardation.

GROSS CHROMOSOMAL DAMAGE

Major chromosomal damage results in very serious disorders and many early spontaneous abortions (Reed, 1975; Witschi, 1971). Such damage includes an extra chromosome, part of a chromosome that is missing or attached to another chromosome, or a chromosome that is completely absent. Such problems seem to occur during ovum formation or division, and some are more frequent among older mothers. Down syndrome is caused by gross chromosome abnormalities, most frequently from an extra chromosome (trisomy of chromosome 21) or some other major abnormality of the 21st chromosome pair. As Chapter 9 describes, Down syndrome usually produces mental retardation and various physical deformities.

The fragile X anomaly is the most common cause of *inherited* mental retardation (Moffitt, Caspi, Harkness, & Silva, 1993; Simonoff, Rutter, & Bolton, 1996). Fragile X syndrome is caused by an abnormal gene (the Fragile X Mental Retardation–1 gene) on the bottom end of the X chromosome. The chromosomal anomaly consists of expanding nucleotide or DNA repeat sequences. While normal individuals show 6 to 50 such repeats, carriers of the disorder show 50 to 200 repeats, and in the full mutation, over 200 repeats can be found in a person with fragile X syndrome (Moffitt et al., 1993). In the full mutation, the defective gene is usually methylated, turning off the gene so that no protein is produced.

Fragile X syndrome boys may have a distinctive large forehead; prominent jaw; low, protruding ears; and large testicles, as described in Chapter 9. The boys typically have mild mental retardation in childhood and moderate retardation as adults. They also show autistic-like hand flapping, hand biting, avoidance of eye contact, speech and behavioral perseveration, and social anxiety (Hagerman, 1996). Girls are usualy less affected than boys because they have two X chromosomes, and the normal X chromosome can partly compensate for the abnormal one. Most of the girls are only mildly retarded and do not become more retarded with age. Intensive study of the fragile X syndrome is helping scientists understand the relationship between a mutation at the DNA level and its widespread effects on cognition and behavior.

HERITABILITY OF PERSONALITY TRAITS

A recent Minnesota study of a small group of identical twins who had been reared apart for many years suggested that personality attributes could be genetically based (Bouchard, 1993). When tested in adulthood, sometimes after many years of separation, twin pairs in the Minnesota study resembled each other remarkably closely not only in their physical appearance, but also in their gestures, interests, and attitudes. Some even dressed alike, independently choosing red caps or the same brand of sneakers for their separate interviews, and others had married highly similar mates (Tellegen, Lykken, Bouchard, Wilcox, Segal, & Rich, 1988). Bouchard and colleagues (1990) attributed about 70 percent of the individual differences found in intelligence to heredity, and about 50 percent of individual differences in personality to heredity, with the effects of family environment being trivial.

However, a similar study conducted in Sweden (Pederson, Plomin, McClearn, & Friberg, 1988) found some marked differences in personality between identical twins reared apart. The Minnesota study results suggested a stronger role for genetics in determining personality than did the Swedish study. Moreover, as Mischel (1993) suggested, some separated-twin similarities are strictly coincidental and occur in unrelated people. The identical twins' strikingly similar physical appearance may have acted to create similar social environments, and their constitutional physical vigor and coordination can play a role in attracting children to athletic or sedentary pursuits. Because of their shared physical attributes, separated male twins who are healthy six-footers may well independently choose to don Nikes rather than wing tips. It is also possible that chance alone or brand name popularity could account for some similarities of dress and other preferences shared by twins. Another weakness in the genetic interpretation of abilities is that identical

This Special Olympics team includes children with Down syndrome and other conditions that previously confined them to the sidelines, while more fortunate youngsters were allowed to compete. They need individualized programs in education and in the world of work, as well as in Special Olympics.

twins sometimes differ markedly. Some pairs of identical twins in the Minnesota study showed unexpected diversity, for example differing as much as 29 points in IQ scores (Tellegen et al., 1993). As yet, there is no known genetic mechanism to produce personality traits or even simple behaviors (Medina, 1966; Rende & Plomin, 1992; Zuckerman, 1995), so it is premature to infer that twin resemblances in psychological characteristics stem mainly from heredity.

"We are not born as extraverts, neurotics, impulsive sensation seekers, or antisocial personalities, but we are born with differences in reactivities of brain structures and levels of [neural activity] regulators." (Zuckerman, 1995, p. 332)

Heritability of Temperament. Rather than inheriting particular personality traits or psychiatric disorders, peo-

ple may inherit temperament types. Temperament may be genetically determined and may act as a precursor to certain types of behavior disorders. Infants have characteristic levels of emotionality, activity, and sociability or shyness, called temperament (Kagan, 1995). That is, some infants show frequent episodes of irritability, fear, and distress, while others are usually sunny and placid (Buss & Plomin, 1984). Infants also differ in their sociability and the intensity and tempo of their activity. It is possible that, given a difficult family situation, a highly active and difficult infant might be particularly likely to stress a mother causing her to act irritably and punitively. The mother's negative behavior could create a hostile rearing environment that teaches and reinforces aggression that could lead to conduct disorder. In this way, a genetically determined characteristic such as difficult temperament could produce behavior that creates environmental risk, psychopathology, and, in this case, problems with aggression. Thus, genetic predisposition could actually create environmental risk by leading to aggressive, avoidant, or risk-taking behavior (Rende & Plomin, 1992). However, this possibility remains to be demonstrated in controlled research. For the present, there is very little evidence that early temperament predicts longer-term adjustment patterns (Institute of Medicine, National Academy of Sciences, 1989).

Arguing whether psychological disorders have mostly an environmental or a genetic origin is fruitless in most cases. The task of weighing nature versus nurture is virtually impossible, because of the immense cellular and molecular complexity of the brain. There are more than 100,000 interconnecting neurons mutually influencing one another in unknown ways. It is humbling to learn that so little is known about neural activity: "Today we understand only a little about the simplest connections in one nerve in a garden slug" (Medina, 1996, p. 4). Furthermore, experience alters brain functioning. Research on behavioral genetics is complicated by the susceptibility of brain biochemistry to alteration from the effects of various types of experiences encountered in childhood.

GENETIC BASIS OF SCHIZOPHRENIA AND AUTISM

The challenge is even more difficult to identify a genetic basis for disorders of thinking and emotion such as schizophrenic and autistic disorder. Because the serious psychotic disorder called schizophrenia seems to run in some families, researchers have speculated that there is a possible genetic basis for this disorder. Schizophrenia is a serious psychotic disorder characterized by unusual, inappropriate emotional expressiveness and marked defects in logical thinking and problem-solving. Schizophrenia rates are highest in people most closely related to a person with schizophrenia, for example, among children of schizophrenic parents and especially among those who have both affected parents and siblings. However, schizophrenia is relatively rare, even among relatives of people with the disorder. If one twin has schizophrenia, then so does the other in 25 to 50 percent of identical twins, but just 5 to 15 percent of fraternal twins are both schizophrenic (Rende & Plomin, 1992). The greater shared risk of schizophrenia for identical twins is not easily explained, since their resemblance or concordance rate of less than 50 percent is not high enough to implicate only genetic causes, which would require a concordance rate nearer to 100 percent. On the other hand, the greater

Identical twins may look so much alike that they are mistaken for each other, even by close friends and family members. Their social environments are the most similar for any pairs of siblings, which may account for some of their behavior similarity.

similarity in identical over fraternal twins challenges a purely environmental explanation.

Establishing that a disorder follows a pattern expected if it is inherited is a first step toward discovering the disorder's genetic basis, but such evidence is not conclusive. The greater shared genetic material of identical over fraternal twins or other siblings has been used to argue for a genetic basis of disorders that are shared more often by identical twins than other sets of siblings or unrelated children. Some early studies were flawed because the clinicians who diagnosed one member of a twin pair knew whether the other twin had schizophrenia, thus potentially biasing the results. Further, the effects of environmental differences were not ruled out. Family environment was assumed to be as similar for fraternal twins as for identical ones, which may not be the case. Twins who are identical in appearance are very likely to be mistaken for each other and treated more similarly than are fraternal twins whose resemblence is less (Kringlen, 1976). Finally, the similarity in schizophrenia rates remains low, even in identical twins, so factors other than genetics must be at work.

Autistic disorder presents a similar picture of familial resemblance. More recently, researchers have discovered high concordance rates within close relatives of people

Fraternal twins are no more biologically similar than any pair of siblings. They are simply conceived at the same time. Some fraternal twins look less alike than this pair.

TABLE 2-4 HERITABILITY OF AUTISM

Relationship	Observed Concordance Rate
Identical twins	36% to 95.7%
Fraternal twins	0% to 23.5%
Non-twin siblings	2%
Unrelated people	Approximately 0%

NOTE: Prevalence rates of Autistic Disorders are 2–5 cases per 10,000 individuals (American Psychiatric Association, 1994), so the concordance rate between non-twin siblings is approximately 50 percent higher than between unrelated individuals. SOURCES: American Psychiatric Association. (1994). *Diagnostic and statistical manual of mental disorders (DSM-IV)*. Washington, DC: Author; August, G. J., Stewart, M. A., & Tsai, L. (1981). The incidence of cognitive disabilities in the siblings of autistic children. *British Journal of Psychiatry, 138*, 416–422; Borden, M. C., & Ollendick, T. M., Development and social subtypes in autism. In B. Lahey & A. E. Kazdin (Eds.), *Advances in clinical child psychology* (Vol. 14, pp. 61–106). New York: Plenum; Folstein, S., & Rutter, M. (1988). Autism: Familial aggregation and genetic implications. *Journal of Autism and Developmental Disorders, 18*, 3–30; Ritvo, E. R., Freeman, B. J., Mason-Brothers, A., Mo, A., & Ritvo, A. M. (1985). Concordance for the syndrome of autism in 40 pairs of afflicted twins. *American Journal of Psychiatry, 142*, 74–77.

with autistic disorder, a rare condition which strikes very early in life and is marked by social unresponsiveness, inappropriate emotional expressions, and is frequently accompanied by mental retardation (see Table 2-4).

Twin research does not provide conclusive evidence of autistic disorders because the number of twins studied tends to be very small, and identical twins who resemble each other in the disorder under investigation are more likely to be included in studies than are fraternal twins, diagnosis is inexact, and twins may not have been correctly identified as identical or fraternal (Borden & Ollendick, 1992). Therefore, evidence from twin studies is only suggestive and must be confirmed by molecular genetics research.

COMPLEXITIES OF BEHAVIORAL GENETICS

Some types of genetic disorders are easily understood and detected, but others are not so straightforward. Certain disorders are produced by the action of several gene pairs rather than just one or two and perhaps also by environmental conditions interacting with genetic factors. For example, the damaging effects of PKU occur from a combination of genetic predisposition and the specific diet the child consumes. Multiple genes are suspected to be reponsible for conditions such as some reading disorders, schizophrenia, Tourette's syndrome, and some affective

disorders such as manic-depressive syndrome. Further, a person's genotype (genetic makeup) may not be fully realized in his phenotype (observable characteristics and behavior). Genes differ in *penetrance* or the degree to which they produce observable body and behavior characteristics. Some, such as those determining eye color, are difficult to counteract by any known environmental manipulation, while others, such as those determining height, can be radically affected by nutrition or other environmental factors. The combination of the operation of multiple genes and of differing penetrance levels make it difficult to verify a possible genetic basis for many types of psychopathology.

In addition, whole groups of genes can appear at different locations on chromosomes or even on different chromosomes, making their presence and action elusive. For example, in some families susceptibility to manic-depressive affective disorder appears to be transmitted by a gene mutation on the X chromosome and linked to the chromosomal location for colorblindness (Baron et al., 1987; Mendlewic, Linkowski, Guroff, & Van Praage, 1979). But this linkage does not occur in all groups of people. In other groups, manic-depressive illness is related to a mutation elsewhere, on chromosome 11 (Egeland et al., 1987). These apparently contradictory findings leave the genetic predisposition to bipolar, manic-depressive disorder still clouded in mystery (St. George-Hyslop, Haines, Farrer, Polinsky, Van

Broeckhoven, Goate, McLachlan, Orr, Bruni, & Sorbi, 1990; Williams, 1991). Ultimately, however, human gene maps may make it possible to identify virtually any single gene or group of genes that cause disorders to be genetically transmitted within families (Institute of Medicine, National Academy of Sciences, 1989). PKU and fragile X syndrome are examples of such disorders, but they are far outnumbered by more complex, less easily defined disorders with heterogeneous genetic and environmental bases. Nevertheless, the search for the potential genetic origins of complex psychiatric disorders continues at a rapid pace. As one prominent researcher explained, "It is reasonable to expect success in the search for psychiatric genes. The search, however, may not lead to a quick clear result, but rather, may be long with many starts and stops along the way" (Kelsoe, 1992, p. 216).

Comparing Explanations of Psychopathology

Each explanation of disordered behavior is produced by a particular thinker or group of theorists working at a particular time and place. Each construction has some merit, and many are championed by enthusiastic proponents who make expansive claims about the theory's power and usefulness. At present, explanations of psychopathology are increasingly likely to be biologically based because of the startling scientific discoveries being made in genetics and biochemistry. In the mid 20th century, when experimental psychologists were making major discoveries about learning and memory in laboratory animal research, accounts of human psychopathology featured learning and memory processes. In contrast, theorists who dealt with troubled people focused on their clients' inner conflicts and on improving their self-esteem.

Each theory is best suited to its era and the type of problems upon which it was originally based; extensions to dissimilar groups at different dates do not always completely succeed. Theorists have commonly focused on adults and ignored children's special characteristics. Some theories of adult psychopathology seem strained when they are applied to children. For example, the humanists' belief in the power of self-actualization and the beneficial effects of nondirective counseling do not typically apply well to undersocialized children who treat others callously, seriously disturbed psychotic children,

or retarded ones. Rogers' writings are not particularly helpful in teaching children necessary social or academic skills. Skinner's learning approach has produced powerful methods for changing the behavior patterns of the preceding groups of children but is less helpful in dealing with crises in self-identity, parental rejection, and emotional problems. Advances in physiological and biochemical research have revolutionized our understanding of some of the genetically based physical disorders and some types of mental retardation, but as yet provide only hints about a biological cause of major psychological disorders such as depression, schizophrenia, autism, and hyperactivity. Recent striking achievements in molecular biology suggest that research in this area could prove illuminating and have practical clinical significance in the future. However, there is also abundant evidence that unhealthy environments produce troubled children who fail to achieve their potential. At present, most theories specialize in the explanation of particular types of behavior disturbances and no theory adequately covers them all. An all-embracing theory probably would have to consider the vast network of physical and social contributors to problems throughout the life span.

SUMMARY

Theories provide general explanations for events such as the development of abnormal behavior. There is debate whether any theory is any more valid than another, but approaches rise and fall in popularity according to their merit. Criteria for evaluating theories include extensiveness, parsimony, empirical validity, internal consistency, testability, and practical utility. In addition, developmental theories differ in their views of maturation as qualitative or quantitative change, of an organismic or mechanistic concept of the child, and of the degree to which early experiences affect development.

Freud's psychoanalytic theory views personality as composed of id, ego, and superego systems. Psychic energy for mental activity arises in the primitive, selfish id. The more realistic ego balances id impulses, situational constraints, and perfectionistic superego demands to determine behavior. Defense mechanisms help the ego reduce tension to a bearable level. Personality development can be halted or impeded by overgratification or trauma at any early stage of personality development (oral, anal, or phallic). Erikson's ego theory extends psychoanalytic models to include social and cultural factors and provides a developmental view of the healthy personality. Contemporary object relations theory emphasizes the importance of relationships with significant others in early childhood. The child forms an internalized representation of self and other that guides later self-evaluation and relationships with other people.

The experimentally based learning approaches of Skinner and Bandura stress the continuous contribution of environmental events in determining behavior. Skinner's operant conditioning approach sees the ultimate causes of behavior in reinforcing and punishing events. Bandura and the social cognitive (social learning) group maintain that a degree of self-control is possible and that both one's expectations of self-efficacy and the probability of success determine behavior.

Rogers' humanistic person-centered theory stresses the achievement of self-understanding, self-acceptance, and self-actualization. This goal is brought about through parental unconditional acceptance of the child and positive regard from others, which lead to the child's self-regard. Criticism and rejection lead to defensiveness and low self-esteem, which produce psychopathology.

Biological explanations speculate that genetic, biochemical, or other physical defects lead to abnormal behavior when combined with certain environmental characteristics. Known genetic abnormalities produce single or multiple-gene disorders and gross chromosomal abnormalities. Despite rapid advances in genetic research, previously unsuspected complexities plague the field, such as different genetic bases for the same psychiatric illness in different groups, apparent genetic contributions to behavior that influence an individual's social environment, lasting effects of experience on biochemical functioning, and low reliability in psychiatric diagnoses, particularly in disorders of children.

CHAPTER 3

RESEARCH METHODS USED TO
STUDY CHILD BEHAVIOR DISORDERS

Key Terms

Concept of control. Holding all variables constant between experimental conditions except the independent variable so that any differences observed can be attributed to the treatment influence.

Cross-sectional designs. Designs in which comparisons are made between different groups of subjects at different ages. Often used in developmental studies of children.

Dependent variable. The behavior or performance observed to assess the impact of treatment, sometimes called dependent measure. Often multiple dependent variables are used.

Descriptive research. Research that attempts to describe certain groups or situations. No manipulation is involved.

Difference research questions. Research questions that compare treatments or conditions to determine if there is a difference.

External validity. Pertains to how well the results of a study generalize to other subjects, measures, and settings that were not actually involved in the research.

Group experimental designs. Research designs in which groups of subjects are compared to determine the effects of treatments.

Independent variable. Refers to the factor under study and manipulated by the researcher. Also called experimental variable.

Internal validity. Pertains to the degree to which all systematic influences have been controlled or held constant except the independent variable.

Longitudinal designs. Designs in which a sample of subjects is observed repeatedly over an extended period of time to measure change. Often used in developmental studies.

Quasi-experimental designs. A type of experiment in which a researcher compares groups that have preexisting differences (e.g., on IQ) rather than actually manipulating conditions. Those preexisting differences represent the independent variable.

Relationship research questions. Questions aimed at determining the degree to which two or more phenomena relate or vary together. Also called correlational research.

Reliability. Pertains to the consistency with which observers record the same behavior type, level, or performance score from simultaneous observations.

Time-series designs. Refers to experimental designs in which a researcher manipulates the experimental variable over different phases of treatment conditions (e.g., baseline, treatment, baseline) and records many repeated observations. Often used with a small number of subjects or a single subject.

CHAPTER OVERVIEW

As you read this volume you will encounter many references to research studies on various topics. The quality of these investigations will vary greatly with some providing reliable results while others are less dependable, perhaps even misleading. This chapter will introduce you to the fundamentals of research methods so you can better evaluate the quality of research articles you read. After reading the chapter, you can expect to be able to answer a variety of questions such as: Was an appropriate control group or condition used (or did improvement in speech occur because of maturation or some other factor)? Was an appropriate dependent measure employed (or did the researcher observe behaviors unrelated to drug abuse or use unreliable measures)? Only well-conducted research can answer important clinical questions asked by parents and faced daily by professionals. Do children grow out of phobias or do phobias persist into adulthood? Are drugs or psychotherapy more successful in the treatment of childhood schizophrenia? What are the most sensitive and accurate measures of children's emotions? We can guess at the answers to such questions, but children's lives are too important to base their treatment on such guesses. The most careful and very best research scrutiny is required.

Most children display both desirable and undesirable behaviors from time to time. It is often difficult to determine which actions can be considered normal and which we should be concerned about as deviant and requiring intervention. The boundaries of normalcy are fluid and are determined largely by societal values. Additionally, the source of societal values is rather difficult to identify precisely. As mentioned in Chapter 1, a child's behavior is often judged in terms of (1) a comparison to age-mates' behavior, (2) the intensity and persistence of any problem behavior, and (3) the degree to which behaviors are culturally appropriate. Thus, it seems that normalcy judgments are primarily made by comparing a child's behavior with that of a majority of peers. This raises the question of how we obtain information regarding behavioral norms (and deviations from these norms).

In order to know how most people behave, we must have information that is gathered *systematically*. We cannot rely on casual observations alone, since such procedures will not produce reliable information that will be the same at different times with various observers. Informal observation, such as we might casually undertake while shopping, is likely to be very selective and quite inaccurate. We may only notice certain individuals (such as those who dress strangely) or certain behaviors that seem different or inappropriate. Such observation will be very unsystematic and the resulting information will be incomplete. Consequently, we must turn to a process that emphasizes the systematic acquisition of information—namely research.

Like most terms, *research* has different meanings for different people. For our purposes research will be broadly defined as a systematic method of inquiry, a systematic way of asking questions and obtaining information. This is a rather simple definition with the emphasis focusing on the term *systematic*, or proceeding in a methodical, planned fashion. Certainly there are many ways for one to obtain information. Every day we make decisions and act based on information. More often than not, our attention is focused mainly on the particular decision to be made or the action to be taken, and frequently in a limited, highly focused manner (such as the driving need to buy *that* stereo equipment *today*). In research, the focus is on objective, systematic information gathering. The process may not produce a soaring emotional state for most people in the same way as impulse buying, but it does tend to result in more rational decisions.

As noted previously, research is a process whereby we systematically gather data regarding some important practical or theoretical question. If research is planned and executed in a technically sound manner, the results should provide an objective answer to the question. In some quarters it is fashionable to question the value of research or to make jokes about the utility of research findings. While such pursuits are amusing, it is important to remember that many items and processes that now make our daily life easier were once the results of some research that was perhaps thought silly at one time.

We are all consumers of research whether we are conscious of it or not. Scientific investigation has contributed immeasurably to the world around us. It influences the production of our food, clothing, medication, modes of transportation, the way we write term papers or go on reducing diets; and the development of many other products and procedures used in daily life. Too frequently we encounter poor quality products that supposedly have been developed and evaluated with care. Consequently, we are skeptical when advertisements say that a product has been scientifically evaluated and is unsurpassed in quality. Having been misled in the past, we may become suspicious of any scientific claims. However, with some knowledge of the characteristics of good research, consumers can make more informed choices, whether personal or professional.

This chapter attempts to make you a better informed research consumer by increasing your ability to evaluate psychological and educational research studies. We are dependent on research of many types, not only on material products, but on educational and therapeutic or rehabilitation programs as well. For example, parents of a child with attention-deficit disorder with hyperactivity (ADHD) must make decisions regarding a treatment program for their child. Likewise, teachers and other professionals must make decisions concerning educational or other treatment programs for children. Box 3-1 illustrates an investigation on the effects of training parents of ADHD children to help their children with their social difficulties (Sheridan, Dee, Morgan, McCormick, & Walker, 1996). In this study the mothers of five boys diagnosed as having ADHD were subjects, and the mothers' acquisition of selected social training skills was measured. Such research studies are necessary in order to determine if parents can be effectively trained to participate in their children's treatment program.

BOX 3-1   EXAMPLE OF A RESEARCH STUDY THAT COULD INFLUENCE THE COMPONENTS OF A TREATMENT PROGRAM

Part of this study investigated the effects of training mothers of young boys diagnosed with ADHD to help their children with their social problems. Parents were trained in the three target skill areas of debriefing, problem-solving, and goal-setting. Debriefing in this study was defined as a method of interacting and conversing with children in a supportive and nonthreatening manner to learn about their social experiences and set the stage for problem-solving. Problem-solving was defined as a child-focused process wherein parents learn how to guide and support their child's efforts to resolve their social difficulties. For purposes of this study, goal-setting was defined as a strategy to assist children in establishing goals for themselves.

Figure 3-1 summarizes the data from one mother who participated and completed the study. These data indicate that this mother improved in her social training skills across all three target behaviors, and that debriefing and problem-solving skills were maintained during follow-up. The goal-setting skill, while reflecting an increase during the training phase, was not maintained during follow-up.

Box 3-1 (continued)

These results suggest that parents can learn and demonstrate certain social training skills that may be useful in working with their ADHD children. The data also suggest that two of the three skills remain evident during follow-up, after training has been terminated. However, the post-training durability of the third skill (goal-setting) was not demonstrated in this study.

FIGURE 3-1   Percentage of debriefing (DB), problem-solving (PS), and goal-setting (GS) skill objectives met by parent subject number 5 in naturalistic (home) setting.

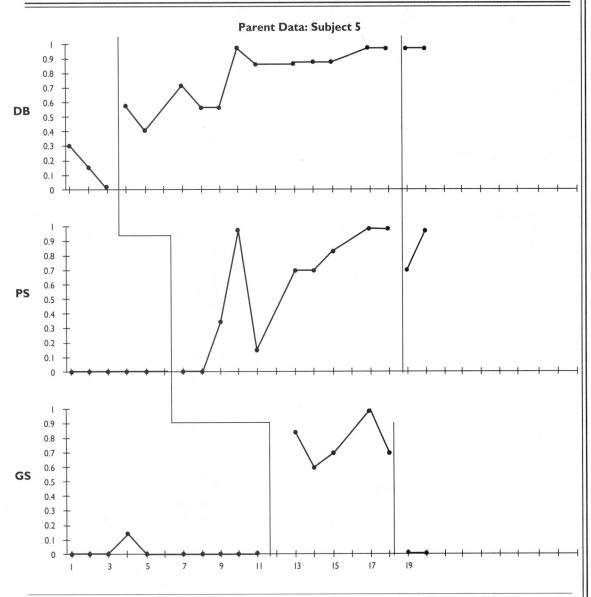

SOURCE: Sheridan, S. M., Dee, C. C., Morgan, J., McCormick, M., & Walker, D. (1996). A multimethod intervention for social skills deficits in children with ADHD and their parents. *School Psychology Review, 25,* 57–76.

TABLE 3-1 Differences Between Scientific Inquiry and Commonsense Reasoning

Area of Difference	Scientific Inquiry	Commonsense Reasoning
Use of theories and concepts.	Studied systematically.	Studied informally and unsystematically, if at all.
Level of proof required.	Very stringent and based on agreed-upon principles.	Loose and variable.
Control demanded.	High degree.	Little or none.
Interest in relationships between phenomena.	Systematic, constant study of relationships.	Unsystematic, often only interested in those of personal relevance.
Types of explanations regarding phenomena.	Couched in the observable, logical, empirically testable.	Often extend beyond the empirically testable to metaphysical explanations.

SCIENCE AND COMMON SENSE

There are many popular misconceptions and negative stereotypes regarding science and scientists—for example, that scientists are unrealistic dreamers, space cadets, or arrogant "ivory-tower eggheads" incapable of relating to the "real" world. (Unfortunately, it is as easy to think of negative stereotypes of scientists as it is to call up a different set of stereotypes about athletes or politicians.) This view implies that there is little relationship between science and common sense (a notion explicitly stated by some). Although there are some important differences between the two, it would be incorrect to conclude that they are totally unrelated.

In one sense science is an extension of common sense that emphasizes *systematic* question-asking. Generally speaking, common sense is characterized by a much less systematic approach to problems than is the scientific method. Common sense might dictate doing different things in different historical eras or in various cultures. Common sense might dictate doing things in a traditional way, such as spanking unruly children ("spare the rod and spoil the child"). Someone using the scientific approach would be more inclined to study the immediate and long-term behavioral effects of spanking as contrasted with other methods of controlling disobedience. Table 3-1 summarizes some of the ways in which science and common sense differ.

THE RESEARCH PROCESS

In general, research can be conceptualized as a process that begins with a question and progresses through a sys-

tematic series of steps aimed at obtaining an answer to that question. Obviously procedural details will vary greatly depending on the particular discipline of the researcher involved and even between investigations within a given discipline. However, the general process remains essentially unchanged.

Research Questions

Recall that the research process begins with the formulation of a question. Knowing what type of research question is being investigated is very important to understanding a research study. There are as many different specific types of research questions as there are studies and investigators. We can, however, place the general types of research questions in psychology into three basic categories: *descriptive* questions, questions regarding *differences*, and questions about *relationships* or *correlations*. *Descriptive* questions ask about the nature of a phenomenon. Such questions are aimed at describing a particular group or a type of individual with regard to certain characteristics. (For example, descriptive research might attempt to describe the behavioral patterns characteristic of individuals with anorexia or ask: What is the average IQ of psychotic children?) These questions are not simple to answer since they require samples of subjects who are truly representative of the group of interest, such as all autistic children or all depressed ones, or particular subgroups such as autistic children of normal-range IQ or depressed adolescents. *Difference* questions ask: Is there a difference? Investigations addressing difference questions may compare groups (for example, is there a significant difference in academic performance between the group that received individual tutoring and the group that received structured group instruction?), or they may compare a group's or an individual's behavior before and after treatment has been applied (as in the study described in Box 3-1). *Relationship* questions ask to what degree two or more phenomena relate or vary together. These are often termed correlational questions (after the correlational statistical analyses used). A correlational study might explore the relationship between annual family income and the frequency of mental health problems of children. Simply stated, the question might read: As family income varies, what tends to happen to the frequency of youngsters' mental health problems? (To put it another way, as income increases does the frequency of child mental health problems tend to increase or decrease?)

It was noted that these represent *general types* of research questions investigated in psychology and other behavioral sciences. Certainly there are many variations within these general categories, many studies that include combinations of these questions, and situations in which the distinctions between the types of questions are blurred. However, for initial instructional purposes regarding research methods, it is helpful to view research questions at this general level. It is important to be able to identify the type of question being addressed in order to more easily understand a study.

Research Paradigms: Distinctions, Advantages, and Limitations

Scientists working in psychology and education often classify research into a variety of methodology categories or paradigms. These paradigms have varied over the years in terms of popularity and use in different disciplines. Currently, distinctions between the following method categories warrant discussion: experimental and nonexperimental approaches, and quantitative and qualitative approaches. Each is applicable in certain situations and selection of a particular approach or method will depend on the training of the investigator, the question under investigation, and the setting in which a study is conducted. All of these methodologies have contributed substantially to our understanding of child behavior disorders. The serious student should at least become acquainted with all of these approaches in order to be knowledgeable regarding research on children's problems.

EXPERIMENTAL/QUANTITATIVE AND NONEXPERIMENTAL/QUALITATIVE

Distinctions

In some ways, experimental and nonexperimental research approaches are mirror images of one another. Experimental research is most often thought of in terms of tightly controlled studies in which the investigator manipulates some treatment or condition that the subject(s) experience. Investigators using nonexperimental research methods tend to observe, analyze, and describe phenomena as they exist naturally rather than manipulating treatments or conditions. Experiments often involve a great deal of control over the research environment and conditions under which subjects participate (for example, research may take place in a lab with no one allowed to intrude on the experimental setting and noise, light, and temperature levels may be held constant). Nonexperimental research, on the other hand, does not typically impose as much control and may take place in a more natural environment such as a classroom, playground, or home.

The bulk of research conducted in psychology and education has historically utilized what most would term *quantitative methodology*. For the most part, this research has asked questions, developed hypotheses, manipulated experimental variables, and precisely measured outcomes in a manner that can be reduced to some numerical representation (such as the number of correct responses, the number of tantrum outbursts, and so on). However, another approach to conducting research known as *qualitative methodology* has gained popularity in psychology and education during the past 10 to 15 years. As described by Lancy, "qualitative research has gone from being fringe, marginal, unscientific, to fashionable ... " (1993, p. 24). Lancy's choice of words is important, most notably the term *fashionable*. Methodologies and terminology often grow and diminish in popularity (become more or less fashionable), without a clear, crisp language to describe what is being discussed. Quantitative and qualitative research methodology distinctions are mired in just such a circumstance. A more appropriate question might be, why are researchers abandoning one experimental paradigm and adopting a different approach? Often, a new technique shows promise of revealing information about the origin of some behavior that more familiar approaches have not clarified.

The methodological label suggests that one method (quantitative) collects data that are numerically based whereas the other (qualitative) collects some other sort of data (e.g., the case history or natural history of some behavioral problem in a child, a family, or a small set of cases). Whereas this is true to some extent, this is not the only difference that is inherent in distinctions between the methods. Qualitative researchers are also more likely to study subjects in their natural context, trying to understand the subjects' perceptions of reality around them—sometimes termed phenomenological reality (Borg, Gall, & Gall, 1993). This approach to research emphasizes an unwillingness to intervene in naturally occurring phenomena, whereas quantitative methods are more likely to manipulate experimental variables, situations, and other matters pertaining to the study. (In part, this rings familiar from the experimental-nonexperimental discussion presented above.) Researchers employing quantitative methodology will often undertake investigations to test theories with the questions, hypotheses, and theories being the points of departure for the study. Qualitative researchers, on the other hand, are more likely to let the theories, hypotheses, and questions emerge from the environment and subjects being studied. Whereas quantitative-experimental studies test hypotheses, case studies more likely generate hypotheses for testing. Likewise, researchers employing qualitative methodology are more likely to have a preference for definitions to emerge as the study progresses, which would not be acceptable for most quantitative researchers, who first develop their tests or observational procedures, assess their adequacy, and then make their observations.

The emergence of qualitative research methodology in psychology and education has been prompted by a desire to learn more about the complexities of naturally occurring human behavior than traditional quantitative approaches have permitted. The tension between controlled experimental and observational case methodology has generated heated debates heavily laced with stimulating intellectual and personal attacks (Borg, et al., 1993; Fraenkel, & Wallen, 1993; Lancy, 1993). It is important to remember that this transition period is still under way. As we gain more experience, the "methodology wars" will diminish and research methodology will eventually be strengthened by adding qualitative elements to the arsenal of quantitative, scientific investigatory tools.

Advantages and Limitations

Each of the above mentioned research approaches have certain advantages and limitations when examined in isolation. Some of these are inherent in the general approaches, whereas others are specifically relevant to particular methods or strategies within these general approaches. In all cases, a researcher must weigh the merits of each procedure and determine the most appropriate method and specific procedures to be employed.

One major advantage of experimental research over nonexperimental methods involves the use of control. An investigator using experimental methods exercises a greater degree of direct control than when using nonexperimental methods. The experimental researcher attempts to control or hold constant all influences except the treatment variable that is being manipulated. Because experimental research involves the use of control in this manner, an investigator can be more confident in attributing his or her results to the treatment variable. If the only known difference between two groups of children is the treatment they receive, then posttreatment differences in their behavior can likely be attributed to the type of treatment received. Experimentation is also characterized by more control of the research setting, as noted above, which minimizes the possibility of results being influenced by extraneous events such as merely the expectation that a treatment would be effective.

The limitations of experimental research can be viewed in the same context as the advantages discussed above. Because of the high degree of control, experimental studies are frequently conducted in a rather artificial environment. Obviously the degree of artificiality varies, since experiments may be executed in a contrived laboratory setting or they may be conducted in a field setting that approximates the subjects' natural environment. Results may be substantially altered by an artificial environment if the setting is sufficiently unusual that subjects perform differently than they would normally. For example, children who have spent most of their time at home may be unusually active or frightened if they are brought to a laboratory or clinic (especially if they see unfamiliar adults in white lab coats, which could indicate that they are doctors who might give injections).

A second limitation of experimental research also concerns the issue of artificiality. Experimental investigations often involve people (experimenters and other subjects), activities, and materials that are unfamiliar to the subjects. Some experiments utilize exotic apparatus that one would never encounter outside a research laboratory. (How often do you think a rat finds a lever to press for food in his or her normal living area?) Such stimuli might influence the subjects' performance so that they perform uncharacteristically, therefore researchers must demonstrate that the experimental setting and procedures don't alter participants' behavior.

As stated earlier, nonexperimental research does not involve the use of direct control to the degree evident in experiments. This is both an advantage and a limitation. On the positive side, many nonexperimental methods do not create an artificial environment that would influence subjects' responses. In fact, some nonexperimental investigations are specifically aimed at studying subjects in their natural environment. Obviously, not all nonexperimental research is conducted in this manner, and in some cases the presence of observers makes those observed somewhat uneasy and constrained in their behavior. Thus, an observer's presence, no matter how unobtrusive, can affect those observed.

The relative absence of control is a limitation to the degree that it contributes to unreliable data. For example, it is quite likely that the data obtained in a case study are substantially influenced by the biases of the interviewer, especially if a structured protocol of questions is not used. Without the control imposed by a consistent set of questions, information may be obtained only in areas that a particular interviewer deems important, which would contribute to incomplete and perhaps unreliable data. Different interviewers would obtain dissimilar information from the same informants. Also bias can be evident in how the interviewer asks even the standard questions or, for example, gives IQ test instructions. That is why researchers are so careful to train their examiners to attain a high standard in their work. Nothing is so fundamental to research in psychology as the reliability of measurement (Li, Rosenthal, & Rubin, 1996). In addition, examiners and raters are tested to ensure that they are accurate. In this text, qualitative case studies more often appear in boxes, as interesting examples of atypical behavior or of psychotherapy approaches. Quantitative and experimental studies are more often cited in the body of the text, as the source of facts.

It is important to understand that there are advantages and limitations to all research approaches and that no single strategy provides a perfect solution to all of the challenges of collecting information. Scientists must select a method or set of methods of choice and be fully cognizant of the strengths and limitations inherent in that approach. Some of the advantages and limitations pertaining to quantitative and qualitative methodology are reminiscent of the discussion just completed for experimental and nonexperimental methods. However, there are also some fundamental paradigm differences that also emerge as strength/limitation choices to which researchers must be alert.

Qualitative research is characterized by naturalistic inquiry or the investigation of phenomena in a natural situation. This is a strength in the sense that subjects should behave as they normally would and not be substantially influenced by the process of being studied. The limitation to this approach we have encountered before. The lack of control imposed may be seen as problematic by quantitative researchers who are more accustomed to regulating or restricting the stimuli that influence their subjects. Qualitative researchers also tend to emphasize inductive analysis by submerging themselves in the details of the data in order to let the questions and relationships emerge rather than beginning with clear definitions and testable hypotheses. This again reflects a control issue. Qualitative researchers claim that the knowledge gained is limited if the questions are determined a priori as experimenters do. More quantitatively oriented researchers find the lack of structure in case studies disconcerting and reflective of a lack of rigor. Qualitative research emphasizes the collection of data in nonnumerical form, which means that extensive verbal descriptions and visual representations (e.g., video) may be what is recorded. These types of data represent a strength in that they provide a richer information base than data that are limited to numerical representations of behavior. For example, in addition to describing a child's anxiety attacks, a case study might include information on the child's early development, family relationships, school adjustments, and other matters. The limitations of such data are that they require lengthy analyses in a form that is not well-understood by quantitatively oriented researchers and for which there is no standard method.

The brief discussion of qualitative/quantitative advantages and limitations above illustrates one of the major difficulties with this paradigm transition in psychology and education. There are some very fundamental differences in approaches to inquiry by researchers who use

---

BOX 3-2 MARGARET MEAD'S REPORTING OF SAMOAN SEXUAL BEHAVIOR

Margaret Mead's research on the Samoan culture has long been a classic, widely known both within and beyond the disciplinary boundaries of cultural anthropology (Mead, 1928). One of the areas that received the most widespread interest in this research was Mead's reporting of Samoan sexual behavior. It was Mead's assertion that young Samoans made the smoothest sex adjustments in the world and that young females deferred marriage "... through as many years of casual love-making as possible" (Freeman, 1983, p. 226). Based on her conversations with young Samoan women, it was Mead's conclusion that premarital sex was commonplace and a casual pastime. This perspective of Samoan culture became so prevalent that one author characterized it as "institutionalized premarital sexuality" (Honigmann, 1963, p. 273). As time passed, however, certain questions began to be raised regarding this aspect of Mead's report. In fact, what began to emerge as a characteristic Samoan behavior rather than recreational sex were reports of "recreational lying," especially about sex (Freeman, 1989).

As other researchers probed this topic, evidence began to accumulate that perhaps Mead's questions to her informants about sexual behavior had produced responses that should not have been accepted at face value. Testimony in 1988 by one of Mead's actual participants indicated that the sexual questions touched on a taboo topic and embarrassed the young Samoan women. Their responses (indicating a common acceptance of premarital sex) were presented in what they intended to be a joking manner. However, unaware of the intent, Margaret Mead took these answers seriously and did not challenge their stories, nor did she obtain corroboration from other sources. Such an error highlights dramatically the need for triangulation, or cross-checking information through multiple sources to provide confidence that data obtained in qualitative research are valid.

REFERENCES
Freeman, D. (1983). *Margaret Mead and Samoa: The making and unmaking of an anthropological myth.* Cambridge, MA: Harvard University Press.
Freeman, D. (1989). Fa'apua'a Fa'amu and Margaret Mead. *American Anthropologist, 91,* 1017–1022.
Honigmann, J. J. (1963). *Understanding culture.* New York: Harper & Row.
Mead, M. (1928). *Coming of age in Samoa.* New York: Morrow.

---

qualitative methodology as compared to those trained with a quantitative orientation. The differences are much more than just divergent types of data. Although there are researchers who conduct poor quality research using both quantitative and qualitative methods, the standards for rigor are more widely accepted in regards to quantitative methods. Critical standards of rigor are not yet evident for qualitative methodology applications in psychology and education (Lancy, 1993), which increases the vulnerability of such investigators to accusations of poor quality science. Errors or questionable results appear even in disciplines where qualitative methods have long been used because of the reliance on informants as the fundamental source of data. Box 3-2 illustrates a case of such questions being raised about work in cultural anthropology.

Research Paradigms: Descriptions and Illustrations

NONEXPERIMENTAL RESEARCH

If you are observing a third-grade boy to see how he gets along with his classmates, you are engaging in nonexperimental research, at least informally. Nonexperimental research methods involve observation, analysis, and description of phenomena rather than the manipulation of treatment variables as is done in experimentation. A variety of specific procedures may be viewed as nonexperimental. We will also find elements of some of these procedures being employed under the rubric of qualitative methods. Each has certain distinctive features as well as unique advantages and limitations. In this section, we will briefly examine certain nonexperimental research methods that are of particular importance in the study of child behavior disorders.

Observation. Observation is a data collection method that actually crosses a variety of methodological boundaries. It may be used in both experimental and nonexperimental research and is also employed in qualitative and quantitative approaches to investigation. It is discussed initially in this section because manipulation of a treatment variable is not inherent in the observation process. Observation has been viewed by some as a distinct research method because of its tradition of usage by certain disciplines. However, in our current discussion, it is best examined as a data collection strategy that may be used in several methods.

Observation is used in both qualitative and quantitative research, although with some differences in the manner employed.

Observation techniques vary greatly depending on the type of investigation and setting in which a study is conducted. One variation involves the degree to which an observer participates in the activities of the group being studied. For example, qualitative researchers have often used what is known as participant observation, wherein the individual collecting the data actually participates in the setting or activities being observed. Such procedures are vastly different from investigations in which a nonparticipant observer collects the data. As suggested by the terminology, nonparticipant observers try to be as inconspicuous as possible and do not actually become involved in the social interactions under investigation. Researchers in psychology have tended to use procedures in which the observer participates very minimally or not at all, and often is not even seen by those being observed (for example, observations made through a one-way mirror or by means of audio or video recordings). Such procedures are employed not because we are unscrupulous snoopers,

but because we do not want research participants' behavior to change because they are acutely aware of being observed. Teenagers and preteens may become agonizingly self-conscious about being observed, at least initially. In contrast, babies show no apprehension unless they are in the stranger-anxiety age range. Similarly, preschool and kindergarten children are delightful to observe because they adjust to nonintrusive observers' presence very rapidly, minimizing the influence on behavior.

The influence of known or evident observers on subjects' behavior has been demonstrated frequently in the psychological literature. For example, Russell, Russell, and Midwinter (1992) found that observer presence had a substantial effect on family members. These investigators also reported that there may be a differential influence on particular family members, with fathers potentially being more influenced than mothers. Researchers employing nonparticipant observation do so because they are very concerned about the subjects' behaving as naturally as possible (a factor that is particularly important in some types of studies). This seems achievable if subjects become accustomed to the observer to the point that behavior returns to a natural state. However, many people may never behave completely naturally when they are aware of being observed.

Observation procedures may also vary in the amount of structure imposed on a study by the researcher. Structure may be imposed either on the environment or on the observer. For example, data may be recorded in a completely unstructured environment such as the natural setting in which the subjects live while they routinely engage in their normal activities. On the other end of this continuum, data may be collected in an environment that is very structured, artificial, and very foreign to the subjects (e.g., a contrived laboratory setting). Similarly, observer procedures may vary on a continuum of structure. Data may be recorded in a totally unstructured fashion (e.g., field notes recorded anecdotally without any guidelines) or they may be recorded in a very structured and prescribed fashion (e.g., standardized protocol or checklist used for counting disruptive behavior frequency).

Case Studies. Case studies represent a second nonexperimental research method frequently used by qualitative researchers (Lancy, 1993). Case studies characteristically involve an in-depth examination of the behavior of an individual or a small social unit such as a family. Case studies in psychology are traditionally characterized by a lack of experimental controls (Kazdin, 1992). The researcher collects observations, perhaps in psychotherapy sessions, but does not introduce different types of treatment or record the client's reaction to various treatments. The focus of such a study may vary depending on the nature of the research question. Usually the researcher attempts to determine all of the factors or influences that are important in a subject's development and current behavior. Data collected often include developmental history, including physical, psychological, and social aspects of the person's development. The case study's purpose is to determine why an individual has reached his or her current status. An investigator describes the subject and attempts to reconstruct his or her past history and the nature and sources of any for present problems.

For the most part case studies address descriptive questions, either as a preliminary investigation, to verify a theory, or to understand and trace the history of a be-

havior disorder as it develops in a child. In so doing, a case study may provide an in-depth clinical picture of the individual as illustrated by the case of John reported by Eaves (1992), presented in Box 3-3. As suggested by the information in Box 3-3, case studies are usually quite detailed and lengthy. They are important in the study and treatment of child behavior disorders, but not highly rigorous from a scientific standpoint.

Case studies are rich in the depth, complexity, and quantity of information typically obtained. This also creates a limitation, however, because case studies usually describe only one or, at most, a few subjects such as those in a family. The information may not apply to other individuals or situations different from those studied. That is, the information may not generalize to other individuals. Another limitation of the case study approach involves possible bias on the part of the investigator or of informants such as the client or family members. In many cases, there are no objective records of the client's past interactions. Information must come from the individual client or perhaps from interested third parties such as parents or other relatives. Such data may be biased because informants are aware of the existing problem and consequently interpret earlier events differently than they would without such knowledge (e.g., viewing previous normal play incidents as abnormal because the child has now been labeled as emotionally disturbed). Data bias or inaccuracy may also occur because of faulty memory on the part of the informants. Individuals providing information may selectively remember certain types of incidents, they may be able to recall only more recent events, or parents or teachers may confuse one child's reactions with those of another child. Case study data may also be biased by the investigator's or therapist's interpretations. Information for a case study comes from the patient or other informants and is necessarily filtered through the investigator before it is recorded. Such data are quite vulnerable to the biases and expectations of an investigator and may be entered into the records in a manner that is incomplete or inaccurate to some degree. It should also be noted that case study methodology is viewed as having certain limitations from a qualitative research perspective in that there is not total adherence to certain elements of the qualitative paradigm. For example, Lancy notes that "Questions or issues are at least partly predetermined. What one studies is carefully delimited in advance" (1993, p. 142). Some qualitative researchers find this

BOX 3-3   THE CASE OF JOHN: AFFECTIVE AND COGNITIVE INDIFFERENT BEHAVIOR IN AUTISM

John's unusual development was noticed at an early age by his parents. Almost from birth he seemed remote and uninvolved with the world around him. His mother, Barbara, became concerned when John failed to engage in the bonding characteristics she had so enjoyed when nurturing his two older siblings. For instance, he was an indifferent eater, often nursing only a few moments at a time; sometimes he rejected his mother's breast entirely, even when he should have been hungry. In addition, when he was picked up by one or the other of his parents, he showed neither the usual anticipatory response nor the infant smile familiar to every parent. Instead, he seemed entirely content to be left alone in his cradle.

Other early signs of emotional development were also absent. Both Barbara and her husband, Tom, agreed that their son seldom made eye contact with either of them. Even when they positioned themselves directly in front of his gaze, they had the chilling sensation that John was looking "through" them rather than at them. His lack of interest in social contact with his parents—indeed, with all human contact—was manifest in many other ways. His usual facial expression was described by his family as "unconcerned" or "just a blank." Although he did not usually resist hugging and cuddling by his family, there was no mistaking that such expressions of affection held little attraction for him. At other times, particularly when some solitary activity was interrupted, John showed displeasure by resisting; on rare occasions, he displayed true emotion through crying and temper tantrums when an activity was interrupted. Although he had considerable contact with age peers, as well as with his two siblings, John showed no interest in them, preferring his solitary activity to cooperative play.

As John grew into childhood, peculiar physical symptoms came to characterize his behavior. He spent long periods staring intently at the palm of one hand. Gradually, he would become agitated and, with a wide-eyed, hysterical look on his face, begin shaking both hands up and down rapidly. He often held his fingers and hands in a stiff, distorted posture; such behavior was frequently accompanied by an odd flicking motion of his index finger. Other common physical activities included rocking back and forth or side to side, mouthing unfamiliar objects, and an activity that his family members referred to as "dangling." John usually dangled his mother's hair, which was often worn in a pony-tail style, but he was attracted to any similar hanging material. For instance, he often grasped a venetian blind cord, jerking it up and down, causing it to bounce or "dance."

Objects had always captured John's attention more readily than people. Yet, he seldom manipulated objects in expected ways (for example, toy cars and dolls were held upside down as often as right side up). Also, the objects that John cherished most were often far outside the realm of usual childhood playthings. For John, the opportunity to listen to the sound made by a piece of cellophane was the equivalent to a day in the park to most children. Further, he generally showed far more interest in the texture of objects than do most children. In fact, he spent a significant proportion of time touching materials or rubbing them against his cheek. A favorite texture was that of pencil erasers and other rubbery objects, but soft, cloth fabrics were also favored. It was a rare occasion when he did not have either an eraser or a piece of cloth within easy reach.

Although John's physical appearance was normal, even attractive, and people said he had an "intelligent look," as he grew older it became all too obvious that his cognitive development was severely diminished compared with that of his age peers. For instance, he never developed speech; he was entirely mute. Nor did he show any real interest in activities demanding cognition at any level. For instance, magazines, books, movies, and television rarely engaged his attention more than momentarily.

A more troubling attribute was John's increasingly severe self-injurious behavior. As a child of 4 or 5 years of age, he developed a tendency to strike his chin with a closed fist. At first, the blows carried little force and were not alarming. By the time he was 9 years of age, his repertoire of self-destructive behavior had grown to a shocking extent. He continued to hit himself in the chin (and other parts of his face and head), but the force of the blows had become much more severe. Further, he now frequently banged his head against any available stationary object. Beyond that, he bit the back of his right hand so often that he had developed a thick callus.

Observation revealed that John's self-injurious behavior was most often displayed when his parents or his teacher asked him to engage in behavior that he disliked. Examples of requests that marked occasions of self-injury included (1) cleaning up around his desk at school, (2) making eye contact with an adult, (3) eating with appropriate utensils, (4) changing an activity, and (5) bedtime preparations. The list of occasions was extensive; the common thread seemed to be John's (usually successful) attempt to gain control over others in his environment by exhibiting alarming self-injurious behavior.

SOURCE: Eaves, R. C. (1992). Autism. In P. J. McLaughlin & P. Wehman (Eds.), *Developmental disabilities: A handbook for best practices* (pp. 68–81). Boston: Andover Medical Publishers.

disquieting and are more inclined to have the questions emerge as the investigation progresses.

EXPERIMENTAL RESEARCH

As noted earlier, experimental research is characterized by manipulation of the treatment or condition under study. The factor under study, manipulated by an experimenter, is known as the *independent variable* (also called the experimental variable). If, for example, we were interested in determining the effectiveness of a new treatment for childhood autism, then our independent variable might be "type of treatment." We might be comparing a new treatment with one that had been used previously, for example, contrasting the effects of these different treatments on autistic behavior. As we manipulate a treatment, we must have some way of measuring its effect. Perhaps we want to count the number of times per hour that a child exhibits what is considered "autistic behavior" (which must be defined operationally, perhaps as bizarre hand or body movements, lack of interest in other people, bizarre speech content, etc.). The measure or means by which we determine a treatment's effect is known as the *dependent variable*. So we manipulate an independent variable (e.g., treatment type) to observe its effects on the dependent variable (counting the frequency with which the behavior occurs under different treatment conditions, or the score an individual receives on a depression scale).

Quasi-Experimental Designs. The discussion presented above illustrates a type of investigation in which a researcher literally manipulates the experimental variable (treatment) and observes the effect of that manipulation on one or more dependent variables. Such a study might be conducted by sampling a group of autistic children and then randomly assigning half of them to one group and the other half to a second group. The groups would be very similar in their behavior and other characteristics (because we randomly assigned the children to the groups) until after the two treatments were applied. There are, however, situations in which a researcher cannot manipulate the independent variable in a literal sense. This might be the case if we were interested in comparing the performance on some task of children with mental retardation and their normal peers. In this example, the focus of study is on performance differences between the two populations, and our independent variable might be labeled "subject classification" (those having retardation

versus those who do not). The researcher does not actually manipulate the independent variable since the intelligence differences were preexisting and impossible to alter. Investigations like this are known as *quasi-experimental* studies in which subjects cannot be randomly assigned to groups, while those where an independent variable is literally manipulated are viewed as "true experiments" (or simply, experiments).

Quasi-experimental studies have particular limitations that do not pose problems in true experiments. We just used the example of comparing subjects of normal intelligence with those having mental retardation on some task performance. As we design such a study, our aim is to control or hold constant everything except the independent variable. There are, however, other influences that cannot be readily controlled. Each group has a history of having mental retardation or being of normal intelligence. That history carries with it a myriad of experiences that cannot be precisely assessed or controlled. For example, the subjects who do not have mental retardation are likely to be healthier and more self-confident than those who are diagnosed with mental retardation. Thus, if we obtain results that suggest differences, we must be cautious in the way findings are interpreted. Although we would like to attribute differences to the independent variable (in this case, mental retardation), some of the experiential factors (e.g., general health status, social rejection, or vitality) might also differentially affect the subjects' performance. This is a continuing problem with quasi-experimental studies and one that researchers must constantly address. It does not, however, preclude the use of such designs in psychology and other behavioral sciences, but requires that we proceed with caution. There are many areas of great interest where the only means of investigation involves quasi-experimental designs, and they have provided enormous amounts of useful information over the years.

Longitudinal/Cross-Sectional Designs. Frequently the study of child behavior disorders is undertaken within a developmental framework. That is, we may be interested in how a particular disorder develops or the developmental course of children's behavioral problems. In these cases the investigations often use a span of time, such as several years, as the independent variable. Two basic approaches have been commonly employed in such research, *longitudinal designs* and *cross-sectional designs.* Longitudinal studies select a sample of subjects, test or

Longitudinal research collects data on the same youngsters over an extended period of time.

observe them, and follow these same subjects for an extended period of time, repeating the assessment intermittently. For example, a researcher may be interested in observing the development of social skills in youngsters with mental retardation as they progress from age 3 to age 15. Cross-sectional investigations, on the other hand, simultaneously sample different groups of subjects who are at several age levels (e.g., 3 to 5, 6 to 8, 9 to 11, 12 to 15) and compare the dependent measure scores (e.g., social skills scores or self-esteem) across the age groups. In both longitudinal and cross-sectional studies, there is an attempt to draw conclusions regarding the developmental trajectory of the dependent variable being measured. In both strategies, time or age serves as the independent variable. Classification of these approaches as experiments is not easy (illustrating that most classification schemes are somewhat arbitrary). Longitudinal studies typically do not involve manipulation of an independent variable, but only repeated observations or measurements over time. Cross-sectional investigations seem to fit the quasi-experimental mold where preexisting differences (e.g., age groups) are present at the time of assessment.

Longitudinal and cross-sectional designs also have certain advantages and limitations that must be considered in developmental studies. As noted previously, longitudinal investigations measure the same subjects repeatedly, usually over an extended period. This permits observation of change in the same individuals as they develop, which is a distinct strength of the longitudinal approach with regard to interpretations of a developmental nature. A potential problem with this procedure

is that subjects' development may be altered by the repeated assessments as they become more "test wise," or that events such as war or economic depressions may affect their development (which would mean that one would not be evaluating development *only*). Thus, it is important to assess the performance of other comparison groups as well as the group of particular interest because all would receive the same repeated testing. Another limitation often encountered in longitudinal studies is subject attrition. As an investigation proceeds over an extended period of time, it is not uncommon for a certain portion of the subjects to be lost because they move, refuse to continue, or die (if the time period is really protracted, we may also have investigator attrition). This may make data collected toward the end of a study different from data collected earlier because of the particular characteristics of the lost subjects rather than because of an actual developmental trend. Thus, we may not actually have the *same* group of subjects at the conclusion of our study. Moreover in really lengthy longitudinal studies, the measures originally used may become outdated and fail to address matters of contemporary concern. Finally, such studies often are prohibitively expensive, so most longitudinal studies now are limited to no longer than 4 to 5 years.

Cross-sectional studies are more convenient to conduct than longitudinal investigations since subjects from several age levels are sampled and typically assessed once at about the same time. This circumvents the difficulties with subject attrition and possible effects of repeated testing. However, other problems are found in cross-sectional developmental studies. One of the most serious limitations is inherent in the cross-sectional approach—the fact that different cohorts or groups are being compared. There is a strong tendency to interpret differences between groups as representing developmental trends in the same manner as longitudinal conclusions are drawn. Such inferences must be viewed with great caution since differences may be caused by factors that are not a result of development. In some cases, the age range from the youngest to oldest groups is so great that sociocultural or historical changes have been substantial (e.g., groups were born in such different times that social mores regarding childrearing have changed, or prevailing teaching practices or permissiveness levels have changed). For example, people's behavior differed before and after the appearance of television, AIDS, computers, synthetic drugs, and so on. Consequently, differences between the groups could be due to development, sociocultural variations, or a combination of the two. Developmental interpretations from cross-sectional studies must be made with great care, although such designs remain an important part of our research methodology in psychology if employed prudently.

Time-Series Designs. Thus far, the examples of experimental research have primarily involved investigations in which groups of subjects might be studied. Traditionally, such studies have been conducted with no fewer than 10 subjects in each group (often more). There is yet another type of experiment that characteristically does not compare groups of this size—*time-series designs.* Time-series experiments involve investigations in which an indepen-

dent variable is manipulated across two or more phases. Treatment is actually manipulated (e.g., applied, then withdrawn, then reapplied) and the dependent variable is monitored. Time-series studies are often used to assess the effect of treatment on the behavior of a small number of subjects or even a single individual subject. If treatment manipulation reliably changes the subject's behavior, then one can conclude that the treatment is effective. Time-series designs have provided researchers with a powerful tool for investigating the effects of treatment in applied settings when limited numbers of children with similar problems might be available for study, something that is not always possible in large group studies. Box 3-4 illustrates such an experiment in which two autistic children were treated for specific fears. There are several variations in time-series design formats that we discuss more completely later.

Time-series designs have an advantage over group experiments because *many more measurements* are collected on the same individuals over some period of time. In group experiments, there is often only one test or measurement after treatment has been applied. In cases where multiple measurements are obtained in group studies, they often constitute only two or three repeated assessments. Even in longitudinal studies, the measurements are far fewer than those typically obtained in time-series investigations. In time-series studies, many observations are made (perhaps several daily) under both untreated and treated conditions. These experiments are occasionally termed continuous measurement studies because of the ongoing data collected from a subject over time. This represents an important strength since one can actually

---

BOX 3-4 TREATMENT RESEARCH FOR AUTISTIC CHILDREN'S PHOBIAS

Two young boys with autism were selected for this intervention because of severe fears that interefered with their daily routine. Kenny (age 4 1/2) had an irrational fear of going outside into the yard alone with the door to the house closed. Ronnie (age 6) exhibited extreme fear at the sign and sound of running shower water. When presented with their dreaded situations, both boys would exhibit extreme avoidance and fear behaviors (e.g., physical resistance, crying, shaking, facial grimaces).

Treatment was undertaken in the boys' respective homes since that was the setting where the fears occurred. In both cases their mothers served as the therapists and were trained in behavioral intervention methods. They were taught how to model approach behavior and also methods of reinforcement so they could reward the youngsters when they did approach the feared settings. Uses of these techniques were discussed, and the mothers also had opportunities to practice implementation in role playing situations. Experimental procedures included a sequence of successive approximations toward each boy's final goal of either approaching a running shower (Ronnie) or going outside into the yard alone with the door closed (Kenny). Baseline data were collected before the interventions were begun, and then the treatment was initiated. Three measures were recorded on each boy: (1) the number of approach steps completed, (2) the number of fear verbalizations and vocalizations, and (3) a rating of the overall appearance of fear. The accompanying figure summarizes the data on these measures for both Kenny and Ronnie.

Box 3-4 (continued)

FIGURE 3-2 **Summary of Data for Kenny and Ronnie.**

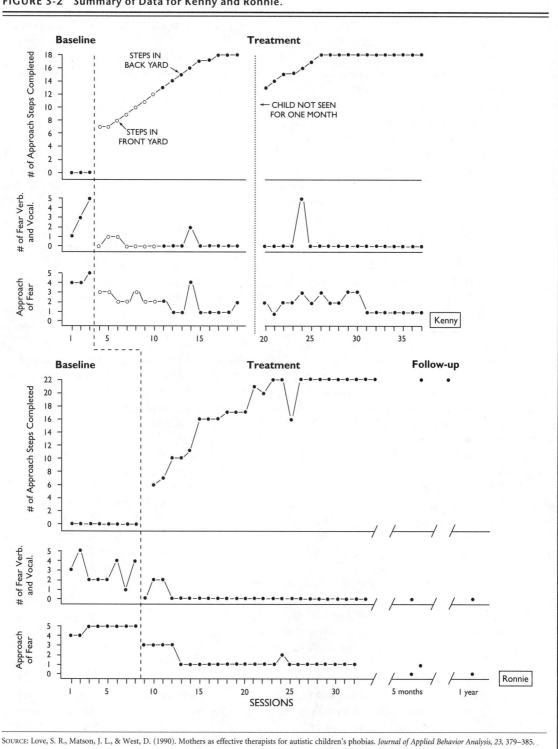

Source: Love, S. R., Matson, J. L., & West, D. (1990). Mothers as effective therapists for autistic children's phobias. *Journal of Applied Behavior Analysis, 23*, 379–385.

observe the *process of change* as well as determine the end product. On the other side of the coin, time-series experiments have been criticized because of the small number of subjects that are studied (often only one). The concern here involves the generalizability of data obtained on only one or a few individuals. Can one third-grade boy with a conduct disorder tell us how children with conduct disorders will generally respond to a particular treatment? Additionally, the types of subjects frequently studied in time-series research are often quite atypical—those that really need treatment because their problems are severe. How do we know that the results would be similar if other people were tested? Basically we do not—unless several replications of the same investigation with different subjects show very similar results. For example, a particular medication may have disastrous side effects in only 1 in 10,000 patients. Testing only a few children may fail to reveal such a rare but potentially lethal reaction.

Group experimental studies represent a mirror image of time-series designs in terms of strengths and limitations. More subjects are included in the group study so that the concern about generalization is lessened. We are more likely to obtain a representative sample of behavior from 30 to 60 subjects than we are from one to three. Another issue arising from group experiments, as they are frequently executed, relates to the small number of measurements that are obtained. If, for example, an experiment is conducted on highly similar groups, different treatments are applied, and subjects are then tested, we have only one sample of behavior—that provided by the test after experimental treatments have been administered. Any posttest differences observed could have been produced by existing pretreatment differences. It is certainly possible that this one assessment involves atypical performance and the researcher would not be aware of it. This concern is somewhat offset by the fact that many subjects are usually tested. It is unlikely that all individuals (or even a substantial number) would be behaving in an extremely atypical fashion unless all had some contagious disease or all were subjected to some stress such as an earthquake or fire.

There are strong designs and weak ones, procedures that produce reliable results and others that might prove misleading. The particular advantages and limitations of specific experimental designs could more than fill this entire book. Interested readers should consult any of the various available volumes on research design (Bailey, 1994; Drew, Hardman, & Hart, 1996; Kazdin, 1992; Kratochwill & Levin, 1992). The limitations of experimental research cannot be discounted as inconsequential nor should they be viewed as insurmountable difficulties. Experimentation remains one of our most powerful tools in the search for causes and most effective treatments of behavior disorders. These limitations can be circumvented to a substantial degree if a researcher is cautious and thorough in planning prior to execution of an experiment. Table 3-2 summarizes advantages and limitations of different research strategies within the general quantitative approach.

QUALITATIVE RESEARCH

As noted earlier, the emergence and acceptance of qualitative research methods in psychology and education is still under way and in many ways continuing to evolve. This results in considerable variation regarding definitions and application standards for these fields of study. What is commonly accepted in cultural anthropology is not well understood in cognitive psychology.

The general term *qualitative research* actually refers to a family of investigatory procedures with a variety of features that are predominantly characterized as being different from experimental and quantitative methods. For example, qualitative research may collect data that are not in numerical form. The data or information may be verbal (words) or visual (e.g., video) and the analysis of the data may occur without reducing those words or video sequences to numbers. This is distinguished from quantitative research in which the investigator may review verbal responses or video clips, but in doing so he or she will tend to count events (such as correct responses or tantrums). The events are thereby reduced to a numerical representation and analysis of those numbers is the means of determining results. Thus, qualitative researchers have an inclination to use narratives as their data form; quantitative researchers tend to use numerical representations of events. It should be noted that some qualitative researchers also use numbers and some experimenters examine themes of interactions, so this distinction is not totally consistent.

The fundamental purpose of qualitative research is one of understanding subjects as they function in their natural environment. Given this purpose, qualitative researchers strongly prefer investigating events and people

TABLE 3-2   ADVANTAGES AND LIMITATIONS OF DIFFERENT QUANTITATIVE RESEARCH STRATEGIES

Strategy	Advantages	Limitations
Case Study	Considerable depth and breadth of information on a given patient's problems.	Data may be biased or inaccurate if informant is biased or does not remember accurately, or if investigator holds a strong bias.
Cross-sectional	Much more convenient to execute than longitudinal studies.	Group differences may make developmental inferences difficult or incorrect.
Experimental (generally)	Exercises considerable control to minimize effects of extraneous factors.	Amount of control exercised may create artificiality and alter subjects' behavior.
Group experimental	Use of many subjects promotes greater confidence in generalizability of results.	Few measurements on subjects does not permit observation of change process.
Interview	Data may be rich and informative because interviewer can probe and interrogate further when answers are unclear or incomplete.	Data may be biased or inaccurate because of interviewer bias and interaction between respondent and interviewer.
Longitudinal	Permits observation of subjects' development over an extended period of time.	Repeated assessment may alter subjects' performance; subject attrition may be substantial over the extended time period.
Nonexperimental	Less exercise of control permits observation of subjects' behavior over an extended period of time.	Less exercise of control may generate unreliable or uninterpretable data.
Observational	Permits precise behavioral descriptions of subjects' behavior and changes caused by intervention.	Data may be inaccurate if observer is biased, or unreliable if observer is not trained or if target behaviors are defined ambiguously.
Quasi-experimental	Permits the study of populations that are different prior to the investigation.	Difficult to control for preexisting differences other than the independent variable.
Questionnaire	Economical means of obtaining data from a large, geographically dispersed sample if distributed by mail.	Data obtained may be limited by format of questionnaire or biased by low response rate.
Time-series	Many measurements on same subject permit observation of change process as treatment is manipulated.	Often criticized for using small number of subjects, which may limit generalizability of results.

without altering the natural state of the environment. They are generally not willing to tamper with what occurs normally, although their very presence may change their subjects' behavior. Related to this approach, some qualitative researchers undertake studies without specific questions or hypotheses being developed, only general questions about a group or setting may be in place at the outset. It is presumed that one can study an environment and that the specific questions and hypotheses will surface. Once again, this is considerably different from experimental and quantitative research in which it is essential that questions, hypotheses, and definitions be specified prior to beginning the investigation.

Judging the validity of information in qualitative research is accomplished in a manner that is very different from other methods examined earlier. The validity of data is determined by cross-checking information sources, or triangulation. If the same information is obtained from multiple sources, it is presumed to be valid or accurate data. For example, if different psychotherapists agree that depressed children display extreme conflict over dependency, others place more credence in the claim. Validity in experimental research is based on the concept of control—if all influences are held constant except one, which is manipulated (the treatment or experimental variable), then it is presumed that the treatment was the causal factor. Since qualitative researchers are unwilling to manipulate or tamper with the natural environment, triangulation among independent observers is the only means of assessing validity.

TABLE 3-3   MAJOR DIFFERENCES BETWEEN QUANTITATIVE AND QUALITATIVE RESEARCH

Quantitative Methods	Qualitative Methods
Preference for precise hypotheses stated at the outset.	Preference for hypotheses that emerge as study develops.
Preference for precise definitions stated at the outset.	Preference for definitions in context or as study progresses.
Data reduced to numerical scores.	Preference for narrative description.
Much attention to assessing and improving reliability of scores obtained from instruments.	Preference for assuming that reliability of inferences is adequate.
Assessment of validity through variety of design procedures with reliance on statistical indices.	Assessment of validity through cross-checking sources of information (triangulation).
Preference for random techniques for obtaining meaningful samples.	Preference for expert informant (purpose) samples.
Preference for precise descriptions of procedures.	Preference for narrative/literary descriptions of procedures.
Preference for design or statistical control of extraneous variables.	Preference for logical analysis in controlling or accounting for extraneous variables.
Preference for specific design control for procedural bias.	Primary reliance on researcher to deal with procedural bias.
Preference for statistical summary of results.	Preference for narrative summary of results.
Preference for breaking down of complex phenomena into specific parts for analysis.	Preference for holistic description of complex phenomena.
Willingness to manipulate aspects, situations, or conditions in studying complex phenomena.	Unwillingness to tamper with naturally occurring phenomena.

SOURCE: Fraenkel, J. R., & Wallen, W. E. (1993). *How to design and evaluate research in education* (2nd ed., p. 380). New York: McGraw-Hill.

Qualitative research methods deviate from those that have customarily been employed in psychology in some very fundamental ways. As with other techniques, we have highlighted only certain features of these inquiry approaches. The interested reader may wish to consult volumes that focus more exclusively on qualitative research (e.g., Lancy, 1993; Patton, 1990).

It is not surprising that the emergence of qualitative approaches to investigation is viewed with a certain level of suspicion by some who are only experienced with experimental quantitative research. To many, however, the most important issue is collecting solid information, irrespective of method employed. For these researchers, the approach in each study is to exploit the advantages and take precautions to minimize or eliminate the impact of methodological difficulties. Table 3-3 summarizes major differences between quantitative and qualitative research paradigms.

FUNDAMENTALS OF DESIGNING RESEARCH

Previous sections have alluded to the process of designing or planning an investigation, an essential step in research.

No investigation that is designed poorly or planned in a haphazard fashion can generate results that are very reliable or useful. The importance of this crucial step cannot be overemphasized regardless of which approach is being employed. The purpose of the present section is to provide background regarding the fundamentals of designing experimental research. This emphasis is not meant to discount the value of nonexperimental and qualitative research in studying child behavior disorders. However, space limitations preclude a more complete examination of all research methods.

The Concept of Control

Earlier, we alluded to the concept of control in discussing experimental research. It warrants specific attention here because it is so central to a well-designed experiment. Many different factors can influence children's behavior including their intelligence, language skills, motivation, relationship with the examiner, and so forth. The object of experimentation is to identify those factors that actually do affect a child's task performance and to eliminate the other factors. The concept of control involves *eliminating the systematic influence of all variables except the one being studied*. For example, perhaps we want to compare the effectiveness of two treatment programs. In this case we have decided to conduct a group experiment. One group will receive treatment A whereas the second will receive treatment B (the independent variable would thus be type of treatment). The concept of control would dictate that all factors must be equivalent for both groups except the independent variable (treatment). That is, the groups must be equivalent with regard to any factors that may influence the results (e.g., age, sex, problem severity, etc.). Procedures must also be similar for the two groups except for any procedural details that are actually part of the treatment characteristics. Unless these matters are held constant, or controlled, we will not be able to attribute any differences to the effect of our treatment. For example, we might not be able to infer that subjects in group A performed better than those in group B because of the treatment (say, for example, individualized instruction) if group A also had more time to complete the task than group B did. The concept of control is basic to experimental design—a notion we will encounter repeatedly.

Designing Time-Series Experiments

Time-series experiments (which trace behavioral changes over time) are very powerful research tools for studying child behavior disorders. Frequently, we are faced with a situation in which an individual child has a particular problem that requires identification and treatment. As behavioral scientists we are interested in exploring the nature of the problem and finding an effective treatment. At the same time, as clinicians we have an immediate need to solve the problem for this particular child. Time-series designs are particularly well suited for situations in which there is a scientific purpose and an immediate clinical need at the same time. With disorders that strike less than 1 child in 1,000, it may not be feasible to use a group experiment to find a group of children with the same problem in order to investigate the nature of the difficulty. Additionally, by the time that all this has been accomplished, we may have neglected a clinical responsibility for the *individual child*. Time-series designs provide a means by which we can treat individuals and at the same time systematically collect scientifically sound information regarding the effectiveness of a treatment. It is well beyond the scope of this chapter to examine all the details involved in time-series research, but we will pro-

vide an overview of fundamental design concepts and examine a few basic design formats. Interested readers may wish to consult volumes that are devoted exclusively to time-series experimentation (e.g., Kratochwill & Levin, 1992).

A few preliminary points need discussion before we examine time-series design formats. As noted earlier, in time-series experiments there are usually a number of performance measures in each phase of the experiment. These are typically obtained by repeated observations of the child's behavior over a period of time. The observations may be conducted over a series of sessions, days, weeks, or some other time dimension that is appropriate given the nature of the experiment. Obviously, a researcher will not merely observe the child in a casual or unsystematic fashion. It is crucial that the investigator has a clear definition that includes a detailed description of how the behavior will be observed or measured. This is known as defining the *target behavior(s)*, the target for change which will be used as a dependent variable. Suppose a child has a tendency to be inattentive to teacher's instructions. Most likely that problem involves a behavior or several behaviors that are causing serious difficulties. The behaviors that are selected to be modified or eliminated become the target behaviors. Our dependent variable might be the number of times those behaviors occur in a 10-minute interval. Rarer behavior, such as temper tantrums or running away, may be counted over longer intervals, such as days or weeks.

We have mentioned that there are different phases in time-series experiments. How does a researcher determine when to change phases, such as from baseline observations to treatment introduction and observation? This is one of the most important points to consider in designing, executing, and evaluating time-series experiments. Phase changes should occur only when a researcher has obtained enough measures or observations to permit an adequate sample of behavior and when the behavior's rate is stable or generally predictable (e.g., shows a regular pattern such as increases at night or on the weekends). The purpose of changing phases is to demonstrate behavior change in the child. Both as researchers and clinicians we want to be able to attribute any observed behavior change to the new condition or treatment. This cannot be done with any confidence unless the data are stable prior to phase change. Basically this means that prior to beginning an experiment we

FIGURE 3-3   Hypothetical data display from an A-B experiment in which a student's rate of disruptions is examined with and without reinforcing on-task behavior.

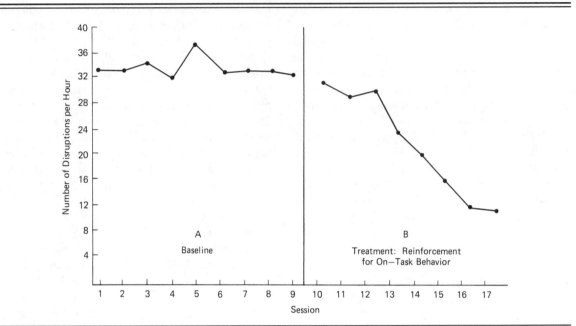

cannot determine exactly how many sessions or data points will be involved in any single phase. The determination of when phases can be changed must be made when the data collected provide a stable estimate of behavior rate (Gelfand & Hartmann, 1984). Related to this point, it is also crucial to have reliable observations and to know the *level* of reliability present in a set of data. That is, how accurate and replicable the behavioral observations are. Without such information, one may be making judgments based on inconsistent scores or performance observations that may lead to incorrect treatment decisions (Hartmann, 1982). Most time-series investigations that are well designed and executed will (or should) provide detailed reliability information. This may be represented by the percent of occasions on which two observers agree that the target behavior has occurred.

THE A-B DESIGN

The A-B design is no longer used to any great extent because of serious weaknesses, which we will examine later. It is discussed here only because of its conceptual simplicity in order to promote a basic understanding of more elaborate time-series designs.

There are two phases in the A-B design configuration, baseline (the A portion) and intervention (the B portion). Figure 3-3 illustrates a data display from an A-B experiment. As suggested by Figure 3-3, baseline data are collected for a period of time (sessions one through nine) until a stable estimate of behavior is obtained. Data in this phase represent the performance level or behavior frequency exhibited by the subject in an untreated condition. After a stable rate of baseline behavior has been established, the intervention phase is introduced. This is represented by sessions 10 through 17 in Figure 3-3.

A cursory inspection of the data in Figure 3-3 might suggest that the treatment was effective. The baseline data are extremely stable and after the intervention is initiated the rate begins to decrease dramatically. The rate continues to decrease and stabilizes with a few minor variations. However, this data display illustrates nicely the serious problems with an A-B design. Assessment of the strength of our treatment depends on attributing a behavior change to the intervention. The major difficulty with an A-B design is the absence of supporting evidence for such an assumption. Although the behavior did change coincidentally with intervention, other influences could have

FIGURE 3-4 Hypothetical data display of a reversal design.

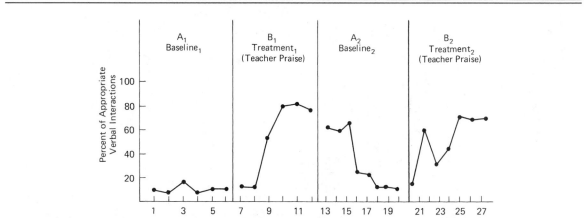

occurred simultaneously, which might have had the same effect (if this is true, the concept of control would not be operative). For example, suppose that on day 10 or 11 of the experiment in Figure 3-3 the child's parents began to administer a medication aimed at reducing the child's hyperactive behavior. Or, the parents could have begun to treat the child more warmly and consistently at the same time as the child's psychotherapy began. If the experimenters are unaware of this, they may believe the reduction in disruptive behavior is explained solely by their treatment (reinforcement of "on-task" behavior). The design itself does not provide assurance that the independent variable was the influential factor.

THE REVERSAL DESIGN

In order to circumvent the difficulties just described, behavioral researchers have extended the A-B format to include a reversal phase (A_1-B_1-A_2). Figure 3-4 illustrates a data display from a reversal experiment. This figure shows that a reversal design is an extension of the simple A-B design discussed above. Procedures during phases A_1 and B_1 are essentially the same as before. However, after the behavior stabilizes in B_1, a further phase change is initiated. The A_2 or reversal phase involves removal of treatment and returning to baseline conditions with the hope that the child's baseline performance rate will be recaptured. Following this same line of reasoning, the A_2 phase is continued until the data stabilize once again, after which treatment is reinstituted in the B_2 phase.

There are a number of reversal variations, although the basic format usually involves three or four phases (i.e., A-B-A or A-B-A-B).

A reversal design provides much greater evidence regarding the influence of intervention than an A-B design. Ideally the data will follow the basic pattern of change illustrated in Figure 3-4 (let's hope so if it is *your* study although it isn't always the case). If this occurs, a researcher can be relatively confident that the independent variable is *the* factor influencing behavior. It is unlikely that other events would occur simultaneously with *each* phase change.

Despite its strengths, the reversal design does have certain limitations. Confidence regarding the effect of an independent variable rests primarily on the reversal of the target behavior in phase A_2. If reversal does not occur, the researcher has little evidence regarding the influence of intervention. Suppose an experiment is conducted using a reversal design and the data obtained appear as in Figure 3-5. We have little reason to believe from these data that the independent variable (treatment) is controlling the target behavior. There may be several explanations of why the data do not reverse.

First, the target behavior may not be under the control of the independent variable (e.g., the treatment) and the change in rate from A_1 to B_1 may be the result of some outside influence, for example, some other program introduced by a teacher or parent. In fact, with data such as those in Figure 3-5, we are in a position that is just as

FIGURE 3-5 Example of an A-B-A experiment that does not reverse the child's behavior rate.

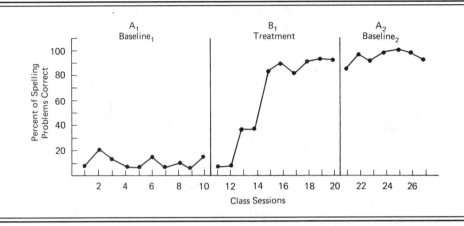

weak a demonstration as a simple A-B design. Another explanation might be that the treatment is so powerful that the influence is not reversible even when baseline conditions are reestablished in A₂, as when a disruptive, resistant child has learned some method of self-control and uses it consistently thereafter. A third explanation might relate to the target behavior itself. Some behaviors are not reversible, particularly those that involve skill acquisition. It is extremely difficult to reverse certain skills such as the ability to read or the familiar example of riding a bicycle or swimming. It is apparent that in Figure 3-5 the unfortunate experimenter selected an inappropriate design to study the target behavior.

One further comment should be made regarding the use of reversal designs. The experimenter in Figure 3-5 demonstrably used an inappropriate design since the target behavior was not likely reversible. There are other occasions when a reversal design should not be employed. In some circumstances it may be undesirable or even dangerous and unethical to reverse treatment conditions. For example, we may be working with a child who is exhibiting self-injurious behavior. If we implement a treatment to eliminate those behaviors, it would be very undesirable to reverse the conditions so as to produce a renewed high rate of self-injury, even though only temporarily.

THE MULTIPLE BASELINE DESIGN

Multiple baseline designs are very useful for time-series experiments in which reversal configurations are not appropriate or behaviors are unlikely to reverse. In these designs, data are recorded on two or more behaviors simultaneously or on a single behavior in two or more settings simultaneously. Treatment is introduced in a staggered or sequential fashion, as in the example in Figure 3-6—in the different settings separately and in a staggered or sequential fashion. In this example, the same behavior (a child's tantrums) is treated in three different locations. First the child receives a program to reduce temper tantrums in the classroom. Then treatment is implemented in the home setting. Reference to Figure 3-6 suggests that the multiple baseline design resembles conducting several A-B experiments but at different points in time. The change from baseline to treatment for each of the target settings is timed sequentially, so that the behavior in setting 2 (playground) remains in baseline while treatment is applied to temper tantrums in setting 1 (the classroom), and so on. In *all* cases, the phase changes must occur only after stable data are evident in the target settings or behaviors under study. The strength of multiple baseline designs is based on the staggering of phase changes. If the independent variable (treatment) is influencing the target behaviors, there should be a pattern of sequential change that reflects the consecutive application of intervention (as in Figure 3-6). For example, if separate behaviors are studied, then the data on behavior 2 should remain stable throughout the time that baseline conditions exist for *that* behavior (even though treatment is applied to behavior 1 during that period). If the treatment is effective, the child's behavior should improve when (and only when) that particular behavior is treated and should not reverse.

FIGURE 3-6 Data display from a hypothetical multiple-baseline experiment.

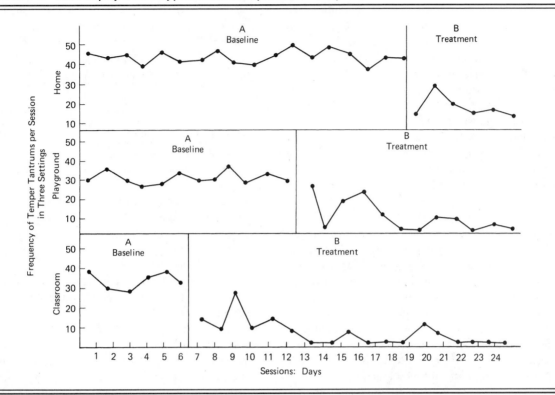

As with most basic design formats, there are a number of variations in multiple baseline experiments. They can be used with separate behaviors and environments, as previously described. In addition, this design is also suitable when the same behavior and the same treatment are studied with two or more subjects (multiple baseline across subjects). In this instance, treatment is applied to different children in a staggered fashion much as we described for settings and behaviors. The multiple baseline design is very flexible, as is suggested by these examples. It is a very powerful design that in recent years has been of increased interest to behavioral researchers. Moreover, multiple baseline procedures do not involve the reinstatement of troublesome behaviors, a particularly important consideration in the treatment of disturbed children.

Designing Group Experiments

Traditional group experiments comparing the performance of an experimentally treated group and an untreated control group have been used in psychological research for many years. As noted earlier, this type of experiment differs in several ways from the time-series designs just discussed. Obviously more subjects are used to participate in each group. Also, far fewer assessments are usually obtained, either one assessment following treatment or before and after the treatment. Frequently the experimental groups are formed, treatment is applied, and a single performance or behavioral measure is then administered (we are not advocating this routinely, however). As indicated in the diagrams presented earlier, time-series experiments usually involve many data points collected or observations made over a number of sessions. Various types of designs are used in group experiments. Only a few of the basic formats will be examined here.

We will discuss two basic types of experimental designs: (1) a comparison of several groups or (2) a pretest-posttest comparison performed on the same group (repeated measures design). In this context, a separate group design refers to investigations in which a different group receives each of several experimental conditions (i.e., group A receives one treatment and is compared with group B, which receives a second treatment). Because the different groups are composed of different subjects, the performance scores in one group are not influenced by performance scores in the other and so are independent of each other. This is distinguished from a pretest-posttest study in which the same subjects are being assessed twice. Because the same individuals are being tested in both the pretest and the posttest, scores in the posttest are clearly *not* independent from those on the pretest. The point of interest is the magnitude of change from pre to post.

One point about terminology should be made here. The terms *experimental variable* and *independent variable* are often used interchangeably and refer to the same concept—the factor being studied that differentiates the groups or is manipulated. For the remainder of this chapter we will use the term experimental variable to avoid confusion with the notion of independence mentioned above. An experimental variable may be either independent (as in the two-group example above) or may involve repeated measures (which makes the comparison non-independent, as with the pre–post example).

Another important factor in group experimental designs involves the number of experimental variables being studied. Group experimental designs may be aimed at studying one, two, or more experimental variables, depending on the nature of the investigation (e.g., an experiment that studies the effects of two types of therapy on males and females has two experimental variables—gender and type of treatment). Next we discuss group experiments both in terms of the independence factor and the number of experimental variables under investigation.

DESIGNS WITH ONE EXPERIMENTAL VARIABLE

Perhaps the simplest group design involves those studies with one experimental variable, often called *single factor designs*. Figure 3-7 presents a diagram of a single factor study in which three separate groups are compared. Since this experiment includes three different groups, each of which receives a different treatment, it is a separate group or independent comparison. As indicated in Figure 3-7, the experimental variable is the "method of treatment"

FIGURE 3-7 Diagram of a hypothetical group experiment design with one variable (an independent comparison).

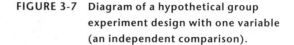
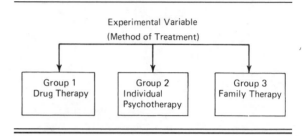

and three types of treatments are being compared (drug therapy, individual psychotherapy, and family therapy). It is important to remember that an experiment such as this requires that the groups be equivalent on all important variables other than the one being tested, in this case, the method of treatment. Thus, subjects may be randomly assigned to groups. You will recall that this is the important *concept of control*, which allows us to attribute any significant behavioral differences observed to the effect of the experimental variable. In this example, we randomly assign individuals to groups prior to initiation of the treatment, administer the treatment, and then test the subjects in each group. If we obtain performance scores that are substantially different between groups, then we will probably conclude that the performance differences are due to the different treatment methods.

Single factor experiments may also include repeated measures of a group's performance. Figure 3-8 illustrates a study with one experimental variable in which a single group's performance is measured repeatedly. The experimental variable in this example is the learning stage (early, midway, late); the same subjects' performance is assessed three times (at the beginning of the study, after the first 10 learning trials, and, finally, after the second 10 trials), which generates three data points that will be compared. The scores from each of the three measurement occasions are conceptually the same as our separate conditions in the earlier example of an independent comparison. As before, the concept of control would require that, to the degree possible, the only difference between measures one, two, and three is the experimental variable—the learning stage. Such experiments have often been used to determine if children make different types of errors at different stages of learning new material.

FIGURE 3-8 Diagram of a hypothetical experiment design with one experimental variable (learning stage) and three repeated measures.

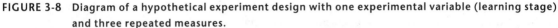

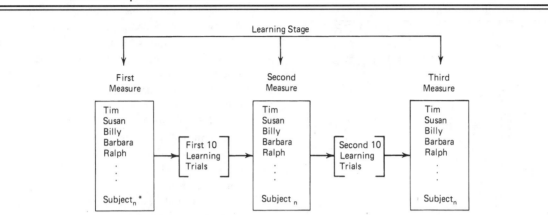

Subject$_n$ is a notation that refers to the last subject in a group

DESIGNS WITH MULTIPLE EXPERIMENTAL VARIABLES

Group experiments may also include two or more experimental variables (such studies are also termed "multifactor designs"). Although there are many variations of multifactor designs, we examine only a few basic ones. Figure 3-9 illustrates a study that investigated two experimental variables simultaneously. This experiment studied the effects of two experimental treatments (variables) on the performance of adolescents with mental retardation: (1) reward anticipation (subjects in one condition anticipated a reward for good performance whereas those in the second condition were not anticipating a reward) and (2) performance expectancy (subjcts in one condition were given information that led them to believe they would surely succeed whereas those in the second condition were given information that would suggest success was unlikely). Thus, there were two conditions under each of these experimental variables. As shown in the figure, there were four separate groups, one for each condition, which indicates that both experimental variables (reward anticipation and performance expectancy) represent independent comparisons. Occasionally it is desirable to have repeated measures on one experimental variable while the second is independent. Such a study might compare two types of psychotherapy (e.g., treatments A and B) on different groups of subjects as the independent experimental variable. In the same study, a second experimental variable might assess the

durability of treatments by testing the same subjects repeatedly over several weeks after treatment ends. This second experimental variable is a nonindependent comparison because the same subjects are tested repeatedly. Designs that employ both independent and repeated measures on experimental variables are known as *mixed* designs.

As noted earlier, there are a great many variations in group experimental design although the variations must all contain the essential feature of control. It is possible to study more than two experimental variables simultaneously with many combinations of independent and repeated comparisons. We have also mentioned the use of quasi-experimental designs with preexisting differences such as the child's age or gender as a focus of the study. A more complete examination of these topics may be found in Cook and Campbell (1990).

COMMON DESIGN MISTAKES

Classic textbook examples are seldom found outside the environment in which they were contrived—in classroom lectures and textbooks. This is the case in research design just as it is in other areas of study. The designs we have presented often must be altered to answer a particular research question or to suit a set of circumstances. In many cases, factors are encountered during research execution that may threaten the soundness of an investigation and require design or procedural changes. As

FIGURE 3-9 Diagram of an experimental design with two experimental variables (both independent comparisons).

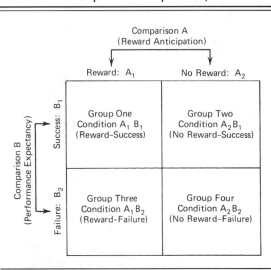

SOURCE: R. F. Welch and C. J. Drew (1972). Effects of reward anticipation and performance expectancy on the learning rate of EMR adolescents. *American Journal of Mental Deficiency, 77,* 291–295. Reprinted by permission.

examples, the more disturbed, resistant families may drop out of therapy, raters may become unreliable, or a school may withdraw from a study. Some problems such as these can be prevented by careful planning. This section examines some common design mistakes.

Internal and External Validity

Validity is a term used in many different contexts and is misused perhaps as often as it is properly employed. We are limiting the use of this term to two aspects of research design. Internal and external validity represent two crucial concepts in research design and are major criteria by which investigations are evaluated. These have been important in experimental research methods for many years (Campbell, 1957; Campbell & Stanley, 1963) and continue to be central concepts in research design (Cook & Campbell, 1990). *Internal validity* refers to the technical soundness of an investigation in terms of control; that is, how well designed is this study? Experiments that are internally valid are those that have controlled all systematic influences except the one under investigation (i.e., the experimental variable). *External validity*, on the other hand, speaks to the issues of generalizability, or how well results can be generalized to other subjects, settings, and treatments.

Both internal and external validity are important although they may be incompatible in certain circumstances. In some situations, the achievement of adequate internal validity requires conducting an investigation in a controlled or contrived laboratory setting. For example, one might best assess the social perception of juvenile delinquents in a laboratory, but at the risk of their giving uncharacteristic performances. To the extent that such efforts create an artificial environment and influence subjects' performance, the generalizability of results may be reduced. That is, subjects may respond differently in a laboratory than in their homes or schools. The reverse may also be true and studies may be representative but poorly controlled. Research is a process of constant compromise in order to achieve an appropriate balance between internal and external validity. The notion of an "appropriate balance" may well vary greatly from study to study. Particularly in the early stages of a research program, internal validity may be the primary concern, whereas later as the fundamental knowledge base grows, more attention may be given to external validity and the issue of to whom the results will apply. In all cases, however, care must be taken not to sacrifice internal validity to a point where the value of any knowledge gained is diminished. Campbell and Stanley (1963) emphasized the importance of internal validity by noting that "*internal validity* is the basic minimum without which an experiment is uninterpretable" (p. 175, emphasis in the original). That is, researchers might be confident that children benefit from psychotherapy given by experts in university clinics. However, less experienced and less adequately trained therapists in the community might not be equally successful in treating child clients.

A number of factors can threaten the internal validity of an investigation and total elimination of all possible threats is often impossible. Nearly every study could be strengthened in some fashion. From a practical standpoint, a researcher's task is to eliminate or minimize the influence of as many problems as possible. Those internal validity problems that cannot be eliminated in a particular study must be accounted for as the results are interpreted.

Internal validity pertains very specifically to the important concept of control mentioned previously. Without control of confounding extraneous influences, a researcher will not be able to attribute results to the experimental variable. For example, suppose we are investigating the effects of a new treatment for obesity. Certainly, if differences are evident we want to be able to say that our treatment probably generated the participants' weight loss. This would not be possible if, say, some other treatment for obesity that was advertised on TV was also carried out by an overweight participant at the same time (which is common for the overweight) and thus became a rival explanation for the results. For example, in addition to a reducing diet, a subject might try fasting or drinking a low-calorie concoction.

Similarly, we would not be able to determine the effects of our treatment if the scales were adjusted (changed or recalibrated) between two measurements of the subjects' weight. In either case, differences may be caused by our treatment or by the other factors, which would not permit us to say, with confidence, what caused the change. We have mentioned only a few threats to internal validity. Interested readers, and particularly those who must complete an undergraduate or graduate thesis project, should consult texts that more completely examine these topics (e.g., Cook & Campbell, 1990; Drew, Hardman, & Hart, 1996).

Related to internal validity concerns are the influences of placebo effects. Placebo effects are those in which changes in subjects' behavior or performance may be observed simply because they are in an experiment and not because of any particular impact of a treatment or intervention. Because of such influences, it may be difficult to attribute changes in subjects to treatment. Such a situation was evident in the study by Wermuth, Davis, Hollister, and Stunkard (1977) which investigated the treatment of bulimia (see Chapter 10). These investigators found a substantial improvement when they administered inactive pills to subjects and therefore were not able to determine that improvement was due to actual medication. Placebo effects present a substantial challenge to researchers studying child behavior disorders since they are likely to be present in some form and to some degree in nearly all therapeutic interventions. Additionally, placebos may be quite potent, in some cases actually altering disorders that are quite severe (Kazdin, 1992) through a beneficial impact on clients' expectations and behavior.

As stated earlier, external validity refers to the generalizability of results that can also be threatened by a number of factors. The basic notion of external validity is that the experimental results must be applicable to subjects, materials, and settings other than those used in the particular experiment. We may not be able to accomplish this if there are substantial differences between the subjects, materials, or setting of the experiment and those in the world outside the experiment. For example, if the sample of subjects is substantially different from the population at large (or the population to which a researcher wishes to generalize), then the results will likely *not* be generalizable. This is a problem when only a few people from a target group, such as mothers of autistic children, volunteer to participate in a study. The volunteers may be more highly educated and their children less seriously disturbed than the remainder of the group of interest. Similarly, the environment in which a study is conducted, such as a brightly lit, sparsely furnished, sterile laboratory equipped with one-way viewing windows, may be unusual or different from the subjects' routine environment. If this is the case, subjects may behave differently than usual and the results would not likely generalize to their homes, schools, and neighborhoods. As before, several major types of factors have been identified as threats to external validity, and interested readers may wish to consult more detailed discussions of these topics (e.g., Cook & Campbell, 1990; Drew, Hardman, & Hart, 1996).

The examination of threats to internal and external validity highlights the importance of thorough planning prior to the execution of a study. Effective planning requires training, foresight, and meticulous attention to detail. Often more time is spent on planning than actually conducting an investigation. Without such initial efforts, an investigation may provide inaccurate information that is of little or no value in the treatment of behavior disorders in children. As a consumer of research, one must keep possible threats to internal and external validity in mind when examining the results of a study. Often the use of common sense alone can help readers to spot errors that invalidate research studies.

Avoiding Pitfalls

Researchers have several methods of avoiding the threats to validity mentioned previously. Employing the appropriate experimental design can be useful since some designs are particularly vulnerable to certain problems. Procedures employed during the actual execution of a study can also be very important in minimizing weaknesses in internal and external validity. Techniques for subject selection and assignment to groups or treatments are vital and powerful procedural tools to strengthen internal and external validity of investigations.

Behavioral researchers seldom study an entire population. In most cases, it is necessary to select a sample of individuals from a given population to serve as subjects. This immediately increases the importance of carefully defining and describing the subject population. Unless this is accomplished, an investigator does not know which individuals are potential subjects and to what population the results should generalize. Population definition is of crucial importance as a foundation of external validity and for selecting an appropriate sample. Many sampling procedures are available and choice of an appropriate procedure depends on the specific nature of an investigation. Space restrictions preclude a detailed examination of all sampling techniques that may be employed. Once again, interested readers may wish to consult one of the volumes that is solely devoted to sampling (e.g., Cochran, 1977; Sudman, 1976).

One of the most generally used methods of selecting subjects is known as *simple random sampling*. This procedure, like sampling in general, is aimed at obtaining a sample of subjects that will be representative of the population under study. To accomplish this goal, researchers use a selection process in which each individual in the population has *an equal chance* of being chosen to participate in the investigation. Since each person has an equal chance of selection, it is assumed that the subject sample characteristics will represent those that exist in the population. Certainly this is an *assumption* and random sampling does not totally *ensure* a representative sample, particularly if small groups are studied. (If a very small number of subjects are sampled from a large population, it is unlikely that all or most of the variety of characteristics are represented in that sample.) However, random sampling procedures do decrease the probability that some systematic bias is operating in the selection process. Even if the resulting sample is found to be unrepresentative in some important way, statistical corrections can be used to control for the differences. The most simple and effective technique for selecting a random sample involves using a random number table (available in most statistics texts), assigning subjects to groups according to whether each successive random digit is odd (group 1) or even (group 2), or using some variation of this procedure.

We have repeatedly stressed the importance of group equivalence on the characteristics other than the experimental variables (the fundamental concept of control, which is essential to internal validity). The basic tool that a researcher can use to accomplish group equivalence is subject assignment. In addition to *random assignment*, researchers can use *experimental matching*. Experimental matching basically involves procedures wherein a researcher forces group equivalence on some characteristic(s) thought to be important for the particular study being conducted. For example, if chronological age (CA) was thought to be important, groups might be formed by matching children on CA. This is often accomplished by replacing subjects or switching group assignment for given subjects until the average CA is the same for the treatment and control groups.

Random assignment procedures (usually accomplished by using random number tables) have become favored over experimental matching. In fact, some researchers believe that matching should be employed only as a last resort, if ever. There are many reasons for favoring random assignment over experimental matching. Perhaps the most compelling relates to the characteristics on which equivalence is desired. Experimental matching requires a clear knowledge of those factors on which control is to be exercised. In one sense, it is nearly a declaration that "these are the important factors and others are not." By selectively placing subjects (i.e., switching, replacing), there is a substantial possibility that the groups will be made different on some factors in addition to those being matched. The major strength of random assignment procedures is that, because of the nature of the process, there is little reason to expect any *systematic* differences between the groups. Thus, the researcher is probably forming equivalent groups on those factors that are known to be important and those that are as yet unidentified as being important for control (a nice touch and good insurance for the durability of your internal validity).

ETHICAL ISSUES IN CONDUCTING RESEARCH

Ethical issues are vitally important in psychology because the field centrally involves people working with other people and controlling aspects of their lives. When children's behavior is given a diagnostic label and is treated, ethical problems may arise. Educational, medical, and mental health professionals are the caretakers, the treatment specialists, and generally the professionally authorized arm of society that addresses human concerns. As such they must be especially concerned about fairness and avoiding harm to clients. Researchers must not take unfair advantage of their responsible positions. They must act ethically or they may be punished by their professional societies or state licensing offices, criminally and civilly.

Ethical concerns hold a place of particular importance in psychological and other behavioral research because of the nature of the research undertaken. To investigate patterns of normal and abnormal behavior, we do invade, look, and explore into the lives of others. We do this not for personal curiosity or advantage, but in order to find causes of problems and more effective treatments. Because psychological research involves people's lives, great care must be taken to ensure fairness to those being studied. A researcher's task is not limited to the design and execution of a technically sound investigation. Constant vigilance must be maintained regarding ethical issues as they pertain to research procedures and related professional activities, especially in the area of child behavior disorders. Consequently, each national professional society requires members to abide by written codes of ethics. Institutional review boards or human subjects committees oversee research ethics, as do federal offices, school district research participation committees, and others. The typical child research project is scrutinized by at least three such bodies in order to protect the welfare of participating children and their families. In addition, public agencies and research sponsoring agencies require that researchers obtain informed, written consent from participants or their parents. Participants are also informed that they may withdraw from the study at any time without penalty.

Concern for research ethics is not new although it has emerged more prominently in recent years. Most professional organizations now have ethical codes of conduct for their members. Some have made a practice of investigating allegations and expelling individuals from membership for breaches of ethical conduct (e.g., the American Psychological Association). Additionally, federal agencies funding research activities typically have regulations regarding appropriate and ethical treatment of subjects. Complete volumes have appeared regarding research ethics (e.g., Sieber, 1992) and as we shall see, the issues can be complex ones, far exceeding the scope of this chapter. Interested readers may wish to consult any of a number of references for a more complete examination of ethical issues in research (e.g., Fisher & Tryon, 1990; Kimmel, 1988; Sieber, 1992).

Probably the most conspicuous concern in research ethics relates to the protection of the physical and psychological welfare of subjects. This concern has emerged because of two major influences: periodic though rare cases of flagrant abuse of research participants' rights and a generally heightened societal sensitivity regarding individual rights. Ethical issues related to subjects are of particular concern in psychological research, especially in terms of subjects' fully informed consent to participate in a research project, which is seen by some as the cornerstone of ethical research (Baumrind, 1990).

Consent in research may be viewed simply as a means by which subjects openly declare whether or not they wish to participate in an investigation. Upon further inspection, this apparently simple process involves a number of complexities. To be valid, consent must include three elements: *capacity, information,* and *voluntariness.* All three elements must be present for consent to be meaningful; the researcher must also be aware that consent is not permanent. It may be withdrawn at any time, which means that participants must be allowed to discontinue their participation whenever they wish to do so and without penalty of any type whether psychological or material.

Capacity refers to a person's ability and legal authority to consent to participate in a research project. Although a 12-year-old boy who is a juvenile delinquent may have the ability to decide whether to agree to participate in an investigation, he does not have the legal authority to do so since he is considered a minor. His parent or legal guardian must grant consent for him to participate, but he must also agree that he wants to do so. This issue is even more sensitive and difficult when subjects with psychosis, mental retardation, or very young children are studied. Because they lack the capacity to determine whether they should participate, their caretakers and the investigators must take special pains to protect them from exploitation. At the same time, caretakers must bear in mind that progress in treatment can come about only through procedurally sound research, and so participation is desirable, in the public interest, and may be advantageous for participants who receive a thorough assessment, a new intervention, or monetary compensation for their participation.

The second element of consent involves *information.* Speaking in the context of mental retardation research, Turnbull (1977) explained:

> *". . . the focus is on* what information is given and how it is given *since it must be effectively communicated (given and received) to be acted upon. The concern is with the* fullness *and* effectiveness *of the disclosure: is it* designed to be fully understood, and is it fully understood? *The burden of satisfying these two tests rests on the professional." (p. 8, emphasis in the original)*

This places a great burden on behavioral researchers and causes particular problems with certain types of studies in which examination of the consent information may alert subjects to what the hypothesis is, which may make them act unnaturally.

Voluntariness, the third element of consent, is, once again, more complex than it may appear on the surface. Clearly a generalized notion of voluntariness would suggest that subjects in a study must agree to participate of their own free will. This also places a great deal of responsibility on researchers in the study of child behavior disorders. Certainly there should not be any constraint or coercion, either explicit or implicit. In some cases even a reward for participation may be coercive, such as might be the case when paying destitute families or altering time of probation for prisoners serving as subjects.

Researchers working in child behavior disorders must be particularly cautious regarding ethical practices. In many cases, meeting the requirements of the three elements of consent present considerable difficulty (Siegel & Ellis, 1985). First, consent must be obtained from a child's parents, guardian, or other agent who is legally responsible and authorized to act on his or her behalf. Even then, a researcher must be confident that the consentor's interests are not at odds with what may be the best interests of the child, which is not *always* the case (Drew, Hardman, & Logan, 1996). A nervous or autocratic parent might desire an inappropriately quiet and timid child. In nearly all cases it is also necessary to obtain consent from the child as well, despite the fact that there is no legal requirement to do so. Ethical appropriateness often goes far beyond what is legally necessary as illustrated by the material presented in Table 3-4.

Thus far, we have discussed ethical considerations related to subject consent for participation. This is an important topic but one must keep in mind *why* consent is addressed so centrally when examining research ethics. One of the major concerns in behavioral research ethics relates to harming participants. Individuals must not be harmed by serving as subjects in any study. Obviously we do not want to physically harm subjects but the notion of harm also extends to such matters as psychological stress, social embarrassment, and many other areas. This is a difficult and complex consideration involving several questions. Ordinary living is not stress-free. A researcher must judge how much added stress would prove harmful, whether we cannot create *any* stress, and many other issues. If pushed to their conceptual limits and interpreted in an extremely literal manner, these considerations would significantly detract from our ability to conduct psychological research (or perhaps eliminate it). Of course there is *some* stress for subjects participating in most investigations, and we cannot take a position that there must be absolutely *no* psychological infringement. It is necessary for us to balance carefully the concepts of harm and the potential risk for harm as we undertake each study. For this reason we have independent review boards (e.g., Human Subjects Committees, Institutional Review Boards) operating in most agencies that examine research proposals and attempt to protect subjects' rights. The questions involved are complex and there are no simple answers. One must turn to professional guidelines (e.g., American Psychological Association, 1992) and our colleagues for guidance.

Another ethical issue in psychological research (related to harm in some senses) involves *privacy,* the degree to which we invade our subjects' privacy. Privacy has been long treasured in Western society. When we collect and analyze information (data) on subjects, we are invading their privacy to some degree. Although total privacy does not exist, each of us has some concept of the degree to which we want to share certain matters with others outside our close circle of family and friends, and the form in which that sharing is acceptable. As we saw with harm, privacy issues must be carefully balanced with a need to conduct research that will help us solve people's problems. Clearly it is an invasion of privacy to secretly tap someone's telephone, but is it also an invasion to observe them in a public place such as a supermarket or a school play yard? Once again there are no simple an-

TABLE 3-4   ETHICAL CONSIDERATIONS PRESENTING PARTICULAR PROBLEMS IN RESEARCH
WITH BEHAVIOR DISORDERED CHILDREN*

Consent Element	Guideline	Problem	Potential Solution
Capacity	Subjects must be mentally and psychologically able to give consent and also be of legal age to give consent.	Children with behavior disorders are not typically of the legal age to give consent. In many cases, they are also unable to give consent by virtue of mental or psychological limitations.	Consent must be obtained from the legal guardian of the child who has the authority to make legal decisions for the child. The child should also give consent, despite the fact that it is not legally required in most cases.
Information	Subjects and legal guardians must be fully informed regarding purposes and procedures of the study. The information must be understood.	Subjects with behavior disorders may have particular difficulty understanding the information, regardless of how well it is communicated.	Researchers must be certain that the legal guardians understand the information and make every attempt possible to make the children understand.
Voluntariness	Subjects and guardians must give consent of their own free will, without explicit or implicit coercion of any type. They must be aware that they can withdraw consent at any time.	Subjects and guardians may feel some degree of coercion simply because the researcher may represent a power figure for them. Similarly, the children may feel coerced if guardians consent.	Researchers must be very sensitive to any evidence of reluctance to consent or desire to discontinue participation. This is true for both subjects and guardians.

*NOTE: Additionally, subjects and guardians have the right to expect guaranteed confidentiality of information obtained by a researcher, as well as the right to nonharmful treatment, knowledge of results, and full compensation for the time the subject spends participating.

swers, and the best that one can do is to be sensitive and remain vigilant to procedures that may unduly or unnecessarily invade privacy.

Deception is also a topic that often surfaces in examining research ethics. Deception relates to a misrepresentation of information regarding the purpose, nature, or consequences of an investigation. Such a misrepresentation may occur because of either omitting information or giving false information. Either, if serious and potentially harmful to subjects, is unethical. It would seem that the answer to such a problem is quite simple—don't do it. However, like so many other topics, matters aren't quite that simple. Deception in one form or another is rather widespread in psychological research. In many cases it seems that researchers do not fully inform subjects about the purpose of the study, such as withholding details about the purpose of a treatment. Menges (1973) indicated that only 3 percent of the psychological investigations he examined provided *complete* information to the participating subjects. In some cases it appears that informed consent forms are written at a higher reading

level than is appropriate for the subjects being investigated, which raises serious questions regarding the effectiveness of some subjects' consent (Ogloff & Otto, 1991). The issue of deception in research remains very controversial as it should (e.g., Baumrind, 1985; Sieber, 1992). There are a number of reasons why this is so and why we find such startling figures as those noted above. In many cases certain psychological research cannot be conducted or would be extremely difficult with *totally* nondeceptive procedures. There are circumstances when we would expect full information might change our subjects' behavior or performance. For example, if we were studying the amount of influence friends have on opinions concerning drug use, complete information about the purpose of the investigation might alter one's susceptibility to such influence. Additionally, there are situations in which the focus of a particular study actually requires deception or it is a part of the investigation. These types of studies would then fall into the categories of being deceptive—so are they unethical? We cannot answer this so simply. Deception must be considered in relation to

Institutional review boards examine research protocols to protect the rights of human subjects.

the risk of harm and other issues as we have seen before and may require discussions with experienced colleagues, school personnel, and ethics boards.

Ethical matters are of particular concern to researchers working in child behavior disorders. Children and adolescents are often more "at risk" or more vulnerable to being taken advantage of by thoughtless or uninformed investigators than are adults. Beyond this fact, the nature of many of the problems that require study with such populations further complicate our ethical considerations. Research on child behavior disorders thus presents a considerable challenge—one of improving our knowledge base for more effective treatment while simultaneously providing the necessary protection for a vulnerable group. Is it ethical to single out a child with learning disabilities or a seizure disorder for study and observation, even treatment in a classroom, and thus draw more attention to his or her disorder? When is it justified to try a new, unresearched treatment on a child?

How accurate must an assessment technique or diagnostic test prove to be before it should be used routinely? Is it better to base our choices of treatments on clinical experience rather than on controlled research tests? If a researcher discovers a promising treatment, can it ethically be withheld from control subjects in order to study its effects? Both design considerations and ethical questions affect our answers to such questions.

SUMMARY

Research is a major source of objective information regarding causes and treatment of child behavior disorders. Because information produced from research is systematically and objectively collected, it tends to be more accurate and reliable than that obtained by casual observation and commonsense reasoning. Research procedures are much more systematic and the requirements of evidence are much more stringent than those used in more informal information seeking. Therefore, some knowledge of research principles is important for those who are consumers of research and are attempting to make decisions about treatment of children with behavior disorders.

Psychological research may be classified into several general types including experimental, nonexperimental, quantitative, and qualitative. These categories of research types are not mutually exclusive and, in fact, overlap in some of the strategies employed. Nonexperimental research tends to be descriptive whereas experimental research often examines causal relationships through manipulations of participants' behavior. Qualitative research tends to use data expressed in nonnumerical forms (e.g., words) and studies subjects in their natural environment. Quantitative research analyzes data in the form of numbers and is more likely to manipulate naturally occurring events in order to achieve control. Each approach is appropriate for different research questions and settings and also has certain advantages and limitations that must be considered. Even within each general approach there are a variety of specific designs or methods that may be used depending on the circumstances of the particular study being planned.

The planning of an investigation is crucial to the soundness of a study and the reliability of results obtained. In selecting an appropriate research design, there are many procedural matters that must receive attention. The design and procedures must minimize threats to the study's validity. When an experimental study has high internal validity, the results can be attributed to the experimental variable rather than some other source. With high external validity, research findings can be generalized to the larger population from which the research participants were drawn. These types of validity are essential for research to be dependable and meaningful. In addition to being concerned about validity, a researcher must take precautions to avoid ethical violations in the process of conducting a study. Behavioral scientists face some particularly difficult ethical issues when studying child behavior disorders since children (and their caretakers) may lack the capacity to make informed judgments about the advisability of participating in research projects. In all cases, children as well as adults must be allowed to terminate their research participation at any time they choose. We now take the opportunity to terminate this chapter. Students who have found these concepts fascinating may well become the researchers of tomorrow. Those who have found it completely uninteresting and largely unintelligible may find graduate work requiring research and statistics to be a real trial. There are more important and valid tests of one's career interests, of course, but most graduate research programs in clinical and counseling psychology, nursing and medicine involve training in research theory and practice. Practitioners must be knowledgeable consumers of research in order to keep pace with new developments.

CHAPTER 4

SOCIAL CONDITIONS AND
CHILDREN'S PROBLEMS

Key Terms

Invulnerables. Stress-resistant, resilient children who are at high risk for physical and mental disorders, but who thrive and develop normally despite their unhealthful environments.

Lead abatement programs. The removal or encapsulation through sealing of lead contaminants. Also, the removal and replacement of lead-coated areas and building components such as windows.

Low birthweight. A baby's weight at or below 2,500 grams at birth, with associated immature development, health, and viability risks. Babies weighing less than 1,500 grams at birth are classified as very low birthweight.

Socioeconomic status (SES). A measure of social class that takes into account a person's formal education, individual or family income level, residential neighborhood, and general social standing.

F
ew people now believe that children are so psychologically resilient that they will develop normally under all conditions. This chapter deals with children whose adverse living circumstances have deprived them of the opportunity to grow up mentally and physically healthy. There are literally millions of such disadvantaged children around the world, and they are found in America's wealthiest cities as well as in backwoods shanties. This chapter examines their plight and suggests ways of improving their lives, drawing upon the research findings on the effects of early intervention programs and the experiences of the few individuals who have thrived and had happy, productive lives despite hardship and adversity. This chapter portrays the family factors and environmental conditions that interfere with healthy physical and psychological growth, describes their effects on children, and shows how such tragedies can be averted through individual, group, and governmental action. In particular, we consider the effects of extreme poverty, discrimination, structural changes in the family, and family conflict and dissolution. Although these factors are considered separately, it is important to realize that they are very often combined to devastating effect in people's lives. For example, discrimination based on gender, ethnicity, or disabilities are strongly associated with economic and educational victimization, inadequate health care, and a high rate of mental and physical disorders. It is easy for the victims of one type of socioeconomic ill to fall prey to others also, usually as a result of poverty. Most of those at the very bottom of the social ladder cannot make their way up to a safer, more privileged position. Ironically, of all who suffer, it is usually the infants and children who suffer the most and receive the least governmental help. This chapter suggests that their psychopathology stems not from genetic factors or individual problems for the most part, but arises in the debilitating conditions in which they grow up. This chapter highlights social conditions that affect millions of young people and endanger the national economic, social, and governmental structures. Also featured are many successful or promising media, educational, and community programs dedicated to helping high-risk children and families.

FAMILY PROBLEMS AND CHILD MENTAL HEALTH

Although it is impossible to pinpoint the causes of many childhood problems, we know that children exposed to greater adversity have increased chances of developing academic-intellectual retardation and behavioral problems of some sort. An English study (Rutter, 1978; Rutter, Yule, Quinton, Rowlands, Yule, & Berger, 1975) identified six family problems commonly associated with children's psychiatric disorders. The family risk factors were: (1) marital discord or a broken home, (2) low income as indicated by the father's unemployment or holding an unskilled or semiskilled job, (3) overcrowding in the home (e.g., a large family living together in cramped living quarters), (4) maternal depression, anxiety, or other emotional problems, (5) the child's removal from the home or placement in foster care, and (6) the father's having an arrest and court record. Surprisingly, none of these factors taken *alone* increased children's psychological problems. However, when the family had two of the risk factors rather than a single one, the probability of the child's being disturbed rose *four* times. So having just one family risk factor quadrupled the child's chance of psychological disturbance. When even more risk factors were present, the child's adjustment risk rose dramatically.

A longitudinal study of children who grew up on the Hawaiian island of Kauai (Werner & Smith, 1992) yielded similar results. Adults who were less well adjusted (had a criminal record or irrevocably broken marriage) by the time they were 30 years old were likely to have been born to an unmarried mother, separated from the mother in their first year of life, lacked stable substitute child care as infants while the mother worked, had a sibling less than two years younger, had a father who was permanently absent in their early childhood, or experienced family disruptions such as unemployment of the breadwinner, illness, or major moves (Werner, 1989). In general, the father's mental illness or drug addiction endangers children's adjustment just as much as psychopathology of the mother (Phares & Compas, 1992).

Male and female children differed in the life period at which they were most vulnerable. Adult adjustment and criminality of *men* was more determined by risk factors in their *infancy and early childhood* (e.g., below-normal early physical development, an unwed mother, lengthy major family disruptions, and the birth of a sibling before the boy was 2 years old). In contrast, *women* were more affected by negative experiences during their *adolescence*, such as their mother's prolonged absence during a separation or divorce, their father's alcoholism or mental illness, conflicts with peers and parents, especially the father, teenage pregnancy or marriage, and severe financial problems (Werner & Smith, 1992).

The same types of factors adversely affect children of all groups. When a family is dysfunctional, poor, and ill-housed and parenting is inadequate because parents are psychologically disturbed, missing, or have criminal records, then the child is at high risk of developing behavioral problems. Undoubtedly, families with several risk factors also live in poor, deteriorated neighborhoods with substandard schools and high crime levels, so the neighborhood as well as the family fosters child psychopathology. The poorer the family's situation and the more stressful their lives, the greater are the child's chances of becoming disturbed.

Different ethnic and cultural groups combat the ill effects of poverty and family disruption in varied ways. The low income sector of the African-American community contains many single mothers and jobless men, but has a resilient and extended family network in which several generations may share a residence (Wilson & Tolson, 1990). Single mothers may alternate living alone, cohabiting with a man, and living with parents or relatives. Their extended families help with childcare. Informal adoptive arrangments may be made with grandparents, aunts and uncles, older siblings or cousins who care for the children, sometimes for years, when parents cannot do so. In a hostile and threatening environment, the African-American extended family offers children a steadying, nurturant refuge.

No one is totally invulnerable to the effects of a bad environment, but some children escape psychological harm, perhaps because of genetic advantages, a temperament that allows them to withstand stress, or care provided by some nurturant and stable adult such as a parent, grandparent, teacher, or family friend. These stress-resistant or "invulnerable" children seemingly miraculously manage to overcome handicaps such as severe child abuse or a strong family history of schizophrenia or criminality (Garmezy & Streitman, 1974). Many researchers hope to identify protective factors in the lives of the resilient children and use this information to develop programs to protect other children who do not have the same natural advantages. Little is yet known about how these fortunate children manage to escape the fate of many others in similar situations, because study of this phenomenon has just begun and the results from specific, small studies may not be widely generalizable. However, the high-risk children in the Kauai study who proved to be resilient were *highly achievement oriented* and stayed in school rather than dropping out. Most listed career or job success as their number one objective rather than striving primarily for happy marriages and children (Werner, 1989). As Table 4–1 illustrates, the resilient individuals tended to have *at least average IQ scores*, indicating average or higher intelligence, had acquired academic skills such as math and reading, and showed healthy levels of self-confidence. Those who were identified to be at high risk for mental health and

Research shows that even if a child's parents are unavailable, uncaring, or abusive, a child can thrive if loved and cared for by someone else.

academic achievement problems during childhood, but who succeeded nevertheless, had several attributes in common:

1. physical vigor, determination, and an attractive disposition that elicited positive responses from others;

2. parent substitutes such as grandparents or older siblings who replaced unavailable, dysfunctional, or rejecting parents; and

3. an external support system such as church fellowship, youth groups, or interested and involved teachers that rewarded them for competence and provided stability and meaning to their lives (Werner & Smith, 1992).

Even these hardy children suffered some ill effects of adverse environments. Many of the resilient had physical problems probably related to stress, such as eating disorders and high blood pressure. Those who had temporarily become delinquents in their teens tended to come from intact families, while those who continued as lawbreakers came from less stable families. This Hawaiian study highlights the importance of schooling and academic resources for poor children and the value of functional families in facilitating children's psychological development.

Helping Children Deal with Uncontrollable Stress

Instruction in coping skills can help children adapt to negative events in their lives that they cannot control (Nolen-Hoeksema, 1992). Children cannot usually bring

TABLE 4-1 CHARACTERISTICS OF RESILIENT CHILDREN AND ADOLESCENTS

Physically healthy and vigorous

Easy temperament, not dull, irritable, or difficult

Positive school experiences, skilled in reading and mathematics

At least average or above average intelligence

Achievement oriented and ambitious

Self-confident

Identifies with resilient models and sources of support

Does not affiliate with delinquent peers

Sense of humor

Lower in novelty-seeking or sensation-seeking

Internal locus of control, sees events as controllable

Good relationship with at least one parent figure (parent, stepparent, grandparent, other relative, interested teacher)

Community support, involved with a church or cultural group, youth group, or school group

SOURCES: Fergusson, D. M., & Lynskey, M. T. (1996). Adolescent resiliency to family adversity. *Journal of Child Psychology & Psychiatry, 37*, 281–292; Luthor, S. S., & Zigler, E. (1991). Vulnerability and competence: A review of research on resilience in childhood. *American Journal of Orthopsychiatry, 61*, 6–22; Werner, E. E. (1989). High risk children in young adulthood: A longitudinal study from birth to 32 years. *American Journal of Orthopsychiatry, 59*, 72–81; Werner, E. E., & Smith, R. W. (1992). *Overcoming the odds: High risk children from birth to adulthood*. Ithaca, NY: Cornell University Press.

their embattled parents together or reverse other major negative events. However, they can be taught strategies for coping with many uncontrollable events by applying techniques from cognitive behavioral therapy (described in Chapter 14). For example, interpretations help children to stop blaming themselves when their distressed and overburdened parents fight or become irritable with their children. Or they may be taught to use *positive imagery* and *distraction* to see them through difficult or painful situations, such as dental surgery or even completing homework. In such situations, they may bridge a delay until a burdensome task is completed or a stressful procedure is done through picturing a positive outcome, or a distressed family worried about a parent's health problems can go to the beach together. Sometimes families are so defeated that they cannot do simple, distracting activities that would make them feel and cope better. Another method to use to cope with uncontrollable stress is to *develop reasonable proximal goals*. For example, a child cannot bring divorced parents together, but can have satisfying interactions with each parent. If children learn to cope with unreversible situations rather than

clinging to the unrealistic hope of recovering the past, they adapt better. In very poor households, a child cannot become rich overnight, but can be helped to realize that helping around the house and doing paid jobs such as babysitting will be a realistic goal that will help the family.

> *"The basic idea is to help children focus on things they can control and ways they can improve themselves so that they are not at risk for becoming despondent and helpless because they are not achieving their greatest fantasies." (Nolen-Hoeksema, 1992)*

POVERTY AND HEALTH RISKS TO CHILDREN
Prenatal Development

Extreme poverty can handicap children even before birth. The statistics are unmistakable on this point. According to the U.S. Bureau of the Census (1994), only 5 percent of white upper class infants have some complications at birth, compared with 15 percent of low SES whites and *51 percent of the nonwhites*, who have very low incomes as a group. That is, a baby's chances of low birthweight are 10 times higher if the baby is nonwhite and poor than white. This section attempts to explain some of these huge income-related differences in infant health, such as being born to mothers who are too young or old. Women who live in poverty are likely to have little formal education, begin childbearing too early before they are fully physically mature, and have many, closely spaced pregnancies. Consequently, their babies may be premature, frail, and small for their gestational age (low birthweight). Factors associated with poverty and birthweight below 2,500 grams include poor maternal nutrition, stress, inadequate prenatal care, smoking, and drug abuse (Institute of Medicine Committee to Study Outreach for Prenatal Care, 1988; Tarnowski & Rohrbeck, 1993). Undernourished babies who are small, weigh little, and have a small head circumference for their gestational age have higher mortality and sickness rates, have more congenital anomalies (birth defects), are growth delayed in childhood, and have more neurological disorders than normal (Magrab, Sostek, & Powell, 1984). Babies also can suffer from their mothers' childhood dietary insufficiencies. Early malnourishment later produces mothers who are shorter, weigh less, and are less adequately physically developed than average. During pregnancy and later during labor, these women are more likely to have complications that may damage their babies. Women who live in poverty tend to have larger families and may continue to have children long after their prime childbearing years. Mothers over the age of 40 are themselves at greater risk during childbearing, and the incidence of certain chromosomal abnormalities in the baby increases with maternal age. For example, as Chapter 9 explains, the chances of a woman bearing a Down syndrome child increase rapidly in her 30s and 40s. Risks to mothers and infants are increased further because the poor often have grossly inadequate prenatal health care, which leads to higher infant and maternal mortality rates for women regardless of age. Many such women are malnourished throughout their lives and their inadequate diets continue during their pregnancies. These women are subject to dangerous complications during pregnancy and delivery.

Counteracting Early Malnourishment.
Mild to moderate protein and energy malnutrition, diet quality, and food shortages all adversely affect children's cognitive development. Such malnourished infants are small and delayed in motor abilities, so they are cared for as though they were younger, which reduces the stimulation they receive. Some researchers believe that the limited stimulation, in turn, limits malnourished infants' cognitive and verbal development (Pollitt, Gorman, Engle, Martorelli, & Rivera, 1993). Better nutrition alone may not benefit malnourished children's cognitive development, but improved diets combined with home stimulation programs may promote rebound growth in children, both physically and cognitively (Sigman, 1995). These special nutrition and improved care programs significantly benefit children, and the benefits include improved family living conditions (Ricciuti, 1993). Fortunately, even mothers who lack formal schooling can profit from instruction in child care. Families from poor neighborhoods in Bogota, Colombia, were given food supplements for their children, a home visit intervention to stimulate their children's learning and development, or both. Home visiting and dietary supplementation in combination reduced severe growth retardation when the children were age 6, an effect that lasted for three years after the intervention (Super, Herrera, & Mora, 1990). Surprisingly, just the home visiting program alone signifi-

cantly improved the children's growth, testifying to the positive effects of maternal instruction.

Simple provision of food for hungry children, while humane and praiseworthy, has not achieved the original goal of boosting public health and national economic development in an enduring fashion. Even when special food distribution programs can be mounted, they have proved infeasible except as an emergency measure to combat famines. The actual gains in children's growth and mental status proved much more modest than was hoped for (Ricciuti, 1993; Super et al., 1990). Both diet and care must improve if malnourished children are to thrive.

Maternal Education Programs.
The best educated mothers tend to have the healthiest infants. In the context of world poverty, *maternal education* may consist of only a few years of formal schooling, yet even this limited amount of formal education is associated with better infant survival and healthy development rates. We do not know why even a few years of schooling should be so beneficial. Perhaps better educated women are more likely to seek prenatal care and later medical services (Zill, 1983), so their children generally are healthier than the children of less educated neighbors. Perhaps the healthier and more vigorous women are more likely to receive educations or perhaps education provides subtle psychosocial advantages even though incomes of the educated are no higher than those of their neighbors.

> "The poor woman having a baby may be at risk because of her age, her nutritional status, her probable poor growth, her excessive exposure to infection in the community which she inhabits, her poor housing, and her inadequate medical supervision, as well as because of complex interactions between these and other potentially adverse influences." (Birch & Gussow, 1970, p. 175)

Maternal Immaturity.
The United States' embarrassingly low ranking in maternal and infant health (18th place in 1995 in maternal illness and death) is attributable to a high rate of teenage pregnancies and low use of contraceptives (Hilts, 1995). Two conditions that are more common among infants of very young mothers are extreme prematurity and very low birthweight (1,500 grams or less), which endanger the baby's life. Babies who

TABLE 4-2   PROBLEMS SOMETIMES ASSOCIATED WITH BELOW NORMAL BIRTHWEIGHT AND PREMATURITY

Irritability, withdrawal, anxiety, apathy
Cerebral palsy
Congenital deformities
Epilepsy
Severe mental retardation
Brain damage and other neurological disorders including cerebral palsy, and spina bifida
Autism and other serious developmental disorders
Vision defects
Hearing defects
Retarded physical growth
General poor health
School achievement problems
Hyperactivity, attention deficits

SOURCE: Bauerfeld, S. L., & Lachenmeyer, J. R. (1992). Prenatal nutritional status and intellectual development: Critical review and evaluation. In B. Lahey & A. E. Kazdin (Eds.), *Advances in clinical child psychology* (Vol. 14, pp. 191–222). New York: Plenum.

survive with subnormal birthweights of below 2,500 grams or about 4 pounds are more likely than normal-weight babies to develop serious physical, mental, and behavioral problems during childhood, as shown in Table 4-2. Babies are more likely to be healthy if their mothers are healthy, are in their prime years to bear children, and if they receive good medical care.

Poverty and Infant Development

The risks associated with poverty continue throughout development. Children from very low income families suffer from many problems including lower intellectual development and school achievement, increased school dropouts, and high rates of emotional and behavioral problems (Huston, 1993; McLoyd & Wilson, 1991). During adolescence, poverty is related to juvenile crime, early pregnancy, and school dropout (Garbarino, 1992). At least some of these harmful effects can be traced to parental inexperience, lack of education, heightened stress, or psychopathology. Poor children from unstable families, who had histories of birth complications or had mothers with low IQ scores, scored from 19 to 37 points lower on an intelligence test than did poor children with-

out birth complications or adverse family factors (Werner & Smith, 1992). In contrast, middle-class children with birth complications show much smaller IQ score reductions. The more economically advantaged children are more likely to have stable families and mothers who are brighter and better educated. Thus a safe, supportive, and intellectually stimulating environment can compensate to some extent for early physical damage.

In contrast, a disorganized and impoverished household may further endanger children who have had a poor start in life. Box 4-1 portrays the desperate situations of poor Brazilian families as they endure the early deaths of their children.

Lead Poisoning in Low Income Neighborhoods

In 1993, the U.S. Department of Health and Human Services pronounced lead poisoning to be the most hazardous health threat to children under the age of 6. The Environmental Protection Agency recently estimated that 3 million U.S. children have blood lead levels high enough to possibly affect their intelligence, physical health, and adjustment (Tesman & Hills, 1994). Lead exposure can reduce children's verbal and nonverbal intellectual performance and produce hyperactivity, distractibility, irritability, lethargy, emotional flatness, antisocial behavior, impulsivity, and decreased attentiveness. Until the 1980s, lead was widely used in household paint, gasoline for motor vehicles, and solder for food cans, cooking vessels, and water pipes. Lead also occurs naturally in some soils and water supplies and in smelter waste dumps, and heavy concentrations of lead persist in many neighborhoods, especially those with substandard housing. Lead emissions are being controlled, but not eliminated. The average lead level in children's blood fell by 77 percent between 1976 and 1991, but is still high in certain areas (Needleman, Riess, Tobin, et al., 1996). Children who live in inner-city neighborhoods are particularly susceptible to lead exposure even today because they live in old, dilapidated structures with chipped and peeling lead-based paint or play in yards contaminated with lead. Older dwellings are dangerous because 74 percent of all housing units built before 1980 contain lead-based paint, which toddlers are likely to ingest in their normal hand-to-mouth activities (Centers for Disease Control, 1991a). In addition, low income children's in-

---

BOX 4-1 Psychological Aspects of High Infant Mortality

Poor South American parents are fatalistic about high infant mortality. They may not name their babies until they are 6 months to a year old and likely to survive, and parents treat infant deaths with resignation. Anthropologist Nancy Scheper-Hughes studied the attitudes toward childbearing and children of mothers in Alto do Cruzeiro, Brazil, a hillside settlement of desperately poor, displaced farm laborers. She found that the average woman had experienced 9.5 pregnancies; 1.4 miscarriages, abortions, or stillbirths; and 3.5 deaths of children younger than 5 years. Like many other women around the world, Brazilian mothers dislike breastfeeding and discontinue it as soon as possible, preferring to feed their infants a nonnutritious gruel of cereal, milk, and sugar. With only foul and contaminated water, unprotected against parasites and infectious diseases, and given inadequate shelter and food, many infants sicken and die.

How do mothers cope with the probable deaths of their babies? Scheper-Hughes found that they withdraw their interest and minimize their contact with babies who appear weak or unresponsive, develop severe diarrhea, or otherwise seem to lack "the will to live." These parents believe that fragile youngsters cannot hope to survive in the harsh world of the slums, so it is futile and a waste of scarce family resources to fight a baby's wish to die. The mothers told Scheper-Hughes that "if a baby *wants* to die, it *will* die." Some babies are seen as fighters and some are not. Interestingly, these mothers also recognize that their children are endangered by their miserable living conditions ("The water we drink is filthy with germs;" "They die because we can't keep them in shoes or away from this human garbage dump we live in."). Their explanations of child mortality reflect both knowledge about the danger of their adverse physical conditions and a fatalistic detachment about their children's fate.

Source: Scheper-Hughes, N. (1985). The 1985 Stirling Award Essay. Culture, scarcity, and maternal thinking: Maternal detachment and infant survival in a Brazilian shantytown. *Ethos, 13,* 291–317.

---

expensive high fat, low calcium and low iron diets increase their lead absorption (Tesman & Hills, 1994).

High lead levels damage various organ systems including the kidneys, liver, gastrointestinal tract, and nervous system, producing convulsions, brain damage, and mental retardation. The amount of damage is directly related to blood lead levels (Jacobson & Jacobson, 1996). Although the immediate effects of low-level lead ingestion may be difficult to detect, even smaller amounts of lead may produce lowered social and academic functioning, hyperactivity, and may aggravate the psychotic behavior of autistic children (Tesman & Hills, 1994). Higher lead levels produce more obvious behavioral effects. One study (Needleman et al., 1996) found that 11-year-old boys with high levels of lead showed more physical complaints, distractibility, delinquency, and aggression than those with lower lead levels. Lead was related to behavior problems of all types, but especially to delinquency and attention problems.

Yet lead exposure is a nearly entirely preventable problem. What is being done to protect children? *Lead abatement programs* are needed to reduce lead hazards in children's homes, child-care centers, schools, and other places where children congregate. Effective lead abatement procedures include: (1) *replacement* of lead paint-covered windows and other parts of buildings, (2) *encap-*

sulation or sealing with a substance that prevents any access to lead paint or dust (ordinary paint does not do this), and (3) *lead paint removal*, which requires trained workers and is itself hazardous to workers and residents. Unfortunately, abatement is very expensive and does not always produce lowered blood lead levels (Lin-Fu, 1992). Parent education programs may be required (Kimbrough, LeVois, & Webb, 1994). Parents in some high lead neighborhoods were trained to wash children's hands before meals and bed, keep their fingernails clipped short, and offer children a well-balanced, low fat diet, which reduces lead retention. Parents were also instructed in methods for removing chipping and peeling paint and constructing barriers to keep children away from heavily leaded areas. This program dramatically reduced the children's blood lead levels (Kimbrough et al., 1994). Additional measures are needed to protect children and ensure that all can develop without preventable problems.

Poverty, Education, and Childrearing Practices

In addition to the physical dangers imposed by their environments, many poor children receive less than optimal care. Very young and inexperienced mothers may not know how to care for their babies, or may be indifferent to their children's welfare because they are psychologically still children themselves. Field (1980) studied a group of lower-SES African-American teenage mothers with premature babies. These young mothers did not know what to expect of their infants and treated them rather like dolls that could neither see nor hear but could only eat, cry, and wet. The teen mothers benefited from being taught about the actual abilities and needs of newborns and how to interact with them (Field, Widmayer, Stringer, & Ignatoff, 1980). The young women wanted to be good mothers, but lacked the knowledge and experience necessary to do so. Other poor mothers are experienced in childcare, but are so overburdened and depressed that they have little time, attention, or energy for it.

Whether a family is rich or poor, factors that seriously stress the parents tend to decrease the quality of their interactions with their children (Gelfand & Teti, 1990). Two types of parenting impairment may negatively affect children: (1) parental rejection of children, and (2) poor child management skills. A mother's rejection, negativity, intrusiveness, and withdrawal from interactions with children tend to produce angry, unhappy, and withdrawn infants and children (Cohen & Campbell, 1992; Davies & Cummings, 1994). Further, parents can be poor at managing their children. That is, parents can be inept at discipline, monitoring, and controlling their children in skilled and positive ways. Parental laxness can produce aggressive, defiant, and even delinquent children, while overly harsh discipline is associated with children's aggression, impulsivity, poor peer relations, and also delinquency (Davies & Cummings, 1994). Parent training interventions can help with both types of parenting impairment, rejection, and poor child management, as Chapter 14 describes.

Rich and poor parents may differ in their childrearing philosophy. Impoverished mothers may believe that life is so harsh that they must avoid spoiling their children or making them "soft" and overly dependent on others. These mothers may ignore their children at times or belittle their complaints in order to accustom them to uncaring, hostile environments, which is greatly at odds with the recommendations of child development authorities. Middle-class mothers are more likely to be hyper-vigilant caretakers who attempt to protect their children from all forms of danger. But would such training be equally valuable for children who live in the least affluent, most dangerous neighborhoods? Less protected children may indeed be better prepared for life's difficulties in poor neighborhoods.

Capable, responsive mothers are more successful at teaching their children skills to help them succeed at school. Such mothers provide the verbal and physical stimulation that enables their children to perform well. Preschoolers' psychological development thrives in homes in which: (1) the mother is emotionally and verbally responsive to and involved with the child, (2) the child has appropriate play materials, (3) the mother avoids restricting or punishing the child, (4) the child's schedule and physical surroundings are well-organized, (5) the child's routine provides variety such as outings, visitors, and parties (Bradley & Caldwell, 1978). The mother's involvement and responsivity, and the availability of play materials in the home are the two best predictors of children's IQ scores at 54 months (Bradley & Caldwell, 1976). It is much easier for privileged middle-class women to provide this type of family atmosphere than for hard-pressed low-SES mothers to do so.

Well-educated, upper income mothers often clearly explain to children how to perform tasks, how to reason out problems, tell them the names of things, and set up situations positively so their children can solve problems. In contrast, when their child gives an incorrect response, lower SES mothers may simply indicate that it is wrong ("This is not a horse. What's this?"). This type of response is much less encouraging and informative than the typical educated mother's reaction ("Well, it looks like a horse, but look here, what are these? Horns! Does a horsie have horns? Who has horns?" [Child says "Cow."] "That's right, Torrey, it's a cow!"). In general, less educated parents are uncertain about their ability to teach their children and so stress correctness rather than experimentation, emphasizing children's obedience to authority and to the rules. They are more likely to issue an abrupt command than to explain how to perform a task, and they are more likely to begin teaching the child without reflecting on how best to do so or taking the child's developmental level into account.

Much of our evidence on socioeconomic class differences in childrearing comes from fairly contrived laboratory observations of parent-child interactions. Less educated parents find such situations particularly threatening and may behave in untypical, constricted ways. Nevertheless, clinical observations suggest that the

Children in homeless families have more than their share of health, educational, and adjustment problems and a less secure future than other children.

same SES-related differences probably hold true in children's everyday life and may explain why many poor children fail to achieve their academic and cognitive potential. Ironically, many affluent families hire low-income, relatively uneducated women as nannies and babysitters, which appears not to disadvantage their children.

It should be emphasized that these child performance findings refer to the *averages* for groups of rich and poor families. There is great variability within both wealthy and poor groups. Not all poor children are cognitively disadvantaged nor do all richer ones score higher on IQ tests. Nevertheless, as a group, economically disadvantaged children have harsher, less stimulating environments that cause them to lag behind their middle-class agemates in cognitive development.

Fortunately, these social class differences can be appreciably reduced if low income mothers feel a sense of personal control or self-efficacy and encourage their children to spend time with them and work with them (El-

der, 1995). The outlook for low income, inner city children is further improved if their parents have supportive marriages, so the increasing rate of single parenthood is a further risk factor (Elder, 1995). A later section of the chapter describes some programs designed to aid the development of America's poorest children.

Homeless Children

To people who cherish the comfort, protection, and traditions of their homes, being without a home is almost unthinkable. Yet homelessness is increasing, even among previously stable employed families with regular incomes. The dramatic increase of homelessness in America, even in otherwise affluent cities, has produced widespread concern for the psychological development of homeless children (Institute of Medicine, National Academy of Sciences, 1988; Link, Phelan, Bresnahan, et al., 1995). On any particular night, over 100,000 children may be homeless, and children represent over half of the members of homeless families (U.S. Conference of Mayors, 1989). To be homeless is to be transitory, with no permanent address, so research on the adjustment of homeless children has been slow and difficult to conduct with families who continuously move in and out of shelters, typically staying there only a few weeks at a time. It also is necessary to separate the effects of lacking a home from effects of low income and SES alone. A study of homeless and comparable, but housed, poor minority families in Minneapolis found that the homeless children are exposed to greater stress and have fewer resources because of lower incomes (Masten, Miliotis, Graham-Bermann, Ramirez, & Neemann, 1993). Both housed and homeless poor children had high rates of problem behaviors, particularly of the externalizing or antisocial type. Whether homeless or not, these impoverished children were most likely to develop adjustment problems if they (1) experienced major stressful life events, such as the death of a close family member, parental separation or divorce, or witnessing or experiencing physical abuse, (2) had psychologically distressed mothers, or (3) had other cumulative risk factors such as living in a single-parent household or being placed in foster care. Simply, *homeless children were more likely to experience stressors of all these types, so they were more likely to have academic and adjustment problems.* This group of families in the Midwest had been homeless for a relatively short time, and it is probable that chronic homelessness for extended time periods is even more harmful for children. Both economic and social welfare measures are needed to prevent the predictable deterioration of the physical and mental health of homeless children and families.

ETHNIC MINORITIES AND DISCRIMINATION
Discrimination and Problem Development

Mental health experts (cited in Tarnowski & Rohrbeck, 1993) agree that the higher rates of disturbance experienced by economically disadvantaged minority children are attributable to low family income rather than family ethnicity. Compared to mainstream, white children, minority children bear much more than their share of pov-

erty. The degree of disadvantage experienced by minority youth has actually increased in recent years. Following income gains made as a result of a supportive social and governmental climate in the 1960s and 1970s, the relative income of children, particularly African-American children, decreased markedly during the past 20 years. Recently, 40 percent of European-American single-mother families and 60 percent of African-American and Latina single-mother families had incomes below the poverty line (U.S. Bureau of the Census, 1992). The proportion of African-American and Hispanic children (Hispanics can be of any race) living in poverty increased dramatically during the 1980s. In the six years from 1979 to 1985, the rate of poverty for black children increased by 7 percentage points, from 36 percent to 41 percent, while the corresponding increase for whites was only 1 percent, growing from 12 percent to 13 percent (Duncan, 1991). This means that compared to whites, three times as many African-American children were classified as very poor, lacking the nutrition, health care, educational advantages, travel opportunities, and other amenities enjoyed by the middle class. Moreover, black children were poorer for longer periods of time than the whites were, and much more likely to have single mothers with very low incomes. Such families readily fall into extreme and irreversible poverty following family breakups, involuntary cutbacks in family members' work hours, and disability of the household head, usually the mother (McLoyd, 1990).

It is a myth that there are more poor minority than white families and children. Since the great majority of the U.S. population is white, there are many more impoverished white children than children of color. Unlike their ethnic minority counterparts, though, white children are more likely to be poor *temporarily*, when their parents divorce or become unemployed, and then regain at least some of their previous income. White families are better able to make economic recoveries for several reasons:

1. Whites are more likely to have better-paid jobs. Well-paying blue collar jobs are being eliminated and poverty-level jobs are replacing them. The nature of the economy is changing, and the major growth is in low paid service jobs in service stations, supermarkets, and fast food restaurants, replacing more economically attractive job opportunities in manufacturing for semiskilled labor.

This affluent life is beyond the reach of many families. Opportunities to move up into the middle class are rare for people of color in today's society because they have less access to superior health care, healthful environments, good schools and jobs, and material possessions.

People who lose higher paying manufacturing jobs typically cannot find comparably well-paid work, and so sink into chronic poverty even if they hold jobs.

2. The percent of children living in impoverished, single-mother households has increased and is now at a higher level in the United States than in comparable countries (Huston, 1994). African-American children are especially likely to grow up in an impoverished mother-headed household. Prior to the time they become adults, African-American children can expect to spend more than five years in poverty contrasted with less than 10 months for the average white child (Hernandez, 1994).

3. The American social "safety net" for poor families is failing; government cash benefits for poor fam-ilies with children are being reduced, so the poorest families are getting even poorer, which further re-duces their chances of recovery (Strawn, 1992). The heritage of racial discrimination in employment, education, and family stability produces stress and economic hardship for minority children. As we have seen, poverty results in excess infant and child deaths; physical, intellectual, and social handicaps; and wasted lives.

The conditions associated with poverty are responsible for America's poor showing in international comparisons of child illness and mortality rates. The United States has rated between 13th and 18th in the world in infant mortality for the past decade. Japan and the northern European nations have regularly surpassed the United States in this important indicator of child welfare. Very significantly, the U.S. ranks only 25th in the world in preventing low birthweights, bettered even by China despite its poverty and nonindustrialized economy. China's surprisingly good showing may be attributable to population control programs that discourage early marriage, early childbearing, and large families. In the United States, the high birth rates among people of color, inadequate prenatal care for the poorer mothers in these groups, and youthfulness of many minority mothers work together to produce excess stillbirths, premature and underweight babies, and high infant mortality rates. The high health risk status of children of color continues in later years. Deaths from childhood diseases such as measles, diptheria, and scarlet fever are six times higher among African Americans than whites. Black children from poor families also have far higher rates of ill health in general, higher abandonment, more father absence, excess levels of learning problems and school dropouts, malnutrition, neglect, dental problems, lead poisoning (as previously noted), some types of drug abuse, and teenage pregnancies (U.S. Bureau of the Census, 1994). As adults they suffer far higher rates of psychiatric disorders than whites. African American men, who experience alarming rates of unemployment and ill health, consistently have the highest rates of mental disorders of any group. Most of such problems stem from poverty and discrimination.

Protective Factors for Children of Color

Parental education aids children. The mathematics achievement test scores of a large sample of black and Hispanic elementary schoolchildren were found to be comparable to those of whites if their mothers had comparable amounts of formal education (Stevenson, Chen, & Uttal, 1990). The researchers reported that the achievement level of black and Hispanic elementary schoolchildren was not substantially lower than that of white children from similar families, and the mothers were very concerned about their children's achievement. In fact, the African-American and Hispanic mothers were even more concerned about their children's education than were white mothers, and they stressed the value of homework, competency testing, and lengthened school days. These results point up the importance of maternal education

and commitment to their young children's education. Unfortunately, during adolescence, peer group pressures strongly discourage academic achievement for large numbers of Hispanic and African-American students, so their earlier educational gains may be erased when they enter their teens (Steinberg, Dornbusch, & Brown, 1992).

Hispanic youngsters are likely to come from families who immigrated from rural Mexico, Cuba, Puerto Rico, and Central and South America, where family unity, sharing resources, and a de-emphasis on individual achievement are prized. Although diverse in terms of their backgrounds, Hispanic children are more likely to experience close family and community ties, and their parents are more likely to stay together than to divorce. These cultural advantages are weighed against other factors that may impede their academic success. Hispanic children of recent rural immigrants are encouraged to obey their parents and contribute to family and group goals rather than strive to win in the types of individual competitions often found at school and in the workplace (Foster, Martinez, & Kulberg, 1996). Although recent, low income immigrants value formal education, they may have limited personal experience in the schools, which reduces their ability to help their children succeed (e.g., in aiding their children with their homework). Further, children whose families primarily speak Spanish are likely to have artificially low scores on standard intelligence tests developed for English-speakers, even if they are very bright, so they experience school achievement problems, are less likely to be promoted, and ultimately drop out of school, which blights their employment futures. When they are given the benefits of appropriate, high quality schooling and health care, low SES Hispanic children and children of other immigrant groups have succeeded at occupations formerly closed to them (Elder, 1995).

Race, Socioeconomic Status, and IQ

Abject poverty and hopelessness are sometimes misattributed to character flaws or to racial differences favoring the majority group. Families of color tend to be among the poorest in the nation, their school attainment is generally low, high proportions of their children receive special education, and many are at the very bottom of the

---

BOX 4-2 HURRAY FOR BIG BIRD! HOW "SESAME STREET" HELPS KIDS LEARN

The Public Broadcasting Service show for preschoolers "Sesame Street" gets high ratings for its educational impact on children, particularly those from low income families (Huston & Wright, 1994; Mifflin, 1995). When the show was first aired 25 years ago, critics feared that it might encourage young viewers' aggression, decrease their tolerance for slower paced classroom instruction, increase their impulsivity, and have other harmful effects. This time, the critics were wrong. Instead, "Sesame Street" is a solid hit with educators and parents as well as young viewers. Researchers Aletha C. Huston and John C. Wright (1994) reported that "Sesame Street" differs from entertainment programs by incorporating techniques that promote learning, such as a particular song to signal a segment involving classification. These educational techniques aided regular child viewers to perform better on tests of verbal and math performance even as late as age 7, which was long after they ceased to watch the program (Mifflin, 1995).

In this case, what children enjoy is also good for them. Not only do young educational TV viewers enjoy watching their favorite "Sesame Street" characters (remember Oscar the Grouch, Big Bird, Kermit and others?), but they are better prepared for school. Studies of children's television viewing attest to the great value of "Sesame Street" for children, particularly low SES children who might otherwise begin school academically disadvantaged.

SOURCE: Huston, A. C., & Wright, J. C. (1994). Educating children with television: The forms of the medium. In D. Zillmann, J. Bryant, & A. C. Huston (Eds.), *Media, children, and the family: Social scientific, psychodynamic, and clinical perspectives.* (pp. 73–84). Hillsdale, NJ: Erlbaum. Mifflin, L. (1995, May 31). Study finds educational TV lends preschoolers even greater advantages. *The New York Times*, p. A18.

---

socioeconomic status scale (Hernandez, 1994). There are significant exceptions within each ethnic minority group with a thin layer of middle-class families attaining higher education, wealth, and social recognition, but such cases are disappointingly few. Why don't the poor and the minorities help themselves? One, older, now discredited explanation was that such groups were constitutionally or genetically less able than the more successful whites. This type of explanation was commonly voiced in the 19th century to account for the social disadvantage of poor whites, women, and minorities, and still persists in such controversial books as *The Bell Curve* (Herrnstein & Murray, 1994; but see Sternberg, 1995, and Steven Jay Gould's book, *The Mismeasure of Man*, 1981, for a stinging rebuttal of these views). Sternberg (1995) criticized *The Bell Curve* for arguing, without a sound research basis, t' one ethnic group is inferior intellectually to another and that the difference is mostly genetic. How does the minority child succeed in the white-dominated world? The challenge is great, because the American Indian, black, or Hispanic child from a poor family must become bilingual and bicultural, simultaneously learning the speech and customs of white middle-class society as well as his own. Economically disadvantaged children get some help from public broadcasting programs. The popular Public Broadcasting System program "Sesame Street" helps many children learn vocabulary, numbers,

and a broad range of facts that prepare them for school (see Box 4-2). Many more such educational television programs are needed for economically disadvantaged children of various ages.

Guns and Youth. High violence rates in core metropolitan areas add to the danger to children and teens, and the school is no safe haven. According to a national survey (CDC, 1991), 4.1 percent of all students and 21.4 percent of African-American male students said they had carried a gun in the past 30 days. And school dropouts were more likely than others to carry a gun (Public Health Service, 1994). More than one-third of a recent national sample of high school students said that they knew someone who had been hurt or killed by gunfire (O'Donnell, 1995; Scanlan, 1993).

Devaluing Schools and Good Students. An added disadvantage for some minority teens is their peers, who belittle studying and academic activities. Students with anti-academic classmates must escape or defy extreme peer pressures in order to succeed academically. Some African-American teenagers report that they must become "loners" or seek friends from other ethnic groups in order to excel academically without being shunned or victimized by peers who despise school and scholars as giving in to the white system (Phinney, 1990).

African-American students are likely to be caught in a conflict between doing well in school and being acceptable to their peers (Phinney, 1990).

Teacher Burnout. Overburdened teachers in very low income schools have too many troubled students and pitifully inadequate resources. Consequently, the teachers often believe their task is hopeless and inadvertently discourage children's attempts to achieve in school (Wagner, 1972). With deprivation and cultural difference both playing a role, it is hardly surprising that few very poor children receive the educations that could equip them to escape the poverty of the barrio, the farm, the black ghetto, or the Indian reservation.

Programs for Poor Families

Recognition of this relentless cycle of poverty has led to the development of intervention programs aimed at improving the educational and vocational prospects for poor children. These programs, their relative merits, and degree of success are discussed next.

In recent years, funding levels for programs for the poor were much reduced because of increased federal debt and growing resistance to taxation, priority given to military weapon systems spending, and growing political conservatism. Some influential reformers, such as Marian Wright Edelman of the Children's Defense Fund, attempt to arouse the public about the dangers of poverty and illness to children. They speak publicly and hold organized demonstrations, such as the June 1, 1996, Stand for Children demonstration by 200,000 people at the Lincoln Memorial in Washington, DC. Nevertheless, conservative groups that disapprove of the lifestyles of the poor, especially unmarried mothers, seek to limit or remove the government assistance now available for them and their children.

Some recent federal welfare-to-work programs have aimed to equip teenage mothers for parenthood and independent living. Under the Family Support Act of 1988, teenage mothers faced mandatory school and work requirements designed to enforce job training and employment so they would not remain on welfare. A research study of this type of program (Aber, Brooks-Gun, & Maynard, 1995) found that participants' attendance at school and job training programs increased, and that there was a modest (3 percent) increase in the number

who were employed. However, since their welfare payments shrank because of their employment earnings, the program did not improve their economic well-being. The program did not affect their family planning, either. Two years after they enrolled, two-thirds of the mothers had become pregnant again, commenting that they had not meant to do so, but it had "just happened."

Many poor families with children in the United States receive governmental assistance and welfare payments, although less so than the poor in most other industrialized nations. The health, early education, and general standard of living of the poorest people in the United States improved from the 1950s to the 1980s, yet now all national statistics show that the income gap between the very rich and the poorest groups has widened greatly and continues to increase (U.S. Bureau of the Census, 1994). In short, despite welfare programs, the poor (many of whom are children) are getting relatively poorer while the richest segment of society amasses even more wealth (Huston, 1994). The aged have made significantly greater economic gains than have poor children, perhaps because older people have developed powerful voting blocks, and children cannot vote. As a result, children are the poorest age group, with an amazing 27 percent of all American children below the age of 18 living in poverty (Hernandez, 1994). There is little reason to expect improvement soon. Poverty has proved the most stubbornly persistent among children in female-headed families, particularly among African Americans. Single black mothers are unlikely to marry, so they are particularly dependent on the resources of the community to help ensure the educational and social development of their children (Elder, 1995).

Head Start. In a technologically advanced society, education is the key to more desirable jobs and a higher standard of living, yet poor children tend to receive low quality educations in the country's unsafest, least adequately staffed and equipped schools, so they cannot advance economically. In response to this harsh truth, compensatory education programs were developed to increase the social mobility of the poor and equip them to become economically self-sufficient and productive citizens. Head Start is such a program, primarily for low income preschool children ages 3 to 5, enrolled in half-day sessions for one school year (some enroll for 2 years). Programs vary across the nation, with some fullday and

Children love to learn, especially if they are enrolled in small classes, their classrooms are rich in stimulation, and they have skilled teachers.

home-based services, but all are required to offer early childhood education, health screening and referral, mental health services, nutrition education and hot meals, social services for the family, and parent involvement. Policy Advisory Councils, composed of parents, program staff and community representatives, are responsible for operating the programs. In 1992, over 600,000 children and families were enrolled in Head Start programs, which is fewer than in the late 1960s but considerably more than in the late 1980s (Zigler & Styfco, 1993). In addition to Head Start, the Follow Through program for children in the early elementary school grades and services offered under the Elementary and Secondary Education Act of 1965 all provided special services for poor students and aimed to give them a fairer start in life. Although it was originally feared that such programs were not helpful (Levin, 1977), subsequent evaluations revealed that children at risk for educational and social failure benefited significantly, even several years following their Head Start

participation (Zigler & Styfco, 1994). This means that Head Start children outperform other low income children in preschool and also in elementary school. They are less likely to be retained in a grade, placed in special education classes, or drop out; their language development is better; and they sometimes maintain their superiority on achievement test scores into the later grades (Collins, 1983; Lazar & Darlington, 1982). Moreover, the children who benefit the most from Head Start are the most needy, their parents are the least educated, more come from single-parent families, and they began Head Start with the lowest IQ scores.

Praise for Head Start is widespread, but not unanimous. Head Start has been criticized as a waste of tax dollars for not permanently increasing children's IQs, grades, and their ultimate employability (Hood, 1992). Although Head Start does not permanently raise children's IQ scores, it may have enduring benefits on their school adjustment and social competence (Zigler &

Muenchow, 1992), a not inconsiderable legacy. Head Start has proved to be a heartening success, with solid public support, reflecting the program's great popularity among children, parents, educators, and the population in general.

Older children need similar programs to improve their schools. One such program is the Chicago Child Parent Center and Expansion Program, a federally funded extended early intervention for economically disadvantaged, mostly African-American children (Reynolds, 1994). This is a "follow-on" program to continue the early success of Head Start in promoting school competence in poor children. The effort is to provide continuing comprehensive services in grades 2 and 3 to reinforce preschool learning, involve the parents, and coordinate schooling and social services. This relatively inexpensive program was remarkably successful in promoting high achievement in reading and mathematics, and reduced retention in a grade. In fact, the children in the program outscored the Chicago schools' average in reading and mathematics by one month, as compared with a large lag for similar children not enrolled in the program. More such efforts will pay rich social and educational dividends.

Juniper Gardens Children's Project. Low-SES children have less help from their families with language and academic skill development, which helps explain their poor school performance relative to middle-class youngsters. As they grow older, they experience a progressive, cumulative deficit in total hours of school-related skills learning, which results in lower school grades, school failure, and increased dropout rates. The Juniper Gardens Children's Project in Kansas City involves schools, parents, and university staff in developing programs to prevent school failure in low-SES children. B. F. Skinner's functional analysis of behavior provided the basis for detailed, individual programs specifying contingencies of reinforcement for the children and their teachers, giving them much additional, productive learning time. Peer tutoring was used very effectively to boost the children's study time and achievement. Over a four year period, the low-SES peer-tutoring groups significantly improved in reading, language, and mathematics, and were no longer statistically different from a higher-SES comparison group (Greenwood et al., 1992).

"Neither Head Start nor any preschool program can inoculate children against the ravages of poverty. Early intervention simply cannot overpower the effects of poor living conditions, inadequate nutrition and health care, negative role models, and substandard schools. But good programs can prepare children for school and possibly help them develop better coping and adaptation skills that will enable better life outcomes, albeit not perfect ones." Zigler & Styfco, 1994, p. 129

FAMILY DISCORD AND DIVORCE

Family strife may be no more common now than in the past but today's unhappy marriages are more likely than ever to be dissolved through separation and divorce. In 1970 there were 35 divorced persons for every 1,000 living in intact marriages, while in 1990 there were 142 divorced persons per 1,000 married persons (U.S. Bureau of the Census, 1991). The marriage rate is declining while the divorce rate is increasing, and more than five times more children were born to unmarried mothers proportionately in 1990 as in 1960. The increase in rates of children born to single women seems due more to couples' inability to afford to marry and set up a household than to any change in their values, morals, or aspirations (Usdansky, 1996). Two-parent families continue to be the rule; in 1991, 71.1 percent of family households with children were headed by couples, as compared with just 28.9 percent with a single parent (U.S. Bureau of the Census, 1992). Nevertheless, many children each year witness the divorce or separation of their parents. Since most divorces occur in families containing children and adolescents, there is widespread concern about possible harmful effects of divorce on child adjustment and development. Certain groups are more likely than others to be affected by parental separation, abandonment, and divorce. Black children, poor children, and those whose parents have never completed high school are particularly likely to live in single-parent, mother-headed households (U.S. Bureau of the Census, 1994). As previously described, these families are among the nation's poorest, least healthy, and least well-protected. The children also receive the nation's least adequate schooling. This means that many children who are experiencing family conflict must also endure poverty and associated hardships.

Why Are Single-Parent Families Increasing?

As we enter the 21st century, 50 to 60 percent of all children will live with only one parent for a year or more before they reach age 18 (Glick, 1984). More and more children of divorced or separated couples live with their mothers and see their fathers rarely, if ever. In 1970, just one-third of black children were living in mother-headed households compared with two-thirds in 1991 (58 percent). At present, African Americans have the highest rate of single motherhood, followed by Hispanics at 28.7 percent, representing a distant second, and whites at 19.3 percent, which, although the lowest rate, is increasing (U.S. Bureau of the Census, 1992). Fewer than 4 percent of children live in single-parent households with their fathers, but this represents a startling *tripling* in 20 years of the number of father-headed single-parent families (U.S. Bureau of the Census, 1992). There are several possible explanations for the substantial increase in single-parent families including:

1. Romantic love and individual fulfillment are now the major reasons for marriage. Previously, couples married largely for economic and family reasons (Keniston, 1977), which might provide less exciting but more stable bases for matrimony. Since marriage is now expected to bring happiness, people are likely to abandon their partners when they fall out of love or fail to find sufficient happiness. Today's motivations for marriage seem to be transitory, based on unstable characteristics, such as physical attractiveness, and are therefore inherently unstable.

2. Women have become more independent economically and socially. Changing employment opportunities for women make them more financially independent than ever before. Now, women can find work or at least obtain welfare payments to support themselves and their children. They need not stay in unhappy marriages.

3. A divorce is now less expensive and easier to obtain, because of more permissive legislation, and divorce is widely socially accepted. Previously powerful traditions and church, legislative, and financial obstacles effectively inhibited couples from seeking divorces. These social and legal barriers are eroding.

4. It is becoming increasingly common for unmarried women to keep their babies and rear them, often with the help of their own parents. This is a startling change: in 1970 only 6.5 percent of one-parent families were headed by a mother who had never married, compared with 30.7 percent in 1991. This revolutionary move toward unmarried motherhood is found in most groups from religious fundamentalists to movie stars. However, never married mothers are most common among African Americans, with the majority (54.2 percent) of black children under the age of 18 living with never married mothers in 1991 (U.S. Bureau of the Census, 1993). Neighborhood families, their own families, and popular entertainers set the example, and teenagers follow to become unmarried mothers. Welfare regulations penalize father-present households, further discouraging parents from wedding. And with high divorce rates, many young people see no permanent advantage to marriage. All of these factors push the rate of single parenthood upward.

5. Changes in the composition of the U.S. population are increasing the overall divorce rate at present. In the 1970s vast numbers of baby boomers reached the ages at which they married and had children, and subsequently they began to divorce and remarry. As this group passes through the divorce-prone years, the national divorce rate will increase only because there are so many individuals in this age cohort. Thus, population demographics alone accounts for some of the high divorce rate and the growth of single-parent households.

6. The expense of families. With the loss of the better paid blue collar jobs in the United States, young couples have a much harder time setting up a household and supporting children. As a result, many fewer marry, even when the woman becomes pregnant.

Thus, powerful social forces work to promote single parenthood. Some of these influences, such as the increased employability of women and the possibility of leaving a miserable relationship, seem socially progressive. Others, such as marrying and divorcing on a whim or impulsively deciding to have a baby without considering the associated responsibilities, appear to be immature and unrealistic, while economic factors are largely uncontrollable. Together, these changes are creating a social revolution with results that are as yet uncharted.

Effects of Divorce on Children

Divorce is often wrenching and emotionally devastating, at least in the short run. Its effects on children vary depending largely upon the amount of acrimony before and after the divorce, and how much the couple come to dislike or even hate each other. A high level of parental antagonism and fighting has a powerful negative effect on many children. Further, how well the children fare emotionally depends on the divorced father's availability to the children, his willingness to provide for their economic support, how well the mother copes with the situation both psychologically and financially, and the ages and sexes of the children. With such a diversity of possible family situations, it is not easy to predict how divorce will affect individual children. However, divorce is unlikely to promote children's adjustment under most circumstances. Only when the divorce produces increased harmony because of the separation of bitterly embattled parents do children appear to benefit psychologically. Serious prolonged marital distress and conflict are related to many different negative child outcomes, including withdrawal, poor social competence, depression, health problems, problems in school work, and aggressive, externalizing behavior (Katz & Gottman, 1993).

After the marriage dissolves, the vast majority of children live with their mothers. If living with just one parent has different effects from growing up in a traditional two-parent family, then many children may be at psychological risk. Black children as a group could be at higher risk for adjustment problems because they are particularly likely to grow up in the low-income households of their divorced or single mothers (U.S. Bureau of the Census, 1994). However, it is unlikely that the greater share of black youth could rightly be classified as disturbed simply because so many of them are reared in single-parent households. Perhaps the support provided by the many extended families in the African-American community and the extensive participation of grandmothers in child-rearing counteract the harmful effects of father absence (Peters & McAdoo, 1983). Alternatively, children might simply adapt to their parents' divorce. Nevertheless, the overwhelming research evidence is that parental conflict disturbs children, whether or not it involves divorce (Amato & Keith, 1991). Moreover, type of marital conflict is associated with type of child dysfunction. When both parents are hostile toward each other during marital disputes, their children later tend to exhibit mild forms of antisocial behavior, whereas couples in which husbands are angry and emotionally distant during conflicts have children more probable to show later anxiety and social withdrawal (Katz & Gottman, 1993).

Although both girls and boys are negatively affected by parental conflict, sons are more likely than daughters to develop disturbed behavior. When parental conflict is building prior to a divorce, boys may develop problems in controlling their aggression and become highly impulsive (Frick, 1994). These problems in impulse control and hostility are very similar to the behavior patterns boys display following a divorce (Hetherington, Cox, & Cox, 1979, 1982), which suggests that the parental strife rather than the separation from the father after the divorce might produce the boys' problems. Girls generally seem to have fewer divorce-related adjustment problems, and when they do, they are more likely to develop anxiety and withdrawal rather than aggression. It is unclear why boys tolerate family turmoil less well than girls do. Perhaps boys are more likely to respond aggressively to stress of any type, including family conflict. In general, more boys than girls are referred to psychiatric and psychological clinics, and boys' most common problems are externalizing and involve aggression and hyperactivity (see Chapter 1 for a discussion of this point). Thus, boys' greater tendencies to develop problems in aggression control seem to be potentiated by the stress surrounding the breakup of their parents' marriages. An additional contributor to boys' externalizing problems after family breakup may be increased peer influence resulting from decreased parental supervision (Barber & Eccles, 1992). Peer influences are considerably more deviant and antisocial than are the activities condoned by adults, so additional exposure to peers will often produce heightened antisocial behavior for older children and adolescents. To exacerbate the boys' post-divorce problems, research shows that following a divorce, mothers may be at a loss as to how to manage their suddenly defiant and disobedient sons. The erratic, inconsistent parental discipline that often accompanies family dissolution, and the over-stressed mother's inability to provide firm and reasonable management, may stimulate the development of boys' conduct problems (Hetherington et al., 1982). In most cases, the children's post-divorce adjustment improves over time, and their longer range status approximates that of children from intact families. Authorities now agree that children in single-mother families are not as different from children in families with both parents as was previously believed, and both groups contain children who are disturbed and others who are normally adjusted (Barber & Eccles, 1992). When families function well and support healthy child development, children thrive regardless of whether they come from single-parent or two-parent families, whether their parents are well or physically challenged, and whether the parents have a heterosexual or same-sex orientation. The current consensus of mental health professionals is that there are many different possible pathways to good development, of which the two-parent nuclear family is only one alternative (Patterson, 1992).

> *A divorced mother says, "I resent the tube telling me, and my kids, that 'children of divorced parents don't make good peer relationships and do poorly in school, and they're likely to live a life of crime.' That's gar-bage! . . . we have crazy people running around who grew up in the so-called normal family." (Arendell, 1986, p. 100)*

HOW DOES PARENTAL DIVORCE AFFECT CHILDREN OF DIFFERENT AGES?

There is no single definitive research study of how parental divorce affects children of different ages, but some research suggests that there are age-related effects.

Effects on Preschoolers. Divorce can upset preschool children; clinical reports indicate that they respond with bewilderment, fretfulness, and heightened aggression, at least temporarily (Wallerstein & Kelly, 1975). Any type of stress is likely to produce temporary regression in toddlers and preschoolers so they become less mature in eating, sleeping, and toileting. The adjustment of many preschool children significantly deteriorates during the first year after their parents' divorce, but delays do not typically persist (Hetherington et al., 1978, 1979).

Parents are concerned about how long their children's post-divorce adjustment difficulties may last. One carefully conducted study by Hetherington and her associates (Hetherington et al., 1978; Hetherington, Cox, & Cox, 1982) revealed that the first year is the worst for both parents and children, with decreasing child problems thereafter. However, some children continue to have adjustment problems two years or more later. Some of the

boys studied by Wallerstein and Kelly (1980) still seemed troubled as long as five years after their parents had divorced. On the more positive side, most adolescents who experienced parental divorce approved of their parents' decision to separate, and reported that they matured faster as a result of the divorce (Reinhard, 1977). In retrospect, most adults interviewed in one study concluded that having their parents divorce during their childhood had little if any effect on their own subsequent adult adjustment (Kulka & Weingarten, 1979). In the majority of cases, children eventually adjust to their new family situations.

Effects on Children. School age children may develop academic problems as well as social ones. In some samples, children's grades and their ability and achievement test scores may decline after the divorce when the father leaves the family (Hetherington et al., 1979). Children in the late elementary school grades are particularly likely to experience school achievement problems and emotional disturbances (Shinn, 1978). However, children in father-absent homes perform better on verbal than math tests and, in some cases, outperform children in traditional families on verbal measures (Barber & Eccles, 1992).

Effects on Adolescents. If anything, adolescents may be better able to cope with the divorce than younger children (Barber & Eccles, 1992; Kurdek & Berg, 1983; Zill, 1983). If true, this may be because of adolescents' greater autonomy from the family as compared with younger children. In a clinical study of developmental differences in children's responses to divorce, Wallerstein and Kelly (1974) found that the adolescents who were least affected by their parents' divorce were those who were able, from the beginning, to maintain some distance from their parents' problems and whose parents either willingly or reluctantly allowed them to do so. Their psychological independence from their embattled parents helped to insulate them from the stressful family situation. After reviewing the research on the influence of divorce and single parenting on adolescents, Barber and Eccles (1992) concluded that children in single-mother families are not so different from those in traditional, two-parent families as was once believed. Particular family circumstances, such as family income adequacy, the mother's satisfaction with her job, conflict with the father, and her relationship with her children all help determine the children's adjustment.

Adjustment to Divorce

It may be a contradiction in terms to speak of an amicable divorce, yet some are less contentious than others, and the more reasonable, less hostile divorcing couples tend to have less disturbed children. The father's attitude is very important for boys' post-divorce adjustment. Divorced fathers who are warm toward their sons and who spend time with them immediately following the divorce seem to help their sons' adjustment (Hetherington et al., 1978, 1979). These fathers' boys showed higher IQ scores and fewer achievement problems than did sons whose fathers were less warm and less available. Nevertheless, the usual pattern of cognitive abilities in which boys perform better on quantitative skills and less well on tests of verbal skills may disappear or be reversed for children in father-absent homes. When the father is absent, boys may no longer perform better in math than in reading and composition. It is possible that fathers promote sons' math achievement because they, more than mothers, effectively assist the boys with mathematical homework. In the group studied by Hetherington et al., the divorced father's influence declined over time, and after two years the mother's adjustment seemed to be the most important influence on the children. Mothers who were ineffective and under much stress had children with more problems. Women who were disorganized and poor disciplinarians had children, especially boys, who were inattentive, distractible, obtained lower IQ scores, and had poorer school grades than children of better-functioning divorced mothers. And divorced mothers who were satisfied with their jobs reported greater well-being for themselves and their children (Coverman, 1989).

Programs for Divorced Parents and Children

Because divorce is so prevalent, there should be many programs to help troubled divorced parents and their children. Unfortunately, there are few such services and families are mostly left to their own devices. Useful programs might assist divorced mothers in improving their parenting skills and providing warm, consistent guidance for their children, especially the boys. In one such effort (described in Hetherington & Parke, 1979), a behaviorally oriented counseling program helped mothers cope with their children through parenting classes in effective child management techniques. The mothers also had access to a 24-hour telephone consultation crisis line for advice and reassurance. These services increased the divorced mothers' feelings of competence and control and helped them to interact with their children in a more reasonable, controlled, and effective manner. Their sons responded with improved, better-controlled, and more acceptable behavior. Various behavioral parent training programs, including those developed by Patterson and Webster-Stratton, both of which are described in Chapter 14, can be useful in preventing and treating children's problems associated with parental conflict and divorce (Kendziora & O'Leary, 1993). The parent training approach shows great promise, can be utilized by most clinicians who specialize in treating children and families, and could easily be made widely available if funding were provided.

Some schools also offer special psychological services for children upset by parental discord. Special school services may be necessary if the children's school performance suffers severely from family disruption and they develop high absence and truancy rates, become aggressive, or their academic performance declines. Boys may particularly profit from a predictable, organized school environment with consistent standards and structured behavioral consequences (e.g., expertly designed and conducted point systems, positive reinforcement for appropriate behavior, and consistently delivered negative consequences for misbehavior). Girls may require a warm, responsive setting in which they are expected to act maturely and instructed in how to do so (Minuchin & Shapiro, 1983). Some schools attempt to recruit male teachers and classroom volunteers of the same ethnicity as the disturbed boys to provide a steadying influence and credible role models. One school-based group problem prevention approach, the Children of Divorce Intervention Program, provides timely intervention for kindergarten and elementary schoolchildren (Pedro-Carroll, Alpert-Gillis, & Cowen, 1992). In weekly group sessions, school social workers help children use group discussions and role-playing employing puppets. The students also are helped to learn to express and understand their feelings and develop competencies such as asking for help when necessary and problem-solving. Parents are assisted in seeking needed social services and joining support networks. Parents and teachers like the program and find it helpful, but further, more rigorous evaluations by independent observers must be conducted in order to demonstrate the program's worth.

Sometimes the court refers especially combative divorcing couples for counseling because they quarrel so violently over child custody, financial arrangements, and visitation rights. Therapists typically interview each parent individually, then see them together to help them negotiate with each other more reasonably and effectively. Children who are troubled by a divorce may be included in the joint treatment sessions with their parents, but only after the parents have gained some measure of emotional control. Some couples prefer group therapy together with others with similar problems, and may participate in self-help groups such as Parents Without Partners. The intervention of trained therapists and the support of other divorced parents can help family members to gain objectivity in dealing with a difficult family situation.

SUMMARY

This chapter focused on family and social factors that handicap children both physically and psychologically, including poverty and associated risks of malnutrition; environmental hazards such as lead exposure; high-risk childbearing without prenatal care, good nutrition, or non-optimal timing of pregnancy; educational inadequacy; and the transmission of impoverishment to future generations. Impoverished children are handicapped in multiple ways, beginning with higher mortality and morbidity, and dietary insufficiency potentially leading to intellectual deficits, as when a high fat, high carbohydrate diet leads to greater retention of lead in body tissues. Further, poor children typically receive substandard

schooling, in part because their ill-educated parents cannot negotiate with the schools on their behalf or effectively guide their learning. Children of color may be particularly ill-served if they are administered standard intelligence and achievement tests developed for use with white, middle-class children. Such testing often miscategorizes low-SES minority children as below average in intelligence because they may differ in language, their expectations regarding testing, background knowledge presumed by the test, and their familiarity and comfort with the testing situation. Schools may have unreasonably low expectations about the academic achievements possible for low-SES children, particularly minorities. Compensatory programs such as "Sesame Street" on TV, Head Start, and the Juniper Gardens Children's Project demonstrate that poor children's situations are far from hopeless. The study of resilient children provides further clues for developing prevention programs aimed to increase children's coping skills.

Children may be harmed by their parents' divorce economically if they live with their impoverished single mothers who receive little if any child support, and they suffer psychologically, if the divorce was surrounded by acrimony. Boys are more likely to be affected by parental conflict and to develop externalizing problems with aggression. However, boys' verbal skills may increase in single-mother families. Girls may develop internalizing problems, become apprehensive, and withdraw. However, divorce does not invariably produce child adjustment difficulties, especially if the father remains available to the children and the conflict is not severe. More recent research suggests small differences between children in single-parent and two-parent families. Family therapy, divorce counseling, school programs for children of divorce, and self-help groups can improve families' adjustment during times of transition.

CHAPTER 5

DISORDERS OF SOCIAL BEHAVIOR

Key Terms

Attention-Deficit/Hyperactivity Disorder. An attention deficit disordered (ADHD) child has primary behavioral difficulties in (1) not being able to attend to tasks for extended periods of time, (2) acting before thinking about the consequences (impulsivity), and (3) fidgety or excessive motor activity.

Coercion. The coercive process in a negative interaction between a child and an adult in which increasing aversive behavior occurs. At some point in the interaction the child may become so aversive (e.g., tantrum, argue, aggressive) that the adult withdraws his or her demand and thus negatively reinforces the child's aversive behavior.

Conduct disorder. A conduct disordered child has primary behavioral difficulties in (1) rule-breaking behavior, (2) aggression, and (3) a disregard for the rights of others.

Juvenile delinquent. Most juvenile delinquents display some of the behavior of attention deficit disordered and conduct disordered children. However, juvenile delinquents are also defined as breaking some type of law.

Oppositionally defiant disorder. An oppositionally defiant child generally exhibits (1) high rates of noncompliance, (2) tantrumming behavior, and (3) arguing.

C H A P T E R   O V E R V I E W

P roblem behaviors that affect society, the environment, and other people directly are particularly difficult to prevent or to treat. These problem behaviors have been called "externalizing" behaviors because they are directed outwardly toward the social environment (Achenbach, 1982, 1991; Walker, 1995). They can be contrasted with internalizing problem behaviors (e.g., anxiety, fears, depression) which primarily affect the child and have less obvious impact on the social environment. Examples of externalizing behavior might be the student's physically attacking a teacher, a child who deliberately sets a home on fire, or a neighborhood gang who robs a store. These are all examples of externalizing behaviors that are likely to bring a strong negative reaction from the community. Frequently, this reaction enmeshes a child or adolescent in a correctional system or results in his expulsion from school.

Externalizing problem behaviors are the most common reason for a child's referral for help by teachers and parents (Kazdin, 1985, 1989; Walker, 1995). But treatment success is modest. Children who are aggressive, argumentative, and noncompliant have poorer long-term outcomes than most children with other behavior disorders (Morris, Escoll, & Wexler, 1956; Robins, 1979; Rutter, Tizard, Yule, Graham, & Whitmore, 1976; Walker, O'Neill, Shinn, Ramsey, Patterson, Reid, & Capaldi, 1986). These antisocial behavior problems portend later problems in adulthood including alcoholism, criminal behavior, marital difficulties, and poor work histories (Kazdin, 1989). Yet, many professionals and educators tend to underestimate the long-term seriousness of externalizing-social disorders (Carter, 1987; Jenson, 1975). These children are not likely to outgrow their problems. The reverse is actually true because adults who were socially disordered as children are more likely to develop serious adjustment problems such as hospitalizations for a mental disorder, arrest, multiple job changes, and divorce (Kazdin 1989; Robins, 1979).

The terms commonly used by schools, juvenile courts, and mental health clinics to describe children with externalizing-social disorders include: antisocial, attention deficit hyperactivity disorders, aggressive, oppositional disorders, socially maladjusted, conduct disorder, and delinquent. These labels are not mutually exclusive and overlap in many areas. This chapter will review the major types of externalizing-social disorders starting with Attention-Deficit/Hyperactivity Disorder, followed by conduct disorder and oppositionally defiant disorder, and finally with juvenile delinquency. All of these conditions are related to some extent. However, we will define each condition precisely and review its possible causes, the effectiveness of current treatments, and long-term outcome.

ATTENTION-DEFICIT/ HYPERACTIVITY DISORDER

Attention-Deficit/Hyperactivity Disorder (ADHD) is one of the most frequently referred psychological disorders of childhood (Barkley, 1990; Langhorne, Loney, Paternite, & Bechtoldt, 1976). However, a great deal of confusion has existed about the condition's definition and name. However, writers agree that ADHD is more prevalent in males than in females with the ratios ranging from 3-to-1 for males to 9-to-1 for females, depending on the definition used by a particular research group (Goldstein, 1995; Ross & Ross, 1982). Similarly, the overall prevalence of ADHD is estimated to be approximately 3 to 5 percent of the school-age population, but this estimate varies widely depending on the criteria used to define the condition (Barkley, 1990). The developmental course of ADHD is fairly stable with onset of the condition probably occurring at 2 to 3 years of age in 50 to 60 percent of the cases (Barkley, 1990). The majority of the cases are not referred for professional help until the child first enters school and experiences difficulty in that setting. A sizable minority of mothers (30 percent) report early difficulties with their infants who later develop ADHD. These infants are described as colicky, irritable, hard to manage, and as having a difficult temperament (Barkley, 1990). Most children who develop ADHD in childhood continue to have some adjustment difficulty in adolescence and early adulthood (Wallandar & Hubert, 1985; Weiss & Hechtman, 1993). It is a myth that ADHD changes dramatically in adolescence. However, to better understand this condition it is first important to understand how it is defined.

Defining Attention-Deficit/ Hyperactivity Disorder (ADHD)

This condition historically has had several different labels including hyperkinesis (high rate of movement), minimal brain dysfunction (MBD), and recently Attention-Deficit/Hyperactivity Disorder (ADHD). The plethora of names has been unfortunate and confusing. These terms have implied high rates of motor activity, some type of brain dysfunction, and difficulty in paying attention. However, since 1994 when the DSM IV was published by the American Psychiatric Association (see Chapter 12),

the primary focus of this condition has been on poor attending and hyperactivity-impulsivity. Table 5-1 lists the currently accepted definition of ADHD.

INATTENTION

It can be seen from the definition in Table 5-1 that *inattention* is a central characteristic of this disorder (Weiss & Hechtman, 1993). Descriptions of ADHD children often include such statements as, "He can never concentrate on his schoolwork because he is staring out the window or disturbing his neighbor," or "She never listens to instructions. It goes in one ear and out the other." Clearly, when compared to nondisabled children, ADHD children have more difficulty attending to a task for a sustained period of time and working independently (Barkley, 1986; deHass & Young, 1984). In addition, these children may also have difficulty screening out irrelevant or extraneous stimuli (Cantwell, 1975). Even if an ADHD child tries to attend, he may be distracted by a common classroom noise such as a truck passing outside the school window or another child tapping her pencil.

IMPULSIVITY

Inattention is important but it does not completely define the ADHD condition. Other characteristics are also important. For example, the definition of ADHD in Table 5-1 lists *impulsivity* as an important characteristic of the ADHD condition. The word "impulsivity" suggests poor self-control, excitability, and the inability to delay gratification or to inhibit urges. Examples of impulsivity include "such behaviors as jumping into the deep end of a swimming pool without knowing how to swim, running into the street in front of cars, climbing on dangerous rooftops and ledges, and blurting out tactless statements" (Cantwell, 1975). Some of these behaviors are dangerous and result in accidents (Barkley, 1990) such as automobile accidents for ADHD adolescents (Hechtman, Weiss, Perlman, & Amsel, 1984). In essence, impulsivity is characterized by acting before weighing alternative responses (Kagan, 1966; Kendall and Braswell, 1985). One approach to assessing impulsivity is to have a child scan an array of different line drawings and identify the one that is identical to a comparison drawing (see Figure 5-1). For instance, children would be shown the picture in Figure 5-1 and would have to pick a bear from the bottom group

TABLE 5-1 Diagnostic Criteria for Attention-Deficit/Hyperactivity Disorder

A. Either (1) or (2):

   (1) six (or more) of the following symptoms of **inattention** have persisted for at least 6 months to a degree that is maladaptive and inconsistent with developmental level:

   Inattention
   (a) often fails to give close attention to details or makes careless mistakes in schoolwork, work, or other activities
   (b) often has difficulty sustaining attention in tasks or play activities
   (c) often does not seem to listen when spoken to directly
   (d) often does not follow through on instructions and fails to finish schoolwork, chores, or duties in the workplace (not due to oppositional behavior or failure to understand instructions)
   (e) often has difficulty organizing tasks and activities
   (f) often avoids, dislikes, or is reluctant to engage in tasks that require sustained mental effort (such as schoolwork or homework)
   (g) often loses things necessary for tasks or activities (e.g., toys, school assignments, pencils, books, or tools)
   (h) is often easily distracted by extraneous stimuli
   (i) is often forgetful in daily activities

   (2) six (or more) of the following symptoms of **hyperactivity-impulsivity** have persisted for at least 6 months to a degree that is maladaptive and inconsistent with developmental level:

   Hyperactivity
   (a) often fidgets with hands or feet or squirms in seat
   (b) often leaves seat in classroom or in other situations in which remaining seated is expected
   (c) often runs about or climbs excessively in situations in which it is inappropriate (in adolescents or adults, may be limited to subjective feelings of restlessness)
   (d) often has difficulty playing or engaging in leisure activities quietly
   (e) is often "on the go" or often acts as if "driven by a motor"
   (f) often talks excessively

   Impulsivity
   (g) often blurts out answers before questions have been completed
   (h) often has difficulty awaiting turn
   (i) often interrupts or intrudes on others (e.g., butts into conversations or games)

B. Some hyperactive-impulsive or inattentive symptoms that caused impairment were present before age 7 years.

C. Some impairment from the symptoms is present in two or more settings (e.g., at school [or work] and at home).

D. There must be clear evidence of clinically significant impairment in social, academic, or occupational functioning.

E. The symptoms do not occur exclusively during the course of a pervasive developmental disorder, schizophrenia, or other psychotic disorder and are not better accounted for by another mental disorder (e.g., mood disorder, anxiety disorder, dissociative disorder, or a personality disorder).

Code Based on Type:

   314.01 Attention-Deficit/Hyperactivity Disorder, Combined Type: if both Criteria A1 and A2 are met for the past 6 months.

   314.00 Attention-Deficit/Hyperactivity Disorder, Predominantly Inattentive Type: if Criterion A1 is met but Criterion A2 is not met for the past 6 months.

   314.01 Attention-Deficit/Hyperactivity Disorder, Predominantly Hyperactive-Impulsive Type: if Criterion A2 is met but Criterion A1 is not met for the past 6 months.

Coding note: For individuals (especially adolescents and adults) who currently have symptoms that no longer meet full criteria. "In Partial Remission" should be specified.
SOURCE: Reprinted with permission from the *Diagnostic and statistical manual of mental disorders.* Fourth Edition *(1994).* Washington, DC: American Psychiatric Association, pp. 83–85. Copyright 1994 by the American Psychiatric Association.

FIGURE 5-1   Sample item from the Matching
             Familiar Figures Test

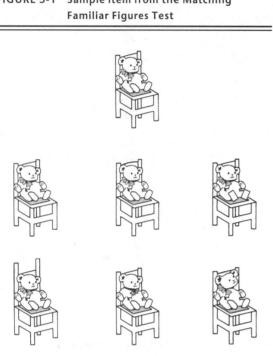

SOURCE: Kagan, J. (1966). Reflection-inpulsivity: The generality and dynamics of
conceptual tempo. *Journal of Abnormal Psychology, 71,* 17–24.

that exactly matches the sample bear at the top. This test is called the Matching Familiar Figures tests, and ADHD children generally make decisions faster with more errors than nondisabled children (Messer, 1976). (Also see Box 5-1.)

OVERACTIVITY

The terms hyperactivity and hyperkinesis refer to high levels of *activity* and energy. Frequently, ADHD children are described as "always on the move," or "bouncing off the walls." Attention-Deficit/Hyperactivity Disorder can be diagnosed with hyperactivity-impulsivity as the predominant characteristic.

The actual methodological measurement of hyperactive children's motor activity ranges from simple observations of behavior to sophisticated measuring devices such as ultrasonic sensors, actometers (readings taken from self-winding wrist watches), and pneumatic cushions that measure movement. Interpretation of activity level measures is difficult because we lack norms specifying average rates of activity for children at different ages

(Ross & Ross, 1982) and the many different types of overactivity (Barkley, 1990, 1996). In the absence of clear-cut norms for different types of motor activity, researchers usually compare motor activity of identified ADHD children with that of nondisabled children. The results are perplexing. It appears that ADHD children are generally indistinguishable from nondisabled peers in unstructured free play situations (Barkley & Ullman, 1975; Routh & Schroeder, 1976).

Perceived activity, however, seems to vary with the type of environment. Situations differ in their structure and the demands they place on the child. As the structure and demand characteristics of an environment increase, then ADHD children begin to stand out and be perceived as being overactive (Jacob, O'Leary, & Rosenbald, 1978). The type of activity must be considered in the assessment of ADHD children. Children's overall levels of activity may not be the critical element in identifying hyperactive children. Instead, it may be whether their activities bring them into conflict over rule breaking with their caretakers (Ross & Ross, 1982; Routh, 1980). A child who fidgets, taps his foot, is unable to keep his hands to himself, and who talks out of turn may constantly come to the attention of the teacher and be perceived as overly active. A child who is engaged in the same amount of motor activity but who is diligently working is judged to be normally active.

Rather than primarily overactive, support can be found that an ADHD child is primarily off-task and impulsive with several associated disruptive behaviors from checklist items that are used to identify ADHD children. Many of these rating scales have a predominance of items dealing with behavior problems such as "quarrelsome, destructive, distractible, or temper outbursts" (Conners, 1969, 1973) rather than just simple activity level (Lahey, Hobbs, Kupfer, & Delamater, 1979). Barkley (1993) has characterized many of these disruptive behaviors generally as a primary deficit in "rule-governed" behavior. ADHD children have difficulty in basically adhering to rules and instructions, which then is commonly interpreted as noncompliant, inattentive, and impulsive disruptive behaviors. These disruptive nonrule-governed behaviors become more pronounced and problematic as the structure and rule demands of the environment increase. Most ADHD children are first identified when they enter school for the first time, a structured, rule-bound environment.

An aspect of impulsivity is the *inability* to wait in order to earn a reward (reinforcer). Often ADHD children are described as being unable to delay gratification and needing instant gratification. Gordon (1979, 1983) conducted a study with hyperactive and nonhyperactive boys in which they had to learn to wait and withhold a response to earn a candy. To earn a candy, the boys had to first press a button,

FIGURE 5-2   The performance of hyperactive and nonhyperactive groups over three time blocks
of a DRL 6-second schedule.

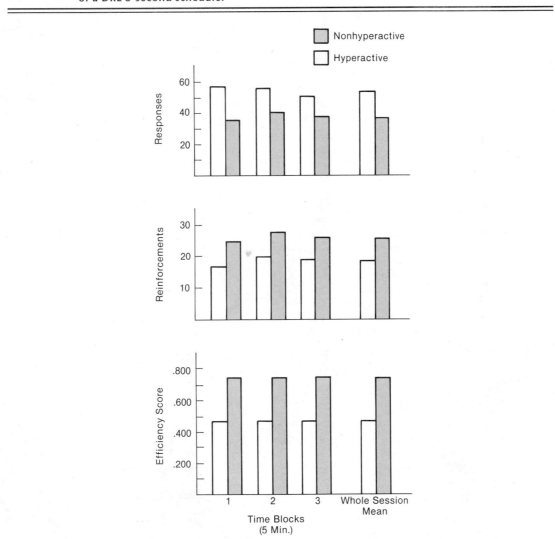

SOURCE: M. Gordon. (1979). The assessment of impulsivity and mediating behaviors in hyperactive and nonhyperactive boys. *Journal of Abnormal Child Psychology, 7,* 317–326. Reprinted by permission.

Box 5-1 (continued)

Box 5-1 (continued)

then wait a period of time (6 seconds), and then press the button again. If they pressed the button too quickly, they lost the candy. This type of procedure is called differential reinforcement of low rates of behavior (DRL-6 second).

The nonhyperactive boys did much better than the hyperactive boys on the waiting task than the hyperactive boys who seemed unable to wait. For example, the nonhyperactive boys: (1) made fewer responses than did hyperactive boys, (2) earned more candies than hyperactive boys, and (3) were overall more efficient in their responding (see Figure 5-2).

One interesting aspect of the study by Gordon (1979) was the behaviors that the boys used to help themselves wait (mediating behaviors) between button pushes. Ninety percent of the hyperactive boys used one of the observable motor behaviors listed in Table 5-2 to help them wait, but only 30 percent of the nonhyperactive boys used behavior mediators. Most (80 percent) of the nonhyperactive

---

TABLE 5-2   A LIST OF OBSERVED MEDIATING BEHAVIORS USED BY HYPERACTIVE BOYS TO DELAY THEIR RESPONDING

Circling DRL response button with finger 9 times
Swinging legs 11, 12, or 20 times
Counting with lip movements
Counting out loud—numbers or ABCs
Blowing on reward box
Singing out loud
Shaking reward box 10 times
Hitting knee with right hand 20 times
Foot-tapping 16 times
Tapping finger 10 times on button box
"Walking" fingers around DRL button 9 times
Stomping with foot 9 or 10 times
Running around table once
Hitting side of box
Jumping jacks 4 times
Hitting collateral (other nonfunctional buttons on console) buttons

SOURCE: M. Gordon. (1979). The assessment of impulsivity and mediating behaviors in hyperactive and nonhyperactive boys. *Journal of Abnormal Child Psychology, 7,* 317–326. Reprinted by permission.

---

boys used nonbehavioral mediators or some type of thinking strategy to pass the time. The more behavioral mediators a child used, the poorer his performance on the waiting task. The more covert or nonbehavioral mediators a child used, the better his performance. The behavioral mediators listed in Table 5-2 are closely related to the fidgety, restless behaviors commonly used to describe the hyperactive child. Gordon (1979) suggests that such physical mediating responses may actually be used by hyperactive children to help control their own impulsivity.

OTHER CHARACTERISTICS OF ADHD

Although the defining characteristics of ADHD primarily include inattention, impulsivity, and fidgety motor behavior, there are also *associated characteristics* that are common to this condition. For example, ADHD children commonly have *social difficulties*, particularly with peers (Barkley, 1995; Cunningham, Siegel, & Offord, 1980; Whalen, Henker, Collins, Finck, & Dotemoto, 1979). They are viewed as being immature, uncooperative, self-centered, and bossy. Most ADHD children have few close

---

BOX 5-2   JAMES, AN ATTENTION-DEFICIT DISORDERED CHILD WITH HYPERACTIVITY

James has been driving his mother crazy since he was an infant. When he was a baby, he was irritable, colicky, and difficult to predict or manage. His mother recalls that he could run before he could walk and that he was constantly getting into things. In fact, he was such an active and exploring preschooler, he poisoned himself and was well known in the emergency room for a series of accidents.

However, trouble really started to occur for James when he entered school. He had difficulty listening to the teacher and staying on task. He had particular problems with acting before thinking. For example, he would raise his hand even before the teacher finished a question and would invariably not know the answer. He would blurt out comments in the classroom, and he seemed incapable of keeping his hands to himself. He always seemed to be on the move, particularly in structured classrooms. In addition to his classroom and academic problems, James also had social problems. His peers did not like him. They commented that he seemed bossy and uncooperative: "He always had to do things his way."

At first, the teacher thought he was immature, and he was retained for a year. This only made things worse. He did not grow out of his problems, and his peers made fun of him for being stupid. James hated school. He became defiant with the teacher and started fights with the other children on the playground.

Things have improved for James since last year. His doctor has him on a stimulant medication, and he spends part of the school day in a resource room classroom. This classroom is particularly good for James because the teacher has a good program that rewards him for being on task and completing work. The teacher also runs a social skills training group, and James is starting to learn how to cooperate with other children. In addition, James' mother and father have taken a parenting class on how to manage ADHD children and things have started to improve at home.

---

friends, they tend to play with younger children, and 50 to 60 percent experience social rejection from their peers. These children are "significantly more often rated as aggressive, annoyingly uncooperative in a group, and easily led by others" (Campbell & Paulauskas, 1979). *Aggressive behaviors* are also found in a sizable subgrouping of ADHD children (Campbell, Breaux, Ewing, & Szumowski, 1986; McGee, Williams, & Silva, 1984; Prinz, Connor, & Wilson, 1981). When aggression is associated with ADHD, the prognosis is generally poorer (Loney, Whaley-Klahn, Koiser, & Conboy, 1981). ADHD children also tend to be *academically deficient* (Barkley, 1996; Cunningham & Barkley, 1979) and tend to have reading deficiencies (Halperin, Gittelman, Klein, & Rudel, 1984). A five-year follow-up study showed that 70 percent of ADHD children repeated at least one grade as compared to 15 percent of nonhyperactive children (Weiss, Minde, Werry, Douglas, & Nemeth, 1971). A high proportion (ranging from 40 to 80 percent) of children labeled as ADHD or hyperactive was also identified as having significant problems with learning and achievement (Barkley, 1990; Hinshaw, 1992).

Possible Causes of ADHD

There is probably no single cause of ADHD. However, in the past decade, a great deal of effort has gone into re-searching the possible multiple causes of ADHD. Some of the research is highly controversial such as the effects of food additives, fluorescent lighting, and sugar. But most of the work has followed more conventional lines of research such as genetics and other biological causes.

ORGANIC BRAIN DAMAGE

Overactivity and poor impulse control have long been associated with the diagnosis of organic brain damage in children. As early as 1908, Tredgold suggested that hyperactivity was linked with brain damage caused during birth by injury or deprivation of oxygen. These early injuries were assumed to go unnoticed until school age, when increased demands were placed on the child (Ross & Ross, 1976). The brain damage hypothesis received additional support from the effect of an encephalitis epidemic that occurred in the United States in 1918. Upon recovery from this disease, many children showed a major shift in behavior and general personality changes. Children who had previously been compliant were now hyperactive, distractible, irritable, deceptive, and were generally unmanageable in school (Ebaugh, 1923; Hohman, 1922; Strecker, 1929).

Other evidence of the possible link between hyperactive behavior and brain damage was provided by brain-injured soldiers (Goldstein, 1942) and children who had suffered head injuries (Strecker & Ebaugh, 1924). Since the injury through disease, birth trauma, or head injury was mostly of a minimal nature without being health or life threatening, the term *minimal brain damage* (MBD) was coined. Some researchers went so far as to assume that presence of hyperactive behaviors and their associated characteristics were sufficient to justify the diagnosis of minimal brain damage (Strauss & Kephart, 1955; Strauss & Lehtinen, 1947). This approach was severely criticized (Sarason, 1949), and attempts to empirically demonstrate the link between brain damage and ADHD have not been successful.

Most children with ADHD do not show "hard" signs or histories of brain damage (Rie & Rie, 1980; Rutter, 1977; Taylor & Fletcher, 1983). Stewart and Olds (1973) estimated that only 10 percent of the referrals for hyperactivity showed a clear history of brain damage. Other reviews set the percentage at fewer than 5 percent of ADHD children showing hard neurological evidence of brain damage (Ferguson & Rapoport, 1983; Rutter, 1983). Similarly, most children with brain damage do not develop ADHD characteristics (Rutter, 1977; Rutter, 1982). Modern computer imaging techniques such as the computerized tomography (CT) scan and the high resolution magnetic resonance imaging (MRI) have been unable to consistently detect structural or neurological damage associated with ADHD, although some structural damage has been found (Denckla, LeMay, & Chapman, 1985; Barkley, 1996). However, a recent study using the positron-emission tomography (PET) scan has shown an 8 percent difference in cerebral glucose metabolism between adult ADHD subjects and nonADHD adult subjects (Zametkin, Nordahl, Gross, King, Semple, Rumsey, Hamburger, & Cohen, 1990). Glucose is a significant energy source in the brain and essential for proper neurological functioning. These findings have also been criticized in the literature as too small a difference to have a major behavioral impact (Reid, Maag, & Vasa, 1993).

The neurological diagnosis of ADHD is difficult to make on the basis of any one clearly defined factor. A modern theoretical explanation of the ADHD theory as explained by Wender (1971, 1972) and as reviewed by Rie (1980) involves the brain's limbic system, which is directly involved in arousal and reward (positive reinforcement). Supporters of this theory propose a deficit in the metabolism of neurotransmitters. Simply stated, a balance generally exists between neurological excitation and inhibition. The ADHD child is presumed to have a defective inhibitory system that results in the child being more active and less sensitive to the effects of positive reinforcement than the normal child. The behavior problems experienced by ADHD children are assumed to be caused by their inability to learn effectively through positive reinforcement. Wender (1971) recommends the use of stimulant medication with ADHD children to restore the balance between the excitatory and inhibitory systems; this balance enhances the effects of positive reinforcement so the learning and behavioral adjustment is facilitated. Reviewers have questioned the research on neurotransmitter balance and ADHD children and the effects of stimulant medication's ability to restore a theorized imbalance (Barkley, 1982, 1985; Ross & Ross, 1982). Ross and Ross (1976) concluded, "There is little empirical support for this theory, and some of its assumptions about high arousal level and defective reward system have been questioned or contradicted."

GENETICS

Several researchers have sought to explain the behavioral characteristics of ADHD children through some type of genetic mechanism. Scientific work in this area is difficult to conduct because the causal effects of heredity and environment are difficult to separate. Researchers have used two basic approaches. First, the incidence of psychiatric disorder in parents of ADHD children is compared to that of families of nondisabled children. Researchers assume that a higher incidence of psychiatric disorder in the families of ADHD children would indicate a possible basis for heritability of the condition. Cantwell (1975) interviewed parents of ADHD children and found that 10 percent of the parents reported they had been ADHD themselves. In addition, 45 percent of these parents said they had some type of psychiatric problem (e.g., alcoholism, sociopathy, and hysteria). Other studies have reported similar results (Lahey, Piacentini, McBurnett, Stone, Hartagen, & Hynd, 1988; Morrison & Stewart, 1971; Morrison, 1980), but caution is necessary in interpreting these studies (McMahon, 1980). For instance, parents who suffer from psychiatric conditions may provide a marginal home life, which may also contribute to the development of ADHD. But in answer to this criticism, comparisons of biological and adoptive parents of ADHD children have been made. In these studies, the ADHD children who were adopted in infancy had no contact with their biological parents after adoption. A higher incidence of psychiatric disturbance was found in the ADHD child's biological parents than in their adoptive parents (Morrison & Stewart, 1971).

The second approach to the study of genetic causes has been to compare genetically identical monozygotic twins and nonidentical dizygotic or fraternal twins. Willerman (1973) studied 54 monozygotic and 49 dizygotic twin pairs by sending their mothers a questionnaire that assessed child activity levels. This study found higher rates of these characteristics in monozygotic twins than in dizygotic twins. Similarly, Goodman and Stevenson (1989) compared the inheritability of ADHD for 127 monozygotic and 111 dizygotic twin pairs. The concordance rates for ADHD were found to be 51 percent for the monozygotic and 33 percent for the dizygotic twins. These researchers suggest that between 30 to 50 percent of the traits of ADHD have an inheritability factor showing genetics plays a substantial role in the cause of ADHD.

Genetic studies of ADHD children indicate that heredity does play a role in the development of the condition. The exact role or genetics, however, is still difficult to determine. Specific genes may cause higher activity levels, inattention, or impulsivity. Or, there may be an interaction effect between combinations of genes. There is no simple answer. Probably there is an interplay of multiple causes such as genetics, biological factors, the environment, and family stresses that increases the vulnerability of a child to the ADHD condition (Barkley, 1985, 1993).

ENVIRONMENTAL FACTORS

Children are subject to a number of stresses such as environmental pollution, exposure to low levels of radiation, ingestion of foods with man-made chemicals, and high divorce rates that did not exist 50 years ago. These environmental stresses have been implicated in the increase in the number of ADHD children. Poisons are a threat to all young children but pose an even higher threat to hyperactive children. Szatmari, Offord, and Boyle (1989) found that 7.3 percent of ADHD children had an accidental poisoning compared to 2.6 percent of nondisabled children. The connection between poisonings and hyperactivity, as pointed out by Ross and Ross (1976), is not an unreasonable one since ADHD children are more likely to "get into things." The "things" may be toxic substances, such as paint, that affect health and behavior.

A common source of lead poisoning is lead-based paint in old buildings. However, lead is also spewed into the environment from industrial pollution such as smelting plants and from the use of leaded gasoline used in automobiles (see Chapter 4). The use of leaded gasoline alone puts approximately 240,000 tons of lead into the air each year in the United States (Ross & Ross, 1982). David, Clark, and Voeller (1972) found that a group of ADHD children whom they studied had greater lead stores in their blood than nondisabled children. The lead in the blood stream was not at toxic levels, but at a subtoxic level that might cause minimal poisoning and contribute to the behavioral symptoms of ADHD. In a similar study, metal toxins (lead, arsenic, mercury, cadmium, and aluminum) concentrations were studied as trace elements in the hair of school-age children in Wyoming (Marlowe, Cossairt, Moon, Errera, MacNeel, Peak, Ray, & Schroeder, 1985). In this study, a significant relationship was found between the accumulation of metals (particularly lead) and increased problematic behaviors as measured by a behavior checklist.

Food additives and diet have recently been given a great deal of publicity as causes of ADHD, particularly by parents and children who value natural or organic foods. The "Feingold Diet" has received the most attention (Feingold, 1975a). This diet restricts artificial food colorings, flavorings, and natural salicylates (an aspirin like compound). Although others were unable to replicate his results, Feingold (1975b) has written that a large percentage (50 percent) of ADHD children show favorable results from the diet, he has testified before the U.S. Senate Subcommittee of Health:

"Following management of children whose primary complaint was hyperkinesis or MBD (minimal brain dysfunction) with diet eliminating all artificial colors and flavors, we again observe the rapid and dramatic response in about 50 percent of cases reported by our earlier patients. Within a few weeks and sometimes days, a complete reversal of the behavioral pattern was observed." (Kolobye, 1976)

Feingold assumed that the ADHD child is allergic to or genetically predisposed to react negatively to these compounds. The problem with Feingold's diet hypothesis is that much of its support has been anecdotal, without adequate scientific evidence. More complete reviews of diet research have generally indicated that diet can play a role in ADHD (Conners, 1980; Harley & Matthews, 1980; Swanson & Kinsbourne, 1980; Trites, Tryphonas, & Ferguson, 1980; Tryphonas, 1979; Varley, 1984). However, the effects are far less dramatic than those reported by Feingold, and the vast majority of ADHD children do not show an improvement on the Feingold Diet (Barkley, 1995). As stated by Goldstein and Ingersoll (1992):

> *"In the past fifteen years, dozens of well-controlled studies published in peer-review journals have failed to find support for Dr. Feingolds' approach." (p. 20)*

In a similar vein, numerous parents report that sugar has a profound effect in producing ADHD behaviors in their children. Although some studies have been conducted with sugar ingestion and ADHD symptoms (Conners, 1986; Prinz, Roberts, & Hantman, 1980), there is no evidence that controlling sugar significantly affects the behavior of ADHD children (Wolraich, Wilson, & White, 1995; Barkley, 1995; Varley, 1984). Sugar should be viewed as energizing an already existing behavioral pattern. Instead of causing a behavior to happen, sugar may merely amplify an already existing behavior pattern, whether the behavior is appropriate or inappropriate.

FAMILY FACTORS

Some studies with ADHD children have shown that their mothers were generally critical, disapproving, unaffectionate, and used severe punishment (Battle & Lacey, 1972). There was some concern that this type of parenting style might actually cause the condition. However, it is now generally agreed that this type of behavior probably was a response to the ADHD child's inappropriate behavior rather then the cause of it (Weiss & Hechtman, 1993). For example, when ADHD children were treated or got older and their behavior improved, then their mothers became less controlling and more responsive (Barkley & Cunningham, 1979; Barkley, Karlsson, & Pollard, 1985). However, ADHD children do leave a mark on parents, particularly their mothers who tend to be less confident, under more stress, socially isolated, self-blaming, and depressed when compared to mothers who do not have ADHD children (Mash & Johnston, 1983). These faults in parenting style and self-confidence do not

cause ADHD, but they can exacerbate the child's behavioral problems (Barkley, 1985, 1995).

Treatment of ADHD

Few childhood behavior disorders have raised such controversy and heated debate as ADHD (Goldstein & Ingersoll, 1992). The treatment of this condition has covered a wide range of approaches including medication, psychotherapy, educational interventions, and diet. Each approach has supporters who are sure that their intervention is the most effective. But over time, few treatments have been scientifically documented to be highly effective (Weiss & Hechtman, 1986, 1993). Traditional psychotherapy, counseling, and play therapy for ADHD children are considered relatively ineffective in altering the child's behavior problems (Mendelson, Johnson, & Stewart, 1971; Menkes, Rowe, & Menkes, 1967; Safer & Allen, 1976). Educational approaches, which have stressed quiet and nondistracting classroom environments and cubicles (Cruickshank, Bentzen, Ratzeburg, & Tannhauser, 1961), have not been significantly effective (Ross & Ross, 1982). The two most promising approaches have been stimulant medications and behavior management techniques.

STIMULANT MEDICATION

The use of stimulants (such as amphetamines) with emotionally disturbed children was first introduced by Bradley (1937). Bradley was a physician at a residential treatment center for children, and he first used benzedrine with children in an attempt to treat severe headaches. To Bradley's surprise, the medication did not affect the children's headaches, but instead it had a dramatic impact on their behavior. Their work habits and school performance improved and their behavior problems decreased. The children referred to the benzedrine tablets as their "arithmetic pills" because the medication improved their classroom performance (Ross & Ross, 1976). Bradley's discovery went relatively unnoticed until the 1950s when stimulant drugs started to be widely prescribed for ADHD children. Controversy erupted over the use of stimulants with ADHD children when it was erroneously reported in the *Washington Post* that as many as 5 to 10 percent of all the elementary-age children in Omaha, Nebraska, were taking the drug (Maynard, 1970). The debate continues today and includes such topics as the general usefulness of stimulants (DuPaul & Barkley, 1990), their effects on mother and child interactions (Barkley & Cunningham, 1979), their effects on academic performance (Barkley & Cunningham, 1978; DuPaul & Stoner, 1994), positive effects on peer relationships (Whalen, Henker, Buhrmester, Hinshaw, Huber, & Laski, 1989), their side effects (DuPaul & Barkley, 1990; Safer, Allen, & Barr, 1972), and their possible abuse (Weiss & Hechtman, 1986).

Even with the scientific debate, today such medications as Ritalin and dextroamphetamine are recognized as changing the behavior of ADHD children. On average 75 percent of ADHD children taking stimulant medication show a behavioral improvement and 25 percent either do not change or get worse (Barkley, 1977; DuPaul & Barkley, 1990). The main immediate improvements for those taking stimulants include improved attending behavior and reduced impulsivity (Barkley, 1985). Fidgety behavior has also been reported as improving, depending on the dosage of the drug (Barkley & Jackson, 1976). However, the medication has failed to reduce activity measures such as the number of times a child is out of his seat or away from his desk. Mothers reportedly needed to exert less control over their ADHD children and responded to them more positively after the children were medicated (Barkley & Cunningham, 1979; Cunningham & Barkley, 1978). One study (Abikoff & Gittelman, 1985) found that after they were placed on the medication, the ADHD children were "indistinguishable" from their nondisabled peers in a classroom.

Academic achievement is critical to the adjustment of ADHD children, both in school and later as adults. As indicated previously, most ADHD children are academically deficient. The exact effects of stimulant drugs on learning and academic performance is unclear; however, evidence indicates that stimulants *do not* improve the long-term academic performance of children (Barkley & Cunningham, 1978; Ross & Ross, 1982; Weiss & Hechtman, 1993). In one series of studies, it was found that stimulant drugs increased attention to work and reduced distractibility in underachieving children (DuPaul, Barkley, & McMurray, 1991). Academic improvement (as measured by a standardized achievement test), however, was not improved by medication, even though both parents and teachers rated the child as academically improved. It appears that ADHD children placed on medication may initially show an improvement in academics

(i.e., over several weeks) (Pelham, Bender, Caddell, Booth, & Moore, 1985) but in the long term (i.e., one to ten years) there is basically no effect of stimulants on academic achievement (Charles & Schain, 1981; Weiss & Hechtman, 1993). Rie and associates (1976b) warned that stimulant medication may mask academic problems because increased attending behavior and reduced classroom behavior problems may be misperceived by teachers as positive changes in achievement. In actuality, the children's learning problems and deficits may be left untreated and unimproved.

The side effects that accompany the use of stimulant medication include insomnia, rebound irritability, decreased appetite, and headaches, all of which are relatively minor and generally temporary. Suppressed growth in height and weight have also been reported (DuPaul & Barkley, 1990; Safer, Allen, & Barr, 1972). However, when children are taken off the drug for the summer, there can be a "rebound" effect in which children tend to grow quickly and compensate for some growth deficiencies. More serious side effects include attributional effects.

With attributional effects, a person ascribes his behaviors to some particular factor. For example, many people believe that a rabbit's foot controls their luck. ADHD children may show a similar attribution effect with stimulant medication (Bugental, Whalen, & Henker, 1977; Whalen & Henker, 1976). An ADHD child may forget her medication in the morning and then assume that she will have a terrible day at school. Rosen, O'Leary, and Conway (1985) reported a case of an ADHD child named Tom who had attributional difficulties in withdrawing from medication. Tom spontaneously stated that "My mother couldn't get me my pills from the hospital. My pills make me get done with my work," and "I get angry without my pill." With a great deal of training and some setbacks, Tom was weaned from the medication and began to attribute his successful behavior to his own self-control. Furthermore, this attributional error can be made by parents and teachers as well as the child. If a child and her parents and teacher attribute all behavioral control to a pill, there can result a lack of teaching or learning; those involved may stop expecting that the ADHD child will develop alternative coping behaviors that may be critical to later adjustment.

Possibly the greatest drawback to the use of stimulant medication with ADHD children is its lack of long-term effectiveness. Clearly, the positive short-term effects of stimulants encourage teachers and parents to use them. A one-year follow-up of ADHD boys receiving stimulant medication together with psychotherapy has been encouraging (Satterfield, Cantwell, & Satterfield, 1979). In the long term, stimulant medication had its greatest effects in (1) reducing serious automobile accidents in adolescence, (2) producing higher self-esteem, (3) providing a more positive view of childhood by adults and peers, and (4) producing better social skills in ADHD children who were treated than in children who were not treated. It did not, however, improve the children's overall academic achievement or the number of grades passed or failed (Weiss & Hechtman, 1993). In virtually all comparisons (social, academic, behavioral) with nondisabled peers, ADHD children who were treated and ADHD children who were not treated with stimulants did poorer. However, ADHD children treated with stimulant medication did significantly improve, especially with better social interactions, improved attention span, and reduced impulsivity. A basic implication is that stimulant medications is a short-term or day-to-day effective tool in the management of ADHD, but several combined therapeutic approaches may be necessary in the long-term management of ADHD (Barkley, 1977; DuPaul & Barkley, 1990).

BEHAVIOR MANAGEMENT

Behavioral techniques used with ADHD children have largely been used in classrooms and homes (Abramowitz & O'Leary, 1991; O'Leary, 1980). Techniques vary, but the most frequently used interventions include (1) positive reinforcement for on-task behavior, remaining seated, and completing assignments; (2) response cost or loss of reinforcement for inappropriate behaviors such as noncompliance, refusal to sit down, and aggression; and (3) cognitive behavior modification that emphasizes self-control and self-reinforcement (see Chapter 14).

A simple system that has been shown to substantially increase on-task behavior is random tones that are recorded on a tape recorder. When the tone randomly sounds and the ADHD child is attending and working, he is reinforced by the teacher socially and with reward points (Pfiffner & Barkley, 1990). This system can slowly be faded so the student marks his own points when the tone sounds (Rhode, Jenson, & Reavis, 1993). Similarly, it was demonstrated through numerous studies that re-

inforcement techniques can be used to improve on-task behavior in ADHD children (as reviewed by Hendersen, Jenson, & Erken, 1986). However, like medication alone, simply improving on-task behavior does not necessarily improve academic performance. Ayllon and Rosenbaum (1977) have suggested that behavioral programs that directly improve academic performance often have the beneficial side effects of reducing disruptive behaviors in ADHD children. Cognitive-behavior modification approaches, which teach self-control, problem solving, and self-reinforcement for appropriate behavior with ADHD children, have been promising (Abramowitz & O'Leary, 1991).

Teaching the parents of ADHD children to design behavioral programs for their children has been demonstrated to be practically effective (Newby, Fischer, & Roman, 1991). O'Leary, Pelham, Rosenbaum, and Price (1976) trained parents to be part of the treatment team and utilize a reward system in the home to reinforce both academic and social achievement of ADHD children in school. Similarly, Barkley (1987, 1995) has developed an 8 to 10 week parent training program that teaches parents to focus on appropriate behaviors and to decrease inappropriate behaviors such as noncompliance and aggression with time out and response cost procedures. The outcome research from this program showed clear improvements in ADHD children's compliant behavior, however, continuous management is required.

Virtually no long-term follow-up data exist documenting the effectiveness of behavioral approaches to the treatment of ADHD (O'Leary, 1980; Ross & Ross, 1982). The cost of doing follow-up studies plus the difficulty in locating subjects are barriers to conducting extensive follow-up research (Mash & Dalby, 1979). This situation is unfortunate since cost effectiveness comparisons are needed to evaluate the different interventions. Clearly, behavioral approaches involve more time and cost more money than do stimulant medication interventions. Both stimulant medication and behavioral techniques appear to be effective in the short term and may be more effective when used in combination (Abramowitz & O'Leary, 1991; Gittelman-Klein, Klein, Abikoff, Katz, Gloisten, & Kates, 1976; Wolraich, Drummond, Salomon, O'Brien, & Sivage, 1978; Hinshaw, Henker, & Whalen, 1984). Stimulants may be more cost effective and better in controlling impulsivity. Behavior therapy may be more effective in improving academic deficits and has fewer negative side effects than stimulants. Both appear to reduce disruptive behaviors and improve attending. The combined effects of both behavioral approaches and medication may be limited (Horn, Ialongo, Greenberg, Packard, & Smith-Winberry, 1990) because their therapeutic effects may vary with different behavior problems. However, no single treatment has been demonstrated to be truly effective in the long term (Weiss & Hechtman, 1993).

CONDUCT DISORDER AND OPPOSITIONAL DEFIANT DISORDER

The term *conduct disorder* is a broad label used to identify a number of aversive and socially disruptive behaviors in children. The definition of *conduct* involves "a mode or standard of personal behavior especially based on moral principles" (*Webster's Tenth New Collegiate Dictionary*, 1994). The key to this definition is a "standard of personal behavior." A breakdown in the social control of a child's personal standard of behavior by a parent, teacher, or society in general leads to insufficiently controlled behavior excesses referred to as conduct disorder. This disorder is an externalizing disorder which affects all the people that deal with the child. The types of problem behaviors associated with conduct disordered children include: aggression (Loeber & Schmaling, 1985a; Patterson 1976a, 1982, 1986), noncompliance (Forehand, King, Peeds, & Yoder, 1975), temper tantrums (Bernal, 1969; Patterson, Reid, & Dishion, 1993), stealing (Loeber & Schmaling, 1985b), firesetting (Kazdin, 1989), and destructiveness (Wolf, 1971).

Characteristics of Conduct Disordered Children

The behaviors listed above are clearly aversive to parents and teachers; however, they are not unique to conduct disordered children. Virtually all children have engaged in some of these behaviors at one time or another during their development. What separates the conduct disordered child from a child with disabilities is the intensity and frequency (excesses) of these behaviors (Quay, 1972; Jenson, Reavis, & Rhode, 1987). Behavioral excesses such as frequent aggression and noncompliance are the most obvious characteristics of conduct disorders. Along with the excesses, however, come a series of deficits. It is easy for parents, teachers, and professionals to focus only on the aversive behavioral excesses and miss treating the behavioral deficits.

One of the most disturbing deficits of conduct disordered children is their poor moral development and lack of empathetic behavior (Goldstein, Glick, Reiner, Zimmerman, & Coultry, 1987; Jurkovic & Prentice, 1977). Many conduct disordered children show little guilt or conscience concerning their destructive behavior. Other writers have described this flaw as more of a deficit in *rule-governed* behavior (Barkley, 1990) or *self-management skills* (Rhode, Jenson, & Reavis, 1993). A child is directed by a social rule that guides the child in how to behave in different situations, particularly unsupervised situations. For instance, a rule might be "honest people do not steal" even when they are unobserved. Conduct disordered children, however, appear to be *contingency governed* (Skinner, 1954) because they respond to the immediate rewards in the environment (e.g., "I will steal it if I can get it now") instead of the social rules. This contingency orientation is reflected in many conduct disordered children's questioning what will happen to them if they misbehave rather than reflecting on the effect the behavior may have on some other person.

Other deficits associated with conduct disorders include *poor social skills* and *academic deficiencies*, particularly poor reading skills (Kazdin, 1989; Hinshaw, 1992; Rutter & Yule, 1973; Semier, Eron, Myerson, & Williams, 1967; Wells & Forehand, 1985). Researchers have shown that one of the strongest correlates to antisocial behavior in adolescents is an academic skills deficiency (Dishion, Loeber, Stouthamer-Loeber, & Patterson, 1984; Short & Shapiro, 1993). Poor academic achievement has been shown to be a causal variable in the relationship between early disruptive behavior and later delinquency (Tremblay, Masse, Perron, Leblanc, Schwartzman, & Ledingham, 1992). Poor school performance is often linked to disruptive classroom behavior, truancy, suspension, and drop out. Once a conduct disordered student is no longer attending school, he or she is usually unsupervised, which further compounds social problems. Walker (1991) has clearly pointed out that school problems, school failure, and lack of supervision are directly linked to a path to prison for many youth. Consider that "Young people, who represent about 20 percent of the

TABLE 5-3 BEHAVIORAL CHARACTERISTICS OF CONDUCT DISORDERED CHILDREN

Behavioral Excesses	Specific Behaviors
Aggression	Physically attacks other (peers and adults)
	Verbally abusive
	Destroys property
	Sets fires
	Vandalizes
	Cruel to animals
	Revengeful
Noncompliance	Breaks established rules
	Does not follow commands
	Argues
	Does the opposite of what is requested

Behavioral Deficits	Specific Behaviors
Moral behavior	Shows little remorse for destructive behavior
	Appears to have no conscience
	Lacks concern for feelings of others
Social behavior	Has few friends
	Lacks affection or bonding
	Has few problem-solving skills
	Acts aggressively and impulsively rather than cooperatively
	Constantly seeks attention
	Poor conversation skills
	Does not know how to reward other peers and adults socially
Academics and school	Generally behind in the academic basics, particularly reading
	Has difficulty acquiring new academic information
	Truant

population, now account for over 40 percent of the reported crimes. Almost half the youth charged with serious offenses are under 15, and 75 percent are boys" (Walker, 1991).

In their social relationships, conduct disordered children are frequently described as being inappropriately competitive, uncooperative, bossy, and defensive about criticism. These children do not know how to be an appropriate leader, how to initiate conversations, and how to socially reward other adults and peers. Loeber and Pat-

terson (1981) reported that 72 percent of the conduct disordered children referred to the Oregon Research Institute for service had poor peer relations. A fundamental problem resulting from poor social skills development is that antisocial children lack the basic ability to solve many social problems (Sheridan, 1995). This lack of rudimentary social problem-solving ability and basic interactive social skills lead to peer rejection and a loss of self-esteem (Patterson et al., 1992). Rejection and the resulting poor self-esteem have several cascading social effects. First, conduct disordered children are often only accepted by other antisocial-aggressive children, building early social alliances and groups that are deviancy based and result in later delinquency (Dishion & Loeber, 1985; Dishion, Patterson, & Griesler, 1994; Cairns, Cairns, Neckerman, Gest, & Gariepy, 1988). This rejection and a need to belong socially may be the roots of later gang behavior. Second, there is a high co-morbidity between conduct disorder and childhood depression (Patterson et al., 1992). Estimates run as high as 50 percent of children showing antisocial behaviors and internalizing-depression (McConaughy & Skiba, 1993).

Table 5-3 lists the behaviors, both excesses and deficits, commonly associated with conduct disordered children. Although the behaviors listed in the table are many and diverse, the basic definitive characteristics of the conduct disordered child are excesses in aggression and noncompliance, with deficits in rule-governed, social, and academic behaviors (see Box 5-3 for a case example).

ANTISOCIAL-AGGRESSIVE BEHAVIOR

We cannot give a concise definition of aggression in the conduct disordered child because experts disagree on its exact definition and causes. However, Table 5-4 lists the basic definition of conduct disorder from the *Diagnostic and Statistical Manual* (DSM-IV) of the American Psychiatric Association (1994). This definition emphasizes a persistent or repetitive pattern of behavior intended to violate the basic rights of others or age-appropriate societal norms or rules. Again, lack of rule-governed behavior is emphasized in this definition with four basic main groupings: (1) aggression toward people or property, (2) destruction of property (see Box 5-4), (3) deceitfulness or theft, and (4) serious violation of rules. Two general types of conduct disorder have been identified that are linked to age. Childhood-Onset Conduct Disorder occurs before age 10, generally showing the early

---

BOX 5-3 BOBBY, A CONDUCT DISORDERED CHILD

Bobby is the type of boy that made his teacher regret Mondays when he would have to go back to teaching. This regret centered on one difficult student, Bobby Jones. This child seemed to be the opposite of what adults wanted in a child. Bobby would go out of his way to do the opposite of what was requested. Adults would have to repeat and repeat what they wanted; then Bobby would argue and fight back. He seemed to have a million excuses why he should not do the simplest of tasks. When pushed, Bobby would respond by fighting or trying to get even. He once destroyed an art project by another boy because he thought he should get a prize. He is also suspected of setting a fire in the classroom last year. But it could not be proven. What is most frustrating about Bobby is that he does not seem to care about others. As long as he gets his way that is all that matters to him. He never shows guilt or remorse for a behavior that hurts another person, even when he is caught red-handed.

Because he is such a troublemaker, other children in the classroom do not like Bobby. They simply stay away from him and would rather not include him in any of their activities because he takes charge and tries to push them around. Bobby's schoolwork also suffers. It is so much trouble to get him to do something that most teachers have given up on Bobby. He is now two years behind in reading.

At home Bobby rules the household. His mother is permissive and has trouble handling Bobby. She just can not set a limit. His father is seldom home. When he is home, Bobby's father is overly strict and wants things changed immediately. Bobby is constantly a source of conflict between his mother and father, and they talk of getting a divorce.

Things have gotten so difficult with Bobby at school that he has been referred to a special education classroom. The incident that seemed to provoke the referral involved Bobby beating a smaller boy for a collection of scratch and sniff stickers. He will be sent to the classroom next week; however, his mother objects to the placement and wants a second chance for Bobby.

---

characteristics of physical aggression, disturbed peer relationships, and early oppositional or noncompliant behavior. The second type is Adolescent-Onset Conduct Disorder, which is characterized by the display of disruptive behavior after age 10. The Adolescent-Onset type is less likely to exhibit overt displays of aggressive behavior and to have better peer relations. However, these adolescents may display many of their misbehaviors in the company of other conduct disordered peers. The children with Childhood-Onset Conduct Disorder have a poorer prognosis than the adolescent type in that they are likely to maintain their disruptive behavior through adolescence and into adulthood.

A central core of aggression (physical and property destruction) and rule violation as a means of controlling others has been investigated by Patterson and Cobb, who labeled it "pain control" or "coercion" (Patterson, 1976a, 1982). Pain control behaviors involve the use of aversive behaviors such as hitting in order to control another person. A common example is frequently seen in grocery stores when a child wants a small toy and the parent refuses. The child may escalate the hostilities and start to engage in a screaming and kicking tantrum until the parent buys the toy to quiet the child and escape the disapproving stares of the other customers. Here, the child has perhaps unwittingly used a tantrum as an instrument to coerce and shape the parent's behavior. Pain control

is so common in conduct disordered children and their families that on average a hit or tease occurs every half hour in these families (Patterson, 1982; Patterson, Reid, Jones, & Conger, 1975). Frequently, noncompliance is at the heart of this pain control-coercive process.

NONCOMPLIANCE

Simply defined, noncompliance is "not doing what is requested" (Patterson et al., 1975), with the request generally being made by a parent or teacher. Noncompliance is one of the most common behavior problems of childhood (Herbert, 1978) and comprises one-third of children's deviant behavior (Wahl, Johnson, Martin, & Johansson, 1974). Patterson, Ray, Shaw, and Cobb (1969), using observers in the homes of antisocial boys, found that on average, one noncompliant behavior occurred every 10 minutes. In normative studies, compliance rates of nondisabled children to parental requests ranged from approximately 60 to 80 percent (Forehand, 1977; Forehand, King, Peeds, & Yoder, 1975). However, compliance rates for clinic referred children who have behavior problems range from only 30 to 40 percent. Developmentally, noncompliance decreases until approximately age 5 (Patterson, 1976), however, for disturbed children after age 5, noncompliance is an extremely stable problem behavior (Achenbach, 1991; Patterson et al., 1992).

TABLE 5-4   DIAGNOSTIC CRITERIA FOR 312.8 CONDUCT DISORDER

A. Repetitive and persistent pattern of behavior in which the basic rights of others or major age-appropriate societal norms or rules are violated, as manifested by the presence of three (or more) of the following criteria in the past 12 months, with at least one criterion present in the past 6 months:

Aggression to People and Animals
   (1) often bullies, threatens, or intimidates others
   (2) often initiates physical fights
   (3) has used a weapon that can cause serious physical harm to others (e.g., a bat, brick, broken bottle, knife, gun)
   (4) has been physically cruel to people
   (5) has been physically cruel to animals
   (6) has stolen while confronting a victim (e.g., mugging, purse snatching, extortion, armed robbery)
   (7) has forced someone into sexual activity

Destruction of Property
   (8) has deliberately engaged in fire setting with the intention of causing serious damage
   (9) has deliberately destroyed others' property (other than by fire setting)

Deceitfulness or Theft
   (10) has broken into someone else's house, building, or car
   (11) often lies to obtain goods or favors or to avoid obligations (i.e., "cons" others)
   (12) has stolen items of nontrivial value without confronting a victim (e.g., shoplifting, but without breaking and entering; forgery)

Serious Violations of Rules
   (13) often stays out at night despite parental prohibitions, beginning before age 13 years
   (14) has run away from home overnight at least twice while living in parental or parental surrogate home (or once without returning for a lengthy period)
   (15) is often truant from school, beginning before age 13 years
B. The disturbance in behavior causes clinically significant impairment in social, academic, or occupational functioning.
C. If the individual is age 18 years or older, criteria are not met for antisocial personality disorder.

Specify **Type Based on Age at Onset:**
   Childhood-Onset Type: onset of at least one criterion characteristic of Conduct Disorder prior to age 10 years
   Adolescent-Onset Type: absence of any criteria characteristic of Conduct Disorder prior to age 10 years

Specify **Severity:**
   Mild: few if any conduct problems in excess of those required to make the diagnosis *and* conduct problems cause only minor harm to others
   Moderate: number of conduct problems and effect on others intermediate between "mild" and "severe"
   Severe: many conduct problems in excess of those required to make the diagnosis *or* conduct problems cause considerable harm to others

SOURCE: Reprinted with permission from the *Diagnostic and statistical manual of mental disorders.* Fourth Edition *(1994).* Washington, DC: American Psychiatric Association, pp. 90–91. Copyright 1994 by the American Psychiatric Association.

The form of noncompliance can be diverse. A child may simply ignore a request made by an adult, often causing the adult to wonder if the child heard or understood the request. Noncompliance can also take the form of delaying, passive resistance, arguing, or giving excuses why a behavior cannot be done. An extreme form of noncompliance is *negativism*, which is "an exaggerated form of resistance, occurring when a child becomes stubborn or contrary, often doing quite the opposite of what the parents wish" (Herbert, 1978). These forms of noncompliance and oppositional behaviors that are persistent for at least 6 months can be classified as a third type of social disorder, oppositional defiant disorder (see Table 5-5). The core of this disorder is negativistic, defiant, disobedient, and hostile behaviors toward authority figures such as parents and teachers. Although oppositional defiant disorder is considered a separate disorder in the DSM-IV, it is a likely precursor to the more serious forms of conduct disorders, especially when the effects of these behaviors are considered. Some researchers see the devel-

---

BOX 5-4 COMPREHENSIVE TREATMENT OF CHRONIC FIRE SETTING IN A SEVERELY DISORDERED BOY

Jim was a 10-year-old boy enrolled in a mental health day program that treated severely behaviorally disordered children. In this program he was treated for a major fire setting problem (Koles & Jenson, 1985). Jim's developmental history was characterized by deprivation, inadequate parenting, chaotic home life, and a series of foster home placements. He was diagnosed as both conduct disordered and attention-deficit disorder. His list of referral problems included stealing, hyperactivity, tantrumming, learning disabilities, aggression, noncompliance, zoophilia, and fire setting. The fire setting had been a problem since Jim was 3, when he burned down the family home. Since his foster placements, Jim had averaged approximately one fire setting every two weeks.

It was assumed that Jim set fires partly because he enjoyed seeing the fires and partly as a reaction to stress. The stress was related to a series of skill deficits in the social and academic areas. In addition, it was assumed that Jim did not fully realize the dangerous consequences of his behavior. His therapy involved a multiple treatment approach that served to educate, relieve stress, and consequate fire setting. It included:

1. *Social problem-solving skills* taught to Jim that involved positive relationships to others, successful classroom adjustment, peer interaction skills, and problem-solving.
2. *Relaxation training* was implemented using basic muscle relaxation techniques to help reduce anxiety.
3. *Oversensitization* was used in which Jim visited a hospital burn unit and interviewed a depressed 10-year-old boy who had suffered burns over 80 percent of his body while playing with matches. He was also given additional information from the burn unit social worker and a fire investigator.
4. *Fire safety education* in which Jim participated in a program through a local fire department that involved film and lecture materials on the destructive effects of fire.
5. *Overcorrection procedures* were used in which Jim collected combustible material in a metal container and set it on fire. He recited a series of statements over and over again during the safe fire (e.g., "fires can kill people," "this fire is safe because it can not spread"). He was then required to scrub the container. The overcorrection procedure served to oversatiate Jim with the fascination of fire setting.
6. *Behavioral contracts* were used to reward no fire setting or mildly punish (e.g., going to bed early) when a fire was set.

After treatment, Jim's fire setting dropped from an average of one every two weeks to virtually zero fires at a one year follow-up. Jim improved his basic social skills and appeared better prepared to handle stressful situations, although some of his inappropriate behaviors such as stealing and family problems have continued.

---

opment of antisocial behavior as a developmental process (Patterson et al., 1993) with early deviant behavior developing into more serious antisocial behavior as the child gets older. In fact, this process may continue well into adulthood. Robins (1966) found that 70 percent of antisocial adults were antisocial as children.

The effects of severe noncompliance and oppositional behavior on others are not difficult to understand: they leave adults with feelings of helplessness and frustration. The expression "out-of-control" has frequently been used to describe the socially disordered child, and its use stems directly from noncompliance and opposition. The lack of conscience, moral concern for others, and rule-governed behavior may be explained partially by the effects of noncompliance in early development. Herbert (1978) speculates that the development of compliance and rule-following behavior is critical to later socialization and moral development. Learning to comply may be an "essential core to morality" in that a child learns to regulate his interpersonal behavior by a set of external

rules and values and not by what happens to please him at the moment. B. F. Skinner (1954) has described a process of culminating steps that lead to self-managed or rule-governed behavior:

Step 1: Learning to comply to requests
Step 2: Learning self-control
Step 3: Learning problem-solving skills

Linked to a failure to learn these rule-governed steps, severe noncompliance may directly disrupt the development of social skills and academic skills of a child (Rhode et al., 1993; Walker, 1995). If the child is uncooperative and lacks problem-solving skills with other children, then the development of basic social and interactive skills may be delayed. If a child does not follow simple directions from teachers, then the development of basic academic and study skills may be retarded. It has been suggested that noncompliance is a "king pin" or central behavior that controls many of the deficits and excesses found in

Childhood tantrums may be viewed by many adults as a disturbing behavior that is difficult to understand. Recent research, however, suggests that tantrums may be a form of pain control used by children in a coercive process.

conduct disordered children (Jenson et al., 1987; Rhode et al., 1993; Walker, 1995). If compliance can be increased in these children, then many of the difficult behaviors such as aggression, arguing, and temper tantrums may improve without directly treating these behaviors (Mace, Hock, Lalli, West, Belfiore, Pinter, & Brown, 1988; Montgomery, 1993). Russo, Cataldo, and Cushing (1981) have shown that if noncompliance can be reduced in children, then other inappropriate behaviors such as crying, tantrumming, and aggression will stop without being directly treated (see Box 5-5).

Other Characteristics of Conduct Disordered and Oppositionally Defiant Children

In addition to the characteristics already mentioned, conduct disordered and oppositionally disordered children have other common characteristics that distinguish them as a clinical group. First, boys are far more likely to be diagnosed as having conduct disorder problems than are

girls (Kazdin, 1985; Wells & Forehand, 1985). Schwarz (1979) estimates that the likelihood for boys to develop conduct problems is 4 to 8 times greater than this for girls. However, the behaviors displayed qualitatively differ between the sexes. Males frequently exhibit more aggression, stealing, vandalism, firesetting, and school related problems. Females tend to display more lying, substance abuse, running away, and prostitution (APA, 1994).

The *Diagnostic and Statistical Manual IV* (APA, 1994) lists the prevalence of rates of conduct disorder at 6 to 16 percent for males and 2 to 9 percent for females. Similarly, for oppositional disorders, the estimate is 2 to 16 percent with no gender difference listed. It is estimated that one-third to three-quarters of all child referrals for services include the problems associated with conduct disorder (Wells & Forehand, 1985). Both conduct disorder and oppositional defiant disorders are some of the most frequently referred conditions to both outpatient and inpatient mental health facilities in the United States (APA, 1994). The exact incidence of conduct disorders

TABLE 5-5 DIAGNOSTIC CRITERIA FOR 313.81 OPPOSITIONAL DEFIANT DISORDER

A. A pattern of negativistic, hostile, and defiant behavior lasting at least 6 months, during which four (or more) of the following are present:
   (1) often loses temper
   (2) often argues with adults
   (3) often actively defies or refuses to comply with adults' requests or rules
   (4) often deliberately annoys people
   (5) often blames others for his or her mistakes or misbehavior
   (6) is often touchy or easily annoyed by others
   (7) is often angry and resentful
   (8) is often spiteful or vindictive
B. The disturbance in behavior causes clinically significant impairment in social, academic, or occupational functioning.
C. The behaviors do not occur exclusively during the course of a psychotic or mood disorder.
D. Criteria are not met for conduct disorder, and, if the individual is age 18 years or older, criteria are not met for antisocial personality disorder.

NOTE: Consider a criterion met only if the behavior occurs more frequently than is typically observed in individuals of comparable age and developmental level.
SOURCE: Reprinted with permission from the *Diagnostic and statistical manual of mental disorders.* Fourth Edition *(1994)*. Washington, DC: American Psychiatric Association, pp. 93–94. Copyright 1994 by the American Psychiatric Association.

in the general population, however, is difficult to determine because of the overlap and developmental natures of the socially disruptive conditions of conduct disorder, oppositional defiant disorder, ADHD, and juvenile delinquency.

Possible Causes of Conduct Disorder and Oppositional Defiant Disorder

Like Attention-Deficit/Hyperactivity Disorder, conduct disorder and oppositional defiant disorder probably have several different causes, all of which can lead to similar behaviors (from this point on, reference to conduct disorder also includes oppositional defiant disorder). Some of these causes are probably genetically based and as old as the human race. The genetic traits include inherited temperament characteristics. In addition, some of the causes are undoubtedly social and involve such variables as modeled violence on television, divorce, or family stress.

Like ADHD, there is probably no single element that causes conduct disorder, but instead is caused by an interaction between many factors. The number of elements and their interactive effects increase the vulnerability of certain children to antisocial patterns of behavior.

INSTINCT AND TEMPERAMENT THEORIES

Instinct theories emphasize that innate, inherited behavior patterns can explain behaviors that are common to antisocial behaviors. Generally, the behavior dealt with by instinct theories includes aggressive behaviors such as fighting or intimidation. Psychoanalytic theory has explained senseless human aggression through an instinct that strives blindly for the destruction of life (Freud, 1933). This instinct, *Thanatos*, has the opposite function in psychoanalytic theory to the life preserving instinct, *Eros* (as reviewed by Baron & Richardson, 1994). However, most psychoanalytic theories of aggression are considered more metaphorical than research based theories of behavior.

Temperament, like instinct, is assumed to be largely inherited (Kagan, 1994; Torgerson, 1976). Unlike instinct, temperament is not considered a rigid behavior pattern that cannot be changed. Instead, it is more a personality style or trait that predisposes a child to act in certain ways. Recently, several researchers have investigated temperament styles in children from very early ages to adulthood (Chess & Thomas, 1983; Graham, Rutter, & George, 1973; Thomas & Chess, 1977; Thomas, Chess, & Birch, 1969). Thomas and associates (1969, 1983) have conducted an extensive study of a child's early temperament and the development of behavior disorders. From infancy to adulthood, 136 New York children were studied extensively on their temperament, which is defined by nine behavioral characteristics (see Table 5-6). The individuals were scored as infants on the nine different temperament characteristics on a three-point scale of high, medium, and low. When the children were approximately 2 years old, 65 percent fell into three basic temperament categories. Ten percent were *difficult children* who cried frequently, were irregular in biological functions, had a high rate of negative moods, had a predominance of intense reactions, were easily frustrated leading to tantrums, negatively withdrew from new stimuli, and were slow to adapt to change. Fifteen percent of the children were *slow to warm up children* who adapted slowly to changes, had a low activity level, and had an initial but not long-lasting tendency to withdraw from change. Finally, the researchers identified 40 percent of the sample as *easy children* who were regular in their habits, adapted well to change, were happy, and approached objects and people with little fear. The other 35 percent of the children studied in this group did not fit into any one of the three categories but shared characteristics across categories.

Although the three temperament categories were broad, they were relatively stable over time and predicted the later emotional status of the children (Chess & Thomas, 1983). Seventy percent of the difficult children studied by Thomas and associates (1969) developed behavior disorders while only 18 percent of the easy children later developed problems. The types of problems ranged from adjustment reaction and depression to conduct disorder.

In the temperament study by Thomas et al. (1969), parents of difficult children initially did not differ from other parents in their childrearing practices and interactions with their children. An unfavorable difference developed, however, for some parents as the difficult children grew older. In effect, the temperamentally difficult child had shaped and molded the parent's negative reactions and attitudes toward the child. A difficult child, however, does not necessarily develop into a conduct disordered child. What is important to note is that difficult children are more vulnerable to stress and have more

difficulty adjusting and adapting (Graham et al., 1973; Rutter, 1983). There seems to be little biological value in having a difficult temperament, particularly in view of the more positive reactions elicited by children with an easy temperament. However, a report by de Vries illustrates why a difficult temperament may have benefit for some children in some situations.

In the study by de Vries, the temperament of the children of the Masai tribe in the sub-Sahara region of Kenya were studied (as reported in Chess & Thomas, 1983). The Masai are a tribe of herders. De Vries assessed the infants of the Masai tribe and identified the 10 infants with the most easy temperament and the 10 with the most difficult temperament. He returned to the tribe 5 months later and found that a severe drought had killed 97 percent of the tribe's cattle herd. When he tried to locate the children he had assessed for temperament, he found the families of 7 of the easy babies and 6 of the difficult ones. The families of the other infants had moved away to escape the drought. Interestingly, of the 7 easy infants, 5 had died, and of the difficult infants, all had survived. When times get difficult, there may be survival value in being a difficult infant. Or, the "squeaky wheel (infant) may get the milk."

Patterson et al. (1993) believes that temperament is a "promising candidate" as a biological risk factor for the development of antisocial behavior in children. However, there is a clear interaction of heredity of temperament

---

BOX 5-5   BEHAVIORAL NONCOMPLIANCE AND ITS RELATIONSHIP TO OTHER PROBLEM BEHAVIORS

Problem behaviors for externalizing-social disordered children seem to revolve around a common set of problems that include noncompliance, tantrums, fighting, arguing, and crying. These problem behaviors may be more than slightly related. In fact, they may revolve around one basic behavior, noncompliance. Russo, Cataldo, and Cushing (1981) investigated the effects of successfully changing noncompliance and then observing the covariation in other problematic behaviors that were not treated directly. This study included three children who had been identified as being noncompliant, hyperactive, and uncontrollable, with at least two other negative behaviors such as aggression, self-injury (SIB), or tantrums. For example Tom, who was 3 years, and 7 months old, was referred for tantrums, aggression (kicking and biting), and self-injury (head banging and hand biting).

The intervention included having the experimenter give the child a command and waiting five seconds. If the child complied, he was reinforced with a small piece of food (e.g., candy, cereal, raisins), physical contact (e.g., hug and a "good boy" or "good girl"). None of the other problem behaviors such as tantrums or aggression were treated. The results of this experiment for Tom are shown in Figure 5-3.

It can be seen that as compliance increased (because it was directly reinforced), the other problem behaviors (crying, self-injury, and aggression) decreased even though they were not directly treated. It appeared for Tom and the other two children in the study that improving compliance also had the side benefit of spontaneously improving the other problem behaviors. This study also showed that "nagging" (repeating a request over and over) made the situations worse by decreasing compliance and increasing problem behaviors.

Box 5-5 (continued)

FIGURE 5-3 Percentage of compliance and the three untreated corollary behaviors (crying, SIB, and aggression) for Tom across experimental conditions and therapists

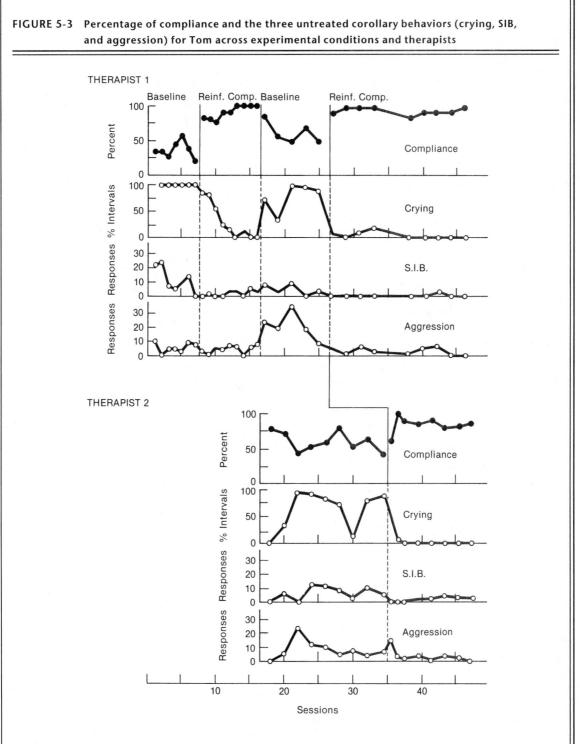

TABLE 5-6   NINE TEMPERAMENT CHARACTERISTICS USED TO ASSESS CHILDREN

1. Activity Level: the motor component present in a given child's functioning and the diurnal proportion of active and inactive periods.
2. Rhythmicity (Regularity): the predictability and/or unpredictability in time of any biological function.
3. Approach or Withdrawal: the nature of the initial response to a new stimulus, be it a food, toy, place, person, etc. Approach responses are positive, whether displayed by mood expression (smiling, verbalizations, etc.) or motor activity (swallowing a new food, reaching for a new toy, active play, etc.). Withdrawal reactions are negative, whether displayed by mood expression (crying, fussing, grimacing, verbalizations, etc.) or motor activity (moving away, spitting new food out, pushing a new toy away, etc.).
4. Adaptability: responses to new or altered situations. One is not concerned with the nature of the initial responses, but with the ease with which they are modified in desired directions.
5. Threshold of Responsiveness: the intensity level of stimulation that is necessary to evoke a discernible response, irrespective of the specific form that the response may take, or the sensory modality affected.
6. Intensity of Reaction: the energy level of response, irrespective of its quality or direction.
7. Quality of Mood: the amount of pleasant, joyful, and friendly behavior; as contrasted with unpleasant, crying, and unfriendly behavior.
8. Distractibility: the effectiveness of extraneous environmental stimuli in interfering with or altering the direction of the ongoing behavior.
9. Attention Span and Persistence: two categories which are related. Attention span concerns the length of time a particular activity is pursued by the child. Persistence refers to the continuation of an activity direction in the face of obstacles to its continuation.

SOURCE: S. Chess and A. Thomas. (1983). *Origins and evolution of behavior disorders: From infancy to early adult life* (p. 42). New York: Brunner/Mazel. Reprinted by permission.

and factors in the environment that may well produce disruptive social disorders. Similarly, Kagan (1994) has suggested that difficult temperament characteristics such as lowered levels of anxiety, inhibition, and fear may only be problematic if these children are raised in permissive families or in neighborhoods where aggression and crime are common. If not, "These boys may become successful politicians, generals, or business executives—roles that also require muted levels of fear, anxiety, or guilt" (Kagan, 1994, p. 252).

PHYSIOLOGICAL AND GENETIC VARIABLES

Several physiological variables may account for the aggression and noncompliance found in conduct disordered children. It has been theorized that an extra male chromosome (XYY) may result in hypermasculinity and enhanced aggression in males. Normally, humans have 46 chromosomes; males have an X and Y chromosome, while females have two X's, XX. The X is the female and the Y is the male chromosome. Some studies have found significantly higher rates of the rare XYY chromosome pattern among prison inhabitants than in the general population. However, on closer inspection, it was found that the type of criminal behavior most frequently associated with the XYY pattern was property offenses rather than aggression or antisocial offenses (Witkin, Mednick, Schulsinger, Bakkestrom, Christiansen, Goodenough, Hirschorn, Lundsteen, Owen, Philip, Rubin, & Stocking, 1976). Witkin et al. (1976) noted that the XYY males probably did not engage in criminal behavior more than XY males, but they were caught and punished more regularly because this condition is associated with intellectual dullness.

The need for stimulation and the physiological reaction that conduct disordered children show may explain some of the behaviors of these children. Some researchers (Fowles & Furuseth, 1994; Quay, 1977, 1993; Shapiro & Hynd, 1993) have suggested that severely conduct disordered children may be motivated by a pathological need for stimulation and reward seeking and are less sensitive to punishment. Thrill seeking aggression and rule breaking may be forms of stimulation seeking which helps relieve a state of boredom. Some research has shown that delinquents high on the conduct disordered dimension do very poorly attending to boring tasks, and they need to relieve boredom through some behavior such as singing and talking to themselves (Orris, 1969).

Thrill seeking and lack of sensitivity to punishment may be a function of neurologically based systems: the behavioral inhibition system (BIS) and the behavioral activation system (BAS) (Gray, 1987; McBurnett, 1992). These systems are supposed to be part of the septo-hippocampal part of the brain that regulates fear and anxiety. A child with a dominant BIS system would be shy, anxious, and withdrawn. A child with an underactive BIS system would seek and respond well to rewards but be somewhat immune to punishment. Quay (1988) has suggested that conduct disordered children have an overactive BAS system, which persistently compels them to seek rewards and thrills, and an underactive or over-powered BIS system, which reduces anxiety and fear and the ability to learn from punishing experiences. Although much of this work is theoretical, several studies have documented psychophysiological measures that support its existence (as reviewed by Shapiro & Hynd, 1993). Recently, two studies have identified a "novelty" seeking gene that predispose individuals to be impulsive, quick tempered, and have a need for extravagant or novel environments (Associated Press, 1996). This research estimates that approximately 15 percent of individuals living in Europe and the United States may carry the novelty seeking gene.

The genetic model of aggression and antisocial behavior is based primarily on the same logic as described earlier for ADHD children (see previous discussion). Studies reviewed by Pollock, Mednick, and Gabrielli (1983) have found higher concordance rates for monozygotic twins than for dizygotic twins for adult criminality in the United States, Europe, and Japan. Similarly, Cloninger and Gottsman (1987) found the concordance rates for adult criminality for Norwegian and Danish monozygotic twins to be 41 to 51 percent and 26 to 30 percent for dizygotic twins. These researchers estimate the heritability of adult criminal behavior at about 54 percent. However, the twin genetic evidence is not as strong for children and adolescents who exhibit antisocial behavior. There appears not to be a significant difference in rates of antisocial behavior between monozygotic and dizygotic twin pairs. It is theorized that biological variables may play a more important role in early onset chronic offenders and later onset offenders (Patterson et al., 1992).

Genetic evidence and stimulation seeking behavior suggest a biological basis for antisocial children's behavior. However, some of the strongest evidence for the causes of antisocial behavior comes from studies of family and social factors in the child's environment. An interplay between a child's environment, vulnerability factors, and biological risk factors all play a part in the development of antisocial behavior.

FAMILY FACTORS

The effects of family influence on the development of antisocial behavior in children are well supported by research evidence. Factors such as childrearing practices, the consistency of discipline, the supportive atmosphere of the family, separation, and divorce all appear to have

some effect in producing aggressive, noncompliant children. Childrearing practices can vary along several different dimensions. Hetherington and Martin (1979) have listed a series of dimensions that include: (1) a *control* dimension from restrictiveness to permissiveness, (2) an *affective-emotional* dimension from warmth to hostility, (3) a *discipline* dimension from consistency to inconsistency, and (4) a *psychological* dimension from love-oriented to power-oriented parenting styles. Two types of childrearing practices, a harsh/abusive parental discipline and parental inconsistency, have been significantly linked to child conduct problems (Frick, 1993; Loeber & Stouthamer-Loeber, 1986).

These extreme forms of parenting styles appear to influence the development of antisocial disorders in children. Parents who are habitually *inconsistent* in rule setting and discipline can leave a child confused regarding the exact limits and consequences for the child's behavior. Parents who use erratic control and are inappropriately permissive are more likely to have aggressive and behaviorally disordered children (Hetherington, Cox, & Cox, 1977a; Hetherington & Martin, 1979; Kazdin, 1985; Patterson, 1982; Patterson et al., 1992). One particular potential pattern identified in the development of aggressive children (Bandura & Walters, 1959) or delinquent adolescents (McCord, McCord, & Zola, 1959) is a lax, permissive mother and a rigid, restrictive father. Other patterns include permissive parents who accept the child's aggression and parents who are rejecting and restrictive (Frick, 1993). The research findings have been summarized by Wells and Forehand (1985):

> In reviewing the results of studies, . . . from behavioral, social, and psychological research, it is striking that one finding is consistent across studies—the extreme importance in the etiology of aggression of parental, particularly maternal, hostility and negativism toward the child, and/or the lack of consistent limits and consequences for negative behavior. (p. 235)

Divorce, separation, substance abuse, depression, and marital conflict are found more frequently in the families of antisocial children than in families of normally adjusted children (Patterson et al., 1992). Boys are particularly affected by divorce, and they are more likely than girls to develop noncompliant and aggressive behaviors after a divorce (Amato & Keith, 1991; Hetherington, 1979; Hetherington et al., 1977b). This sex difference in the development of behavior problems for boys may be related to the loss of the father as an appropriate sex-role model (Hetherington, 1979). The development of anti-social behaviors and delinquency, however, does not appear to be a direct result of divorce or separation but stems from the marital conflict and disharmony leading up to the break between parents (Fick, 1993; Hetherington et. al., 1977b) or the poverty that follows divorce. As Rutter (1979) has stated, "Anti-social behaviors were linked with broken homes not because of the separation involved, but rather, because of the discord and disharmony which led to the break." During the period of marital disharmony, the child may be forced into coalition with one parent and in return be rejected by the other parent, causing intense conflict (Schwarz, 1979). It should also be noted that the a child's antisocial behavior may promote marital disharmony, which in turn is associated with more acting out behavior in the child (Griest & Wells, 1983).

Family variables are only part of the cause for conduct disorder and delinquency. There are also many other variables that contribute to the risk vulnerability of a child's becoming antisocial. A list of these factors is given in Table 5-7 (Kazdin, 1985, 1989). However, there are still two powerful contributors to noncompliance and aggression that need to be discussed: modeling and coercion.

MODELING

Modeling is the acquisition of new behaviors through the observation and imitation of other people's behavior (Bandura, 1973; Kirkland & Thelen, 1977). For antisocial children, acquiring aggressive and noncompliant behaviors may involve the imitation of parents, peers, and possibly some characters from television and films. Bandura and Walters (1959), in studying aggressive adolescent boys, found that their parents repeatedly modeled and reinforced aggressive behavior directed against others. These parents, however, punished aggressive behavior if it was directed against themselves. Parents of nonaggressive boys did not generally condone aggression, and in family conflicts these parents were considerate and used reasoning to handle problems.

Modeling can have some surprising effects on behavior. It is not always essential that the model be another person. Some research evidence has shown that children who see themselves model appropriate behavior on videotape can gain a significant positive effect on their

TABLE 5-7 FACTORS THAT CONTRIBUTE TO ANTISOCIAL BEHAVIOR

Psychopathology and Criminal Behavior in Parents

The risk factor for antisocial behavior is increased when either parent has a psychiatric illness. However, alcoholism or criminal behavior in the father is particularly associated with antisocial behavior.

Parent-Child Interactions

Inconsistent parenting and discipline practices are associated with antisocial behavior. Lax, erratic, or overly harsh punishment practices are related to antisocial behaviors. One pattern is especially associated with antisocial behavior: a lax mother and an overly severe punishing father.

Broken Homes and Marital Discord

Divorce and broken homes can be related to antisocial behavior particularly when there is continuing bitter conflict between parents, reduced income, reduction in the quality of living, and decreased child supervision.

Birth Order and Family Size

Delinquency and antisocial behavior are greater among middle children than they are for first and last born children. In addition, family size is related to delinquency with a greater number of children associated with higher rates of antisocial behavior.

Social Class and Socioeconomic Disadvantage

Delinquency and antisocial behavior are related to poorer living conditions and economic and social disadvantage. However, this effect is not particularly strong across studies.

SOURCE: Adapted from Kazdin, A. E. (1985). *Treatment of antisocial behavior in children and adolescents*, Homewood, IL: Dorsey Press.

behavior. For instance, the study reviewed in Box 5-6 is an example of the powerful effects of behaviorally disordered students reviewing a videotape of only their appropriate behavior in the classroom. This technique is known as "self-as-a-model" and has been used with ADHD students (Clare, 1993), antisocial youth (Kehle, Clark, Jenson, & Wampold 1989), depressed adolescents (Kahn, Kehle, Jenson, & Clark, 1990), and elective mutes (Kehle, Cressey, & Owen, 1990).

BOX 5-6 WATCHING MYSELF AND DOING BETTER: SELF-MODELING

We tend to model behaviors of individuals who are similar to ourselves and individuals who are successful with their behavior. Who could be a better model than ourselves modeling something successful? Self-modeling or self-observation has been used with several different behaviors and conditions such as elective mutism, Attention-Deficit/Hyperactivity Disorder, depression, basketball free throws, swimming, and several others (as reviewed by Clare, 1993). Kehle, Clark, Jenson, and Wampold (1986) used this technique with antisocial behaviorally disordered students in a special education classroom.

Four behaviorally disordered students who were ages 10 and 13 were videotaped in their special education classroom for approximately 20 to 30 minutes. Their baselines of disruptive behaviors (before video intervention) averaged approximately 50 percent of the time and included such behaviors as being off-task, making noise, aggression, not staying seated, making obscene gestures, and talking out of turn (see Figure 5-4). After the videotapes were shot in the classroom they were edited leaving out all of the disruptive misbehaviors, leaving in only appropriate, on-task behaviors for each of the subjects. The first three experimental subjects then viewed their edited, appropriate self-model tape for 11 minutes each with the experimenter. The fourth child, a control subject, viewed an unedited tape, which still included his disruptive behaviors.

The treatment effects were dramatic when the three experimental subjects' behaviors were observed back in the classroom after their five days of self-modeling tape viewing (see Figure 5-4). The fourth control child, however, continued to misbehave until his videotape was also edited and he viewed himself self-modeling only appropriate behaviors. Why did this simple technique work to change such well established misbehavior? Possibly, the effects of a powerful model (yourself) being successful in a chronically successful environment can make a big impact.

SOURCE: Kehle, T., Clark, E., & Jenson, W. R. (1986). Effectiveness of the self-modeling procedure with behaviorally disturbed elementary age children. *School Psychology Review, 15*, 289–295.

FIGURE 5-4   Self-as-a-model results

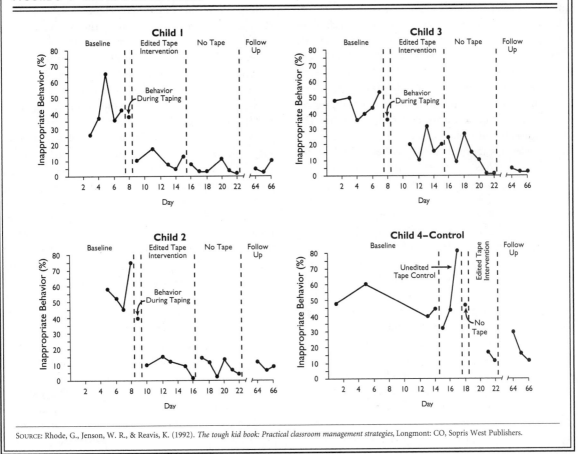

SOURCE: Rhode, G., Jenson, W. R., & Reavis, K. (1992). *The tough kid book: Practical classroom management strategies*, Longmont: CO, Sopris West Publishers.

Violent films and television can provide negative models for children, teaching them new and more sophisticated forms of physical and verbal aggression (Huesman & Miller, 1994; Liebert, Sprakin, & Davidson, 1982; Murray, 1995; Olweus, 1984). There is ample exposure of children to television programming. Nearly 98 percent of American households have television sets and 52 percent have more than one set, one of which is used primarily by children (Nielsen Television Index) (Murray, 1995). An interesting fact is that children in the United States have more televisions per household than indoor plumbing (Washington State University, 1994). On average, American households have the television on 7 hours a day, and children watch 28 hours per week (Andreasen, 1990; Condry, 1989). The average American child will spend more time watching television than any other activity except sleeping (American Pediatric Association, 1990). For example, in a 12 year period, a child in America spends approximately 11,000 hours in school but over 15,000 hours watching television (Murray & Lonnborg, 1995). Research has shown a positive and significant correlation between aggressive behavior and violence on television (Huesmann & Miller, 1994; Paik & Comstock, 1994).

Violence has permeated not only prime time television but has also been included in commercial product advertisements, music videos, and cable television. The average number of violent acts during prime time evening television is approximately 5 per hour. On Saturday mornings (cartoons are children's favorite viewing), the number of aggressive acts is between 20 and 25 (Gerbner & Signorielli, 1990; Gerbner, Morgan, & Signorielli, 1993). By the time children have finished elementary school, they will have witnessed on television 20,000 murders and 100,000 violent acts.

The modeling effects of aggression in filmed violence are well documented (Bandura, Ross, & Ross, 1963; Eron, 1963; Leyens, Camino, Parke, & Berkowitz, 1975; Liebert & Baron, 1972). Filmed violence not only teaches new and unique ways to be aggressive, but it also has a *disinhibitory* effect on aggression in general (Bandura et al., 1963; Comstock & Strasburger, 1990). A child who is exposed to a violent film model will be less inclined to stop or inhibit aggressive behavior when given the opportunity. In addition, repeated exposure to violence over time may *desensitize* or dull a child to the effects of aggression and the signs of pain in others (Baron & Rich-

ardson, 1994; Cline, Croft, & Courrier, 1973; Thomas, Horton, Lippincott, & Drabman, 1977).

Longitudinal research shows the relationship between television viewing as a child and its later consequences. Eron and Huesmann (1984) and Huesmann and Eron (1994) have reported the long-term effects of television violence on hundreds of children studied from 1960 to 1981 (the Rip Van Winkle study). The results show that the effects of violent television is only small in the short run but the cumulative effects over time can be large. Children as early as age 6 show increases in aggressive behavior in relation to television watching, and males around 8 years old (third graders) show the most vulnerability to television violence.

The long-term behavioral effects reported in this study after 22 years are even more impressive. There is a clear relationship to the amount of violent television watched and the number of criminal convictions, aggression against a wife, and traffic violations when these children grow up. For example, Figure 5-5 shows the relationship between serious adult criminal acts and the frequency of television watching (measured at age 8) for males and females. It is not surprising that children with behavior problems preferred aggressive characters, viewed larger amounts of violent material, and were more likely to believe the fictional content of the aggressive material to be true (Gadow & Sprafkin, 1993).

With any correlational study, a circular relationship may exist between the type (aggressive v. nonaggressive) of child and the amount and type of television viewed. However, the evidence mounts with the 1972 Surgeon General's Advisory Committee on Television and Social Behavior linking violent behavior with violent television programs. Then, a decade later, the landmark study from the National Institute of Mental Health (1982) reaffirmed the 1972 findings, and, more recently, another confirming report was published by the American Psychological Association Commission on Violence and Youth (1993).

THE COERCION HYPOTHESIS

The use of aggression and noncompliance to control other people's behavior has been called *coercion* or *pain control* (Patterson, 1974, 1982, 1986; Patterson & Reid, 1970; Patterson, Reid, & Dishion, 1992). Patterson (1976a) assumes that coercive behaviors may stem from instinct, modeling, television viewing, or reinforcement. Infants use coercive pain control by crying to gain a par-

FIGURE 5-5 Relation of TV viewing at age 8 to seriousness of crimes committed by age 30

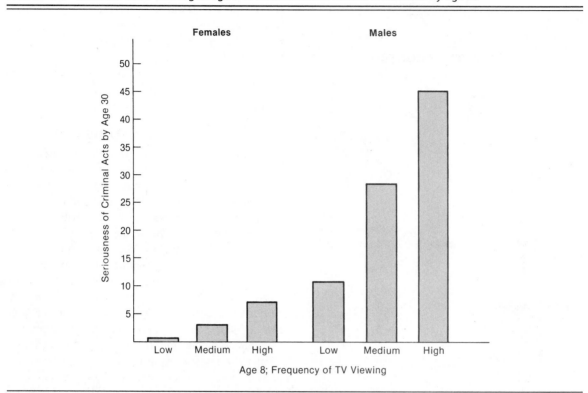

SOURCE: L. D. Eron & R. L. Huesmann. (1984). The control of aggressive behavior by changes in attitudes, values, and conditions of learning. In R. J. Blanchard & D. C. Blanchard (Eds.), *Advances in the study of aggression* (Vol. 1, p. 150). New York: Academic Press. Reprinted by permission.

ent's attention for care and feeding (see previous section on temperament). This type of elementary pain control no doubt has survival value for the infant. More refined coercive behaviors such as tantrumming, teasing, or aggression are learned through modeling and reinforcement of the behaviors. What is important, however, is not necessarily how the aversive behaviors are acquired, but rather how they become so intense and destructive.

All children are coercive at some point; however, antisocial children use coercion much more frequently and much more intensely than other children. Coercive control follows a typical sequence of behaviors in which a demand or request is made to a noncompliant child by either an adult or another child. The child responds to the demand with aversive behaviors rather than compliance. The person who made the original demand withdraws it in order to avoid the child's aversive behavior. Withdrawing the request or demand reinforces (nega-

tively) the problem child and increases the chances that in the future he or she will respond with more intense and aversive forms of behavior (Rhode et al., 1993). The problem child also learns that requests are not to be taken seriously and can be avoided by shows of ferocity (Table 5-8).

The escalation of pain control results in interactions in which family members exchange punishment at high rates (Patterson, 1982, 1984; Patterson et al., 1992). The communication patterns in the family are altered in that it is not open and a general atmosphere of hostility exists. Parents who are caught in this coercive trap are inconsistent disciplinarians. The evidence indicates that children from such families are nearly twice as resistant to changing their problem behaviors when punished than normal children (Patterson, 1976a). Moreover, the children are not as responsive to social praise and reinforcement and lag behind in the development of age-appropriate social skills.

TABLE 5-8   COERCIVE PAIN CONTROL

Teacher	Student

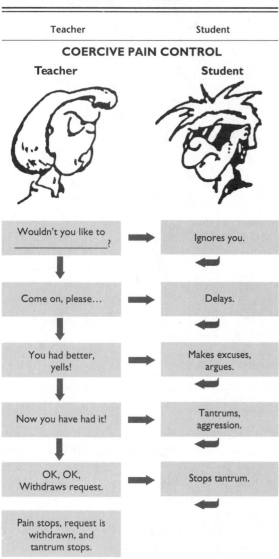

COERCIVE PAIN CONTROL

Teacher	Student
Wouldn't you like to _____?	Ignores you.
Come on, please...	Delays.
You had better, yells!	Makes excuses, argues.
Now you have had it!	Tantrums, aggression.
OK, OK, Withdraws request.	Stops tantrum.
Pain stops, request is withdrawn, and tantrum stops.	

SOURCE: Rhode, G., Jenson, W. R., & Reavis, K. (1992). *The tough kid book: Practical classroom management strategies,* Longmont: CO, Sopris West Publishers.

Treatment of Conduct Disordered and Oppositionally Defiant Children

The very diverse nature of the behaviors that make up antisocial disorders makes the condition difficult to treat. Aggression can take several different forms ranging from physical and verbal aggression to property destruction

such as fire setting. Noncompliance can range from simply ignoring requests to doing the exact opposite of what was requested. In addition, the deficits such as poor social skills, faulty problem-solving skills, a lag in rule-governed behavior, and poor academic skills make each antisocial child a unique and individual case. Clinicians from different backgrounds may set entirely different priorities in treating these problems.

TRADITIONAL TREATMENT APPROACHES

Traditional approaches to the treatment of conduct disorders have involved techniques such as therapeutically induced insight into the origin of the problem, play therapy, catharsis (therapeutically discharging pent-up aggressive energies), or trying to re-bond with the child. Psychodynamic approaches to the treatment of conduct disorders have generally included insight into the development of an underlying conflict usually involving the child's parents and a psychosexual theme (Aichhorn, 1964). In one case study, unstructured play therapy was used to discover the underlying motivations of a 5-year-old girl, Jane, who had developed violent temper tantrumming and noncompliance (Seeberg, 1943). Through 69 play therapy sessions in which Jane could freely express her feelings, a basic unconscious sexual conflict involving her mother was uncovered. Jane was encouraged to release her aggression and jealousy toward her mother in the play therapy situations. Her aggression ceased to be a problem after the play therapy sessions; however, her noncompliance continued.

Catharsis is defined as a therapeutic release of pent-up aggressive drives in a socially acceptable manner. The hypothesis is that aggressive energies build up in a child and must be discharged in some form of aggressive behavior. In treatment, the therapist assumes that one form of aggression can be substituted for and is equivalent to others forms of aggression. For example, a frustrated child who is restrained from hitting a peer who has taken his toy can alternatively release the built-up aggressive impulses by hammering pegs. In this example, hammering pegs is substituted for hitting the other child. The two acts are considered equivalent in that once the pegs are hammered, the aggressive energies are assumed to have dissipated. In treatment contexts, a therapist may urge a conduct disordered child who is violent to punch a "Bobo" doll or fight with rubber foam bats.

The assumed rage release from catharsis therapy is probably a therapeutic myth (Brendtro & College, 1993) and may actually make an antisocial condition worse. The research evidence indicates that catharsis theory does not significantly reduce the aggressive behavior of children (as reviewed by Parke & Slaby, 1982). Rather, as Bandura (1973) has stated:

> "Evidence from research studies of children indicates that, far from producing a cathartic reduction of aggression, participation in aggressive activities within a permissive setting maintains or increases it." (Feshbach, 1956; Freeman, 1962; Kenny, 1952; Mallick & McCandless, 1966; Nelsen, 1969).

Traditional therapeutic approaches to the treatment of antisocial children have not been well researched and those that have been researched have not been found to be particularly effective (Herbert, 1978; Kazdin, 1985). Some approaches that on first inspection seem reasonable, such as catharsis therapy, may actually be counterproductive in controlling aggression and noncompliance. Medication approaches have also not been extensively used with antisocial children because no drug effectively reduces noncompliance or aggression (Shapiro & Hynd, 1993). The most promising approaches to the treatment of antisocial behavior are social learning and behavioral approaches.

SOCIAL LEARNING AND BEHAVIORAL APPROACHES

These approaches can be contrasted with traditional psychotherapy because they emphasize changing observable behavior through direct interventions. Instead of trying to interpret underlying conflict or release stored aggressive impulses, behavioral methods utilize environmental consequences, parent training, contingency contracting, and problem-solving to change disruptive behavior (Kazdin, 1987, 1993; Wells & Forehand, 1981, 1985). Techniques such as point systems, reinforcement, precision request making, and time out (brief withdrawal from a positive environment) are commonly used to deal with aggressive and noncompliant behavior. Often a complete cure is considered unrealistic once antisocial behaviors are well established. Instead, a continued management approach through childhood and adolescence may be necessary. Kazdin (1987) has made the analogy of the treatment of chronic diabetes to antisocial disorders in childhood and adolescence. Both conditions require constant monitoring and treatment with a host of techniques once they are established.

Preventive approaches that combine several different treatment approaches to promote family competence, reduce school failure, and improve social relationships early in a child's life may be an alternative to chronic management. The FAST Track (Families and Schools Together) is a project designed to identify and intervene with high-risk children when they first enter school (Conduct Problems Prevention Research Group, 1992). This model, which combines parent training, home visits, social skills training, academic tutoring, and classroom intervention at an early age, is highly promising. However, the longitudinal data are not yet in on its preventative effectiveness. Nevertheless, each one of the components of the FAST Track model has been used to manage conduct disordered children.

Gerald Patterson and his colleagues at the Oregon Research Institute have spent two decades researching effective behavior change techniques with antisocial children. His research group has seen over 200 families with children who were primarily aggressive and noncompliant. Approximately 50 percent of these children also engaged in truancy, stealing, and firesetting.

The primary treatment approach used with these children is to train parents to effectively reduce their children's "noxious" behaviors (Patterson, 1982; Patterson & Fleischman, 1979; Patterson et al., 1992; Spitzer, Webster-Stratton, & Hollinsworth, 1991; Webster-Stratton, 1983). Treatment in the home consisted of training parents to define and track both deviant and appropriate behaviors; to withdraw reinforcement, or to ignore inappropriate responding, and to use time out for inappropriate behaviors; to construct contracts with specified contingencies for behaviors and to catch the child being *good* and reinforce him for appropriate behaviors. Figure 5-6 shows the rate of obnoxious behavior before treatment averaged 0.7 responses per minute for aggressive boys as compared to 0.45 responses per minute for nonproblem boys. After treatment and at a 12-month follow-up, the observed rate of obnoxious behaviors for the aggressive boys were within normal limits, although the treatment required booster sessions for the parents and children.

The investment of professional time in the Patterson studies was relatively small, particularly when compared to the significant therapeutic gains. Other behavioral approaches have concentrated on improving compliance and reducing aggression by using precision request

FIGURE 5-6   Total deviant behaviors in the home for the treated sample of deviant children (solid line)
before, during, and after treatment and their nondeviant peers (represented as a grid
showing the range of normative behaviors)

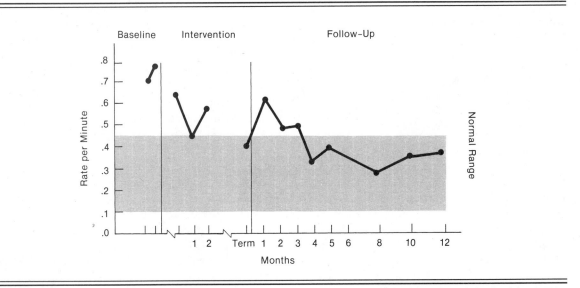

SOURCE: G. R. Patterson. (1974). Interventions for boys with conduct problems: Multiple settings, treatments, and criteria. *Journal of Consulting and Clinical Psychology, 42*, 476.
Copyright 1974 by the American Psychological Association. Reprinted by permission of the author.

making and other behavioral techniques (Forehand &
McMahon, 1981). It appears that these parents get caught
in coercive interactions because they do not use appropriate requests systematically followed by consequences.
The variables that affect child compliance are listed in
Table 5-9. Parents are taught to be specific, give the child
time enough to comply, to use a neutral voice, to make
eye contact, not to use a question format (e.g., "wouldn't
you like to clean your room?"), not to nag, and to follow
compliance or noncompliance with appropriate consequences (Jenson, Reavis, & Rhode, 1987; Rhode et al.,
1993). The outline for a precision request is given in Figure 5-7 (Rhode et al., 1993).

Improving compliance and reducing aggression is insufficient in treating conduct disordered children. The
child's deficiencies must also be treated if a conduct disordered child is to make long-term improvements. Social
skills training programs that improve problem-solving,
conflict negotiation, accepting negative feedback, and
giving positive feedback to others can be effective with
behaviorally disordered children (Morgan & Jenson,
1988; Sheridan, 1995). When the children master these
skills, they are assigned homework to ensure that they

practice the skills. Similarly, academic problems must be
corrected if a conduct disordered child is going to make
a successful adjustment to a school setting.

Behaviorally based direct instruction programs have
been proven effective in teaching appropriate classroom
behavior and basic academic and study skills to behaviorally disordered children (Archer & Gleason, 1992;
Kesler, 1987; Walker, 1995). However, deficits in rule-
governed and problem-solving behaviors are still problematic for antisocial children. One promising approach
has been developed that combines both cognitive and
behavioral techniques to teach problem-solving skills to
antisocial youth (Kazdin, Esveldt-Dawson, French, &
Unis, 1987; Kazdin, Siegel, & Bass, 1992). This approach
emphasizes realistic personal situations with siblings, parents, peers, and teachers, and directly teaches problem-
solving skills through generating alternative solutions,
consequential thinking, and taking the perspective of the
other person. The preliminary evidence from this approach shows that it is significantly superior to traditional
therapeutic approaches and is effective in teaching basic
problem-solving skills to antisocial children (Kazdin et
al., 1992; Kazdin, et. al., 1987).

TABLE 5-9 FACTORS THAT AFFECT COMPLIANCE DURING REQUEST MAKING

1. *Question format:* It is better not to use a question format such as "Isn't it time to . . . ?" It is better to state, "It is now time to . . ." Questions reduce compliance with conduct disordered children.
2. *Eye contact:* It is better to make direct eye contact with a child when making a request.
3. *Distance:* It is better to be one meter or less from a child when making a request.
4. *Two requests:* More than two requests (i.e., nagging) reduces compliance.
5. *Loudness of request:* It is better to give a request in a soft but firm tone instead of a loud voice.
6. *Time:* Children should be given approximately 3 to 5 seconds to comply once a request is given. During this interval, the adult should not give another request, repeat the request, nor engage in an argument with the child.
7. *Nonemotional requests:* It is better to give a request in a nonemotional manner instead of yelling or name calling.
8. *Descriptive requests:* It is better to give a specific descriptive request instead of a global request (e.g., "Clean your room" versus "Clean your room by stacking the toys in the box, books on the shelf, and clothes in the closet."
9. *Consequate compliance:* Consistently reinforce compliance and mildly punish noncompliance.

FIGURE 5-7 Precision request sequence

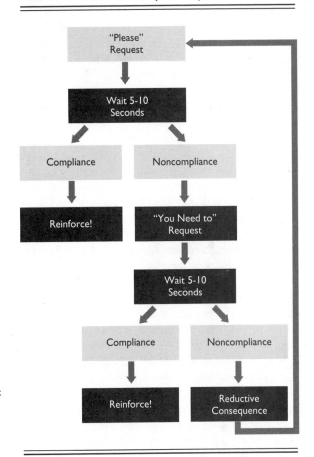

SOURCE: Rhode, G., Jenson, W. R., & Reavis, K. (1992). *The tough kid book: Practical classroom management strategies,* Longmont: CO, Sopris West Publishers.

JUVENILE DELINQUENCY
Characteristics of Adolescent Delinquents

Legally, any person younger than age 18 who engages in unlawful activities is a juvenile delinquent. Thus, delinquent activities can range from occasional illicit drug and alcohol use to a pattern of violence or even murder. Children and teens who are truants from school are considered delinquents, as are juveniles with extensive histories of assault with deadly weapons or drug dealing. As discussed in Chapter 1 on developmental differences in behavior problems, a certain amount of nonconformist, oppositional behavior and minor law-breaking is not uncommon in childhood and adolescence.

Certain types of disruptive behavior are more likely at specific ages. As clinic-referred children become older, their aggressive behavior decreases but their delinquent behavior increases, so they typically go from disobedience

and threats to truancy, theft, and substance abuse (Achenbach, Howell, Quary, & Conners, 1991). The most serious type of juvenile delinquency is associated with diagnosable psychiatric disorders, most often conduct disorder in children and adolescents and antisocial personality disorder in older adolescents and adults. Psychiatrically, only when the antisocial behavior is severe, chronic, and represents a pervasive pattern of disregard for, and violation of, the rights and welfare of others does it constitute conduct disorder or antisocial personality disorder (American Psychiatric Association, 1994). Such antisocial adjustment problems usually begin as a pattern of repeated, persistent exploitation, aggressive attacks, stealing and property destruction in childhood or early adolescence and often continues into adulthood, when the offender graduates into adult criminal activities. The most serious predatory crimes involving robbery, burglary, and violence rarely occur before adolescence, but most are the culmination of an antisocial "career" that began early in life.

Many aggressive young people never qualify as having an externalizing disorder despite engaging in some markedly antisocial behavior. Of a large sample of boys in Pittsburgh, 51 percent of the fourth graders had damaged property, 53 percent had stolen something, 91 percent claimed to have been physically violent, and 21 percent had used illicit substances (Loeber, Stouthamer-Loeber, Van Kammen, & Farrington, 1989). For most boys, such transgressions are occasional rather than typical. Only when their behavior is consistently cruel, predatory, exploitive, and destructive over a period of at least one year is it psychiatrically diagnosable.

Developmental Paths to Delinquency. There are different pathways to juvenile delinquency, depending on the delinquent's use of violence and illicit drugs. The developmental pathway to (1) *Adolescent violent criminality (the aggressive versatile path)*: typically has an early onset during the preschool years and includes conduct problems and hyperactivity combined with impulsivity and attention-deficit problems. School achievement problems and a large repertoire of new and different antisocial problems or innovations are other features (Loeber, 1990); (2) *The nonviolent path*: If violence is not a feature during adolescence, but property and drug offenses occur, problem onset is later, during late childhood or early adolescence, and the youth often has deviant peers; (3) *The illicit drug use path*: Adolescents who use illegal drugs, but are not violent or criminal, are more likely to have had internalizing problems such as shyness or anxiety as children. Frequent commission of any one type of offense, such as stealing, makes it more likely that the youth will progress to committing more serious offenses (Loeber, 1990). There may be a developmental progression from characteristic disobedience, aggression, and destructiveness during childhood to later truancy, stealing, and illicit substance use (Loeber & LeBlanc, 1990). Note, however, that childhood antisocial behavior is common, particularly among boys, and most often leads to normal adult adjustment.

Onset and Course of Delinquency. Adolescents who at an earlier age committed their first offense have a larger total number of offenses and are more likely to become chronic offenders (Farrington, Loeber, Elliott, Hawkins, Kandel, Klein, McCord, Rowe, & Tremblay, 1990). That is, early commission of criminal acts is associated with a worse prognosis than is later initial illegal activity. Nevertheless, other factors are important in delinquent careers, such as the amount of violence or cruelty associated with the illegal act, whether others persuaded the child to act, and whether the act was motivated by considerations of personal gain or by excitement.

Juvenile delinquency is related to the same set of characteristics as the other externalizing or social disorders already discussed. Among a sample of incarcerated delinquents, 85 percent met the diagnostic criteria for conduct disorder, with 19 percent having a secondary diagnosis of attention deficit and hyperactivity (Hollander & Turner, 1985). How does this destructive, and self-destructive, lifestyle begin, and what can be done to prevent societal violence? The roots of violent delinquency lie partly in an increasingly violent society. In the 30 years between the 1960s and the 1990s, the homicide rate among teenagers increased threefold in the United States (Fuchs & Reklis, 1992). Today, homicide is the leading cause of death for young black males (Wilson & Herrnstein, 1985), and one in five of all high school students carries a weapon to class (Will, 1992). Whether the violence rates for U.S. teens escalate rapidly or more slowly and unevenly, the overall upward trend is a cause of justified alarm (Lykken, 1993). Both youths and adults are alarmingly violent. The United States ranks first among 20 industrialized countries in homicide rates per 100,000 inhabitants. The U.S. homicide rate is more than four times greater than the next highest country ("Violence," 1992), and guns are used in two-thirds of the homicides. The public taste for violence seems to have increased. Preferences in movies and television programming are for more and more violent aggression, which stimulates both exact imitation of particular violent acts and generalized aggression, especially among aggressive younger viewers (Bandura, 1969; Gerbner, Gross, Morgan, & Signorielli, 1981). With weapons so readily available and people so willing to use them, it is hardly surprising that many young people grow up violent and callous to the needs and rights of others. "The theory is that firearms

There is strength in numbers for gang members. A youth may be forced to join a gang to avoid being victimized by its members.

have been the teeth that transform bark into bite" (Klein & Maxson, 1989, p. 219).

Gangs. An increase in the number and violence of gangs draws more youths into criminal activities. Gangs seem to have originated as neighborhood play or athletic groups providing a social structure for young people's activities. Some became criminal groups, with an organization, identifiable leadership, territory, and the avowed purpose of engaging in illegal activities (Miller, 1980). However, gangs continued to have a social function, and members spent much of their time simply "hanging out" or congregating together, not necessarily engaging in illegal activities. America's growing involvement in illicit drug use provided an opportunity for criminal activity in drug dealing, much as Prohibition did in the 1920s when alcohol was outlawed and adult gangs controlled alcohol distribution. Then and now, society's demand for illegal substances and activities such as drugs and prostitution stimulated the growth of gangs and gang violence. A major historical difference, though, is that Prohibition era gangsters were adults and today's gangsters are more likely to be juveniles.

Gangs attract many children, particularly boys, with their individual hand signs, graffiti, distinctive clothing, and reputations for toughness and adventure. Even if not attracted to a gang, a schoolchild may have little choice but to affiliate with one gang or another in order to seek protection from extortion and physical assault. Once recruited, the boy will be expected to support and participate in the gang's activities, whether harmless, mildly criminal, or physically assaultive. Girls associated with gangs may be expected to fight other girls and have sex with the boys, which leads naturally to prostitution for many girls. In this respect, affiliating with a gang is somewhat like joining the military: you cannot choose which command to obey. There is no single definition of a gang, because the structure and activities of gangs differ across the country, but today's gangs appear to be more violent and more drug involved than in previous times (Goldstein, 1991).

Family Characteristics. Family factors also are important contributors to juvenile violence and are similar to other disorders reviewed in this chapter. The structure of the family itself appears to affect children's antisocial attitudes and behavior. As though the increasing number of mothers who are single parents did not have enough troubles, their children, especially the boys, may defy them and exhibit more hypermasculine behavior, including aggression, boasting, and risk-taking (Draper & Belsky, 1990). Many children in mother-only households are well-socialized and achievement-oriented, but the risks of inadequate socialization are greater when children become defiant and the mother alone must bear all responsibility for maintaining the family.

In either intact or single-parent families, children are at greater risk for delinquency if there is poor parental monitoring and supervision, harsh and inconsistent discipline, and parental rejection. Large families in which grandparents, parents, and several siblings have criminal records also place children at risk (Goldstein, 1991).

Family Violence. Violent children tend to come from violent homes. In American homes, some 31 percent of the children have been punched or beaten and 11 to 12 percent threatened or attacked with a knife or gun (Mulvihill, Tumill, & Curtis, 1969). Approximately one-quarter of wives have been targets of domestic physical violence (Strauss (1977–1978), and the children are often terrified witnesses to these attacks. They are also increasingly victims, participants, or both, of increasing violence at school, particularly at the elementary school level ("School Crime Rates," 1990).

A growing body of research suggests that early physical abuse and severe bullying may have permanent effects on brain function and behavior. As a result of early, repeated physical attacks, the prefrontal lobes of the brain that ordinarily inhibit aggressive impulses through release of serotonin are damaged, leading to impulsive aggressive outbursts (Goldman, 1995). If this theory is confirmed, a source of at least some forms of delinquency in the neural circuitry will have been identified. It is important to note that it is a *combination* of early and severe mistreatment and resulting brain action changes that produce violent behavior, according to this theory.

Temperament. As with conduct disorder and Attention-Deficit/Hyperactivity Disorder, temperament is an important factor. Research on antisocial behavior in adoptees suggests that there could be some genetic predisposing factor, possibly the child's temperament (Carey, 1991; DiLala & Gottesman, 1991). Although there are no specific genes for criminality or violence, some children may be temperamentally more difficult to socialize than others. One authority (Loeber, 1990) views one dimension of temperament, activity level or hyperactivity, as a critical factor in the etiology of disruptive behavior. Fearless, aggressive, stimulation-seeking children are more likely to engage in delinquent activities (Lykken, 1993). However, they may also be more inclined than more passive children to engage in a heroic defense of family and friends, so circumstances may dictate whether their outcomes are negative or positive.

Schooling. Academic skills deficits often precede and accompany delinquency (Dishion et al., 1984). At times, the seriousness of defiant youngsters' academic achievement deficiencies is underestimated because of their more flamboyant oppositional behavior and truancy, which lead teachers to reject them. Reading difficulties are common among delinquent and pre-delinquent youth (Rutter & Yule, 1978). Since children who cannot read cannot master other academic subject matter, they quickly fall far behind the class and may drop out of school altogether. Normal peers tend to shun classmates who are disruptive, aggressive, and academically deficient, so children who begin to fail in school find it in-

creasingly difficult to associate with well-adjusted peers. Childhood academic failure may substantially contribute to loss of social status at school, poor self-esteem, discouragement, association with more deviant peers, and delinquent behavior (Forehand & Wierson, 1993).

Prevention and Treatment of Delinquency

Should juvenile delinquents be punished or given rehabilitative treatment? Should youths who commit serious crimes be punished as adults, or should we assume that they lack the experience and judgment of an adult and treat them as children capable of moral and behavioral education? As presented in Chapter 1, our society has alternated between issuing minors the same type and severity of punishment as adults, which was typical in the 17th and 18th centuries, and treating them as child victims in need of education and socialization. The present juvenile justice and mental health systems recognize the need for both restriction and education of youths convicted of crimes. Sometimes it is difficult to predict whether an offending youth will receive the punishment for adults or the more protective sentencing for children.

Juvenile Corrections and Institutions. People demand protection from property destruction, theft, and violence. Fagan and Hartstone (1984) observed that America is getting tough on criminals of all ages, and that the previous approach of "aid, encouragement, and guidance" to juveniles is giving way to "punishment, just deserts, and secure confinement." The increasing use of firearms by youthful offenders makes them just as dangerous as armed adults, so it is not surprising that the public is demanding harsher punishment and incarceration for minors. Even though this "get tough" attitude is understandable, it may be ineffective.

Institutional placements include large state training schools, forestry camps, detention centers, long-term youth correctional facilities, and municipal jails. Most institutions hold juveniles awaiting court action, administer diagnostic evaluations, provide temporary housing, and administer correctional punishment. Despite their great expense, the effectiveness and appropriateness of such institutions are questionable. Most importantly, such institutions do not stop crime. Approximately half of all juveniles imprisoned in training schools will later be re-arrested and incarcerated again (Griffin & Griffin 1978). Training schools for juvenile delinquents too often become "crime training centers" in which juveniles learn new and more serious criminal techniques from fellow inmates (Stumphauzer, 1979). It soon becomes a sign of prestige and a rite of passage to graduate to incarceration in a high security juvenile detention center. Salt Lake City delinquents ask each other knowingly whether they've been sent to "Decker Lake" or its equivalent yet. They simply expect to be sent to the high security detention center when they reach the appropriate age and offense level. When they reach that stage, they may find themselves intimidated and physically and sexually assaulted by the other inmates (Bartollos, Miller, & Dinitz, 1976). Nevertheless, institutionalization is the most frequent societal response to juvenile crime.

Perhaps there is nothing inherently wrong with the idea of incarcerating youthful offenders, although much is wrong with the present way it is done. These institutions are typically underfunded, understaffed, poorly managed, and grossly overpopulated, which produces accompanying behavioral control problems. To a considerable extent, inmates' lives are controlled by the fiercest of the other inhabitants rather than by the authorities. In such an environment, antisocial behavior patterns are likely to become stabilized rather than overcome. Attempts to improve inmates' behavior through special programs of milieu therapy, therapeutic communities, self-government, psychodrama, and confrontation therapy routinely fail (Goldstein, 1991), in part because they are hardly ever applied appropriately or consistently.

Behavior Therapy Approaches. The introduction of behavioral interventions in institutional settings has yielded somewhat more positive outcomes, especially in improving the youths' behavior within the institutions. A community-based, family-style intervention called *Achievement Place* places a small group of six to eight delinquents in a private home with teaching parents who are highly trained behavioral psychologists (Phillips, 1968). The model assumes that the delinquent's behavior problems are caused by the lack of specific adjustment skills, and so rigorous training in social skills is necessary (Kirigin, Wolf, Braukmann, Fixen, & Phillips, 1979). The teaching parents' goal is to train the youths in social,

academic, and self-care skills, through acting as appropriate models, and providing highly structured direct instruction using prompts and earned response consequences. Each group home features: (1) a motivational system (token economy and level system), (2) a self-government system that allows the boys to participate in decisions that affect them, (3) a behavioral skills training program, and (4) a relation-building program between the youths and the teaching parents. At first, each boy must earn daily privileges such as television viewing time, sports participation, or extra snacks; later, as he advances through the program, he earns longer-term privileges on a weekly basis. Teaching parents work closely with the children's schoolteachers and each youth brings home a daily report card on his school performance and behavior, and earns points at home for positive reports.

Rigorous evaluations indicated that the Achievement Place program produces impressive improvements in the youths' behaviors at the group home and school. Moreover, Achievement Place produced a much lower rate of reinstitutionalization for up to two years afterwards. Nevertheless, after three years, participants did not differ significantly in recidivism from boys in traditional programs (Kirigin, Braukmann, Atwater, & Wolf, 1982). It appears that they made consistent progress while in the program, but these gains fade when they return to their original homes and neighborhoods. It may be too much to expect of any program to render young people completely impervious to the deviant family and peer influences that induced them to commit offenses in the first place. However, this program's initial results have been so impressive that Boy's Town of Nebraska, a program for juvenile offenders and orphans, has switched to this model and provides long-term training and care.

Interpersonal Skills Training. This approach assumes that juvenile delinquents lack a broad array of interpersonal, planning, aggression management, empathy, and other psychological skills (Goldstein, 1993). Each of these missing skills must painstakingly be taught to the aggressive youth through four techniques—modeling, role-playing, performance feedback, and transfer (generalization)—and maintenance of training (Goldstein, 1993). Each youth has a different profile of skill strengths and deficiencies, so each must be carefully assessed and individually treated by a highly skilled trainer. Training typically occurs in groups of five to seven youths led by two trainers. Training components of various types are administered depending on individual need and include highly detailed instruction in anger control, moral reasoning, problem-solving, accurate perception of situations, stress management, cooperation, recruiting supportive models, and understanding and using group processes. One program component, anger control training, teaches specific alternative skills to respond to provocations. Youths are taught to recognize anger triggers (physiological cues that signal their anger arousal) and reminded to produce covert anger-reducing self-statements and the Hassle Log, to judge progress in various situations.

Clearly, the skills deficiencies of many aggressive youths are immense, and much training is required. This interpersonal skills training approach has had some success, but the challenge is a significant one. Several research evaluations have produced positive outcomes, with aggression reduction, interpersonal skills acquisition, and recidivism reduction (Goldstein, Glick, Irwin, Pask-McCartney, Rubama, 1989). Yet like other treatment programs for delinquents, failure of treatment gains to transfer to everyday life and to be maintained remains a serious limitation. At least the interpersonal skills training approach is educational, humane, inexpensive, and promising as compared to most others.

SUMMARY

Social disorders of children are some of the most common behavior disorders referred for treatment and special education services. The social disorders presented in this chapter included Attention-Deficit/Hyperactivity Disorder, conduct disorder, and juvenile delinquency. ADHD is characterized by poor attending, impulsivity, and fidgety motor behavior. The conduct disordered child is a rule breaker who is noncompliant and aggressive. The juvenile delinquent has many of the characteristics of ADHD and conduct disordered children; however, the delinquent also has engaged in some type of law breaking.

The childhood social disorders stand out because the behaviors that define these disorders are primarily behavioral excesses. All children fight, are sometimes inattentive, and sometimes break rules. However, socially disordered children engage in these behaviors to an excess when compared to their peers. It is easy, however, to focus just on the excesses of these children. These children also have significant deficits. These deficits include poor academics, inappropriate social skills development, and inadequate moral or rule-governed behavior. If the deficits are not treated along with the excesses, these children will then have a poor outcome in adolescence and adulthood.

C H A P T E R   6

Drug Use by Children
and Teenagers

Addiction. In physical addiction, the drug user develops tolerance for the drug, requiring increasingly larger doses to achieve an effect. Also, drug cessation creates a characteristic withdrawal syndrome with effects ranging from unpleasant to life-threatening depending upon the drug. In psychological addiction, the user feels compelled to take the drug, but there is no physical withdrawal syndrome.

Delirium tremens (DT's). In the final stages of alcoholism, abrupt cessation of drinking produces a traumatic withdrawal reaction characterized by fever, tremors, hallucinations, and convulsions, sometimes resulting in death (20 percent of the cases).

Fetal alcohol syndrome. Heavy and prolonged alcohol consumption by a pregnant woman can cause characteristic physical deformities and mental retardation in her fetus, and other behavioral problems after birth. The safe amount of alcohol for pregnant women to consume is unknown.

Prevalence. The frequency of a particular condition within a population, most often given as the number of persons per 1,000, or for rare conditions as the number of persons per 100,000 who have a disorder. Usually presented as *annual prevalence*, or the number of cases found within a specific year, or as *lifetime prevalence*, which is the number of cases occurring within the lifetime of a particular group such as high school seniors.

Psychoactive drugs or substances. Agents that act on the central nervous system, affecting cognition or emotions. Can be either prescription drugs, such as antidepressants or antipsychotics, or nonprescription substances, such as caffeine or cocaine.

Stimulant psychosis. A toxic reaction caused by an overdose of some stimulant drug such as amphetamine. The user becomes excited, irritable, aggressive, irrational, and sometimes dangerous. One such incident makes future ones more likely.

Substance-related disorders. Use of either illegal or harmful but legal substances. Includes substance-use disorders involving dependence and abuse, also substance-induced disorders or harmful consequences of substance use.

This chapter addresses some major issues concerning drug and substance use by youth, including: (1) Why, despite continual exposure to health warnings, are young people so attracted to potentially toxic, possibly addictive and illegal drugs? (2) Which youngsters are most vulnerable and why? (3) Which drugs are widely used and why do preferences change over time? (4) How do drugs affect adolescents psychologically and socially? (5) What can be done to prevent, control, and treat drug misuse and addiction?

DRUGS AND YOUTH: AN INTRODUCTION

Drug use is popular among Americans. In fact, psychoactive substances are more frequently used in the United States than anywhere else in the industrialized world (Botvin & Botvin, 1992). The terms *drugs* and *substances* are used here to indicate nonprescribed use of prescription or nonprescription drugs, as well as substances such as alcohol, tobacco, and the so-called illicit drugs that are illegally obtained, such as marijuana, opiates, narcotics, inhalants, cocaine, hallucinogens, and other synthetic drugs that act on the central nervous system. Drug abuse is ranked as America's most serious problem according to most public opinion surveys (Botvin & Botvin, 1992). Widespread concern centers on the dangers associated with use of drugs by young people and the social and economic effects of drug-related crime. Despite harsh, mandatory sentences for drug dealers and even users, and prevention and treatment programs, young people continue to use drugs.

Theories of Adolescent Drug Experimentation and Use

MOTIVATION TO USE ILLICIT DRUGS

What draws young people to illicit drugs although they are expensive, sometimes difficult to obtain, and their use can bring trouble with parents, teachers, and the law? Many teenagers recognize that drug use could endanger their health and could even prove fatal. Yet there have been only slight decreases in the use of most illicit drugs in recent years, and many youngsters persist in experimenting with whatever drugs are available and in vogue. A number of factors may help to account for drug use, including the drug experience itself, the need to appear daring and adult-like, and the influences of friends and family members. Next we shall consider each of these potential determinants of drug usage.

According to one review (Petraitis, Flay, & Miller, 1995), there are as many as 14 different theories to explain adolescent substance use. However, these multiple theories can be classified in terms of the primary importance each gives to: (1) *cultural or social factors* that can influence drug use, such as permissive or discouraging attitudes or ready availability of drugs; (2) *interpersonal influences*, for example, from parents, other family members, and peers, and (3) *personality characteristics and biological dispositions* that make particular adolescents susceptible to the physiological and psychological effects of drugs. Table 6-1 portrays the factors that may lead to juvenile drug experimentation. Note that these factors are not mutually exclusive, so any particular teenager may experiment with marijuana, for example, because of news coverage about its effects and the people who use it, an older sibling's encouragement to try it, a teen dealer's free sample, and a group of friends who are smoking mari-

---

BOX 6-1   FADS IN KIDS' DRUG USE

Public officials, educators, and parents rejoiced in the 1980s when a dramatic drop occurred in teen drug use. It appeared that the battle against youthful drug use was being won. Yet, after declining for ten years, teenage drug use is increasing again in the 1990s (Associated Press, 1995; Johnston et al., 1995), despite widely available drug education and prevention programs in schools. Illegal drug use among high school seniors reached a low of 41 percent in 1992, but rose dramatically to 48 percent by 1995 (Johnston et al., 1995). Why should adolescents' drug use fluctuate so much from time to time?

1. *Drug prevention programs are neither as available nor as effective as they should be.* This is undoubtedly true, but prevention efforts are increasing, as is their effectiveness, so teens' drug use should not increase.
2. *Parents who have used drugs feel like hypocrites when they tell their kids to avoid drugs.* Also possibly true, but parental prohibitions have rarely deterred teens from trying drugs.
3. *Drug use follows drug availability and expense. When drugs are cheap and easily available, they will be used by many young people.* This is probably true, yet teens avoid particular drugs that are known to be very dangerous or have unpleasant effects, whatever their cost and availability.
4. *Teens prefer the drugs that are momentarily popular with their peers, have effects that are believed to be enjoyable, and convey status in the peer group.* In short, they tend to use drugs that are faddish and in style at the moment.

It is not known for sure exactly why drug use fluctuates over time. Factors such as expense and ready availability play a role, but possibly not a major one. Teen preferences for substances do seem to be a subject of fads based on what other teens and sports and entertainment figures do. If the popular students and stars choose drugs, it will be difficult to prevent teens from following them.

SOURCES: Associated Press. (1995, December 16). Teen drug use rising again. *Salt Lake Tribune.* A9; Johnston, L. D., O'Malley, P. M., & Bachman, J. G. (1994). *National survey results on drug use from the Monitoring the Future Study, 1975–1993.* (1995). *High school senior survey: Monitoring the future study.* Washington, DC: U.S. Government Printing Office.

---

juana together. There are many enticements for junior high and high school students to try drugs.

Social and Cultural Factors

TRANSITION TO ADULTHOOD

Some children consider drinking, smoking, and consumption of illegal drugs to be an indicator of adulthood. Young teenagers can mimic adults and can share some of their experiences vicariously by using illicit drugs long before their parents consider it appropriate for them to do so. It is not unusual to see 13- and 14-year-olds imitating the make-up, hair styles, and clothing of popular musicians. They copy their cigarette, tobacco, and drug habits as well. It has been suggested that among some groups in the United States, using drugs is just one aspect of growing up (Jessor, 1992; Jessor & Jessor, 1977). This interpretation of juvenile drug consumption emphasizes the tumultuous nature of American adolescence, a time during which some teenagers flout religious and conventional values, defy moral and legal strictures, and declare their independence in a very unmistakable fashion. It

should be emphasized that many young people do *not* go through such a phase, and that many of those who do are in later life indistinguishable from their more conforming neighbors. Some substances, such as tobacco, alcohol, and marijuana, are so widely used by adolescents that no particular personality features or family background could possibly typify them all.

Not all groups share the same preferences in drug use. There are ethnic, cultural, age, and sex group differences in patterns of drug use. Some ethnic group differences are described in Box 6-2.

Family and Peer Factors

INFLUENCE OF PEERS

It is extremely rare for a youngster to try drugs unless he associates with drug users. Thus the greater the frequency of drug use in the population, the more likely that the child will become a user herself. The social learning theory approach to child development (Bandura, 1977) stresses the influence of others who act as models for the child to emulate. Even socially condoned parental drug

TABLE 6-1 INFLUENCES ON ADOLESCENT DRUG EXPERIMENTATION AND USE

Cultural Influences

Positive attitudes toward drug use fostered by the culture, subculture, and neighborhood, including high crime and unemployment rates, inadequate schools, readily available drugs, lack of legitimate educational and career opportunities, weak public policies on drug control, advertising, and publicity.

Interpersonal and Family Influences

Influential role models (parents, other family members, or peers) who encourage drug use, greater influence of peers than parents, weak attachment to parents, troubled home life, parental rejection, lack of supervision, and unconventional values of parents.

Personal Characteristics

Impulsivity, aggressivity, instability, risk-taking, and thrill seeking; low self-esteem or self-efficacy, anxiousness, depressed mood, poor coping skills, poor academic and cognitive skills, and greater biological susceptibility to addiction.

SOURCE: Petraitis, J., Flay, B. R., & Miller, T. Q. (1995). Reviewing theories of adolescent substance use: Organizing pieces in the puzzle. *Psychological Bulletin, 117,* 67–86.

usage can promote children's drug experimentation. When parents use alcohol and tobacco, as well as prescribed barbiturates and amphetamines, their children are more likely to become drug users, even despite their parents' disapproval. In such circumstances, the children may come to view their parents as drug-using hypocrites who apply a more lenient standard to themselves than to their families. In other families, drug-using parents are lenient about their children's use, or simply don't care. Either way, family members are extremely influential models of conduct for young people.

Friends are very important too; nearly every study of teenage drug use has reported that users have friends who are users, and abstainers have abstaining friends. This suggests that parents are correct to be disturbed if their children want to associate with the wrong crowd. Friends' use of drugs is one of the most powerful predictors of drug use, and teens are more likely to resemble their friends in drug use than in any other feature except age and sex (Petersen, 1984). However, it is very difficult for parents to dictate their older children's choice of friends.

When parents are heavy users of legal or illegal psychoactive substances and when a teenager's friends use and encourage him to use drugs, he is very likely to do so as well (Huba, Wingard, & Bentler, 1979). Given the models, the motivation to imitate them, and the access to the drugs, it is a rare teenager who can say no.

OTHER FAMILY INFLUENCES

There are exceptions to this rule, but on the whole young illicit drug users tend to come from less traditional families and abstainers are more often found in families with traditional religious and moral values. Such families are less restrictive about their children's choice of friends. They emphasize the child's individuality, freedom, and personal adjustment more than families of abstainers, who value discipline, family cohesiveness, conventional patriotism, and religion. These are only trends, however, and many readers may know of counter-examples in which defiant, heavily drug-using sons and daughters emerge from the most authoritarian, conventional, and pious families in their communities.

Individual Physiological and Personality Factors

PERSONALITY CHARACTERISTICS

Intense clinical and research scrutiny over many years has failed to identify any unique personality characteristics that predict lifetime drug use or dependence. Narcotics addicts have frequently been described as immature, irresponsible, insecure, and egocentric, living only for the moment. However, it is impossible to determine whether they became this way because of narcotics addiction or whether preexisting personality features made them susceptible to addiction. That is, we cannot say which came first—the behavioral characteristics or the drug dependence.

In earlier times, psychotherapists were convinced that drug usage stemmed from a flawed, addictive personality. Freud tied drug addiction to masturbation, homosexual impulses, unconscious, unresolved needs for dependency and oral stimulation, and an unconscious drive toward self-destruction (Salmon & Salmon, 1977). Some contemporary psychoanalysts also view addiction as caused by personality defects, particularly low self-esteem and a craving for unceasing praise and approval (Greenspan, 1977). Early developmental deprivation or overindul-

---

BOX 6-2   CULTURAL DIFFERENCES IN EARLY DRUG USE

A group of 1,000 Seattle fifth-graders was studied to determine early drug use and attitudes about drugs (Catalano, Hawkins, Krenz, Gillmore, Morrison, Wells, & Abbott, 1993). An interesting pattern of ethnic and cultural differences and similarities between African-American and European-American children emerged. Can you predict the results? Answers appear at the bottom of this box.

1. Which group—African-American or European-American fifth-graders, use marijuana more frequently?
2. Do European-American or African-American children use more tobacco and alcohol?
3. In which ethnic group, European Americans or African Americans, are there larger sex differences for boys using more tobacco and alcohol?
4. Are African-American or European-American parents stricter about their fifth-graders' drug use?

As shown below, some results of the Catalano group's study (1993) are surprising. Clear ethnic differences appear and foster earlier initiation into tobacco and alcohol use for European-American children. At this age, the African-American children experience more parental guidance and firm control discouraging their use of illicit substances. Of those children who do engage in drug abuse, African-American girls are as likely as boys to do so, which is a clear contrast to the European-American pattern favoring greater drug use for males than for females. However, risk factors such as availability of drugs, early antisocial behavior, adequacy of family management by parents, and opportunities for involvement in school activities predict substance use in both ethnic groups. Other research (Farrell & Danish, 1993) has shown that impulsivity and poor control of aggression play a major role in drug use by African-American adolescent boys, while peer influences are more influential for European-American youth. It is important to gear prevention efforts to participants' age and ethnicity.

   Answers: (1) Both groups make equally little (5.7 percent) use of marijuana. (2) Significantly more European- than African-American children had used alcohol and tobacco by the fifth grade. (3) For tobacco and alcohol use, many more European-American boys than girls were users, but no sex differences in use were found for African-American children. There were no sex differences in marijuana use in either ethnic group. (4) African-American parents are much stricter in forbidding their fifth-graders' drug use than European-American parents. These early parental prohibitions may be responsible for African-American children's later initiation into use of these substances.

SOURCES: Catalano, R. F., Hawkins, J. D., Krenz, C., Gillmore, M., Morrison, D., Wells, E., & Abbott, R. (1993). Using research to guide culturally appropriate drug abuse prevention. *Journal of Consulting and Clinical Psychology, 61*, 804–811; Farrell, M., & Danish, S. J. (1993). Peer drug associations and emotional restraint: Causes or consequences of adolescents' drug use? *Journal of Consulting and Clinical Psychology, 61*, 327–334.

---

gence is presumed to result in eventual use of drugs. A problem with this theory is that the most searching objective research has failed to identify any particular child or parent characteristics that actually do strongly predispose people to the use of drugs. As mentioned previously, some adolescents with particular, sensation-seeking personalities choose to try drugs, and others with exactly the same characteristics do not. Younger African-American youth who are impulsive, aggressive, and nonconventional engage in earlier drug use, but the causal relationships between these characteristics and drug use are unclear (Catalano et al., 1993). In general, the personality differences found between youthful users and abstainers are not great and include a taste for risk-taking, rebelliousness, dislike for and avoidance of school, and feelings of alienation (Botvin & Botvin, 1995). This syndrome could be termed acute adolescence, because it well describes the stormy transition from childhood into adulthood followed by many young people. However, these behavioral characteristics prove transitory in most cases and hardly constitute a personality type. At present, it appears that social and environmental factors may be better predictors than individual personality features. Growing up in a stressful environment is related to earlier first drug use and later escalation of use to include more dangerous drugs (Wills & Filer, 1996). Problem drinking, drug use, and addiction may be accompanied by various adjustment problems, but are probably caused by a combination of factors such as family influences, peer practices, and the popularity of psychoactive drugs as shown in Table 6-1. The greater the number of risk factors present in a child's life, the more likely it is that she or he will try drugs.

Drug Use Definitions

Following the American Psychiatric Association diagnostic manual (American Psychiatric Association, 1994), the

Students can purchase drugs at school or in their neighborhoods, often from other kids. Are stricter drug laws and harsher penalties needed? Do we need more drug education programs, or should we decriminalize drug use?

general term *substance-related disorders* is used to refer to taking an illegal, toxic, or dangerous substance, including alcohol, nicotine, sedatives, opioids, or other substances. The term substance-related disorders can also refer to health-endangering side effects of taking any prescribed or over-the-counter medication, household toxic agents such as pesticides and antifreeze, and gases such as carbon monoxide and carbon dioxide. All of these agents affect brain functioning, respiration, thinking ability, and mood. In high dosages, some can be fatal.

The definition of a substance-related disorder is very broad and includes substances that are illegal; harmful psychologically, physically, or both; addictive; or are used in a societally disapproved fashion. Consider the case of a 12-year-old boy who recently began to smoke cigarettes. He pays his older friends to supply him with cigarettes and his brothers and friends help conceal his smoking from his parents. The 12-year-old would qualify as having a substance-related disorder under the DMS-IV definition because his activity is legally prohibited and he is misusing a powerful, addictive, dangerous substance. In

contrast, if he took a psychostimulant drug prescribed by a physician for the control of his attention deficit and hyperactivity, no substance-related disorder would be involved, even if the prescribed drug had serious side effects such as sleep disturbance, weight loss, and growth retardation. Thus, to have a substance-related disorder, the person must not only use a psychoactive drug, but the usage pattern must be illegal, socially disapproved, or harmful in some way.

Two groups of substance-related disorders are closely linked: (1) *Substance-use disorders*, which usually but not always include substance dependence and substance abuse. These are disorders in which ingestion of the substance itself constitutes the problem; and (2) *Substance-induced disorders* that constitute a chilling list of the *physical results* of substance use, including substance intoxication and withdrawal syndrome. In addition, substance-induced disorders can produce *psychological problems* such as mood disorder, anxiety disorder, sexual dysfunction, delirium, persisting dementia (thinking disorder), persisting amnesia, and sleep disorder.

Substance dependence (a substance use disorder) has been described in various ways. However, the DSM-IV definition specifies that the individual uses a substance despite significant, related problems and that there is *tolerance* (requiring increasingly larger amounts to achieve an effect), *compulsive drug-taking* despite repeated attempts to stop, and *withdrawal symptoms*. Specific withdrawal symptoms vary with the particular drug of abuse and are highly unpleasant, sometimes causing dangerous physiological and cognitive effects of declining blood level concentrations after prolonged heavy use of the substance. Some substances such as alcohol, narcotics, and sedatives produce obvious withdrawal symptoms (which will be discussed later as each type of substance is described), others such as amphetamines and cocaine produce variable, less apparent withdrawal, and still others such as hallucinogens produce no significant signs of withdrawal.

Both tolerance and withdrawal are usually seen in substance-related disorders, but are *not* required for the diagnosis, as in some cases of cannabis (e.g., marijuana) dependence. In severe cases, vitually all of the person's life centers around the substance, while family responsibilities, friendships, and job performance are sacrificed. At this stage, the person may recognize the serious medical and psychological damage created by the drug, but be unable to stop.

The technical term *substance abuse* differs from dependence in that there is no tolerance, withdrawal, or compulsive use. Instead, DSM-IV defines abuse as *the harmful social and physical consequences of repeated use* such as: (1) serious failure to fulfill major role obligations as a parent, child, spouse, friend, student, or employee, or (2) problems in managing potentially hazardous activities such as driving a vehicle or operating other machinery, and (3) inviting physical injury through aggression and impulsivity, such as engaging in physical fights and disorderly conduct.

DEVELOPMENT OF SUBSTANCE ABUSE DISORDERS

Will today's experimentation with marijuana lead to tomorrow's tragic death from an overdose of barbituates or cocaine? How can widespread use by adolescents be prevented? Traditional approaches featuring presentation of factual information about the dangers of drugs and testimony of former users, mental health experts, and law enforcement officers have not proven effective (Botvin & Botvin, 1995). Many such drug education programs have been ridiculed by high school students for grossly overstating the perils of addiction from using even the milder "gateway" substances such as alcohol and marijuana. From their own experiences and accounts of their friends, most young people believe that experimentation with commonly used drugs does not lead to dependence on dangerous ones. Moreover, they see little point in what they consider to be simplistic slogans, such as "Just Say No to Drugs." Experimental or occasional use does not inevitably lead to heavy use or addiction (Newcomb & Bentler, 1988), yet experimenting with milder drugs can expose some students to greater abuse risks.

The Path to Serious Drug Usage. Typically, people do not begin their drug experiences with narcotics or injected cocaine, but they try more easily obtained, less potent drugs instead. Those who have tried and enjoyed some of the minor drugs are more likely to be drawn to other, potentially more harmful ones than are teens who have never used any illegal substance. Long-term studies of drug use among large groups of high school students show that students' drug usage follows a predictable course (Kandel & Faust, 1975). Most begin by using alcohol and tobacco, which are easily obtained. Often beer or wine are tried first, and then cigarettes or hard liquor. Next they may try marijuana. Some adolescents then graduate from the "gateway" substances to more potent drugs such as LSD, psychostimulants, cocaine, or, for a few, narcotics. Only a small minority of teenagers eventually obtain the most dangerous drugs, but their route from experimentation to heavy drug use is highly predictable. Most begin with familiar substances of abuse and stop there, while a few are drawn to increasingly dangerous and expensive drug habits. Those who begin drug use early (before the age of 15 years) are at increased risk of developing severe drug disorders (Robins & McEvoy, 1990). Further, a teenager's pattern of past drug usage is the single best predictor of future drug consumption (Kandel, Davies, Karus, & Yamaguchi, 1986). Those who experiment with drugs early in life are most likely to continue to use them.

Predictors of Heavy Use. Who is powerfully drawn to psychoactive drug effects? Parents want to know if this could happen to their child and how it might be prevented. To some extent, all young people are at risk, because they are more likely than children or adults to engage in *reckless, sensation-seeking behavior.* Arnett concluded that, "Adolescents are overrepresented statistically in virtually every category of reckless behavior" (Arnett, 1992, p. 339), and drug use is one type of reckless behavior. Other forms of recklessness engaged in disproportionately by the young include minor criminal activity, speeding and other types of dangerous driving, and engaging in high-risk sex. Seeking thrills and adventure is particularly common in pubescent males, and may have both a hormonal and social basis (Arnett, 1992). Combined with a common adolescent belief in one's importance and invulnerability, sensation seeking can lead to dangerous drug use.

Another predictor of progressing to more serious drug usage is the person's *early and heavy use* of a substance at the preceding stage. Thus, the teenager who becomes an early and frequent smoker or drinker is more likely to progress to the use of marijuana than is the classmate who only rarely smokes or drinks. Young people who are strongly attracted to some consciousness-altering drugs are more likely to try other types. However, this progresses to narcotics for relatively few young people.

The research literature reveals that although there are wide individual differences, some children are more likely to begin drug use than others. In particular, those who *feel distant from or rejected by their parents* are more likely to experiment with drugs. In addition, youths who have *problems with aggression toward others have difficulty getting along,* and those with *poor academic skills* are all at higher risk for drug use (Petraitis, Flay, & Miller, 1995).

Families are very likely to blame their child's antisocial friends or *deviant peer group* for the child's drug use. However, recent research findings indicate that *peer influences are less powerful than individual characteristics.* Boys from low-income families who were oppositional, hyperactive, combative, and generally disruptive were particularly likely to develop later substance abuse (Dobkin, Tremblay, Masse, & Vitaro, 1995). These more deviant boys subsequently sought out similar antisocial friends once their drug habits were developed. That is,

youngsters who were already deviant were attracted to deviant peer groups.

> *"Adolescents who, by age 18, had never experimented with any drug were relatively anxious, emotionally constricted, and lacking in social skills." (Shedler & Block, 1990, p. 612)*

In contrast to many other studies, research at the University of California, Berkeley, suggests that adolescents who had experimented with drugs such as marijuana, but not become regular or heavy users, were the best-adjusted. But there can be too much of a good thing. Heavy adolescent drug users tended to be alienated, emotionally distressed, and have poor impulse control. Surprisingly, adolescents who, by age 18, had never experimented with any drug were somewhat anxious, emotionally constricted, and lacking in social skills (Shedler & Block, 1990). In the Northern California social environment, drug experimentation was linked to better adjustment, and both heavy drug use and complete abstinence were unusual and associated with less than optimal adjustment.

In the next section, we examine the use and effects of each of a number of substances and drugs widely available to children and adolescents.

Tobacco

Only in the past 25 years has the general public realized how dangerous tobacco is. The leading illnesses causing death in the United States are cancer, heart disease, and stroke, and cigarette smoking has been proven to be a major risk factor in all three (U.S. Department of Health, Education, and Welfare [DHEW], 1979). Consequently, the prevention of smoking by young people is an important public health concern, because illness and death caused by smoking represent tragic personal losses and high costs to employers, taxpayers, and health systems.

Although there have been ups and downs, smoking rates for all age groups have mostly decreased during the last three decades, perhaps because widely publicized information about the serious health risks related to smoking seems to be having some effect, even on adolescents. Three-quarters of 12th-graders and 82 percent of 8th-graders stated that they disapprove of people who smoke one or more packs of cigarettes per day (National Institute on Drug Abuse, NIDA, 1993). Nevertheless, large numbers of teenagers continue to take up the habit. Young women in particular are taking up smoking, perhaps in part because of clever advertising campaigns aimed at them. Traditionally, smoking has been a male pasttime, but sex role barriers are falling. Sex differences in smoking rates have virtually disappeared. *The Statistical Survey of the United States* (U.S. Department of Health and Human Services, 1993) shows that nearly 4 percent more older males than older females smoke in the 35-year-and-older group, but among 18- to 25-year-olds, approximately equal proportions of males and females smoke.

Women's smoking arouses particular concern because smoking during pregnancy significantly increases their risk of having vulnerable premature or low birthweight babies. Moreover, women's longer average life spans make them especially vulnerable to smoking-related diseases such as cancer, which typically take many years to develop. Thus, although the overall percentage of smokers has decreased, increased smoking among young women is a cause for public health concern.

PATTERNS OF NICOTINE USE

In previous decades, experimentation with tobacco resulted in lifelong smoking habits in about 70 percent of the people who had smoked more than a single cigarette (Hamilton-Russell, 1971). Cigarette advertising and adolescent values both portray smoking as sophisticated, daring, and sexy, so some young people decide to try it for a while and then believe that they will simply stop when they decide to do so. However, large numbers revert to smoking within a few weeks, months, or even years of swearing off cigarettes and do not stop until they develop serious symptoms such as chest pains, shortness of breath, or cancer. Nicotine is a powerful addicting drug, and habitual smokers experience strong cravings for nicotine and a physiological tolerance requiring increasing numbers of cigarettes each day. When they decide to quit, smokers suffer a withdrawal syndrome consisting of irritability, distress, and inability to concentrate.

A very small percentage, roughly 5 percent of smokers, are able to smoke over long periods without becoming addicted. They strictly control their smoking; for example, they refrain from smoking on some days or never

smoke until after dinner (Shiffman, Paty, Kassel, Gnys, & Zettler-Segal, 1994).

The likelihood of addiction and lifelong smoking may not be so great now as in the past because there is much more social, institutional and governmental pressure not to smoke. Smokers are now banished from many public areas, airliners, and entire buildings. Nevertheless, it is much more difficult to stop than most young people think. Some of the most carefully designed and conducted studies of smoking treatment have produced one-year abstinence rates no better than 38 percent on average (Shiffman, 1993). This means that 60 to 70 percent of those who attempt to quit resume smoking within the period of one year after treatment. Most smokers who *persistently* attempt to quit eventually succeed, but often only after many difficult attempts (Lichtenstein, 1982). Addiction is common and prevention and treatment are difficult.

Tobacco companies are combating the reduction in domestic cigarette sales in part by denying that nicotine is addicting, denying that they control the amount of nicotine in their cigarettes, and developing other non-smoked tobacco products, which are also addictive. In a disturbing return to an earlier era, children are now using smokeless, chewing, or spit tobacco. Some 11.4 percent of 18- to 25-year-old men and 5.4 percent of 12- to 17-year-old males say they use smokeless tobacco, although distinctly less than 1 percent of females use it (Statistical Abstract of the United States, 1994). Young people may not yet realize the health risks associated with this form of tobacco, and they can easily observe sports stars chewing and spitting copiously in televised ball games. Substance use is subject to fads, so it is not yet clear whether young men will continue to use spit tobacco as they grow older.

PREVENTION

Research based prevention programs are being introduced to counteract the powerful social influences of parents, family members, and peers who are smokers; reckless adolescent values; and tobacco industry advertisement and product development campaigns. Several such prevention efforts are described in Box 6-3. The reduction in the social acceptability of smoking, the smoking prohibitions and unattractive physical surroundings offered to smokers at the entrances to public

---

BOX 6-3   HOW TO PREVENT TEENAGE SMOKING

Inform them? Scare them? Or what? Early smoking prevention efforts relied on scare tactics, moral exhortations not to smoke, factual information about ill effects, or attempts to enhance teens' self-esteem, all of which were unsuccessful. Teens responded much as one 16-year-old girl did: "They gotta realize they can't *make* kids do anything. Kids rebel against it." Today's smoking prevention programs are more likely to rely on peer leaders, either older or same-age, to deliver the messages. Also, student participants in role playing are less passive and resist offers to smoke cigarettes in a realistic, age-appropriate fashion, rather than what adults imagine they should say. They get social reinforcement in the form of attention and approval for their efforts, which helps to teach and encourage them. Results of such social influence approaches to prevention generally range from a reduction of 33 percent to 39 percent less smoking initiation for at least two years after the program (Botvin & Botvin, 1995). However, the results disappear over time, which suggests that prevention efforts must continue.

   Other prevention approaches feature training in personal and social skills to enhance teens' competence. These programs usually train students in two or more types of skills including: (1) problem-solving and decision-making skills, (2) cognitive skills for resisting negative social influences, such as counterarguments to cigarette ads, (3) self-control skills including self-instruction, goal setting, and self-reinforcement for appropriate behavior, (4) coping strategies, including relaxation exercises, for relieving stress and anxiety, (5) interpersonal skills, such as how to make friends, and (6) assertive skills, such as how to make or refuse requests and how to express feelings and opinions. Participants see these skills modeled or demonstrated, rehearse the skills with feedback on performance adequacy, and complete homework assignments between meetings. Amazingly, all studies published that used the skills training approach reported significant and usually relatively large behavioral effects. Skills training appears to hold great promise in the prevention of substance use.

SOURCE: Botvin, G. J., Schinke, S., & Orlandi, M. A. (1995). School-based health promotion: Substance abuse and sexual behavior. *Applied & Preventive Psychology, 4,* 167–184.

---

places, and the recognized health hazards for others exposed to "second-hand" smoke have greatly reduced smoking's glamorous aura. Today's children are more likely to associate smoking with the sight of smokers huddled outside smoke-free buildings desperately puffing on cigarettes while exposed to the elements than with the image of the Hollywood movie star lighting up, which was common in the 1940s and 1950s.

Alcohol

National surveys reveal very high rates of disapproval of drinking and smoking among teenagers, particularly younger ones, yet students continue to drink alcohol. They usually try alcohol for the first time on average when they are between 12 and 13 years of age (U.S. Department of Health and Human Services, 1992). In 1992, some 87.5 percent of the high school seniors said they had used alcohol at least once, which was a decrease from the 90.7 percent who had tried alcohol in the class of 1988 (NIDA, 1993). Lifetime prevalence rates (defined as a person's ever having tried alcohol) also decreased from 93 percent in 1979 to 89.5 percent in 1990 (NIDA, 1993).

Similarly, the proportion of heavy party drinkers (potential problem drinkers) among high school students has decreased slightly.

Nonetheless, drinking rates among youth remain high, with beer and wine coolers being favorites because of their widespread availability and seemingly low alcohol content. Wine coolers are particularly attractive to young people who like their fruit flavors, sweetness, and attractive colors, which resemble soft drinks. Each year, juniors and seniors in high school drink an amazing 35 percent of all wine coolers sold in the United States and 1.1 billion cans of beer (U.S. Department of Health and Human Services [HHS], 1992).

ASSOCIATED RISKS

There are many dangers from alcohol use by young people. Drinking is often associated with automobile accidents, water-related injuries, drowning, and involvement in violent crimes such as assault, murder, and rape. Often, both perpetrators and victims have been drinking. A national survey of college students revealed that almost one-half who had been victims of crime had themselves used drugs or alcohol before the crime occurred (HHS,

1993). Suicide attempters are more likely to be frequent drug or alcohol users, and drinking is highly associated with adolescents' suicide attempts using firearms (HHS, 1993). Risky sexual behavior that could lead to HIV infection, other sexually transmitted diseases, or unplanned pregnancy also is associated with alcohol use. Dangerous in itself, alcohol drinking exposes young people to risks of many types.

Fetal Alcohol Syndrome

Although both sexes are equally likely to have sampled alcohol at some time, more boys than girls become heavy drinkers during the high school years. This is fortunate because if she becomes pregnant, a young woman's heavy drinking can result in serious damage to her unborn child. Although *occasional* alcohol exposure during pregnancy has not been conclusively demonstrated to be hazardous to the fetus, heavy and prolonged drinking during pregnancy is associated with increased infant mortality, low birthweight, hyperactivity, learning disabilities, and retarded physical and mental development (Smotherman & Robinson, 1996). A rare abnormality called *fetal alcohol syndrome* occurs in prenatal life among the babies of a small percentage of alcoholic mothers or, to a lesser degree, to nonaddicted heavy drinkers, especially those who consume more than six drinks a day over an extended time period (Streissguth, Martin, Martin, & Barr, 1981).

ALCOHOL ADDICTION

Alcohol proves addicting for a smaller proportion of users (2 to 10 percent) than do most other addictive substances (Barry, 1977). Physical dependence seems to play only a limited role in heavy drinking, but alcoholism is often disastrous. Alcoholism is the most common and one of the most harmful forms of substance abuse in the United States today. However good their previous adjustment, alcoholics typically become erratic, undependable, and belligerent, lose their jobs, destroy their marriages, drive away their nonalcoholic friends, and terrorize their families. Even later during adult life, children of alcoholics suffer adjustment problems, with males showing more antisocial and alcoholic disorders and females developing more problems with depression, self-esteem, marital adjustment, and parenting (Chassin, Pillow, Curran, Molina, & Barrera, 1993). Alcoholics may destroy their own health as well. Heavy drinking is associated with liver damage and vitamin deficiency. When

deprived of alcohol, alcoholics may develop an extremely unpleasant, potentially dangerous withdrawal syndrome with such features as nausea, vomiting, agitation, anxiety, sweating, hand tremors, and racing pulse. A small proportion (who may also have other illnesses) develop very dramatic symptoms including grand mal seizures, hallucinations, tremors, and potentially fatal delirium tremens or DT's. Every city has a dilapidated slum section that harbors large numbers of homeless alcoholics.

Unlike addiction to narcotics or most other psychoactive drugs, long-term alcoholism can result in extensive physical deterioration such as permanent brain damage (Korsakoff's psychosis) and cirrhosis of the liver. Unfortunately, it is currently impossible to predict which heavy drinkers can drink safely and which are at increased risk of becoming alcoholics. Social and cultural factors may play a role, since larger proportions of people in some groups develop problems with alcohol than in others in which alcohol use is prohibited or frowned upon for religious or cultural reasons. For example, alcoholism rates for the English and Northern Europeans seem to be higher than for Italians or Jews, probably for cultural reasons.

PREVENTION OF ALCOHOL ABUSE

Legal Remedies

It is ironic that one of the most potentially dangerous of the addictive drugs—alcohol—is also one of the most socially condoned when taken in moderation and is perhaps the easiest to obtain. Many teenagers want to appear to be experienced drinkers, so they overindulge and their drunkeness endangers themselves and others. Communities have found that one way to prevent some of the harmful effects of teenagers' immoderate drinking is to increase the minimum legal drinking age, which is sometimes effective. When states reduced the legal age for alcohol consumption, the rate of alcohol-related auto crashes immediately increased by 10 to 30 percent. In contrast, states that increased their legal drinking age immediately decreased their alcohol-related auto accidents by about the same margin. However, the lower rates were typically not maintained, perhaps because minors easily found illegal sources of alcohol. Legislative changes in the legal drinking age are not controlled experiments, so it is difficult, even impossible, to gauge their effects (MacCoun, 1993). Thus, although raising the legal drinking age would seem to be a very simple preventive interven-

Roadside sobriety tests are commonplace, but they don't prevent teens from drinking and driving. Is this a necessary part of growing up?

tion, its long-term value in reducing accidents and controlling minors' use of alcohol is still under study.

Psychosocial Prevention Programs

Certain types of family constellations foster abstinence, moderation, or misuse. Sons of alcoholic fathers are at high risk of becoming alcoholic themselves. Their alcoholism rate is roughly four times higher than normal (Cadoret, 1987). These boys also have high rates of adjustment problems, particularly hyperactivity, oppositional behavior, conduct disorder, and delinquency (Sher, Walitzer, Wood, & Brent, 1991). It is difficult to discern whether parental alcohol abuse in itself is responsible for the children's problems or whether other, associated factors are influential such as alcoholic parents' high rates of depression, antisocial behavior, marital conflict, and use of harsh physical discipline.

Parental modeling, childrearing competence, and cultural values greatly influence young people's drinking. When parents are heavy drinkers, when they create tension and conflict in the family, and when they have conduct disorders or hold antisocial attitudes, their teenage children are likely to drink heavily. This same family pattern appears in the backgrounds of heavy illicit drug users. One prevention effort, the Michigan State University Outreach Program (Nye, Zucker, & Fitzgerald, 1995), worked with families with alcoholic fathers or preschool-age sons to control the family interaction patterns

believed to put the sons at high risk for aggressive adjustment problems. Family interactions were observed, and parents were taught to monitor and modify their child's behavior and to provide reinforcement for the boys' socially desirable, cooperative behavior. Training of the parents in marital problem-solving was also used because their levels of conflict were high. Results were positive, with the boys' improving their rates of positive behavior and decreasing their negative behavior, particularly when the mother's investment and participation in the program were high. Thus, mothers may play a key role in producing positive outcomes for their children in homes with alcoholic fathers.

Alcohol Abuse Prevention

Some alcohol risk reduction programs for young people focus on information and attitude change rather than on family relations. A six-week skills-training program for small groups and an alternate one-hour individual advice and information interview with a professional counselor both were effective in reducing and maintaining drinking rates over a two-year period (Baer, Marlatt, Kivlahan, Fromme, Larimer, & Williams, 1992). Program content emphasized that keeping alcohol consumption at moderate levels minimized health and social risks, and gave participants nonalcoholic drinks disguised as cocktails to demonstrate that alcohol effects at moderate doses are largely dependent on expectancies, setting, and beliefs. The intended lesson is that alcohol is not necessary in order to have a good time. Students were also trained to monitor their drinking and estimate their own blood alcohol levels. More evaluation is needed, particularly with younger groups, but this prevention approach is well-accepted by participants and seems to be effective.

Marijuana and Hashish

Marijuana and its more potent form, hashish, have been very popular among youth for the past 30 years and remain the most widely used of the illicit drugs with the exception of tobacco and alcohol. The main psychoactive ingredient in marijuana is tetrahydrocannabinol (THC). The THC concentration in marijuana has increased markedly in recent years and is causing an increase in users' panic reactions. The most potent form of marijuana or cannabis is called hashish or hash. Both forms are readily obtainable at most high schools, and even junior high schools, and on the streets. Nevertheless, as with other illegal drugs, their popularity among high school students has varied in recent years. The peak lifetime prevalence (whether someone ever used the substance) of 65.6 percent of high school graduating students was reached in 1981, but decreased to 40.7 percent of graduating seniors in 1992 (National Institute on Drug Abuse, NIDA, 1993), and subsequently increased again. The possible reasons for this fluctuation will be explored later. Nevertheless, students' marijuana usage levels remain extremely high.

EFFECTS OF MARIJUANA

Pharmacologists traditionally considered marijuana to be a relatively mild and nonaddictive drug, with less potential for misuse and overdose than alcohol and many other drugs. However, marijuana products have increased in potency and are now a significant factor in motor vehicle accidents and fatalities (Peterson, 1984). Euphoria, sensory and time distortions, feelings of unreality, increased appetite and eating binges, reduced male sex hormone production, disrupted short-term memory and cognitive performance, and slowed reaction time and impaired visual tracking ability all have been produced by marijuana. Taken repeatedly and in high dosages, as it could be by adolescents, marijuana may create tolerance, requiring increased dosages to achieve an effect, and a withdrawal syndrome (sleep disturbances, restlessness, irritability, decreased appetite, sweating, and weight loss from abrupt elimination of retained body fluids). Quitting typically produces no intense craving for marijuana (Tinklenberg, 1977). Some studies report neither tolerance nor withdrawal effects. However, there may be psychosocial effects. Some users become preoccupied with the drug experience, lose interest in other activities, and reject non-drug-using friends and family members. In the sociology of teenage drug use, peers provide models, sources, and encouragement for dangerous experimentation and continued substance misuse. An additional negative factor in marijuana and hashish use is that the street drugs available to adolescents are sometimes mixed with contaminants and other drugs that could prove dangerous.

Given the hazards of even the seemingly mild illicit drugs, their widespread use among the young presents something of a puzzle to concerned parents and teachers. It is possible that drugs' psychosocial as well as their pharmacological effects support their use. Experimentation with drugs is considered sophisticated and daring by some adolescents, and students can gain status by becoming users. In support of this argument, teenagers tend to overestimate their smoking and drug usage when being interviewed (Botvin & Botvin, 1992). They undoubtedly also exaggerate their drug involvement when talking with their friends in order to appear tougher, older, and more sophisticated. An additional incentive is provided by marijuana's pharmacolocial properties. Users praise its ability to produce a relaxed, mild "high." Smoking marijuana becomes a pleasant group experience, and some people report increased pleasure in music and other sensual experiences, enhanced sexual performance, increased appetite, and mild hilarity. Among the less pleasant effects and those that are less obvious to users are interference with immediate memory and ability to perform classroom tasks, and also dangerous and erratic driving (*Marijuana and Health*, 1980). Other temporary physical effects include disruption of normal sperm production and slight reduction of testosterone production, especially in younger men. Longer-term health effects can include impaired lung function, probably resulting from using smoking as the method of ingestion.

PREVENTION OF MARIJUANA USE

Because marijuana is so widely used, it appears that attempts to outlaw it have proved futile. Harsh laws simply drive the price up, and drug dealers have become big, though illegal, businessmen. Initial attempts to frighten young people into shunning drugs were dismissed by them as lies and gross exaggerations. The 1936 film "Reefer Madness," which was designed to deter drug use, is now viewed as an unintended comedy, a camp classic. Such scare tactics left many young people with an abiding scorn for drug prevention programs. And yet there is some indication that teenagers are not impervious to the health movement that has become popular with their elders. The emphasis on improved nutrition, weight reduction, and vigorous physical excercise may be affecting younger people's attitudes toward illicit drug use. Since 1979, more and more high school seniors have begun to consider regular (but not experimental or rare) marijuana use to be physically and psychologically harmful. At present over two-thirds of high school seniors judge regular use of marijuana to involve great risk. Perhaps the widespread publicity about the health hazards of cigarette smoking have affected attitudes about smoking marijuana as well, or perhaps as yet unknown social and cultural trends are at work. Whatever the reasons, young people's use of marijuana seems to be decreasing.

Inhalants

Inhalants appeal to children who seek a drug experience but lack the money to buy illicit drugs. The inhalants discussed in this section include volatile hydrocarbons such as airplane glue, paint, gasoline, cleaning fluid, and aerosols, which provide poor and younger boys with a way to get high. Inhalants typically are used by 11- to 15-year-olds, especially by whites (*Statistical Abstract of the United States*, 1993). Very few older teenagers or adults use these types of inhalants.

Inhaling volatile hydrocarbons requires no special skills or paraphernalia, and children can easily learn how to do it from friends or even from warnings about the hazards involved. The effects are quick and potent, and include impairment of judgment and feelings of dizziness, elation, drunkenness, and weightlessness (Cohen, 1977). Repeated use can produce dizziness and hallucinations, and long-term, continuous use could damage vital organs. Especially dangerous is the practice of sniffing inhalants inside plastic bags placed over the head, which can lead to death by asphyxiation. Gasoline sniffing can produce sudden death from heart rhythm irregularities (Bass, 1970) or respiratory failure (Comstock & Comstock, 1977). Little research has been done on these products' toxicity because they are not intended to be ingested. Apparently there is no physical addiction, although users can develop tolerance to solvents, which could be perilous and lead to death by poisoning.

Also included as inhalants are the amyl and butyl nitrites, which are referred to as poppers or snappers. These were tried by 1 in every 12 seniors (8 percent) in 1984. However, their use declined, and amyl and butyl nitrates are now rarely tried (1.5 percent of the seniors in 1992) (Johnston et al., 1993).

Hallucinogens

Humans have perhaps always sought to experience elation, strange visual effects, and spiritual experiences by consuming certain plants, mushrooms, and liquids. Today these substances are termed hallucinogens (hallucination-producing agents), even though their effects seem to be primarily emotional and they rarely produce distorted perceptions similar to those in psychotic reactions. Ingestion of LSD-25, (PCP) phencyclidine or Angel Dust (which is officially classified as a narcotic, but is difficult to classify because its effects are so diverse and unpredictable), mescaline, peyote, psilocybin, and related compounds produce altered states of thinking and feeling. Some hallucinogens, such as peyote, are used in religious ceremonies by certain North American Indian tribes.

Following widely publicized experimentation with LSD and other hallucinogens by well-known artists and intellectuals in the 1950s, the use of these substances spread to colleges during the 1960s and eventually included high school students, although not in large numbers. At present, hallucinogen use is most popular among young adults, particularly whites who reside in the West. African Americans find hallucinogens less attractive than people of other ethnic groups (U.S. Department of Health and Human Services, 1993). The high point in adolescents' use of hallucinogens occurred in the 1960s to early 1980s and has since decreased regularly (NIDA, 1993). The decline in young people's use of LSD since the late 1960s may be traced to news reports that it could produce chromosome breakage, suicide, psychosis, and repeated, uncontrollable LSD experiences despite discontinued use. Most of these ill effects eventually were found to be exaggerated, rare, or nonexistent (Brecher, 1972). Nevertheless, they were widely believed and may have discouraged the use of hallucinogens.

LSD stimulates the central nervous system and the sympathetic division of the autonomic nervous system. Users report weird visual sensations (flashes of light, enhanced appreciation of colors, blurring or distortion of vision), mood swings, inability to gauge time, dizziness, weakness, tremors, drowsiness, and uncontrollable thoughts. Some people find this experience exciting and seek it repeatedly, but others find it terrifying. The reasons for these individual differences in reaction could be due to a host of different factors including the drug type, dosage, and purity; the user's drug history and other personal characteristics; and the setting for drug use.

Most hallucinogens are not addicting but do require increasing dosages to produce an effect. There is no perceived compulsion to continue their use, and there are no withdrawal symptoms. A major danger is that the street drugs could be adulterated with dangerous substances. Many young people experiment with hallucinogens only once or a few times and then, having satisfied their curiosity, turn to other drugs or drug abstinence.

Stimulants

COCAINE

In the past decade, cocaine in various forms has become increasingly popular with adolescents and young adults. Once extremely expensive, cocaine is more affordable following the introduction of cheaper cocaine products such as the impure but potent coca paste and crack cocaine sold in inexpensive, rocklike chunks, which are smoked. The great majority of adolescent users first try cocaine in the 10th, 11th, or 12th grade, in contrast to their much earlier use of alcohol, cigarettes, inhalants, and marijuana. High school seniors nationally have decreased their use of cocaine from the 1975 level of 5.6 percent to the 1992 level of 3.1 percent, with an all-time high of 13.1 percent in 1985 (NIDA, 1993). Cocaine users tend to smoke tobacco and marijuana heavily and to be heavy drinkers, and they may use all three substances together. Adolescents who use marijuana heavily are particularly likely to become cocaine users in young adulthood (Kandel, Davies, Karus, & Yamaguchi, 1986). Ethnic groups differ in their drug preferences; for example, crack cocaine is more popular among African Americans than among whites or Hispanics (NIDA, 1993).

EFFECTS OF COCAINE

Whether sniffed, injected, or smoked, cocaine has become a very popular illicit drug. It acts as a central nervous system stimulant and mood elevator. In small dosages, stimulants increase work output, help people resist fatigue, and create a temporary good mood, and users believe that stimulants enhance their intellectual, physical, and sexual performances. Sigmund Freud once enthusiastically recommended it to his fiancee, saying, "It will make the roses return to your cheeks," but he later recognized the drug's dangerous side effects. Many high school students may now display a similar disenchantment with cocaine. In intravenous doses of 16 to 32 milligrams, cocaine produces an intense, very brief euphoria that peaks in 8 to 12 minutes and dissipates in 30 to 40 minutes. Smoking crack has similar, but even more intense effects. Intranasal injestion is slower acting and less

preferred by heavy users because of damage to the lining of the nose. Habituation or tolerance develops after the first few doses together with strong cravings for the drug. Cocaine users experience a stimulant effect for a two or three hour period after cocaine injestion, with rapid heartbeat, high blood pressure, and rapid breathing, followed by a precipitous drop in mood. Chronic cocaine snorters may develop nasal congestion and dripping (rhinitis), and nasal irritation, ulceration of the mucus membranes of the nose, and ultimately perforation of the nasal septum. Ironically, even successful professional and business people can be attracted to this "status drug," and if they continue to use it, can become addicts.

Like other stimulants, cocaine in high dosages can be dangerous or even fatal. People poisoned by an overdose of cocaine may develop a reaction in which they become highly suspicious and paranoid, have hallucinations, could become violent, and experience extreme depression as the drug wears off. Overdoses produce tremors, delirium, and convulsions. Emergency room admissions involving cocaine have increased dramatically in recent years, and there has been growing concern about the health of babies born to addicted mothers (see Box 6-4).

The list of athletes and entertainers who have been hurt or killed by cocaine accidents continues to grow. Cocaine's expense and its use by the rich and famous has lent glamour to cocaine and made it a status symbol. Tragically, a planned heavy dose or inadvertent overdose can also kill, causing acute respiratory failure or circulatory collapse. Moreover, it is addicting, although withdrawal reactions are different from and less severe than those associated with narcotics. Addiction may lead to crime. Young people with low incomes must produce large sums of money regularly in order to support a cocaine habit costing perhaps $200 a day, so they must steal from family, friends, and strangers, or become dealers themselves.

OTHER STIMULANTS

In addition to cocaine, the stimulants include ephedrine (a nonprescription decongestant), the amphetamines including "ice," a concentrated form of crystal methamphetamine, methylphenidate (a mild stimulant called Ritalin, which is prescribed for attention deficit with hyperactivity), and related compounds. Many young people use these substances for their stimulant effects. These effects are similar to those described for cocaine, and

---

BOX 6-4 "CRACK BABIES": EFFECTS OF MOTHERS' USE OF CRACK COCAINE

Recently, nurses and doctors in obstetric units have reported "crack babies," or newborns of mothers who are addicted to crack cocaine. These babies were said to be physically frail and impossible to soothe. But are these neonatal problems attributable to crack or to some other, associated factor such as the mothers' youth, poor health, or lack of prenatal care? Women who are heavy crack users often also abuse alcohol, smoke cigarettes, take other drugs, and live marginal lives. Any one or several of these other problems could result in irritability and fragility in newborn infants.

Theresa Hawley and Elizabeth Disney (1992) produced a social policy report on crack cocaine for the Society for Research in Child Development. The problem of cocaine usage during pregnancy is potentially huge, especially in the inner cities, since 31 percent of the babies delivered in one Detroit hospital tested positive for cocaine exposure (Ostrea, Brady, Gause, Raymundo, & Stevens, 1992). An added concern is the tremendous cost. The average hospital cost for the delivery and care of a cocaine-exposed infant is over ten times the average cost for delivery of a drug-free infant of similar social status (Calhoun & Watson, 1991). Recall, however, that the cocaine-exposed baby's problems could stem from causes other than cocaine itself.

Research on crack effects on babies continues, but the best documented effects on newborns are increased risk of premature birth, which is dangerous for the infant, decreased birthweight, and smaller head circumference, which persists during childhood. Cocaine has a vasoconstrictive effect, which decreases the supply of nutrients to the fetus prenatally and could potentially lead to impaired cognitive and intellectual functioning. Various other physical abnormalities appear to be more numerous among cocaine-exposed children, but the link between the drug and these abnormalities is not yet proven. Some cocaine-exposed newborns seem to show a Neonatal Abstinence Syndrome consisting of irritability, inability to sleep, incessant shrill crying, and other problems that are similar to, but milder than, the neonatal reaction to withdrawal from narcotics. Future studies will reveal whether fetal cocaine exposure produces any enduring problems for children. However, the main lesson of this type of research is clear. Pregnant women should be encouraged individually and through major advertising campaigns to refrain from any unnecessary drug usage.

SOURCES: Calhoun, B. C., & Watson, P. T. (1991). The cost of maternal cocaine use: I. Perinatal cost. *Obstetrics and Gynecology, 78,* 731–734; Hawley, T. L., & Disney, E. R. (1992). Crack's children: The consequences of maternal cocaine abuse. *Social Policy Report, Society for Research in Child Development, 7,* No. 4, whole issue; Ostrea, E. M., Brady, M., Gause, S., Raymundo, A. L., & Stevens, M. (1992). Drug screening of newborns by meconium analysis: A large-scale, prospective epidemiological study. *Pediatrics, 89,* 107–113.

---

cocaine users may resort to the less costly, longer acting amphetamines when they cannot afford the more expensive drugs. At the height of the 1960s drug craze, speed freaks injected large quantities of amphetamine over an extended period of wakefulness. These stimulants produced all of the nasty aspects of *stimulant psychosis* such as agitation, paranoia, and violence. The psychotic behavior disappears days or weeks after stimulant use is discontinued, but can resume if stimulants are used once again. All types of stimulants are very addicting. The abstinence syndrome following withdrawal is characterized by intense depression, agitation, insomnia, nausea, and headaches, all of which can be relieved by proper medical care. Addicts often take sedatives to ease the agitation produced by cocaine and become addicted to the sedatives as well as to the cocaine.

Depressants

Young people most commonly try intoxicants, stimulants, and hallucinogens, but occasionally they add a sedative or depressant such as pentobarbital (Nembutal) or

secobarbital (Seconal). Less frequently, they may use one of the minor tranquilizers such as meprobamate (Miltown or Equanil), chlordiazepoxide (Librium), alprazolam (Xanax), which is the most-prescribed tranquilizer in the United States, diazepam (Valium), or triazolam (Halcion), the country's most popular sleeping pill. Widely available as prescription drugs, tranquilizers and sedatives were illicitly used in the past year by only about 2.9 percent of seniors in the national high school sample (NIDA, 1993). The students chose barbiturates and tranquilizers equally, with methaqualone (Quaaludes) losing popularity over the past decade (NIDA, 1993).

Like alcohol, which is also a depressant, these drugs can produce intoxication, loss of coordination, nausea, giddiness, and aggressive behavior. Taken for short periods, the depressants seem relatively safe. Tranquilizers ordinarily are taken as directed for no more than two months, and sleeping pills for no more than two weeks. But they are highly addictive and produce severe and physically dangerous withdrawal symptoms. Mixing another depressant with alcohol is extremely dangerous. Users develop tolerance, and so require increasing dosages. Ironically, the fatal dose level (the amount that proves deadly) remains constant while tolerance develops. Thus it is easy for users to take fatal overdoses, particularly in combination with alcohol (Cooper, 1977).

Narcotics

Products of the opium poppy (opiates such as opium, morphine, heroin, and paregoric) and synthetic narcotics have long been used to induce relaxation, soothe fussiness, relieve anxiety, stop coughing or diarrhea, and counteract intractable pain. Many 19th-century Americans became addicted to patent medicines that contained morphine. Ironically, these morphine addicts were treated with another highly addictive drug, which was named heroin to denote their heroism in taking the cure. Parents with infants who were difficult to soothe or failed to thrive could give them laudanum—a potent and highly addicting mixture of morphine and alcohol. The passage of legislation prohibiting nonprescriptive use of opiates probably prevented addiction for many, but also had the unintended effect of creating a flourishing illegal trade, so opiate prices soared in response to addicts' demands (Brecher, 1972). Today, narcotics addiction continues to be a major social problem, particularly among desperately poor, inner-city inhabitants.

NARCOTICS ADDICTION

The effects of taking an opioid help explain its popularity. In small or moderate doses, the user feels a surge of pleasure or "rush" followed by a longer period of gratification and release from pain and care during which concerns are forgotten and drowsiness alternates with wakefulness. The addictive power of narcotics is legendary, but perhaps a bit exaggerated, and addiction is not inevitable. There is danger of a possibly fatal overdose as habituation takes place and because it is impossible to determine the dosage in street drugs. Moreover, other long-term effects for addicts are extremely dangerous, including endocarditis, an infection of the heart lining associated with injections; HIV, AIDS and other infections; and tetanus.

Opiates other than heroin were reported to have been used during the past year by 3.3 percent of 1992 high school seniors, with 0.6 percent claiming to have used heroin (NIDA, 1993). This usage rate undoubtedly would be higher if school dropouts were also included in the survey. Moreover, students might conceal its use so these statistics could represent an underestimate of unknown

FIGURE 6-1   The Stages and Cycle of Change

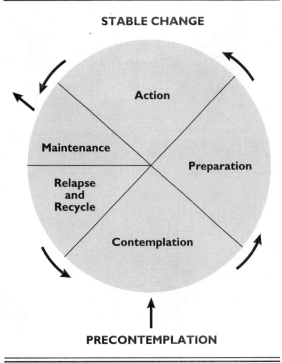

SOURCE: DiClemente, C. C. (1993). Changing addictive behaviors: A process perspective. *Current Directions in Psychological Science, 2,* 101–106. Reprinted with the permission of Cambridge University Press.

magnitude. Nonetheless, like most other illicit drugs, opiates are less appealing to today's youth than in previous decades.

TREATMENT OF DRUG ADDICTION

Drug addiction is very difficult to treat effectively, and relapses are common. Treatment success is elusive because addictions are diseases of denial and the addicted individual is often the last person to recognize the problem. Acknowledging the problem is only the beginning of treatment, and making lasting changes is even more challenging. To break an addiction, it is necessary to become resolute and master skills ranging from avoiding drug-related stimuli to improving interpersonal relations as shown in Figure 6-1 (DiClemente, 1993). To be successful, the addict must first recognize the addiction, become uncomfortable with the consequences of drug abuse, and be determined to do something about it—*the*

When skillfully presented, group therapy is a popular, safe, and moderately effective form of treatment for juvenile substance misusers. No form of treatment, however, is sufficiently powerful to prevent or treat compulsive drug use.

contemplation stage. In *the preparation stage,* the addict makes a firm commitment to try to change and prepares to take specific action. *The action stage* consists of implementation of the plan to cease drug use. Typically, this stage last for three to six months and includes detoxification. *The maintenance stage* is equally difficult, because the user must modify lifestyle to avoid relapse and support abstinence indefinitely. Treatment failures are common, so following relapse, many people recycle, starting the treatment process anew. Sometimes a number of repeats are needed before lasting success is achieved.

Many types of treatment are available, from inpatient detoxification and group therapy to outpatient methadone or drug-free treatments. Some programs are supervised by physicians and other professionals, and others stress self-help in groups of former addicts. Many programs, such as the nonprofessionally directed Alcoholics Anonymous or Cocaine Anonymous, mainly serve adults rather than children or adolescents. Next we describe the major types of treatments available and assess their ef-

fectiveness. Although some of these treatments are chiefly for adults, the emphasis will be on treatment for the young.

Hospitalization and Detoxification

Formerly, narcotics addicts were sent or volunteered to go to federal hospitals in Lexington, Kentucky, and Fort Worth, Texas, to be withdrawn from drugs. These programs featured withdrawal (detoxification) using decreasing doses of morphine and several months of inpatient treatment. Despite their great cost, these programs proved to be nearly useless. Most of those who were treated resumed their narcotics habits soon after their release. Even had hospital programs proved effective, there are now too many addicts to attend to in this fashion.

A similar program for adolescents at Riverside Hospital in New York produced the same disappointing results. Despite three years of inpatient and outpatient treatment, nearly all of those treated later resumed using narcotics. Scandals concerning the availability and use of illicit drugs inside the hospital helped lead to its closure. Treatment authorities now agree that hospital-based, long-term treatment programs are no more effective for most addicts than outpatient treatment, which is far less costly and much less disruptive to addicts' lives (Maisto, Galizio, & Connors, 1991). Nevertheless, short-term hospitalization and detoxification are necessary to manage the dangerous withdrawal symptoms associated with alcohol and barbiturate dependence.

Methadone Maintenance

During the past 20 years, methadone maintenance has been one of the most widely used treatments for narcotics addiction. Proponents of this treatment method view physiological dependence as the most important aspect of narcotics addiction. To combat the physical dependence and prevent withdrawal symptoms, addicts are given daily dosages of methadone, a synthetic narcotic. Methadone must be taken daily, and patients who are doing well may take home two- to three-day supplies. However, methadone itself presents some serious problems. It is highly addicting, can seriously harm a fetus, and must be consumed for years, perhaps for life (Maisto et al., 1991). Methadone's advantage over heroin is that it is legal and it is cheap. Neverthless, a certain amount of methadone is diverted to the black market, and there have been methadone-related deaths, some of which occurred when children or other family members mistakenly drank a mixture of orange juice and methadone stored in the home refrigerator. A longer acting alternative to methadone, LAAM (levo-alpha-acetylmethadol), may prevent such accidents and may allow addicts to travel.

Even its proponents are forced to admit that methadone maintenance has its drawbacks. In addition to the possibilities of accidental poisoning and harm to the fetus, methadone can be combined with other nonnarcotic drugs. Thus, users can concoct a potent chemical cocktail including methadone, alcohol, and stimulants if they wish.

Methadone use is illegal for those under 16 years of age who have not been dependent on narcotics for at least two years. Teenagers younger than 18 years must have their parents' written consent and must have tried and failed in at least two previous attempts at detoxification. Youthful addicts seem to require treatment in a highly structured environment emphasizing instruction in academic, interpersonal, and vocational skills (Biase, 1973). Simply giving them methadone fails to meet their other social, academic, and job-training needs. Methadone programs are more effective when they also include counseling and medical care, and when they allow patients to take the methadone home and tolerate some temporary relapses and missed appointments (Galanter & Kleber, 1994).

Chemical Antagonists

Methadone blocks the euphoria produced by large doses of narcotics only when the methadone is given in even larger dosages then the narcotics (the blockade effect). Consequently, scientists have searched for nonaddictive drugs that would act like methadone. Several narcotic antagonists such as naloxone, naltrexone, and cyclazocine have been tested for effectiveness, safety, and appeal to addicts. All have some unpleasant effects such as nausea, dizziness, drowsiness, depression, and constipation. The chemical antagonists do not appeal to most addicts, so they have limited promise at present and are most often used by well-motivated, well-educated adults.

Antabuse has long been taken by alcoholics as a deterrent to drinking. Antabuse induces feelings of intense sickness and nausea if taken with alcohol, and so prevents drinking. Unfortunately, it is easy for an alcoholic to defeat antabuse treatment either by not taking antabuse or by drinking until the effects of antabuse are overcome by intoxication. A central and still unsolved problem with substance abuse is that it is terribly difficult to motivate addicts to abstain.

Therapeutic Communities

Therapeutic communities are based on the assumption that all addicts are manipulative and have antisocial personalities and that they must be persuaded to realize these tendencies in themselves. Alternatively, behavioral therapists recognize each client's uniqueness and need for individualized treatment (Hickey, 1994). In contrast, in therapeutic communities, addicts are presumed to require regimented residential treatment, close supervision, and critical encounters with staff and fellow addicts involving harsh confrontations with the unpleasant reality of their drug habits. The first of the residential treatment programs was Synanon, which was founded in 1958 by Charles Dederich, himself a former addict. Like Alcoholics Anonymous, Synanon viewed addiction as deriving from a personal weakness. Addicts' manipulativeness was attacked in group sessions featuring confrontations, demands for confessions of hypocrisy and cheating, and group support for abstention. Only highly motivated applicants were accepted following a rigorous screening process, and even then they could not always tolerate the restrictive program, which was run autocratically by ex-addicts. There are many variants of the therapeutic community approach: Other programs such as Odyssey House use professional therapists as staff members, as well as former addicts, and feature group therapy, tutoring sessions, adult education, and vocational training. Length of stay is individually determined, but varies from six to eighteen months in most settings. The older therapeutic communities typically barred all psychoactive drug use, but some multimodal treatment programs now prescribe methadone maintenance as a treatment aid. Recently, therapeutic communities have become more flexible and some have worked with families, allowed the use of psychotherapy and medications, and targeted adolescents or mothers with children (Harvard Mental Health Letter, 1995, August).

Despite their rigor, therapeutic communities are largely unsuccessful as measured by controlled studies. Approximately 75 percent of those who enter programs such as Odyssey House, Phoenix House, Gateway House, and Daytop Village drop out within the first month (Louria, 1977). Many addicts, especially young ones, are unwilling or unable to make the required commitment to long-term, possibly permanent residence in the therapeutic community. Less than 15 percent of those admitted to all types of therapeutic communities graduate from treatment and over half drop out in less than three months (De Leon, 1984).

Drug-Free Counseling Treatments

A number of outpatient counseling programs have been developed for addicts who want help but are reluctant to become dependent on methadone or unwilling to become a permanent resident of a dictatorial therapeutic community. Outpatient counseling on either a group or

an individual basis is the form of treatment offered to most adolescent substance abusers. The procedures used in the drug-free treatments include individual and group counseling, educational and recreational activities, and vocational guidance. Participants are helped to become and to remain free of drug use. However, like the alternative approaches, the drug-free services have an exceedingly high dropout rate. They are probably more suitable for nonopiate drug users than for narcotics addicts, because the client is largely unsupervised and remains in his or her customary environment with access to drugs. Drug-free counseling may be the most appropriate and effective treatment for young non-narcotics users now available, but it leaves much to be desired. All of the drug treatment programs just described seem to have some, though limited, beneficial effects. The therapeutic communities and drug-free treatments produce the lowest rates of re-admission to drug treatment programs (Maisto et al., 1991; Sells, 1979). These treatments also decrease both narcotic and non-narcotic drug use, and improve employment rates. Those addicts who have the best outcomes in all treatments comply better with treatment demands, stay in treatment longer, and do not have serious psychiatric disorders or criminal records.

PREVENTION

Because there has been limited success in treating drug use and addiction, prevention assumes added importance. Yet prevention has also proved to be extremely difficult. The early prevention programs were particularly ineffective and featured scare tactics portraying all illicit drugs as highly addictive and physically and socially ruinous (Donaldson, 1995). Young people then dismissed all official pronouncements even when they were accurate. Today, numerous excellent and accurate drug pamphlets are available from the Do It Now Foundation, the Wisconsin Clearing House of the University of Wisconsin-Madison, and the Addiction Research Foundation, Toronto, Canada. However, even accurate drug information may not deter children from experimentation with psychoactive drugs. It seems that something more than information is needed.

Media campaigns of limited duration often take the form of short public service television or radio messages featuring sports stars who advocate abstinence. These brief announcements are popular with broadcasters and the public, but their effectiveness is very difficult to demonstrate (Johnson et al., 1990). One study assessed the effects on viewers of TV "spot" announcements featuring basketball star Earvin "Magic" Johnson's revelation that he was HIV seropositive because of unsafe heterosexual encounters (Kalichman, Russell, Hunter, & Sarwer, 1993). The announcement attracted interest and many telephone calls for information for about three weeks. This brief surge of interest in HIV and AIDS could provide an opportunity for other education and prevention programs, but taken alone is probably not very effective as a prevention measure. A major problem with media interventions to prevent drug use is that television is primarily a commercial entertainment medium, which greatly limits its use in prevention (Schilling & McAlister, 1990). Most experts believe that such televised presentations must be combined with continuing school- and home-based prevention programs in order to have an impact.

Many present-day prevention programs address participants' emotional and social needs in addition to providing information about drug effects. For example, the Midwestern Prevention Program (Johnson et al., 1990) features a 10-session school and home program in drug use resistance skills training for sixth- and seventh-graders. The training goes beyond a "Just Say No" intervention to provide children with discussion and role playing groups together with their parents and other family members. Parents and children receive instruction in positive communication skills, and community leaders organize a drug abuse prevention task force with mass media coverage. Thus a communitywide drug prevention effort accompanies individual and small group skills training. This program produced significant reductions in tobacco and marijuana use over three years, but did not reduce alcohol consumption (Johnson et al., 1990).

The more successful prevention programs make effective use of social science research on effective influence processes, while the ineffective ones merely present the information in a traditional classroom fashion or simply exhort youngsters to avoid drugs and dealers. Children need to learn how to avoid drug use as well as to recognize its bad effects. The Life-Skills Training Program (Botvin, Baker, Dusenbury, Tortu, & Botvin, 1990) is a school-based cognitive-behavioral prevention program to help eighth- and ninth-grade students resist advertising pressure, manage anxiety, communicate effectively

and assertively, and improve social skills through intensive practice and feedback. Preaching about long-term health risks is minimized, while immediate negative consequences of drug use are stressed. Results showed that the program was effective in reducing use of cigarettes, marijuana, and immoderate alcohol use. The preceding studies show that psychological techniques can be effective in preventing children and teens from dependence on illicit substances, especially if sessions are scheduled several times a week over a period of several weeks, and booster sessions are used later to maintain and enhance program effects (Botvin & Botvin, 1992).

Federal and state authorities often have preferred the seemingly more direct route of denying young people access to prohibited substances and providing stiff penalties for their possession, sale, and use. Some laws specify "Zero Tolerance," barring any minimum level of drugs to trigger arrest and criminal charges. Even a shred of a marijuana cigarette or a single marijuana seed would suffice as evidence. There is no research evidence for the utility of this particular, extremely severe approach. There are minimum age limits on the legal use of alcohol and tobacco, and these limits are sometimes made more restrictive to modify young people's access to these substances. In addition, there is a continuing, unsuccessful effort to cut off the supply of illegal drugs, both nationally by crackdowns on dealers and internationally. Powerful economic incentives exist for drug dealers, and enforcing the law has proven impossible. So as long as the demand and the supply exist and cannot be permanently decreased, our national drug problem will persist.

The apparent failure of the government's tactic to combat drug use by denying users with access to drugs and providing ever-harsher penalties has led critics to advocate legalization of some or all illicit drugs (see Box 6-5). This is not to say that legal prohibitions and punishments always fail. Harsh legal deterrents virtually eliminated amphetamine abuse in Japan following World War II, and widespread opiate use in mainland China was eliminated by the Communist government. However, legal remedies have been less successful in combating drug use in North America, and there is always the possibility that legalization will stimulate young people's use of harmful drugs. Probably, particular historical times and cultures require their own prevention approaches, and there is no single best solution for everyone.

BOX 6-5   THE CASE FOR DRUG LEGALIZATION

Critics of the present U.S. drug policy are calling for the legalization or decriminalization of illicit drug use. In the influential magazine *Science*, published by the respected American Association for the Advancement of Science, political scientist Ethan Nadelmann (1989) made a bold case for repeal of drug prohibition. He called for de-emphasizing our traditional reliance on criminal justice agencies to control drug use and turning to more positive and constructive education, prevention, and treatment alternatives. Most proponents of this plan advocate legal availability of some or all now-banned drugs combined with vigorous efforts to restrict consumption, but not through criminal sanctions. Government funding that is presently directed to prohibiting the production, sales, and use of illicit drugs would instead be devoted to education, prevention, and treatment efforts. Here are the criticisms of the present criminal justice approach to the illicit drug trade:

- It is futile to try to limit availability. Marijuana and opium can be grown in many places all over the world, and the coca plant thrives in most subtropical regions. Criminal gangs or political groups are in control in remote or inaccessible regions of production, and governments are helpless to control production. Labs producing "look alike" synthetic drugs that imitate popular substances can be set up anywhere. Control of drug production is now impossible.
- It is costly in dollars and in lives. At least $10 billion was spent by the U.S. government to enforce drug laws in 1987 (Nadelmann, 1989). Roughly 10 percent of inmates in state prisons are incarcerated for drug law violations, and many more are in city jails. And the numbers are growing. The U.S. Sentencing Commission has predicted that in 10 years, one-half of the federal prison population will be there for drug law violations. The cost of imprisoning them is staggering, and the money to do so is being diverted from worthy causes such as education, health, welfare, highway and building construction, and cultural programs.
- The drug trade brings living wages and large profits to people all over the world. People in poor, drug-producing countries do not see themselves as morally obligated to prevent "rich, decadent" Americans from obtaining drugs. They wish only to earn a living for themselves and their families. Neither U.S. laws nor U.S. foreign policy initiatives are likely to change others' attitudes about the desirability of making money from drug exports.
- Law agencies' raids and arrests have not prevented drugs from reaching the streets. When the heat is on, drug prices go up, so dealers continue to prosper.
- Prohibition of illicit drugs provides an inviting opportunity for organized crime. Illegal profits are flaunted by drug dealers in impoverished neighborhoods, making law-abiding holders of low-paying legitimate jobs appear to be foolish and exploited. Well-heeled dealers are attractive role models for the young. Making drugs legal would take away the exorbitant profits now enjoyed by criminal groups and allow governments to collect billions of dollars each year on drug sales taxes, much as is now done with cigarettes and alcohol.

Nevertheless, there are some convincing arguments against legalization, such as:

- On-the-job productivity of workers who take these drugs while at work would decrease, causing accidents and harming the economy.
- Unless some controls are imposed, many people would be able to take drugs with dangerous, potentially fatal effects. Prices would go down dramatically, so usage might increase. Addiction might become common, especially among the venturesome young, blighting their futures. (Proponents of legalization all oppose selling drugs to children, however.)
- If legalization results in increased psychoactive substance use, highway accidents and fatalities, unsafe sexual encounters, assaults, and other impulsive, risky, and antisocial behaviors will increase. The known effects of psychoactive drugs would produce these costly and tragic outcomes.
- Legalization would not eliminate crime. Criminals would only take up some other socially harmful, prohibited activity, such as illegal sales of prescription drugs, prostitution, or extortion.
- Drug use would be encouraged by the availability of safe, pure, unadulterated drugs as opposed to the often toxin-contaminated street drugs of today, which vary widely and undetectably in dosage levels, with some producing fatal overdoses. Young people know that buying certain types of street drugs is dangerous because they may have been sprayed with dangerous fertilizers, herbicides, or mixed with more powerful substances that produce unpleasant or dangerous effects. Without such threats, usage would be encouraged.

There are additional arguments on both sides of the drug prohibition issue that readers can generate themselves. The major question to address is whether our present approach to treat illicit substance use, manufacture, and distribution as a crime is the best course of action for today's society.

SOURCES: Nadelmann, E. A. (1989). Drug prohibition in the United States: Costs, consequences, and alternatives. *Science, 245,* 239–245; Shenk, J. W. (1995, October). Why you can hate drugs and still want to legalize them. *The Washington Monthly,* pp. 32–40.

SUMMARY

Psychoactive drugs, which affect users' perceptions, mental abilities, and emotions, are found in most households. Drug misuse occurs when these drugs are used by juveniles, overused or used inappropriately, and when outlawed drugs are consumed. Some drugs produce physical addiction or dependence, require increasing dosages to produce an effect, or cause withdrawal symptoms when the drug is discontinued. Addicting drugs include nicotine, alcohol in some cases, stimulants including cocaine, depressants, and narcotics. Some illicit drugs are very quickly addictive, as in crack cocaine, while others are apparently not addictive, such as marijuana, hallucinogens, and inhalants.

Substances such as tobacco, alcohol, and marijuana are used by many high school students. The typical sequence is to proceed from heavy alcohol and tobacco use to marijuana, with some students going on to use cocaine, inhalants, and hallucinogens. There are gender, cultural, and ethnic differences in drug preferences, difference in age of first use, and predictors of drug use. However, most teenagers who misuse drugs have parents and siblings who drink, smoke, and indulge in prescribed or illicit psychoactive drugs. Their families may be stressed and dysfunctional as well. Drug users tend to have drug-using friends, and they and their families may be somewhat less traditional and more permissive than are abstainers. Drug users show accentuated signs of adolescent turmoil, rejecting school and adult authority, although it is difficult to determine whether the rebellion preceded or followed their drug use. There are no personality types that predict drug addiction.

Addictions are extremely difficult to break permanently, especially in the young. Nearly any form of treatment produces decreased use if the full course is followed, but dropout and relapse rates are high for all treatments. Therapeutic communities are aimed mostly at older addicts, and teenagers are given outpatient counseling where they may receive insufficient supervision or support. The limited success of treatment efforts has heightened interest in prevention. Prevention programs based on social influence and skill-building approaches are proving increasingly successful in preventing or delaying first drug use. Fortunately, teen drug use is decreasing possibly because of a greater national interest in promoting health, increasingly sophisticated prevention efforts, and widely publicized drug-related deaths of celebrities.

ANXIETY AND MOOD DISORDERS

Key Terms

Bipolar affective disorder. Serious mood affliction in which depression alternates with excited, seemingly elated periods and with normal mood. Formerly called manic-depressive disorder. Extremely rare in childhood.

Depression (in childhood). A rare affective disorder meeting most criteria for adult depression including sadness, pessimistic attitude, fatigue or overactivity, and somatic complaints. DSM-IV adult diagnostic criteria are used to diagnose child mood disorders, with developmentally appropriate modifications.

Desensitization. Treatment technique that introduces feared and avoided stimuli gradually either in real life (in vivo) or in imagination (systematic desensitization) while the client maintains muscular relaxation.

Guided participation. Modeling therapy in which the client is supervised and physically assisted in gradually making closer approximations to engaging in the feared act.

Learned helplessness. A temporary state of passivity and impaired problem-solving brought about by overwhelming and inescapable, insoluble problems (in animals, inescapable threats such as electric shocks).

Obsessive-compulsive disorder. Recurrent, unwanted ideas (obsessions) and unwilling engagement in repetitive, stereotyped actions (compulsions).

School phobia. Extreme reluctance or inability to attend school arising from fear of some school-related situation, such as evaluation apprehension.

School refusal. Fear and avoidance of school stemming from home influences, school-related situations, or any other factors. Includes, but is not limited to, school phobia.

CHAPTER OVERVIEW

This chapter deals with the problems experienced by children who become psychologically vulnerable, at least temporarily, and develop emotional or mood problems and serious anxiety reactions. In addition to describing the various childhood internalizing disorders (disorders focused on maladaptive thoughts and emotions), we present the long-term prognosis for children with these conditions who receive different types of medication and psychosocial treatment, which are also described.

We begin with a presentation of the most prevalent of these disorders—anxieties and phobias—and explain how these syndromes differ from common childhood worries and fears in their description, timing, intensity, and persistence. School refusal is described for the many readers who work with affected children in schools and clinics. Posttraumatic stress disorder in children is also described. Compulsive rituals and obsessive concerns are compared with similar but normal childhood behaviors. Childhood depression receives major attention because of its dramatic emergence into general psychiatric use during recent years. Promising new cognitive-behavioral prevention and treatment methods are presented. Juvenile suicide is a matter of increasing concern and receives attention here. Much of what is known about childhood depression, obsessive-compulsive disorders, and posttraumatic stress disorders in childhood has been discovered within the past decade.

INTRODUCTION

No child is free from fear and anxiety, despite society's attempts to protect children. Anxiety disorders may be the most common psychological problems in both childhood and adulthood (Anderson, 1994). Stress, anxiety, and depressed mood are unavoidable, but children differ dramatically in the amount of stress they experience, how much support they receive from families and community institutions, and how resilient they are, both physically and mentally. Even healthy, loved, and materially advantaged children may suffer stress from the pangs of rejection by their peers, actual or perceived failure in school, or the marital battles of their parents. Stress and anxiety represent individual, personal reactions to life challenges, and people differ in their *thresholds* for experiencing stress and in their *tolerance* for resisting the debilitating effects of continuing stress. Both stress threshold and tolerance levels depend on a person's enduring character-

istics, such as temperament and general physical robustness, and on more transitory, situational factors, such as major life events including illness or death in the family, moving to a new neighborhood, the birth of a sibling, and employment loss. Some children are much less resilient and capable than others, possibly because of genetic differences in temperament or because of their rearing, a difficult family situation, or other debilitating experiences. These vulnerable children respond to stress with marked anxiety, depression, physical complaints or other maladaptive behavior patterns. They may develop general anxiety or a specific phobia in the form of an extreme, uncontrollable fear of harmless objects such as friendly pets or common experiences such as attending a movie or riding on a bus. Young children's anxious symptoms should not be simply dismissed as harmless, since they tend to persist over several months, even in children younger than 7 years, and correlate with school performance, such as reading achievement (Ialongo,

Edelsohn, Werthamer-Larsson, Crockett, & Kellam, 1994).

ANXIETY DISORDERS
Generalized Anxiety Disorder

Generalized anxiety disorder consists of uncontrollable, excessive anxiety and worry, occurring consistently for at least six months and extending to concerns about many events or activities. Generalized anxiety disorder can occur at any age after infancy and now includes a formerly separate category, overanxious disorder of childhood (American Psychiatric Association, 1994). The child must also show at least one other symptom from a group that includes irritability, restlessness, fatigue, difficulty in concentrating, muscle tension, or sleep disturbance. Such children are frequently perfectionistic about their work and very insecure and unsure of themselves no matter how well others evaluate them, even if they are not being evaluated at all (American Psychiatric Association, 1994). In childhood, this persistent disorder typically begins at around 10 years of age, often co-occurs with depression, and is marked by physical complaints of respiratory distress, racing pulse, trembling, feeling faint, chills, or sweating (Beidel, Christ, & Long, 1991). Of a large sample of children diagnosed with overanxious disorder of childhood, 46 percent were ill for at least eight years and had experienced a previous episode (Keller, Lavori, Wunder, Beardslee, Schwartz, & Roth, 1992).

Generalized anxiety disorder is different from other anxiety disorders in its broad focus over many different situations. The other anxiety disorders are more focused. In *separation anxiety disorder*, children show excessive, age-inappropriate anxiety about any separation from home or a loved one, typically the mother. Such children are so distressed about separation that they insist on knowing where a parent is at all times, phoning incessantly to check on her location. This type of reaction would be normal and expected in an infant or toddler, but is highly unusual in an elementary school-age child. Others may be plagued by persistent, unreasonable worries and feel compelled to engage in repetitive rituals such as prolonged and repeated hand washing (*obsessive-compulsive disorder*) or may become profoundly depressed. Generalized anxiety disorder and specific phobias are the most prevalent of the childhood disorders,

A child who clings to her mother in an age-inappropriate way may have adjustment problems, only one of which is separation anxiety.

and obsessive-compulsive disorders and childhood depression are much less common (McGee, Feehan, Williams, Partridge, 1990). Formerly, young people were very rarely diagnosed with posttramatic stress disorder, but this syndrome is seeing increasing recognition in children who have been emotionally devastated by experiencing or seeing others experience extreme threats in natural disasters or physical assaults. However, diagnosis of emotional disorders in children is difficult because the identification of the condition depends so heavily on self-reported anxiety, fear, or depression, and young children are often unable to tell others about their concerns. New, specialized self-rating scales and interviews and clinicians' increased alertness to the possibility of a child's developing an internalized disorder help in the detection of these conditions.

"Anxious children ... seem preoccupied with concerns about evaluations by self and others and the likelihood of severe negative consequences. They seem to misperceive characteristically the demands of the environment and routinely add stress to a variety of situations." (Kendall, 1993, p. 239)

Childhood Fears and Phobias

It is not surprising that children become fearful in view of their physical and mental immaturity. Compared with adults, children have limited physical strength, knowledge, and skills with which to deal with problems in an often overwhelming world. Small children are vulnerable and can be physically overpowered easily, even by an enthusiastic medium-sized dog. Lacking mature cognitive skills, they may not know what to do in unfamiliar situations such as when they become lost or need help for another reason. These physical and cognitive limitations reduce children's abilities to cope with situations that are easily managed by older people and may make them apprehensive in many situations. Thus, children develop fears because they lack fully developed physical and mental coping skills.

Children also learn specific fears from observing other people's reactions or through being warned to avoid potential dangers. Their parents teach them to shun strangers and dangerous situations. Parents also transmit their own fears to their children by showing visible apprehension about thunderstorms, insects, the sight of blood, reptiles, or medical personnel. Playmates and siblings also serve as fearful models and effective transmitters of common fears of insects, snakes, and large predators such as lions or tigers. Thus, children can acquire fears *directly* from frightening experiences with a particular object or situation or *indirectly* from verbal warnings or modeled fearful reactions of family members or peers. There are many ways to become afraid, which may help explain why so many children are fearful.

Developmental psychologists have estimated that 90 percent of all children develop specific fears during their early years (Macfarlane, Allen, & Honzik, 1954). Older children, teens, and adults typically worry most about social evaluation ("What if I flunk this test and have to leave school?" "Can everyone see me sweating?" "Is my appearance so awful that I should hide?"), while children younger than about 8 years are less concerned about social evaluation. Typically older children fear internalized and abstract threats (Kendall & Ronan, 1990), while young children fear external, physical threats. Most younger children lack the social comparison skills and the ability to take other people's perspectives, which is necessary to formulate interpersonal anxieties (Vasey, 1993). Information on developmental differences in fears

TABLE 7-1 DEVELOPMENTAL CHANGES IN CHILDREN'S FEARS

Age Range	Types of Fears
0–12 months	Loss of support, loud noises, unexpected, looming objects, strangers
12–24 months	Separation from parent, injury, strangers
24–36 months	Animals, especially large dogs, darkness, separation from parent
36 months–6 years	Animals, darkness, separation from parent, bodily harm, strangers
6–10 years	Imaginary beings, snakes, injury, darkness, being alone
10–12 years	Social evaluations, school failure, injury, death, thunderstorms, ridicule
Adolescence	Peer rejection, school failure, war and other disasters, family issues, future plans (especially in boys)

SOURCES: Rutter, M., & Garmezy, N. (1983). Developmental psychopathology. In E. M. Hetherington (Ed.), *Handbook of child psychology* (Vol. 4). New York: Wiley; Morris, R., & Kratochwill, T. (1983). *Treating children's fears and phobias.* New York: Pergamon; Vasey, M. W. (1993). Development and cognition in childhood anxiety: The example of worry. In T. Ollendick & R. Prinz (Eds.), *Advances in clinical child psychology* (Vol. 15, pp. 1–40). New York: Plenum.

and worries is summarized in Table 7-1. Such developmental data help parents and psychologists to determine the likelihood that a particular child's fear is normal or clinically significant.

PHOBIAS

There are several tests for assessing the normality of children's fears, including the timing, duration, intensity, and type of fear:

1. *Age of onset.* Fears may require clinical assessment and treatment when the age of onset is highly unusual, as when a 10-year-old develops a strong aversion to dogs or to strangers. Such fears are common among infants and preschoolers, but not among older children. When a fear reaction arises at a developmentally unusual or inappropriate time, it may represent a phobia rather than a normal childhood fear.

2. *Persistence.* A strong fear reaction that persists long after the usual age of occurrence could be a phobia. The older child who unaccountably continues to

display great fear of harmless stimuli may have a phobia rather than one of the usual childhood fears.

3. *Intensity.* Most minor fears are not abnormal. However, even developmentally common fears may be a matter of clinical concern if they are sufficiently intense as to become incapacitating. When a common fear, such as apprehension about public speaking, is so intense as to foreclose many career choices or to prevent school attendance, it becomes pathological.

4. *Prevalence.* Finally, some types of fear are so unusual that their very occurrence signals abnormality. Older children and adolescents may develop *agoraphobia* (literally, fear of public places), which is the incapacitating fear of certain situations from which escape could be difficult or embarrassing (e.g., leaving the safe confines of their homes and families to attend school or social occasions). This disorder, which is discussed later, precludes school attendance, interferes with social relationships with peers and with holding a job, and clearly is pathological whatever the person's age.

A fear of water is common, but some children develop a full-fledged phobia of water, which requires professional treatment.

DEVELOPMENTAL DIFFERENCES IN FEAR EXPRESSION

The DSM-IV (American Psychiatric Association, 1994) diagnostic criteria recognize developmental differences in the symptoms constituting a phobia. For individuals under age 18, the phobia must persist for at least six months, so a child's short-lived fear will not be mistaken for a clinically significant condition. Further, the fear level must be intense enough to interfere with normal activities such as attending school, riding public transportation, or visiting other public places. Unlike adults, children may not recognize that their fears are excessive or unreasonable, and rarely complain about having phobias. However, when placed in the feared situation, children may express intense anxiety by crying, having tantrums, physically freezing, or clinging. In contrast, adolescents and adults are more likely to experience a *panic attack,* in which they experience several minutes of terror that they are about to perish, have a heart attack or stroke, lose control, or "go crazy." For phobic people of all ages, exposure to the phobic stimulus or situation provokes intense anxiety, which leads to active attempts to avoid the feared situation whenever possible, and the phobia inter-

feres significantly with normal functioning (American Psychiatric Association, 1994).

DEVELOPMENTAL COURSE OF FEARS AND PHOBIAS

Some fears and phobias are more tenacious than others, but it is not known why. Those that tend to persist throughout life include fears of physical illness, agoraphobia, and fears of specific social situations, such as public speaking (Vasey, 1993). Fortunately, most early fears are overcome. Brief psychotherapy can produce significant improvement in most phobic children , and uncomplicated phobias are sometimes overcome even without professional treatment (Agras, Chapin, & Oliveau, 1972). Thus, the prognosis can be quite positive for phobic children, but the general apprehensiveness and low self-confidence that indicate an anxiety disorder are more persistent. Anxiety disorders that begin in childhood often continue into adulthood (Kendall et al., 1992), and only around 20 percent of these phobias are finally overcome (American Psychiatric Association, 1994).

Separation Anxiety, School Phobia, and School Refusal

Separation anxiety is a childhood anxiety disorder consisting of excessive fear and worry about becoming separated from home and a major attachment figure, usually the mother. The DSM-IV (American Psychiatric Association, 1994) diagnostic manual does not recognize either school refusal or phobia as distinct from separation anxiety, but views them as features of separation anxiety for some children. That is, only some of the children with separation anxiety also display school refusal or phobia (Berger, 1988; Last & Strauss, 1990).

School refusal refers to persistent avoidance of school or attendance only when forced because of the child's intense fear and anxiety about going to school. Like the anxious child, the school refuser may be perfectionistic and display excessive concerns about school performance (Ficula, Gelfand, Richards, & Ulloa, 1983). When required to attend school, the child may wake up with a painful stomachache or headache. This often occurs on a Monday after a school vacation, at the beginning of the school year, or after being kept home by a minor illness. When parents agree that the child can stay home from school, the child's physical complaints diminish dramatically, since avoiding school reduces the anxiety. The child predictably becomes anxious and symptomatic again whenever preparing to attend school, so he or she stays home, if the parents allow it. School refusal is not a unitary condition, but can arise from different causes. School refusers can meet diagnostic criteria for various emotional disorders, or for none (Silverman, 1992). The feature school refusers share is the anxious, insistent avoidance of school.

In *school phobia*, which is one type of school refusal, the child's fear is centered on some aspect of the school, such as fear of a particular teacher, of being called on in class, or of entering the classroom. Thus, school refusal is the more general term, while in school phobia, some specific aspect of school is feared. Striking between 1.4 and 17 children per 1,000 (Kennedy, 1965; Rutter, Tizard, & Whitmore, 1981), school refusal is a more frequent childhood problem than some other, better known disorders such as childhood autism (see Chapter 11). School refusal has been reported by investigators around the world, wherever there is formal classroom education, and represents a serious social and economic problem.

School refusal differs from truancy in that the child with school refusal has an emotional disorder and is anxious, depressed, and fearful, especially in social situations, and typically remains at home while avoiding school (Berg, 1981). In contrast, truants tend to be hostile and defiant, avoid home when they are supposed to be at school, and prefer to spend time with friends.

TREATMENT OF SCHOOL REFUSAL

Home study programs are sometimes tried, but may not meet all of the school refuser's academic and social needs. Prolonged avoidance of school can retard a student's academic achievement, create problems in relating to peers and adult nonfamily members, and increase feelings of depression and low self-esteem (Ficula et al., 1983). Eventually, the adolescent's career and social opportunities can be severely curtailed. In *mild acute school refusal*, which tends to affect younger children, there is little or no family discord and initial onset is sudden. Here, the prognosis is excellent, since the child's primary problem is school attendance. The treatment approach is direct and often successful and recurrences are rare. Kennedy (1965) recommended that the fearful child begin by spending just a half hour at school and progressively increase time at school over several days. The child's somatic complaints about headaches, weakness, and stomachaches are dealt with matter-of-factly by scheduling medical examinations before or after school hours. This clever tactic ensures that possible physical illness receives prompt attention, but the child's complaints do not serve as a means for avoiding school.

Severe chronic school refusal has a much less favorable prognosis. Chronic school refusal typically is found in children older than 11 years who come from unstable families. These children may also suffer from depression, negative self-image, and difficulty in getting along with family members (Ficula et al., 1983). Parents who are behaviorally deviant themselves or express negative attitudes toward school are unlikely to help their child return to school. Adolescents with chronic school refusal have a poor prognosis and may also develop debilitating panic attacks and agoraphobia (Rutter & Garmezy, 1983).

Etiology of Phobia

Two major types of explanations of childhood phobias, the psychoanalytic and the learning-cognitive positions, can be distinguished. Both of these theories attempt to explain the origins of anxious, phobic, depressive, and other emotional disorders. Therefore, the following description of theories of phobia formation also apply generally to anxiety reactions, panic episodes, and other reactions involving extreme fear and anxiety or obsessive-compulsive disorder. Theories of childhood and adolescent depression receive separate consideration later.

PSYCHODYNAMIC THEORY: HISTORICAL AND MODERN FORMS

In Sigmund Freud's theory of psychoanalysis (Freud, 1950/1909) phobias were originally attributed to psychologically created tension, anxiety, guilt, sexual jealousy, and rage. In his famous psychoanalytic interpretation of the horse phobia displayed by a 5-year-old boy named Hans, Freud traced Hans' fear of horses to the boy's presumed Oedipal sexual desires for his mother and his rage toward and fear of his father who competed successfully for the mother. Freud argued that all of the child's emotions toward his father were displaced upon a powerful animal that reminded the boy of his father—the horse. His fear also permitted the boy to stay at home with his mother while he avoided the horses in the streets. Under Freud's direction, the boy's father (who was a patient of Freud's) interpreted the psychological nature of his fear to Hans and the boy's horse phobia was overcome. This case provided the model for the psychoanalytic interpretation of children's phobias.

Sigmund Freud's psychoanalyst daughter, Anna, described children's anxieties as originally diffuse and vague, but later compressed into anxiety about one symbolic object, such as a dog, which represents an unconscious fear (A. Freud, 1977). The child believes he fears the symbolic figure (e.g., the animal), but actually he fears becoming overwhelmed by sexual and aggressive feelings and probable retaliation from his parents if he acted on those feelings. Once the child's anxiety is redirected toward the symbolic, external object, he can reduce his anxiety to some extent by avoiding that object. Psychoanalysts believe that the choice of phobic object is not random, but depends upon some actual or fancied resemblance to persons or events featured in the psychological conflict.

Present-day *object relations theory* is a psychodynamic theory based on psychoanalysis, which emphasizes the importance of social rather than sexual attachments to parent figures. In the object relations view, the phobic person unconsciously wishes to be the center of a parent's attention and exclusive love ("Social Phobia," 1994). Since this is impossible, real or imagined rivals for the parent's attention become internalized (*introjected*) images, which are critical and threatening and must be appeased. For example, the child may come to imagine that the father is a rival for the mother's love from the child. Being internalized and therefore inescapable, the child's fear takes the form of excessive self-criticism. In order to reduce anxiety caused by these internalized images, the child focuses the fear on some external object that has a special, symbolic connection with the fear. The child then develops a specific phobia or generalized anxiety as a compromise way of expressing an unacceptable desire in a disguised form that does not stimulate ridicule or retaliation from others. In the example of social phobia, the unconscious fear of provoking the father's jealous rage is interpreted as being transferred to other people, so the child fears being independent or intimate with anyone, and avoids social contacts. Psychodynamic explanations of avoidant behavior continue to draw significant support, especially among practicing clinicians, although research validation is sparse.

SOCIAL LEARNING AND COGNITIVE APPROACHES

Cognitive social theory (formerly called social learning theory) emphasizes the role of modeling or *observational learning* in the development of fearful reactions. The child may never actually encounter a dreaded object such as a tiger or snake, but still comes to fear it mightily. Why? Social learning suggests that the child observes and imitates the fearful reactions of parents, other children, and even of television characters. People also may provide verbal instructions (e.g., "Stay away from that snake! Snakes are so slimy; I can't stand them!"), as well as physical cues such as grimacing, gesturing, or running away. Fears are most likely to be acquired through imitation or verbal instructions (Bandura, 1969). Ironically, children do not necessarily fear things that realistically could harm them. For example, children are much more likely to be hit by automobiles or to drown than to be bitten by a wolf or a snake. Yet they tend to fear snakes and wolves more than cars or bodies of water. Their parents must make special attempts to teach children realistic fears and help them counteract unrealistic ones.

PSYCHOSOCIAL TREATMENTS FOR PHOBIC REACTIONS

Psychoanalytic Treatment. Because psychoanalysts do not view the phobic behavior itself as the child's central problem, they do not advocate treatments based on encounters with feared situations. Rather, the child is encouraged to act out fears and fantasies in play within the warm, accepting atmosphere of the play sessions. The analyst interprets the underlying meaning of the child's fantasies, play themes, and dreams. During the analysis, the child's troubling unconscious feelings are transferred from the parents to the analyst and re-experienced as intense rage or love of the analyst within the safe treatment environment. In treating older, more cognitively mature children and adolescents, the analyst points out the importance and meaning of the transference, which helps the patient to understand and overcome past relationship problems.

Heinecke (1989) offered the example of a young boy named John, who became furious at his mother for being late, making him late for his therapy appointment, thus failing to protect him as he believed a mother should. John's anger was repeated in his relationship with his therapist when the therapist too was a few minutes late. At first, John said it didn't matter and he didn't want to discuss it, but he then began to throw balls at the therapist and a plant in the office provocatively. He seemed to want to communicate some message to the therapist that he could not describe in words. Later, in his free play, John pretended there were two ferocious catlike animals that threatened to destroy each other, which prompted the therapist to interpret John's resistance and the underlying anger as follows: "It is very difficult for you to let me know how angry you were at being kept waiting because your anger might really destroy me and I would in turn destroy you." John: "No, no, no. Let's get on with the game." This type of interpretive therapeutic interchange is thought to free patients from the parental introjections responsible for their incapacitating feelings of guilt and shame. The child's phobic reaction is expected to disappear without specific intervention when his basic psychological conflicts have been resolved and his troublesome misconceptions have been corrected through the analyst's interpretations.

The parent's role is limited to supplying information pertinent to the child's problem, but which the child may be unwilling or unable to discuss. Most parents are con

currently in analysis themselves with another therapist, so treatment of parent and child proceeds in parallel and both may improve together.

Critique of Psychodynamic Treatment. Psychodynamic treatment, either psychoanalysis or analytic play therapy, is very expensive and time consuming, sometimes requiring two or more years of individual treatment sessions (Sterba, 1959), which makes it prohibitively expensive for most families. There have been a number of case reports of successful psychoanalytic treatment of children with phobias, but, as noted in Chapter 3, by themselves, uncontrolled case studies do not provide scientifically accepted evidence of treatment success.

Desensitization and Participant Modeling Therapies. Learning-based methods for treating fear reactions include *systematic desensitization* and *modeling*. Systematic desensitization was first developed for use with phobic adults (Wolpe, 1958) and later adapted for use with adolescents and children (Kendall et al., 1992). The client first is helped to construct a *hierarchy* ranking his fears from the least to the more severe. For example, a mild-intensity fear item for a test-anxious child might be, "You hear about a friend who has a test soon," and the most intense fear item might be, "You are taking a test and you don't remember any of the answers and you know you won't be able to finish in the amount of time left." Then the therapist teaches the client a set of exercises to deeply relax the different muscle groups throughout the body. The *relaxation* is used to counteract the muscular tension associated with fear and anxiety since it is impossible to be tense and anxious and yet relaxed at the same time. Various clever methods have been worked out to teach children how to relax, including training in following simple instructions (e.g., "Stand up and sit down."), playing the child's favorite music, and using bubble-blowing to induce deep breathing (Morris & Kratochwill, 1983). Nevertheless, some children cannot be induced to relax, and others may be unable to conjure up the needed mental images from the hierarchy when instructed to do so. Ideally, the client first imagines the least potent of his fears (e.g., seeing a picture of a classroom) while relaxing his body completely. Then he is helped to imagine increasingly frightening scenes while maintaining a state of relaxation. At the conclusion of treatment, the client should be able to maintain relaxation even while contemplating the most intimidating situations and should be equally calm while encountering these situations in person. Although the imaginal or systematic desensitization procedures have successfully treated adults, there is only mixed research evidence for their effectiveness as the sole form of intervention in the treatment of younger children's fears (Morris & Kratochwill, 1983).

Because children have trouble in imagining fear-provoking situations on cue, they may respond better to *in vivo desensitization*, in which they practice relaxation in the actual situation they fear. All desensitization takes place in gradual steps. For example, the child who fears some aspect of the school might first be brought to the school building while school is not in session, then might visit the building for a few minutes during her favorite school activity, and finally would be able to maintain relaxation during an actual school day. One study found that water phobic children between the ages of 3 and 8 years benefitted more from actual exposure to the water than from vicarious exposure in a systematic desensitization procedure (Menzies & Clarke, 1993). In addition, the in vivo exposure treatment effects were maintained over a three-month period. However, neither systematic desensitization nor in vivo desensitization teach the child how to deal with the situations or objects she fears. Because children so often do lack needed social, athletic, or cognitive skills, they may require treatment other than desensitization.

Guided Participation. This is a very effective method for treating some types of children's specific fears and phobias (Kendall et al., 1992; Rosenthal & Bandura, 1978). In this treatment approach, one or more models demonstrate increasingly more direct and bolder encounters with whatever the child fears. The child can see that there are no untoward results for the models and there is nothing to fear. Moreover, the child learns effective methods for dealing with the dogs, snakes, injections, or other dreaded stimuli. This treatment method is particularly effective when a variety of adult and child models participate and they encounter and overcome several different examples of the feared stimulus (Bandura, Blanchard, & Ritter, 1969; Bandura & Menlove, 1968). To illustrate, two adults and three children might act as models and demonstrate how various people interact with dogs of three different breeds. Modeling displays can conveniently and effectively be presented on film or videotape, making it unnecessary to assemble a large cast of models

and snakes, dogs, medical personnel, thunderstorms, or whatever is needed in the child's treatment.

In guided participation, the fearful child engages in carefully supervised confrontations with the feared situations in a natural context, with gradually increasing performance requirements. For example, after viewing fearless models, snake avoidant children are required to touch the arm of a person who is petting a nonpoisonous snake, to stroke the snake with gloved hands, and finally to lift and handle the reptile (Ritter, 1968). Unlike other forms of therapy, the modeling and desensitization therapies require only approximately 4½ hours of treatment over a series of about four sessions (Gelfand, 1978). Guided participation has been employed mostly with younger children who have highly focused phobias. More evidence is needed concerning stimulus-exposure treatments' effectiveness in relieving other, less focused types of fears and anxieties, for example, fear of social situations, and social and academic evaluation (King, 1993).

Multifaceted Cognitive Behavioral Treatments. Fear and anxiety disorders are not simple phenomena, and complex psychological treatments for them may be required. Kendall's (1993, 1995; Kendall & Southam-Gerow, 1995) multifaceted cognitive behavioral treatment for children is remarkably effective in overcoming children's anxiety disorders. The treatment includes cognitive techniques, such as modifying the child's anxious self-talk (e.g., "I'm helpless, I'm going to throw up or run away and make a fool of myself if I have to go into the swimming pool.") and teaching problem-solving and behavioral strategies, including graded exposure to fear situations, practice in evaluating potentially threatening situations, and reward for successful efforts. The children first participated in graduated imaginal exposure (desensitization) and in vivo exposure to previously avoided situations. Then active interventions to overcome anxious ruminations and develop adequate coping repertoires in the avoided situation are introduced. In problem-solving training, the child is helped to devise appropriate plans for confronting the feared situation, such as recognizing that an unfamiliar teacher will not hurt her, making eye contact with the person, and saying hello. When a situation is no longer perceived as dangerous and fear-provoking, the child is free to act constructively and more effectively. After the treatment, 64 percent of the children in one study no longer met diagnostic criteria for anxiety disorder (Kendall, 1993).

Drug Treatments. Certain classes of drugs have proven to be quite useful in reducing anxiety in adults. The benzodiazepines, usually alprazolam (Xanax) or clonazapam (Klonopin), are prescribed to provide short-term anxiety relief and thus boost the effectiveness of psychotherapy for adults and younger clients, although research support for their use with children is lacking (Kaplan & Hussain, 1995). Other drugs are also used to reduce anxiety. Competitive athletes, anxious student test-takers, and performing musicians may ingest beta-blockers such as propranolol (Inderal), atenolol, nadolol, or timolol, which block the action of the hormone epinephrine (adrenaline) and the neurotransmitter norepinephrine. This suppresses the sympathetic nervous system, which governs fight and flight reactions, and interrupts the anxiety cycle that begins with the person's perception of a pounding heart and cold, shaky hands. With these frightening physical reactions removed, athletes may improve in their fine motor coordination and other aspects of their performance ("Social Phobia," November, 1994). It is not yet established whether these drugs can be used safely and effectively with anxious or phobic children, although some physicians are prescribing them for children.

POSTTRAUMATIC STRESS DISORDER

Devastating events can leave their mark on a child's psychological adjustment. Such events may include experiencing or witnessing others experience severe accidents, assaults, natural catastrophes, or life-threatening illnesses. However, in most natural disasters, only a minority of child victims meet diagnostic criteria for posttraumatic stress disorder (Vogel & Vernberg, 1993). Catastrophic events affect people of all ages, but there may be some gender and developmental differences in reactions. For example, the DSM-IV (American Psychiatric Association, 1994) states that for children, sexually traumatic events can include age-inappropriate sexual experiences without involving either threatened or actual physical injury. Girls report more posttraumatic stress disorder and general psychiatric symptoms, including anxiety and depression, than boys (Vogel & Vernberg, 1993).

Posttraumatic stress disorder sometimes develops immediately, but may appear months or even years following the stressful event, and in children primary symptoms

Natural disasters such as hurricanes can leave children with phobias and generalized anxiety, even children who did not experience the disaster themselves, but only heard about it.

may include disorganized or agitated behavior. Characteristic symptoms include persistent reexperiencing or play reenactment of the traumatic event or avoidance of anything associated with it. Young children are likely to engage in repetitive play expressing some aspects of the traumatic situation, so young auto accident victims may repeatedly enact accidents with toy cars, and may have nightmares, but be unable to report their content. Children also may show difficulty in sleeping, irritability, attention problems, exaggerated startle responses, and become hypervigilant (American Psychiatric Association, 1994). Physical symptoms such as stomachaches and headaches may appear, and young children may regress to baby talk or forget their toilet training and become passive and clinging or defiant (Posttraumatic Stress Disorder: Part I, 1996).

Psychologists have just begun to study children's coping styles in dealing with highly stressful events. One group of researchers (Weisenberg, Schwarzwald, Waysman, Solomon, & Klingman, 1993) found that when under enemy missile attack during the Persian Gulf war, Israeli children who engaged in distraction and avoidance activities ("I talked to the others," "I thought of things not connected to the situation.") were less likely to

---

BOX 7-1   A CASE OF POSTTRAUMATIC STRESS DISORDER IN A YOUNG GIRL

Gail was a healthy, happy 5-year-old before her family's house was engulfed in flames one night. Everyone was asleep, and Gail's mom received second degree burns over much of her body as she just managed to carry her daughter to safety. Her older brother could not escape and died in the fire. Gail's father was away on a business trip at the time.

Gail responded well to medical treatment after the fire, although she couldn't stay in her bed at night and insisted on sleeping with her parents. In fact, she slept very little and had nightmares about monsters when she did get to sleep. Everyone expected Gail to recover emotionally as her mother's burns healed and the family coped with their grief over her brother's death, but 3 months later, Gail had developed severe separation anxiety. She could not tolerate being left alone, even for short periods of time, but was also defiant with her parents and hyperactive. She was fascinated by flames from candles and matches, and would stare at them, while maintaining a rigid posture, until someone extinguished them. Her pediatrician checked her headaches and frequent stomachaches, which prevented her from eating much, but found no physical basis. Gail no longer appeared healthy and happy, and her parents sought psychological treatment for her.

Gail's therapist helped to speed her recovery through modeling appropriate safety procedures in the detection and safe handling of fires, so Gail could gain a sense of mastery and learn coping methods. Gail was also helped to observe candle and match flames and fireplace fires through gradual exposure and relaxation training, and play therapy and coping self-talk were used to increase her feelings of self-efficacy and confidence. She may always have some emotional scars from the fire, but Gail is now a much less anxious, better adjusted child.

---

develop stress reactions than those whose coping was problem-focused ("I kept checking my gas mask," "I constantly checked to see if everyone was okay."). Also, older children tended to use more effective distraction activities than younger children, a developmental difference that was also observed in children involved in a major flood (Burke, Borus, & Burns, 1982). In contrast, child survivors of Hurricane Andrew (one of the worst natural disasters ever to strike the United States), who suffered more posttraumatic stress also reported more coping strategy use of *any* type, but particularly blame and anger directed at other people (Vernberg, La Greca, Silverman, & Prinstein, 1996).

The little research published on treatment of children exposed to disasters indicates that they profit from support from teachers and classmates (Vernberg et al., 1996) and small group discussions led by mental health professionals (Weisenberg et al., 1993). Depending on the circumstances and level of trauma, family therapy, cognitive-behavioral therapy, or play therapy may be used (Vernberg & Vogel, 1993). Box 7-1 describes posttraumatic stress disorder in a young child.

OBSESSIVE-COMPULSIVE DISORDER

Obsessions and compulsions are abnormal thoughts, images, or impulses (obsessions) or repetitive acts (com-

pulsions) that: (1) are unrealistic and dysfunctional, (2) are experienced as unwelcome but irresistible, (3) are experienced as products of one's own mind rather than external in origin, (4) are ritualistic and stereotyped, and (5) are time-consuming (take more than one hour each day) and disrupt everyday activities (DSM-IV, American Psychiatric Association, 1994; Rachman & Hodgson, 1980). *Obsessions* are recurring thoughts, doubts, or fears that the person cannot repress despite their unpleasant nature. Typical obsessive themes of school-age children involve aggression, contamination by contact with supposedly unclean objects, and maintaining order (Clarizio, 1991). Obsessions are neither realistic nor constructive and may even prevent the person from engaging in effective problem-solving. In contrast, *compulsions* are repetitive acts that the person feels forced to carry out over and over again. Both children and adults are more likely to engage in rituals at home than in public and keep their ritualistic behaviors hidden, so some authorities believe that this disorder may be as much as 20 to 40 times more common in youth than officially estimated (Clarizio, 1991).

In order to be diagnosed with obsessive-compulsive disorder, either obsessions or compulsions or both must be present and must constitute the person's major psychological problem (DSM-IV, American Psychiatric Association, 1994; Rachman & Hodgson, 1980). Some young children develop compulsions without obsessions. Constituting less than 2.1 percent of psychiatric referrals

---

BOX 7-2   BRIAN: A BOY WITH OBSESSIVE-COMPULSIVE DISORDER

Other mothers sometimes congratulated her on how neat, obedient, and diligent her Brian was, but Amanda knew there was a problem. Her 12-year-old son had developed an alarming repertoire of head and shoulder movements, a kind of shrugging and head wagging that he repeated over and over again, and she knew that he was desperately afraid of failing in school despite earning good grades. Sometimes he would perform some little routine many times, and seem to be unable to stop. She was frankly worried, but hoped that with time he would grow out of it. Meanwhile, she reassured him nearly every day that everything was okay, but it never reassured him. He didn't seem to trust his parents, telephoned them repeatedly when they went out to dinner, and checked on their whereabouts all the time when the family was at home.

Amanda would have become even more upset if she had known what Brian was thinking. His obsessions were numerous, and he lost sleep because he couldn't stop worrying about failing in school, making a fool of himself, or harming his family. Some of his compulsive routines came from his feelings that his parents would be harmed if he did not continue some action. So he would continue tapping his foot in order to ward off catastrophe or continue arranging objects on his desk until his feelings of panic subsided. The specter of school failure also tortured him, and he was spending longer and longer getting less homework done because his compulsive routines took so much time and attention.

A child such as Brian might benefit from cognitive-behavioral therapy (McCarthy & Foa, 1988). As described in this chapter and Chapter 14, cognitive behavior therapy includes many elements. Family and teachers withhold reinforcing reassurance and attention for inappropriate compulsive behavior. The child is taught relaxation as an alternative response to anxious thoughts and is gradually helped to imagine and enter increasingly anxiety-provoking situations (exposure), but is helped to resist the temptation to engage in the stereotyped routines by the therapist, parents, and teachers. Knowledge about the efficacy of such treatments for children is scarce as yet, but this treatment approach has proved effective with adults.

SOURCE: McCarthy, P. R., & Foa, E. B. (1988). Obsessive-compulsive disorders. In M. Hersen & C. Last (Eds.), *Child behavior therapy casebook* (pp. 55–69). New York: Plenum.

---

for adults (American Psychiatric Association, 1994), obsessive-compulsive disorders have a 2 percent lifetime prevalence in children and adolescents (McGough, Speier, & Cantwell, 1993). Thus, most obsessive-compulsive disorders originate before adulthood. Most very young children insist on certain rituals, which apparently reassure them and provide a sense of security, for example, a familiar bedtime routine of being sung to or read to from familiar books, or a favorite stuffed animal or ragged old security blanket to hug while going to sleep. In contrast to these normal rituals of childhood, pathological obsessive-compulsive behavior often is aimed to reduce severe anxiety and involves unusual activities such as repeated hand washing, bathing, and cleaning already spotless surroundings, as described in Box 7-2. Also, most childhood rituals are dropped naturally as the child becomes older, while obsessive-compulsive routines are more likely to appear in adolescence and young adulthood and persist, accompanied by phobic behaviors. When assessed between two and seven years after they were first diagnosed, 43 percent of one group of children and adolescents still had obsessive-compulsive disorders, and only 6 percent were judged to be markedly improved despite receiving multiple treatments (Swedo, Lenanare,

Rettew, Hamburger, Bartko, & Rapoport, 1993). Compulsive children are particularly likely to engage in rituals involving washing (Rapoport, Swedo, & Leonard, 1992), and may also repeatedly order objects in a particular arrangement, or check on the presence and location of certain objects over and over again. These children may also develop phobias, depression, and neurologic disorders such as Tourette's disorder. In fact, obsessions more often accompany other problems such as depression or phobias than occur alone. This has led some authors to question whether obsessive-compulsive behaviors truly constitute a separate diagnostic entity or are merely one of many alternative expressions of anxiety (Rutter & Garmezy, 1983). Obsessions are likely to persist throughout adulthood (Zeitlin, 1982).

Etiology of Obsessive-Compulsive Disorder

For many years *psychoanalytic theory* provided the generally accepted explanation of this disorder. Maladaptive thoughts and rituals were thought to be caused by anxiety resulting from unconscious psychological conflict. Compulsions were seen as avoidance maneuvers engaged in to reduce anxiety and magically prevent some dread event such as the death of a parent. In the psychoanalytic view, performing the compulsive ritual is imagined by the patient to prevent the occurrence of a threatening event and produces some relief from anxiety. The compulsive act is construed as the child's attempt to control unconscious hostility toward others, particularly the parents (Breuer & Freud, 1955/1925).

More recent *learning-based explanations* stress that compulsive behavior can arise from various sources and can be continued for many different reasons. Factors other than anxiety might contribute to compulsive actions. Children with severe mental retardation may engage in stereotyped movements that draw the reinforcing attention of other people, whether the attention is positive or negative in tone. In some cases, seemingly compulsive behavior is actually maintained by its sensory consequences—the sounds or visual stimulation it produces. One study (Rincover, Newsom, & Carr, 1979) revealed that some children with severe mental retardation or pervasive developmental disorders repeatedly switched the room lights on and off, simply for the sensory stimulation provided by the clicks of the light switch and changes in room illumination. Although the light switching was ritualized and persistent it probably did not constitute true obsessive-compulsive behavior because crucial features of the disorder were missing, such as anxiety if the act was interrupted, hypochondriacal concern, and excessive guilt.

Treatment of Obsessive-Compulsive Disorder

In *behaviorally oriented therapies*, obsessive-compulsive adults have overcome their compulsive behavior through *imagined exposure* to anxiety provoking events followed by *guided, prolonged exposure to the feared stimulus* (Foa, Steketee, & Milby, 1980). Treatment may also take the form of *physical prevention of compulsions* such as excessive hand washing or other ritualistic behavior (Mills, Agras, Barlow, & Mills, 1975; Walton & Mather, 1963). A compulsive hand-washer is instructed to refrain from the ritualistic behavior throughout a three-week treatment period. Contact with water or other cleaning agents is prohibited, except for a 10-minute shower every fifth day, and the process is closely supervised by family members (McCarthy & Foa, 1988). Alternatively, the water

may be turned off, making the ritual impossible to perform. A compulsive object arranger might be deprived of objects to manipulate. Adult and adolescent clients can knowingly agree to these relatively restrictive treatment conditions. It is not yet clear how physical interference or prevention measures should be used with children. Here again there is much to be learned through research.

DRUG TREATMENT AND COMPREHENSIVE MANAGEMENT

At present, obsessive-compulsive disorder is one of the few types of anxiety disorders in children or adolescents for which drugs have been found to be useful. Both clomipramine (Anafranil) and fluoxetine (Prozac) have been found to help reduce compulsive and obsessive behaviors (McGough, Speier, & Cantwell, 1993; Popper, 1993). Some clinicians recommend *comprehensive management* of children's obsessive-compulsive disorders, including behavioral interventions such as cognitive therapy or in vivo desensitization, family support, and medication (McGough et al., 1993). Others caution that because of the danger of harmful physical effects, most drug treatments for children remain experimental and understudied and should be used only after psychological therapies have been tried and failed (Kaplan & Hussain, 1995; Thyer, 1991).

> *"It can be argued that the development of pharmacological interventions is on the cutting edge of research in the treatment of childhood disorders."* (Pelham, 1993)

DEPRESSION IN CHILDREN AND ADOLESCENTS

Depression is one of the most common psychological disorders of adulthood and is multifaceted in both symptoms and etiology. Depression can strike anytime between early childhood and old age, can endure for years, or disappear within months, and depressive episodes may be frequent or only very occasional. In addition to major depression, there are milder forms. *Minor depression* or *subclinical depression*, in which the person feels and appears depressed, but fails to meet all diagnostic criteria for major depression, and *dysthymia* (chronic dysphoric mood for most of the time over two years or more) are more common than major depression. Depression is very rare in early childhood and begins to assume adult prevalence in the middle to late teens and early twenties. Dysthymia may continue for years and may appear with episodes of major depression in a condition termed "double depression." Minor depression typically occurs in reaction to stressful events such as the termination of a relationship or a marriage, the death of a loved one, an illness, or serious financial difficulties. However, clinically significant depression occurs when the person's depressed emotions are devastating, unshakable, out of proportion to the situation, and the person becomes hopeless, despondent, and sometimes nonfunctional. Major depression may follow an identifiable loss or severe stress, as in rejection by a loved one or the loss of a close friend or family member, but there also may be no obvious external precipitating event. The type of mood disorder may vary also; in a *major depressive episode* or *major depressive disorder*, only depression is experienced. In contrast, in *bipolar disorders*, depressive episodes and hyperexcited manic episodes may alternate, with mania usually preceding a plunge into depression. Manic states are characterized by inexplicable exhilaration, greatly increased activity with apparent tirelessness, sleeplessness, impulsivity, irritability, and grandiose, unrealistic thoughts and plans. Bipolar affective disorder, which is sometimes referred to as manic-depressive disorder, rarely occurs in childhood.

Depressive Symptoms

Older teenagers and adults are diagnosed with major depressive episode or disorder when they have severely depressed mood or very diminished interest or pleasure in their usual activities over at least a two-week period, and show a pattern of other problems such as inexplicable, marked appetite or weight change, either insomnia or prolonged sleeping, changed physical activity acceleration or deceleration, marked fatigue, inappropriate feelings of guilt or worthlessness, indecisiveness or inability to concentrate, or unwelcome, recurring thoughts of death or suicide. Any one or several of these symptoms in mild form or temporarily do not constitute depression, and depression itself can range from mild to totally debilitating. Depression adversely affects the person's social, cognitive, and physical functioning—in fact, all aspects of life—and is often accompanied by social relationship difficulties and loss of friends. A formerly competent, decisive person may become hesitant, confused, troubled, avoidant, and unable to make simple decisions. Depressed children and teens resemble depressed adults in many, but not all ways. Table 7-2 presents some of the features of the juvenile forms of depression. For adults, among the most characteristic signs of depression are complaints about one's deficiencies, excessive self-reproach for imagined wrongs, and an unrealistically pessimistic view of self and of life. In extreme cases, the person may become actively suicidal. Dysphoric or sad

TABLE 7-2 DEPRESSIVE BEHAVIORS IN CHILDREN AND ADOLESCENTS

Age Group	Depressive Behaviors
Infants	sadness, weeping, apathy, motor retardation, failure to thrive, vomiting, irritability, developmental delays, feeding or sleeping difficulties
Toddlers and preschoolers	irritability, social withdrawal, negative self-image, peer problems, anxiety, phobias, weeping, loss of interest/pleasure in usual activities (anhedonia), loss of appetite, sleep disturbances, changed activity rates, desire to die, somatic disorders including enuresis, encopresis, asthma, eczema, failure to thrive, aggression, self-endangering behavior
Schoolchildren	irritability, anhedonia, fatigue, somatic complaints, sleeping and eating disturbances, changed activity rates, suicidal thoughts, guilt, low self-esteem, sudden schoolwork problems, aggression, decreased ability to concentrate, phobias, anxiety, separation anxiety problems, depressed facial expression
Adolescents	disturbed sleep, appetite or weight changes, changed activity rates, fatigue, anhedonia, self-devaluation, difficulty in concentrating, indecisiveness, suicidal thoughts or attempts, anxiety, phobias, somatic disorders, excessive emotional dependency, withdrawal, reckless behavior

SOURCES: *Diagnostic and statistical manual of mental disorders* (4th ed.). (1994). Washington, DC: American Psychiatric Association; Herzog, D. B., & Rathbun, J. M. (1982). Childhood depression: Developmental considerations. *American Journal of Diseases of Children, 136,* 115–120; Nottelmann, E. D., & Jensen, P. S. (1995). Comorbidity in children and adolescents: Developmental perspectives. In T. Ollendick & R. Prinz (Eds.). *Advances in clinical child psychology* (Vol. 17, pp. 109–156). New York: Plenum Press; Poznanski, E., Mokros, H., Grossman, J., & Freeman, L. (1985). Diagnostic criteria in childhood depression. *American Journal of Psychiatry, 142,* 1168–1173.

mood, general pessimism, extreme self-criticism, inability to enjoy oneself, and physical complaints about energy loss, and appetite and sleeping problems are all aspects of depression in adults and older adolescents.

Depression in Childhood

The official American Psychiatric Association DSM-IV diagnostic scheme contains no separate category for childhood depression, and, with minor alterations, adult affective disorder criteria are used for children. However, children are much less able to recognize and report their emotions than are adults, so they do not complain about feeling depressed, which is a major indicator of depressive disorder. Adopting the official DSM-IV adult diagnostic criteria yields extremely low rates of major affective disorder in children younger than 6, while depression rates rise during middle childhood and reach adult levels by the late teens. The rate of affective disorder doubles from the ages of 3 through 4 years to 10 through 14 years, when it is 1.7 percent, and increases further to 7.6 percent among 18- to 19-year-olds (American Psychiatric Association, 1994). In a large representative sample of high school students, 2.9 percent met diagnostic criteria for current major depressive disorder or dysthymia, and 20.4 percent, or over 1 in 5, had been depressed at some time during their lives (Lewinsohn & Rohde, 1993). In adolescence, depression frequently accompanies other mental disorders, especially anxiety disorders and conduct disorder (Cole & Carpentieri, 1990). Depression is not just a transitory problem, and relapse rates are high (18.4 percent) for teenagers with major depressive disorders (Lewinsohn, Rohde, & Seeley, 1993).

ASSESSMENT

Improved measures of childhood depression make the condition's diagnosis easier. For example, the Children's Depression Inventory (Kovacs & Beck, 1977), a self-report questionnaire adapted from the much-used Beck Depression Inventory for Adults, is useful in research and clinical practice, as is the Reynolds Child Depression Scale (Reynolds, & Graves, 1989). The Achenbach Child Behavior Checklist (CBCL; Achenbach & Edelbrock, 1978), which also measures depression, is one of the most frequently used tests of child psychopathology and is available in versions to be completed by the parent, teacher, and the child. Clinical researchers frequently em-

ploy the Kiddie-SADS, a children's version of the standard adult interview for research, the SADS, or Schedule of Affective Disorder and Schizophrenia (Endicott & Spitzer, 1978), and other standardized interviews including the Children's Assessment Scale also assess childhood depression. Children can validly report their depressive symptoms using these measures and show high levels of agreement with parents' ratings of the children's depression (Romano & Nelson, 1988).

These measures have revealed higher rates of depression among children than had been previously suspected. Nevertheless, even when the same diagnostic techniques are used over the years, the rates of child and adolescent affective disorder appear to be increasing (Ryan, Williamson, Iyengar, Orvaschel, Reich, Dahl, & Puig-Antich, 1992).

SEX DIFFERENCES IN DEPRESSION

Approximately twice as many women (10 to 25 percent) as men (5 to 12 percent) suffer from major depression over their lifetime (American Psychiatric Association, 1994). Yet during childhood, slightly more boys than girls are diagnosed with mood disorders. By the mid-teens, the sex ratio in depression more closely approximates the twice greater female rate in adulthood. The gender difference in susceptibility to depression seems to emerge around the age of 13 (Lewinsohn & Rohde, 1993). The reasons for the contrasting child and adult gender differences in depression are unknown at present, but both the hormonal and other physical changes of puberty and the social roles of females and males have been suggested as possible causes of the large preponderance of depressed women.

PROGNOSIS

The research results are only tentative at present, but children's depression seems to be relatively persistent and may increase in severity over time. In one study, a remarkably high percentage (69 percent) of a group of clinic children with milder, more chronic dysthymic affective disorder developed a more serious major depressive disorder within five years (Kovacs, Feinberg, & Crouse-Novak, 1984). The long-term prognosis probably depends upon the type and severity of illness, and on family factors such as family disruption, parental marital discord, and parental psychopathology, particularly the mother's depression. One study (Welner, Welner, &

TABLE 7-3 MAJOR PSYCHOSOCIAL THEORIES OF DEPRESSION

Theory	Predisposing Event	Precipitating Event
Psychodynamic	Constitutional overreliance on oral stimulation	Real or imagined loss or rejection
Attachment	Attachment insecurity, early loss	Major loss or rejection
Beck's cognitive theory	Early rejection, loss, or failure	Major loss or disappointment
Reinforcement loss theory	No necessary predisposition	Massive reduction in reinforcement
Learned helplessness	Unavoidable pain or failure	Major loss or traumatic event

Fishman, 1979) found that one-third of a small sample of adolescents who were hospitalized with unipolar depression recovered completely and without further recurrences, while two-thirds either stayed ill or worsened. Those with bipolar reactions typically are more seriously incapacitated and almost all continue to be disturbed. It would be accurate to say that juvenile depression is rare, but seriously incapacitating.

Theories of Depression

HISTORICAL BACKGROUND

Until the past 20 years, most clinicians did not recognize the possibility that children might become depressed. This attitude can be traced to the commanding influence of psychoanalytic theory in the first half of the 20th century. The psychoanalytic view was that children are too psychologically immature to develop depression (Mahler, 1979). Perhaps since the prevailing theory denied the existence of childhood depression, clinicians failed to observe it. Taking a slightly different view, some later clinicians argued that rather than developing depressive symptoms, children had "masked depression," consisting of a wide variety of problems, ranging from hyperactivity to phobias (Cytryn & McKnew, 1974). However, the concept of masked depression proved clinically unhelpful since it was ill-defined and overinclusive. Finally, in view of the mounting volume of clinical accounts of child depression, the American Psychiatric Association recognized depression in children, provided that the adult diagnostic criteria were met (DSM-III, 1980). In recent years, research evidence of developmental changes in depressive symptoms have been incorporated into the DSM criteria (American Psychiatric Association, 1994).

PSYCHOANALYTIC AND ATTACHMENT THEORIES

The early work of Sigmund Freud (1965/1917) and of his colleague Karl Abraham (1966) portrayed adult depression as originating with a constitutional predisposition toward overreliance on oral stimulation as the source of pleasure and reassurance (see Table 7-3, which contrasts the major theories of depression). The person with such a predisposition would develop excessive needs for physical contact, touching and reassurance (Malmquist, 1977). The child would have unusually strong needs for love and affection, making him highly vulnerable to any form of real or perceived rejection. Events such as the birth of a sibling, experiencing harsh weaning methods, or more subtle forms of loss of love and attention from parents could constitute traumatic events and leave a psychological scar. Some blow to self-esteem later in life rekindles the basic conflict that is manifested in depression.

The psychoanalytic explanation of depression has had many proponents, but is very difficult to verify. Private mental events that took place early in childhood are proposed to play a causal role in later depressive reactions, but memories are inexact. It is possible that subtle suggestions from psychoanalysts unintentionally influence their patients' reports of their early experiences. When there is so much opportunity for memory failure and distortions, patients' recollections may prove unreliable indicators of the causes of depression. However, other theories of depression also rely heavily on the patients' reconstructions of early childhood events, and so most theories are difficult to verify.

"Despite its scientific and other imperfections, psychoanalysis provides us with access to deep and often dark layers of personality that are not confronted by other psychological disciplines." (Reiser, 1994)

Attachment theory is a modern-day descendant of psychoanalytic theory, which views experiences occurring very early in life, within the first or second year, as primary determinants of later personality. As initially formulated by Bowlby (1969/1982), attachment theory portrays infants as experiencing severe anxiety if faced with a major separation from their primary caregiver. The separation could be the physical removal of the caretaker or the psychological removal, as when the caretaker becomes clinically depressed and unresponsive or preoccupied with the birth of another child. An intense mourning process follows, which could persist, reflecting an unresolved loss. As a result, the child cannot form a secure, internalized *working model* or mental representation of the major attachment figure to serve as a buffer against psychological devastation experienced when a loss occurs in the future. Working models consist of a person's conscious and unconscious mental representations of others in relation to the self as used to perceive happenings, form expectations of the future, and construct plans for conduct. The internal working model allows the child to form expectations about how others will behave and how lovable, worthy, and competent the self is. Without a healthy internal working model to serve as reassurance, the prolonged absence or psychological unavailability of the parent can lead the child to believe that attachment figures are unreliable and the self is unlovable. The child believes himself or herself to be unworthy of love, rejected, and an emotional orphan. Early experiences of loss and attachment insecurity may form the person's fundamental response patterns and predispose her to the development of depression when other types of loss occur (Ciccetti, Toth, & Lynch, 1995).

BECK'S COGNITIVE THEORY

Disordered thinking is also an important factor in cognitive theories of depression, but unlike the psychoanalysts, the cognitive theorists place no emphasis on unconscious conflict. Early experiences are thought to be important in both types of theories. In Beck's (1974) cognitive theory of depression, the individual is predisposed toward depression by early rejection, by the loss of a parent, or by his own unrealistic and perfectionistic self-expectations.

Beck believes that in later life, depressive reactions may be triggered in cognitively vulnerable individuals by stressful events such as another major loss or disappointment. The depression-prone person mistakenly blames the loss on some personal shortcoming and becomes convinced that she is unlovable, incompetent, and unworthy. Kovacs and Beck (1977) described a *cognitive triad* of distorted depressive thinking regarding: (1) oneself, (2) the situation, and (3) the future. Depressed individuals believe that they suffer from some type of basic defect or character flaw which causes people to reject them. At the same time, they view others as making tremendous, impossible demands on them. They conclude that the situation is their own fault, cannot be improved, and that the future is hopeless. Beck maintains that the disordered and distorted thinking typical of depression can be found in children as well as in adults. As Beck predicted, children diagnosed with depression are likely to have negative schemata or cognitions about the self, the world, and the future as a result of negative evaluations and rejection from parents who overuse punitive parenting procedures (Stark, Humphrey, Laurent, Livingston, & Christopher, 1993). Thus, early loss of various types can predispose children to depression. Nonetheless, most children with adverse, stressful family situations do not develop depression. More information is needed about the various types of factors that produce depression, including possible genetic or constitutional factors, environmental stresses, and personality characteristics.

LEARNING THEORIES

Some explanations emphasize the importance of learning in the production of depressed behavior. The *reinforcement loss* approach maintains that severe reduction of predictable, earned positive reinforcement can produce depressed behavior (Ferster, 1974; Lewinsohn, 1974). Examples are a high school graduate who enters college but is unable to achieve the good grades that had previously reinforced and maintained studying or a child who loses a stressed parent's reinforcing attention or who is separated from a parent who provided the child's major source of positive reinforcement. The significant loss of reinforcement for these individuals may ultimately lead to apathy and depressed affect. Their complaints about feelings of worthlessness, guilt, and suicidal talk may elicit at least temporary reinforcing attention and concern from others.

Lewinsohn and his associates (Lewinsohn, 1974; Lewinsohn, Hops, Roberts et al., 1993) have demonstrated that depressed people are socially awkward and inept.

They avoid others, don't initiate conversation, and respond minimally to others' attempts to initiate interactions, which leads other people to avoid them, thus intensifying their isolation. In Lewinsohn's view, depressed people first suffer extinction, or near total loss of reinforcement for their efforts. Consequently, they display emotional outbursts at first and ultimately become passive and withdrawn. Only changed behavior such as seeking new sources of reinforcement or reestablishing familiar ones, can terminate the depressive reaction. Problems of the reinforcement explanation are that it is not always possible to identify major losses of reinforcement preceding depressive episodes, and that drug treatments restore normal social functioning for many depressed people without provision of a reinforcement-rich environment.

A second learning-based approach to depression is Seligman's (1975) theory of *learned helplessness*. This model portrays early learning of helpless reactions to unavoidable stress as the original cause of depression. Seligman first observed that laboratory animals that had earlier encountered unavoidable shock later could not learn to escape when avoidance was possible. The inescapable shock had apparently interfered with adaptive responding causing a reaction Seligman termed learned helplessness. Similar reactions have been demonstrated in a much less extreme form in children who have encountered unsolvable problems (Dweck, 1977). Seligman reasoned that the passivity, helplessness, and hopelessness of depressed people might be analogous to the learned helplessness demonstrated in laboratory experiments (Abramson, Seligman, & Teasdale, 1978). People experience inescapable stress and uncontrollable tragedies, which might convince them that they cannot control their lives, so they give up helplessly.

The learned helplessness model may not apply well to human depression because, unlike major depression, learned helplessness spontaneously disappears within 72 hours of treatment and animals' "helpless" reaction of freezing does not require any learning, but appears to be an automatic, unconditioned response to inescapable aversive stimuli (Kaufman, 1994). At this point it is impossible to predict which children will become passive in stressful situations and which will resist. There are wide individual differences in how people respond to inescapable noxious events. No inescapable major stress is observable in the life histories of many depressed people, nor do detectable stressors necessarily diminish when they improve, which presents difficulties for Seligman's theory.

GENETIC, BRAIN, AND BIOCHEMICAL FACTORS IN DEPRESSION

Although it is widely believed that there is a hereditary component to depression, there is controversy about exactly what is inherited and through what mechanisms (Baron, Klotz, Mendlewica, & Rainer, 1981; Jakimow-Venulet, 1981; Rutter & Garmezy, 1983). Almost no family behavior genetic studies have focused on child or adolescent depression (Nurcombe, 1992), in part because official psychiatric recognition of the disorder is relatively recent, and a reliable diagnostic syndrome is a necessity for conducting this type of research. Nevertheless, one controlled study of the family history of adults who had prepubertal major depressive disorders, a nondepressive mental disorder, and normals reported that people who were diagnosed with a major depression before 20 years of age had higher rates of major depression, alcoholism, and other psychiatric disorders in first-degree relatives (Puig-Antich, Goetz, et al., 1989). Puig-Antich and colleagues suggested that family members' alcoholism stimulates depression in genetically vulnerable children. This finding of a family history of depression and alcoholism is only suggestive because the transmission could be all or partly psychological or environmental rather than genetic.

The advent of effective antidepressant medication suggested that at least some types of depression might have a biochemical basis and that there may be both receptor and neurotransmitter involvement in hormonal responses in depression. The *neurobehavioral systems approach* to childhood psychopathology attempts to combine neuroscience and ethological explanations of normal and disturbed behavior. Both genetic and environmental factors are studied to identify how and when they exert maximal influence during early development (Collins & Depue, 1992). The neurobehavioral systems model holds that there are biologically based sensitive periods in neural development during which biological and environmental influences interact to affect the emerging emotional and behavioral systems. During prenatal life, the genotype guides the development of the *behavioral facilitation system*, a generalized, nonspecific emotional system that is activated by rewarding stimuli.

The genotype determines the individual's number of dopamine cells (Collins & Depue, 1992), which affect the
intensity of a person's subjective emotional experience
related to rewards. In Collins and Depue's view, the
molding of the behavioral facilitation system through experiences at key stages of development, such as 8 to 18
months, may influence emotional circuitry. It is not
known how amenable these emotional structures are to
change in later life, and early experience could set the
stage for later mood disorders or emotional normality.
Although brain-behavior relationships are under intensive study, the neurobehavioral systems model and other
biosocial models of depression remain highly conjectural
as yet. "There may be multiple biochemical as well as
psychological pathways to depression" (McNeal & Cimbolic, 1986, p. 372).

Treatment of Depression

DRUG TREATMENTS

Antidepressant drugs are less effective for children and
adolescents than for adults. In fact, most authorities state
that antidepressant medications are no more effective
than placebos with childhood and teen depression. In
adults, lithium salts have been dramatically effective in
the treatment of bipolar affective disorders, and major
depression has been relieved through any of an array of
other drugs such as tricyclic antidepressants (primarily
imipramine or Tofranil and desipramine, Norpramin, or
Pertofrane), monoamine oxidase inhibitors (MAOIP),
and the newer selective serotonin reuptake inhibitors, including sertraline (Zoloft) and fluoxetine (Prozac). In
contrast, antidepressant drugs have at best produced
mixed results with children and adolescents, usually not
exceeding placebos (mock medications) in effects (Kaplan & Hussain, 1995; Reynolds, 1994), and some have
dangerous side effects. As yet, none has been clearly
found to be effective in treating child and adolescent depression, although the newer antidepressants (Prozac,
Zoloft, Paxsil, and Welbutrin) are seeing very widespread
use (Stark, Napolitano, Swearer et al., 1996). Tricyclic
antidepressants (the oldest and among the most frequently prescribed antidepressants for adults) are ineffective in treating depression in persons younger than 18
years (Ambrosini, Bianchi, Rabinovich, & Elia, 1993). An
additional drawback is that the tricyclic antidepressants
such as imipramine and desipramine can too easily prove
lethal for children if an overdose is misadministered or

if ingested in suicide attempts. The tricyclic antidepressants, though widely used to treat children's depression
anxieties, phobias, and enuresis, have caused children's
deaths at prescribed, therapeutic doses through cardiac
toxicity and alteration of electrochemical conduction
within heart muscle. Great care must be taken to assess
young patients' tolerance for tricyclic antidepressants and
supervise these drugs' use (Gadow, 1991). Despite their
inefficacy and possible danger, antidepressant drugs are
frequently prescribed for depressed children and adolescents (Jensen, Ryan, & Prien, 1992; Popper, 1992), perhaps because distressed families demand medication for
their depressed children.

Although results of pharmacological treatments for
juvenile depression thus far have been disappointing
(Ambrosini et al., 1993; Pelham, 1993), new medications
are being constantly developed. Adult depression defied
pharmacological treatment until the past few decades, so
there is hope of similar future progress for children and
adolescents. Nevertheless, at present the most promising,
safe, and effective interventions for children's mood disorders are the psychotherapies.

PSYCHOLOGICAL TREATMENTS

Psychotherapies vary in effectiveness in treating depressed children. Conversational nondirective or psychodynamic forms of therapy aimed at uncovering presumed
underlying psychological conflict are more difficult to
conduct with depressed children than depressed adults.
This is because young children may find it difficult or
impossible to understand and describe their feelings of
depression, anxiety, and concern. Various types of play
therapy (see Chapter 14) may be used to help depressed
youngsters, but surprisingly little information about play
therapy effectiveness has been published (Russ, 1995).
The most recent developments in child psychotherapy
have centered on more highly structured behavioral
approaches.

Some recent, well-conducted, controlled experiments
indicate that *cognitive-behavioral therapy* can help young
people to effectively manage their depression. As developed by Lewinsohn and colleagues (Clarke, Hops, Lewinsohn et al., 1992; Lewinsohn, Clarke, Hops, & Andrews,
1990), cognitive-behavioral intervention is conducted in
small groups of three to eight adolescents in 16 sessions
over an eight-week period. The treatment is designed to
reduce the adolescents' self-consciousness and feelings of
being different, so the intervention resembles a class in

which therapists teach adolescents skills to help them learn to control their depressed mood. Brief readings, structured learning tasks, short quizzes, and homework assignments are familiar and acceptable to them since these activities are not stigmatizing and resemble normal classroom routines. Course content emphasizes that depression results from life stress and that students will master new skills to deal more effectively with stress and gain control over their moods. Teen clients are informed that some of the skills taught, such as relaxation or self-control tactics, may not be useful to them personally, and they may select which techniques to use, because they know their situation the best. The intervention teaches adolescents how to relate to peers, how to increase the number and quality of enjoyable activities in their lives, how to set and how to achieve realistic goals for change. In addition, depressed teens are taught relaxation training, how to increase positive thoughts and decrease depressive thoughts, and basic problem-solving skills, which the teens and their parents may be instructed to practice together. Finally, the teens are taught how to avoid becoming depressed again, which is personalized for each adolescent's own situation.

The content of the teen depression course is research-based, and the results have been excellent. In two research studies, between 54 percent and 67 percent of the treated teenagers no longer met DSM criteria for an affective disorder as compared with only 5 percent to 48 percent of those in a wait-list control group, and they continued to improve in the months following the cognitive-behavioral treatment (Lewinsohn & Rohde, 1993). Individualized "booster" sessions are offered at four-month intervals over a two-year period in an attempt to prevent relapses, although these sessions did not reduce relapse rate. This work indicates the importance of basing therapies on psychological principles, adapting the intervention to the developmental characteristics of the client group, and rigorously assessing treatment outcomes.

PREVENTION

The cognitive-behavioral methods used to treat juvenile depression have also proven impressively effective in preventing depressive symptoms. One study (Gillham, Reivich, Jaycos, & Seligman, 1995) identified children who were at risk for future depression because of current depressive symptoms, parental conflict, or both. High risk children were trained in cognitive and social problem-solving skills. In the cognitive component, children were

taught to identify negative beliefs—for example, that no one liked them or that they were hopelessly stupid in school—to assess the accuracy of these beliefs. Then they were helped to generate more realistic alternatives, such as that others don't like them if they don't behave in a friendly fashion and that they can improve. In the problem-solving program, the children were taught to approach problems deliberately by thinking before acting, generating many possible solutions, and to carefully weigh the pros and cons of each option. Other skills they learned included techniques for coping with their parents' fighting, negotiation, assertiveness, and relaxation. Compared to a control group, the prevention group reported significantly fewer depressive symptoms through a two-year follow-up period, and the prevention effects grew larger over time. Moderate to severe symptoms were reduced by one-half. This successful program indicates that something can be done to reduce or prevent children's susceptibility to depression, which greatly improves their lives.

SUICIDE

Contrary to popular belief, children do make serious suicide attempts, some of which are fatal. Suicide is very rare in children younger than 12 years, but is the sixth leading cause of death among children between the ages of 5 and 14, and increases to become the third leading cause of death for 15- to 24-year-olds (Wilson, 1991). Suicide looms large as a cause of death in young people in part because they are generally very healthy and unlikely to die from disease. The death rate from suicide rises significantly in early adolescence beginning around the age of 14. Annually, about 3 percent of older adolescent girls and 1 percent of older adolescent boys make a serious suicide attempt (Clarke, 1993). Suicide rates increase regularly with increasing age throughout life, peaking among the elderly, who may be suffering from increasing disability or incurable disease. Suicide rates for youth are increasing, possibly partly because of physicians' greater alertness to the problem.

Characteristics of Suicidal Youth

Adolescents who attempt suicide have been studied (Lewinsohn, Rohde, & Seeley, 1993) and found to share a number of problems. Adolescents with the following features were more likely to attempt suicide: Adjustment problems, past psychiatric disorders, depressive thought patterns, inadequate coping styles, school or health problems, and past suicide attempts. Female adolescents had more risk factors, showed greater vulnerability to the risk factors, and were somewhat more likely to attempt suicide than male teenagers. The more risk factors a teenager had, the more probable was a suicide attempt (Lewinsohn et al., 1993).

In the adult population more women attempt suicide, but more men actually succeed in killing themselves, perhaps because men tend to use more lethal methods such as firearms. Women more commonly employ methods such as overdoses of prescription drugs, which act slowly, making a change of intention or rescue possible. Now, however, women are increasing their use of firearms in suicide attempts.

Suicide methods differ with age. Children younger than 12 years of age tend to choose nonlethal methods in suicide attempts, such as throwing themselves down stairs, from the roof, or eating soap; there are virtually no reports of children this age using firearms for suicide (Pfeffer, 1981). Perhaps the greater use of firearms related to age and gender arise from adult men's greater access to and proficiency in the use of deadly weapons. In addition, men may be more determined to succeed. During childhood, however, there is no marked preponderance of male suicides.

Motives for Suicide

Most adult suicides are attempted and committed by depressed people, and the same is true for children and adolescents (Clarke, 1993). Since suicidal thoughts and behavior are symptoms of depressive disorders, the connection between suicide and depression is understandable. However, many suicidal youngsters are not depressed (Reynolds, 1994), and 42 percent of one large sample of adolescent suicide attempters lacked a history of major depression (Andrews & Lewinsohn, 1992). Completed suicide is more often associated with depression, while suicide attempts can reflect a host of different motivations, including revenge, jealousy, demands for attention, and other hostile and manipulative intentions (Lumsden, 1980). Suicidal thoughts appear to increase when a person suffers from several disorders (King , Pfeffer, Gammon, & Cohen, 1992), especially conduct dis-

order, drug and alcohol abuse, and borderline personality disorder (a pattern of intense, unstable relationships, unstable self-image, impulsivity, anger, and recurrent suicidal gestures or behavior).

Families of children who become suicidal are more likely to have parents and other family members who are depressed or otherwise psychiatrically disturbed. Child suicide is also linked to the death of someone close, and to the child's own adjustment problems (Reynolds, 1994; Shafi, Carrigan, Wittinghill, & Derrick, 1985). Suicidal family members create emotional turmoil at home and they can unknowingly serve as self-injurious models for the children. Alternatively, the child may be unwanted, abused, feel valueless, or be locked in serious conflict with parents. Whatever the reason, the child comes to feel a deep, hopeless despair and pessimistic doubt that improvement is possible. The most common problems of suicidal children are depression and hopelessness, but also impulsive anger and hostility (Wilson, 1991).

Young children's beliefs about suicide may appear bizarre, but they are understandable given the children's cognitive immaturity. Most children under 9 years do not understand that death is universal, irreversible, and unavoidable (Childers & Wimmer, 1971). They may envision returning to enjoy seeing their family regret having treated them badly or may think that at the last minute they will be able to fly and thus avoid death after having plunged from a high place. Many children who commit suicide previously discussed, threatened, or attempted suicide in order to wring sympathy from unresponsive adults.

Suicide is a social as well as a psychological phenomenon. Adolescent suicide rates differ dramatically in different historical periods and cultures. There have been highly localized outbreaks or epidemics of suicide, as when several teenagers at the same school commit suicide during a short time period, or among intellectual groups as in the *Sturm and Drang* literary movement when young men in 19th-century Germany considered suicide a romantic and heroic death. In recent years an epidemic of suicide occurred among young Native American men on certain Indian reservations, including the Wind River Indian Reservation in Wyoming. Among the Hopi youth, suicide has become a matter of concern, and higher suicide rates occur among families who reject traditional tribal ways of life and make traditionally disapproved of marriages. Such families become identified as deviant, which probably puts pressure on the children (Levy & Kunitz, 1987). For young men living in the decaying, violent inner-cities, wildly reckless and violent gang behavior verges on the self-destructive and in some instances may have suicidal overtones. Glorifying highly risky, melodramatic behavior, particularly when combined with heavy alcohol and drug use, can prove deadly. Whole cultures and nations vary in suicide rates. When suicide is honored as a tradition, as in Japan, rates tend to be high, even among youth, but in Catholic countries where suicide is forbidden for religious reasons, suicides are much rarer. Suicides are increasing in many parts of the world, perhaps partly because of improved public health record keeping and because religious and cultural prohibitions are loosening.

Prevention of Teen Depression and Suicide

One of the most effective suicide prevention measures may be removing firearms from homes and neighborhoods so children and teens cannot use them to kill themselves or attack others. Taking similar precautions to restrict young people's access to potentially lethal types of prescription drugs and other substances would further reduce suicide risk. However, these straightforward preventive measures are unlikely to be widely adopted in the near future because many states are reducing rather than increasing their restrictions on the general availability of firearms. In addition, drugs that could be fatally misused are commonplace.

Readers should know how to help individuals who have threatened or attempted suicide. First, it is important to attend to and properly interpret the threat or gesture. Suicide threats cannot be dismissed, even when they seem minor or manipulative, because people who make threats show significantly increased rates of suicide. In one study, 55 percent of suicide victims had previously made suicidal threats, 85 percent had expressed suicidal ideas (as opposed to 18 percent of a group of nonsuicidal adolescents), and 40 percent had made previous suicide attempts (Shafi et al., 1985). Such findings indicate that any suicidal talk, threats, past attempts, or suspicious "accidents" should be taken seriously. Second, act decisively to protect the person from self-harm. This may require

notifying the family or actually accompanying the suicidal person to a clinic or hospital emergency room for medical care until the acute danger of suicide has passed. Do not be dissuaded if the person appears calm and says that she or he is no longer suicidal. That may not be true.

The goal in suicide prevention is to remove all means to commit suicide until the person calms down, receives professional counseling, and can assess the situation more realistically. Thus, there must be no access to dangers such as weapons of any type, motor vehicles, high places, drugs, poisons, and other means to commit suicide. Ironically, the suicide attempter will nearly always feel better and abandon self-destruction, sometimes after only a brief period. Those who are quietly determined to commit suicide are the most difficult to identify and treat. Nevertheless, prompt, decisive intervention can save lives.

SUMMARY

Anxiety disorders are suspected when children's fears are very unusual in age of onset, intensity, persistence, and type. Simple phobias are thought to stem from observational learning or direct instruction from others. Most common childhood fears are overcome without professional treatment, but true phobias and anxiety disorders are considerably more persistent. School refusal is found worldwide, and in its simple, acute form is easily treated by the child's carefully managed return to school. Severe school refusal is resistant to treatment and is related to long-range adjustment problems. Posttraumatic stress disorder can occur at any age, and in children involves disorganization, agitation, nightmares, and repetitive play reenactment of the traumatic situation. Treatments for children's phobias and anxiety disorders include learning-based therapies such as in vivo desensitization, relaxation, participant modeling, and cognitive-behavioral therapies, including positive self-talk, reinterpreting the situation, and self-control. Treatments combining these cognitive and behavioral components are particularly effective.

Obsessive-compulsive disorders are extremely rare during childhood, but become more common during adolescence. Compulsive-like rituals may be motivated by anxiety, by the sensory consequences they produce, or by the attention they attract. There has been little scientific study of the treatment of obsessive-compulsive disorders in children, but clomipramine hydrochloride (Anafranil) medication has proven helpful in reducing symptoms.

Children can become clinically depressed and are diagnosed using criteria for adult depressive disorders, but children are more likely than adults to show somatic complaints, irritability, and social withdrawal. As many as one-third or more of child psychiatric clinic patients are depressed, and many also suffer from anxiety and have conduct problems. Depression is variously attributed to unconscious conflict originating early in life (psychodynamic theory), to loss of customary reinforcing activities (operant learning explanation), to learned helplessness (Seligman's theory), or to distorted thinking linked with early loss (Beck's cognitive theory). The condition is rare earlier than puberty, and research on treatment effectiveness has only begun. However, group cognitive-behavioral therapy provides a promising treatment for depressed adolescents. As yet, antidepressant medication is relatively ineffective with children and teenagers.

Suicide is extremely rare before the ages of 10–12 years, but the rate rises dramatically in early adolescence and increases throughout life. Juvenile suicide is associated with depressed mood, but also with conduct disorder, substance abuse, and borderline personality disorder. Suicide rates are affected by social and cultural factors as well as by the availability of lethal methods such as guns and some prescribed medications. Suicide attempts can be prevented in the short term by withholding access to the means to injure oneself, alertness to suicidal talk and attempts of any type, and by firm insistence that the youth obtain professional help and be temporarily hospitalized, if necessary.

C H A P T E R   8

LEARNING DISABILITIES

Key Terms

Auditory association. The act of associating or relating ideas or information that is presented verbally.

Auditory blending. Combining the parts of a word into an integrated whole.

Auditory discrimination. The process of distinguishing between different sounds.

Dyslexia. A severe type of learning disability that impairs the ability to read, sometimes totally.

Haptic perception. Relating to the sensation of touch and information received through body movements or position.

Hyperactivity. An excess of activity in inappropriate circumstances, also referred to as hyperkinesis. Often accompanied by attention deficits.

Neurological dysfunction. Presumed malfunctioning of the neurological system. Often the affected individual exhibits behavioral signs of brain injury.

Perceptual disorder. A deficiency or abnormality in the reception and/or interpretation of stimuli.

Visual discrimination. The process of distinguishing among visually presented stimuli.

S obbose yu obened yur buk to pegn reding the chapter and this is what you saw. You begin to feel the tension building in your stomach and that tightness in your forehead, slightly over your right eye, begins to grow. Soon it will be a headache, the Mother of all headaches. Won't it ever get easier? Why is it so hard? Tonight will end at 2:30, it has to even though you absolutely have to get through 10 pages. The whole chapter will take at least a week and a half to cover.

For some of your fellow students, this chapter may look like the material in the paragraph above. They are otherwise bright and capable students who must struggle with academic work that many students and teachers take for granted. They may have been diagnosed as having a learning disability and may even be among the 1 percent of the population that have been given the label of dyslexia, a very severe type of learning disability that involves tremendous difficulty in learning to read (Bender, 1995). Jeanne is one of those students who have been recognized as having learning disabilities. She describes her academic life in Box 8-1 at a time when she was a junior, having just completed an upper-division psychology course on child behavior disorders.

Learning disabilities is relatively new as a diagnostic label when compared to most childhood disorders. Although people have encountered learning difficulties in the past, their problems were likely mistaken for signs of low ingelligence, which is incorrect. The term *learning disabilities* was first proposed in 1963 by Dr. Samuel Kirk, one of the pioneers in the field of special education. Kirk's statement on learning disabilities defined the field. He described a type of disorder that had been previously recognized and studied, but had never been given sufficient organized, formal attention to provide a solid information base. The children being discussed did not fit neatly into any major category of disability condition recognized at the time. They do not have mental retardation—in fact, they often are of normal or above average intel-

ligence. They exhibited a wide variety of behavioral characteristics. However, a common theme recurred in the stories that their parents exchanged. Many of these youngsters were failing in school; they were often having difficulty in reading, spelling, and mathematics. Simply stated, these children had learning disabilities; their problems largely defied the existing diagnostic and treatment techniques available during the 1960s, the time the label was proposed. In recent years, the concept of learning disabilities has had an extremely important influence on special education, which makes the study of youngsters with learning disabilities all the more exciting. Today, children with learning disabilities are the largest group of children with disabilities in the United States, with a growth in the number of children diagnosed with learning disabilities that has been unparalleled by any other area of exceptionality (U.S. Department of Education, 1994).

DEFINING LEARNING DISABILITIES

There has been considerable disagreement and variation regarding the definition of learning disabilities over the years. Kirk (1963) introduced the term in response to growing pressure for a *commonly accepted term* in order to focus efforts for research and program funding. He was very cautious with his language as he proposed the

---

BOX 8-1   JEANNE'S STORY

NOTE: *The following is a statement prepared by an upper-division psychology undergraduate student who has learning disabilities. She tells her story in her own words of how she is coping with this condition and succeeding in college.*

Throughout elementary I sensed a problem but never understood what this problem was.

I watched as the teacher would do math problems on the board totally understanding exactly what was going on. An assignment would be given and I'd start my work. The only problem was I couldn't remember anything I had just been taught. It was gone—there was no memory of it.

I would try and try but for some reason I could not retrieve the concepts I understood previously. Too embarrassed to ask for help, I would sit at my desk and write numbers at random, pretending to be finishing my assignments. Every night I would bring home my math and ask my father to help me. Sometimes with his help I could figure it out (after being told the same thing over and over again). Other times I would get upset, he would get upset, and it was a disaster that followed. Dad just couldn't figure out why something so easy caused me such difficulty.

After a while I quit bringing my math book home and found other ways of compensating for my problems. I just felt stupid.

Another problem I experienced was often times I would transpose numbers and end up getting problems wrong. I would switch 27 to 72 and that looked right to me.

My self-esteem was lowered and anxiety would take over. I didn't want anyone to see how "stupid" I was so I used a lot of energy trying to convince teachers and friends of my good strengths.

I learned early what these strengths were and focused attention to the strengths, trying to hide my weaknesses.

I remember on one occasion a test the whole class was taking. It was a math test with multiple-choice answers. We figured out the problems and then filled in the bubbles. I did very well at guessing and ended up in the top math group. The only reason I made it through that year was due to a boy in the class. I confided in him that I didn't understand, and he allowed me to copy his homework every day.

To be honest I have no idea how I made it through math in junior high and high school. In high school my algebra teacher was also one of the football coaches. The class was the last period of the day and the football team practiced then also. He would come in, give the assignment, give a few examples, and usually leave. There was a group of us who would stay in the room and work out the problems together. Thinking about it I realize that group is what helped me the most. Many times they would go over and over problems and sometimes I just had to copy someone's work and try to figure it out.

I was on the high honor roll all three years in high school and no one realized how much I really struggled.

College was never a thought of mine. It actually never crossed my mind.

I married, had three children, and 10 years later decided to attend college for the first time. In the back of my mind I told myself, "I'll go as far as I can; then, when its time to take my math requirements, I'll quit."

When I first started college I bought a mini taperecorder and taped the lectures. I would review the tape when I returned home and fill in missed material in my notes. I made cards to review the material by testing myself. I was doing well, much to my surprise.

It seemed as though I had learned to compensate well, and I had strengthened myself in other areas.

I heard about a program at the university about math anxiety and decided to call. I met with a counselor and signed up for a math class with a group called Student Support Services. They offered tutoring and support.

I tried to bluff my way through this class only to realize this couldn't be done in college. Many times I asked myself what I was doing there.

I met with my math instructor after class almost every day doing problems. He would work them out on a board while explaining every step along the way. Sometimes he would ask me to do the problem. "I can't" I would answer, and he followed with "Yes you can, I'll help you." He would have me explain why I was doing each calculation and tell me if it was right or wrong. This man had a lot of patience with me and we worked many hours together.

Finally I went in to his office one day and admitted to him that I see some things backwards. He said he could tell something was wrong. I asked how he knew and he said several times he witnessed me switching numbers around.

From that time on he would read the problem to me to copy. That really helped a lot.

Jeanne

term learning disabilities and was extremely concerned about the intended purpose—the need for a label that would be useful for research, behavioral management, or personnel training. These concerns went largely unheeded, and the field expanded in an uncontrolled fashion. Children with a wide variety of problems were labeled as having learning disabilities, and definitions often were either very loose and vague or were tailored to cover those who were already being served in order to justify their special treatment. Hammill (1990) mentions 11 different alternative definitions that are used in the field of learning disabilities and other authors have found similar definitional variation. For example, definitions by people who have learning disabilities vary a great deal. Reiff, Gerber, and Ginsberg (1993) investigated definitions used by 60 individuals with learning disabilities who were considered to have adapted successfully as adults. Among these subjects there were 57 different definitions of learning disabilities.

It is clear from the discussion presented thus far that defining learning disabilities is not a simple task. Perhaps the most widely accepted legal definition is presented in the Individuals with Disabilities Education Act (IDEA) of 1990:

> Specific learning disability means a disorder in one or more of the basic psychological processes involved in understanding or in using language, spoken or written, which may manifest itself in an imperfect ability to listen, think, speak, read, write, spell, or to do mathematical calculations. The term includes such conditions as perceptual handicaps, brain injury, minimal brain disfunction, dyslexia, and developmental aphasia. The term does not include children who have learning problems, which are primarily the result of visual, hearing, or motor handicaps, of mental retardation, or of environmental, cultural, or economic disadvantage." (Section 5(b) (4) of P. L. 101—476)

In many ways this definition resembles Kirk's 1963 statement, which introduced the term learning disabilities. It is clearly very broad and quite vague in many respects. It would certainly make a behaviorist or diagnostician uncomfortable for it fails to specify the behaviors characteristic of learning disabilities. However, it is important to remember that this definition is set in the form of a law—one that must necessarily be broad in order to apply to many different settings, children, and purposes.

Learning disabilities is a general educational term. Although it may serve certain administrative purposes satisfactorily, the term learning disabilities is insufficiently specific for research purposes and even for instructional uses. The term can be effectively used only as a generalized referent or umbrella term because it encompasses a variety of specific types of problems (Hardman, Drew, & Egan, 1996; Smith, 1994). In fact, some of the narrowly defined *types* of learning disabilities, such as dyslexia, are still too broad and have themselves been characterized as a collection of different syndromes or subcategories. This view is reflected by the American Psychiatric Association in DSM-IV where the term *learning disorders* is employed and combined with more specific terms such as disorders in reading, mathematics, and written expression as well as a general category of "learning disorder not otherwise specified" (American Psychiatric Association, 1994). Box 8-2 outlines the descriptions of learning disorders in DSM-IV. In the field of learning disabilities, definitions, causes, and behavioral characteristics often become confusingly intertwined. In some instances children may exhibit similar behavior, such as not following directions, but each child's behavior stems from a different cause. In other cases the reverse is true—the same cause may generate different behaviors. Perhaps nowhere is the complexity of the human organism as evident as it is with learning disabilities.

PREVALENCE

The field of learning disabilities continues to grow at a phenomenal rate. However, because of imprecise use of the label it is difficult to determine how many children actually do have learning disabilities at any one time. Epidemiological studies that would provide empirical evidence concerning prevalence of learning disabilities have not been undertaken to the same degree as in other areas of disabilities. As we will see later, definitions of learning disabilities have varied greatly over time and between geographical locations. This imprecision, of course, makes even gross estimates of frequency unreliable.

In addition to a phenomenal growth rate in prevalence, learning disabilities have always varied greatly in estimated prevalence with some estimates being so high as to be alarming and questionable. For example, Smith (1994) noted learning disability prevalence figures ranging from 2 to 20 percent (1 in 5) of all schoolchildren.

BOX 8-2 DSM-IV LEARNING DISORDER DESCRIPTIONS

DIAGNOSTIC FEATURES

Learning disorders are diagnosed when the individual's achievement on individually administered, standardized tests in reading, mathematics, or written expression is substantially below that expected for age, schooling, and level of intelligence. The learning problems significantly interfere with academic achievement or activities of daily living that require reading, mathematical, or writing skills. A variety of statistical approaches can be used to establish that a discrepancy is significant. *Substantially below* is usually defined as a discrepancy of more than 2 standard deviations between achievement and IQ. A smaller discrepancy between achievement and IQ (i.e., between 1 and 2 standard deviations) is sometimes used, especially in cases where an individual's performance on an IQ test may have been compromised by an associated disorder in cognitive processing, a comorbid mental disorder or general medical condition, or the individual's ethnic or cultural background. If a sensory deficit is present, the learning difficulties must be in excess of those usually associated with the deficit. Learning disorders may persist into adulthood.

DIFFERENTIAL DIAGNOSIS

Learning disorders must be differentiated from *normal variations in academic attainment* and from scholastic difficulties due to *lack of opportunity, poor teaching,* or *cultural factors.* . . . *Mathematics disorder* and *disorder of written expression* most commonly occur in combination with *reading disorder.* When criteria are met for more than one learning disorder, all should be diagnosed.

READING DISORDER

DIAGNOSTIC CRITERIA

A. Reading achievement, as measured by individually administered standardized tests of reading accuracy or comprehension, is substantially below that expected given the person's chronological age, measured intelligence, and age-appropriate education.

B. The disturbance in criterion A significantly intereferes with academic achievement or activities of daily living that require reading skills.

C. If a sensory deficit is present, the reading difficulties are in excess of those usually associated with it.

MATHEMATICS DISORDER

DIAGNOSTIC CRITERIA

A. Mathematical ability, as measured by individually administered standardized tests, is substantially below that expected given the person's chronological age, measured intelligence, and age-appropriate education.

B. The disturbance in criterion A significantly interferes with academic achievement or activities of daily living that require mathematical ability.

C. If a sensory deficit is present, the difficulties in mathematical ability are in excess of those usually associated with it.

DISORDER OF WRITTEN EXPRESSION

DIAGNOSTIC CRITERIA

A. Writing skills, as measured by individually administered standardized tests (or functional assessments of writing skills), are substantially below those expected given the person's chronological age, measured intelligence, and age-appropriate education.

B. The disturbance in criterion A significantly interferes with academic achievement or activities of daily living that require the composition of written texts (e.g., writing grammatically correct sentences and organized paragraphs).

C. If a sensory deficit is present, the difficulties in writing skills are in excess of those usually associated with it.

LEARNING DISORDER NOT OTHERWISE SPECIFIED

This category is for disorders in learning that do not meet criteria for any specific learning disorder. This category might include problems in all three areas (reading, mathematics, written expression) that together significantly interfere with academic achievement even though performance tests measuring each individual skill are not substantially below that expected given the person's chronological age, measured intelligence, and age-appropriate education.

SOURCE: Reprinted with permission from the *Diagnostic and statistical manual of mental disorders.* Fourth Edition (1994). Washington, DC: American Psychiatric Association, pp. 46–53. Copyright 1994 by the American Psychiatric Association.

Regardless of which prevalence rate one accepts, learning disabilities clearly represent a very large proportion of all exceptional children served in the schools. During the 1991–92 school year, there were over 4.9 million identified exceptional children being served and over 2.2 million or about 45 percent of these were labeled as having learning disabilities (U.S. Department of Education, 1994).

The history of the learning disabilities field can provide at least two important lessons. First of all, the power of organized parent groups became evident as perhaps never before. Certainly this was not the first group of parents ever to organize but it may well have been the most potent. Parents of those with mental retardation also achieved a great deal, but they had the advantage of a field that was relatively well established. Parents of children with learning disabilities created a massive focus of activity nearly overnight and demanded services for their children. Previously, many parents blamed their underachieving children's lack of application for their school failures. Now a more socially acceptable and nonjudgmental explanation was provided—learning disabilities. Unfortunately, society's demand for services for children with learning disabilities appeared before effective instructional technology had been developed. This brings us to our second point: while growth of the field of learning disabilities was indeed rapid, it was undisciplined. There was no solid, systematic program of scientific investigation on which to base programs of personnel preparation. However, there was an increasing demand for qualified personnel, as suggested by the statistics cited above. Frequently the individuals pressed into service had little or no training. This occurred in all institutions and professional groups—teachers, psychologists, and university faculty. Consequently, instructors were often hired more on the basis of their interest in the problem than for actual knowledge or experience. This situation led to some very predictable outcomes. Programs were more often based on misconception than solid principles of instruction or diagnosis derived from research. And the children involved suffered. Classes for students with learning disabilities quickly became dumping grounds for children with all types of difficulties.

Thus, there are a number of difficulties that emerge from developing a massive program of activity without a firm conceptual base and a foundation that will facilitate scientific knowledge acquisition. The field of learning dis-

abilities is still plagued with the residue from these early errors. Research design and measurement problems continue to trouble investigators working in the area (Drew, Hardman, & Hart, 1996). Such difficulties have unfortunate consequences for the growth of a reliable knowledge base about people with learning disabilities. They also substantially detract from the progress of information related to interventions and improving treatment (Conte & Andrews, 1993; Ohtsuka, 1993).

DESCRIBING AND CLASSIFYING LEARNING DISABILITIES

Children with learning disabilities have often been described as having a mild disorder and exhibiting many different behaviors (Smith, 1994). As isolated incidents, such behaviors as reversing letters or not focusing attention may not be abnormal except when they recur or when they occur in combinations that substantially handicap children's daily performance. It has been said many times that all of us have learning disabilities to some degree or in some fashion in that our perceptions and memory are fallible. This saying may be an attempt to make learning disabilities seem less threatening by viewing it as a variant to counteract any harm done by labeling some children as having learning disabilities.

There are some striking differences between the literature on learning disabilities and that focusing on other disorders. It is not uncommon for descriptions of children with learning disabilities to be void of references to actual research and seem often to be based on unsystematic clinical observations that are presented as "common knowledge" but are marked by ambiguities. In some cases the actual behavior of the children seems to be ignored or overlooked in favor of relying on stereotypes, such as a child being viewed as generally overly active rather than merely overly active in certain circumstances. On the other hand, since parents, teachers, and psychologists often agree on many elements of behavioral descriptions for children with learning disabilities, it appears that learning disabilities do exist. We will describe behaviors that are commonly discussed by those who are working with children labeled as having learning disabilities. Often these syndromes do not have a firm empirical base, although where such evidence exists we will so indicate.

Further, it is useful to remember that normality is socially defined by many sources, as was discussed in Chapter 1.

As noted earlier, learning disabilities has often been viewed as mild disorders (Hardman et al., 1996). There has been little empirical study of learning disability severity although the topic has continued to appear in the literature (e.g., Binney, 1992; McKinney, Montague, & Hocutt, 1993; Salyer, Holmstrom, & Noshpitz, 1991). The literature in learning disabilities has also begun to address subtypes of the generic disorder, although emergence of a widely accepted classification scheme for subtyping has not occurred (e.g., Bender, 1995; Bender & Golden, 1990; Bowers, Risser, Suchanec, & Tinker, 1992; McIntosh & Gridley, 1993; Raviv & Stone, 1991).

Hyperactivity

Hyperactivity is frequently one of the first behavioral characteristic mentioned in descriptions of learning disabilities by teachers (Hardman et al., 1996). It is often reported that such children cannot sit still for more than a very short time, fidget a great deal, and are, in general, excessively active. Such behavior is often viewed as one of the "soft" signs (or indirect indicators) of neurological dysfunction. Hyperactive behavior or hyperkinesis has been examined in considerable depth in Chapter 4, which addresses social disorders in children. However, hyperactivity must also be briefly considered in the context of learning disabilities because it is perhaps the most common behavioral characteristic associated with children who are labeled as having learning disabilities (Carlson & Bunner, 1993; Sandler, Hooper, Watson, & Coleman, 1993).

It is important to note that not all children labeled as having learning disabilities are hyperkinetic (Faraone, Biederman, Lehmman, & Keenan, 1993; Zentall & Ferkis, 1993). Additionally, the *stereotype* of hyperkinesis seems to have led many to expect and consequently to see hyperactivity in children with learning problems. Although hyperkinesis is commonly viewed as involving a *general excess* of activity, evidence suggests that this may be incorrect and that we might find it more fruitful to look at the *appropriateness* of a child's behavior in particular settings. Hyperkinetic children seem to exhibit higher inappropriate activity levels than their normal counterparts under structured circumstances, such as might be found in certain types of classroom instruction (Bender, 1995;

Smith, 1994). However, most research indicates no difference between hyperactive and other children in unstructured situations such as play and other nonacademic settings. That is, hyperactivity is most apparent in situations in which sitting and attending to a task are required.

Clearly hyperactivity is common in children with learning disabilities. However, observations of hyperactivity alone are not sufficient to lead to a diagnosis of learning disabilities and not all children with learning disabilities are hyperactive (Semrud-Clikeman, Biederman, Sprich-Buckminster, & Lehman, 1992). Further, a generalized superficial view of hyperactivity is not likely to be of great value in treatment since it seems to be somewhat situation specific, that is, in some contexts these children may be overly active, but not in others. Research aimed at clarifying the relationship between hyperactivity and the other constellation of attributes associated with learning disabilities is essential if we are to advance our understanding and treatment of this population.

Perceptual Problems

Children labeled as having learning disabilities often have perception problems. Abnormalities of perception have played an historic and prominent role in clinical and research descriptions of such youngsters. In fact, the field of learning disabilities seems to have grown out of the early work of Werner and Strauss (1939, 1941) and Goldstein (1936, 1939) who were studying the perceptual, cognitive, and behavioral effects of brain injury. The notion that perceptual disorders are related to learning disabilities enjoyed considerable popularity over the years. Interest in this view has diminished somewhat recently because of failure to establish a clear connection between perceptual problems and neurological dysfunction. However, attention to perceptual difficulties in children with learning disabilities has not completely dissipated and some interest continues to focus on neurological bases of learning difficulties (e.g., Bigler, 1992; Grace & Malloy, 1992; Weinberg & Harper, 1993).

Despite the assessment and conceptual difficulties, perceptual and neurological problems represent a rather appealing explanation for some of the behaviors exhibited by children with learning disabilities (e.g., the inability to copy from a chalkboard or to recognize properties that distinguish geometric shapes like circles and triangles). In a general sense, children with perceptual

Reversal of letters is characteristic of some type of learning disability.

disorders do exhibit behaviors suggesting a disruption in sensory processing. Such problems may involve the interpretation of sensory information or problems during the input of stimuli. Regardless of the particular etiology involved, children with learning disabilities have difficulty in processing sensory information.

VISUAL PERCEPTION PROBLEMS

Humans receive information from the environment through a number of sensory systems differing in efficiency and accuracy. Children with learning disabilities often display difficulties in visual perception, which has ramifications for a variety of academic functions (e.g., Chittooran, D'Amato, Lassiter, & Dean, 1993; Faigel, Doak, Howard, & Sigel, 1992; Snow, English, & Lange, 1992). Children with visual perceptual problems may exhibit a variety of specific deficiencies that can seriously interfere with school achievement. They may see a visual stimulus only as unconnected parts rather than as a whole or integrated pattern. For example, a child may see unrelated lines as illustrated in Figure 8-1 rather than an integrated pattern representing a letter in the alphabet. Consequently such a child may have difficulty identifying letters in the alphabet, inescapably leading to problems in academic performance (Smith, 1994).

Visual perceptual disorders may also take the form of deficits in *figure-ground discrimination.* Figure-ground discrimination, which most of us master easily, is the process of distinguishing a visually presented object from its background. In school a child with this type of disorder may have problems focusing on a given word or line on a printed page. This particular example raises certain questions that we will encounter throughout this chapter, which have plagued the perceptual theorists specifically and workers in learning disabilities generally. Does the inability to focus on or identify a particular word provide substantive evidence of a perceptual problem—specifically a figure-ground discrimination difficulty? It is conceivable that the child merely has an attention problem (another characteristic often attributed to children labeled as having learning disabilities). It is also possible that the child cannot remember the word

FIGURE 8-1 Example of a visual perception problem

Unrelated Parts

Normal Perception

(memory problems have also been frequently attributed to such children). Perhaps the child has not been effectively taught the word (an instructional deficiency). There is no question that these all may be reasonable explanations for the same behavior, and it is difficult to determine which are operative in an individual case (Bender, 1995). This discussion also emphasizes the relative scarcity and imprecise nature of research information currently available. Clearly, research efforts in the area of learning disabilities must be intensified and become more analytical than has been the case previously.

Children with learning disabilities are frequently described as having difficulty in visual discrimination (the

ability to detect objects visually or discriminate one visual stimulus from another). Such problems may result in several behaviors that are often encountered by these youngsters and their teachers. The children may not be able to discriminate between certain letters or words (e.g., W and V, sit and sat). They may exhibit letter reversals that logically relate to a visual discrimination problem (e.g., horizontal reversals of such letters as b and d, vertical reversals of letters such as b and p). Discrimination errors such as those noted above are not unusual in all younger children and normally decrease with age, so it may not be easy to determine whether a problem exists. For the most part, frequent reversals and transpositions in children who are beyond the age of about 7 or 8 may suggest a potential problem warranting investigation (Hardman et al., 1996).

We have described a number of problem behaviors shown by children with learning disabilities and often attributed to disorders of visual perception. Certainly we have not examined all visual perception problems that have been described in the literature—our purpose is to be illustrative rather than exhaustive. Some youngsters have also been characterized as having problems of perception in other sensory areas, notably auditory, haptic, or tactile, and physical position perception. Although they have received somewhat less attention, they warrant brief discussion to provide a more complete picture of the perceptual difficulties associated with learning disabilities.

AUDITORY AND HAPTIC PERCEPTION PROBLEMS

Auditory perception involves the ability to recognize, organize, and interpret stimuli that are received through the sense of hearing. Difficulties in four different components of auditory perception have often been reported in children with learning disabilities. Singly or in various combinations these include problems in discrimination, association, memory, and blending. Since auditory stimuli represent a substantial source of information in school (as do visual stimuli), problems in auditory perception may be a significant performance handicap to learning. For example, children with difficulties in *auditory discrimination* may not be able to distinguish between the sounds of certain syllables or words. Young children with this problem may also have difficulties in identifying particular other sounds such as the doorbell, and in distinguishing between that sound and another. Children who have difficulties in *auditory blending* may be unable to blend the phonic elements of a word together into a consolidated whole as they say the word (e.g., an inability to blend the phonemes "m-a-n" to form the word *man*). Auditory association and memory are of obvious significance because of the way in which much of our schooling occurs. A child who has difficulty in *auditory memory* may not be able to recall information that is presented verbally, such as is often the case with learning the alphabet, the days of the week, and the months in the year. Children with *auditory association deficits* often cannot make simple associations between ideas or information items that are presented verbally (e.g., simple analogies).

We may encounter children who have a particularly difficult time with information presented either through the visual or the auditory sensory systems. When such problems are identified, it often becomes necessary to teach material through alternate modes of presentation. Depending on the nature of the disorder, one may choose to present material predominantly in an auditory mode (such as using tape recordings of books for an individual who has visual perception problems). For those with deficiencies in auditory perception, visual presentation alternatives may be helpful. Unfortunately, we seldom find individuals with a "pure" deficit in only one perceptual system, which complicates instructional treatments based on auditory deficit theories (Bender, 1995).

Children with learning disabilities may also have problems in *haptic perception*, which includes both tactile and kinesthetic sensation. These deficiencies are not common, but are thought to play important roles in certain school-related activities (Smith, 1994). Haptic perception involves the process of obtaining information via the tactile (sensation of touch) and kinesthetic systems (body sensation from movement and/or position). Handwriting is thought to rely partially on haptic perceptual abilities in that a child must receive tactile information relative to holding the pencil and kinesthetic sensation regarding movement during the process of writing. Children with difficulties in this area may be unusually slow writers, have problems with regard to spacing and forming letters, may not be able to stay on the lines, and may show a variety of other difficulties that combine with perceptual disorders described earlier. It is difficult to discriminate haptic perception problems from clumsiness or carelessness, which makes misdiagnosis likely.

COMMENTS

Previously we raised questions concerning the amount of empirical evidence available pertaining to children labeled as having learning disabilities. As we conclude the discussion of perceptual problems, this issue must be mentioned once again. *Perceptual dysfunction* cannot be observed directly, but is inferred from the child's behavior. Such behavioral deficits have often been reported by teachers and clinicians working with these children. However, the reader must be cautioned that explanatory theories such as neurological dysfunction are largely deduced by analogy and are not directly observable. We do know that certain children exhibit various constellations of behaviors that are similar to the behavior of other subjects such as adults with known cerebral injury. However, they also resemble younger children in their behavior more than youngsters their own age, suggesting that general physical immaturity may play a role. For the children who are our immediate concern, knowledge is mainly inferential and diagnoses are subject to more error than is the case for conditions such as conduct disorders, anxiety, or phobias.

Memory/Information Processing

The ability to remember what one learns is essential to daily life and central to successful performance in school. Memory and other cognitive processes are complex phenomena that have been studied by experimental psychologists for decades. Because it is difficult to study thought processes directly, we theorize about the manner in which these functions occur based on a person's observable behavior. Most of our theories are several steps removed from what is observed. Memory might provide one of the best examples of the intuitive process of theory construction and the difficulties involved in developing and studying such theories. Memory is the end product of several cognitive steps. In a very simplified sense, one must perceive a stimulus, process (encode) the information, store the information, and, finally, retrieve the information and somehow indicate that it has been retrieved (recognize or recall the information).

SHORT- AND LONG-TERM MEMORY

Memory has been studied intensively but still is only partially understood. This limited understanding must be kept in mind as we discuss this topic. Theories regarding the manner in which the memory functions have varied over the years. Earlier theories focused a great deal of attention on differences between long-term and short-term memory. Initially the concepts were defined simply in terms of the time interval between learning and recall. These distinctions soon became viewed as primitive, and much contemporary memory research no longer examines performance simply in terms of short-term versus long-term memory (STM v. LTM). The learning/memory phenomenon is now more often conceptualized in terms of information processing and schema models. Information processing involves consideration of the interrelationships of perception, attention, storage, and retrieval of information. Schemas (sometimes termed schemata) refer to associations between related items of information that facilitate remembering—concepts around which bits of information are clustered (Lefrancois, 1995).

Children labeled as having learning disabilities have long been informally characterized as having memory and other information processing problems (Lorsbach, Sodoro, & Brown, 1992; Swanson, 1993). Frustrated teachers continually bemoan the fact that such children may learn something one day and have forgotten it by the following day. This type of behavior occurs so often in children with learning disabilities that some consideration is clearly warranted here. The clinically reported memory difficulties have been so frequent that they have led to a variety of commonsense theories (e.g., the "leaky bucket" hypothesis, in which you teach the child a fact but memory failures result in performance failure later). All of these factors make the study of memory in those with learning disabilities even more fascinating and also makes the problems of such individuals more perplexing.

It is paradoxical that memory problems have been so evident in the clinical descriptions of children with learning disabilities and yet formal research examining this topic has been rather scanty. This research deficit is even more striking since the memory research efforts in normal and other deviant populations have been so intense. Studies of memory characteristics of children with learning disabilities have yielded conflicting findings. Some research has found no differences between the memory performance of youngsters with learning disabilities and their nondisabled counterparts, while other investigations have shown that those with learning disabilities perform more poorly (Kraker, 1993; Lorsbach et al., 1992; Swanson, 1993). Thus, there are continuing clinical reports of poor memory, but these are not clearly confirmed by research results. The evidence has led some writers to suggest that children labeled as having learning disabilities may have different rather than generally deficient memory and cognitive abilities (Kraker, 1993; Short, 1992; Swanson, 1993), a notion that has held considerable appeal in the field for some time. This perspective has led to the development of specific instructional emphases that are very focused toward children's specific problems rather than viewing those with learning disabilities as generally cognitively deficient (e.g., Garnett, 1992; Zentall & Ferkis, 1993).

ATTENTION PROBLEMS

It was suggested earlier that children with learning disabilities may have an attention problem that limits their information processing abilities. Teachers frequently report that these children are unable to sustain attention to lengthy tasks (short attention span), are distractible, and often daydream (Leviton, Bellinger, & Allred, 1993). However, much of the experimental research related to cognition has addressed the issue of *selective* attention problems, that is, the inability to focus attention on important stimuli and screen out or ignore irrelevant stimuli (Richards, Samuels, Tumure, & Ysseldyke, 1990). This has been examined by studying what is known as *incidental learning.* In most learning tasks there are certain stimuli that are important and central to acquiring the information (e.g., the idea presented in the narrative on a printed page). Other stimuli are unimportant, in fact irrelevant, to acquiring the information (e.g., the page numbers, the location of a certain passage on a page, or the color of the book cover). In selective attention, the reader tends to ignore the irrelevant stimuli (or at least attends to them to a lesser degree) and focuses on the stimuli that are central to the task, the words in the text. Evidence suggests that some children having learning disabilities do not employ selective attention to the same degree that children without learning disabilities do (Zentall & Ferkis, 1993). Children without learning disabilities tend to recall more central information than their peers with learning disabilities, while children with learning disabilities often equal or surpass their classmates without learning disabilities in recalling *irrelevant* information, which does not aid them in school tasks. Delineating problems with attention continues to be of significant interest in the learning disabilities field as research on their information processing difficulties proceeds (Swanson, 1991, 1992).

Academic Achievement

Many individuals with learning disabilities encounter significant problems in academic achievement. In fact, the emergence of learning disabilities as a field of exceptionality was driven by the continuing academic problems that such youngsters experience. Academic achievement difficulties are typically the reason children with learning disabilities are identified in the primary grades. Such difficulties persist throughout their formal schooling, including college (Wilczenski, 1993; Yanok, 1993), although the ranks of college graduates and successful people contain many with learning disabilities.

READING

It is estimated that 85 to 90 percent of the students with learning disabilities have reading disabilities (Bender, 1995). The specific nature of these reading problems vary greatly. In some cases children have difficulties with basic word knowledge and word recognition. When most readers encounter a familiar word, they recall it readily. However, unfamiliar words require special attention. Consequently it is important for us to know some basic rules regarding spelling patterns and pronunciation to derive meaning when we confront new material. Using such knowledge, we can often sound out the letters, search our memory for similar words, and roughly determine the meaning of novel words. This process is particularly difficult for many students with learning disabilities (Hardman et al., 1996). While good readers know rules of syntax, common prefixes, and suffixes; can generalize letter patterns; and are able to draw analogies rather flexibly, others are not so fortunate. Students with significant reading disabilities have trouble with this process and can only do so slowly and laboriously when they can accomplish it at all. On a positive note, students with reading disabilities can be taught such skills with specific training in the process, which improves their reading substantially (Billingsley & Ferro-Almeida, 1993; Englert & Palincsar, 1988).

The ability to use contextual cues to derive meaning is another important component of reading and one that distinguishes good from poor readers. Skilled readers tend to be quite proficient at inferring the meaning of an unknown word from the contextual information around it. For example, a five-letter word beginning with an "h" may be identified as horse in a story about a farm. Poor readers, on the other hand, experience difficulty using context to facilitate word recognition and reading. However, specific instruction on using contextual clues improves performance (Smith, 1994; Sorrel, 1990).

Effective use of contextual information requires that a person be able to perceive what the context is—that is, be able to discern and use the important ideas in the text. Students with learning disabilities encounter considerable difficulty perceiving and using the organization of important ideas in text material, frequently concentrating of peripheral details and information. For instance, they may focus on supporting characters in a piece of literature, seemingly exaggerating their importance in the overall plot far beyond what was intended by the author (perhaps not remembering much about the central personality). This problem can also be addressed by focused instructional intervention with students having learning disabilities. Teaching specific learning strategies such as organizational and summary skills, mnemonic use, and problem-solving can counter such difficulties and substantially enhance reading performance (Nelson, Smith, & Dodd, 1992; Scruggs & Mastropieri, 1993; Vauras, Lehtinen, Olkinuora, & Salonen, 1993; Wong, 1993).

WRITING AND SPELLING

It is not unusual for children with learning disabilities to exhibit problems in their writing performance that affect their academic achievement. Handwriting difficulties may include very labored, slow writing and problems with forming and spacing of letters. Additionally, such students often have poor spelling skills and rather immature composition (Smith, 1994). Some researchers connect the handwriting proficiency of students with learning disabilities to their reading abilities (Seidenberg, 1989). Part of this logic derives from evidence indicating that children with learning disabilities do *not* write more poorly than their normally achieving classmates who are reading at a comparable level (Grinnell, 1988). However,

further research is definitely needed to investigate the relationship between poor writing skills and reading ability.

Poor spelling abilities are often attributed to children with learning disabilities. These youngsters seem to commit numerous errors such as frequent letter omissions, extraneous letter inclusions, and letter-order errors. Some of their spelling seems to reflect developmentally immature mispronunciations (e.g., spilt for spilled) (Smith, 1994). Current literature suggests that the spelling abilities of children with learning disabilities generally follow the developmental patterns of their nondisabled peers, although progress at a slower rate (Bender, 1995). Additional research is also needed in order to more clearly understand the spelling abilities of students with learning disabilities.

MATHEMATICS

Students with learning disabilities often experience difficulties with some very basic arithmetic skills. They frequently encounter problems with simple counting, writing numbers, and mastering fundamental math concepts (Fuchs, Fuchs, & Bishop, 1992; Zentall & Ferkis, 1993). Some students omit numbers when counting while others can count but do not grasp what the numbers mean with regard to value. Predictably, students with learning disabilities encounter problems in circumstances where more than one digit is involved (i.e., working with numbers greater than 9), which requires an understanding of

---

BOX 8-3   SELF-INSTRUCTION ON COPING WITH MATH ANXIETY

This study investigated the efficacy of a coping strategy for reducing math anxiety in children with learning disabilities. The coping strategy was based on cognitive behavior modification (CBM). Twenty children from grades 4 through 7 participated, half were children with learning disabilities and the remaining were normally achieving children. The two groups were balanced for age and sex. The categorization of learning disabilities was primarily based on a discrepancy between measured intelligence and achievement. All of the subjects with learning disabilities had average to above-average intelligence (WISC-R) and evidenced academic deficits of 1 to 2 years, but they did not have sensory handicaps, mental retardation, or cultural or environmental disadvantage. The normally achieving students were randomly selected and had an overall average academic performance profile.

An instructor provided subjects with directions for completing the mathematics tasks and modeled the completion of sample problems. In the process of completing the sample task, three levels of self-talk were demonstrated that focused on affect-laden (emotional) statements designed to inhibit or enhance performance. The first type of self-statement was a neutral or task-specific statement: "I have to carry that number here." The second and third types of self-talk were two levels of task-approach statements: a positive statement ("I'm doing just fine, I got that part finished") and a negative statement ("I'll never get this, I'm too dumb"). Following the modeling procedure, the students engaged in a 10-minute discussion that focused on the kinds of things they said to themselves while completing a mathematics task. After the discussion, subjects were assigned to a desk and taught how to operate a tape recorder and a clip-on microphone. Once they were comfortable with the equipment, they were provided with a math task and instructed to think out loud, verbalizing everything that occurred to them.

Box 8-3 (continued)

Box 8-3 (continued)

The design for the study included a pretest, intervention, and posttest. Pretest data were collected during two 45-minute sessions on two consecutive days following the first instruction described above. The second pretest period was preceded only by a verbal reminder to think aloud throughout the entire time of working on the mathematics tests. The intervention procedure was applied to the students with learning disabilities only and involved weekly sessions lasting from the first week of May through the second week of June. Intervention included presentations on the role played by self-talk in performance. Cue cards were provided that outlined stages in the coping process and sample self-statements to assist in applying the strategies (see Table 8.1). Posttest data were collected twice, once on the day following the last intervention session from both groups of students and a second time as a maintenance check two weeks later.

TABLE 8-1   CUE CARDS 1 AND 2

Cue Card 1:
Steps in the coping process

(a) Assessment of the situation
    Label and plan
(b) Recognizing and controlling the impulse of negative thoughts
    Recognizing that negative thoughts hurt my work
    Controlling by replacing
(c) Reinforcing
    Pat yourself on the back for a good job

Cue Card 2:
Coping self-statements

(a) Assessment of the situation
    What is it that I have to do?
    Look over the task and think about it.
(b) Recognizing and controlling the impulse of negative thoughts
    Recognition:
    Okay, I feel worried and scared . . .
    I'm saying things that don't help me. . . . I can stop and think more helpful thoughts.
(c) Confronting/Coping/Controlling
    Don't worry. Remember to use your plan.
    Take it step by step—look at one question at a time.
    Don't let your eyes wander to other questions.
    Don't think about what others are doing. Take it one step at a time.
    When you feel your fears coming on . . . take a deep breath, think "I am doing just fine. Things are going well."
(d) Reinforcing
    I did really well in not letting this get the best of me.
    Good for me. I did a good job.
    I did a good job in not allowing myself to worry so much.

The dependent measures were self-talk data and performance data on fraction problems. Typewritten transcripts of the recorded audiotapes were produced following the completion of each session. Coders who knew nothing about the children rated them on the three levels of self-talk (positive, neutral, negative) in operational terms. These raters achieved a very high, 93 percent, level of agreement. Self-talk data are summarized by the two pretest and posttest sessions in Figure 8-2.

FIGURE 8-2 Comparisons of qualitative self-talk (a) (Pretests 1 and 2); and comparisons of self-talk for learning disabled and average achievers (b) (Posttests 1 and 2).

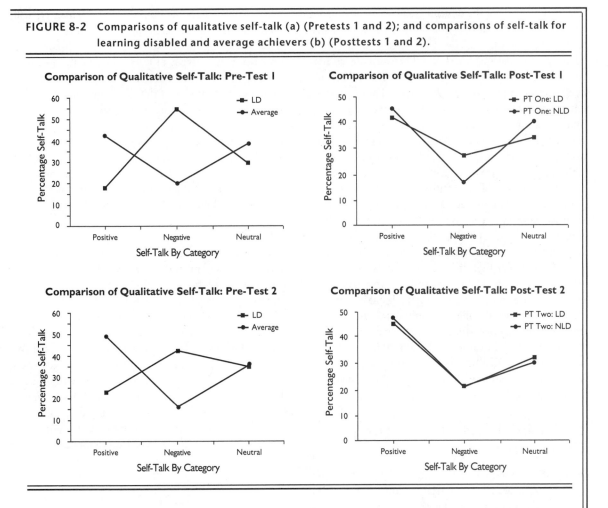

Although both groups generated similar amounts of total self-talk in both pretest sessions, normally achieving students produced significantly more *positive* self-statements than did the children with learning disabilities. Conversely, students with learning disabilities produced significantly more *negative* self-statements than normally achieving students during both pretest sessions. Pre-post comparisons indicated that the children with learning disabilities improved their self-talk. That is, after training, these children engaged in significantly more positive and significantly less negative self-talk during posttest sessions. As illustrated in Figure 8-2, the patterns of self-talk by children with learning disabilities more closely approximated those of their normally achieving peers during posttest sessions. Additionally, the students with learning disabilities significantly improved their percentage correct scores on math problems from pre- to posttest measures. Correlation coefficients between all subjects' positive self-talk and math performance was found to be moderately positive (.60 and .61 for pretests 1 and 2, and .43 and .54 for posttests 1 and 2). That is, when subjects engaged in positive self-talk, their math performance tended to improve.

SOURCE: Adapted from Kamann, M. P., & Wong, B. Y. L. (1993). Inducing adaptive coping self-statements in children with learning disabilities through self-instruction training. *Journal of Learning Disabilities 26*, 630–638.

place value. Many of the difficulties encountered in math by students with learning disabilities are not isolated from difficulties they experience in other academic areas. Identifying spatial and size relations between objects represent consistent problems for such students and become central in math performance. Problems that look different at first glance may have the same answer (e.g., 3 + 3 and 4 + 2) and those that may appear very similar have different answers (e.g., 3 + 3 and 3 + 2). Likewise many arithmetic problems involve word problems and require significant reading, which results in poor math performance for poor readers (Smith, 1994). Academic difficulties experienced by students with learning disabilities, such as those in math, seem to be accompanied by a number of related problems, which may also contribute to poor performance. Understandably, math anxiety appears to be rather high in such youngsters (Kamann & Wong, 1993). Box 8-3 summarizes an investigation of a coping strategy aimed at reducing math anxiety in children with learning disabilities. Results of this intervention appeared to improve students' math anxiety and also moderately related to improved math performance. Research on the difficulties encountered by students with learning disabilities in mathematics is badly needed, particularly research on intervention effectiveness.

Social and Emotional Characteristics

Much of the literature on learning disabilities spotlights difficulties in academically related skills and abilities. However, it is not unusual for these youngsters to also experience emotional and interpersonal difficulties (Dalley, Bolocofsky, Alcorn, & Baker, 1992; Pearl & Bryan, 1992). Their learning problems relate to low self-esteem and negative emotional consequences in a rather circular fashion, with learning difficulties seemingly contributing to emotional difficulties which, in turn, may affect motivation and academic efforts (Abrams, 1991; Bryan & Bryan, 1991; Deci, Hodges, Pierson, & Tomassone, 1992; Gresham, 1992). They may have difficulty interacting with others because of misperceived social cues and problems in discriminating some of the subtle nuances of interpersonal interaction.

There has been increasing research interest in the study of the social and emotional dimensions of learning disabilities. Social and emotional factors have not been included in definitional considerations, which typically affect funding for research and intervention, although there has been some interest in studying self-concept as a predictor of subtypes of learning disability (Bender & Golden, 1990). Much remains to be investigated regarding the emotional side of this disability, and research in the area is still maturing. At this stage, the emotional components of learning disabilities appear to be serious, including adolescent depression, suicide, and even possibly psychosis and serious violence (Huntington & Bender, 1993; Nestor, 1992). There is also some indication that there is substantial emotional residue for these individuals in adulthood (Denckla, 1993).

COMMENTS

In concluding this section, it is important to restate a notion that was mentioned previously. It remains our contention that the term *learning disabilities* is a broad, umbrella-type label that may include many different specific problems. Clinicians and researchers alike may observe any of a variety of difficulties, in combination or singly, in an individual child carrying such a label. We have discussed several characteristics that have been attributed to and studied in children with learning disabilities. We have not, however, elected to *characterize* such individuals because learning disabilities vary so widely in their nature and severity. It is our opinion that in doing so we would inevitably err in some fashion.

DEVELOPMENTAL FACTORS

Theories of human development have played an important role in the study of learning disabilities for many years. For example, theories regarding developmental delays have been involved in researchers' frustrated attempts to derive a single, comprehensive theory relating to the causation of learning disabilities (i.e., that all learning disabilities can be explained in terms of developmental delays). Developmental theory has been appealed to because performance of such children in a number of areas resembles that of younger normal children (e.g., Reid, 1988; Smith, 1994). It has been suggested that youngsters with learning disabilities show differences and delays in neurological development (Grace & Malloy, 1992; Weinberg & Harper, 1993). In some cases, evidence supporting such a developmental lag has been found as

Learning disabilities can lead to intense frustration, as suggested by this youngster's behavior. Identifying the actual problem is often not easy.

a peripheral result in studies focusing primarily on other topics (e.g., language, handedness, attention, visual impairment), which is not surprising since for the most part neurological status can only be inferred from behavior (Miller, 1990; Ross, Lipper, & Auld, 1992; Sonksen, Petrie, & Drew, 1991). Other researchers, however, have assessed behavior with the basic intent of studying neurological involvement (e.g., Bigler, 1992; Grace & Malloy, 1992). Although studies are few and seldom examine precisely the same behaviors, there is considerable evidence suggesting neurological immaturities and developmental lag in children with learning disabilities. It also appears that such youngsters are most dissimilar from their normal counterparts at younger ages and converge more with their classmates as they become older.

Children with learning disabilities have often been described as exhibiting extremely uneven abilities across skill areas. Their mental and behavioral development progresses in an irregular fashion and thereby proceeds very unevenly in some cases. In skill areas that are sig-

nificantly delayed, these children's behavior often resembles that of younger normal children (Smith, 1994).

ETIOLOGY

We have described a wide variety of specific problems during our examination of children with learning disabilities. Given the range of performance deficits, it is hardly surprising that a variety of known and hypothesized factors may cause or contribute to the disability. The behaviors found in children with learning disabilities have been explained in several fashions. Hypothesized causes of learning disabilities have included such factors as birth injuries, nutritional abnormalities, poor self-image, developmental delay, poisoning by environmental elements, genetic defects, and poor teaching. As we discuss causation in learning disabilities, it is important for the reader to remember that precise knowledge is often absent and that much of what we are describing represents theory, hypotheses, analogies, and inferences drawn from other populations, situations, or information. Thus, conclusions are tentative and subject to change as new and improved information becomes available.

Neurological Damage

We already noted the assumption that learning disabilities may be caused by brain damage or some other type of neurological problem (e.g., Bigler, 1992; Hardman et al., 1996). Opinions regarding this perspective vary greatly. Some authors have taken a very strong position favoring a neurologically based explanation whereas others question its validity. In most circumstances, the existence of neurological damage as a cause is presumptive and credible supportive evidence is lacking (Bender, 1995; Miller, 1990). This has led many professionals to discontinue the pursuit of neurological bases of learning disabilities. Until technology advances permit more precise assessment of neurological status, neither of the above theoretical extremes can be verified. Most likely there are some children labeled as having learning disabilities whose problems are based on neurological damage. It is also probable that others with the same global label and similar abnormal behavior do not have any neurological dysfunction. At present, we cannot determine any specific neurological problem for the vast majority of children with learning disabilities.

There are a variety of factors that could result in the neurological damage suspected in some children with learning disabilities. For example, difficulties encountered as a child may have developed prenatally and could result in such damage (e.g., low birthweight, inadequate gestational age at birth, Rh blood incompatibility between the mother and fetus, or serious maternal infection). Similarly, abnormalities during the birth process may also cause neurological damage (inadequate oxygen supply to the baby or abnormal positioning of the fetus during delivery). Or, damage may occur after birth, as when a child has convulsions from a high fever (Drew, Hardman, & Logan, 1996; Miller, 1990). These are merely examples of factors that may have a significant impact on the neurological status of an individual. They are also relevant to childhood disorders other than learning disabilities and are discussed more completely in Chapter 9, which examines mental retardation, and in Chapters 4 and 5, in material on poverty-related risks to development.

Genetic Causation

The possibility that learning disabilities are inherited often concerns parents. There is some evidence that genetic factors may play a role since learning disabilities tend to run in families, but once again it is unlikely that any such cause can be identified for most or all learning disabilities (Bender, 1995; Smith, 1994). Part of the support for genetic causation is derived from research on identical and fraternal twins (Bonnet, 1989; Eme, 1992; Light & DeFries, 1995; Smith, 1989). Such research has suggested that both twins have learning disabilities more often among identical pairs, who are genotypically identical, than fraternal twins.

The higher incidence rates for both identical twins than for fraternal twins suggests that there may be some genetic contributions to the development of learning disabilities. However, the problems of separating the influence of genetics and environment always persist. A case could also be made that abnormal behaviors in one family member may be reflected by other family members as a result of learning or family expectations and standards. Even the identical twin results could be caused by their very similar environment. While it is true that such children have the same genetic composition, it is also true that they share the same environment, even prenatally. Identical twins most often share chorionic membranes and the same placenta. Consequently, prenatal damage such as that caused by oxygen insufficiency could easily affect both twins similarly. With fraternal twins, such damage might not impact both babies in the same manner since they have two chorions and two placentas. This point is important since, if subjects in twin studies are selected on the basis of one having learning disabilities and that condition being due to a prenatal accident of some sort (e.g., oxygen deprivation, nutritional abnormality), the identical sibling of that fetus would likely have been subjected to the same condition; a fraternal sibling, however, may have developed in a different environment. There has also been some speculation that the postnatal environment of identical twins is also more similar than that encountered by fraternal twins (Schonemann & Schonemann, 1994). Any or all of these possibilities *might* explain the results of these studies. Although the evidence suggests some genetic influence (Faraone et al., 1993), one certainly cannot ignore environmental explanations.

Environmental Influences

From our discussions of child behavior disorders throughout this text, it is clear that the environment may influence a child in many significant ways. Although the area of learning disabilities involves certain intriguing notions of a neurological and developmental nature, the environment must also be viewed as a potentially important contributor. In this sense the environment is conceived quite broadly. Certain maternal conditions are significant during the prenatal period (e.g., dietary inadequacies, smoking, alcohol and drug consumption), and these factors create the environment of the unborn child. Likewise, a number of environmental influences after birth have been mentioned as potentially causing learning disabilities (e.g., poverty, neglect, food additives, ingesting lead, inappropriate or poor school instruction). Thus, both prenatal and postnatal environmental influences have been identified as causative of learning disabilities (Bender, 1995; Morgane, Austin-LaFrance, Bronzino, & Tonkiss, 1993; Richards, Symons, Greene, & Szuszkiewicz, 1995). Deficient general sensory stimulation and specific language deficiencies have also been implicated as causative in learning disabilities (Seidenberg, 1993; Smith, 1994).

The environment also appears to play a significant role in learning disabilities with regard to the motivation with which such youngsters approach much of their schoolwork. Poor motivation has long been ascribed to these children with characterizations of inattentiveness, poor concentration, and minimal task persistence. Such behavior has led to descriptions of some children with learning disabilities as learners who, because of long-term, repeated academic failures, develop a helpless feeling or learned helplessness about schoolwork and do not see themselves as in control of their own learning (Smith, 1994). It is difficult to determine whether this is a cause (etiology) or effect (resulting behavior). These children have likely entered school with certain difficulties, and the environment has contributed to a vicious cycle of failure and poor motivation that exacerbates the problems. Motivational considerations are of vital concern in the schooling of all children although they are even more crucial in teaching youngsters with learning disabilities, many of whom have experienced repeated failure (Anderman & Maehr, 1994; Cameron & Pierce, 1994; Short, 1992). Motivation, learning strategies, self-reliance, and social competence all appear in discussions of the school environment and its interaction with students having learning disabilities (e.g., Billingsley & Ferro-Almeida, 1993; Deci et al., 1992; Dalley et al., 1992; Nelson et al., 1992).

TREATMENT

We have seen that the area of learning disabilities has sorely tested the definitional and explanatory capacity of education and behavioral science. However, this testing process has also provided a substantial service to the field. Throughout history, behavioral scientists and educators have often sought single concept theories that efficiently explain all of the behaviors exhibited by a particular group of individuals. In most cases, such efforts are destined to fail, a point that is perhaps more evident with learning disabilities than any other behavior disorder. The conceptual and explanatory problems associated with this area have served as a constant reminder to behavioral scientists that it is probably not useful to search for *one single* theory or *one single* treatment for use with a diverse group of individuals. Learning disabilities is an umbrella that includes many specific disorders and one must approach treatment in that manner.

Treatment of individuals with learning disabilities also requires careful consideration of the age of the person being treated (Denckla, 1993; Spekman, Goldberg, & Herman, 1992). Interventions that are effective with adolescents and adults having learning disabilities will differ somewhat from those for children. The specific components of a suitable intervention for a youngster of 7 will clearly be different than those employed for someone who is 13, 16, or 20 years of age. Individuals with learning disabilities who are in their adolescent or young adult years are likely to resemble others of the same age in their social and behavioral characteristics, such as alcohol consumption, recreational interests, and sexual activity (McCusker, Clare, Cullen, & Reep, 1993; Sigler & Mackelprang, 1993). All of the factors complicating the lives of nondisabled adolescents (e.g., achieving individuality, romance, sexuality and hormonal development, occupational choices) are present for those with learning disabilities (e.g., Nass & Baker, 1991; Tallal, 1991). These young people are also susceptible to antisocial peer pressure and the prospect of gang activities, related misconduct, and violence (Nestor, 1992; Pearl & Bryan, 1992).

Clearly it is important to include age considerations into the equation when determining intervention plans.

Drug treatment has frequently been used for learning disabilities, especially to control hyperactivity. Some type of psychostimulant such as Ritalin (methylphenidate) or Dexedrine (dextroamphetamine) may be administered although a number of different drugs may be used depending on the response of the individual child (Carlson & Bunner, 1993). Medication is effective in some respects, such as in improving children's classroom behavior, but not in others, such as enhancing academic achievement or social adjustment on a long-term basis (Swanson et al., 1993). Further, medication may have unfavorable side effects and concern has been expressed regarding potential abuse including unauthorized use of the child's psychostimulant medications by other family members (Levy, 1989).

Despite the frequent prescription of drugs for learning disabilities, the complexity of determining which medication to administer highlights both our poor understanding of the disorders and the drugs and their action. It is not always possible to predict which specific medication will perform properly for a given child, sometimes resulting in the need to undertake trial sessions on more than one medication. Identifying an effective medication and an appropriate dosage level can prove difficult. In some cases psychostimulants have been administered in very high doses, which causes serious concern regarding potential toxic effects (Swanson et al., 1993). More typical doses may result in only minor side effects such as insomnia, some headaches, and mild irritability. For the most part, these effects are insignificant and temporary, although there is considerable variation among individuals. Most current literature suggests that there appears to be distinct benefits to the use of medication. However, parents' and physicians' expectations regarding *generalized* improvement are often exaggerated far beyond what the existing research evidence will support (Swanson et al., 1993). While the child's classroom behavior seems to be improved, long-term academic enhancement is not evident (Carlson & Bunner, 1993). Thus, a medication may control the hyperactive behavior, but we certainly have not "cured" a learning disability by administering the drug. The child most likely still has learning problems, if for no other reason than that he or she is behind academically. Academic deficiencies may adversely affect the child's self-image and treatment by others.

Behavioral interventions are also used extensively with individuals having learning disabilities. Such treatment programs may be aimed at enhancing academic skills or modifying other behavior in some fashion. In many cases behavioral procedures are used to supplement medical treatment, although they are also used as a primary therapy tool for a wide variety of purposes. Distinguishing between behavioral and instructional intervention is not always simple and often inconsequential. Both entail altering behavior and acquiring skills, and those that are most effective typically employ the most fundamental principles of learning—strategic use of stimuli and controlling the consequences of behavior, such as reinforcement (Hardman et al., 1996). For some students, it also is important to teach them to take increased responsibility for their own learning, which often includes self-monitoring and the use of learning strategies (Bender, 1995). Learning strategy interventions may be packaged in formats that have considerable appeal to young students with learning disabilities such as the GET IT strategy described in Box 8-4 (Welch & Sheridan, 1995).

Behavioral treatment procedures are frequently employed to intervene in social skills areas for some youngsters who suffer frustration and emotional consequences of failure (Bender & Golden, 1990; Huntington & Bender, 1993). For example, Bender (1995) describes a young student with learning disabilities named Thomas who exhibited social-behavioral problems in the form of public swearing at his classmates who walked by him to retrieve their assignments. It was determined that Thomas was receiving considerable attention from both his peers and the teacher who would respond to his outbursts. In Thomas' case, baseline data led to a decision to remove him from the source of attention by placing him in a timeout corner when he swore and instructing his classmates not to respond to his swearing in any fashion (e.g., giggling or laughing). As a result, Thomas' swearing was basically reduced to very low levels within a 10-day period of intervention and continued at an acceptably low rate even upon returning to preintervention conditions. In this example, the behavioral intervention was relatively simple although very effective, making the classroom environment much less frustrating for the teacher and potentially more effective for all students. It should also be noted that for some individuals, residual emotional problems require supplementary counseling and other mental health assistance in order to provide a

---

BOX 8-4   THE GET IT STRATEGY: TEACHING RESPONSIBILITY FOR LEARNING

The GET IT strategy is characterized by its developers as a cognitive learning strategy for reading comprehension, although it can easily be modified for use in a number of instructional contexts. This program is a video-mediated package developed with the clear intent of appealing to the student. It is patterned after television game shows and combines real-life student situations from the perspective of the student. Part of the presumed appeal of the GET IT package is that it portrays life through the eyes of the student rather than as adults conceive it.

The GET IT program attempts to teach basic learning strategies and responsibility to the student. The title is a mnemonic supplied to assist students to remember the components and associated tasks as follows:

G: Gather the Objectives (or GET objectives).
E: Execute the search for objectives.
T: Take notes.
I: Inspect inventory of objectives.
T: Test your comprehension.

GET IT accentuates interactive student participation. It has been employed effectively with students in a number of settings. Larsen-Miller (1994) studied the program with sixth-grade students identified as having learning disabilities in an integrated setting. Her data suggested that students made significant gains in reading comprehension and knowledge about the parts of a textbook, and demonstrated more positive attitudes toward reading after use of the program.

SOURCES: Welch, M., & Sheridan, S. M. (1995). *Educational partnerships: An ecological approach to serving students at risk.* San Francisco: Harcourt Brace; Larsen-Miller, L. (1994). *An investigation to determine the effects of a video-mediated metacognitive reading comprehension strategy in a complementary environment.* Unpublished Master's Thesis, University of Utah.

---

comprehensive treatment program (Dalley et al., 1992; Faigel, Doak, Howard, & Sigel, 1992).

From an instructional perspective, perhaps the most empirically based treatment approach involves the use of applied behavior analysis principles, which consist of specific and precise use of stimuli and consequences as noted above. As we know from other portions of this text, applied behavior analysis permits identification and modification of a wide range of behaviors. Based on the pioneering work of B. F. Skinner, this approach focuses primarily on observable performance (or behaviors) and de-emphasizes underlying causation such as internal mental, anatomical, or biochemical abnormalities. Such a treatment approach has great appeal since its specific format can be modified and applied to a wide variety of problems in many contexts.

There has been a considerable shift in approaches to instructional intervention with students having learning disabilities in the past few years. The field of learning disabilities has, since its inception, been one of the most controversy-ridden areas in education and psychology with regard to instructional intervention. The various theories of causation have had enthusiastic proponents and have often represented "warring" factions competing

for funding and public favor. This tendency continues to date, although a movement has begun toward focusing on each child's distinctive instructional problems rather than forcing a generalized concept on learning disabilities.

Intervention literature in learning disabilities is now beginning to address treatments aimed at specific problems such as writing, mathematics, reading, spoken language, and attention deficits (Berk & Landau, 1993; Choate & Rakes, 1989; Enright, 1989; Fuchs, Fuchs, & Bishop, 1992; Rakes & Choate, 1989). Some instructional interventions have pinpointed precise difficulties within these areas, such as problem-solving, and problem-attack strategy training (Sigler & Mackelprang, 1993; Welch & Sheridan, 1995). Such academic intervention is clearly more specific and narrow than was once employed with individuals having learning disabilities, all of whom were once thought to need training in physical coordination or training in letter recognition. However, thorough academic treatment also includes attention to the individual in his or her broader context. In this regard, academic intervention will often be accompanied by treatment of problem behaviors and social skill instruction in order to provide more comprehensive programming that will

Individual tutoring may help youngsters with learning disabilities perform in their academic subjects.

promote the student's inclusion in the academic mainstream (Jones, Bender, & McLaughlin, 1992).

THE PROGNOSIS

The prognosis for those with learning disabilities as adults is brighter than ever before, even though it includes some facets of life that are less than positive. On the optimistic side, more trustworthy research literature is available on adults with learning disabilities than ever before. Like many other long-lasting disability conditions, the literature on learning disabilities has historically focused more on childhood and the younger years than adolescence and adulthood. Now research on learning disabilities is increasingly investigating adults (e.g., Denckla, 1993; Roffman, Herzog, & Gershba-Gerson, 1994) and addressing matters related to post-secondary

schooling (e.g., Dickey & Satcher, 1994; Ruhl & Suritsky, 1995; Shafrir & Siegel, 1994). The learning difficulties of this population persist in college (Ryan, 1994; Wilczenski, 1993), and there is an elevated interest in designing instructional programs to meet the needs of college students with learning disabilities (Hildreth, Dixon, Frerichs, & Heflin, 1994; Yanok, 1993). Although the world has not magically opened up to accept people with learning disabilities in all fields, there is clearly more interest and potential than a few years ago (Bender, 1995). The Americans with Disabilities Act of 1990 (ADA) requires that appropriate academic adjustments must be provided for college students who are diagnosed as having learning disabilities. The aim of this legislation is that reasonable accommodations must be made to ensure meaningful access to higher education for these students. ADA is broad and offers little guidance regarding how accommodations

---

BOX 8-5 MATHEW'S STORY

NOTE: *The following is a statement prepared by an upper-division psychology undergraduate student who has learning disabilities. Mathew tells his story in his own words, recounting some of his school experiences, his diagnosis, and how his learning disabilities affect his academic efforts.*

Imagine having the inability to memorize times tables, not being able to "tell time" until the ninth grade, and taking several days to read a simple chapter from a school textbook.

In elementary and high school, I was terrified of math classes for several reasons. First, it did not matter how many times I practiced my times tables or other numerical combinations relating to division, subtraction, and addition, I could not remember them. Second, I dreaded the class time itself for inevitably the teacher would call on me for an answer to a "simple" problem. Multiplication was the worst! Since I had to count on my fingers to do multiplication, it would take a lot of time and effort. Do you know how long it takes to calculate 9x7 or 9x9 on your fingers? Suffice it to say too long, especially if the teacher and the rest of the class is waiting.

When I was a sophomore at a junior college, I discovered important information about myself. After two days of clinical cognitive testing, I learned that my brain is wired differently than most individuals. That is, I think, perceive, and process information differently. They discovered several "wiring jobs" that are called learning disabilities. First, I have a problem with processing speed. The ability to bring information from long-term memory to conscious (into short-term memory) takes me a long time. Second, I have a deficit with my short-term memory. This means that I cannot hold information there very long. When new information is learned, it must be put into long-term memory. This is an arduous process requiring the information to be rehearsed several times. Third, I have a significant problem with fluid reasoning. Fluid reasoning is the ability to go from A to G without having to go through B, C, D, E, and F. It also includes drawing inferences, coming up with creative solutions to problems, solving unique problems, and the ability to transfer information and generalize. Hence, my math and numerical difficulties.

Perhaps the most unique piece of information I learned was that I have scotopic sensitivity to light. This means that the eyes are overly sensitive to light and glare, which tires them rapidly.

With all of this knowledge, I was able to use specific strategies that will help me in compensating for these neurological wiring patterns. Now I tape all lectures rather than trying to keep up taking notes. I take tests in a room by myself and they are not timed. Anytime I need to do mathematical calculations I use a calculator. To compensate for scotopic sensitivity, I use transparent blue-green plastic sheets when I read textbooks and I use green paper when I write assignments, etc.

Mathew

---

are to be considered in individual circumstances (Scott, 1994). Requests for adjustments are evaluated on a case-by-case basis. Consideration is given to the individual's abilities, and in many cases, time limits may be adjusted and extra tutorial assistance provided as described by Jeanne earlier in Box 8-1. It is also the case that examination approaches may be altered, such as using verbal examinations in some situations (Nester, 1993).

We have suggested that the adolescent and adult years are not without trials for those with learning disabilities and some of the information does not suggest an optimistic prognosis. There is considerable evidence that our instructional system fails a substantial portion of adolescents with learning disabilities. For example, the dropout rate of these youngsters is quite high. Some evidence suggests that 47 percent of those with learning disabilities drop out of school by age 16 (Gartner & Lipsky, 1989). For those that make it through secondary school and at-

tend college, there is also a tendency to discontinue schooling prior to completion and before the general population (Wilczenski, 1993). For those that do continue, there is a constant campaign to adapt to the needs of the academic environment while continually requesting reasonable instructional accommodations from that environment when required by the disability. This is a constant process and often the requests for accommodation are met with great skepticism by faculty and others in higher education who know little about learning disabilities (Shea, 1994). While most of us only had to manage the process of learning the information in college, students with learning disabilities clearly have a much more demanding task, but with understanding and practical assistance from family, friends, and teachers, they can succeed. Box 8-5 provides a glimpse of such a student and what life is like for one person with learning disabilities who, by most people's standards, is experiencing substantial success in life. Like Jeanne, who we met earlier, Mathew is a junior psychology major and scheduled to graduate within a year. He has a good academic record, participates actively in class projects and discussions, and is planning to attend graduate school in the field of social work. Both Jeanne and Mathew volunteered their stories to help readers realize that with accurate diagnosis, the ADA, and help from student disabilities services and instructors, learning disabilities can be dealt with and students can succeed in school—even at academically demanding colleges and universities.

SUMMARY

Learning disabilities is a label of relatively recent origin (within the past 30 years) that has generated considerable confusion and controversy. The individuals so labeled exhibit an extremely diverse set of learning and behavioral problems beyond those typical for people at their level of tested intelligence. They may be average or above average in intelligence but often have pronounced difficulties in reading, math, and other school subjects. They are often, but not always, characterized as hyperactive as children. People with learning disabilities have also been described as having perceptual difficulties, memory problems, and attention deficits. Individuals with learning disabilities may exhibit various combinations of these characteristics and may be impaired to varying degrees depending on the nature of their problem(s), their age, and the setting. Interventions for people with learning disabilities may include the administration of medication, behavioral treatment, and/or specially designed instructional programs developed to address academic problem areas. School-based learning is challenging for them and may require extraordinary effort and application. In many cases, a comprehensive treatment program will involve multiple interventions aimed at addressing several areas of difficulty simultaneously.

C H A P T E R   9

MENTAL RETARDATION

Key Terms

Adaptive behavior. The ability to respond constructively and independently to demands of the social environment in relation to general expectations of one's age level and cultural group. Adaptive skill areas specified in the AAMR definition include: communication, self-care, home living, social skills, community use, self-direction, health and safety, functional academics, leisure, and work.

Appropriate supports. Terminology used in the AAMR definition of mental retardation that refers an assortment of services, settings, and people who can assist and support the needs of the individual with mental retardation.

Gestational age. Refers to the prenatal age of a developing fetus based on the time of fertilization (such as 24 weeks).

Incidence. Refers to the rate of occurrence (number of new cases) of a disorder that are identified during a specified time period (e.g., one year).

Prevalence. Refers to the total number of cases of a disorder existing at a particular point in time.

Primary prevention. Actions taken before the onset of a condition that prevent the undesirable outcome from occurring (such as preventing maternal drug abuse, which thereby prevents the unborn infant from being damaged).

Secondary prevention. Actions initiated that reverse or shorten the interval that a problem exists (such as controlling the diet of a person with phenylketonuria, which minimizes the damage to the central nervous system).

Significantly subaverage intellectual functioning. Terminology used in the AAMR definition of mental retardation referring to an IQ standard score equal to or less than approximately 70 to 75.

Tertiary prevention. Actions taken to minimize the unfavorable effects of a condition, thereby improving the person's functioning (such as specialized training to enhance language skill development).

CHAPTER   OVERVIEW

Mental retardation is a disorder that has been recognized perhaps longer than any other that we currently study in psychology. Written documents from ancient Egypt made oblique reference to the condition as early as the 1500s B.C., and it may have been implicit in law codes of Babylonia nearly 1,000 years earlier (Scheerenberger, 1983). In addition to its lengthy history, mental retardation is relatively common. It occurs in the families of the wealthy and prominent (including that of the late President John F. Kennedy) as well as in less advantaged families. Although prevalent, mental retardation is often misunderstood. Many have a stereotyped notion that all children with mental retardation are extremely dull and physically different, as is the case with some but not all people having mental retardation (e.g., the hydrocephalic and Down syndrome individuals). On the contrary, many such children can cope with the demands of daily life and have no distinctive physical characteristics that would set them apart from others.

DEFINING MENTAL RETARDATION

Defining mental retardation is not as simple as it might seem on the surface. In the past, many definitions became popular and then faded into scientific obscurity as others emerged. Part of the difficulty in defining the condition relates to the central role of intelligence in mental retardation. It has been commonly accepted that those with mental retardation have a lower level of intelligence than is typical in the general population. Consequently, definitions of mental retardation have reflected many facets of the long-standing controversy regarding the nature of intelligence and the degree to which it can be altered by experience. Additionally, many disciplines have each yielded different perspectives, definitions, and terminology regarding mental retardation, further complicating the issue. Psychologists, sociologists, anthropologists, educators, medical personnel, and others have undertaken research in the area, but only relatively recently have serious efforts been made to conceptualize mental retardation from a multidisciplinary viewpoint. As we will see in later sections, classification systems still vary to some degree from one profession to another; each system em-

phasizes the treatment orientation or scientific perspective associated with its specific profession.

Perhaps the most widely accepted definition of mental retardation has been presented by the multidisciplinary American Association on Mental Retardation (AAMR) (1992). This definition has undergone many revisions and refinements over the years which have yielded the following formulation: "Mental retardation refers to substantial limitations in present functioning. It is characterized by significantly subaverage intellectual functioning, existing concurrently with related limitations in two or more of the following applicable adaptive skill areas: communication, self-care, home living, social skills, community use, self-direction, health and safety, functional academics, leisure, and work. Mental retardation manifests before age 18" (AAMR, 1992, p. 1). Four assumptions are considered essential to application of this definition. They are:

1. Valid assessment considers cultural and linguistic diversity as well as differences in communication and behavioral factors [all of which can affect performance];
2. The existence of limitations in adaptive skills occurs within the context of community

BOX 9-1 AAMR DEFINITIONAL EXPLANATIONS

Mental retardation refers to substantial limitations in present functioning. Mental retardation is defined as a fundamental difficulty in learning and performing certain daily life skills. The personal capabilities in which there must be a substantial limitation are conceptual, practical, and social intelligence. These three areas are specifically affected in mental retardation whereas other personal capabilities (e.g., health and temperament) may not be.

It is characterized by significantly subaverage intellectual functioning. This is defined as an IQ standard score of approximately 70 to 75 or below, based on assessment that includes one or more individually administered general intelligence test developed for the purpose of assessing intellectual functioning. These data should be reviewed by a multidisciplinary team and validated with additional test scores or evaluative information.

Existing concurrently. The intellectual limitations occur at the same time as the limitations in adaptive skills.

With related limitations. The limitations in adaptive skills are more closely related to the intellectual limitation than to some other circumstances such as cultural or linguistic diversity or sensory limitation.

In two or more of the following applicable adaptive skill areas. Evidence of adaptive skill limitations is necessary because intellectual functioning alone is insufficient for a diagnosis of mental retardation. The impact on functioning of these limitations must be sufficiently comprehensive to encompass at least two adaptive skill areas, thus showing a generalized limitation and reducing the probability of measurement error.

Communication, self-care, home living, social skills, community use, self-direction, health and safety, functional academics, leisure, and work. These skill areas are central to successful life functioning and are frequently related to the need for supports for persons with mental retardation. Because the relevant skills within each adaptive skill area may vary with chronological age, assessment of functioning must be referenced to the person's chronological age.

Mental retardation manifests before age 18. The 18th birthday approximates the age when individuals in this society typically assume adult roles. In other societies, a different age criterion might be determined to be more appropriate.

The following four assumptions are essential to the application of this definition. These statements are essential to the meaning of the definition and cannot be conceptually separated from the definition. Applications of the definition should include these statements. Each statement has clear implications for subsequent assessment and intervention.

1. *Valid assessment considers cultural and linguistic diversity as well as differences in communication and behavioral factors.* Failure to consider factors such as the individual's culture, language, communication, and behaviors may cause an assessment to be invalid. Sound professional judgment and the use of a multidisciplinary team appropriate to the individual and his or her particular needs and circumstances should enhance the validity of assessments.

2. *The existence of limitations in adaptive skills occurs within the context of community environments typical of the individual's age peers and is indexed to the person's individualized needs for support.* Community environments typical of the individual's age peers refer to homes, neighborhoods, schools, businesses, and other environments in which persons of the individual's age ordinarily live, learn, work, and interact. The concept of age peers should also include consideration of individuals of the same cultural or linguistic background. The determination of the limitations in adaptive skills goes together with an analysis of supports that can include services that the individual needs and supports in the environments.

3. *Specific adaptive limitations often coexist with strengths in other adaptive skills or personal capabilities.* Individuals frequently have strengths in personal capabilities independent of mental retardation. Examples include: (a) an individual may have strengths in physical or social capabilities that exist independently of the adaptive skill limitations related to mental retardation (e.g., good health); (b) an individual may have a strength in a particular adaptive skill area (e.g., social skills) while having difficulty in another skill area (e.g., communication); and (c) an individual may possess certain strengths within a particular specific adaptive skill, while at the same time have limitations within the same area (e.g., functional math and functional reading, respectively). Some of a person's strengths may be relative rather than absolute; thus, the strengths may be best understood when compared to the limitations in other skill areas.

4. *With appropriate supports over a sustained period, the life functioning of the person with mental retardation will generally improve.* Appropriate supports refer to an array of services, individuals, and settings that match the person's needs. Although mental retardation may not be of lifelong duration, it is likely that supports will be needed over an extended period of time. Thus, for many individuals, the need for supports will be lifelong. For other individuals, however, the need for supports may be intermittent. Virtually all persons with mental retardation will improve in their functioning as a result of effective supports and services. This improvement will enable them to be more independent, productive, and integrated into their community. In addition, if individuals are not improving significantly, this relative lack of improvement should be the basis for determining whether the current supports are effective and whether changes are necessary. Finally, in rare circumstances, the major objective should be to maintain current level of functioning or to slow regression over time.

SOURCE: *Mental Retardation: Definition, Classification, and Systems of Supports* (9th ed., pp. 5–7). Washington, DC: American Association on Mental Retardation. Copyright 1992 by the American Association on Mental Retardation. Reprinted by permission.

TABLE 9-1   1992 AAMR ADAPTIVE SKILL AREAS

Skill Area	Portrayal
Communication	The ability to understand and communicate information by speaking or writing, through symbols, sign language, or nonsymbolic behaviors such as facial expressions, touch, or gestures.
Self-care	Skills in such areas as toileting, eating, dressing, hygiene, and grooming.
Home-living	Functioning in the home including clothing care, housekeeping, property maintenance, cooking, shopping, home safety, and daily scheduling.
Social	Social interchange with others including initiating and terminating interactions, responding to social cues, recognizing feelings, regulating own behavior, assisting others, and fostering friendships.
Community use	Appropriate use of community resources including travel in the community, shopping at stores, obtaining services such as gas stations, medical and dental services, using public transportation and facilities.
Self-direction	Making choices, following a schedule, initiating contextually appropriate activities, completing required tasks, seeking assistance, resolving problems, demonstrating appropriate self-advocacy.
Health and safety	Maintaining own health including eating; identifying, treating, and preventing illness; basic first aid; sexuality; physical fitness; and basic safety.
Functional academics	Abilities and skills related to learning in school that also have direct application in life.
Leisure	Developing a variety of leisure and recreational interests that are age- and culturally appropriate.
Work	Ability that pertains to maintaining part- or full-time employment in the community including appropriate social and related work skills.

SOURCE: Adapted from *Mental Retardation: Definition, Classification, and Systems of Supports* (9th ed., pp. 40–41). Washington, DC: American Association on Mental Retardation. Copyright 1992 by the American Association on Mental Retardation. Reprinted by permission.

environments typical of the individual's age peers and is indexed to the person's individualized needs for supports;

3. Specific adaptive limitations often coexist with strengths in other adaptive skills or other personal capabilities; and

4. With appropriate supports over a sustained period, the life functioning of the person with mental retardation will generally improve (AAMR, 1992, p. 1).

Some of the terminology in this definition is rather general and abstract. However, the AAMR manual includes explanations of key terms and extensive commentary on the concepts. This material is reproduced in Box 9-1.

The 1992 AAMR definition departs from earlier efforts in several ways. One important difference involves the manner of viewing intelligence measures. The AAMR definition focuses on intellectual functioning primarily at the time of diagnosis and largely turns matters of adaptive skills and needed environmental supports for classification and program planning. From a measured intelligence standpoint, a person either has mental retardation or does not—a standard score on an intelligence test of

70 to 75 or below indicates mental retardation. This level of intellectual functioning, coexisting with limitations in two or more of the specified adaptive skill areas, fulfills the requirement for a diagnosis of mental retardation.

Adaptive behavior has been part of the conceptualization of mental retardation for over 30 years, although assessment has never reached a satisfactory level of precision (Frankenberger & Harper, 1988; Jacobson & Mulick, 1992). The 1992 AAMR definition uses specified adaptive skill areas rather than referring to a more generic concept of adaptive behavior (see Table 9-1). Although these designated skill areas are more specific, adaptive skills have proved difficult to measure (e.g., Borthwick-Duffy, 1994; Jacobson, 1994; MacMillan, Gresham, & Siperstein, 1993).

DESCRIBING AND CLASSIFYING MENTAL RETARDATION

Because of different definitions in the mental retardation field over the years, there have been similarly varied bases for describing and classifying such individuals. Chapter 12 addresses classification of child behavior disorders in a more complete and general fashion. This section specifically examines descriptive classifications of mental retardation. We will emphasize the complex nature of the mental retardation diagnosis as well as the multidisciplinary nature of the field. Readers should remember that all descriptions and classifications are useful in some circumstances but may be dysfunctional in others, in which case they should not be used.

The term *mental retardation* is an extremely general label which includes a very heterogeneous population. Scientifically, it is necessary to specify the type of individual being studied. From a practical standpoint there is also a need to be more specific, since different types of retardation require different approaches to treatment and service delivery. Classification schemes in mental retardation provide a common vocabulary and serve as a convenient means for communication about the work under way, whether it be research or clinical treatment. Mental retardation involves many fields of study, each with its own terminology and descriptive system, and so several classification schemes warrant discussion.

Historically, the characteristic most typically associated with mental retardation has been reduced intellectual functioning. The *severity* of the intellectual impairment has long been a common means of describing and classifying those with retardation. As we mentioned earlier, the AAMR (1992) uses measured intelligence as one part of its definition of mental retardation but employs it only in the initial diagnosis and no longer classifies intelligence by severity. The American Psychiatric Association has also revised its definition of mental retardation in DSM-IV to be nearly identical with that of AAMR (American Psychiatric Association, 1994). However, the DSM-IV classification model continues to use measured intelligence to group those with mental retardation. DSM-IV includes four severity classifications plus a fifth for circumstances in which the individual's intelligence is untestable. The classifications are as follows: (1) IQ 50–55 to approximately 70 is *mild mental retardation*, (2) IQ 35–40 to 50–55 is *moderate mental retardation*, (3) IQ 20–25 to 35–40 is *severe mental retardation*, (4) IQ levels below 20 or 25 is *profound mental retardation*, and (5) *mental retardation, severity unspecified* is for situations where there is a presumption of mental retardation but the person's intelligence is not testable with standardized

instruments (because the individual functions too low, is not cooperative, or is too young) (American Psychiatric Association, 1994, p. 40).

AAMR (1992) employs four broad dimensions for the diagnostic-classification process as well as in planning interventions. These dimensions include: (1) Dimension I, intellectual functioning and adaptive skills; (2) Dimension II, psychological/emotional considerations; (3) Dimension III, physical health and etiology considerations; and (4) Dimension IV, environmental considerations. The diagnostic process concentrates on Dimension I (intellectual functioning and adaptive skills). This process involves three criteria which, if met, results in a diagnosis of mental retardation. To receive such a diagnosis an individual must have an IQ of 70 to 75 or below as measured on an appropriately standardized instrument, significant deficiencies in at least two of the adaptive skill areas (see Table 9-1), and be under 18 years of age.

Once a diagnosis of mental retardation is determined, the classification process then turns to the other dimensions. For Dimension II, an assessment of the person's mental health is undertaken and strengths and limitations are assessed. This evaluation is based on behavioral observations and clinical assessment using multiple data sources such as interviews, psychometric instruments, and structured observation. Dimension III evaluation provides a description of the individual's general physical health and the etiology of the mental retardation, if known. Finally, under Dimension IV the classification provides a description of the environmental considerations for the individual—both the current circumstances and that which would be optimal for promoting the person's growth and development. The last element of the AAMR model involves developing a profile of supports needed for the person's individual intervention plan. These supports are outlined in four levels: (1) intermittent (episodic, often crisis-related), (2) limited (time-limited but consistent, not episodic), (3) extensive (regular in some environments), and (4) pervasive (continuous and intense, across environments). Throughout the process of diagnosis, classification, and intervention planning, the AAMR model requires an interdisciplinary team to be involved to provide the most thorough evaluation possible. Attention is directed to cultural differences both in assessment procedures as well as intervention planning, although some concerns have been raised that this new definition may further expand the

TABLE 9-2 DSM-IV ETIOLOGICAL OR PREDISPOSING FACTORS

Predisposing Factor	Examples	Percent of Clinical Cases*
Heredity	Chromosomal aberrations (e.g., Down syndrome, fragile X), inborn metabolic errors (e.g., Tay-Sachs), single-gene abnormalities (e.g., tuberous sclerosis).	5%
Early alterations of embryonic development	Chromosomal changes (e.g., trisomy 21 Down syndrome), prenatal toxic damage (e.g., infection, maternal alcohol consumption).	30%
Pregnancy and perinatal problems	Fetal malnutrition, prematurity, trauma, viral and other infections.	10%
General medical conditions acquired in infancy or childhood	Infections, traumas, and poisoning (e.g., lead).	5%
Environmental influences and other mental disorders	Deprivation of nurturance, social, linguistic, and other stimulation, and severe mental disorders (e.g., Autistic Disorder).	15–20%

*Percentage does not equal 100 because no clear etiology is identifiable for about 30 to 40% of those seen in clinical settings.
SOURCE: Reprinted with permission from the *Diagnostic and statistical manual of mental disorders*. Fourth Edition (1994). Washington, DC: American Psychiatric Association, p. 43. Copyright 1994 by the American Psychiatric Association.

overrepresentation of minorities being diagnosed with mental retardation (Macmillan et al., 1993).

Etiology (cause) has traditionally provided a basis for classification of mental retardation that has addressed medically related matters. The DSM-IV approaches etiology as factors that predispose a person to having mental retardation. Five classifications are outlined with a notation that "etiological factors may be primarily biological or primarily psychosocial, or some combination of both" (American Psychiatric Association, 1994, p. 43). The five major predisposing categories are summarized in Table 9-2.

The AAMR (1992) document examines etiology from two major standpoints, one being the type of factor involved and the second, the timing of the influence. From the first perspective (type of factor), four categories are involved including: (1) *biomedical*, associated with biological process (genetic disorders, nutrition); (2) *social*, matters related to social and family interaction such as poverty and limited schooling; (3) *behavioral*, possible causal behaviors (e.g., maternal substance abuse); and (4) *educational*, influences related to the availability of educational resources that foster growth mentally and in adaptive skills. The second major perspective (timing of the influence) is addressed primarily from a prevention or intervention position and is arranged in three levels. These prevention levels include: (1) primary prevention, where intervention is undertaken before the problem begins or that prevents the occurrence of mental retardation

(e.g., maternal substance abuse programs); (2) secondary prevention, where intervention reverses the effects or shortens the duration of a problem that already exists (e.g., nutritional treatment programs for phenylketonuria); and (3) tertiary prevention, where intervention restricts unfavorable effects of a problem and improves his or her functioning (e.g., habilitation or education programs) (AAMR, 1992, pp. 71–72).

Each classification system discussed has certain strengths and weaknesses. Clearly, each has a different purpose and its usage may be limited to a particular discipline or situation. Although there may be some overlap, the systems presented differ in many ways. An individual with mental retardation may be classified in several different fashions at different times depending on the system employed, the situation, and any of a multitude of other contingencies (e.g., the services available in a particular community, evaluation by psychologists as opposed to a physician). Some who would prefer a single approach to classification have criticized this practice. However, a single approach to classification is not possible given all of the different reasons for classifying mental retardation (e.g., legislative, administrative, instructional).

PREVALENCE

How many children have mental retardation? As was the case in defining the condition, answering this question is not as simple as it may seem on the surface. First of all, a complete census of the population would be neither simple to conduct nor economically feasible. Some direct census investigations have been undertaken over the years (e.g., Birch, Richardson, Baird, Horobin, & Illsley, 1970; Lemkau & Imre, 1969; Mercer, 1973), although for the most part we have relied on estimates based on expected percentages of retardation in the general population. Regardless of approach, the definition of retardation plays a central role in the outcome. Obviously whenever the definition is altered, there may be a substantial difference in the number of individuals considered as having mental retardation.

As we examine the magnitude of mental retardation, recall our earlier discussion distinguishing between incidence and prevalence (incidence is the number of new cases identified in a specific period and prevalence is the total number of cases present at a given time). This is important here because much of the literature about mental retardation has either ignored the distinction or used the terms loosely and interchangeably. The number of people considered to have retardation is therefore somewhat variable. Particularly among those with mild disabilities, a person may be identified as having retardation at one point in time (e.g., school years) and no longer be functioning at that level at a later time (e.g., during adulthood). Additionally, it should be noted that precise data regarding either prevalence or incidence are very difficult to obtain.

Estimates of the prevalence of mental retardation have typically ranged from 1 to 3 percent of the general population (Drew, Hardman, & Logan, 1996). The U.S. Department of Education estimated that 12.3 percent of all children with disabilities in the U.S. public schools (ages 6–21) have mental retardation (U.S. Department of Education, 1993). Translating these estimates into actual numbers, over 554,000 individuals with mental retardation received services under the Individuals with Disabilities Education Act (IDEA) during the 1991–92 school year (U.S. Department of Education, 1993). Using the 3 percent prevalence figure, Hardman, Drew, and Egan (1996) estimated the general population with mental retardation to be in excess of 7 million people. Clearly, we are faced with an imprecise answer to the question regarding mental retardation prevalence. Prevalence rates differ depending on the definitions being used, assumptions employed, and may even vary in different geographical locales (e.g., different states). The preva-

lence estimate depends on the frame of reference (i.e., distinctions between incidence and prevalence), the environmental setting, and perhaps other unknown factors.

DEVELOPMENTAL FACTORS

One can hardly discuss mental retardation without discussing child development. Study of retardation's causation, classification, treatment, and prognosis immediately immerses one in studying the developmental process. The purpose of this section is to examine how development plays a role in mental retardation. In the section that follows this one, we examine the etiology of mental retardation during prenatal, neonatal, and childhood periods. The prenatal period is vital to normal development. During gestation, toxins, accidents, or other unfavorable events can occur that place the unborn baby at risk for mental retardation. These often involve maternal health problems or genetic abnormalities that influence fetal growth and development.

In diagnosing child psychopathology, it is important to establish *when* the onset of a particular condition occurred. Very often the timing of an infection or a chromosomal or physical accident will determine the impact of that incident. For example, *when* a debilitating accident occurs often affects the manner in which a youngster adapts to being paralyzed. It may also dictate the type of treatment administered and its success rate. These same types of considerations are evident in mental retardation. When a mother contracts German measles (rubella) determines the impact of the disease on her unborn child. If rubella is contracted by the pregnant mother during the first three months of gestation, there is considerable risk that the developing fetus will develop mental retardation. There is somewhat less danger later in the pregnancy, although even then such diseases usually involve some risk.

During the first trimester (the first three months of pregnancy), the tissue development of an unborn baby is progressing very rapidly. It is during this time that the foundation of physical development is primarily established, although one certainly does not discount the rest of the period. The basic material for what will later become the central nervous system (e.g., brain, spinal cord) is rapidly being established along with such vital organs as the visual and auditory systems, and many other parts

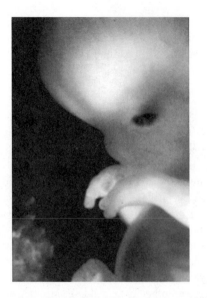

Slightly over 2 months and about 1½ half inches long, this fetus is developing very rapidly and is also very vulnerable.

of the young baby that are extremely important to its ability to function. When the tissue is developing at its most rapid rate, it is *most* vulnerable to the effects of detrimental influences such as rubella. If the central nervous system tissue being formed at this time is damaged by infection, genetic accident, or factors such as maternal nutrition, all such tissue that subsequently develops may be damaged. For example, if the mother contracts German measles at the time that her unborn child is first (and most rapidly) developing tissue related to visual organs, the child has a much higher probability of being born with a visual defect than if the disease is contracted at a later time. This same child may also develop mental retardation, perhaps severely, since the essential foundation for the central nervous system development is also being formed at that time and all prenatal development beyond that point is affected. Thus, the prenatal basis of the physiological development of a child is crucial and is affected by the timing of both fortunate and less fortunate events. This timing rule is very important in the prenatal study of mental retardation. It is important to determine when a vital organ system is developing most rapidly and when the foundation for later development is being established.

Mental retardation also may arise during early childhood. Physiologically, the baby is obtaining essential sub-stances for life such as nutrition and oxygen from the environment. The baby is also affected by environmental stimulation (noises, light, persons), which has great importance for subsequent development of mental functioning, speech, and social development. If the child's environment is basically supportive and stimulates proper development, there is a high likelihood that he or she will develop normally. However, if the environment impedes or interferes with the child's development, the child could develop retardation. As before, although from a different standpoint, the timing of unfortunate circumstances (or accidents) may have serious consequences. For example, if some infection is contracted by the newborn or young child causing deafness prior to development of language, it may well affect all subsequent language development. Similarly if the early environment is insufficiently stimulating, mental retardation may result.

Mental retardation can be prevented by timely treatment in some cases. An illustration of this can be found in phenylketonuria (PKU), which is an inherited metabolic disorder. In this condition, infants are unable to process phenylalanine properly. Phenylalanine is found in many common foods such as milk, and the inability to metabolize it results in an accumulation of substances that damage the central nervous system and mental retardation develops. However, if dietary treatment is implemented early and consistently, before the damage occurs or is serious, mental development can proceed normally.

ETIOLOGY

The causes of mental retardation are many and varied. In some cases, pathology of a physiological or biological nature can be identified. However in many more, causation is unknown. The purpose of this section is to provide an overview of the origins of mental retardation.

Prenatal and Neonatal Causation

GENETIC FACTORS

Genetic abnormalities were discussed in Chapter 2 in relation to a variety of disorders including certain types of mental retardation. Genetic anomalies (abnormal genetic makeup) may present various complications that ultimately result in mental retardation. *Down syndrome* represents one of these prenatal conditions. On an overall basis, Down syndrome occurs about 1 to 1.5 times per 1,000 live births (Dykens, Hodapp, & Evans, 1994). Actually there are three types of Down syndrome, each resulting from a different type of chromosomal error. The most common cause of Down syndrome is known as *nondisjunction*, in which an extra chromosome exists at the 21st position in the *G* group. This condition is also known as "trisomy 21" because of the three chromosomes in that position. Figure 9-1 illustrates a chromosomal configuration for a Down syndrome female with trisomy 21.

Such a condition occurs because of improper cell division during the formation of the egg or the sperm. Because the error occurs prior to fertilization, its impact on the developing embryo is substantial and the damage severe. The probability of a nondisjunction error resulting in trisomy 21 is dramatically elevated for mothers over 40 years of age. Evidence suggests that the risk of a Down syndrome birth after age 40 is approximately 18 in 1,000 births, whereas it is only 0.69 per 1,000 for mothers in their early 20s (Cahalane, 1989). Recent years have witnessed intensified research on improving fetal diagnostic techniques and a reduction in pregnancies among older women (Haddow, Palomaki, Knight, & Williams, 1992). There has been a resulting decline in the incidence of Down syndrome births.

Down syndrome may also be caused by a second chromosomal aberration involving material in the 21st pair in the *G* group. This condition is known as *translocation* and occurs when material from the 21st pair detaches (actually breaks off) and fuses to another chromosome pair. For example, the material may fuse with the 14th or 15th pair of the *D* group. This imbalance of genetic material causes about 9 percent of all Down syndrome infants of mothers under 30 years of age and 2 percent born to mothers over 30 (Drew et al., 1996). This represents a very different incidence pattern than nondisjunction Down infants. Nondisjunctions may well be a genetic accident that occurs as a function of age or health. Translocation has been demonstrated to be inherited in about one-third of the cases.

The third type of genetic abnormality resulting in Down syndrome is known as *mosaicism*. This condition is distinctly different from nondisjunction and translocation in that it represents an accident that occurs after fertilization which produces an infant with a mixed chromosomal makeup; some tissues have cells that are af-

FIGURE 9-1   Chromosome configuration of a Down syndrome female with trisomy 21

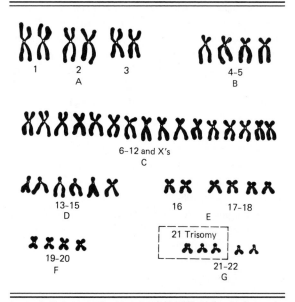

SOURCE: Smith, D. W., & Wilson, A. A. (1973). *The child with Down syndrome (mongolism)* (p. 6). Philadelphia: W. B. Saunders. Reprinted by permission of the publisher.

fected whereas others have the normal genetic configuration. Often cells with an abnormal makeup involve the 21st pair as in those conditions discussed earlier. However, the involved tissue and resulting damage is highly dependent on when the error occurs during the development of an embryo. The level of mental retardation may vary from mild to more severe impairment. Some children with mosaic Down syndrome have even been reported in the normal range of functioning, which may illustrate dramatically the interaction between genetic and environmental influences. Down syndrome has historically received a great deal of attention in the research literature on mental retardation. Interest continues on a variety of topics such as motivation (Ruskin, Mundy, Kasari, & Sigman, 1994), developmental adaptive behavior (Dykens et al., 1994), motor performance and movement (Chiarenza, 1993; LeClair, Pollock, & Elliott, 1993), and family matters such as sibling behavior and family conflict (Cuskelly & Gunn, 1993; Seltzer, Krauss, & Tsunematsu, 1993).

Fragile X syndrome is another genetic abnormality that results in mental retardation about once in slightly over 1,000 newborns, more frequently in males than females. The condition is called "fragile X" due to the fact that the X chromosome of an affected individual will show a fragile spot when grown in an experimental culture. Like Down syndrome, those with fragile X syndrome may vary in measured intelligence with some functioning in the lower range of average, especially when they are younger (Lachiewicz, Spiridigliozzi, Gullion, Ransford, & Rao, 1994). Individuals with fragile X syndrome exhibit a broad array of aberrant characteristics including behavioral problems (e.g., hand flapping, biting, hyperactivity), some difficulties with aggression, language deficiencies, and, potentially, learning disabilities (Kauffman, 1993). Males with fragile X syndrome also appear to have autistic-like behaviors and also show a number of schizophrenic features (Kerby & Dawson, 1994). Fragile X is receiving growing attention in the research literature on behavior and personality characteristics although there is some concern that intervention methods are more based on clinical observation than on controlled research (Simensen, 1993).

MATERNAL CHARACTERISTICS

Maternal age seems to be associated with aspects of the baby's health other than Down syndrome. Spontaneous abortions occur more frequently in mothers who are very young (under 15), particularly if there have been multiple pregnancies. Likewise, the risk to mother and infant is substantially increased for mothers over 35 to 40 years of age. Spontaneous abortion is *least* likely to occur between the maternal ages of 20 and 30, which has been translated by many to mean that these are the prime childbearing years (Creasy, 1990). Although the mother's age is certainly important, other maternal influences also appear related to infant prematurity. For example, adequate nutrition may be one of the most important factors influencing general fetal health and well-being (Chez & Chervenak, 1990; Grand, 1992; Jack & Culpepper, 1991). Maternal nutrition deficiencies may have a significant impact on fetal development, as discussed in Chapter 3. Logic and the most fundamental knowledge of physiology would suggest that poor maternal nutrition endangers early mental development. However, the specific relationship between nutrition and mental development remains unclear (Ricciuti, 1993).

Sometimes the unborn fetus may be inadequately nourished regardless of the mother's nutritional status. Conditions such as maternal *thyroid deficiency, chronic*

diabetes, and *anemia* may substantially affect the development of the fetus and result in premature birth. Conditions associated with prematurity substantially increase the possibility of intellectual impairment of the baby. If, for example, the mother has a vascular insufficiency, the blood supply to the fetus may be inadequate, limiting the basic flow of nutrients and oxygen. Maternal diabetes may have similar effects. The impact is mainly dependent on the severity of the mother's condition and on the success of its medical treatment. However, maternal diabetes is always considered to create some degree of risk to the baby, who should be monitored for birthweight and gestational age problems as well as for other complications (Claireaux & Reed, 1989).

Serious damage to the fetus may be caused by *incompatible blood types* between the mother and the unborn baby. Perhaps the best-known form of this condition involves the *Rh factor*. This difficulty may be encountered if the mother's blood is Rh negative and the fetus has Rh positive blood. The mother's system may become sensitized to the fetus's Rh positive blood and begin to produce antibodies that cause serious damage to the fetus. Sensitization of the mother may occur if the Rh positive blood from the fetus enters her circulatory system, which commonly happens during delivery, or if Rh positive blood has been used in a transfusion given to the mother. Typically the first born is not at risk unless maternal sensitization occurs following a transfusion to the mother (Mahnovski & Pavlova, 1989). However, subsequent pregnancies present considerable fetal risk unless the mother receives medical treatment. The babies in these successive pregnancies are often damaged in the later stages of gestation as the mother's antibodies seek to destroy the Rh positive red blood cells, which are essentially a foreign substance in the maternal system. This can result in several conditions including *erythroblastosis fetalis* (a severe form of anemia) and *hyperbilirubinemia*. The latter condition occurs because of accumulating bilirubin from red blood cell hemoglobin, which may be so concentrated that it damages the brain tissue and causes mental retardation. Fortunately, treatment for Rh incompatibility has advanced substantially and many babies have been saved.

A variety of *maternal infections* may also increase the risk of harm to the unborn fetus, particularly if they occur during the first trimester of pregnancy. The likelihood of spontaneous abortion or severe defect in the infant is considerably greater when the mother has an infection accompanied by elevated fever (*febrile* infection). Such conditions may be especially problematic since the mother's illness may be very mild or even not recognizable but still may result in rather serious harm to the fetus. This makes both research and treatment difficult. Also, viral infections may result in serious difficulties during pregnancy although they do not always damage the fetus. German measles (rubella) is perhaps the viral infection most widely recognized as causing mental retardation. Once again the risk to the fetus is greatest in cases in which the mother contracts rubella during the first trimester of pregnancy. There is a significant risk to the fetus if she has rubella during early pregnancy, and there is a continued but lesser risk during the later months of pregnancy. It should be noted that mental retardation is not the only damage that results from congenital rubella. Deafness is the most frequent outcome; others include cerebral palsy, cardiac difficulties, blindness, seizures, and other neurological problems (Brendt & Beckman, 1990).

Syphilis is an infection caused by bacteria (the spirochete bacterium) transmitted by sexual contact. Maternal infection with syphilis may have a serious impact on the development of a fetus, particularly if the infection continues past the 18th week of gestation. In this condition, the bacteria cross the placenta and actually infect the developing fetus, causing damage to the central nervous and circulatory system tissues. Although treatment of syphilis has progressed over the years, venereal disease in general remains a serious problem. Often conditions are unreported, either because of embarrassment or because the symptoms are mild and subside. The danger to the unborn fetus remains, however, and may result in spontaneous abortion, stillbirth, mental retardation, and many other difficulties for the infected baby. Treatment may prevent such outcomes *if* implemented prior to the 18th week; the damage inflicted after this time is likely to be permanent.

Toxoplasmosis is another infection that may result in severe problems for the unborn fetus. This condition is caused by a protozoan infection that is carried in raw meat and fecal material. One of the major hazards of toxoplasmosis is that in the mother, the infection may be so mild that it does not cause serious concern, perhaps no more so than a common cold. Fetal impact may be dramatic, however. It should be noted that if the mother is exposed prior to conception, the danger to the fetus is minimal, but toxoplasmosis becomes a problem if the exposure occurs during pregnancy (Drew et al., 1996).

Clearly, maternal infection may cause a wide variety of complications leading to mental retardation, other defects, and even stillbirth. The fetus may also be endangered by a number of other substances introduced into the mother's system from the outside. Chemicals, drugs, alcohol, smoking (discussed in Chapter 6), and radiation all may cause difficulties for the fetus. In some cases the detrimental effects are well known whereas in others, the data may only be suggestive. For example, some consequences of maternal alcohol abuse during pregnancy is fetal alcohol syndrome (FAS) or the less severe fetal alcohol effects (FAEs). FAS is a leading cause of mental retardation and is particularly unfortunate because it is preventable (Short & Hess, 1995; Williams, Howard, & McLaughlin, 1994). Prenatal risk is heightened whenever almost any foreign elements enter the mother's system.

ATYPICAL BIRTH

Thus far we have discussed several factors that may operate during the prenatal period to place the fetus in danger of retardation. A comprehensive examination of all possible influences that may operate during this period is far beyond the scope of this chapter; complete chapters and volumes have been written providing information on this crucial part of life development (e.g., Johnson, 1988; Little, 1990). The final period of this phase, the birth process, also subjects a baby to risk of mental retardation. Historically, certain schools of thought viewed the process of birth, even an easy birth, as an extremely traumatic psychological event. Early psychoanalysts (notably Otto Rank and Sigmund Freud) attributed many later life difficulties, such as anxiety and depression, to repercussions from the shock of birth trauma. Birth is stressful to mother and infant alike. However, current thinking focuses much more narrowly on the physical trauma of atypical births than did earlier theories.

The *position of the fetus* in utero is very important in terms of potential birth complications. Figure 9-2 illustrates a normal fetal presentation with the head being positioned toward the cervix and the face down (with the mother lying on her back). Other fetal positions substantially raise the probability of damage. For example, the

FIGURE 9-2   An example of normal fetal position

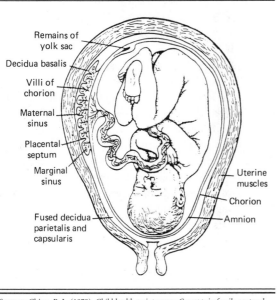

Remains of yolk sac
Decidua basalis
Villi of chorion
Maternal sinus
Placental septum
Marginal sinus
Fused decidua parietalis and capsularis
Uterine muscles
Chorion
Amnion

SOURCE: Chinn, P. L. (1979). *Child health maintenance: Concepts in family-centered care* (2nd ed., p. 109). St. Louis: C. V. Mosby. Reprinted by permission of the publisher.

FIGURE 9-3   Example of breech fetal position

SOURCE: *Dorland's illustrated medical dictionary* (1974). (25th ed., p. 1253). Philadelphia: W. B. Saunders. Copyright 1974 by W. B. Saunders Company. Reprinted by permission of the publisher.

problematic *breech presentation* occurs when the buttocks (rather than the head) are positioned toward the cervix. Figure 9-3 illustrates the breech fetal position. Several difficulties may result from a breech birth. Unless the fetus can be turned, the head will exit through the birth canal last rather than first. This occurs during the later stages of labor when the contractions are stronger and more rapid than during early labor. Breech birth may place a great deal of stress on the head of the fetus. In a normal delivery, the head moves through the birth canal slowly, permitting a gradual process of molding of the skull. But in a breech presentation, molding of the head may be rather rapid and perhaps incomplete, causing mechanical damage to the brain tissue. Damage may also occur because of the abnormal pressure (it is more intense and it is brought to bear on a head that is in a reversed position).

The breech position may cause difficulties other than possible mechanical damage. Since the fetal head is the last portion to exit, the baby must obtain its oxygen solely from the umbilical cord until delivery is completed. This may cause two difficulties. First, the cord may be too short to remain attached while the head is expelled. Un-

der such circumstances the placenta may become detached from the uterine wall, eliminating the oxygen supply to the fetus. This becomes particularly problematic if the head does not pass through the pelvic girdle fairly easily and quickly. The fetal head will be tightly confined in this portion of the birth canal, especially since the normal molding process is not occurring. If such difficulties arise, the baby may become *anoxic* (oxygen-deprived) and experience severe tissue damage. Anoxia may also occur if the cord is long enough but becomes pinched between the baby's head and the pelvic girdle. In such circumstances the oxygen supply may be cut off in the same manner as if the placenta had detached. In current medical practice, a breech baby is seldom delivered through the birth canal because of the risks described above. Even turning the fetus is dangerous, both because it is difficult and because of the possiblity of entangling the umbilical cord and the body. In many cases a fetal breech position baby will be safely delivered by Caesarean section.

FIGURE 9-4   Example of shoulder fetal position

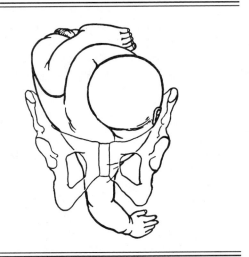

SOURCE: *Dorland's illustrated medical dictionary* (1974). (25th ed., p. 1253).
Philadelphia: W. B. Saunders. Copyright 1974 by W. B. Saunders Company.
Reprinted by permission of the publisher.

Figure 9-4 illustrates another abnormal fetal position that results in serious difficulties. In the *shoulder* presentation, a shoulder or arm proceeds down through the pelvic girdle before the rest of the fetus. This type of presentation makes delivery through the birth canal difficult and frequently impossible. Sometimes it is possible to reposition the fetus, which may make delivery routine. However, as noted previously, *in utero* repositioning may prove difficult; Caesarean section is often favored when extremely unusual fetal positions are present.

In this discussion of the birth process and mental retardation, we should mention yet another area of risk: the length of time for delivery. (Prospective parents should take heart, however, because advances in medicine have made childbearing safer than ever before.) Even if the fetal position is normal in all respects, the *time the delivery takes* can be very important. It was noted previously that during early stages of labor, contractions are typically less frequent and intense than those occurring later in delivery. This progression of intensity and frequency serves a very important purpose. In the early stages of labor, the fetus begins to move into the birth canal and the pelvic girdle begins to stretch. ˙ ˙ normally positioned fetus, the head also begins to be molded to fit through the birth canal. This is possible since the fetal skull is not solid. There are seams in the bony struc-

ture that have yet to grow together; these facilitate the molding process (thus, the temporarily misshapen heads often observed in newborn infants). The lower intensity of early labor permits the molding to occur gradually. The pressure of molding is absorbed by fluid surrounding the baby's brain, protecting it from injury. However, if labor proceeds very rapidly, time may not permit adequate molding of the skull. Generally, deliveries following a labor of less than two hours are considered *precipitous birth*. In these instances, there is an increased risk of brain injury and mental retardation.

The average labor time for a normal delivery is about 7 to 12 hours, although there is great variation in labor time for normal births. Difficulties may also result in deliveries in which labor is unusually prolonged. One of the complications that may accompany prolonged labor is similar to that associated with precipitous birth. If advanced labor (intense and frequent contractions) continues for a long period, a great amount of pressure is placed on the skull of a fetus. This pressure may rupture membranes and blood vessels, causing tissue damage and mental retardation. A second danger of prolonged labor is oxygen deprivation (anoxia) to the fetus or even a stillborn baby. Labor that continues substantially beyond the normal time span may place a fetus at risk if the placenta begins to detach, cutting off the baby's oxygen supply before delivery is completed.

NEONATAL CHARACTERISTICS

Two neonatal characteristics are highly related to a child's risk of developing retardation—*birthweight* and *gestational age*. Gestational age refers to the age of a fetus calculated from the time of conception. Low birthweight and inadequate gestational age at birth are perhaps the most common risk factors (Creasy, 1990). Infants with these two characteristics may be endangered in a wide variety of ways. They may have mental retardation or be retarded in their physical development; they may be highly vulnerable to infections or other diseases and have a higher probability of dying as an infant. Premature infants have inadequate birthweight and low gestational age.

COMMENTS

The preceding discussion may have been anxiety-provoking for the reader who is studying mental retardation for the first time, or is a prospective parent. We regret provoking anxiety, but it may be unavoidable or could even be helpful. The student of mental retardation cannot ignore these anxiety-arousing topics but must maintain an appropriate objective perspective. *The vast majority of pregnancies proceed normally and produce normal babies.* Today more than ever, medical advances have increased the safety of the mother and baby. You will recall that the prevalence of mental retardation is estimated as between 1 and 3 percent of the population. Mental retardation that is caused by prenatal influences, including abnormalities in the birth process, is quite infrequent and some is now preventable, as we shall point out later.

Causation During Infancy and Childhood

GENETIC FACTORS

In some cases, a newborn infant may already be in serious difficulty even though damage is not apparent at birth. A number of genetic disorders cause problems during infancy and later in a child's development. The first genetic disorder we will discuss actually overlaps the prenatal and early stages of infant development. Phenylketonuria (PKU) is an inherited metabolic disorder that occurs in about 1 of every 10,000 live births. Affected infants lack the ability to process phenylalanine, a substance found in certain foods such as milk. This results in an accumulation of toxic levels of phenylpyruvic acid (or phenylalanine), which severely damages the central nervous system (CNS). If the condition remains untreated, dramatic and serious intellectual impairment results (Nielsen, Lou, & Guttler, 1988). Most individuals with untreated PKU have IQs below 50 and are unable to speak. Many cannot master such basic tasks as bowel control and walking; they often exhibit generally aberrant behavior.

We mentioned that PKU causes damage in both prenatal and neonatal stages of development. Prenatal damage occurs with a pregnancy in mothers who themselves have PKU (Lowitzer, 1987). In such circumstances the fetus is exposed to a high level of phenylalanine, which damages the fragile developing nervous system. Prenatal diagnosis of PKU is now possible although the technique is not widely used (Cahalane, 1989). The neonatal PKU condition presents a different situation and one in which great treatment progress has been achieved. In these cir-

cumstances, the mother is a carrier but does not have PKU herself. PKU children born to such mothers develop symptoms after birth. When they encounter phenylalanine in their diet, their enzyme deficiency prevents proper processing of the substance and toxic-level accumulations occur as described before. As we have noted, the resulting damage will be severe if the condition is untreated. Fortunately such outcomes are unnecessary today because of advances in early diagnosis and treatment through dietary management (Steele, 1989).

Maple syrup urine disease is another genetic disorder in which there is metabolic deficiency. In this case the diagnostic label is more representative of a symptom than of the disease process. Affected infants tend to excrete urine that has a distinctive odor resembling maple syrup. Maple syrup urine disease may cause severe intellectual impairment, although more often than not the condition is fatal. Menkes, Hurst, and Craig (1954) originally described a family in which four out of six infants died of the disorder during the first few weeks of life. These babies exhibited a variety of difficulties, and their urine had the distinctive odor of maple syrup. The cause of this condition has been linked to metabolic deficiencies of three separate amino acids causing extreme CNS damage in the newborn. As with PKU, treatment may require dietary control although it is complicated by the fact that three amino acids found in many different foods are involved in the problem. In an untreated state maple syrup urine disease is lethal—few untreated infants survive more than a few weeks. Even treatment is risky since so little is known about it.

Galactosemia is another genetically linked metabolic disorder that may produce mental retardation during early infancy. With this condition there is difficulty in carbohydrate metabolism, unlike the two previously discussed disorders of protein and amino acid metabolism. Infants with galactosemia are unable to properly process certain sugar elements in milk. The results of such a condition, if untreated, are toxic damage to the infant's liver, brain, and other tissues. Again, treatment consists of dietary control (elimination of milk and other foods containing lactose) at a very early age, which may successfully prevent substantial damage. Untreated, galactosemia may cause permanent and serious intellectual impairment (Drew et al., 1996).

The reader should not interpret the discussion thus far as suggesting that all postnatal genetic disorders are metabolic in nature. Some are sex related in which the aberration occurs in the sex chromosome portion of the genetic material (e.g., Turner's syndrome, Klinefelter's syndrome, Lesch-Nyhan syndrome). Other genetic disorders may produce a variety of physical and functional manifestations. The interested reader may wish to consult a medically oriented volume for more complete information (e.g., Eden & Boehm, 1990; Reed, Claireaux, & Bain, 1989), since a comprehensive examination of genetic disorders related to mental retardation is quite technical and is beyond the scope of this chapter.

Most schemes for classifying events have certain failings in common—there are nearly always examples that do not neatly fit the classification system. This is exemplified by the first disorder we discussed, PKU. Although we have chosen to examine the topic in the subsection on postnatal disorders, we have seen that it also occurs prenatally in certain cases. The same is true of the next few conditions to be discussed—some overlap exists between prenatal and postnatal causes of retardation.

In the very early stages of prenatal development, tissue begins to differentiate, setting the stage for formation of various organs. We mentioned in the earlier section on developmental factors that this is a very vulnerable period for the unborn because of the vital development under way at the time. One event of great importance is the development of the neural tube, which eventually becomes the spinal and brain areas. This occurs quite early, with a groove being evident by the 17th or 18th day (gestational age); closure of the tube is normally completed between the 25th to 28th day. Substantial deviations in the closure process can result in serious outcomes that are typically labeled as *clinical defects* because the causes of such problems are unclear.

One closure-related clinical defect is known as *anencephaly*, which appears when there is improper closure at the head end of the neural tube. Anencephaly occurs early and results in incomplete development of the forebrain portion of cerebral tissue (in fact, the tissue often degenerates as gestation proceeds). Infants born with anencephaly typically die shortly after birth. Improper closure at other parts of the neural tube may also cause damage to the central nervous system in the form of a condition known as spina bifida. In such cases, incomplete closure of the spinal column may permit the spinal cord tissue and meninges (tissue covering) to protrude or bulge from their normal position. The type and extent of damage may vary depending on the longitudinal position of the affected area. Paralysis of the body below the damaged area is not uncommon and may prevent control of excretory functions. Infections may result and progress up the spinal cord tissue causing brain damage. Although typically not as serious as anencephaly, any incomplete closure of the neural tube may produce mental retardation as well as other disabilities.

Hydrocephalus is a clinical defect that may or may not be related to improper closure of the neural tube. In a generic sense, hydrocephalus refers to an increase in cerebrospinal fluid volume in the skull from any cause. With incomplete neural closure, the cerebral tissue does not assume its proper position in the skull cavity and is replaced by fluid. In such conditions, an excess of fluid in the skull is merely a symptom and is not the major difficulty in terms of brain damage. The primary problem results from the improper neural closure wherein the spinal cord begins to fuse with surrounding tissue at the opening. As the body grows in length, the upper cerebral tissue is actually pulled into the spinal area.

Hydrocephalus more commonly results from defects in the production or absorption of cerebrospinal fluid. The central nervous system has a circulatory system for the distribution of cerebrospinal fluid. This fluid plays a number of important roles, one of which is to provide a protective layer between the brain tissue and the bony structures of the skull and spine. As this fluid circulates, a certain amount is produced anew and a similar amount is absorbed. If more is produced than is absorbed, an excess of fluid accumulates, putting pressure on the brain and causing brain damage and mental retardation. This may occur in two fashions, depending on age and skull development. During early infancy the skull is in sections and is not solid. An excess of fluid accumulating in the skull cavity at this time will place outward pressure on the skull, spreading the sutures and enlarging the head. The fluid production-absorption imbalance may also occur after the suture lines have begun to fuse. Obviously in such circumstances an adequate expansion of the skull cavity will not be possible. Hydrocephalus under both of the preceding situations places excess pressure on the brain, typically resulting in damage and mental retardation. The degree of impairment may vary from very severe to only mild. In some cases, treatment is possible if the condition is discovered early and immediate surgery undertaken to implant devices to drain excess fluid.

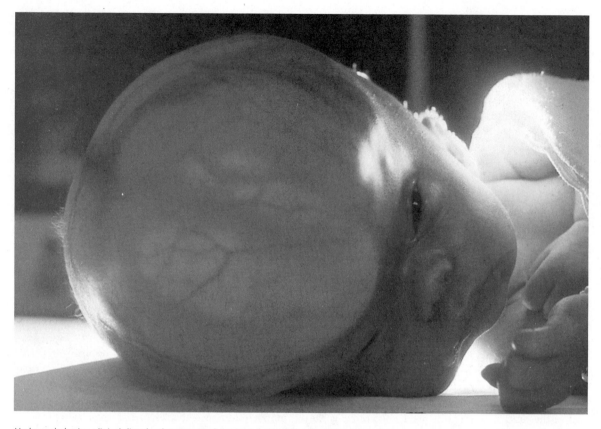

Hydrocephalus is a clinical disorder that may result in mental retardation if not treated early.

PSYCHOSOCIAL FACTORS

Infancy and the early childhood years are an extremely important period in an individual's development in a number of ways. Certain aspects of physiological development must be completed during these years or they will never occur. Additionally, during this time the infant is acquiring many of the skills and behaviors essential to intelligent behavior. The environment plays a vital role in this development although we know painfully little regarding *precise* impact in many cases. Our most solid evidence of environmental influence has been found in situations where there is severe abuse and neglect. Clearly, such deprivation has a serious impact on the young child's development and may result in severe developmental lag and mental retardation (see Chapter 4). Our knowledge about the precise influence of less extreme environmental conditions is more limited. During the postnatal period a complex constellation of social and physical factors comprise the child's environment. These include socioeconomic status, verbal and teaching interactions typical in the family, achievement motivation, exposure to toxic substances such as lead, and nutrition, to name only a few.

The list of potential psychosocial causes of retardation is huge and many risk factors occur together so that it is often difficult to trace the origins of retardation in mild cases. This is particularly unfortunate since, as noted earlier, the majority of mental retardation cases fall into this group. Many individuals who have mild retardation come from low socioeconomic environments with circumstances of poverty and other characteristics described in Chapter 4. In the absence of other evidence (e.g., identifiable physiological abnormalities) and with the potency of sheer numbers, it is difficult to avoid drawing strong conclusions regarding environmental causation. However, investigation of causes with this part of the population with mental retardation quickly become very complex and involve sociological as well as psycho-

Poverty and its associated factors of poor health care and malnutrition may seriously interfere with a child's intellectual development.

logical influences. Additionally, satisfactory resolution of the historical "nature-nurture" argument remains forthcoming.

TREATMENT

This section will examine a variety of techniques employed in working with children and adolescents having mental retardation. The term "treatment" should be interpreted cautiously, not in a literal sense, for it does not necessarily lead to "cure." Substantial progress has been made in preventing certain types of mental retardation, notably those with biomedical causes. (Prevention of retardation where there appears to be an environmental cause is a serious societal problem that is discussed fully

in Chapter 4.) Additionally, in some cases we are now able to arrest the progress of damage that would become more serious if untreated, as in the case of dietary treatment for PKU. However, although some prevention is possible, mental retardation is not amenable to cure as the term is generally interpreted; that is, it cannot be reversed.

The medical profession has played a significant role in the field of mental retardation. This is particularly true in cases that are identified prior to the beginning of formal schooling. Several factors contribute to this involvement. First of all, mothers are typically under the care of physicians during pregnancy and the newborn infant is also under close medical scrutiny. Difficulties that arise during this time naturally come to the attention of the physician, especially since they usually stem from physiological problems of some nature. Medical personnel are influential during a child's early years for yet another reason. Prior to the time the child enters school, the family is more likely to have a relationship with a physician than with a representative of any other discipline. Whereas it is not uncommon to have a family doctor, it would be rather unusual to have a family psychologist, and unless the family is very poor, they would not likely have a family social worker. Consequently, if a child of 3 or 4 years of age seems a little slow in mental development, the family physician is a probable contact even if the condition seems more mental than physical.

Prenatal Intervention

Earlier we discussed Down syndrome, a form of mental retardation caused by chromosomal abnormalities that can be diagnosed in utero. This is accomplished by drawing a sample of the amnionic fluid (amniocentesis) and performing a chromosomal analysis. Such procedures carry some risk to the baby and are not recommended on a routine basis for every pregnancy. Amniocentesis may, however, be undertaken with certain high-risk pregnancies (e.g., advanced maternal age, prior birth of a Down child).

When we speak of "treating" Down syndrome, the term treating is being used loosely and arouses a certain amount of controversy. If diagnosis indicates that the fetus has Down syndrome, nothing can be done to *treat* the baby to prevent retardation. The genetic error exists in the cell structure and subsequent cell division will include the chromosomal aberration. The parents may decide to terminate the pregnancy through a therapeutic abortion in order to avoid giving birth to a Down child. Recent years have witnessed a decrease in the prevalence of Down syndrome babies, which has partially been attributed to the availability of amniocentesis and legal abortions. Preventive measures of this type have become increasingly popular because of the emotional distress and great continuous financial expense involved in rearing a permanently disabled child.

The issue of abortion is, of course, highly controversial. Even more debatable are practices of allowing such children to die once they are born by withholding medical treatment (unrelated to their retardation) that would permit them to continue living (e.g., surgery to correct an intestinal obstruction). These practices, as well as others (e.g., active termination of the life of nonviable neonates), are not uncommon (Drew et al., 1996). A decision involving such alternatives raises many moral and legal questions and is agonizing for both parents and professionals. The physical and emotional outcomes of a decision to terminate life in such circumstances must be carefully measured against the impact of giving birth to and raising a child with Down syndrome or other serious disability that is identifiable at or before delivery. Medical personnel must be extremely sensitive to the needs of parents during the decision-making process; the parents should also be made aware of the resulting medical actions and potential legal ramifications. In many cases other professionals (e.g., psychologists, clergy) are called in to assist in this difficult time.

We previously noted that Rh incompatibility between mother and fetus can lead to mental retardation. Fortunately, over the years medical science has made dramatic progress in treating this condition. When an Rh incompatibility exists, doctors can monitor the fetal condition by periodically analyzing the amnionic fluid (Mahnovski & Pavlova, 1989). If the fetus reaches a critical state, one of several actions may be taken. In the later stages of pregnancy, it may be possible to induce labor and deliver the baby early. As soon as delivery is completed, the infant is usually treated with an exchange transfusion which supplies fresh and healthy blood. Obviously, such a procedure may not be possible if gestation has not progressed sufficiently to permit the infant to survive. But in such a situation the fetus must still have fresh blood. In some cases this has been successfully accomplished by conducting an exchange transfusion through surgically extending a fetal leg through an incision in the mother's abdomen. However, perhaps the most dramatic development has involved transfusions conducted completely on an intrauterine basis. This is typically accomplished by inserting a long needle through the mother's abdomen directly into the peritoneal cavity of the fetus. The fetus then receives a transfusion of blood that is compatible with the mother's antibodies and fetal development can proceed without damage to the unborn child.

An additional treatment has been developed in which an Rh negative mother is injected with Rh_o immune globulin (commercially known as RhoGAM). As we mentioned earlier, Rh incompatibility often does not present a problem during the first pregnancy if the mother has not become sufficiently sensitized to produce antibodies in damaging quantities. The mother should be injected with RhoGAM within the first 72 hours after she gives birth to her first baby. She will then be desensitized and can begin a subsequent pregnancy without antibodies being present. Treatment with RhoGAM is necessary for each pregnancy for Rh negative mothers.

Earlier we discussed PKU, an inherited metabolic disorder that can lead to mental retardation. Recall that PKU infants cannot properly process phenylalanine, which then accumulates in the body to a point that the central nervous system is damaged. PKU can be diagnosed early through routine screening procedures. If a baby is identified as having PKU early (prenatally or within the first few days after birth), the level of phenylalanine in the system can be carefully *controlled* through dietary restrictions. If it is initiated in time, control of the phenylalanine may prevent an accumulation from seriously damaging the central nervous system (Cahalane, 1989; Steele, 1989). If, however, treatment is not initiated promptly, irreparable damage may occur (Langenbek, Lukas, Mench-Hoinowski, & Stenzig, 1988). Although PKU may be one of the most studied genetic disorders related to mental retardation, the exact manner in which accumulated phenylalanine damages the CNS tissue is currently unclear. At least research on this disorder has led to an effective clinical diagnosis and treatment program and a consequent reduction in the number of impaired individuals.

Medical personnel often serve important roles in the general prevention of high-risk pregnancies. As we discussed earlier in this chapter, many conditions may contribute to such circumstances (e.g., maternal malnutrition) and when they occur the probability of mental retardation is increased. Routine health care becomes very important in identifying and treating high-risk mothers and infants. The medical profession is joined in such efforts by social workers, nutritionists, and others who work as a team to provide comprehensive care for needy families.

Postnatal Intervention

There is a great deal of interest in infant stimulation programs for those children who are identified early as having problems. In some cases, such efforts are used with children who are at risk because of prenatal or later en-

vironmental circumstances. In others, the infants may be clearly identified as having retardation because of a condition present at birth (e.g., Down syndrome). This type of treatment often involves psychologists, behavioral therapists, educators, and parents. Although each program has different characteristics, the basic notion is to provide the infant with a stimulus-rich environment through systematic, planned stimulation of all sensory modalities. The goal of such treatment is to accelerate development beyond what may be expected in the normal environment. Research on infant stimulation is logistically difficult and there is limited evidence regarding its lasting impact. However, the concepts have great intuitive appeal, and some long-term results appear promising (Bailey & Wolery, 1989; Hardman et al., 1996). One of the most prominent projects, the Carolina Abecedarian Project, involved comprehensive intervention in a variety of family environmental areas as well as direct infant stimulation (Ramey & Ramey, 1992). As with most research of this nature, results are still emerging but they seem to be favorable with respect to improving intellectual and social functioning.

Children with mental retardation frequently show distinct deficits in language development. Treatment efforts in this area have emphasized establishing an imitative repertoire of language skills as well as generalization of language skills from one environment to another (Drew et al., 1996). Although results have varied to some degree, language treatment appears to offer a promising line of investigation and potential treatment, and more children with mental retardation are learning to speak appropriately than was thought possible in the past. Teaching procedures have included demonstrating the required sounds and then rewarding children's closer and closer approximations to normal speech. Although effective, the process is extremely tedious and requires a devoted set of teachers and parents who are willing to spend a great deal of time teaching their children with retardation. Box 9-2 presents a study investigating the effectiveness of an augmented language system in promoting peer-directed interactions.

Treatment takes on a different character as the child with mental retardation begins formal schooling. As we mentioned earlier, many children are not identified as having retardation until they enter school. This is particularly true for a large portion of those who are mildly handicapped. Although their development may have

BOX 9-2   CAN YOUTH WITH SEVERE MENTAL RETARDATION BE TAUGHT TO SPEAK?

Thirteen young males (ages 6.17 to 20.42 years, mean age of 12.25) with moderate to severe mental retardation served as subjects in this study. They all had little or no functional speech at the beginning of the investigation. They participated in a two-year study learning symbols and using a system of augmented language (SAL) designed to supplement the severely limited language abilities present. The SAL included a symbol-embossed computerized keyboard that produced synthesized speech, a symbol vocabulary, and teaching procedures to encourage communicative attempts on the part of the subject. The symbol vocabulary was individualized for each subject based on information from parents and teachers. Teachers and parents were trained in three one-hour sessions regarding the use of the SAL device. The device was then integrated into each subject's ongoing activities at home and school. Data were collected via 30-minute observation probes during two school years (18 the first year and 19 the second); both home and school settings were employed for data collection. Data were collected by a nonparticipant observer using a coding log designed to record the content and context of each communication event. Audio tapes were used to supplement the data collected by observer recording. Communication success was the primary dependent variable.

Figure 9-5 summarizes a portion of the results relating to peer-directed utterances. These data indicate that the use of the SAL increased the percentage of successful peer-directed utterances when the target students interacted with peers having mental retardation, but not when the peers did not have mental retardation. The difference between the percentage of successful utterances directed to peers with mental retardation when using the SAL (87%) and when not using the SAL (31%) underscores the importance of the SAL when both peers have mental retardation.

FIGURE 9-5   Success of peer-directed utterances by peer status with and without SAL

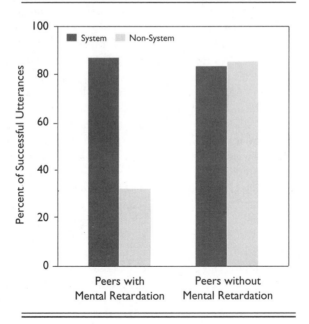

SOURCE: Adapted from Romski, M. A., Sevcik, R. A., & Wilkinson, K. M. (1994). Peer-directed communicative interactions of augmented language learners with mental retardation. *American Journal on Mental Retardation, 98,* 527–538.

been somewhat slow, their skills were adequate to adapt (if only marginally) in the preschool environment. However, as they enter the schools, they are expected to perform in those skill areas that are most difficult for them.

Depending on the type and extent of the child's mental retardation, some of the medical and behavioral treatments discussed earlier may still be under way during the school years. Medication may be administered on a continuing basis if the child has difficulties that warrant such treatment. The behavioral therapist may continue working with children of school age to shape social skills or to teach them to speak appropriately. The type of treatment and instructional programming will be largely determined by an assessment of individual needs.

One of the traditional approaches to instructing children with mental retardation in school has been to separate them from their nonhandicapped classmates. This has been accomplished by the use of both special schools and self-contained classes in regular schools. In the former arrangement, children having retardation receive instruction in a separate school, operated exclusively for the handicapped. Self-contained classes represent a somewhat less dramatic separation, with classes for children with mental retardation being operated within a school that also houses children without disabilities. In past years, these arrangements were the primary service delivery patterns for most, if not all, children identified as having retardation. Most recent trends have substantially altered the use of segregated approaches such as special schools and self-contained classes. Investigations over the past decade suggest that students with mental retardation benefit substantially from placement and interaction with their nondisabled peers (McDonnell, Wilcox, & Hardman, 1991; Meyer, Peck, & Brown, 1991).

The favored means of instruction now aims to minimize separation of handicapped and nonhandicapped children. With this system, those with mental retardation are instructed with their normal classmates to the degree that is feasible based on each individual child's level of functioning. Mildly handicapped children may receive instruction in a regular classroom with additional special assistance or they may be in the regular class part of the time and receive specialized instruction part of the time in what is known as a resource room. In general, the more severely the child is disabled, the greater is the likelihood that instruction will be undertaken in a setting apart from the regular educational environment. However, most recent thinking and practice has advocated working with even severely affected youngsters in instructional settings as close as possible to those of their peers without disabilities (Hardman et al., 1996; Stainback & Stainback, 1990).

The more integrated pattern of instruction has become a major focus of attention for educators since the mid-1970s. The popularity of this perspective is often attributed to the enactment of Public Law 94-142, federal legislation which has now been supplanted by the passage in 1990 of the Individuals with Disabilities Education Act (IDEA). Although the idea was promoted by federal legislation, the integration movement predates P.L. 94-142 by a considerable period of time. In fact, the federal legislation is probably best viewed as the culmination of a trend that began long before the law was conceived.

Educational service delivery for students with disabilities has long been conceived as reflecting a variety of options, ranging from more to less restrictive environments. The continuum of services varying from segregated to integrated is based on the functioning level of the child. Figure 9-6 illustrates this model as conceived for all students who are exceptional, ranging from severe disabilities to gifted and talented. The basic concept suggests that children with mental retardation should receive the least restrictive possible instruction and placement; that is, their schooling should be like that of normal children to the degree that this is possible. As this notion gained popularity, the terms *least restrictive alternative* and *mainstreaming* began to emerge, and the term *inclusion* is now commonly found in the literature. As this concept has gained popularity, integration efforts have been undertaken with more severely involved children that would not have been even considered a decade ago (Hardman et al., 1996).

As we examine the least restrictive alternative concept, it is important to realize that the notion has many legal connections outside the context of education for children with mental retardation. The least restrictive alternative principle has its basis in criminal law (e.g., *Jackson v. Indiana*, 1972), which holds that it is cruel and inhuman to dispense punishment that is disproportionately harsh in relation to the crime committed. The link between criminal law and educating children with mental retardation may seem tenuous at first glance. However, legal scholars have placed a great deal of emphasis on the relationship of this law to treatment of mental retardation. Throughout the years, there have been many cases of litigation involving education of those with mental

FIGURE 9-6   Educational service options for students who are exceptional

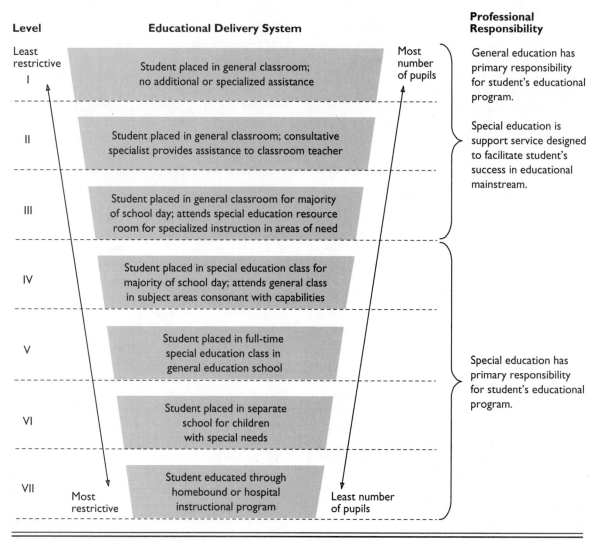

Level	Educational Delivery System		Professional Responsibility
Least restrictive		Most number of pupils	General education has primary responsibility for student's educational program.
I	Student placed in general classroom; no additional or specialized assistance		
II	Student placed in general classroom; consultative specialist provides assistance to classroom teacher		Special education is support service designed to facilitate student's success in educational mainstream.
III	Student placed in general classroom for majority of school day; attends special education resource room for specialized instruction in areas of need		
IV	Student placed in special education class for majority of school day; attends general class in subject areas consonant with capabilities		
V	Student placed in full-time special education class in general education school		Special education has primary responsibility for student's educational program.
VI	Student placed in separate school for children with special needs		
VII	Student educated through homebound or hospital instructional program	Least number of pupils	
Most restrictive			

SOURCE: Hardman, M. L., Drew, C. J., Egan, M. W. (1996). *Human exceptionality: Society, school, and family* (5th ed., p. 29). Boston: Allyn & Bacon.

retardation. Furthermore, federal legislation such as IDEA is not as innovative in educating those with disabilities as some would suggest. Drew, Logan, and Hardman (1992) catalogued over 200 different major pieces of federal legislation enacted between 1827 and 1981 that focused on this area, and the number has surely grown since that time.

Dramatic changes such as integrating instruction for the handicapped into the educational mainstream never occur without controversy. The movement toward educational integration was prompted by two major influ-ences occurring during the past 25 years: (1) shifts in social policy that aligned educating students having disabilities with the general social integration of people of color, and (2) research showing the beneficial effects of integrating disabled and nondisabled youngsters (Hardman, 1994; McDonnell et al., 1991; Meyer et al., 1991). Box 9-3 provides some additional information regarding the push to integrate, and a brief sketch of one young man who made it out of special education but likely would never have been placed there if IDEA had been in force earlier. Educational integration of normal children

---

BOX 9-3   HE PROBABLY WOULD NOT HAVE BEEN IN SPECIAL EDUCATION

Billy Hawkins is an exception, he moved *out* of the world of special education prior to the time that federal law required disabled students be educated with their nondisabled peers to the degree possible. Billy Hawkins spent the first 15 years of his life labeled as having mental retardation. Now Billy Hawkins holds a Ph.D. and is an administrator in higher education in the state of Michigan. Billy Hawkins is an African-American. During the period of time that he was classified as having mental retardation, Dr. Hawkins was in a special education class separate from his peers in general education. If IDEA had been in force, he would most likely not have been in special education to begin with.

IDEA is aimed at including youngsters with disabilities in the educational mainstream and guarding against ethnic discrimination. Overrepresentation of children of color in special education is still a concern as we approach the 21st century. According to a 1993 report by *U.S. News & World Report*, disproportionately high numbers of minorities in special education continues at a level beyond what would be expected based on population demographics. According to this report, nearly 80 percent of U.S. states have an over-representation of African-American students in special education. The passage of IDEA in 1990 is a hopeful move toward rectifying this problem. Plus we have the efforts of Billy Hawkins and others who are exerting great effort to see that children receive an appropriate education.

SOURCE: *U.S. News & World Report*, December 13, 1993.

---

with those having mental retardation is part of a larger issue relating to mental retardation which has been called *normalization*. The normalization principle goes far beyond the context of education and refers to placement, residential arrangements, and treatment for individuals with mental retardation at all ages. The normalization principle essentially broadens the integration effort into the daily lives of those with mental retardation, making their conditions and circumstances as close as possible to the norms of mainstream society. This notion has been most prominent in arguments against mass institutionalization of large segments of those with mental retardation.

Debate regarding the placement of individuals with retardation in residential institutions has been intense and continuing. Often the arguments have been based on compassion or on practicality. There is great variation from one institution to another—some provide good treatment whereas others are quite dismal. Those that fall in the latter category have prompted much of the anti-institutionalization furor. Much of the case against institutional placement for people with retardation has focused on the institutions with extremely bad conditions and treatment. Such perspectives raise the immediate question of how those with mental retardation fare outside an institutional setting. It is not surprising that some individuals with mental retardation manage rather well whereas others encounter some difficulty (Edgerton, 1990; Schalock & Genung, 1993). Successful placements depend on both community circumstances as well as the

personal competencies of the individual with mental retardation (Chen, Bruininks, Lakin, & Hayden, 1993). Community integration of those with mental retardation has many unresolved issues. Topics of concern emerging in the literature are much different than previously existed, but are logical outcomes of greater community immersion for those with mental retardation. For example, we must now ask questions about life expectancy of those with mental retardation who live in the community, their health care, and their sources of supports as family caregivers become aged (Criscione, Kastner, O'Brien, & Nathanson, 1994; Heller & Factor, 1993; Kastner, Nathanson, & Friedman, 1993).

PREVENTION

Prevention of mental retardation has been a goal of professionals in the field for many years. Because of the varied causes of mental retardation, prevention efforts are extremely diverse and some approaches have involved extremely controversial methods. In some cases, preventing mental retardation requires courses of action that are unacceptable to some segments of the population.

As we have seen, there are a number of prenatal causes of mental retardation. In some cases, these involve health problems or disease states that affect the developing fetus through the mother during pregnancy. Certain causes have become less of a difficulty than they once were because of immunizations that are routinely undertaken with a large portion of our general population (e.g., rubella). To the extent that these are effective in reducing the occurrence of maternal difficulties during pregnancy, they become important steps in preventing mental retardation.

Maternal nutrition and personal habits may also have an adverse impact on a developing fetus in certain cases. In some instances, high-risk maternal conditions have existed long before the pregnancy. One example is found in maternal malnutrition, which is often a long-standing condition that has serious effects on the central nervous system of the developing fetus. Such problems become especially severe when expectant mothers do not consult health care advice or have no access to prenatal medical care (Drew et al. 1996).

A close relationship between medical personnel and new parents is important in the prevention of mental retardation. As we have seen in the section on causation, a number of conditions may lead to development of mental retardation very quickly after birth unless they are recognized through monitoring, assessment, and early intervention. For example, PKU screening is now routinely undertaken when a baby is born and the family is in contact with a physician. When a baby is identified with PKU, treatment can be successfully undertaken through dietary control, thereby preventing damage to the central nervous system.

Prenatal screening and diagnosis can also lead to preventive intervention that may be highly controversial from a moral and ethical perspective. Procedures are available that permit detection of certain types of fetal damage in utero, which may present those involved with a difficult decision regarding continuation of the pregnancy. Although therapeutic abortion is legal and is much more accepted than it once was, such actions still present dilemmas for many people. In addition, there is greater public awareness of the problems attendant to intervening or withholding treatment from newborn babies that are grossly defective at birth. Decisions to withhold treatment and thereby "prevent" mental retardation are difficult and have many ramifications beyond any specific case being considered.

SUMMARY

Mental retardation has long been recognized and studied scientifically for many decades. Despite this lengthy history, problems and variations regarding definition and classification have persisted even into recent times. Although definitional differences significantly affect prevalence figures, estimates of the number of those with retardation have generally ranged from 1 to 3 percent of the general population. Classification schemes used in the field of mental retardation have included etiology, adaptive behavior, severity of intellectual deficit, and educational expectations. Each definition and classification approach has certain advantages and limitations depending on its purpose.

Causation of mental retardation is as varied as the types and levels of severity of the condition. Mental retardation may result from abnormalities during pregnancy, birth, and infancy. During the prenatal period, mental retardation may result from genetic aberrations or environmental difficulties that influence the health of the mother and the fetus. Also, the birth process may result in damage that can cause mental retardation. After birth, mental retardation may be caused by environmental influences that limit the opportunity to develop or by trauma or physical accident.

Treatment of mental retardation has been as diverse as its causes and behavioral characteristics. Some treatments have involved biological and medical interventions whereas others have focused on psychological and behavioral methods. A variety of medical intervention are employed. For example, in the case of Rh incompatibility, the infant may receive a transfusion of blood that is compatible with the mother's in order to minimize the development of damaging antibodies. After the baby is born, the mother may also receive an injection of RhoGAM to reduce the mother's sensitization to the baby's incompatible blood, thereby reducing antibody production and protecting future pregnancies. Medical intervention may also include such matters as prescribing a controlled diet for a child with PKU to minimize or circumvent central nervous system damage. Psychological and behavioral interventions may include intense stimulation during infancy to promote mental growth, special training in language skill development, and special education once the youngster enters school. Current research supports instruction of children with mental retardation in settings with their peers who do not have mental retardation to the degree possible.

C H A P T E R   1 0

HABIT DISORDERS

Key Terms

Anorexia nervosa. A condition of self-inflicted starvation accompanied by compulsive exercising.

Bulimia. Uncontrolled binge eating followed by purging (often vomiting).

Encopresis. Refers to abnormal or unacceptable patterns of fecal expulsion by children beyond the age of toilet training and who lack organic pathology.

Enuresis. Chronic inappropriate wetting by children who do not evidence physical disorders and who are old enough to be toilet-trained.

Insomnia. A condition where the person encounters continuing substantial difficulty falling asleep or maintaining sleep throughout the night.

Narcolepsy. A disorder involving involuntary and inappropriate sleeping spells.

Obesity. A condition where an individual is extremely overmweight (20 percent or more) and has an excess of body fat, to a degree that it impairs health and social interactions.

Phonological disorder. Refers to a disturbance in speech-sound production which results in a failure to use speaking sounds that are developmentally expected.

Somnambulism. Refers to episodes of activity during sleep, more commonly known as sleepwalking.

Stuttering. A disturbance in the fluency and rhythm of speech with intermittent blocking, repetition, prolongation of sounds, syllables, words, or phrases.

T
he disorders discussed in this chapter have been viewed in a variety of manners in the psychopathology literature. Theories have focused on a wide array of viewpoints ranging from primarily physiological to psychological as researchers have explored both causation and symptoms. It is not unusual to encounter perspectives representing a mixture of organic and psychological components. All of these views are correct to some degree because the disorders presented here have varying elements depending on the case. We have chosen to examine these problems as habit disorders because of the strong perspective of learning that surfaces in one fashion or another in each condition. In taking this approach, it is not our intent to discount the influence of physiology when relevant, and the reader will encounter considerable attention to such factors. In many cases, research has indicated that the most effective treatment is found in combinations of physiological and behavioral interventions.

Some habits are very desirable and important to human functioning (e.g., the nearly automatic behavioral movements involved in typing a paper). Other habitual behaviors may not be desirable but are so inconsequential that they would not be viewed as a disorder (e.g., nail biting). The topics reviewed here represent extreme deviations from normal behaviors that are unusual in their form or frequency and usually require treatment. They are also behavioral patterns that parents frequently identify as topics of concern.

EATING DISORDERS

Nearly all parents periodically complain about their childrens' eating behavior. Such concerns often focus on the parents' beliefs or preferences about proper eating habits for children. The parents complain that their youngsters do not eat enough, that they do not eat the "right" food, or that they do not eat at the proper time or place or with the prescribed implements. It is important at this point to remember that individual behaviors vary substantially within the range of what would be considered normal. More often than not, child eating behavior falls within the normal range of variation, even though parents are concerned. We will examine three conditions in this section: obesity, anorexia nervosa, and bulimia. The DSM-IV does not categorize obesity as an eating disorder because it has not been demonstrated to be consistently related to psychological or behavioral problems (American Psychiatric Association, 1994). There is no ques-

tion, however, that obesity represents a serious health problem.

Obesity

Obesity is not as easily defined as one might think (Kraemer, Berkowitz, & Hammer, 1990). In general, individuals are thought obese who have an excess of body fat and weigh approximately 20 percent more than is considered normal, based on published expected weights such as the Metropolitan Life Insurance tables. Obesity presents a number of difficulties for those so affected. Evidence suggests that obesity is increasing in prevalence among the population of the United States and is related to a number of serious health problems as well as psychological and social difficulties (e.g., Allison, 1995). Estimates suggest that 5 to 10 percent of the preschool population are obese, rising to 27 percent by ages 6 to 11 and 22 percent in the teen years. Further, the prevalence of

Obesity is increasing among children and often presents serious health risks.

obesity among children has increased 54 percent during the last 20 years (Foreyt & Goodrick, 1995). In addition to cardiovascular disease, individuals who are obese may also experience increased risk for hypertension, diabetes, sleeping problems (notably obstructive sleep apnea), depression, and social adjustment (Alfonso, 1995; Johnson, 1994; Sloan & Shapiro, 1995; Stoohs, Guilleminault, & Dement, 1993; Wing, 1993; Wing, Shiffman, Drapkin, & Grilo, 1995). A severely obese person has three times the risk of dying than a person of normal body mass (Abraham & Llewellyn-Jones, 1992). Consequently we address obesity as a serious problem to both physical and mental health. Part of the gravity of obesity lies in the fact that it is not easily treated. Theories regarding causes of obesity are conflicting and many treatment attempts have been disappointing in the long run (Kirsch, Montgomery, & Sapirstein, 1995). Those who lose substantial amounts of weight often are plagued by a continual battle of regaining.

CAUSATION

Theories regarding causation of obesity vary and often appear to be in conflict (Braet & Verhofstadt, 1994; Foreyt & Goodrick, 1995; Robinson, 1994). One view suggests that obesity is a hereditary or constitutional condition. Support for this perspective is partially derived from cellular differences between obese and nonobese individuals as well as between those who are obese as children and those who become overweight as adults. For example, physiologically there seem to be two types of obesity, hyperplastic and hypertrophic. *Hyperplastic obesity* occurs when an individual has an abnormally high number of fat cells (nonobese people tend to have about three billion such cells whereas hyperplastic obese counterparts may have double that number). *Hypertrophic obesity* occurs when individuals are overweight primarily because of extremely enlarged fat cells rather than because of a larger than normal number of fat cells. Obesity that is primarily hyperplastic seems to develop in childhood while hypertrophic obesity is more an adult disorder. Such causation, however, remains speculative since the distinction regarding onset does not always hold. Biological or physiological explanations feature the inheritance of a tendency toward obesity or slimness. Many times we hear statements such as "Johnny inherited his fatness from his parents" or "Sally is slender just like her mother." But these remain unsubstantiated popular beliefs, involving oversimplified explanations.

Many researchers and therapists working in the area view learned behavior as an important causal factor in obesity (Foreyt & Goodrick, 1995; Wilson, 1994). There is little question that food consumption in contemporary society serves social as well as physiological purposes, for children and adults (Brown, 1991). Although eating is a behavior that is under voluntary control, many dimensions of adult eating appear almost automatic and involuntary. A variety of family and social influences may lead to overeating and obesity (e.g., Agras, 1995). For example, parents socially reinforce their children for eating, perhaps consuming more than they physiologically need at the moment. Children are frequently admonished to "clean their plate" for one reason or another (e.g., it is socially appropriate, the cook may feel hurt, or some convoluted logic regarding necessary guilt because of depriving "all those starving children" elsewhere). Can such influences contribute to obesity? Does obesity developed during childhood destine an individual to obesity as an adult?

Much of the literature suggests that obesity in youngsters does predict adult obesity. Evidence suggests that overweight babies tend to be obese during childhood and adolescence and that this progression continues to adulthood (Agras, 1995; Graber, Brooks-Bunn, Paikoff, &

Warren, 1994; Kirschenbaum & Fitzgibbon, 1995). Abraham and Llewellyn-Jones (1992) reported data indicating that as high as 41 percent of infants "who were obese at the age of 1, were obese as adults" (p. 147). Other estimates place the chances of an obese 12-year-old being of normal weight when reaching adulthood at only 1 in 4, and the normal weight probability diminishing to about 1 in 28 if the obesity persists through adolescence (Foreyt & Goodrick, 1995). This is not a highly optimistic outlook for obese youngsters. Certainly more research is needed in this area but the probabilities are compelling.

Recent literature on obesity and other eating problems illustrates both the importance of research and the need for more sophisticated theoretical perspectives that can tolerate multiple and interactive causation (e.g., genetic and environmental) (Agras, 1995; Brooks-Bunn, Graber, & Paikoff, 1994; Brownell & Wadden, 1992; Ponton, 1995). A wide variety of factors remain to be clarified with regard to their effects on weight and, ultimately, relationships to obesity. For example, although folklore persistently supports the notion that stress-induced eating may lead to obesity, research in the area of stress and eating remains unclear regarding the nature of this relationship (Greeno & Wing, 1994).

TREATMENT PROCEDURES

Weight loss is a difficult process and one that attracts a great deal of attention in the lay public. One has only to count the lengthy paid advertisements on television to determine that this is a topic of high interest. Solutions and treatments for overweight conditions that might seem uncomplicated on the surface, such as dieting and exercise, are neither simple nor reliable in the context of obesity (de Peuter, Withers, Brinkman, Tomas, & Clark, 1992; Lowe, 1993). Although specific strategies for treating obesity are many, they can generally be categorized into two broad groups: behavioral therapies and medical treatments.

As a general rule of thumb, treatment for obesity must be approached in a systematic fashion and in a manner that raises the probability of success. Current thinking suggests that a multidisciplinary team is a more effective means of addressing the complexities of obesity than employing what may be limited tools available to a single profession (Alger, 1992). Certain characteristics of the person being treated also tend to lend themselves to a greater or lesser probability of successful treatment

(Foreyt & Goodrick, 1994; Wardle, 1995). For example, eating patterns may be quite important. Obese people who eat three meals a day as opposed to "grazing" at various times throughout the day tend to respond more favorably to treatment (Sitton, 1994). Likewise, people who exhibit the more structured three meals per day seem to experience better success than those who omit meals such as breakfast (Sitton & Miller, 1991). It is also not surprising that a history of binge eating does not lend itself to predicting successful obesity treatment (Alger, 1992; Hart, 1991; Sitton, 1994). Recent literature on obesity is addressing assessment more than ever before (e.g., Allison, 1995; Wardle, 1995). Monitoring treatment progress and predicting success is an important element in obesity management in order to reduce the frequency of failures in a field where success has not been as high as desired.

Medical treatments for obesity have long held considerable appeal because of what appears to be a simple and rather rapid process. In many cases, the concept of taking a pill to provide a solution for a difficult problem is enticing to the lay person. Unfortunately, the drugs available that suppress appetite often have a number of undesirable side effects, and lost weight is frequently regained once the medication is discontinued (Abraham & Llewellyn-Jones, 1992; Sitton, 1994). A variety of amphetamine-based medications have been popular in both over-the-counter form and by prescription to suppress appetite. For many people, such drugs may serve to reduce appetite but they also may produce a heightened level of irritability and disrupt sleep. Dexfenfluramine is a medication aimed at increasing the secretion of the brain hormone serotonin which, in turn, reduces the desire for food, particularly carbohydrates. Dexfenfluramine has been used as a medical treatment for obesity with some degree of success, although weight tends to be regained when patients terminate the medication (Weintraub, 1992).

Surgical interventions also have been used as medical treatments for obesity, particularly for individuals who suffer from the most severe forms. Recent surgical approaches have favored strategies that restrict stomach capacity either through the use of stapling procedures or inserting balloon-type devices into the gastric cavity (Bull & Legoretta, 1991). Both of these procedures are aimed at reducing gastric volume, thereby producing a perception of being full after eating relatively small amounts of food. Complications have plagued both types of treatments (e.g., infections, apparatus failures), and some believe that such approaches should be employed only when other therapies have been unsuccessful (e.g., Sitton, 1994).

Behavioral therapies tend to focus on managing eating behavior rather than addressing other causes of obesity (e.g., Agras, Telch, Arnow, & Eldredge, 1995; Moreno & Thelen, 1995). While behavioral treatment of obesity does not completely discount physiological factors, it does focus on those contingencies in the environment that can be manipulated to alter habits related to energy intake and expenditure. One of the most prominent features of behavioral therapies relates to the development of self-monitoring capacity by the obese individual (Foreyt & Goodrick, 1995; Sitton, 1994). Self-monitoring allows the person to become conscious of behaviors that contribute to undesirable eating, which can then be targeted for modification. In many cases, the individual being treated must keep careful records of what is eaten, when it was eaten, who was present, and what feeling predominated at the time. Social and environmental circumstances can become cues for eating, which may also become targets for control and/or change. It is also important to modify the consequences of eating such that there is some type of reward for eating in a manner that promotes weight reduction. Such a process basically involves cognitive-behavioral restructuring in order for the person to be able to effectively lose weight, revise their image of themselves and their environment, and maintain the loss (Agras et al., 1995; Rosen, Orosan, & Reiter, 1995). Maximally effective treatment requires that the specific features of any treatment program must be tailored to the individual and his or her environmental context (Brownell & Wadden, 1991; Schwartz & Brownell, 1995).

Although behavior therapies have been somewhat successful in treating obesity, maintenance of weight loss continues to be a difficult problem. Relapse prevention is an essential element of any comprehensive treatment program for obesity (Sitton, 1994). Behavioral patterns leading to obesity are not developed overnight, but over a considerable period of time. Further, as time progresses and the condition persists, such habits become a part of one's life. This is clear from the mixed success regarding weight loss in many cases and even more so by the incredible difficulty obese children experience in maintaining a weight loss. Continued research on the effective treatment of obesity and maintenance programs is essential for promoting a healthy lifestyle.

Anorexia Nervosa

Anorexia nervosa is a condition of self-inflicted starvation that occurs most often in adolescent females with most cases developing before age 25. The average age of onset is about 17 and there appears to be peaks in frequency at 14 and 18 (American Psychiatric Association, 1994). Only a very small percentage of individuals with anorexia are male and about 90 to 95 percent are female (Shafer & Garner, 1995; Tso, 1992). Although anorexia nervosa used to be very rare, it appears to be occurring much more frequently in recent years (Marx, 1994). Some writers have estimated that for adolescent females and young women, between 5 and 10 percent are affected with anorexia, and in certain social contexts the figure may be as high as 20 percent (Abraham & Llewellyn-Jones, 1992; Tso, 1992). The increased prevalence may result from the tremendous influence of the broadcast media and the value contemporary society places on slenderness (Myers & Biocca, 1992). This reasoning is persuasive given the predominance of female patients and the increasing prevalence of the disorder, particularly in industrialized, highly developed countries (Fabrega & Miller, 1995; Kinoy & Holman, 1992; Solberg & Strober, 1994). It also seems to occur more frequently in families that might be considered above average socioeconomically, and further evidence suggests that individuals in higher social classes have a greater desire to be thin (Marx, 1994). The slogan "You can't be too rich or too thin" appears on T-shirts and other items in expensive catalogues. Although the societal line of logic is compelling and likely accurate to some extent, it is too easy to chastise society. The disorder is complicated and can be life-threatening in some instances (e.g., the case of the well-known singer Karen Carpenter). About 10 percent of the anorexic patients who are hospitalized experience complications leading to death (American Psychiatric Association, 1994; Shisslak & Crago, 1992). Individuals with anorexia frequently demonstrate the binge-purge patterns such as those found in bulimia, which leads to inclusion of such a subtype category in the DSM-IV (American Psychiatric Association, 1994; Shafer & Garner, 1995). As we shall see in the following paragraphs,

---

BOX 10-1 TRACY

Tracy came to therapy at the age of 19 in her sophomore year of college, where she was getting good grades. She had a boyfriend from high school but had made few friends at college. Tracy stood 5'6" tall and weighed about 98 pounds. She had started losing weight deliberately about two years earlier, although she had been thin even then, weighing about 120. She just started eating less and less; losing weight became the most important thing in her life, although she couldn't explain why. When she came to me, Tracy was frankly unhappy about the prospect of gaining weight, but she was also frightened by feelings of fatigue, the loss of her period for over six months, and her difficulty in being able to concentrate on schoolwork.

As the younger sister of an unpredictable, rebellious, angry girl, Tracy felt obligated to be a "problem-free" child for her parents. She had witnessed countless fights between her parents and sister and listened endlessly to her parents complaining about her sister. Tracy was praised by her parents for being a good student, responsible, and considerate. Tracy had become entirely oriented toward pleasing others. She learned to hide her negative feelings, conceal different opinions, and become exceptionally intuitive about other people's wishes and needs.

Whenever possible, Tracy kept her problems to herself. She carried her silence even to the point of telling no one when she was attacked and raped on the way home from school when she was 14.

As high school graduation grew closer, Tracy began to restrict her food intake. She counted calories constantly, began to eliminate whole food groups from her diet, and spent hours inspecting her body for fat. She knew that she was afraid to go away to college. She feared that her mother would become depressed without her. She felt guilty about starting a life of her own and confused about what her parents really wanted her to do about going to college. Tracy did not realize that her overwhelming terror of making a mistake played a major part in her anorexia nervosa.

Family and friends expressed concern about Tracy's weight loss, but she held them off with excuses and with promises to gain. She decided on her own to pursue psychotherapy because of worries about her physical health. After Tracy and I discussed her diagnosis of anorexia nervosa, we agreed to the following treatment plan: a complete medical evaluation by a physician familiar with eating disorders; weight gain at the rate of 1 to 2 pounds a week; a target weight of 122; weekly "weigh-ins" at the doctor's office (in a hospital gown after voiding, and supervised by the doctor or nurse); and psychotherapy once or twice weekly, depending on her progress.

Tracy took over one-and-a-half years to reach her target weight. She would gain and lose. For a long time, she described her food intake as "huge," when in fact she was eating under 2,000 calories per day (on which she could not gain). Her fatigue and poor concentration, which she correctly understood as the effects of malnutrition, helped motivate her to stop restricting her food.

Psychotherapy centered on three broad topics: (1) her "addiction" to food restriction and how to recover from it, (2) her feelings about her family and about herself as a part of her family, and (3) her body image problems.

Tracy was able to grasp the concept of "addiction to restriction" very easily. She also saw that she would have to learn new coping skills in place of her "addiction." She remained, however, very guarded on the topic of her family. She was able to express some resentment toward her sister, but she just couldn't acknowledge any negative feelings toward her parents. Her body image problems had a lot to do with the rape at age 14. Tracy did come to feel and express her reactions to that trauma—her self-blame, her shame, and last of all, her anger.

Tracy achieved her goal weight and maintained it for over six months before ending her psychotherapy. She would return to anorexic ways of thinking when pressured or stressed, but she could resist the temptation to restrict her food. She had also expanded her social network at school, was able to participate in "fun things," share intimate stories with friends, and be silly when she felt like it.

SOURCE: Wagner, S. (1992). Eating disorder treatment stories: Four cases. In R. Lemberg (Ed.), *Controlling eating disorders with facts, advice, and resources* (pp. 58–59). Phoenix, AZ: Oryx Press.

---

causation may be complex and difficult to identify. Also, anorexia nervosa is not totally a phenomenon of recent vintage. One of the most often cited graphic descriptions of the disorder was published in 1689. In this work, Morton characterized an individual as being so thin that she was "like a Skeleton only clad with Skin" (cited in Tso, 1992, p. xi).

For the most part, individuals identified as suffering from anorexia seem to be driven by a need to be thin or, more specifically, by an obsession to avoid being fat (Srinivasagam, Kaye, Plotnicov, Greeno, Weltzin, & Rao, 1995). This results in a sharp reduction of food intake and is often accompanied by an almost frantic, compulsive exercise routine (Alexander-Mott, 1994; Shafer &

Garner, 1995). These behaviors occur despite the fact that few patients have a history of being overweight. In fact, most descriptions of them as children include terms such as "problem-free" almost to a point of being overly docile and conforming. This was the description given of Tracy, the young woman described in Box 10-1, by Wagner (1992). Often they are excellent students and appear to have few problems or disorders of any kind. They are frequently characterized as perfectionists, intellectually superior, overly sensitive, hold a negative perception of themselves, and manifest compulsive behaviors such as repetitive cleaning rituals (Bastiani, Rao, Weltzin, & Kaye, 1995; Gillberg, Rastam, & Gillberg, 1995; Thiel, Broocks, Ohlmeier, & Jacoby, 1995). Not all cases of anorexia nervosa have compulsive features, although such elements are very prominent in the literature on this disorder. The DSM-IV diagnostic criteria for anorexia nervosa are summarized in Table 10-1.

After they recover, most anorexics can describe environmental contingencies that prompted and precipitated their unusual eating behavior. Often the behavior was triggered by some rather common or trivial event that made them feel too heavy or not respected. The onset of the disorder is usually quite sudden; eating is reduced and a rigorous exercise regime begun. Frequently, as weight loss and exercise compulsively continue, family members reportedly make note of the fact that the youngster is becoming too thin or is beginning to look emaciated. Despite these cues, anorexics often deny such viewpoints, continue to exercise and eat very little. The high activity level typically continues until the individual reaches such a weakened state that it can no longer be continued. Weight loss criteria in DSM-IV is only 15 percent below normal, although the loss may range much higher in individual cases (Alexander-Mott, 1994; American Psychiatric Association, 1994). Physiological changes go far beyond the reduction of body fat to include a wasting of muscle tissue and alterations of the bone marrow, as well as a variety of other problems associated with starvation (Shafer & Garner, 1995). Menstruation ceases in female patients or becomes extremely painful, and often the protective layers of flesh diminish so completely that it is painful to sit on a hard surface such as a wooden chair or in a bathtub. Frequent bruising also occurs as the disorder progresses. Clearly anorexia may become a serious problem, as suggested by the mortality rate cited earlier, not one easily dismissed.

TABLE 10-1 DIAGNOSTIC CRITERIA FOR ANOREXIA NERVOSA

A. Refusal to maintain body weight at or above a minimally normal weight for age and height (e.g., weight loss leading to maintenance of body weight less than 85% of that expected; or failure to make expected weight gain during period of growth, leading to body weight less than 85% of that expected).

B. Intense fear of gaining weight or becoming fat, even though underweight.

C. Disturbance in the way in which one's body weight or shape is experienced, undue influence of body weight or shape on self-evaluation, or denial of the seriousness of the current low body weight.

D. In postmenarcheal females, amenorrhea, that is, the absence of at least three consecutive menstrual cycles. A woman is considered to have amenorrhea if her periods occur only following hormone (e.g., estrogen) administration.

Specify Type

Restricting Type: During the current episode of anorexia nervosa, the person has not regularly engaged in binge-eating or purging behavior (i.e., self-induced vomiting or the misuse of laxatives, diuretics, or enemas).

Binge-Eating/Purging Type: During the current episode of anorexia nervosa, the person has regularly engaged in binge-eating or purging behavior (i.e., self-induced vomiting or the misuse of laxatives, diuretics, or enemas).

SOURCE: American Psychiatric Association. (1994). *Diagnostic and statistical manual of mental disorders (DSM-IV)* (4th ed., pp. 544–545). Washington, DC: Author.

A very interesting problem is how youngsters can be victimized by anorexia nervosa. Most of their clinical descriptions would lead us to believe that they should receive a great deal of reinforcement for all of their "good" and conforming behavior. Further, while the events that reportedly precipitate the disorder vary greatly in magnitude, they often seem too trivial to trigger such a dramatic outcome (Marx, 1994). Causation of anorexia nervosa remains somewhat unclear. Some writers have attributed the disorder to genetic factors, hormonal and endocrine problems as well as malfunction of the hypothalamus (Braun & Chouinard, 1992; Morley, Flood, & Silver, 1992; Park, Lawrie, & Freeman, 1995). Others have postulated psychological problems (Gillberg et al., 1995; Heebink, Sunday, & Halmi, 1995; Irwin, 1993; Thiel et al., 1995). Perhaps the most common view of causation stresses environmental influences, often including parental behaviors and the impact of family relations or other life-stress situations (Sohlberg & Strober, 1994; Steiger, 1993). Further research is clearly needed along all lines of etiological possibilities.

Many of the physiological problems associated with anorexia nervosa will reverse under treatment, but treatment is often complex and must focus on both physical and psychological factors. One of the immediate needs is to correct the individual's nutrition problem and achieve medical stabilization. This can be difficult since many patients will resist; but it is essential in order to begin reversing the physical deterioration (Goldner & Birmingham, 1994). A variety of therapeutic procedures have been employed for this process including hospitalization, psychotherapy, drug treatment, force feeding, behavior modification, and information feedback to the patient regarding the effects of eating (Rockwell, 1992; Shafer & Garner, 1995; Vaz-Leal & Salcedo-Salcedo, 1995). Treatment must address a variety of factors since the weight and nutrition problems may be symptomatic of other difficulties. Therapists often focus on the relationships among family members, particularly if the youngster is still living at home (DiNicola, 1993; Vaz-Leal & Salcedo-Salcedo, 1995). Often such treatment is aimed at changing parental expectations for conforming, obedience, and achievement striving since these children seem to try too hard to meet parental expectations. Therapy approaches seem to include combinations such as those noted above and often include family counseling (Dare, Eisler, Colahan, & Crowther, 1995; Dare, LeGrange, Eisler, & Rutherford, 1994). Even under intense therapy regimens, this is a difficult disorder to treat. Women long-recovered from anorexia still score significantly higher than peers who were never affected on measures of persistent perfectionism and exactness, tendencies thought to contribute to the condition (Srinivasagam et al., 1995). Clearly, anorexia nervosa is not a simple disorder. Treatment seems most effective when a combination of methods is used to address the many problems of an anorectic teenager.

Bulimia

Bulimia is an eating disorder in which there are frequent episodes of uncontrolled binge eating alternating with purging of what has been consumed. During such eating binges, a person may ingest enormous quantities of food in a very short time period. Although estimates vary widely, it has been reported that bulimics may consume between 1,200 and 55,000 calories in a single binge, and with some individuals binging on a daily basis (Weiss, Katzman, & Wolchik, 1994). These people may not be able to control such eating binges despite the fact that they typically view it as being abnormal (Pike, Loeb, & Walsh, 1995). Powerful feelings of guilt and self-disgust regarding binge eating may then lead to purging (through vomiting or laxatives) and periods of fasting. This behavior is also largely out of control. For example, because of increased tolerance, laxative use may reach an extremely high level, over 100 doses daily for some individuals (Kinoy & Holman, 1992). The DSM-IV diagnostic criteria for bulimia are summarized in Table 10-2.

Bulimia has often been thought to be closely related to anorexia nervosa (Abraham & Llewellyn-Jones, 1992). On the surface, behaviors of the two disorders appear similar. However, the DSM-IV has outlined distinctions between them that allow for differential diagnosis and classification. Individuals with bulimia are often close to an appropriate weight and are able to maintain that approximate level, whereas the binge-eating/purging type of anorexic is not so characterized, being significantly underweight. It is quite possible for a person to be clinically diagnosed as having binge-purge type anorexia nervosa at one point and later to be classified as bulimic, if such matters as weight returning to normal and menses becoming rather regular (American Psychiatric Association, 1994; Rastam, Gillberg, & Gillberg, 1995). Common to both anorexia and bulimia is an extreme concern with body weight and fear of becoming fat. Individuals with bulimia exhibit a considerable fluctuation between gaining and losing weight, whereas anorexics are characterized only by extreme, life-threatening, weight loss.

It is very difficult to accurately determine the prevalence of bulimia because affected individuals are extremely secretive about the extreme binging and purging, and social eating behavior is usually controlled and appropriate (Parry-Jones, 1994). Unless an individual admits a problem exists, the disorder is difficult to detect since bulimics' body weight and condition are typically within the normal range. Like anorexia, bulimia is a disorder that primarily affects young females with males being diagnosed infrequently. Estimates indicate that about 1 to 3 percent of adolescent and young adult females are affected by bulimia (American Psychiatric Association,

TABLE 10-2 DIAGNOSTIC CRITERIA FOR BULIMIA NERVOSA

A. Recurrent episodes of binge eating. An episode of binge eating is characterized by both of the following:

(1) eating, in a discrete period of time (e.g., within any 2-hour period), an amount of food that is definitely larger than most people would eat during a similar period of time and under similar circumstances.

(2) a sense of lack of control over eating during the episode (e.g., a feeling that one cannot stop eating or control what or how much one is eating).

B. Recurrent inappropriate compensatory behavior in order to prevent weight gain, such as self-induced vomiting; misuse of laxatives, diuretics, enemas, or other medications; fasting; or excessive exercise.

C. The binge eating and inappropriate compensatory behaviors both occur, on average, at least twice a week for 3 months.

D. Self-evaluation is unduly influenced by body shape and weight.

E. The disturbance does not occur exclusively during episodes of anorexia nervosa.

Specify Type:

Purging Type: During the current episode of bulimia nervosa, the person has regularly engaged in self-induced vomiting or the misuse of laxatives, diuretics, or enemas.

Nonpurging Type: During the current episode of bulimia nervosa, the person has used other inappropriate compensatory behaviors, such as fasting or excessive exercise, but has not regularly engaged in self-induced vomiting or the misuse of laxatives, diuretics, or enemas.

SOURCE: Reprinted with permission from the *Diagnostic and statistical manual of mental disorders.* Fourth Edition (1994). Washington, DC: American Psychiatric Association, pp. 549–550). Copyright 1994 by the American Psychiatric Association.

1994). Bulimia seems to emerge more frequently among certain populations than others. For example, for women of college age, the prevalence seems to be considerably higher, ranging from nearly 4 to just under 20 percent (Weiss et al., 1994). These young women also seem to have a history of eating problems (Tordjman, Zittoun, Anderson, & Flament, 1994), as well as other difficulties including depression (Alpert, Maddocks, Rosenbaum, & Fava, 1994; Andrews, Valentine, & Valentine, 1995; Walters & Kendler, 1995) and obsessive-compulsive behaviors (Thiel et al, 1995).

The causes of bulimia are somewhat unclear at this time. People with bulimia seem to have a preoccupation with food and a persistent urge to eat—they live a life that largely revolves around food and eating. Nearly any incident may trigger an episode of binging, not unlike the behavior of alcoholics (Sundgot-Borgen, 1994). As noted above, those with bulimia seem to have more evidence of affective disturbance than most people. Additionally, they seem to evidence a higher level of substance abuse and some report a history of sexual abuse (Alpert et al., 1994; Holderness, Brooks-Gunn, & Warren, 1994; Pope, Mangweth, Negrao, & Hudson, 1994). There is also considerable interest in cultural and social pressures as both triggering and long-term causal agents (Kenny & Adams, 1994; Myers & Biocca, 1992; Stice, 1994). Clearly, there is a need for additional research on the causal factors contributing to bulimia. Although we know that some individuals are more at risk than others (e.g., young females, certain athletes), there is much we do not know regarding the causation (Sundgot-Borgen, 1994; Thompson & Sherman, 1993).

There have been a variety of treatments employed for bulimia with varying degrees of success. From the outset, it is necessary for a medical evaluation of the individual to be undertaken. There are a number of medical complications that may require attention initially (Sansone & Sansone, 1994). For example, there may be ruptures in the gastric or esophageal areas due to the vomiting, there may be metabolic complications either from the vomiting or the abuse of laxative agents, or there may be musculoskeletal problems that are derivatives of overexercise. Any of these may require some type of medical attention. There are also serious dental complications found in many bulimia sufferers (dental erosion), although these are not amenable to treatment since they are irreversible (Sansone & Sansone, 1994). At any rate, medical stabilization or treatment may be required prior to directing attention to the bulimic condition itself (Crow & Mitchell, 1994). It should be noted that those bulimics exhibiting the most severe symptoms over a longer period of time are the most difficult to treat.

Treatment approaches to bulimia have included administration of medication, and various combinations of counseling and behavioral management. In some cases, medication that has shown limited or mixed results with anorexia, such as antidepressants, seem to be somewhat more effective for bulimia (Advokat & Kutlesic, 1995). Antidepressants appear to produce a decrease in binge eating in about 70 percent of the patients, although some have noted that behavioral therapies appear somewhat more effective (Crow & Mitchell, 1994). The various strategies used in behavioral approaches are many, but typically self-monitoring is a prominent feature, as it is with anorexia treatment. A range of cognitive behavioral therapies, using basic behavioral management principles, have been shown to be quite effective with bulimic patients (Fairburn, Norman, & Welch, 1995; Wilson & Fairburn, 1993). Initially these approaches involve interrupting the disordered eating, followed by examination of connections between cognition and eating, followed by self-monitoring training and alterations in the reinforcement contingencies (e.g., cues, thoughts or cognitions, consequences). Once advances have been made, therapy may begin a shift to relapse prevention and perhaps development of support groups and/or family involvement (Dodge, Hodes, Eisler, & Dare, 1995; Manley & Needham, 1995). Continued treatment research is important in order to more clearly determine relative effectiveness between features of the treatments.

TOILETING PROBLEMS

Periodically, most parents express concern regarding their child's toileting behavior, particularly when the youngster is being trained to perform this natural function in a socially appropriate manner. The process of toilet training often generates a certain amount of frustration and stress for parents and children alike. For the most part, problems encountered in toilet training are transient and appropriate patterns of behavior are developed by the time a child is 2 to 4 years of age. However, for a small percentage of children this does not occur. For such children, toileting remains problematic beyond the normal age at which we expect these behaviors to have been habituated and may continue into and beyond the elementary school years.

It is somewhat surprising that more research has not been undertaken on toileting behaviors. The question of the best time for beginning training has not yet been completely resolved. Obviously the appropriate age will vary from child to child—a statement that holds true for all behaviors. Around age 2 seems to be the commonly accepted time when serious efforts should be directed toward shaping these behaviors, although the pendulum has swung widely between early and later ages for the last century in the United States (Luxem & Christophersen,

1994). Customary ages for undertaking toilet training vary considerably between and within cultures around the world (e.g., Hackett & Hackett, 1994; Ojha & Pramanick, 1992; Pathania & Chaudhary, 1993). Problems with waste elimination should likely include a perspective that extends beyond the child to consider the family and cultural context. Such a notion is not unusual in a discussion of habit disorders generally and has received considerable attention in the literature on toileting problems.

Encopresis

Encopresis is a toileting disorder that involves repeated, unacceptable patterns of fecal expulsion in inappropriate locations (e.g., in clothing or on the floor) by a child who is 4 years of age or older, who does not exhibit organic pathology (American Psychiatric Association, 1994). This generic label includes several different types of conditions. On one dimension, encopresis can be viewed in terms of retentive and nonretentive problems. Retentive encopretics are characterized by an excessive retention of fecal material whereas nonretentive encopresis involves uncontrolled expulsion of feces (incontinence) resulting in soiled clothing and bedding. Another dimension relates to whether or not control of fecal expulsion has been established and then ceased (known as discontinuous or secondary encopresis), or whether control has never been reliably established (continuous or primary encopresis). It is easy to see how such subcategories represent very different disorders even though the behaviors may appear similar in some cases. These distinctions are very important when we are trying to establish causation and treatment.

Encopresis incidence estimates vary rather widely although most figures range between 2 and 3 percent (Christophersen & Rapoff, 1992; Mellon & Houts, 1995). The DSM-IV places prevalence estimates at approximately 1 percent of all 5-year-olds (American Psychiatric Association, 1994). Encopresis occurs more frequently in males than females and a rather substantial proportion of those affected are of the discontinuous type. Although statistics differ depending on the source, about 60 percent of all encopretics involve children who have established control and then cease to exercise it (Mellon & Houts, 1995). Obviously, encopresis represents a difficult and frustrating problem for all involved including the child, parents, and peers. Some difficulties extend far beyond the unpleasant process of cleaning up the mess and the embarrassment of having an accident (Bernard-Bonnin, Haley, Belanger, & Nadeau, 1993; Dwivedi & Bell, 1993). In many cases the negative impact on the child's self-image and sense of personal worth is devastating (Buchanan & Clayden, 1992). It also takes little imagination, however, to see how encopresis can generate myriad negative emotions in caretakers, which can work against treatment.

TREATMENT

Treatment of encopresis has generally followed one of the three major theoretical perspectives of the problem: medical, psychoanalytic, and behavioral (Thapar, Davies, Jones, & Revett, 1992). Medical treatment tends to emphasize direct physical control of fecal matter using enemas, laxatives, stool softeners, along with modified diet and sometimes pediatric counseling. In some cases, medication (e.g., imipramine, senokot) has been employed to control bowel actions although most authorities view encopresis as a combined biobehavioral problem and employ combinations of treatment procedures (Christophersen & Edwards, 1992; Houts & Abramson, 1990; Smith, 1994). For example, biofeedback treatment has been of some interest and shown to be most effective when combined with rather standard medical care such as enemas, laxatives, and diet modification (Cox, Sutphen, Borowitz, & Dickens, 1994). It is generally thought that clinicians must attend to environmental as well as physical factors in order to effect a cure. The psychoanalytic view of encopresis regards the behavior as a symptom of inner conflicts and tends to employ psychological treatment that emphasizes interpretation of the child's play, the older child's acquisition of insight, and counseling of parents and the child. Evidence regarding the success of psychotherapy is very sketchy primarily because of the virtual absence of adequate research on the approach.

The primary focus of behavioral treatment is the establishment and maintenance of appropriate toileting behavior through manipulating environmental consequences. For the continuous encopretic, this becomes a process of teaching control skills that presumably have never been learned. For the discontinuous cases, it becomes a matter of reestablishing and maintaining such

behaviors (Mellon & Houts, 1995). Many procedural variations have been used with an impressive success rate. For the most part, treatment studies can be grouped into three general categories: (1) those that primarily give positive reinforcement for appropriate control, but no punishment for soiling; (2) those that punish the child who soils; and (3) those that employ a combination of positive reinforcement and punishment. One of the major strengths of the behavioral studies is that they provide specific procedural descriptions for use by clinicians and caretakers. The specificity of behavioral approaches makes evaluation and replication of treatment procedures easier than with other theoretical perspectives. Behavioral treatments of encopresis appear promising, as noted earlier. However, there is great variation in the circumstances surrounding each case and interventions are successful to the degree that every individual case is precisely evaluated and an individualized treatment program implemented. Assessment procedures should include complete medical examinations in order to provide comprehensive information regarding the physical status of the child. Further research that is scientifically sound is badly needed in the area of encopresis. Not only are the investigations of encopresis scarce, relative to other disorders, a substantial portion of the published research lacks important methodological features that enhance the scientific soundness of the data (Houts & Abramson, 1990; Mellon & Houts, 1995).

Enuresis

Enuresis is probably more widely recognized as a toileting problem than encopresis. Certainly it is a more frequent topic of informal conversation among parents as well as a subject examined in the professional literature. In part there is good reason for this since enuresis is more common (Christophersen & Rapoff, 1992; Popper & Steingard, 1994). DSM-IV cites prevalence figures of 7 and 5 percent for males and females, respectively, at 5 years of age, reducing to 3 percent (males) and 2 percent (females) at age 10 (American Psychiatric Association, 1994). Nocturnal enuresis refers to chronic inappropriate nighttime bed wetting by children who do not evidence physical disorders. Diurnal enuresis refers to wetting during the daytime. There is considerable difference of opinion regarding the minimum age at which such behavior

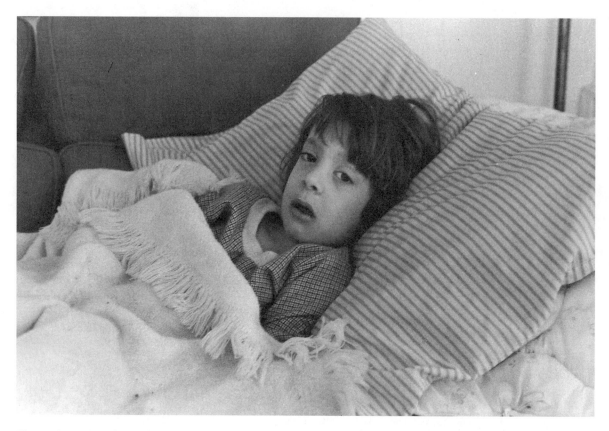

Nocturnal enuresis can be very frustrating for both parents and children.

should be considered problematic. However, most clinicians view urinary incontinence after about 3 to 5 years of age as a problem.

Although early literature considered encopresis as the fecal equivalent of enuresis, there is no solid evidence of a relationship between the two disorders. A child with enuresis may or may not be also encopretic. The major focus of research on enuresis has been on nocturnal occurrences and the disorder has often been labeled as functional nocturnal enuresis. Because of this trend in the literature, the present section will emphasize the nighttime behavior. This is not meant to suggest that inappropriate urination may not also occur during the day. But in this context it is interesting to consider the connection between sleep and urinary incontinence.

There are three generic classes of theories regarding causation and related treatment: medical, psychodynamic-psychoanalytic, and behavioral. Considerable attention has been given to enuresis in relation to the influence of sleep patterns. It is reasonable to think that enuresis might occur only during deep sleep when a child is unaware of and does not react to the physiological need to void. Certainly there are individual differences that would explain why some waken and void themselves in the toilet, and others do not. There are other speculations relating sleep cycles and sleep abnormalities to enuresis (Friman & Warzak, 1990; Norgaard & Djurhuus, 1993). For example, some authorities believe that children with enuresis often have an inadequate release of an antidiuretic hormone during certain sleep stages that may be accompanied by a deficient muscular inhibition (Houts, 1991; Mellon & Houts, 1995). These two physiological processes combined could lead to a lack of control and nighttime wetting. However, they remain as areas in need of further investigation in order to further understand enuresis and its treatment.

The psychodynamic perspective interprets enuresis as a symptom of some inner conflict (Mishne, 1993). This notion is consistent with the fundamental psychoanalytic view of disorders and has been encountered in our earlier discussion of encopresis. Effectiveness of psychoanalytic treatment has been poorly documented, and there is little research evidence to support a success rate significantly different from that of subjects receiving no treatment. Medical explanations of enuresis have included developmental or maturational lag, genetic influences, abnormalities of the urinary tract, and a deficit in cortical control (Peltzer & Taiwo, 1993; Warzak & Friman, 1994). Obviously some of these could be interrelated and treatment can be implemented only with some.

A variety of medications have been used over the years to treat enuresis. Use of one family of drugs, amphetamines, is related to the sleep cycle causation perspective. Amphetamines are stimulants and are thought to make it easier for the enuretic to awaken, either by raising the average depth of sleep or making the individual more easily aroused. This line of reasoning connects enuresis with deficiencies in cortical inhibition and arousal deficits in sleep. Although the logic is reasonable, the evidence does not suggest that stimulants are consistently effective in the treatment of enuresis. Although medication has certainly been effective in some cases of enuresis, the results are not consistent and evidence clearly indicates that other treatments, or certainly combinations of therapies, are preferred (Houts, Berman, & Abramson, 1994; Kaplan & Hussain, 1995; Thompson & Rey, 1995).

Behavioral approaches to treating enuresis mainly focus on the environmental contingencies related to urination. Specific treatment procedures have been combined with varying degrees of success. Electric devices have been developed to sound a bell or buzzer when urine causes a circuit to close. These urine alarms have been used in mattress pads and in training pants. Alarm devices have long been used since the 1930s and remain popular for the treatment of enuresis. Often combined with other therapy components, many authorities view urine alarms as a treatment of choice (Friman & Vollmer, 1995; Houts et al., 1994; Warzak & Friman, 1994).

In most instances, it appears that combining various procedures is the most effective approach to treating enuresis (e.g., Thyer, 1995; Warzak & Friman, 1994). Here again, the nature of any given program is best determined by a careful analysis of the specific child's characteristics. It should be noted, however, that all treatment approaches suffer from less than complete success and a certain percentage of cases can be expected to relapse and need retreatment.

SLEEP DISORDERS

Many parents voice dissatisfaction or concern about their children's sleep patterns at one time or another. Research suggests that sleep disturbances are relatively common among many different age groups ranging from children to young adults (Coren, 1994). Some evidence suggests that as high as 30 to 45 percent of very young children exhibit sleep disturbances (Van Tassel, 1985). Nightmares, for example, tend to peak in frequency between 3 to 6 years of age, with virtually all children experiencing some episodes during this period (Leung & Robson, 1993). Sleep behavior is of considerable concern to parents although, fortunately, a considerable portion of sleep disorders are considered minor.

Several different stages or states are involved in the normal sleep cycle. It is worthwhile examining these briefly prior to discussing sleeping disorders. Sleep consists of two distinct states. REM sleep is a period during which rapid eye movements occur and an individual dreams. The second state, known as NREM sleep, is not characterized by rapid eye movements and is made up of four distinguishable stages based on brain-wave activity. Stage 1 of NREM sleep represents the transitional period between wakefulness and sleep. Stages 2, 3, and 4 are characterized by differences in amount and type of brainwave activity and are generally spoken of as increasing "depth" of sleep. Normal sleep patterns begin with NREM sleep and progress from stage 1 through stage 4 during the first 90 minutes or so of the night. Around this point, the first period of REM sleep occurs and is typically brief, lasting from 5 to 15 minutes. Normal sleep is characterized by repeated cycles of REM and NREM sleep as well as the various stages of NREM sleep. Stage 1 usually accounts for only about 5 percent of a total night's sleep; stage 2, about 40 to 60 percent, and the remainder being stages 3 and 4. Most of the stage 3 and stage 4 sleep occurs during the first two cycles of NREM sleep. In normal sleep the cycles are not random and are, in fact, cyclic. The early portion of a night's sleep tends to rather predictably follow the stages of awake, stage 1, stage 2, stage 3, stage 4, stage 3, and stage 2. At this point the first REM period occurs and then NREM stages recycle (2, 3, 4, 2) followed by another REM period.

FIGURE 10-1 Sleep cycles

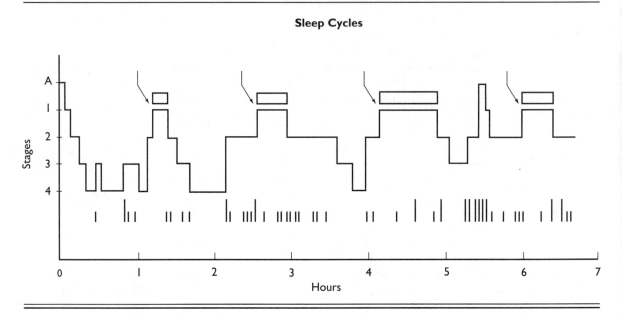

Illustrated pictorially in Figure 10-1, these sleep cycles and stages become important to us since certain sleep disturbances tend to occur predominantly during particular sleep states.

The American Psychiatric Association classifies sleep disorders into several categories according to causation in DSM-IV. Our major interest here is in primary sleep disorders, which are those that are not believed to be caused by other mental disorders, the physiological result of a general medical condition, or a sleep disorder resulting from substance abuse. DSM-IV includes two categories of primary sleep disorders, *dysomnias*, which are those that related to abnormalities in the "... amount, quality, or timing of sleep," and *parasomnias*, which are those associated with "... abnormal behavioral or physiological events occurring in association with sleep, specific sleep stages, or sleep-wake transitions" (American Psychiatric Association, 1994, p. 551). We will examine selected sleep disorders in both dysomnia and parasomnia categories.

Parasomnias

Parasomnia disorders are sleep disruptions associated with specific parts of the sleep cycle, stages of sleep, or

sleep-wake shifts. Parasomnias represent "... activation of physiological systems at inappropriate times during the sleep-wake cycle" (American Psychiatric Association, 1994, p. 579). They pertain to cognitive processes or cerebral function, and may also involve the motor system, such as in sleepwalking (Binnie & Prior, 1994). People affected by parasomnias tend to complain about atypical behaviors *during* sleep rather than incidents of insomnia or unusual sleepiness during the day (Mindell, 1993).

NIGHTMARES AND NIGHT TERRORS

Nightmares and night terrors are disorders in the parasomnia category. There is considerable dreaming during normal sleep and dream sleep receives continuing attention in the literature (e.g., Hobson & Stickgold, 1994; Stickgold, Pace-Schott, & Hobson, 1994; Travis, 1994). As all of us know from experience, dreams can be either pleasant or unpleasant. Most children have occasional bad dreams and nightmares that result in wakefulness and fear (Leung & Robson, 1993). However, for some children, these sleep disturbances are frequent, persistent, and intense, which are then considered to be serious enough to be considered disorders. We will discuss two sleep disorders in this section, nightmares and night terrors. Specific research on the prevalence of nightmares

Although the eyes may be wide open in terror, this youngster may not remember the night terror episode.

and night terrors has been relatively infrequent to date (Coren, 1994). Prevalence estimates for the two conditions place the frequency of nightmares between 10 and 50 percent for children 3 to 5 years of age, and 1 to 6 percent among children for night terrors (American Psychiatric Association, 1994). Nightmares and night terrors may appear somewhat similar, but only on the surface. As we examine them more closely distinctions become quite evident.

Nightmares and night terrors tend to happen at different times of night and during different sleep stages. Nightmares generally occur during REM episodes, stage 1 sleep, and during the latter part of the night (Bearden, 1994; Kinzie, Sack, & Riley, 1994). This is the stage when dreaming typically occurs, which may suggest that nightmares differ from other dreams mainly in content. On the other hand, night terror incidents seem to occur during the first two hours of sleep and arise out of stage 4, a NREM state (Dahl, 1992; Horne, 1992). As indicated

above, stage 4 NREM sleep is not a period during which dreaming normally takes place. It is considered to be the stage of deepest sleep. This suggests that night terrors are distinctly different phenomena from ordinary dreams.

There are a number of differences between a child's behavior during nightmares and night terrors. For example, children experiencing night terrors typically sleep through the episode even though their behavior is extremely agitated. Often their eyes are wide open, as though they were staring at something in terror; they make grimaces; they exhibit considerable physical movement, sometimes running about the room frantically; and they may also shout and scream. Parents often watch such activity helplessly, unable to quiet their children with reassurances or awaken them. Nightmares present a very different picture. Children's movements and verbalization are much more subdued, typically restricted to moaning and slight movements in bed. Beyond this, children having nightmares most often are already awake by the time their parents arrive. From this description one might conclude that night terrors are merely more fearful episodes of nightmares, perhaps more dramatic in content. Further examination of such events would not support such a deduction.

In most cases, nightmares are followed by a period during which the child is awake, recognizes people and surroundings, can provide a coherent account of what has transpired, and can remember the contents of the dream. Night terrors are followed by instant and peaceful sleep, lack of recognition of people and surroundings, and, frequently, complete amnesia regarding both content and occurrence. Further, children experiencing night terrors often hallucinate; those with nightmares do not. Night terrors may be rather prolonged (15 to 20 minutes) whereas nightmares tend to be of a much shorter duration (1 to 2 minutes). At this point, there is little question that nightmares and night terrors are distinctly different phenomena. Either may, however, present a serious difficulty depending on the circumstances and the persistence of the problem. The DSM-IV diagnostic criteria for both nightmares and night terrors are summarized in Table 10-3.

Causation for nightmares and night terrors remains largely unknown at this time, although some theories have proposed a variety of rather elaborate notions such as sexual impulses that are not understood by the individual or causation by experiences in a previous life (Mills, 1994). Nightmares and night terrors have also been associated with a variety of other conditions such as bronchial asthma, milk intolerance, night-time feeding, and genetic disposition (Horne, 1992; Leung & Robson, 1993; Mitrani, 1993). Nightmares have been observed as a side effect of the use of certain drugs such as anabolic steroids (International Society of Sport Psychology, 1993). With both nightmares and night terrors, there appear to be multiple causes possible, with nearly any event or condition that alters the normal sleep cycle being suspect. Treatment for both nightmares and night terrors have included the application of a variety of medications such as paroxetine, clonazepam, and fluoxetine (e.g., Lepkifker, Dannon, Iancu, & Ziv, 1995; Lillywhite, Wilson, & Nutt, 1994) and psychotherapies including hypnosis (e.g., Alpert, 1994; Kingsbury, 1993; Nagy, 1995). Results of these therapies have been rather mixed, with some claims that cognitive-behavioral strategies appear to offer the most consistently useful treatment ap-

---

TABLE 10-3   DIAGNOSTIC CRITERIA FOR NIGHTMARES AND NIGHT TERRORS

Nightmare Disorder

A. Repeated awakenings from the major sleep period or naps with detailed recall of extended and extremely frightening dreams, usually involving threats to survival, security, or self-esteem. The awakenings generally occur during the second half of the sleep period.

B. On awakening from the frightening dreams, the person rapidly becomes oriented and alert (in contrast to the confusion and disorientation seen in sleep terror disorder and some forms of epilepsy).

C. The dream experience, or the sleep disturbance resulting from the awakening, causes clinically significant distress or impairment in social, occupational, or other important areas of functioning.

D. The nightmares do not occur exclusively during the course of another mental disorder (e.g., a delirium, posttraumatic stress disorder) and are not due to the direct physiological effects of a substance (e.g., a drug of abuse, a medication) or a general medical condition.

Sleep Terror Disorder

A. Recurrent episodes of abrupt awakening from sleep, usually occurring during the first third of the major sleep episode and beginning with a panicky scream.

B. Intense fear and signs of autonomic arousal, such as tachycardia, rapid breathing, and sweating, during each episode.

C. Relative unresponsiveness to efforts of others to comfort the person during the episode.

D. No detailed dream is recalled and there is amnesia for the episode.

E. The episodes cause clinically significant distress or impairment in social, occupational, or other important areas of functioning.

F. The disturbance is not due to the direct physiological effects of a substance (e.g., a drug of abuse, a medication) or a general medical condition.

SOURCE: American Psychiatric Association. (1994). *Diagnostic and statistical manual of mental disorders (DSM-IV)* (4th ed., pp. 583, 587). Washington, DC: Author.

---

proach (Blanes, Burgess, Marks, & Gill, 1993). The search for effective and parsimonious treatment continues, as illustrated by the procedure outlined in Box 10-2 (Brody, 1996). As with other therapies, this strategy requires systematic research in order to establish the extent of its effectiveness. Past experience with therapies for sleep dis-

---

BOX 10-2   A NOVEL THERAPY FOR NIGHT TERROR

Dr. Bryan Lask, consulting psychiatrist at the Hospital for Sick Children in London, has reported on an effective nondrug treatment for night terrors in children.

Since most such episodes occur within the first hours of sleep when parents are still awake, he suggests that parents note the time they happen for five successive nights. Then he instructs them to wake the child 10 to 15 minutes before the terror typically occurs, keep the child up for 4 or 5 minutes and then let the youngster return to sleep.

Dr. Lask suggests that parents continue this process until the terrors cease, which is usually within a week. If the night terrors recur, which usually happens only once, Dr. Lask recommends that the process be repeated.

SOURCE: Condensed from Brody, J. E. (1996, January 17). Personal health. *The New York Times*, p. B8.

---

orders suggests that the treatment of choice depends on the individual circumstances of the affected person to some extent.

SLEEPWALKING DISORDER (SOMNAMBULISM)

It is estimated that between 1 and 5 percent of all children have repeated episodes of somnambulism or sleepwalking (American Psychiatric Association, 1994). Somnambulism and night terrors have a number of common features and it is not unusual to find both problems in the same child. Sleepwalking occurs during NREM sleep in stages 3 and 4. (Unlike normal children, somnambulist children will often start to sleepwalk if they are stood upright during stage 3 and 4 sleep—something that will not occur in normal children.) Sleepwalkers typically do not remember the incident and are very difficult to awaken. Their eyes are open and they appear to be walking with a definite purpose, although they show very little emotion. Somnambulism can create particular problems since the children can place themselves in danger by walking in unsafe places such as balconies and stairways. Essentially their senses are not functioning in a manner that would protect them from falling or other types of accidents.

Somnambulism is most often attributed to some type of emotional stress (e.g., Bucci, Chiarelli, & Spagnolo, 1994; Mutzell, 1994). Frequently some specific accident or other stressful incident is reported to have preceded the sleepwalking (Garland & Smith, 1991). Treatment has taken a number of approaches with varying degrees of success. A variety of different medications have been employed with highly varied results, seeming at times to almost be idiosyncratic (Appelberg, Rimon, Nikkila, & Ahlroth, 1989; Lillywhite, Wilson, & Nutt, 1994; Kavey

& Whyte, 1993). Both psychoanalytic and behavioral therapies have been employed with variable success, with relapses being relatively common (Cuisinier & Hoogduin, 1991). The treatment of somnambulism remains largely unexplored relative to many other childhood disorders.

Dysomnias

Dysomnias are sleep disorders where the affected individual has significant and chronic difficulty related to the ". . . amount, quality, or timing of sleep" (American Psychiatric Association, 1994, p. 553). Those affected by a dysomnia may experience substantial problems going to sleep or maintaining a sleep state for a sufficient period to be restorative. Dysomnias may also be found in individuals who seem to fall asleep at inappropriate times, such as during a conversation or when they are driving an automobile. While the former may only be embarrassing, the latter circumstance presents some clear dangers to the person involved as well as to others. We will focus on the two dysomnias mentioned above, insomnia and narcolepsy.

PRIMARY INSOMNIA

Most of us have experienced circumstances when we have difficulty falling asleep, even repeatedly to a point where we are very tired over a period of time. Insomnia as a primary disorder, however, involves such a problem that has a duration of at least a month, causes substantial impairment in several areas of functioning, and is not related to substance effects or a general medical condition (American Psychiatric Association, 1994). The disorder of primary insomnia seems to begin in the early adult years and is relatively rare during childhood or adolescence. The pattern of insomnia seems to vary, with younger adults experiencing greater difficulty falling asleep, whereas older individuals complain more often of problems sleeping through the night. Although prevalence data are incomplete, insomnia patterns seem to vary among populations with physical and mental health problems (e.g., Harris, Gorelick, Cohen, & Dollear, 1994; Hohagen, Kappler, Schramm, & Rink, 1994; Soldatos, 1994). Persistent insomnia seems to increase with age and is more frequent among women (Brabbins, Dewey, Copeland, & Davidson, 1993; Koenig, O'Connor, Guarisco, & Zabel, 1993). Prevalence data place some estimates of insomnia as high as 30 to 40 percent among adults, although only 15 to 25 percent of those seeking treatment in clinics are identified as having primary insomnia (American Psychiatric Association, 1994).

Causes of insomnia are varied as one would expect. Some evidence suggests that cognitive anxiety or worrying is a significant contributor to insomnia (Lichstein & Fanning, 1990). Seemingly related to this notion is evidence suggesting that stress, anxiety, and panic attacks are more frequent among individuals with serious insomnia conditions (Lepola, Koponen, & Lienonen, 1994; Partinen, 1994; Stepanski, Glinn, Zorick, & Roehrs, 1994; Soldatos, 1994). General relationships between insomnia and substance abuse (e.g., alcohol, drugs) are also found in the literature, although such circumstances do not fit the DSM-IV definition of primary insomnia (Dufour & Fuller, 1995; Ettorre, Klaukka, & Riska, 1994; Hinsberger, Sharma, & Mazmanian, 1994).

Treatments for insomnia difficulties have varied widely and shown highly variable results (Regestein & Monk, 1995). Medication has been employed in a number of fashions with mixed results. Drugs have been used as a means of manipulating the sleep cycle, as a sedation, and a hypnotic (Hohagen, Montero, Weiss, & Lis, 1994; Nakra, Gfeller, & Hassan, 1992; Parrino, Spaggiari, Boselli, & DiGiovanni, 1994). Other treatment procedures involving self-help videos supplemented with therapist guidance have shown promising results (Riedel, Lichstein, & Dwyer, 1995). Nonpharmacologic treatments have the advantage of reducing harmful side effects and placing the patient in greater control. In most cases, comprehensive behavioral treatment packages have shown strong success and may be tailored more directly to the individual's specific needs (Chambers, 1992; Lichstein & Riedel, 1994).

NARCOLEPSY

Narcolepsy is a disorder in which individuals encounter "sleep attacks" at times when they are trying to stay awake (e.g., during the day). Narcolepsy has often been thought of as excessive sleep, but more correctly should be viewed as inappropriate sleep incidents. The term inappropriate is not meant to suggest a value judgment—narcoleptic incidents can prove physically dangerous and socially embarrassing. They may take place at any time or place, when the individuals are walking, standing, driving an automobile, or at the dinner table (Aldrich, 1992; Broughton & Broughton, 1994; Cohen, Ferrans, & Eshler, 1992). Often the episodes are brief, lasting about 15 minutes or even much less. Patients usually describe the incident in terms of an irresistible urge to sleep. Some are aware that an attack is about to occur, experiencing dream images or hallucinations just before an episode, whereas others experience the episodes without any warning (Aldrich, 1990). Still others are able to avoid sleep by concentrating intensely on remaining awake.

Estimates regarding the prevalence of narcolepsy vary from 0.02 to 0.16 percent in the general adult population or about 10 in 1,000 at the most (American Psychiatric Association, 1994). These figures would suggest that there are as many as 250,000 individuals in the United States suffering from narcolepsy. It is unclear how many narcoleptics are children, although the onset of the problem seems to occur predominantly between the ages of 10 and 20. The cause of narcolepsy has largely eluded researchers to date. One factor that has been identified relates to disturbances of REM sleep. Unlike most people, narcoleptics seem to begin their nocturnal sleep in a REM state. As indicated earlier, in normal people, initial sleep begins with several NREM stages followed later in the cycle by REM sleep. Narcoleptics do, however, seem to have relatively normal *amounts* of REM and NREM sleep during the night. Treatment of narcolepsy has primarily focused on drug therapy with benefits from using stimulants such as amphetamines, although some complications and side effects may appear (Mitler, 1994; Parks, 1994). Attention to nonpharmacological treatments, such as behavioral management and diet alteration, are only recently emerging in the literature and considerable research is needed to establish effectiveness (Broughton & Mullington, 1994; Garma & Marchand, 1994).

SPEECH DISORDERS

Definitions of speech disorders have varied considerably in type and specificity. The definition used here represents a synthesis of definitions derived from several authorities (e.g., Silverman, 1995; Van Riper & Emerick, 1990). For our purposes, defective speech or a speech disorder (which are terms often used interchangeably) refers to speech behavior which is sufficiently deviant from normal or accepted speaking patterns that it attracts attention, interferes with communication, and adversely affects communication for either the speaker or listener. As before, we are focusing on behavior deviations that clearly exceed the normal range of variations.

Prevalence estimates of children with speaking disabilities have varied greatly; consequently, many authors either avoid this topic or are extremely vague in their discussions. The most frequently quoted figure in the speech pathology literature suggests that about 7 to 10 percent of the population are affected (Hardman, Drew, & Egan, 1996). In the 1990–91 school year, 21 percent of all children ages 0 to 21 who received services in programs for those with disabilities were classified as having speech or language impairments (U.S. Bureau of the Census, 1993). Speech and language impairments were cited as the second most frequent disability receiving special services under the Individuals with Disabilities Education Act in 1991–92 (learning disabilities was most frequent) (U.S. Department of Education, 1994). Both incidence and prevalence consistently vary as a function of age. The incidence of speech disorders is roughly 12 to 15 percent for children in kindergarten through 4th grades, reduces to about 4 to 5 percent in grades 5 through 8, and remains somewhat constant thereafter unless therapeutic intervention is undertaken (Hardman et al., 1996). In some cases treatment results in a change, whereas in others the children outgrow a disorder or "self-correct" their problems. Service patterns vary over time, between types of disorders, and authorities disagree greatly on the impact of intervention early in the elementary years (e.g., Felsenfeld, Broen, & McGue, 1992; Silverman, 1995). Once again, we are faced with the reality that prevalence is socially rather than absolutely defined.

Identification and classification approaches to speech disorders have varied depending on etiology and the treatment perspective being employed. Rather than examine classifications completely, we will select from rather traditional categories and attend to speech disorders that are related to habit. Specifically, we will discuss problems of delayed speech, phonology or articulation, and stuttering. Readers interested in a more comprehensive examination of speech disorders should consult other sources (e.g., Aronson, 1990; Case, 1991; Love, 1992; Silverman, 1992, 1995; Van Riper & Emerick, 1990).

Delayed Speech

Very young children are typically able to communicate to some degree through gestures, noises, squeals, and other means prior to the learning of speech and language (Tiegerman, 1993a). Most such behaviors tend to be dropped as they learn the process of speaking. However, in some cases children develop speaking skills much later than is normally expected. As we begin this discussion, it is important to remember that we are examining deviations from normal that are *significant* or *extreme*. As we listen to children and adults, we note considerable variation in speaking ability or performance—some people are quite skilled and articulate (those "silver-tongued" individuals) whereas others are less facile ("tongue-tied"). This normal range of skill is *not* the focus of the current discussion. In order to examine delayed speech, it is helpful to review the typical development of speech. Box 10-3 summarizes certain landmarks of normal language and speech development in children.

We noted previously that, in some cases, maturation may serve as a natural cure for certain speech problems. Most young children make a certain number of errors in their speech that do not typically persist. For example, they may delete final consonants ("buy" for bike) or unstressed syllables ("nana" for banana), and they often substitute certain sounds for others ("tit" for sit, "dup" for soup). Often these errors are considered amusing and cute, and it is not uncommon for parents, siblings, or other individuals to focus attention on such errors, for example, by imitating the child's pronunciation to others or by speaking in "baby talk" with the child. These behaviors may inadvertently promote speech disorders.

BOX 10-3   NORMAL LANGUAGE AND PRELANGUAGE DEVELOPMENT

Age	Behavior
Birth	Crying and making other physiological sounds.
1 to 2 months	Cooing as well as crying.
3 to 6 months	Babbling as well as cooing.
9 to 14 months	Speaking first words as well as babbling.
18 to 24 months	Speaking first sentences as well as words.
3 to 4 years	Using all basic syntactical structures.
4 to 8 years	Articulating correctly all speech sounds in context.

SOURCE: Drew, C. J., Hardman, M. L., & Logan, D. R. (1996). *Mental retardation: A life cycle approach* (6th ed., p. 197). Englewood Cliffs, NJ: Prentice-Hall.

Although the precise nature of the impact remains unclear, modeling is thought to influence natural verbal development and is used in interventions (Gardner, 1989; Owens, 1995; Weiss, 1993).

Delayed speech represents a failure of speech to develop at the expected age. Some children with delayed speech develop little or no expressive speech beyond vocalizations that are not interpretable as conventional language. Such children may continue to communicate nonverbally through gestures or they may use nonspeech vocalizations extensively long after such behavior is typical. Others can speak a little but their proficiency is limited for their age, and they mainly use nouns without qualifying or auxiliary words.

ETIOLOGY OF SPEECH DELAYS

Delayed speech is a term that is applied to inadequate proficiency that may be caused by any of a number of influences ranging broadly from heredity to environment. Such disorders may stem from experience deprivation, such as when a child is raised in an environment that provides little opportunity for learning to speak or circumstances that actively interfere with mastering speaking skills (Hardman et al., 1996). Delayed speech may be the result of sensory deprivation from an anatomical defect such as a hearing loss (Lonigan, Fischel, Whitehurst, & Arnold, 1992; Radziewicz & Antonellis, 1993). Other factors that may contribute to cases of delayed speech include neurological problems (e.g., cerebral palsy) and serious emotional disturbances like childhood schizophrenia, autism, or less severe problems such as negativism (e.g., Cohen, Davine, Horodezky, & Lipsett,

1993; Davis, Fennoy, Laraque, & Kanem, 1992). Our focus in this discussion will be on speech delays that may be caused by the establishment of faulty habits, which in turn are the result of abnormal or unsatisfactory learning circumstances (e.g., experience deprivation, reinforcement contingencies that do not promote speaking) (Tiegerman, 1993b).

The term negativism relates to a set of behaviors or conditions that may contribute to delayed speech. When children are developing speech, great pressure is being exerted by parents for them to learn many other skills as well. During this period, children are expected to learn how to eat properly, to go to bed when it is expected, to control excretory functions, and many other behaviors that characterize adults. These demands exceed some children's tolerance level so that they may be unable to perform as expected by parents and others. Certain children respond negatively to such a situation by refusing to perform—one very effective type of refusal is refusing to talk. It is quite easy for a parent to punish some types of refusal (e.g., refusal to eat or to go to bed) but it is not as simple to handle a refusal to talk. A child cannot easily be forced to talk and may be able to communicate needs quite adequately through gestures. In still other circumstances, children are frequently punished for talking because parents view it as inappropriate or inconvenient (e.g., it is too loud or badly timed because the parents are conversing, watching television, or reading). Consequently it is easy to see how the habit of not speaking may be learned—it is reinforced at times, it is a method of avoiding punishment at others, and it may be a means of expressing refusal to perform that does not place one in great jeopardy of being punished. If such circumstances persist over a sustained period of time when speech is typically developed, the result may be a child with a significantly delayed speech problem. Not only has the child failed to learn speaking skills but in some cases he or she has learned *not* to speak (Hardman et al., 1996).

If the child's failure to speak is a form of rebellion, the reward contingencies in the environment must be altered. It must be made more reinforcing for the child to speak than not to do so. Additionally, the child must be taught the skills of speaking that have not heretofore been learned. It may also be necessary to alter child behavior patterns that are only indirectly related to the speech delay such as eating and going to bed. Clearly, if the problem persists over a period of years, it becomes increasingly difficult to treat because the delay is more pronounced and the behaviors become more firmly habituated by continued and increasingly complex reinforcement contingencies.

Another category of causation in delayed speech is experience deprivation in which the environmental circumstances limit the opportunity to learn speaking skills and/or actually interfere with such learning. Environmental contingencies must exist in a configuration that will permit and promote children's learning to speak. This certainly does not mean that the family home life has to become a contrived miniature language class on a continuing basis. Most households function routinely in a manner that will foster a child's speech acquisition (e.g., encouragement to name objects and reinforcement for response). There are, however, some households that do not promote language acquisition, and significantly delayed child speech may result. In some cases, conversation is unusually infrequent in the child's home. Such circumstances may exist if parents rarely speak with each other or the child. Consequently, the child does not have much speech modeled and perhaps receives little reinforcement for speaking and vocalizing. The basic principles of learning would suggest that learning will be retarded in such an environment, and the outcome may well be delayed speech. There might be additional difficulties in the family, which may contribute to the child's problems in learning to speak. The relationship between the parents may be rather tense or troubled, which results in a low frequency of verbal communication and also causes anxiety or fear in the child. Perhaps the parents'

talking that *does* occur consists largely of arguing and threatening. This could easily compound the difficulty of infrequent modeling by adding a component of punishment or aversive stimulation. The child's learning may be further interfered with if speaking is often associated with punishment (e.g., when the father speaks and the mother shouts obscenities in response).

There are other circumstances in which there is limited speaking that are quite different from those described above but where the net result may be quite similar. An example may be found when a child with normal hearing capacity is born to deaf parents (either one or both). The parents' primary method of communication may be through signing and gestures. There may be little child speech learning in this type of environment or, at best, the child's speech proficiency may be significantly delayed. It should be emphasized that the outcomes of such circumstances are extremely variable. As a personal example, one of the authors knows of four brothers with normal hearing who were born to parents who were deaf and had been so from a very early age. The parents used sign language but little or no verbal communication. All of the boys (now adults) learned to speak quite well and, although they experienced some minor problems in school, have distinguished themselves in a variety of fashions. One holds a Ph.D. degree in special education from a major university; a second has both an M.D. and Ph.D. (the latter earned at a well-known European university); the third is an able public servant; and the fourth began his rise to the heights of achievement as an inventor and has become a millionaire. We would all be fortunate to be so successful but it is important to remember that this is an exceptional story. An introspective recollection by one of the brothers published in Hardman et al., (1996) suggested a variety of exceptional influences such as unusually close relationships with their grandparents that led to a favorable outcome in this particular case. Substantial speech delay is not uncommon in hearing children born into an environment where verbalization is unusually infrequent on account of parental deafness.

Delayed speech caused by experience deprivation may occur in situations much different from those described above where verbal conversation is infrequent. There are some homes where there is a great deal of verbalization and noise but it occurs in a very confused and unsystematic fashion. From a habit or learning disorder perspective, such an environment may seriously impede the acquisition of speech at the time when it is normally learned. Learning a skill is a rather delicate process, particularly in its early stages. Stimuli must be presented in an uncomplicated, systematic fashion and without competing or distracting stimuli so a child can focus on the important features and discriminate those that are central from those that are not important (Nelson, 1993a; Tiegerman, 1993b). Additionally, when an appropriate behavior occurs it needs to be reinforced (and this process must be repeated consistently for learning to progress). A chaotic environment probably will not provide such contingencies and may produce delayed speech.

Children learning to speak will tend to take the route that requires the least effort. Thus, if there is little need to speak it is unlikely that the child will do so, and in some homes a child has little need to speak. Such conditions are often described in other terms (e.g., the overprotective parent) but viewed from a learning perspective there simply may be little need to learn speech. Let us use a fictitious illustration to complete this examination, although many of us have informally observed situations that may have similar features. As children begin to develop speech and interact with those around them, they communicate in several ways. They may imitate, express pleasure or displeasure, and request with sounds, gestures, facial expressions, and body posture. Reciprocal interactions between parents and infants is very important in this early time, and it is not uncommon to encounter parents who want to satisfy all of their child's needs (Tiegerman, 1993a, 1993b). There are extremes wherein parents anticipate a child's desires or needs and quickly provide for them by responding to gestures or nonspecific vocalizations. They may rush to feed their children, procure toys for them, and meet a multitude of other needs in response to a mere gesture or cry. By doing this they may teach (reinforce) such behaviors and delay speech development, whereas the child might have to perform more exacting tasks (such as asking for water) to obtain reinforcement in other circumstances. It is easy to see how such behaviors, in extreme form, could teach a child to meet needs in a fashion other than speaking. Delayed speech can result from this type of situation although it is not necessarily so.

TREATMENT OF SPEECH DELAYS

Speech delay caused by experience deprivation can be treated through the fundamental principles of learning;

in theory this is a simple task, but implementation can be very difficult. Alteration and precise control of stimuli and reinforcement contingencies may be quite complex. Considerable success has been evident in direct teaching interventions that alter the stimulus-reinforcement contingency in order to promote more normal speech development (Owens, 1995). Obviously, alternative methods, procedures, and perspectives are useful in order to enhance individualization (e.g., Ratokalau & Robb, 1993), and may well involve collaboration between speech clinicians, teachers, and parents (Nelson, 1993a, 1993b; Weiss, 1993). The approach will always depend on the specific details of the problem(s) and the viewpoint of the therapist.

Phonological Disorders

Phonological disorders in DSM-IV were previously classified as articulation disorders and are the most frequently occurring category of all speech disorders (American Psychiatric Association, 1994). Disorders of articulation represent the majority of cases encountered by public school speech clinicians (Edwards, Cape, & Brown, 1989; Patton, Kauffman, Blackbourn, & Brown, 1991), with some estimates ranging as high as 80 percent (Van Riper & Emerick, 1990). An articulation disorder is basically a disturbance in speech-sound production. In most instances, such problems in children are *functional articulation disorders*, that is, they are not caused by any readily apparent organic defect. In a certain number of cases, articulation difficulties follow a developmental path; as the child grows older articulation errors often diminish or are eliminated. This has led some public school officials to contend that speech clinicians should not give as much attention as they do to articulation problems, particularly when children are very young. Certainly there is some logic to such a position as fiscal and human resources become increasingly scarce. However, some articulation errors are not caused merely by immature speech development. Articulation performance is likely to improve with development until about the age of 9 or 10. Problems that exist beyond that point are likely to persist unless therapy intervenes; such disorders can become increasingly difficult to remedy if permitted to continue untreated, and affected individuals may suffer residue of the disorder for years (Felsenfeld, Broen, & McGue, 1992).

As with other speech disorders, defective articulation may be caused by a variety of factors. Some cases are due to brain damage or nerve injury (often referred to as dysartia); others are caused by physical deformity (such as malformed mouth, jaw, or teeth structures); some are thought due to heredity; and many cases represent learned behaviors (Love, 1992; Silverman, 1995). Those caused by defective learning (functional disorders) constitute a significant problem since a small proportion of articulation errors can be attributed to identifiable organic flaws. However, there are also many causes for functional articulation disorders. The stimulus and reinforcement contingencies that result in such problems are as variable as those that promote or permit speech development in general. Perhaps the modeling by parents is inappropriate, such as babytalk; although the influence of babytalk has been questioned, the literature suggests that the nature of parental speech is influential on children's linguistic maturity (e.g., Gardner, 1989; Owens, 1995; Weiss, 1993). It may be that household reinforcement for accurate speech production is unsystematic. In many instances, it is less important to precisely determine the causes of functional articulation disorders than the causes of organically based disorders, which may be amenable to surgical correction (Denny, Marks, & Olif-Carneol, 1993; Yoshida, Michi, Yamashita, & Ohno, 1993). However, the influential contingencies cannot be ignored since treatment must focus on altering the causal environment if it still exists. The essential task is one of rearranging learning contingencies so that more appropriate speech patterns can be acquired and generalized to diverse environments. A variety of behavior modification procedures have been successful in improving articulation problems of habit (Silverman, 1995). Generalization of appropriate learning is obviously important to the child's overall speech performance (Elbert, Powell, & Swartzlander, 1991; Gray & Shelton, 1992), and treatment may, once again, involve collaboration among teachers, parents, and speech therapists (Gardner, 1989; Weiss, 1993; Nelson, 1993a, 1993b).

Stuttering

Stuttering is a disorder of fluency and is perhaps the most widely recognized of all speech problems. Stuttering represents a disturbance in the fluency and rhythm of speech with intermittent blocking, repetition, or prolongation of sounds, syllables, words, or phrases. Nearly all of us at one time or another have known or encountered an individual who stutters, and most of us personally exhibit such behaviors occasionally even though we are not stutterers. Furthermore, nearly all young children stutter at times as they develop their speaking abilities. For the most part these are normal nonfluencies that disappear as the child grows older and progresses in speech development. However, these normal behaviors play a prominent role in certain theories of stuttering.

Many people think of stuttering almost automatically when they consider speech disorders in general. This is not surprising since in stuttering the interruptions in the flow of speech are very evident and easily remembered. Additionally, stuttering makes listeners very uncomfortable. Often listeners try to "help" the stutterer by filling in the relevant words when a block occurs. It is clear that the communication process creates a considerable degree of discomfort for both the stutterer and listener. Consequently people tend to remember stutterers better than those with other speech disorders. Despite the prominence of stuttering, it is among the least prevalent of speech disorders (Van Riper & Emerick, 1990). Although prevalence statistics are notoriously variable and inaccurate, stuttering consistently appears as a speech disorder that occurs rather infrequently when compared to other problems.

ETIOLOGY OF STUTTERING

The causes of stuttering have been investigated for many years. Scientists in the past have often searched fruitlessly for a single cause. Fortunately, more current thinking has discarded this oversimplified perspective in favor of a view that stuttering may have a variety of causes (Ivanova, Lapa, Lokhov, & Movsisyants, 1991; Schulze & Johannsen, 1991; Silverman, 1995). Present theories about the causes of stuttering can basically be divided into three types: those that address it as an emotional or neurotic problem (i.e., wherein stuttering is a behavioral manifestation of some emotional difficulty); those that view it as a constitutional or neurological problem; and those that view stuttering from a learning perspective.

There is decreased interest in attempting to find a constitutional cause of stuttering, although a few studies still appear in the literature. Some investigators have explored neurological dysfunction generally, whereas others have focused more specifically on such factors as cerebral dominance problems and cortical organization. Results have been mixed. Some evidence has suggested that individuals with fluent speech may have different brain organization than those who stutter (Ivanova et al., 1991). There has also been some suggestion that those who stutter use different parts of the brain in information processing (Webster, 1988). Other researchers have found some support for the notion that cerebral dominance problems may be present to a greater degree in those who stutter than those who are fluent (Rastatter & Loren, 1988). And lastly, some have speculated that the separate neural systems controlling various speech production components may be out of synchronization in those who stutter (Perkins, Kent, & Curlee, 1991). Thus, the research that has continued to address to neurological causation of stuttering has shown variable results with rather divergent theoretical outcomes.

Studies have also explored a variety of possibilities other than those listed above. Some literature has examined the notion that heredity may play a role in stuttering and linked this line of thinking to sex differences in the incidence of the disorder (male stutterers outnumber females about 4 to 1). Some authors have suggested that the hereditary influence exists because of higher incidence of stuttering within certain families, studies of parental disfluency, and twin studies where shared genetic material exists (e.g., Lewis & Thompson, 1992; Poulos & Webster, 1991; Van Riper & Emerick, 1990). As we know, however, it is often difficult to separate the impact of heredity and environment generally, as well as in speech disorders (Drew, Hardman, & Hart, 1996). Often this can only be accomplished under specific genetic analysis thereby specifying causation (such as in certain types of Down syndrome). Other researchers have studied quite different etiological possibilities. For example, some have explored causal implications of the emotional dimensions of parent-child interactions (Schulze & Johannsen, 1991) although little support has emerged supporting emotional causation. Emotional causation has also been of interest in speculation that the stuttering child may experience demands that exceed his or her capacity to respond (e.g., Adams, 1990). Once again the research has been fragmentary and support for such a view has not emerged in a substantial manner.

The learning theory approach to stuttering is not new but has attracted increased attention over the years. Stuttering tends to emerge most often between 3 to 5 years of age (Yairi & Ambrose, 1992; Yairi, Ambrose, & Niermann, 1993). Some have contended that stuttering, in its fully developed form, is a learned and more severe outgrowth of normal nonfluency in the early years which increases. The hypothesis is that a child may develop stuttering behavior if substantial attention is directed to normal nonfluencies during the early development of speech. Considerable interest in this perspective continues (e.g., Gagnon & Ladouceur, 1992; Onslow, 1992), although it should be noted that there are also critics of this view (e.g., Silverman, 1992). Considerable evidence in the literature supports the notion that at least some stutterers are the victims of habit disorders. As noted, this view holds that most young children exhibit a certain amount of nonfluency as they learn and develop speaking skills and that stuttering disorders may often be an outgrowth of that nonfluency. The difference between normal nonfluency and stuttering is likely to be indistinguishable at first. However, when attention is drawn to the nonfluencies rather than the fluent statements, an unfortunate set of learning contingencies may be formed that result in stuttering. Even within the learning theory view of stuttering, there is considerable difference of opinion concerning the functioning and precise form of these contingencies. Each case must be examined and treated individually.

TREATMENT OF STUTTERING

Treatment of stuttering has been as varied as the theories of causation. Psychotherapy has met with limited success. Other procedures have been used to focus on the rhythm process of speech such as using a metronome to establish a beat, as well as relaxation therapy to overcome tenseness (Van Riper & Emerick, 1990). In all cases, results have been mixed. Some success has been evident using play therapy, creative dramatics, parental counseling, and working with teachers and classmates (Cooper & Cooper, 1992; Zebrowski & Schum, 1993). Treatment of stuttering has increasingly included behavioral therapy that attempts to teach the affected individual fluent speaking patterns as well as minimizing relapses (Gagnon & Ladouceur, 1992; Onslow, 1992). Individualized treatment programs appear essential, focusing on the stimulus and reinforcement contingencies in the child's environment. With certain children it is important for them to learn to monitor and manage their stuttering, perhaps through speaking more slowly and in a rhythmic fashion. For others it appears that they must also be aware of physical factors such as breathing. Stuttering is a complex disorder and effective treatment may also be rather intricate.

SUMMARY

In this chapter, we have examined a very diverse range of habit disorders that present significant difficulties in a child's development. Many of these create problems that sorely test the resources and patience of families as well as professionals. In discussing the causes and treatments of habit disorders, we have all too often had to rely on terms such as "unclear," "unknown," and "unsuccessful." We are painfully aware that parents who seek assistance in solving their children's problems frequently receive conflicting opinions and advice. This further emphasizes the need for systematic and rigorous research that will provide a more solid information base for effective clinical treatment, a fact that is encountered repeatedly in this book.

A great deal of attention has been given to eating problems. Although a seemingly simple problem on the surface, both physiological and psychological research has shown that it is an extremely complex disorder. A variety of treatments have been employed for obesity and evidence of effectiveness has largely been disappointing. Anorexia nervosa is a complex eating disorder and has received increasing attention in the recent literature. Primarily a problem occurring in adolescent females, anorexia is a condition of self-inflicted starvation. Health complications can be extremely serious, even resulting in death in a certain percentage of cases, and treatment is quite difficult. Bulimia, or the "binge-purge" syndrome, is characterized by episodes of gorging followed by purging via vomiting or laxatives. Thought to be related to anorexia, bulimia is beginning to emerge as a distinct disorder. Research and treatment of bulimia is difficult partially because this covert behavior is guarded by those affected in a shroud of secrecy that is often preserved because of normal weight maintenance.

We also discussed toileting problems, and attention was especially focused on encopresis and enuresis. Encopresis represents problematic patterns of fecal expulsion, whereas enuresis refers to wetting difficulties. These disorders have been thought to be related although evidence for this view is lacking. Treatment can be very difficult, and relapses are frequent.

Included in our discussion of habit disorders were sleep problems, a common difficulty. Researchers have studied several different stages of sleep, which may be involved in different ways with sleep disorders. Night terrors, nightmares, and somnambulism are particularly difficult problems. Research seems to indicate that different stages of sleep are related to these conditions as well as to different characteristics with respect to episodes of sleep disturbance. More research in the area of sleep disorders is clearly needed since the behaviors can be quite pronounced in some cases and are difficult to treat.

Speech disorders are the last topics discussed in this chapter. Speech disorders reportedly affect 7 to 10 percent of the general population, although research evidence has suggested great geographic variation. Delayed speech and articulation disorders were discussed. Stuttering is probably the most widely recognized speech difficulty. However, it actually is found in a much smaller percentage of the population than other types of speech disorders, such as articulation problems. Treatment of speech disorders varies greatly depending on the type and, often, the characteristics of the individual case. In some instances it is relatively simple, whereas in others it may be complex, lengthy, and of limited effectiveness. Learning based treatments have met with particular success in the treatment of selected speech disorders.

C H A P T E R I I

PERVASIVE DEVELOPMENTAL
DISORDERS AND CHILDHOOD
SCHIZOPHRENIA

Key Terms

Asperger's disorder. A type of pervasive developmental disorder in which the affected individual exhibits severe impairment of social interactions, the development of repetitive patterns of behaviors, interests, and activities, but without the significant language delays characteristic of autism (American Psychiatric Association, 1994).

Autism. A pervasive developmental disorder that is characterized by an early onset and difficulties in socially relating to other people.

Childhood disintegrative disorder. A type of pervasive developmental disorder in which the affected individuals experience a significant regression in several areas of functioning following at least two years of normal development. Affected areas may include language and communication skills, social skills, motor skills, and bowel or bladder control.

Childhood schizophrenia. A childhood psychotic disorder that is characterized by a late onset and may include thought disorders, hallucinations, delusions, disorganized speech or behavior, movement or motor disturbance such as catatonic-type immobility, and/or unusually flat affect.

Pervasive developmental disorders. A general category of disorders, typically evident in the early years, characterized by severe and pervasive impairment in several developmental areas including social interaction, communication, or stereotyped behavior, interests, and activities (American Psychiatric Association, 1994, p. 65).

Rett's disorder. A type of pervasive developmental disorder in which individuals seemingly have normal development through about the first five months but thereafter experience a slowing of development, a loss of purposeful hand movements followed by the development of stereotyped hand activity, accompanied by serious impairment of language development.

CHAPTER   OVERVIEW

P
ervasive developmental disorders and childhood schizophrenia are categories of disorders that include some of the most damaging and debilitating of all childhood disability conditions. Pervasive developmental disorders are typically apparent in a child's early years of life and may include severe developmental disturbances in communication and social skills as well as evidence of stereotyped behavior such as prolonged periods of manipulating objects and apparently meaningless repetitive body movements. Childhood schizophrenia tends to emerge from 7 to 15 years of age and often involves hallucinations, delusions (unreasonable false beliefs), and thought disorders (e.g., illogical or disturbed thinking).

Included among pervasive developmental disorders in DSM-IV are autism, Rett's disorder, childhood disintegrative disorder, Asperger's disorder, and pervasive developmental disorder not otherwise specified (American Psychiatric Association, 1994). Children diagnosed with one of the pervasive developmental disorders may exhibit combinations of bizarre, incomprehensible behaviors that seem to be extremely abnormal, such as a child who lives in a fantasy world, hears strange voices, and completely screens out reality.

Pervasive developmental disorder is a relatively new term, first used as a classification category in DSM-III and continued in DSM-IV (American Psychiatric Association, 1994). The term *pervasive developmental disorder* suggests that the condition emerged early in the child's development, and it affected all (pervasively) of the child's developing systems (i.e., social, language, cognitive). In some types of developmental disorders, the child was never really normal, but was either born with the condition or developed it very early. In others, there is a period of apparently normal development followed by a regression or the development of abnormal behavior or physical symptoms. This chapter will review the basic pervasive developmental disorders with particular attention given to autism since it is the most frequently occurring of the specific disorders in this category. DSM-IV does not include a specific category for childhood schizophrenia, relying largely on adult criteria for circumstances when it appears earlier. Childhood schizophrenia is examined in this chapter because of its interesting comparisons with pervasive developmental disorders, particularly autism. For example, children diagnosed with schizophrenia may also exhibit behaviors that are extremely abnormal, may be affected by hallucinations, and display a certain level of withdrawal or peculiar social interactions. Although there are certain surface similarities, there are also a number of distinctions, as we will examine later.

PERVASIVE DEVELOPMENTAL DISORDERS

A number of developmental areas are affected by pervasive developmental disorders. The DSM-IV noted that "severe and pervasive impairments" are evident in social interaction skills and communication, which are often accompanied by stereotyped interests, behavior, and activities. These impairments reflect substantial deviation from what would be expected given the individual's mental age or developmental level (American Psychiatric Association, 1994, p. 65). Perhaps the most widely known of these disorders is autism.

Autism

Autism is a widely recognized condition although it develops rather infrequently, only about 2 to 5 occurrences in 10,000 individuals (APA, 1994; Fombonne & du Mazaubrun, 1993; Ritvo et al., 1989). Autism has only recently been addressed by federal legislation as a category of disability in the Individuals with Disabilities Act of 1990 (IDEA). However, the term *autism* has been used in psychological literature for many years. Bleuler (1911) first introduced the term in describing adult patients who were socially withdrawn, although Kanner (1943) first applied the label to children who were socially aloof and self-isolated from a very early age. Kanner also studied the same group of youngsters from their early childhood through adulthood giving detailed descriptions of their adjustment and placements.

Autism has received a great deal of public attention in the past few years. Popular awareness of the disorder has been enhanced substantially by the release of the award-winning film *Rain Man* in the late 1980s and by written descriptions appearing in sources more widely read than scientific journals (e.g., Sacks, 1993, 1994). One extraordinary example is found in the autobiographical account by Williams (1992), which provides a view of autism not often available to those of us studying the disorder. A short excerpt from that volume is found in Box 11-1, which describes part of Donna Williams' early world. Clearly, Donna Williams is not typical of those with autism, although accounts such as hers serve very well to educate all of us regarding the disorder.

Youngsters with autism often do not return their parents' efforts for affection or eye contact.

Federal regulations for IDEA define autism in the following manner: Autism means a developmental disability significantly affecting verbal and nonverbal communication and social interaction, generally evident before age three, that adversely affects educational performance. Characteristics of autism include—irregularities and impairments in communication, engagement in repetitive activities and stereotyped movements, resistance to environmental change or change in daily routines, and unusual responses to sensory experiences. (U.S. Department of Education, 1991, p. 41271)

The DSM-IV includes most of the early characteristics described by Kanner such as abnormalities in social in-

---

BOX 11-1   A View from the Other Side

"I discovered the air was full of spots. If you looked into nothingness, there were spots. People would walk by, obstructing my magical view of nothingness. I'd move past them. They'd gabble. My attention would be firmly set on my desire to lose myself in the spots, and I'd ignore the gabble, looking straight through this obstruction with a calm expression, soothed by being lost in the spots. *Slap.* I was learning about 'the world.'

I learned eventually to lose myself in anything I desired—the patterns on the wallpaper or the carpet, the sound of something over and over again, like the hollow thud I'd get from tapping my chin. Even people became no problem. Their words became a mumbling jumble, their voices a pattern of sounds. I could look through them until I wasn't there, and then, later, I learned to lose myself *in them.*

Words were no problem, but other people's expectations for me to respond to them were. This would have required my understanding what was said, but I was too happy losing myself to want to be dragged back to something as two-dimensional as understanding.

'What do you think you're doing?' came the voice.

Knowing I must respond in order to get rid of this annoyance, I would compromise, repeating 'What do you think you're doing?' addressed to no one in particular.

'Don't repeat everything I say,' scolded the voice.

Slap. I had no idea what was expected of me.

For the first three and a half years of my life this was my language, complete with the intonation and inflection of those I came to think of as 'the world.' The world seemed to be impatient, annoying, callous, and unrelenting. I learned to respond to it as such, crying, squealing, ignoring it, and running away."

Source: Williams, D. (1992). *Nobody nowhere: The extraordinary autobiography of an autistic* (pp. 3–4). New York: Avon Books. Excerpted with permission.

---

teraction with others, impaired communication skills, and unusual responses to many facets of the environment. However, the DSM-IV also notes that the condition is characterized by an onset before 3 years of age, although a diagnosis of autism is not prevented for circumstances in which characteristics are found after age 3. Under such circumstances, the category of atypical autism would be used. The diagnostic criteria for autism used by the American Psychiatric Association in DSM-IV are summarized in Table 11-1.

It should be noted that, while Kanner was accurate in describing the autism syndrome in general, he was wrong about the intellectual ability of these children. He thought that children with autism had good intellectual development based on the observation that some of the children had an exceptional cognitive ability (splinter skills) in one area such as memory or calendar dates. However, it is now recognized that most children with autism have lowered intellectual functioning, with about 75 percent having measured IQs below 70 (Kauffmann, 1993; Sue, Sue, & Sue, 1990). Even the few children with exceptional splinter skills generally exhibit developmental retardation in most other areas.

Rett's Disorder

Rett's disorder differs from autism in a number of ways. Whereas autism occurs more frequently in males than females, Rett's disorder appears only in females (American Psychiatric Association, 1994). Rett's disorder also tends to emerge after a period of seemingly normal development, typically appearing between 5 months and 4 years of age. For children affected with Rett's syndrome, there is a diminishing of some skills that previously developed in a normal fashion. Purposeful hand skills are often replaced with stereotyped movements that resemble hand washing. Growth of the head, which appears normal at first, decelerates and there may be an appearance of seizure disorders. Children with Rett's disorder also tend to have serious impairments in language development as well as retardation in motor skills, often exhibiting poor coordination in walking. Diagnostic criteria are outlined in Table 11-2.

Rett's disorder occurs infrequently with some estimates suggesting a prevalence of 1 in 15,000 infant females (Tridon, Schweitzer, & Six, 1989). This level of occurrence makes large-scale research efforts quite

TABLE 11-1 DSM-IV CRITERIA FOR AUTISM

A. A total of six (or more) items from (1), (2), and (3), with at least two from (1), and one each from (2) and (3):
1. Qualitative impairment in social interaction, as manifested by at least two of the following:
    a. Marked impairment in the use of multiple nonverbal behaviors such as eye-to-eye gaze, facial expression, body postures, and gestures to regulate social interaction.
    b. Failure to develop peer relationships appropriate to developmental level.
    c. A lack of spontaneous seeking to share enjoyment, interests, or achievements with other people (e.g., by a lack of showing, bringing, or pointing out objects of interest).
    d. Lack of social or emotional reciprocity.
2. Qualitative impairments in communication as manifested by at least one of the following:
    a. Delay in, or total lack of, the development of spoken language (not accompanied by an attempt to compensate through alternative modes of communication such as gestures or mime).
    b. In individuals with adequate speech, marked impairment in the ability to initiate or sustain a conversation with others.
    c. Stereotyped and repetitive use of language or idiosyncratic language.
    d. Lack of varied, spontaneous make-believe play or social imitative play appropriate to developmental level.
3. Restricted repetitive and stereotyped patterns of behavior, interests, and activities, as manifested by at least one of the following:
    a. Encompassing preoccupation with one or more stereotypic and restricted patterns of interest that is abnormal either in intensity or focus.
    b. Apparently inflexible adherence to specific, nonfunctional routines or rituals.
    c. Stereotypic and repetitive motor mannerisms (e.g., hand or finger flapping or twisting, or complex whole-body movements).
    d. Persistent preoccupation with parts of objects.
B. Delays or abnormal functioning in at least one of the following areas, with onset prior to age 3 years: (1) social interaction, (2) language as used in social communication, or (3) symbolic or imaginative play.
C. The disturbance is not better accounted for by Rett's Disorder or Childhood Disintegrative Disorder.

SOURCE: Reprinted with permission from the *Diagnostic and statistical manual of mental disorders.* Fourth Edition (1994). Washington, DC: American Psychiatric Association, pp. 70–71. Copyright 1994 by the American Psychiatric Association.

difficult. Some reports suggest there are neurological and neurochemical abnormalities among those having Rett's disorder, although further research is essential for a solid information base to emerge (Gorbachevskaya, Yakupova, Kozhushko, & Bashina, 1992; Myer, Tripathi, Brase, & Dewey, 1992; Wenk, Naidu, Casanova, & Kitt, 1991). There has also been some recent interest in the study of blood chemistry among children with Rett's syndrome, although substantial trends have yet to surface in these data as well (e.g., Leboyer, Bouvard, Recasens, & Phillippe, 1994; Plioplys, Greaves, Kazemi, & Silverman, 1994). Although little is currently known about causation, children having the disorder typically have rather severe mental retardation and the degeneration seems progressive.

Childhood Disintegrative Disorder

Childhood disintegrative disorder is also characterized by an initial period of normal development, but in this case

it is more extended than that found in Rett's syndrome. In childhood disintegrative disorder, the developmental regression begins after at least two years before which the child develops in an age-appropriate fashion (most often the onset is between 3 and 4 years of age). The period of normal development is marked by typical social relationships, communication skills and adaptive behavior. As summarized in Table 11-3, childhood disintegrative disorder results in significant loss of previously acquired skills in areas such as language and social interaction and in physical matters such as motor skills and bowel or bladder control. The behavioral features and social interaction levels begin to appear like those found in youngsters with autism, although the clinical features of the two disorders are distinct in the literature (Hiroshi, Michiko, & Miyake, 1992; Malhotra & Singh, 1993). Previously known as Heller's syndrome and disintegrative psychosis, childhood disintegrative disorder is very rare and may be associated with other medical conditions, although it is not clear that illness is a triggering mechanism in causation (Hiroshi, 1989; Volkmar, 1992).

TABLE 11-2 DIAGNOSTIC CRITERIA
FOR RETT'S DISORDER

A. All of the following:
   1. apparently normal prenatal and perinatal development
   2. apparently normal psychomotor development through the first 5 months after birth
   3. normal head circumference at birth
B. Onset of all of the following after the period of normal development:
   1. deceleration of head growth between ages 5 and 48 months
   2. loss of previously acquired purposeful hand skills between ages 5 and 30 months with the subsequent development of stereotyped hand movements (e.g., hand-wringing or hand washing)
   3. loss of social engagement early in the course (although often social interaction develops later)
   4. appearance of poorly coordinated gait or trunk movements
   5. severely impaired expressive and receptive language development with severe psychomotor retardation

SOURCE: Reprinted with permission from the *Diagnostic and statistical manual of mental disorders*. Fourth Edition (1994). Washington, DC: American Psychiatric Association, pp. 72–73. Copyright 1994 by the American Psychiatric Association.

Asperger's Disorder

Another pervasive developmental disability receiving increased interest recently is known as Asperger's disorder. Asperger's disorder is characterized by severe impairment in social interaction accompanied by the emergence of a narrow pattern of behavior and activities. Terms used to describe these features in those with Asperger's syndrome include pedantic, repetitive, and concrete language and behavior combined with emotional lability, inappropriate or poor social functioning, and facial expressions that are exaggerated, overstated, or not reflecting appropriate affect (Ryan, 1992; Taiminen, 1994). The diagnostic criteria for Asperger's disorder employed in DSM-IV are summarized in Table 11-4 (American Psychiatric Association, 1994). Although the language is characterized as perhaps pedantic and concrete, Asperger's disorder is not characterized by clinically significant delays of language development. Likewise, the development of cognitive skills and self-help or adaptive behavior skills are also not significantly delayed; the children are simply socially unresponsive and their behavior involves what most would call significantly eccentric features that interfere with schooling and adult life (Gross, 1994; Szatmari, 1991).

TABLE 11-3 DSM-IV CRITERIA FOR CHILDHOOD
DISINTEGRATIVE DISORDERS

A. Apparently normal development for at least the first 2 years after birth as manifested by the presence of age-appropriate verbal and nonverbal communication, social relationships, play, and adaptive behavior.
B. Clinically significant loss of previously acquired skills (before age 10 years) in at least two of the following areas:
   1. expressive or receptive language
   2. social skills or adaptive behavior
   3. bowel or bladder control
   4. play
   5. motor skills
C. Abnormalities of functioning in at least two of the following areas:
   1. qualitative impairment in social interaction (e.g., impairment in nonverbal behaviors, failure to develop peer relationships, lack of social or emotional reciprocity)
   2. qualitative impairments in communication (e.g., delay or lack of spoken language, inability to initiate or sustain a conversation, stereotyped and repetitive use of language, lack of varied make-believe play)
   3. restricted, repetitive, and stereotyped patterns of behavior, interests, and activities, including motor stereotypes and mannerisms
D. The disturbance is not better accounted for by another specific Pervasive Developmental Disorder or by Schizophrenia.

SOURCE: Reprinted with permission from the *Diagnostic and statistical manual of mental disorders*. Fourth Edition (1994). Washington, DC: American Psychiatric Association, pp. 74–75. Copyright 1994 by the American Psychiatric Association.

Although motor delays and clumsiness are occasionally included in descriptions of children with Asperger's disorder, research does not suggest that this is a reliable distinguishing characteristic (Ghaziuddin, Butler, Tsai, & Ghaziuddin, 1994). Although Asperger's disorder is associated with general medical conditions (American Psychiatric Association, 1994), determination of causal factors or physical abnormalities remain unclear (David, Wacharasindhu, & Lishman, 1993).

The subtypes of pervasive developmental disorders as presented in DSM-IV represent an interesting set of disorders. The utility of distinguishing between these subtypes for diagnosis and treatment is a question that will be determined over time, just as the effectiveness of DSM-IV as a tool remains to be determined. There is considerable interest, however, as reflected in the recent literature on DSM-IV development and utility (e.g.,

TABLE 11-4 Diagnostic Criteria for Asperger's Disorder

A. Qualitative impairment in social interaction, as manifested by at least two of the following:
   1. marked impairment in the use of multiple nonverbal behaviors such as eye-to-eye gaze, facial expression, body postures, and gestures to regulate social interaction
   2. failure to develop peer relationships appropriate to developmental level
   3. a lack of spontaneous seeking to share enjoyment, interests, or achievements with other people (e.g., by a lack of showing, bringing, or pointing out objects of interest to other people)
   4. lack of social or emotional reciprocity
B. Restricted repetitive and stereotyped patterns of behavior, interests, and activities, as manifested by at least one of the following:
   1. encompassing preoccupation with one or more stereotyped and restricted patterns of interest that is abnormal either in intensity or focus
   2. apparently inflexible adherence to specific, nonfunctional routines or rituals
   3. stereotyped and repetitive motor mannerisms (e.g., hand or finger flapping or twisting, or complex whole-body movements)
   4. persistent preoccupation with parts of objects
C. The disturbance causes clinically significant impairment in social, occupational, or other important areas of functioning.
D. There is no clinically significant general delay in language (e.g., single words used by age 2 years, communicative phrases used by age 3 years).
E. There is no clinically significant delay in cognitive development or in the development of age-appropriate self-help skills, adaptive behavior (other than in social interaction), and curiosity about the environment in childhood.
F. Criteria are not met for another specific Pervasive Developmental Disorder or Schizophrenia.

SOURCE: Reprinted with permission from the *Diagnostic and statistical manual of mental disorders*. Fourth Edition (1994). Washington, DC: American Psychiatric Association, p. 77. Copyright 1994 by the American Psychiatric Association.

Volkmar, Klin, Siegel, & Szatmari, 1994; Szatmari, Archer, Fisman, & Steiner, 1994).

CHILDHOOD SCHIZOPHRENIA

Potter (1933) described childhood schizophrenia based on many of the characteristics of adult schizophrenia. He commented, however, that children "cannot be expected to exhibit psychopathology with all the elaborations of the adult." Stated simply, since children do not have the language complexity, intelligence, or maturity of adults, their psychotic symptoms are different. Potter developed a six-point classification system that listed a lack of interest in the environment, withdrawal into a fantasy world in which everyday experience has little meaning, a defect in logical thinking, and emotional reactions ranging from a stupor to extreme unexplained excitement. What primarily characterized these children was their withdrawal into a *fantasy world* and their *illogical, disturbed thinking*.

Modern classification of schizophrenia does not differ a great deal from Potter's early description of the con-

dition. As noted earlier, the DSM-IV does not have a specific category for childhood schizophrenia. The adult criteria for schizophrenia are used for children and adolescents; these criteria are listed in Table 11-5. As seen from this list, emphasis is placed on delusions, hallucinations, disorganized speech, and behavioral and affective disturbance. According to DSM-IV, "the essential features of the condition are the same in children, but it may be particularly difficult to make the diagnosis in this age group. In children, delusions and hallucinations may be less elaborated than those observed in adults, and visual hallucinations may be more common (American Psychiatric Association, 1994, p. 281).

DIFFERENCES AND SIMILARITIES BETWEEN AUTISM AND CHILDHOOD SCHIZOPHRENIA

Several researchers have examined the fundamental differences between autism and childhood schizophrenia (e.g., Caplan, 1994; McKenna, Gordon, & Rapoport,

With an IQ well above average, this youngster with schizophrenia has continuing episodes of hallucination.

1994). It appears the primary difference between infantile autism and childhood schizophrenia is reflected in the cardinal characteristics of the two conditions. Autism is defined as basically a condition in which socially relating to other people is greatly disturbed. Childhood schizophrenia, on the other hand, is described primarily as a condition characterized by thought disorder and hallucinations. It should be noted that both autism and childhood schizophrenia can occur in the same child.

Other fundamental differences also exist. First, there is a marked difference when the two conditions occur during childhood. Infantile autism has a peak age of onset before age 2½, while schizophrenia appears in later childhood and early adolescence. If a child has not developed autism by 5 years of age, he or she probably never will. The greatest risk factor for childhood schizophrenia, however, is from 7 to 15 years of age. Autism develops early, disrupts basic development areas (i.e., social, language, and intellect), and continues into adulthood with

little change in its clinical course. Childhood schizophrenia develops late, leaves many of the developmental areas untouched, and runs a varied course with episodes of improvement and relapse. Additional differences between autism and childhood schizophrenia are listed in Table 11-6. The characteristics of these two conditions will be contrasted in more detail when individual features of social skills, language, intelligence, and self-stimulatory behavior are discussed. However, some areas of commonality of characteristics for these two conditions should also be discussed.

These two conditions are similar in that they are both rare. As mentioned earlier, most estimates and research have shown the general prevalence of autism to be approximately 2 to 5 in 10,000 (APA, 1994; Fombonne & du Mazaubrun, 1993; Ritvo et al., 1989). Some evidence suggests a much higher prevalence ranging from 10 to 14 cases per 10,000 (Bryson, Clark, & Smith, 1988; Cialdella & Mamebe, 1989; Ohtaki, Kawano, Urabe, & Komori, 1992) although such variance is most likely attributable to variation in the diagnostic criteria employed. There also appears to be some difference in prevalence due to gender, with males having autism outnumbering females between 2 to 1 to 4 to 1, particularly at higher levels of functioning (Fombonne & du Mazaubrun, 1992; Ohtaki et al., 1992; Volkmar et al., 1993). Similarly, schizophrenia is rare in childhood and adolescence. The incidence rate for schizophrenia in adulthood and adolescence is 2 to 4 per 1,000 and approximately 1 in 1,000 for children. Both autism and childhood schizophrenia occur more frequently in males, generally with a ratio of approximately 4 males to every female (Gorwood, Leboyer, Jay, & Payan, 1995; Joseph, 1994; Volkmar et al., 1993). However, this male and female difference disappears for schizophrenia in late adolescence when the ratio is nearly equal.

Social Skills

The inability to form personal relationships and to relate socially to other human beings is considered the basic core characteristic of children with autism (Cohen, Volmar, Anderson, & Klin, 1993; Ricks, 1989; Rutter, 1991; Szatmari, Bartolucci, & Bremner, 1989). Infants with autism are frequently described by their mothers as being noncuddly babies who seldom laugh, often become stiff and rigid when they are picked up, or are unresponsive

TABLE 11-5   DSM-IV CRITERIA FOR SCHIZOPHRENIA

A. *Characteristic symptoms:* Two (or more) of the following, each present for a significant portion of time during a 1-month period (or less if successfully treated):
  1. delusions
  2. hallucinations
  3. disorganized speech (e.g., frequent derailment or incoherence)
  4. grossly disorganized or catatonic behavior
  5. negative symptoms, that is, affective flattening, alogia, or avolition
  Note: Only one Criterion A symptom is required if delusions are bizarre or hallucinations consist of a voice keeping up a running commentary on the person's behavior or thoughts, or two or more voices conversing with each other.

B. *Social/occupational dysfunction:* For a significant portion of the time since the onset of the disturbance, one or more major areas of functioning such as work, interpersonal relations, or self-care are markedly below the level achieved prior to the onset (or when the onset is in childhood or adolescence, failure to achieve expected level of interpersonal, academic, or occupational achievement).

C. *Duration:* Continuous signs of the disturbance persist for at least 6 months. This 6-month period must include at least 1 month of symptoms (or less if successfully treated) that meet Criterion A (i.e., active-phase symptoms) and may include periods of prodromal or residual symptoms. During these prodromal or residual periods, the signs of the disturbance may be manifested by only negative symptoms or two or more symptoms listed in Criterion A present in an attenuated form (e.g., odd beliefs, unusual perceptual experiences).

D. *Schizoaffective and Mood Disorder exclusion:* Schizoaffective Disorder and Mood Disorder With Psychotic Features have been ruled out because either (1) no Major Depressive, Manic, or Mixed Episodes have occurred concurrently with the active-phase symptoms; or (2) if mood episodes have occurred during active-phase symptoms, their total duration has been brief relative to the duration of the active and residual periods.

E. *Substance/general medical condition exclusion:* The disturbance is not due to the direct physiological effects of a substance (e.g., a drug of abuse, a medication) or a general medical condition.

F. *Relationship to a Pervasive Developmental Disorder:* If there is a history of Autistic Disorder or another Pervasive Developmental Disorder, the additional diagnosis of Schizophrenia is made only if prominent delusions or hallucinations are also present for at least a month (or less if successfully treated).

Classification of longitudinal course (can be applied only after at least 1 year has elapsed since the initial onset of active-phase symptoms):
  Episodic With Interepisode Residual Symptoms (episodes are defined by the reemergence of prominent psychotic symptoms); *also specify if:* **With Prominent Negative Symptoms**
  Episodic With No Interepisode Residual Symptoms
  Continuous (prominent psychotic symptoms are present throughout the period of observation); *also specify if:* **With Prominent Negative Symptoms**
  Single Episode in Partial Remission; *also specify if:* **With Prominent Negative Symptoms**
  Single Episode in Full Remission
  Other or Unspecified Pattern

SOURCE: Reprinted with permission from the *Diagnostic and statistical manual of mental disorders.* Fourth Edition (1994). Washington, DC: American Psychiatric Association, pp. 285–286. Copyright 1994 by the American Psychiatric Association.

to physical contact and affection (Capps, Kasari, Yirmiya, & Sigman, 1993). Other mothers describe their infants (before they were diagnosed as having autism) as exceptionally "good" babies because they were so undemanding and did not need the mother's constant attention. This lack of social relatedness is reflected in the child's later social development. Many children with autism do not develop appropriate play skills. For instance, they would rather spin the tires on a toy instead of play with it appropriately. Most children with autism also do not

form normal friendships with other children. They are social isolates (Cohen, Volmar, Anderson, & Klin, 1993; Rutter, 1991).

The research in the social behavior of autism has expanded in the past few years. Much of this research has focused on eye contact and gaze aversion, the approach and avoidance of children with autism, play skills, and social skills training. However, social interactions remains one of the most difficult research areas because of the difficulty in explicitly defining and reliably recording

TABLE 11-6 DIFFERENCES BETWEEN INFANTILE AUTISM AND CHILDHOOD SCHIZOPHRENIA

Infantile Autism	Childhood Schizophrenia
Early onset (before 30 months)	Late onset (late childhood–adolescence)
Early abnormal development	Develops normally and then withdraws into fantasy world
Poor social interaction skills (poor eye contact, social avoidance, lack of play skills)	Dependency on adults but interacts socially
No hallucinations or delusions	Hallucinations and delusions
Mentally retarded	Normal intelligence
Language disturbance (muteness, pronoun reversals, echolalia)	Good language development
Steady course of the disorder	Variable course
Concrete thinking	Thought is disordered (illogical, jumps from one topic to another)

social behaviors. A nondisabled child will frequently initiate social contacts and will generally not avoid contact initiated by other people. However, children with autism systematically avoid play situations and engage in solitary and uncooperative activities. These children do not show the necessary social imitation skills needed to engage successfully with other children. Many autistic children relate to other people as "objects" instead of people, often pushing or pulling them by the hand to get what they want (Sue et al., 1990).

The social behavior of schizophrenic children with late onset also is characterized by social withdrawal and avoidance of others (Asarnow, Tompson, & Goldstein, 1994). However, this social withdrawal is of a different nature and occurs later in the child's development and is not a direct, overt avoidance of all social contact as in autism. These children may be bizarre in their social interactions or withdrawn into a fantasy world.

Language

Disturbance of language is a basic symptom of childhood autism (Davis, Fennoy, Laraque, & Kanem, 1992; Hall, 1992; Van-Lancker, Cornelius, & Needleman, 1991). The exact nature of the language disturbance distinguishes autistic children from nonpsychotic children who have language difficulties. For example, many prelanguage skills are absent in children who are later diagnosed as autistic. Patterns of babble that normally occur in children before 2 years of age frequently do not develop in children with autism. Many of these children who do not babble or respond to sound have intact auditory systems. Similarly, many autistic children do not show age-appropriate gesturing skills and verbal imitation skills, both of which are considered to be prelanguage skills in most children. A significant percentage (28 to 61 percent depending on the study) of autistic children do not develop language skills and are mute at some point during their childhood. If a child with autism develops language, it is generally late and the child shows a poor vocabulary, unusual speech content, simple speech structure, and a monotone quality. Many children with autism seem to use language as a noncommunicating, self-stimulatory behavior (Hardman, Drew, & Egan, 1996). In some cases they interpret language in a very concrete manner, as in the case where a mother of a young boy with autism asked him to "crack a window" and let some air in the room. The youngster actually took an object and broke the window.

Frequently, autistic children exhibit echolalic speech—they repeat sentences or questions addressed to them (Loveland, McEvoy, & Tunali, 1990; Nientimp & Cole, 1992; Tirosh & Canby, 1993). A child might have *immediate echolalia* or "parrot speech" in which the most recently heard speech is repeated, as illustrated in the description by Donna Williams in Box 11-1. Another example might be when a child with autism is asked his or her name, the child might simply repeat, "What's your name?" Some children with autism demonstrate *delayed echolalia* in which something heard hours or days ago is repeated. In such cases, a child might repeat something that was heard days before and is totally out of context, which sounds quite bizarre. Experiences of happiness, sadness, and excitement are typically absent from the language of many autistic children. Inflection and change of emphasis on certain key words containing emotional meaning are missing, which results in a flat, monotonous manner of speaking.

The type and quality of language of autistic children can be sharply contrasted with the language of schizophrenic children. First, the language of autistic children is generally delayed or disrupted in its normal

---

BOX 11-2 TEMPLE GRANDIN

I phoned Temple from the Denver airport to reconfirm our meeting—it was conceivable, I thought, that she might be somewhat inflexible about arrangements, so time and place should be set as definitely as possible. It was an hour and a quarter's drive to Fort Collins, Temple said, and she provided minute directions for finding her office at Colorado State University, where she is an assistant professor in the Animal Sciences Department. At one point, I missed a detail and asked Temple to repeat it, and was startled when she repeated the entire directional litany—several minutes' worth—in virtually the same words. It seemed as if the directions had to be given as they were held in Temple's mind, entire—that they had fused into a fixed association or program and could no longer be separated into their components. One instruction, however, had to be modified. She told me at first that I should turn right onto College Street at a particular intersection marked by a Taco Bell restaurant. In her second set of directions, Temple added an aside here, said the Taco Bell had recently had a facelift and been housed in a fake cottage, and no longer looked in the least "bellish." I was struck by the charming, whimsical adjective "bellish"—autistic people are often called humorless, unimaginative, and "bellish" was surely an original concoction, a spontaneous and delightful image.

SOURCE: Sacks, O. (1993). A neurologist's notebook: An anthropologist on mars. *The New Yorker,* December 27, 1993/January 3, 1994, p. 110.

---

development. The language of schizophrenic children does not consistently show impaired development (Asarnow, Asamen, Granholm, & Sherman, 1994). Second, the language of autistic children is confused and the content is impoverished. Schizophrenic children generally use correct language structure to communicate bizarre thoughts. Unlike autistic children whose mutism or strange use of language sets her or him apart as different, the bizarre meaning and fantasy of the schizophrenic child's language content are abnormal.

Intelligence

The majority of autistic children evidence lowered intellectual functioning as measured by standard intelligence tests (Kauffmann, 1993; Sue et al., 1990). While early literature suggested that these youngsters had difficulty with imitation, more recent work suggests that this may be a deficiency in information processing (Smith & Bryson, 1994). The intellectual capacity varies considerably among those with autism as indicated by the high functioning of the young woman in Box 11-2. Such individuals, however, are rare and do not reflect the general population of those with autism. Further, even with individuals such as Temple Grandin, described in the box, there are hints that something is different in their functioning.

It is easy to be fooled by some autistic children's abilities. About 10 to 15 percent of the individuals with autism exhibit what is known as "splinter skills," which are fairly narrow areas of functioning in which they seem to

excel. These splinter skills are particularly notable because they represent islands of relatively high capacity surrounded by low functioning in other areas. Historically, the presence of splinter skills led to descriptions of people with autism as having savant tendencies and even to the use of the term "Idiot Savant" in past years.

In contrast to the lower IQs typical of children with autism, those who developed schizophrenia later in childhood tend to show intelligence in the near normal range (Kauffmann, 1993). The nature of intelligence also seems to be different for children with autism and those with schizophrenia. The majority of children with autism have mental retardation with particular deficits in verbal and reasoning skills. Children with schizophrenia, however, show less retardation and overall better intellectual development in all areas.

Self-Stimulatory and Self-Injurious Behavior

Self-stimulatory, or stereotypic behavior, is a repetitive, apparently purposeless behavior that occurs in normal, psychotic, and developmentally disordered children. Self-stimulatory behavior is not unique to childhood behavior disorders. Everyone self-stimulates, and it is interesting to watch a group of people. Some people without disabilities unconsciously pull their hair, bite their finger nails, wiggle their feet, or tap pencils. What distinguishes these common forms of self-stimulation behavior from abnormal self-stimulation is exaggeration in form, the frequency, and appropriateness of the behavior for a particular environmental setting. For example, a child with autism may spend hours spinning coins, gazing at lights, rocking, twirling, or flapping hands (Powers, Thibadeau, & Rose, 1992; Stahmer & Schreibman, 1992; Zissermann, 1992). All of these behaviors have a social and educational cost for such children.

In some cases self-stimulation may become self-injurious, which is much more destructive, causing concern for parents and others around the youngster (Konstantareas & Homatidis, 1989). Common forms of self-injurious behavior in autistic children include head banging, face slapping, scratching, and biting. The motivational factors for self-injurious behaviors are similar to those of self-stimulation. For example, the sensory feedback received from self-inflicting a wound may be reinforcing (Stahmer & Schreibman, 1992). Other important factors that may motivate self-injurious behavior include inappropriate but well intended concern and attention from others, which may serve to reinforce the behavior and self-injury as the child tries to avoid compliance to requests (Kauffmann, 1993).

A number of problems are associated with self-stimulation and self-injury: some people are frightened or repelled by the behaviors, and the behavior may interfere with a child's attention and learning new tasks (Stahmer & Schreibman, 1992). It also may disrupt previously learned behaviors and displace socially acceptable behavior of various types (Bodfish, Crawford, Powell, Parker, Golden, & Lewis, 1995; Powers et al., 1992).

Differences in self-stimulatory and self-injury behavior between children with autism and those having schizophrenia have not been thoroughly investigated. Both forms of behavior can occur in both types of conditions. One basic difference is the frequency of occurrence. Children with autism will engage in self-stimulating and self-injurious behavior generally at much higher rates than children with schizophrenia. However, certain types of self-stimulation appear in common between autism and schizophrenia. For example, *hand regard* or gazing is not an uncommon form of self-stimulation for both children having autism and schizophrenia.

Stimulus Overselectivity

Stimulus overselectivity is a perceptual disability in which a child focuses on only a part of a stimulus, perhaps an irrelevant cue or at least one that is not a central feature (Hardman et al., 1996). Overselectivity has been studied mostly in children with autism. Although it has been found to be particularly evident in those with lower IQs, it is also of considerable interest in children who are considered to be high-functioning (Myles, Anderson, Constant, & Simpson, 1989). Stimulus overselectivity interferes with learning many of the basic stimulus discriminations needed to adjust to the environment. For example, normal children use a number of cues to learn discriminations between correct and incorrect responses. For the most part they focus on central features that are most vital to the discrimination. Children with autism, however, may focus on irrelevant or peripheral cues that are not distinctly different between the alternatives, and therefore are not central to discriminating between correct and incorrect.

Stimulus overselectivity hinders children with autism as they attempt to learn complex discriminations in language and some of the subtle choices involved in developing social skills (Cohen et al., 1993; Mesibov & Stephens, 1990). It may also help explain the common characteristic of autistic children's need to keep their environments the same or unchanging. This "insistence on sameness" characteristically involves requiring the house furniture arrangement to stay exactly the same or a daily schedule or travel route to remain unchanged (Gordon, State, Nelson, & Hamburger, 1993; Levinson & Reid, 1993; Norton & Drew, 1994). If they are changed, the child may tantrum and persistently try to return the situation to its previous state. Overselectivity may help account for this need for sameness because the child has learned to rely on an irrelevant characteristic (e.g., a chair's position or a particular arrangement) to help discriminate and map their environment. Stimulus overselectivity has not been studied extensively in schizophrenic children although there is some indication that it is present in chronic adult schizophrenics (Kauffmann, 1993).

Family Characteristics

There has long been speculation concerning the families and parents of children with autism and schizophrenia. Some have characterized the parents, particularly mothers, of children with autism as being rather cold and rejecting (e.g., Bettelheim, 1967). Such theories have been couched primarily in the context of causation. Although some literature continues to explore psychodynamic theories related to autism, most of the focus relates to topics such as the child's fears and newborn anxieties (e.g., deBenedetti-Gaddini, 1993; Haag, 1993; Weininger, 1993). The view that parents of children with autism, as a group, are characteristically rejecting and cold does not receive much support in the literature.

Family members of children with schizophrenia and autism are quite often faced with considerable stress, which may result in emotional distress (Hardman et al., 1996). Even the physical demands are significant. For example, a child with autism may sleep for only a few hours per night, making physical fatigue a substantial life component that may contribute to emotional stress levels (Norton & Drew, 1994). The family routine is likely disrupted significantly and high stress levels have been associated with some depression and affective disruptions among mothers (Bristol, Gallagher, & Holt, 1993; Cook, Asarnow, Goldstein, & Marshall, 1990; Donenberg & Baker, 1993; Gillberg, Gillberg, & Steffenburg, 1992). Siblings may have difficulty adapting to their parent's stress levels and the amount of attention provided to the child with the disability, and may manifest some depression symptoms (Bagenholm & Gillberg, 1991; Gold, 1993).

ETIOLOGICAL THEORIES: AUTISM AND CHILDHOOD SCHIZOPHRENIA

Theories regarding the causes of autism and childhood schizophrenia can generally be divided into two broad categories: psychodynamic (those based on the psychoanalytic school of psychology) and those related to biological causation. While considerable research has addressed causation, information to date has not established a solid basis for understanding these disorders fully. In both cases there appears to be an array of symptoms with potential causes from both biological and environmental influences (e.g., Reichelt, Knivsberg, Lind, & Nodland, 1991).

Psychodynamic Theories of Cause

Freud contributed some of the earliest theoretical work toward an explanation of schizophrenia. Later refinements of Abraham (1955) maintained that the development of schizophrenia was brought about by a regression or fixation of the *libido* (sexual energy) at an early primary stage. This stalling of normal development presum-

ably produces a withdrawal of personal and object relationships into an *autoerotic* state of self-stimulation.

As noted above, some have portrayed the parents of children with autism as highly intellectual, cold, rejecting individuals with little interest in people or human warmth (Bettelheim, 1967). This view suggests that causation of autism relates to the child withdrawing from such rejection and erecting defensive barriers to the outside world to avoid psychological pain. Such reasoning is used to explain the child's behavior, which appears to primarily involve interactions with an inner world and little attention to the outside environment involving people. As noted earlier, little attention has been given to this viewpoint in recent times, although psychodynamic literature continues to focus on other matters (e.g., deBenedetti-Gaddini, 1993; Haag, 1993; Weininger, 1993).

Biological Theories of Cause

Biological theorists view the causes of autism and schizophrenia as functions of birth trauma, viral infections such as German measles, and metabolic problems. Genetic factors have also attracted considerable attention in searching for the causation of autism (e.g., Bailey, 1993; Bailey, Bolton, Butler, & le Couteur, 1993; Prior, 1989) although establishment of a solid data base is still in progress (Cammisa & Hobbs, 1993; Cuccaro, Wright, Abramson, & Marstellar, 1993). Many of these biological conditions also contribute to an increased incidence of seizures, low birthweight, abnormal neurological measures (electroencephalograph, EEG, and computer tomographic brain scan, CT), mental retardation, and poor motor development (Elia, Musumeci, Ferri, & Bergonzi, 1995).

In recent years, major advances in computer guided brain imaging have given scientists a literal cross-section picture of the brain of an individual with autism. Computer tomography (CT scans) uses a series of cross-sectional X-rays to produce lifelike pictures of the brain at different depths. The results on individuals with autism have shown some abnormal brain structures (Dawson, Finley, Phillips, & Lewy, 1989; Siegel, Asarnow, Tanguay, & Call, 1992), but the results have not been consistent in the type of abnormality and between individuals. One area of the brain that has appeared abnormal in some cases is known as the vermis and is located in the cerebellum, which might account for some of the cognitive anomalies found in autism. However, further study is needed and some researchers find such abnormalities less appealing than genetic causation (e.g., Bailey, 1993).

Disease and its effects on the central nervous system have been suspected of causing autistic-like symptoms in children. For example, there has been considerable interest in the relationship between congenital HIV and autism (Moss, Brouwers, Wolters, & Wiener, 1994; Museti, Albizzati, Grioni, & Rossetti, 1993). Likewise, the Herpes simplex virus has been suspected of attacking the neurological system and resulting in autistic symptoms (Fotheringham, 1991). Such neurological impairment is also linked to anaerobic infections in young children (Brook, 1995). However, despite such an array of potential damaging assaults, no single disease trauma has been consistently identified as being the causative agent (Cammisa & Hobbs, 1993).

Genetic factors can be involved in the development of a clinical condition in basically two ways. First, direct damage to the genetic material itself such as the chromosome structure that holds the genes can cause a defect. Second, an abnormality can be coded in the genetic material and passed on as an inherited characteristic. In the late 1960s, a new condition was discovered that was thought to have a major implication for autism. The condition, known as fragile X syndrome, plays a role in the cause of mental retardation and also appears in a percentage of males having autism (Bailey et al., 1993; Drew, Hardman, & Logan, 1996). Although inferences from earlier research suggested that fragile X might be a significant causative factor in autism (e.g., Coleman & Gilbert, 1985), more recent literature indicates that it appears in a relatively small percentage of youngsters with autism (Bolton, Pickles, Butler, & Summers, 1992; Hasimoto, Shimizu, & Kawasaki, 1993).

Substantial advances have been made in research on the roles of genetics in autism and childhood schizophrenia (e.g., Bailey, 1993; Nigg & Goldsmith, 1994). Considerable information has been gained by examination of twins in both disability conditions. Twin studies are typically undertaken when genetically identical twins (monozygotic) are compared to fraternal twins (dizygotic or nongenetically identical) to determine if there are differences in autism. A higher incidence for monozygotic twins would suggest a genetic base for the condition. Although evidence from such research suggests a genetic link (Bailey, 1993; McKenna et al., 1994; Nigg & Gold-

smith, 1994), there remains a great deal of work to be done in order to clarify the causative mechanisms involved. For example, chemical imbalances such as an excess of dopamine may contribute to schizophrenia. Sometimes termed the dopamine hypothesis, this may occur because dopamine receptors are overly sensitive or because an actual excess of dopamine is present (Sue et al., 1990). In either case, the condition is seen as genetically transmitted. Identifying a genetic linkage is much easier than understanding how such a condition developmentally results in autism or childhood schizophrenia (e.g., Cammisa & Hobbs, 1993; Cuccaro, Wright, Abramson, & Marstellar, 1993).

Both the autism and childhood schizophrenic genetics studies suggest a polygenic recessive gene-model (involving many genes from both parents) as a cause for some of the case. It also seems that the disorders reflect spectrum disorders in which there are varying levels or severity evident as well as the appearance of a disorder in one member of the family while others might be unaffected (McKenna et al., 1994). Although biological evidence is mounting, it would be incorrect to suggest that all autism and childhood schizophrenia is genetically based. It is more likely that there are multiple causes that lead to one type of condition, especially autism. Many researchers now believe that multiple biological causes are involved (Bailey, 1993; Cammisa & Hobbs, 1993; Gillberg, 1990a, 1990b).

TREATMENT

Treatments for autism and childhood schizophrenia are varied and controversial. The controversy comes from desperate attempts to treat some of these conditions that historically have had very poor outcomes or appear to be based on questionable evidence (Hardman et al., 1996). It is not difficult to imagine trying almost any reasonable approach to save a self-injurious child or one who has not directly communicated with you as a parent. All the major approaches including psychoanalytic treatment, behavioral interventions, and medical approaches have been used with autistic and schizophrenic children.

Psychoanalytic Approaches

The basic aim of psychoanalytic oriented treatment of autistic and schizophrenic children is to repair ego

This youngster echoes what he hears, a behavior known as echolalia.

damage resulting from a dysfunctional maternal-child relationship, causing the child to withdraw into a private world (deBenedetti-Gaddini, 1993; Weininger, 1993). The analyst totally accepts the psychotic child's behavior and allows him or her to regress to earlier developmental states so that the disrupted normal development can be reexperienced. Often based on the early work of Bettelheim (1967), treatment frequently attempts to reduce environmental stresses generated by parental relationships. Although some interest in such treatment approaches continues, it has diminished substantially in the current literature (Zimmerman, 1994).

Psychoanalytic treatment approaches to autism and childhood schizophrenia were basically early pioneering efforts at treatment. However, their overall effectiveness in improving a child's behavior is questionable. The length of time required for treatment is very long and considered not cost effective by most hospitals and treatment agencies. Most important, the psychoanalytic assumption that parents cause the conditions is fundamentally in error. Such an assumption adds a great burden to a family in treatment and separates parents from the treatment process. Parents can be valuable assets to a comprehensive treatment approach.

Behavioral Approaches

Behavioral treatment appears attractive to many clinicians and educators because it is evaluative in its basic approach, treats problem behaviors directly, and includes parents as part of the treatment team (Kauffman, 1993). The basic behavioral approaches follow a consistent pattern. First, empirical data are gathered on the target be-haviors (problem or abnormal behaviors) before the treatment intervention is started. This pretreatment sam-ple (baseline) is then used as a standard to evaluate the treatment effects. If the treatment is not effective, it is either changed or stopped. The behaviorist treats behav-ior that is happening here and now and can be measured. Behavioral excesses, such as self-stimulatory behavior, tantrums, self-injury, bizarre speech, or aggressive be-haviors, are treated by ignoring the behavior and rein-forcing an incompatible behavior, or by direct punish-ment techniques, such as loss of tokens or the use of time-out (Chapman, Fisher, Piazza, & Kurtz, 1993; Ramm, 1990). Behavioral deficits such as poor eye con-tact, failure to speak, and impoverished social skills are remedied by teaching and reinforcing appropriate behav-ioral replacement skills (Davis, Brady, Williams, & Ham-ilton, 1992; Durand & Carr, 1992).

Possibly the most dramatic effects of the use of be-havior management has been in the treatment of severe self-stimulation and self-injury (Chapman et al., 1993; Ramm, 1990). Behaviors such as head banging, scratch-ing, biting, and face slapping can lead to disfigurement and blindness. Behavioral techniques such as time-out, overcorrection, and differential reinforcement of zero rates of behavior (DRO) have been effective in reducing self-injury.

Central among the important gains in treating autistic children have been the inclusion of parents as active members of the treatment team. Parent training has been successful in teaching parents to decrease their child's inappropriate behavior and to teach needed adjustment and self-help skills. Including parents is important be-cause it gives them skills to successfully manage their child's behavior in home settings, which decreases the probability the child will be institutionalized. Parental participation in behavioral treatment programs has shown promising results (Krantz, MacDuff, & McClanahan, 1993; Lemanek, Stone, & Fishel, 1993), making them important partners in the improvement of their child rather than identifying them as a causative agent. Such approaches represent an important step to-ward normalization for both the youngster and the family (Nientimp & Cole, 1992).

One of the most controversial treatments emerging in recent years is used with individuals having autism, fo-cusing specifically on their communication problems.

Known as facilitative communication, this procedure was developed initially in Australia and employs typing as a means of communication (Biklen, 1990, 1992). The therapist-facilitator provides physical support by touch-ing the student's arm, providing interpersonal support through light pressure. The advocates of facilitative com-munication have been enthusiastically supportive al-though other researchers have not been able to obtain results suggesting its effectiveness. A number have raised serious questions regarding the soundness of facilitative communication and the research evidence supporting its use (Simpson, 1993; Szempruch & Jacobson, 1993). Challenges have included suggestions that the facilitative therapist rather than the person with autism is doing the communication (Cummins & Prior, 1992; Thompson, 1993; Wheeler, Jacobson, Paglieri, & Schwartz, 1993). Clearly, further objective research using sound scientific methodology is needed to clarify the effectiveness of fa-cilitative communication.

Behavioral techniques employing the basic principles of applied behavior analysis are effective, but they do not cure autistic or schizophrenic children. They effectively manage problematic behaviors and teach needed survival behaviors (e.g., Carr & Carlson, 1993; Chapman et al., 1993). Their main treatment effect is in successfully keep-ing children in the community with their families and not in institutions. These techniques are also more hu-mane since good behavior management practice incor-porates whole families in the treatment process.

Medical Approaches

Medical treatment of autistic and schizophrenic children has included a number of different therapies including psychosurgery, electroconvulsive shock, and drug thera-pies. Most of the more drastic approaches such as psy-chosurgery and electroconvulsive shock have been aban-doned because of the possible harmful side effects and doubtful therapeutic effects (Hardman et al., 1996; Kauff-man, 1993). The more controversial drug therapies used with autistic and schizophrenic children include D-lysergic acid (LSD-25) and megavitamin treatment with vitamin B.

The major advances in medication-based treatment for schizophrenic children have been the use of antipsy-chotic and other medications often directed at control-ling behavior and managing symptoms (Gordon, Frazier,

McKenna, & Giedd, 1994; Rapoport, 1994; Spencer & Campbell, 1994). The major antipsychotic medications work well with psychotic adults and are more effective with older autistic and schizophrenic children (McClellan & Werry, 1992). These medications help reduce bizarre speech, aggression, and appear to "organize" the child's behavior. The antipsychotic medications have also been found to be effective in reducing self-injurious behavior, particularly if they are used in combination with behavioral techniques (Brady, 1993; Carr & Carlson, 1993; Menage, Thibault, Berthelemy, & Lelord, 1992; Nelson & Pribor, 1993; Osman & Loschen, 1992). However, the difficulties with antipsychotic medication used with children is its overuse or as a sole treatment approach. Most authors agree that no single medication can effectively treat the heterogeneous symptoms found in autism or childhood schizophrenia (e.g., Harty, 1990; McClellan & Werry, 1994). Side effects of overuse include drowsiness, which reduces the ability to learn, and, if used for an extended period of time, troublesome involuntary motor movements (dyskinesia).

Medications used for treatment of individuals with autism often include antipsychotic, serotonergic, and dopamine drugs (Gualtieri, 1992). As described with schizophrenia, specific symptoms tend to be treated with particular medication, such as using clomipramine with obsessive-compulsive behaviors (Gordon et al., 1993). Decreasing self-injurious behavior and diminishing social withdrawal have also been effectively accomplished with medication (Menage et al., 1992; Nelson & Pribor, 1993; Panksepp & Lensing, 1991). Despite evidence for successful treatment in some children, other research on the effectiveness of medication has shown small or no improvement in the autistic symptoms (Ekman, Miranda-Linne, Gillberg, Garle, & Wetterberg, 1989; Oades, Stern, Walker, & Clark, 1990; Sherman, Factor, Swinson, & Darjes, 1989). Continued research on the use of medication with those having autism is important.

As a treatment for autistic and schizophrenic children, medication is a relatively inexpensive, less time-consuming than psychological interventions, and can be administered by just a few staff members. These benefits are also the drug's most damaging drawbacks. It is too easy to medicate a difficult child and let him or her languish in the back room of a treatment facility. States of stupor induced by high doses of drugs reduce aggression

and bizarre forms of behavior. However, a drug-induced stupor interferes with learning and wastes precious time during which a child might be learning new language and self-help skills. Also, medication has no long-lasting effects. Once the drug is withdrawn, the symptoms reappear. Drugs can best be used in moderate dosages, under close medical supervision, and in conjunction with other forms of therapy.

PROGNOSIS

Neither children with autism nor schizophrenia improve a great deal as they grow older (e.g., Remschmidt, Schulz, Martin, & Warnke, 1994). Although specific treatment programs may substantially improve functional skills and independent functioning, what is functional for one individual may include traditional academics while another individual learns basic self-help or self-protection skills (Chapman et al., 1993; Dalrymple, 1989; Handlan & Bloom, 1993). Intelligence is one of the most important predictors of future outcome for children with autism. Intelligence is a very stable characteristic and typically does not improve with treatment or special education programs. Near normal intelligence while the child is young predicts better adjustment in adulthood, although even higher functioning individuals with autism tend to retain some self-stimulatory behavior and exhibit concrete thinking. Language seems to be a critical element in making predictions when IQs are above 50. If the child's IQ is above 50 and he or she exhibits a severe language disability (but the child does speak), then the prognosis is fair. If the child has only a mild language disorder and normal nonverbal intelligence, the prognosis is good. Unsurprisingly the long-term prognosis for individuals with autism is as variable as the unique characteristics they present (Kanner, 1992). Long-term planning by parents of children with autism requires a great deal of foresight and effort, typically with help and involvement from multiple agencies (Gray, 1993; Moreno & Donellan, 1991; Norton & Drew, 1994).

Institutionalization frequently harms children with autism or schizophrenia. Individual treatment programs and educational opportunities are minimal in many large hospitals. Kanner (1992) did a 28-year follow-up study of a group of autistic children, several of whom were placed in institutions, with foster parents, or on farms.

TABLE 11-7 FACTORS RELATED TO POOR AND GOOD
OUTCOMES FOR CHILDREN WITH
AUTISM AND SCHIZOPHRENIA

	Poor	Good
Infantile autism		
Language before age 5		X
IQ normal		X
IQ below 50	X	
Discharge to institution	X	
Discharge to trained parents		X
Early intervention		X
Comprehensive treatment services		X
Childhood schizophrenia		
IQ above average		X
IQ below average	X	
Onset before age 10	X	
Acute onset		X
Slow onset	X	
Identifiable precipitating event		X
Good social skills		X

The results clearly showed that placements in large institutions led to a deterioration in social skills and general functioning, and was tantamount to a "life sentence" in the institution. The farm placements, however, produced some of the best and longest-lasting adjustments; the autistic children had routine farm chores that made them useful, and they were generally accepted by small communities despite their peculiarities.

Childhood schizophrenia has a course and outcome that is different between those with early onset as compared to those who have symptoms emerging later. Youngsters with earlier manifestations of symptoms appear to have a relatively poor prognosis (Remshmidt et al., 1994). The earlier the onset, before age 10, the lower the chance of a favorable recovery. Additionally, a slow developing condition, which takes a great deal of time to manifest itself completely, appears associated with poor adjustment in childhood. This slow or insidious onset is contrasted with an acute (fast) onset, which is often precipitated by a stressful event, such as a family member's death or parental divorce. Table 11-7 summarizes the prognostic indicators for both autism and childhood schizophrenia.

SUMMARY

Pervasive developmental disorders, as defined in DSM-IV, include autism, Rett's disorder, childhood disintegrative disorder, Asperger's disorder, and pervasive developmental disorder not otherwise specified. This chapter has examined childhood schizophrenia and pervasive developmental disorders, with particular attention given to autism since it is the most frequently occurring of the pervasive developmental disorders.

Most researchers and clinicians now consider autism and childhood schizophrenia to be separate disorders with several basic differences. Autism is primarily characterized as a disorder in relating to other people, which generally develops before 30 months of age. Problems in social behavior can include poor eye contact, avoidance of social interactions, and a lack of basic social skills such as smiling or showing empathy. Along with problems in social relations, children with autism also have language problems. They exhibit high rates of self-stimulatory behavior or self-injurious behavior, and three-fourths have mental retardation. High rates of self-stimulatory behavior, poor intellectual functioning, and a lack of language skills limit a child's ability to relate to other people.

In contrast to autism, childhood schizophrenia is characterized primarily as a thought disorder that develops late in childhood. Hallucinations, an inability to connect thoughts logically, jumping randomly from topic to topic, and a withdrawal into a fantasy world are common for the schizophrenic child. Unlike many children having autism, children with schizophrenia generally develop good language skills and have near normal intelligence. Periods of improvement and relapse are characteristic of the child with schizophrenia, while autism runs a steady course with little overall change in the behavioral symptoms from childhood through adulthood.

As with most of the severe behavior disorders of childhood, autism and childhood schizophrenia appear not to have a single cause but are complex in their origins. Birth complications, disease, and genetics are suspected of contributing to the development of autism and schizophrenia. The origins of these conditions appear primarily to be biological in nature, although environmental factors can interact to improve or worsen their courses. Parents do not cause autism or childhood schizophrenia as once was thought.

Effective treatment approaches have been slow in coming for autism and childhood schizophrenia. These children typically do not profit from long-term separation from their families and community and placement in large institutions. Promising new approaches for these children emphasize getting them into treatment at a young age and including family members as part of the treatment effort. Structured behavior therapy approaches are effective in reducing many bizarre behaviors and teaching more appropriate and adaptive behaviors. Medication may also be effective in reducing problematic behaviors in some cases. However, it should be emphasized that both medication and behavior therapy only manage the behavioral symptoms of these conditions and do not produce cures. The long-term effectiveness of these approaches is promising but they have not yet been studied extensively. Variables that appear to best predict later adjustment include the child's intelligence, language usage, and age of onset of the condition.

CLASSIFICATION OF CHILDHOOD

BEHAVIOR DISORDERS

Key Terms

Axes. Dimensions along which categories may be arranged. For example, in a classification system, there may be separate dimensions or axes for psychiatric diagnostic categories and for problems in living, or for mental and physical disorders.

Classification. The ordering of objects or behaviors into groups containing a common set of characteristics.

Comorbidity. The co-occurrence of two or more disorders in the same individual at the same time, for example, simultaneous occurrence of anxiety and depression.

Diagnosis. The actual assigning of objects or behaviors to groupings within a classification system or nosology.

Reliability. A determination of how consistently a classification system measures phenomena. For example, a classification system with good reliability consistently places the same types of behaviors into the same grouping.

Validity. A classification system's ability to measure what it proposes to measure. For example, if the developers of a classification system propose that a system is capable of grouping and classifying childhood behavior disorders, then the system has good validity if it is able to group most childhood behavior disorders encountered by clinicians and researchers.

T his chapter considers the manner in which related disorders are grouped together conceptually and distinguished from less closely related disorders. First, we debate the necessity for such groupings and consider how classification may aid in the study, prevention, and treatment of psychological disorders. Negative effects of classification, such as negative labeling, are also considered. Various classification systems are reviewed, with special attention to the most widely used system, the American Psychiatric Association's *Diagnostic and Statistical Manual of Mental Disorders* (1994), abbreviated as DSM-IV. Alternative systems, including behavioral and educational classification schemes, are also examined.

OVERVIEW OF CLASSIFICATION

Classification is the key to understanding large groups of events. Every day we classify people, objects, events, and situations so that we can understand and relate to them better. Without classification, we would be left in a sea of unrecognizable, unique events. We have all been in situations in which little or nothing is familiar—for example, one's first day at a large university among strangers. However, over time we learn to recognize people and to classify them as friends, colleagues, rivals, students who have shared classes, and interesting people we want to know. In effect, we have classified the environment, understand it, and feel comfortable with it.

All learning requires classification of new objects into familiar groups (Brunner, 1963; Brunner, Goodnow, & Austin, 1956). Classification has proved particularly useful in the diagnosis and treatment of physical disease. After recognizing a disease, physicians can often predict its course, identify its probable origin, and recommend an appropriate course of treatment; in several cases, disease prevention is even possible. For example, German measles (rubella) can be identified readily from laboratory tests and from the appearance of symptoms such as a skin rash. If rubella strikes a woman during the first three months of pregnancy, her unborn child can be born

deaf or blind and may be mentally retarded. However, because physicians can accurately classify rubella, it can be treated and even prevented. Preferably, women can be vaccinated to prevent the occurrence of the disease. In this instance, proper classification of a physical disease leads to effective treatment and prevention procedures; without classification, German measles would be just another skin rash.

Like physical illnesses, behavioral or psychological disorders can be identified through classification procedures. However, each child has a unique set of problems. In addition, the "symptoms" or behavioral indicators that are associated with psychological disorders are not as discrete and identifiable as the symptoms for rubella. Individuality, uniqueness, and ambiguous symptoms are the enemies of any classification system. These systems require general characteristics that are readily identifiable. However, even with these difficulties, major advances have been made in the classification and diagnosis of children with adjustment problems. These classification advances have facilitated the understanding, treatment, and possibly the prevention of some of these disorders.

"There is considerable disagreement concerning what constitutes an optimal diagnostic system for psychopathology in children and adolescents. Nonetheless, there [is] good agreement that these taxonomic dif-

ficulties have been a critical factor impeding child psychopathology research progress to date." (Jensen et al., 1993, p. 553)

Classification: What Is It?

Classification is more than a description of phenomena. It goes beyond description and involves the grouping or placement of objects or behaviors into distinct classes or sets. Sokal (1974, p. 116) has defined general classification procedures of all sciences as "the ordering or arrangement of objects into groups or sets on basis of their relationships. These relationships can be based on observable or inferred properties." Sokal's definition suggests that there must be some general or common feature that identifies objects and determines their placement within a set of categories. These common features or relationships are specified in a classification rule or *operational definition* (Bridgman, 1927). Good operational definitions include a set of objective criteria or rules that can be used to decide whether a particular case belongs within a specific category (Hempel, 1965). An operational definition serves as a judgment test to determine whether an object or behavior belongs within a certain category.

Satisfactory operational definitions provide clearly stated objective criteria that can be understood and used similarly by various people. Ambiguity and personal interpretation are held to a minimum by good operational definitions. For example, IQ scores might be used as part of the operational definition to classify mentally retarded children. An IQ score below 70 on a standard intelligence test can be used as one criterion to identify mental retardation. This part of the operational definition of retardation seems to work well with children at the extreme ranges of the IQ continuum. For instance, an IQ score of 150 is certainly not a sign of mental retardation, and an IQ score of 20 probably indicates retardation if the test was properly administered. Difficulties develop, however, toward the midpoint of this retardation continuum, or at values around 70. If a child has an IQ of 70 and performs poorly at school but is well adjusted and competent in his nonacademic everyday life, then it is unclear whether the child meets the IQ criterion for retardation or not. As the example demonstrates, operational definitions are never perfect, and there often are borderline cases in which they break down. In that case, it is helpful to have multiple criteria for disorders.

Good operational definitions for classifications systems share several characteristics. First, they specify many points of comparison, not just one, as in the IQ test example. Second, the definitions are clear and objective. The characteristics specified in the definition should be measurable and, if possible, directly observable. Third, the definitions should be used similarly by everyone. In properly classifying mental retardation, for example, examiners use multiple criteria including IQ scores below 70 to 75, measures of adaptive behavior (behavior needed to function independently), and a time span within which the condition first occurred (before 18 years, the developmental period of childhood or adolescence) (Drew, Hardman, & Logan, 1992).

Classification and Diagnosis

We have already defined classification as the ordering of objects or behaviors into sets or groups using operational definitions. An *identification* or diagnostic process is the actual assigning of objects or behaviors to groupings within a classification system (Sokal, 1974). A diagnostician may identify an unknown mental disorder by matching the child's observable behavioral characteristics with the operational definitions included in a diagnostic classification system. *Diagnosis* permits the practitioner to identify the child's problem and administer appropriate treatment. However, true scientific classification goes beyond simply describing something and leads to diagnosis and understanding. Literally, *diagnosis* means to distinguish or differentiate (R. E. Kendall, 1975) or, as Achenbach (1974, p. 568) has stated, "to reduce uncertainty."

Diagnosing a behavior disorder is, then, the process of using an accepted classification system to match a person's atypical behavioral characteristics to a set of operational definitions. In clinical practice, this process allows a clinician to assign a child's behavior to a particular subcategory of the classification system. The matching and assigning of behavior to a subcategory results in naming or diagnosing the child's behavior disorder. This process yields a *differential diagnosis* that distinguishes a specific diagnosis from other diagnostic categories within a classification system.

It should be clear from this discussion that a *child* is not diagnosed by the classification process; only the child's *disorder* is diagnosed (Rutter, 1965). Reducing

---

BOX 12-1   LESSONS IN CLASSIFICATION FROM ALICE IN WONDERLAND

We know him as Lewis Carroll, but that was his pen name. The actual author of *Alice's Adventures in Wonderland* was the Reverend Charles Dodgson, a 19th-century English mathematics teacher at Christ Church, Oxford University. Carroll's inspired nonsense has delighted generations of children with its wealth of puns, jokes, and logical dilemmas. The following exchange between Alice and the Cheshire Cat illustrates the difficulty involved in classifying people as sane or insane.

> "In *that* direction," the Cat said, waving its right paw round, "lives a Hatter: and in *that* direction," waving the other paw,
> "lives a March Hare. Visit either you like: they're both mad."
>> "But I don't want to go among mad people," Alice remarked.
>> "Oh, you can't help that," said the Cat; "we're all mad here. I'm mad. You're mad."
>> "How do you know I'm mad?" said Alice.
>> "You must be," said the Cat, "or you wouldn't have come here."
>> Alice didn't think that proved it at all; however, she went on: "And how do you know that you're mad?"
>> "To begin with," said the Cat, "a dog's not mad. You grant that?"
>> "I suppose so," said Alice.
>> "Well, then," the Cat went on, "you see a dog growls when it's angry, and wags its tail when it's pleased. Now *I* growl
> when I'm pleased and wag my tail when I'm angry. Therefore I'm mad."
>> "*I* call it purring, not growling," said Alice.
>> "Call it what you like," said the Cat.

In contrast to characters in Wonderland, real-life mental health workers cannot make up their own criteria for insanity. Clinicians must have a research-based, shared, well described, and widely used system for classifying behavior as normal or pathological. However, as shown by various recent reports of mistaken hospitalizing of sane individuals in mental institutions, context makes a difference in classification of behavior. Even normal behavior is more likely to be classified as disturbed when displayed by someone who has been identified as having an adjustment problem.

SOURCE: Carroll, L. *Alice's Adventures in Wonderland.*

---

individuals to diagnostic terms such as autistic, retarded, or hyperactive sounds demeaning, robbing them of their individuality and implying that they will never improve. It is particularly inappropriate to classify children in terms of disorders because, even more than adults, children can be expected to grow and change over time. Further, all classification systems are imperfect and can lead to inappropriate labeling. It is a mistake to believe that any child conforms exactly to the behavioral description of a diagnostic category. Each child is unique, and exceptions are the rule in the classification of children's psychological disorders.

The Purpose of Classification

Having a commonly understood language is essential to the success of any human enterprise. Diverse and geographically distant groups can communicate readily if they share a common language. Classification systems provide a shared language for science. In the absence of such a common terminology, scientific communication will be beset with confusion and misunderstanding (Rutter, 1965). With agreement on a common classification language, clinicians in different locales can communicate with each other, information can be shared, and the development of scientific theory can progress (Blashfield & Draguns, 1976b). Without a common classification language, we have a clinical Tower of Babel in which no one speaks the same language.

Ideally, a classification system helps to unify the study of behavior disorders so that terminology is standardized, communication is facilitated, and facts can be established concerning the behavior disorder's etiology (origin or cause). These conditions are rarely met, and even with extensively studied problems, such as mental retardation, the lack of a single core conceptualization of the condition impedes the training of service deliverers and inhibits the development of prevention and treatment pro-

BOX 12-2   MORE LESSONS IN CLASSIFICATION FROM ALICE IN WONDERLAND

The following passage from *Alice* illustrates the importance of using commonly understood and agree upon rules of evidence. This is important in classification, because otherwise users would compose their own criteria on the spot much as the unfortunate King of Hearts attempts to do in this interchange with a gigantic Alice who had eaten a magical mushroom and grown to tremendous size.

> At this moment the King, who had been for some time busily writing in his notebook, called out. "Silence!" and read out from his book, "Rule Forty-two. *All persons more than a mile high to leave the court.*"
>
> Everybody looked at Alice.
>
> "I'm not a mile high," said Alice.
>
> "You are," said the King.
>
> "Nearly two miles high," added the Queen.
>
> "Well, I shan't go, at any rate," said Alice; "besides, that's not a regular rule: you invented it just now."
>
> "It's the oldest rule in the book," said the King.
>
> "Then it ought to be Number One," said Alice.
>
> The King turned pale, and shut his notebook hastily. "Consider your verdict," he said to the jury, in a low trembling voice.

SOURCE: Carroll, L. *Alice's Adventures in Wonderland.*

grams (Drew et al., 1992). Good classification systems can also help identify a disorder's *prognosis* (probable outcome), and its likely response to different types of treatments. However, these benefits are not easily realized and apply only to a limited portion of child psychopathology. The development of classification systems for childhood behavior disorders is recent, and such systems have been criticized for their imperfections (Hallahan & Kauffman, 1986; Hobbs, 1975a). But standard classification schemes mostly benefit psychologically disordered children.

In most cases, the causes of childhood behavior disorders are not known, probably because many of these conditions have varied and complex causes (see Chapter 2). Various causes may produce the same type of behavior disorder, and different behavior disorders may result from similar causes. Accurate classification can aid in ferreting out contributing causes of behavioral disturbances (Chess & Hassibi, 1978; Rutter, 1965; Zubin, 1967). For example, classifying autistic children by strict diagnostic guidelines has helped pinpoint two potential causes of infantile autism: (1) transmission of a recessive gene and (2) a fragile X chromosome break (Levitas et al., 1983; Ritvo, Freeman, Mason-Brothers, Mo, & Ritvo, 1984). Similarly, studies of children classified as having attention-deficit disorder have shown that some of these children have neurological abnormalities, which suggests that the condition may in part be caused by physical abnor-

malities (as reviewed by Ross & Ross, 1982; Rutter, 1965). Although these studies are preliminary, they are important in helping unravel the complex causes of behavior disorders. Without accurate classification, this research would not be possible.

Accurate prognosis, or prediction of a disorder's outcome, is facilitated by classifying children into diagnostic categories. This is important because most parents want to know the likely outcome for their children. Will they develop normally, or will they continue to have difficulty throughout their lives? These prognostic determinations are made by scientific researchers who accurately classify children and then employ longitudinal studies to evaluate the children's adjustment in later years (Patterson, 1983; Robins, 1966, 1979; Walker et al., 1986; Weiss & Hechtman, 1986; Werner & Smith, 1992). For example, if a study follows three children with different diagnoses—a child with autistic disorder, a child with social phobia, and a child with severe conduct disorder—we can predict the likely outcomes for each of these children within some margin of error. If the autistic child is also severely mentally retarded and has no expressive language, the likely outcome in adulthood is poor (DeMyer et al., 1973). The likely outcome for the child with social phobia is relatively good in adulthood, in comparison to the prognosis for the severely antisocial-aggressive child with conduct disorder (D. P. Morris, Soroker, & Burruss,

1954; H. H. Morris, Escoll, & Wexler, 1956; Robins, 1966, 1979; Walker et al., 1986). All of these predictions can be in error, especially when they are made for individual children rather than groups of children. We cannot say for sure that a particular child will have a good or bad outcome even if accurately classified. However, given accurate classification and good longitudinal research, statistically accurate predictions can be made for most children so classified.

Another advantage to accurate classification of a childhood behavior disorder is to predict the child's probable response to a particular treatment. The number of children with attention-deficit disorder who respond to stimulant medication, and the effects of this medication over time, can be predicted (Ross & Ross, 1982; Weiss & Hechtman, 1986). Phenylketonuria (PKU) provides another excellent example of the advantages of reliable classification. PKU is produced by an inherited enzyme defect, which results in improper oxidation of particular protein substances and damage to the nervous system that causes mental retardation. Before PKU was identified through urine and blood tests, it was responsible for 1 percent of people institutionalized because of severe retardation (Liebert, Poulos, & Strauss, 1974). Correct classification of this disorder has led to an effective treatment (placing the child on a special diet) that prevents mental retardation. However, if the condition is not diagnosed in infancy and the child's diet is not meticulously controlled, the child's prognosis is very poor, and permanent retardation is extremely likely. Thus, in addition to providing a common language for clinicians and scientists, a good classification system may permit reliable predictions regarding a behavior disorder's cause, course, and response to treatment. In practice, however, classification has had little effect on the treatments children receive, which depend largely on whatever is available or temporarily popular among clinicians (Achenbach, 1985).

Possibly one of the least obvious but most important reasons for the classification of behavior disorders is to attract funding for the treatment and research of children suffering from specific psychological disorders. Typically, children's disorders must be classified or labeled according to an acceptable system in general use before treatment programs in clinics, hospitals, and schools can be provided (Chess & Hassibi, 1978; Gallagher, Forsythe,

Ringelheim, & Weintraub, 1975). Funding makes treatment services possible through insurance payments and government funding of services in the schools. Similarly, research into the causes and treatment of behavior disorders is often directed to children with specific diagnoses such as learning disabilities. Various federal agencies and private foundations specify by diagnostic categories (such as infantile autism, childhood drug dependency, depression, and stress-related disorders) the types of research projects they are willing to fund.

In summary, the development of classification systems helps to establish a standard scientific language that can be used by clinicians and researchers in their daily work. Classification aids in the identification of causes of behavior disorders, establishment of prognosis, and the development of effective treatment methods. Moreover, classification often determines whether private and government funds are provided for treatment and research on behavior disorders. But classification systems are imperfect when used with complex, highly individualized, naturally occurring behavior. It is important to understand how to judge the adequacy of classification systems.

Criteria for Behavior Classification Systems

Good classification systems share several features. A good system can be used with high reliability or consistency by different diagnosticians. It includes a manageable number of behavior disorders, and it describes, as closely and as concisely as possible, how these disorders exist in nature. A classification system should also be useful to clinicians and researchers so that it is utilized for its practical information and not as a mere mechanism to secure treatment and research funds. In addition, since the nature of psychopathology changes with age, classification systems for use with children should be flexible enough to address issues of growth and development.

RELIABILITY

Reliability depends on consistency. Gelfand and Hartmann (1984) have clarified the term reliability as follows: A friend or acquaintance, if unreliable, is inconsistent; thus little confidence can be placed in her. In contrast, a reliable friend behaves consistently and can be depended on. The key term here is *consistency*. A behavior classifi-

---

BOX 12-3   MATHEMATICS DISORDER?

The DSM-IV system has been criticized for being over inclusive and describing some "disorders" that are so common as to qualify for normality rather than abnormality. Mathematics disorder is one such condition. Here are the diagnostic criteria for 315.1 Mathematics Disorder:

A. Mathematical ability, as measured by individually administered standardized tests, is substantially below that expected given the person's chronological age, measured intelligence, and age-appropriate education.

B. The disturbance in criterion A significantly interferes with academic achievement or activities of daily living that require mathematical ability.

C. If a sensory deficit is present, the difficulties in mathematical ability are in excess of those usually associated with it. (American Psychiatric Association, 1994.)

Most readers will either qualify for having this "disorder" or can think of many other people who do. Even today, mathematical ability is sex typed as more appropriate for males than females. Thus, large numbers of women and girls would meet the criteria, although their behavior patterns are completely normal for females. Thus mathematics disorder seems to represent an error of over inclusion in the DSM-IV.

SOURCE: Reprinted with permission from the *Diagnostic and statistical manual of mental disorders*, Fourth Edition. (1994). Washington, DC: American Psychiatric Association. Copyright 1994 by the American Psychiatric Association.

---

cation system is not reliable (is inconsistent) if under similar conditions the same behaviors are not classified the same way. For example, during reading times (similar conditions) in Mrs. Jones' classroom, a child's hitting others, moving about the room without permission, and talking out of turn might be equally likely to be diagnosed as exhibiting unsocialized aggression or hyperactivity. We would call this procedure unreliable. For example, if one clinician observes the same child misbehaving on two separate occasions and arrives at two different diagnoses, we would say that the system's *test-retest reliability* is poor. A different type of reliability involves two clinicians. If two clinicians observe the same behavior simultaneously and arrive at two different diagnoses, we would conclude that the *interrater* reliability of the classification used is questionable.

The possible causes of low reliability have been researched by several investigators (as reviewed by Blashfield, 1984). These causes include poor training of clinicians in the use of the classification system, the inconsistency of the patient's behavior, and inadequacy of the classification system (Helzer et al., 1977; Ward, Beck, Mendelson, Mock, & Erbaugh, 1962). Few data are available on the reliability of classification systems devised especially for children (Achenbach, 1980; Quay, 1979). The fact that children change and develop rapidly over time presents a particular problem for diagnosti-

cians. What was diagnosed as a problem at one point may be radically changed in six months, as we have discussed in Chapter 1. Operational definitions that are unclear and overlap (share descriptive terms or symptoms with other operational definitions) greatly reduce interrater reliability (Zigler & Phillips, 1960, 1961). For example, if a classification system has separate categories for an oppositional child and a conduct-disordered child (i.e., noncompliant and aggressive), then it may be difficult to reliably select a diagnosis because of the commonalities and shared terms for these two categories (Werry, Methven, Fitzpatrick, & Dixon, 1983). In the DSM-IV, care is taken to distinguish between oppositional behavior, in which a child resists work or school tasks that require self-application out of unwillingness to conform to others' demands, and conduct disorder, in which there is a clear, hostile invasion of the basic rights of others and purposeful violation of social norms. Nevertheless, clinicians find it difficult to decide whether a child's behavior is best classified as oppositional defiant, conduct disordered, or hyperactive and impulsive because interpersonally aggressive actions typify all three subcategories.

The number of categories included in a classification system also affects its reliability. When a system has only a few broad categories, such as psychotic and neurotic disorders, then its reliability can be quite good. However, as the similarity and number of categories increase, the reliability of the system decreases, because clinicians are required to make finer and more difficult discriminations between categories (Rutter & Shaffer, 1980; Ward et al., 1962; Zubin, 1967). Child psychiatric classification reliability appears to be only fair. The interrater reliability of the most frequently used classification systems with children has been reported to be approximately 50 percent (Cantwell, Russell, Mattison, & Will, 1979; Mattison, Cantwell, Russell, & Will, 1979). However, better interrater scores have been reported with older children and certain distinctive categories (Strober, Green, & Carlson, 1981).

VALIDITY

Validity can be defined as a classification system's ability to measure what it proposes to measure. In a sense, validity explains how well a measure describes reality (Howell, Kaplan, & O'Connell, 1979). Validity may be described here as a classification system's accuracy in identifying behavior disorders, as compared to other systems that are known to identify the condition accurately. For example, if a team of experienced clinicians observes and rates a child as depressed, but a classification system's definition does not fit the child's behavior, then the validity of that system would be in doubt. This system of validity is called *concurrent validity*, because a currently accepted standard (the judgments of the team of experienced clinicians) is used to judge the classification system. Concurrent validity is critically important if a new system is going to be accepted and used (Blashfield, 1984; Blashfield & Draguns, 1976a, 1976b; Sundberg, 1977).

Another test for validity is how well a classification system predicts the course and outcome of a behavior disorder. A classification system that accurately identifies infantile autism and has good predictive validity might make the following predictions: (1) autism is a lifelong condition with few changes; (2) the course of the condition is steady, with few improvements or remissions; and (3) management of the condition is improved if the child has some communication skills and near-normal intelligence (is not retarded). Such a classification system provides outcome predictions in addition to identification and labeling.

Reliability and validity often go hand in hand. A system has to have some degree of reliability before it can be either descriptively or predictively valid. Although there is some disagreement in the literature (Carey & Gottesman, 1978), it is generally accepted that a reasonable level or reliability is needed before a system can be tested for validity. In a sense, reliability sets an upper limit on the validity of a system; without good reliability, a system cannot be valid. A system, however, can be highly reliable, but can have low validity (Spitzer & Fleiss, 1974). When this is the case, it generally means that reliable but irrelevant selection criteria, which are in fact unrelated to the conditions, have been used.

SCOPE AND COVERAGE

The scope of a classification system is the breadth of its coverage (Blashfield, 1984; Blashfield & Draguns, 1976a, 1976b; Cromwell, Blashfield, & Strauss, 1975). *Scope* refers to a classification system's ability to cover either a broad or a narrow spectrum of clinical conditions. If a system has 100 percent or extremely broad coverage, it has a category for every possible problem presented by patients. If a system has only 10 percent coverage (narrow coverage), then it can classify only 10 percent of the cases presented by patients and leaves the rest unclassified. It may seem that classification systems should have the broadest possible coverage, but broad coverage is not always entirely desirable. With broad coverage, there may be many overlapping categories with similar terms, and this reduces reliability (Blashfield, 1984). Excessively broad coverage also produces what are known as "wastebasket" categories. These are broadly defined categories that are designed for idiosyncratic or exceptional cases that do not fit any other category. An example of such a broad category is adjustment disorder in the American Psychiatric Association's (1994) *Diagnostic and Statistical Manual of Mental Disorders,* Fourth Edition (DSM-IV); it is used for troubled individuals when other diagnoses do not apply (see Box 12-4).

Overly narrow coverage also creates problems. With narrow coverage, a system's reliability can be quite high, because the operational definitions of the categories are very specific and limiting. The system's validity can also be quite high, but only for a few conditions. If too many conditions remain unclassified because the system is not appropriately flexible, then clinicians and researchers will shun the system. The acceptance and use of a system in making classification decisions are referred to as its *utility* (Hartmann, Roper, & Bradford, 1979). For example, if 50 percent of behavior problems are not covered by the

---

BOX 12-4 DSM-IV DIAGNOSTIC CRITERIA FOR ADJUSTMENT DISORDER

A. The development of emotional or behavioral symptoms in response to an identifiable stressor(s) occurring within 3 months of the onset of the stressor(s).

B. These symptoms of behaviors are clinically significant as evidenced by either of the following:
1. marked distress that is in excess of what would be expected from exposure to the stressor
2. significant impairment in social or occupational (academic) functioning

C. The stress-related disturbance does not meet the criteria for another specific Axis I disorder and is not merely an exacerbation of a preexisting Axis I or Axis II disorder.

D. The symptoms do not represent bereavement.

E. Once the stressor (or its consequences) has terminated, the symptoms do not persist for more than an additional 6 months.

Based on predominant symptoms, subtypes of adjustment disorders are coded, including: with depressed mood, anxiety, mixed anxiety and depressed mood, disturbance of conduct, mixed disturbance of emotions and conduct, and unspecified type. Disturbances that last less than 6 months are classified as acute, while those that last longer are classified as chronic.

[Our comment: This category allows the classification of any behavior that affects social or occupational functioning and is assumed to be the results of some "stressor." The diagnostician is left to define what a stressor is, and then decide whether the patient's behaviors are in excess of the normal and expected reaction to that stressor and what the *predominant* symptom is. This is a difficult if not impossible task. Clearly, reliability and possibly validity are sacrificed with such a classification, and what is left is broad coverage and a general label, "adjustment disorder."]

SOURCE: Reprinted with permission from American Psychiatric Association. (1994). *Diagnostic and statistical manual of mental disorders* (4th ed., pp. 300–301). (1994). Washington, DC: Author. Copyright 1994 by the American Psychiatric Association.

---

classification scheme, then little is gained by using the system. A classification system must cover enough conditions to make it useful to practitioners.

PARSIMONIOUS AND MUTUALLY EXCLUSIVE DEFINITIONS

Good classification systems employ parsimonious and mutually exclusive definitions (Quay, 1979). Parsimonious definitions use as few terms as possible to describe behavior disorders. The excessive use of terms tends to confuse users and reduces reliability. Similarly, the reliability of a classification system is increased when definitions are as mutually exclusive as possible (that is, when one definition is clearly different from others, with few shared terms). When key terms are shared by two or more definitions of behavior disorders, diagnosticians cannot tell which definition to use. For example, if the word *anxiety* is the key term in a description of phobic reactions and a description of adjustment reactions, then the diagnostician cannot be sure which label to apply.

Classification systems are never perfect. They are always affected by factors such as reliability, validity, coverage, utility, parsimony, and the mutual exclusiveness of definitions. All of these factors then interface with the

level of training and personal preferences of clinicians and researchers using the system. Imperfect systems and the human factor will invariably produce some degree of error. But these systems are necessary in our research, clinical, and educational systems.

> "There is considerable disagreement concerning what constitutes an optimal diagnostic system for psychopathology in children and adolescents. Nonetheless, there [is] good agreement that these taxonomic difficulties have been a critical factor impeding child psychopathology research progress to date." (Jensen et al., 1993, p. 553)

CLASSIFICATION SYSTEMS

Accurate classification systems for children's behavior disorders are relatively new phenomena. The first clinically useful system was developed for adult disorders by a German psychiatrist, Emil Kraepelin, in 1899. For the next 50 years, children were not formally included in classification systems. However, during this time a common group of child behavior disorders was recognized. In 1928, Wickman asked 511 elementary school teachers and 30 clinicians to assess the serious behavior problems of schoolchildren. The teachers reported that conduct problems such as stealing, lying, and inappropriate sexual behaviors were rated as the most serious. In contrast, clinicians rated personality problems such as social withdrawal, depression, and fearfulness as the most serious problems. Other studies (Mutimer & Rosemier, 1967) have found similar results: Teachers most frequently identified aggression, disobedience, and destruction of property as serious problems, while clinicians viewed withdrawal, depression, and phobic reactions as the most serious problems. This classification dichotomy of "acting-out" problems and "withdrawal" problems is echoed in all modern classification systems, whether they are statistically, medically, behaviorally, or educationally based.

Statistically Based Classification Systems

A great deal of research has been done on childhood behavior disorders using multivariate statistical methods called *factor analysis* and *cluster analysis*. These sophisticated statistical techniques are used to identify clusters or factors of characteristics that are related or intercorrelated. For example, a factor called *hyperactivity* might include the characteristics of inattention, impulsive behavior, high rates of motor activity, and poor academic success, all of which occur in the same children. Generally, these characteristics are reported by parents or teachers when a child is referred for help, or they may be compiled from behavior checklists that are filled out by teachers.

The development of powerful computers in the 1960s made possible the extensive use of multivariate statistics in developing classification systems for childhood behavior disorders (Dreger, 1982). Peterson (1961) studied 400 cases that were referred to a child guidance clinic and derived 58 items that were descriptive of behavior disorders in children. These items were then assembled into a behavior checklist, and 831 elementary school-age children were then rated by teachers for behavior problems. Factor analysis demonstrated that the majority of problems of children in schools could be accounted for by two major dimensions: *aggression* (behavior disorders) and *withdrawal* (personality disorders). Minor dimensions were later isolated and included *inadequacy-*

immaturity (hyperactivity) (Quay & Quay, 1965), *juvenile delinquency* (Quay, 1964), and *childhood psychosis* (Quay & Peterson, 1975); the last of these was rarely encountered.

Several other studies (Patterson, 1964; Walker, 1970, 1982; Wirt, Lachar, Klinedinst, & Seat, 1977) have found similar factors or clusters of childhood problems. Possibly the most extensive statistical investigation of childhood behavior disorders has been the work of Achenbach and Edelbrock (Achenbach, 1966, 1978, 1982; Achenbach & Edelbrock, 1978, 1979) using the Child Behavior Checklist and Profile (CBCL). This research was conducted on hundreds of children who were observed and rated by their parents and teachers. One group of children had been referred for psychological problems, and the other group (the controls) were nonhandicapped children. Factor analysis of these ratings produced two broad factors: *internalizing* symptoms and *externalizing* symptoms. The internalizing symptoms were emotional difficulties such as anxiety, phobias, overinhibition, fearfulness, worrying, and somatic problems (physical complaints such as headaches and stomachaches). The externalizing problems were directed toward the environment and other people, and included aggression, disobedience, fighting, and, to a lesser extent, hyperactivity. These researchers also found that problems varied with age and between males and females. This research is discussed further in Chapter 13.

The multivariate classification systems have gained in popularity over the past few years for several reasons. First, these systems are empirically derived, which means that the problems are first rated by parents and teachers. Then, a rigorous statistical procedure defines which characteristics are interrelated (intercorrelated) and validly form "real" diagnostic clusters. This process is different from other systems (to be discussed shortly), which have used the judgment of a committee of clinicians to decide behavior disorder categories. Second, most multivariate classification systems are developed through the use of standardized behavior checklists, which many clinicians and educators find easy to use. Third, independent investigators have repeatedly found similar clusters of behavior disorders. For instance, most multivariate classification research has found the broad-band behavior disorders of internalizing and externalizing problems with the associated narrow-band problems of aggression, hyperactivity, delinquency, depression, withdrawal, phobias, and others. This type of independently replicated finding adds support to the validity of these systems.

Psychiatric Classification Systems

Some of the most frequently used classification systems are based on a medical model. A pure *disease model* or *medical model* assumes that abnormal behavior is caused by an underlying organic problem, such as a brain lesion, chemical imbalance, genetic abnormality, or infection (Blashfield, 1984; Wing, 1978) (see Chapter 2). The abnormal behavior is assumed to be a symptom produced by some abnormal organic or psychological condition, and proper treatment of the disorder requires removing its underlying cause or disease.

This disease model also assumes that observing, describing, and classifying disorders will lead to discovering the biological causes and cures of abnormal behavior patterns (Draguns & Phillips, 1971). This careful strategy of observation and classification has produced dramatic advances in general medicine and some advances in psychiatry. For example, following the accurate diagnosis of syphilis, syphilis spirochetes were discovered to enter the central nervous system and to cause general *paresis* (a pattern of physical and mental breakdown). However, despite intensive efforts with new biological diagnostic tools such as computerized tomography (image-enhanced brain X-ray scans), researchers have been unable to identify physiological causes for the vast majority of behavior disorders.

The *Diagnostic and Statistical Manual of Mental Disorders (DSM-IV)* specifies that these disorders can indicate a behavioral, psychological, or biological dysfunction. To qualify as a mental disorder, a condition must be associated with present distress or disability; significantly increased risk of pain, disability, or death; or produce an important loss of freedom, as when phobias keep a person confined to the house. The reaction must be beyond that expected or culturally appropriate for stressful circumstances such as the death of a loved one or the loss of a job (American Psychiatric Association, 1994, p. xxi).

Since 1952, the American Psychiatric Association has employed expert task forces to develop and revise its official nomenclature (naming system for disorders)—the DSM diagnostic manuals. Committees of experts decide through a process of discussion and compromise what

disorders should be included and how they should be defined. The committee process is very different from the development of multivariate classification systems, discussed earlier, which is closely bound by the research data.

In 1952, the first edition of the DSM (DSM-I) was published as a unifying, standard classification system for adult psychiatric disorders. The need for such a system became apparent during World War II, when large numbers of U.S. men were mobilized to fight, and over 90 percent of the psychiatric cases referred to military psychiatrists did not fit any existing classification system (Ullmann & Krasner, 1965). However, the DSM-I proved inadequate for children because it included only two basic categories: adjustment reaction (infancy, childhood, and adolescence) and schizophrenic reaction, childhood type. Clinicians who worked with children found these classification categories overly general and incomplete.

In 1968, a second edition of the DSM (DSM-II) was introduced, which included more categories for children's disorders. However, the operational definitions were still nonspecific and difficult to apply. The clinician was given little direction in deciding whether a child must have all or most of the symptoms described in a particular category in order to receive a particular diagnosis (Fish, 1969; Spitzer, Sheehy, & Endicott, 1977). The diagnostic ambiguity of the categories and the overuse of "wastebasket" categories, such as "adjustment reaction" for a variety of problems (Cerreto & Tuma, 1977), made this system unsatisfactory for use with children. A system was needed that added more specific and useful information and went beyond merely indicating a mental disorder.

The 1980 DSM-III classification system was a radical departure from previous systems (Spitzer & Endicott, 1978; Spitzer et al., 1977) in that each disorder was defined *without* assumptions about its cause. This atheoretical approach aimed to prevent the classification system from representing one, possibly biased theoretical perspective. The DSM-III also included many new categories of childhood behavior disorders, such as attention-deficit disorder, conduct disorder, infantile autism, pervasive developmental disorders, and others.

Further, the DSM-III was a *multiaxial* classification system instead of a categorical system in which a child could receive only one diagnostic label. The multiaxial system provides a set of dimensions (axes) that are coded

TABLE 12-1 DSM-IV CLASSIFICATION: AXES I AND II CATEGORIES AND CODE NUMBERS

Disorders usually first diagnosed in infancy, childhood, or adolescence

Learning Disorders

315.00	Reading disorder
315.1	Mathematics disorder
315.2	Disorder of written expression
315.9	Learning disorder, not otherwise specified

Motor Skills Disorder

315.4	Developmental coordination disorder

Communication Disorders

315.31	Expressive language disorder
315.31	Mixed receptive-expressive language disorder
315.39	Phonological disorder
307.0	Stuttering
307.9	Communication disorder NOS

Pervasive Developmental Disorders

299.00	Autistic disorder
299.80	Rhett's disorder
299.10	Childhood disintegrative disorder
299.80	Asperger's disorder
299.80	Pervasive developmental disorder NOS

Attention-Deficit and Disruptive Behavior Disorders

314.xx	Attention-Deficit/Hyperactivity Disorder
	.01 Combined type
	.00 Predominantly inattentive type
	.01 Predominantly hyperactive-impulsive type
314.9	Attention-Deficit/Hyperactivity Disorder NOS
312.8	Conduct disorder
	Specify: childhood-onset or adolescent-onset type
313.81	Oppositional defiant disorder
312.9	Disruptive behavior disorder NOS

Feeding and Eating Disorders of Infancy and Early Childhood

307.52	Pica
307.53	Rumination disorder
307.59	Feeding disorder of infancy or early childhood

Tic Disorders

307.23	Tourette's disorder
307.22	Chronic motor or vocal tic disorder
307.21	Transient tic disorder
	Specify: single episode or recurrent
307.20	Tic disorder NOS

Elimination disorders

	Encopresis
787.6	With Constipation and Overflow Incontinence
307.7	Without Constipation and Overflow Incontinence
307.6	Enuresis (Not Due to a General Medical Condition)
	Specify: Nocturnal Only/Diurnal Only/ Both

Other Disorders of Infancy, Childhood, or Adolescence

309.21	Separation Anxiety Disorder
	Specify if Early Onset
313.23	Selective Mutism
313.89	Reactive Attachment Disorder of Infancy or Early Childhood
	Specify Inhibited or Disinhibited Type
307.3	Stereotypic Movement Disorder
	Specify if With Self-Injurious Behavior
313.9	Disorder of Infancy, Childhood, or Adolescence NOS

Mental Retardation (Coded on Axis II)

317	Mild Mental Retardation
318.0	Moderate Mental Retardation
318.1	Severe Mental Retardation
318.2	Profound Mental Retardation
319	Mental Retardation, Severity Unspecified
307.60	Functional enuresis (84)
	Specify: primary or secondary type
	Specify: nocturnal only, diurnal only, nocturnal and diurnal

The preceding conditions are usually first diagnosed before adulthood, but the DSM makes no clear distinction between childhood and adult disorders. Children may receive the diagnoses listed here or elsewhere in the DSM-IV, for example for cognitive, substance-related, schizophrenic, anxiety, or sexual and gender identity disorders.

BOX 12-5   BOBBY: EXAMPLE OF A CHILD WITH GENERALIZED ANXIETY DISORDER

Bobby is a 10-year-old whose worried mother has come to see the school counselor. She has been concerned because he has been getting more quiet and withdrawing from everyone. Bobby is a shy child who prefers playing alone rather than with the neighborhood kids. He had a persistent problem with enuresis, wetting his bed at night regularly until he was 8, but overcame it. Bobby has had some language difficulties, particularly pronouncing certain words clearly. In addition, Bobby's parents have had marital difficulties. His mother was not worried until recently, when he began telling her he didn't want to go to school because he didn't think his schoolwork was good enough. He is a studious child who gets good grades, but derives no pleasure from it. The teacher told his mother that he never plays with other children, but she believed that he was just shy. However, 6 months ago when the family had a small reunion, Bobby began sobbing and saying that he didn't want to go with his parents and older brother. Bobby has always been friendly with the family; although shy, he used to like seeing them all. When his mother began asking Bobby what was wrong, he said that he was afraid and too tired to go. Lately, he has also been telling her he feels lonely. When she suggests that he play with some children in the neighborhood, he says he can't and goes to his room, where she often finds him crying. When she talks to him, he says he wants friends but is too afraid.

The multiaxial DSM-IV diagnosis for Bobby would be as follows:

Axis I: 300.02 Generalized Anxiety Disorder (Previously termed Overanxious Disorder of Childhood). Also 315.39 Phonological Disorder

Axis II: None

Axis III: None

Axis IV: Parents have marital difficulties

Axis V: Current Global Assessment Functioning (GAF): 60, Moderate

---

SOURCE: Carter, C. (1987). *School psychologists' perceptions of internalizing and externalizing behaviorally disordered children.* Unpublished doctoral dissertation, University of Utah. Adapted by permission.

---

along with the principal psychiatric diagnosis. Axis I is the principal psychiatric diagnosis and either the child's main problem or the problem for which the child was referred (for example, attention-deficit disorder with hyperactivity); Axis II includes mental retardation and personality disorders (which are rare in children); Axis III includes any significant physical disorders (such as allergies); Axis IV includes any notable psychosocial stressors (for instance, divorce of parents); and Axis V is the diagnostician's rating of the child's level of adaptive functioning (intellectual and social functioning). The multiaxial approach used in DSM-III was continued in slightly modified form in DSM-IV, which was published in 1994. DSM-IV categories first diagnosed in childhood and adolescence appear in Table 12-1.

Here is an example of a multiaxial DSM-IV diagnosis for a hyperactive child with reading difficulties and severe family problems:

Axis I: 314.01   Attention-Deficit/Hyperactivity Disorder, combined type (Child has the necessary number and type of symptoms of both inattention and hyperactivity-impulsivity, present before age 7 years, shows clinically significant impairment at school and at home.)

Axis II: None (No mental retardation or personality disorder.)

Axis III: Physical condition—allergies, 477.9, Rhinitis, allergic

Axis IV: Psychosocial stressor: Divorce of parents in the past year

Axis V: GAF = 35 (Highest level of adaptive functioning during past 6 months; functioning marginally, failing at school.)

Another example with background information, is given in Box 12-5 for a severely anxious child.

Other medical classification systems include those of the Group for the Advancement of Psychiatry (GAP) (1974) and the *International Classification of Diseases* (ICD), developed by the World Health Organization (WHO). (See Table 12-2 for a brief explanation of these systems.) But in the United States, the various editions

TABLE 12-2   Group for the Advancement of Psychiatry (GAP) and International Classification of Diseases (ICD) Systems

A. Group for the Advancement of Psychiatry (GAP) System

The GAP system was developed in 1966 as a psychoanalytically based classification system composed of nine separate categories. The GAP categories are far less elaborate than the DSM categories that specify exact types and number of symptoms required for specific diagnoses. The GAP categories are:

1. Healthy response of early childhood developmental crisis type—acute, mild, manifested by separation anxiety and clinging behavior.

2. Reactive disorder of early childhood—acute, moderate, manifested by regressive encopresis, thumb-sucking, and withdrawn behavior.

3. Developmental deviation of later childhood—delayed maturational pattern type, chronic, moderate, manifested by impulsive behavior, low frustration tolerance, continued enuresis, reading disability, and persistence of prelogical thought processes.

4. Psychoneurotic disorder of later childhood—phobic type, acute, severe, manifested by ritualistic behavior, counting compulsions, and obsessive rumination.

5. Psychotic disorder of later childhood—schizophreniform type, chronic, severe, manifested by autistic behavior, associative (thought) disorder, resistance to change, whirling, echolalia, ritualistic behavior, and panic states.

6. a. Psychophysiologic skin disorder of later childhood—chronic, moderate, manifested by neurodermatitis and excoriations.

    b. Personality disorder—overly inhibited type, chronic, severe, manifested by withdrawn behavior, learning inhibition, and hesitant speech.

7. Brain syndrome of early childhood—chronic, moderate, manifested by hyperkinesis, impulsive behavior, distractibility, and difficulties in coordination.

8. a. Mental retardation of adolescence chronic, mild.

    b. Psychotic disorder schizophrenic type, chronic, moderate, manifested by autistic behavior, associative (thought) disorder, and continuing enuresis.

Because it is so closely tied to the psychoanalytic model of psychopathology, the GAP system has fallen into disuse. Research, education, and treatment resources are tied to features of other classification systems, so even excellent competing classification systems see little use.

B. World Health Organization (WHO) ICD System

The WHO has developed a series of classification systems for diseases, with the intent of standardizing the diagnosis of medical disorders internationally. The basic classification systems have been gathered together in a volume called the *International Classification of Diseases* (ICD). The mental disorder component of the ICD is called *The ICD-10 Classification of Mental and Behavioural Disorders*. The system is multiaxial, with four primary axes: (1) clinical psychiatric syndromes, (2) intellectual level, (3) associated biological factors, and (4) psychosocial influences. The ICD-10 was designed to coordinate and share subcategory code numbers with DSM-IV. The numerical codes and terms from DSM-IV are based on those in ICD-9 and ICD-10. Both the ICD and the DSM systems are widely used throughout the world.

Sources: WHO. (1992). *The ICD-10 classification of mental and behavioural disorders: Clinical descriptions and diagnostic guidelines.* Geneva: Author; WHO. (1993). *The ICD-10 classification of mental and behavioural disorders: Diagnostic criteria for research.* Geneva: Author; Group for the Advancement of Psychiatry. (1974). *Psychopathological disorders in childhood: Theoretical considerations and a proposed classification* (p. 216). New York: Jason Aronson. Copyright 1974 by the Group for the Advancement of Psychiatry. Reprinted by permission.

of the *Diagnostic and Statistical Manual of Mental Disorders* (DSM) of the American Psychiatric Association have been the standard for mental health workers, who rarely use the other systems.

Evaluation of DSM-IV

The DSM-IV is clearly superior to its predecessors. It is based on research findings, was systematically field tested for applicability to thousands of psychiatric patients by large groups of clinicians before the final version was adopted, and includes more categories for childhood behavior disorders than previous DSM editions. Its multiaxial system provides contextual information useful in formulating treatment plans in individual cases. However, the system has its critics. The "atheoretical" nature of the DSM has been criticized by several researchers who feel that the system is in fact theoretically based on the medical model (Faust & Miner, 1986; Morey, 1991). Because the American Psychiatric Association is a society of

M.D.'s, it would be reasonable to expect that their diagnostic manual would display a stronger biological and medical emphasis than would be likely for systems devised by clinical psychologists, social workers, or educators. Moreover, the DSM-IV includes problems (e.g., mathematics disorder, disorder of written expression) that are educational rather than psychiatric in nature, and might best be left out of the domain of a psychiatric disorder. Another criticism is that for some of the classification categories, the necessary empirical validation (the system's concurrent or predictive validity) is lacking or open to debate (Morey, 1991).

Like the earlier versions of the DSM, the validity and reliability of the broad DSM-IV axes have also been criticized. For the broadest diagnostic categories (for example, mental retardation or mood disorders), the interrater reliability of the DSM-III-R and DSM-IV was acceptable (Cantwell, Russell, Mattison, & Will, 1979; Mattison, Cantwell, Russell, & Will, 1979; Werry et al., 1983). However, for the finer discriminations demanded by a multiaxial system, the reliability and validity of the system fell to lower levels (Fernando, Mellsop, Nelson, Peace, & Wilson, 1986; Foa & Kozak, 1995; Werry et al., 1983). Geographically, local definitions of diagnostic categories seem to arise. For example, in the DSM-IV field trials of the categories for mood disorders, practitioners within a single hospital or city system had good to excellent agreement in identifying major depression (Keller, Klein, Hirschfeld, Kocsis, McCullough et al., 1995). However, when different sites were compared across the United States, diagnosticians' agreement fell to fair to good levels, and the test-retest agreement in identifying the same disorder as present over a six-month interval was only poor to fair for major depression. This means that local norms for assigning diagnoses are agreed upon by different clinicians at the same hospital or clinic, but that clinicians in Ohio, for instance, do not agree closely with those in California in assigning diagnoses. Further, a patient diagnosed with major depression or schizophrenia at one time is unlikely to receive the same diagnosis half a year later, instead being classified as having a personality disorder or addictive disorder, thus indicating low predictive validity for the diagnosis (Carson, 1991). Since diagnosticians must attempt to identify a particular child's specific disorder, low reliability for the individual disorders presents a considerable problem. As a remedy, published training guides for diagnosticians

have been developed (La Bruzza & Mendez-Villarnubia, 1994; Rapoport, 1996).

Unfortunately, the multiaxial approach, while richly informative about individuals, is difficult to use, requiring that the diagnostician inquire more deeply and broadly into the patient's life than is usually feasible. Also, some of the axes are problematic. Axis II, which contains a strange combination—mental retardation and the personality disorders—is particularly disliked by users and thought to be in need of revision. The DSM-IV advises users that the etiology and treatment of the Axis II disorders (mental retardation and personality disorders) are not fundamentally different from the other types of disorders. The intent in separating these two classes of disorders from the others was to prevent their being overlooked by diagnosticians (American Psychiatric Association, 1994). It is difficult to see how clinicians could possibly overlook severe mental retardation or personality disorders such as antisocial, paranoid, or histrionic personality disorder (the last of which is marked by excessive emotionality and attention seeking). The decision to place mental retardation and the personality disorders apart from the other conditions seems misguided. Nevertheless, it is true that a child with mental retardation could also suffer from a number of other psychological disorders, which would warrant separate diagnoses.

Other innovative aspects of the DSM-IV have also been questioned. Axes IV (psychosocial and environmental problems) and V (global rating of functioning) appear to be helpful in understanding an individual, but may not in fact help because they have questionable reliability and validity (Maser, Kaelber, & Weise, 1991).

Despite continued efforts to improve the DSM, a survey of its acceptance by 1,000 practicing psychiatrists and residents (psychiatry students in training) produced disquieting results (Jampala, Sierles, & Taylor, 1986). In this survey, 35 percent of the psychiatrists and 20 percent of the residents said they would stop using the DSM if it were not required. One of the serious faults uncovered in this survey was that the diagnostic categories did not apply to nearly half of the patients, and consequently, the practicing psychiatrists "do not believe in the validity of the DSM-III criteria." In response, the developers of DSM-IV took care to consult with practitioners as well as researchers in order to enhance the DSM's usefulness.

Additional reliability and validity research is needed on many aspects of the DSM-IV, particularly the subcategories, or specific disorders. This nomenclature represents a serious and sophisticated effort to provide a vehicle for clinical, educational, and research communication for practicing clinicians and educators from a variety of disciplines. Since the DSM was primarily designed by more than 60 task force committees working with expert consultants, rivalries of various types, theoretical preferences, and the developers' personal preferences may have affected the inclusion or exclusion of some categories. It is difficult to eliminate bias and professional politics in such a process, especially if empirical evidence is scanty.

Behavioral Classification

Behavioral classification offers a strikingly different alternative to classification based on multidimensional statistical studies or a medical model. The behavioral model focuses on the patterns of behavior of an *individual* child, rather than groups, and assumes no underlying causes of problem behaviors (Goldfried & Kent, 1972; Hartmann et al., 1979; Nelson, 1983; Ullmann & Krasner, 1969). According to the behavioral view, responses are interpreted as samples of what a person does in particular situations, rather than as signs of a disorder a person has developed (Nelson, 1983, p. 196). What is important to the behavioral classification process is how the abnormal behavior is maintained by the environment. Identifiable contextual factors are presumed to maintain both desirable and undesirable behavior patterns. Some disorders such as autism and some mental retardation may be caused by an organic dysfunction, but even these behaviors can still be managed to some extent by environmental manipulation. In behavior therapy, very little emphasis is placed on how the problem developed. Rather, behavioral clinicians develop painstaking descriptions of specific, individual behavioral responses that make up behavioral classifications.

To answer the question of how behaviors are maintained, the clinician performs a *functional analysis* of the child's behavior (Bijou & Peterson, 1971). A functional analysis attempts to determine the environmental events that produce the deviant behavior. For example, a mother may tell her child that it is time to go to bed (the *antecedent event* that occurs immediately before the target behavior), at which time the child may scream, "NO,

In a functional analysis of a child's tantrums, the parent utters a request, "It's time to go home now.", and the child refuses, kicks, and cries. Should the parent then insist or give in?

don't wanna!" and throw herself down on the floor and kick her legs (undesirable behavior), which is followed by the mother relenting and letting the child stay up longer (an immediate positive consequence of the tantrum). We can see from this example that the antecedent event sets the occasion for the response and that the consequence acts to increase or decrease the occurrence of the response. It is easy to forecast that this little girl will refuse to go to bed on future nights. This behavioral classification system has been called the ABC system (A = antecedent, B = behavior, and C = consequence).

The behavioral classification system puts a high premium on identifying target clinical behaviors, which are then accurately measured, sometimes for periods of weeks or more (Kanfer, 1985; Kazdin, 1985; Kratochwill, 1985; Mash, 1985). Inferred qualities such as anxiety or emotional trauma, which cannot be directly observed, are de-emphasized by most behaviorists. The behavioral clinician deals with tantrums or oppositional behavior rather than with presumed hostility or Oedipal conflicts. However, cognitively oriented behavior therapists (P. C. Kendall & Urbain, 1981; Mahoney, 1974; Meichenbaum, 1977) focus on clients' verbal reports of internal cognitive and emotional states (such as the child's reports of fearfulness or impulses to run around during class time) and then attempt to modify those dysfunctional cognitions. Instructing children in more confident, assertive thoughts and behavior is expected to bring behavioral improvements (see Chapter 14).

Behavioral approaches emphasize observation and precise measurement of behavior. This is done by classifying a child's problem as a *response excess* (too high in frequency—for example, throwing tantrums several times a week), *response deficit* (deficient in frequency—for example, delayed language skills), or caused by inappropriate *stimulus control* (the right response but emitted in the wrong environment—for example, using singing and telling jokes during a test in the classroom) (Bijou & Peterson, 1971; Kanfer & Saslow, 1965). In the behavioral approach, the detailed description of each selected desirable or undesirable behavior becomes important, including the *topography* (the physical description of the response), *frequency* of occurrence, *duration*, and *amplitude* (response intensity) (Tryon, 1976).

With their emphasis on setting events, behavioral descriptions, and consequences, good behavioral classification systems also take into account other important variables. Kanfer and Saslow (1965) have developed a formal model for behavioral diagnosis, which is given in Table 12-3. This model classifies problems as response excesses and deficits, but also includes an analysis of the biological, social, and cultural surroundings, which could be affecting the child's behavior. The behavioral classification system is more closely tied to an individualized treatment strategy than are alternative classification systems such as the DSM-IV. The child's behavior is observed frequently and precisely, and if a treatment strategy is not effective, it is changed until a more effective intervention is found.

Behavioral classification has several distinct advantages. Since behavioral systems emphasize direct measurement of observable behavior, the reliability of these systems is generally good. There are few inferred characteristics or assumptions that might reduce reliability by producing observer disagreement. The validity of behavioral systems is also high, because the behaviors to be classified and the functional analysis to be performed are based on a particular child's behavior occurring in the natural context of the child's everyday life. However, direct assessment done in the problem environment can

TABLE 12-3 KANFER AND SASLOW'S BEHAVIORAL GUIDE TO A FUNCTIONAL ANALYSIS OF INDIVIDUAL BEHAVIOR

The functional analysis of individual behavior is based on intensive observation and evaluation of the situational factors that influence the occurrence of particular target behaviors. The analysis features:

1. *Initial analysis of the problem situation:* The client's major complaints are categorized into classes of behavioral excesses and deficits. Each behavior is described in terms of frequency, intensity, duration, and appropriateness of form. As an additional indispensable feature, the behavioral assets of the patient are also listed so they can be used in a therapy program.
2. *Clarification of the problem situation:* Consideration is given to people and circumstances in the client's environment which tend to maintain the problem behaviors and how these behaviors affect the client and others in the environment. Attention is given also to the consequences of changes in these behaviors that may result from intervention.
3. *Motivational analysis:* Assessment is made of what types of stimuli reinforce the client and how these reinforcers could be used in an intervention program. Attention is given both to pleasurable stimuli that the client views positively and to aversive stimuli that the client fears or avoids.
4. *Developmental analysis:* What are the limitations of the client's physical condition (defective vision, hearing, residual illness, etc.) or physical environment (urban versus rural, ethnic, socioeconomic status, etc.)? Could these biological and developmental variables relate to the client's current problem?
5. *Analysis of self-control:* To what extent and in what situations can the client control his problem behavior? Can the client's self-controlling behavior be used in an intervention program?
6. *Analysis of social relationships:* Who are the most significant people in the client's environment? Assess how these relationships influence each other, and how important people in the client's environment can participate in the intervention program.
7. *Analysis of the social cultural-physical environment:* The client's behavior is compared to the norms of the client's environment. Such a comparison allows an assessment of how the client's behavior is viewed by others in his environment, how this view will change as the environmental setting changes (e.g., school, home, friends, or work), and what the limitations of the environment are.

SOURCE: Kanfer, F. H., & Saslow, G. (1965). Behavioral analysis: An alternative to diagnostic classification. *Archives of General Psychiatry, 12,* 848–853. Adapted by permission.

have drawbacks caused by the intrusion of an observer, which can inject artificiality into the situation (*observer reactivity*). Behavioral classification also places high value on the individual and describes each problem uniquely rather than attempting to fit the child's problem into some preconceived group of disorders. This is in direct contrast to classification systems that try to fit individuals into predefined categories.

One study investigated the reliability of using behavioral classification by over 100 experienced, doctoral-level clinicians (Wilson & Evans, 1983). The clinicians assessed three written case descriptions of three common childhood disorders: fearfulness, conduct disorder, and social withdrawal. The members were asked (1) to describe their impressions of the major difficulties characterizing each child, (2) to state treatment goals, and (3) to rank-order treatment goals. The overall reliability between clinicians in selecting a first-priority behavior for treatment was only 38 percent, indicating considerable variability in selecting behaviors for treatment. Surprisingly, 22 percent of the behavior therapists participating in this study also used loose psychodynamic and intrapsychic terminology (for instance, "internalized hostility," "insecure child," "poor self-concept") in their behavioral classification of the cases. This study demonstrates the strength of traditional concepts of psychopathology and shows that practicing behavior therapists may have some difficulty in reliably using purely behavioral descriptions.

Others have criticized the behavioral classification approach for failing to deal with human aims and values (Shoben, 1966), which are important but not directly observable. The emphasis on observation and measurement has been viewed by some clinicians as mechanistic, possibly missing the richness of human thought and emotion that other systems try to take into account. A complete divorce from labels and formal psychiatric diagnosis has also been difficult for most behaviorally oriented clinicians. Even major behavioral textbooks (Bellack, Hersen, & Kazdin, 1982; Morris & Kratochwill, 1983; Ullmann & Krasner, 1969; Yates, 1970) feature traditional psychiatric groupings and headings (for example, depression, infantile autism, schizophrenia, phobias) (Draguns & Phillips, 1971).

In many clinical settings where behavioral classification and assessment are used, it is not uncommon to see a formal diagnosis from the DSM coupled with a behavioral classification or description. This joint use of the two systems has been encouraged by some authorities (Taylor, 1983) and is generally unavoidable, because insurance companies, federally funded programs, and school systems usually require a formal psychiatric diagnosis before they will fund treatment efforts. The major advantage of behavioral classification is in its practical treatment application to treatment of individual children who may suffer from troublesome problems that defy ready classification in the DSM.

Educational Classification

More behaviorally disordered children are identified at school and classified with special educational classification systems than with any other type of system. Teachers spend considerable time with children and have significant opportunities to observe many of the children's problems. Problems such as aggression toward peers and teachers, anxiety-based avoidance of school (school phobia), and attention problems are common examples of behavior disorders that are exhibited in schools. However, even though they are frequently used, educational classification systems are poorly constructed and include a confusing mixture of medical, psychoanalytic, and behavioral concepts.

Categorical educational classification systems are designed by state boards of education and are used primarily by local school districts for funding purposes. Funds to schools are tied to the number of children classified as handicapped, resulting in classification systems with extremely broad coverage. Common categories included in such educational classification systems include mental retardation, learning disabilities, communication disorders, physical handicaps, and behavior or emotional disorders. The federal definition of a severe emotional disturbance (behavior disorder) is found in the regulations of the Education for All Handicapped Children Act of 1975 (P.L. 94-142):

(i) *The term means a condition exhibiting one or more of the following characteristics over a long period of time and to marked degree, which adversely affects educational performance:*

(a) *An inability to learn which cannot be explained by intellectual, sensory, or health factors;*

(b) *An inability to build or maintain satisfactory interpersonal relationships with peers and teachers;*

(c) Inappropriate types of behaviors or feelings under normal circumstances;

(d) A general pervasive mood of unhappiness or depression;

(e) A tendency to develop physical symptoms or fears associated with personal or school problems.

(ii) The term includes children who are schizophrenic. The term does not include children who are socially maladjusted, unless it is determined they are seriously emotionally disturbed. (Education for All Handicapped Children Act of 1975, Section 121a.5)

In contrast to the classification schemes described previously, this definition lacks precision, provides no guidelines for assessment, and excludes many subcategories of disturbance that are included in other approaches. The educational classification system omits any reference to severity, so children with barely discernible problems are classified together with those who are unable to function in a school setting. State definitions for the classification of behavior disorders generally are patterned after this federal definition because of funding requirements. If a child fits this definition, then the state educational system becomes eligible for federal funds to serve that child. Consequently, a significant number of low achievers who are not otherwise disturbed are referred for testing and subsequently inaccurately identified as learning disabled or seriously emotionally disturbed, mainly in order to qualify them for special education services (Welch & Sheridan, 1995). Approximately 9 percent of students eligible for special education services in 1990 were classified as having a behavior disorder (U.S. Office of Education, 1991). The basic components of most state definitions are found in Table 12-4 (Cullinan, Epstein, & McLinden, 1986).

The federal and state definitions of behavior disorders (see Table 12-4) have been severely criticized (as reviewed by the U.S. Department of Education, 1985). Some educators feel that the federal definition is so vague that it defies reliable use (Kauffman, 1982; Walker, Reavis, Rhode, & Jenson, 1985). Kauffman (1982) complained that "One is forced to conclude that the federal definition is, if not claptrap, at least dangerously close to nonsense" (p. 4). This definition includes children who have internalizing problems (such as physical symptoms, fears, depression, and unhappiness), but inexplicably ignores children with externalizing problems with the control of

TABLE 12-4 STATE DEFINITIONS OF EMOTIONAL OR BEHAVIORAL DISORDERS

1. *Disorders of emotion/behavior:* The student's emotions or behaviors are generally improper, immature, or show evidence of a specific form of disturbance.
2. *Interpersonal problems:* Limitations in developing and/or maintaining satisfactory social relations with peers or adults.
3. *Learning/achievement problems:* The student is having achievement or learning problems, or, further, his or her emotional or behavior disorders are causing such problems.
4. *Deviation from norm:* Emotions or behaviors are unusual, inappropriate, or inferior with respect to some standard.
5. *Chronicity:* The problems are of long standing.
6. *Severity:* The problems are extremely serious or intense, or exhibited across several situations.
7. *Etiology:* The problems are clearly attributed to some causal phenomenon.
8. *Prognosis:* Special education and services are reserved for students who are most likely to improve.
9. *Exclusions:* Conditions that exempt the student from being defined as behaviorally disordered, even though he or she may evidence social, emotional, or learning problems like those previously mentioned.
10. *Special education needed:* The student is not suited for regular education or will be served more appropriately through some type of special services.
11. *Certification:* The student's eligibility for special services is based on approval by some designated individual or group, or is determined through specific assessment procedures.

SOURCE: Cullinan, D., Epstein, M. H., & McLinden, D. (1986). Status and change in state administrative definitions of behavior disorder. *School Psychology Review, 15,* 383–392. Reprinted by permission.

aggressive, antisocial behavior (Jenson, 1985). This definition does not include "socially maladjusted" children, and so bars them from special educational services for the emotionally disturbed.

Clearly, this definition ignores the fact that most of the behaviorally disordered children referred for special education are socially maladjusted. Also, there are no studies on the reliability of educational classification systems! No one knows for sure how reliably these systems are applied, or whether they are used in a capricious or biased manner.

It is ironic that the most frequently used classification system has poor validity and completely unknown reliability. Educational classification appears to be a convenient fiction developed to provide a vehicle for public funding for special education services for a large and diverse group of children. Providing services for needy children is a commendable aim, but the system developed to achieve it should not be based on scientific subterfuge. Educational categories are created by governmental and administrative edict, rather than by research on the actual nature of schoolchildren's psychological disorders, which makes this classification system useless for estimating the extent of need for services or for developing improved services (MacMillan & Kavale, 1986). That is, the current educational classification system impedes rather than promotes research on schoolchildren's disorders. Once a child is educationally classified and placed, then other, better systems such as behavioral classification are generally used for educational and treatment purposes.

The U.S. Congress is currently considering new legislation that would revise and, we hope, improve the definitions of behavior disorders to be considered in the classroom. In the past, the official definitions have made little educational or scientific sense.

THE EFFECTS OF LABELING THROUGH CLASSIFICATION

Labeling, or diagnosis, is the end product of most classification processes. Such labeling should reduce uncertainty and should permit the beginning of research or treatment for a child. This is the ideal situation; in reality, however, labeling a child's behavior might produce several unanticipated harmful side effects.

The label of mental illness can adversely affect other's perceptions of a child's potential (Hobbs, 1975a; Jones, 1972; Mercer, 1975). An adolescent who has been labeled a delinquent may be distrusted by others and denied employment opportunities. Minority children who are incorrectly labeled as mentally retarded may be segregated into special education classes and denied the opportunities of regularly placed students. A child labeled as autistic or schizophrenic may be given up as hopeless and sent to languish in a large institution. Those labeled as having minimal brain dysfunction may cease trying to improve their own behavior, which they attribute to brain damage. In all of these situations, people react more to the labels than to the actual characteristics of the children. It is assumed that the labels accurately describe the

children. In essence, labeled children are depersonalized (Blashfield & Draguns, 1976b), and all of their special qualities and unique personality are ignored.

Opportunity is important to all of us, particularly in education and employment. Rather than opening doors to treatment and returning to normalized environments, labeling can restrict or lock a child into dead-end placements. Gallagher (1972) estimates that only 10 percent of all children placed in special education classes and schools in large cities ever return to regular education placements. Nationally, only 45 percent of children labeled as behaviorally disordered are educated in regular or resource classrooms. The majority are placed in restrictive settings, such as self-contained classrooms, special schools, or homebound/hospital placements (U.S. Department of Education, 1985).

In her research on mentally retarded children in California, Jane Mercer found that in the 1970s only 19 percent of the special education students were ever mainstreamed or returned to regular school (cited in Krasner, 1976). A large percentage of children labeled as mentally retarded either dropped out of school without an adequate education (23 percent), were eventually expelled or sent to other restrictive placements such as institutions (46 percent), or were eventually deemed too old to complete the school program (12 percent). If used inappropriately, classification labels can lock many doors that lead back to normal environments.

The *self-fulfilling prophecy* is another possible aspect of labeling. In this process, a child's behavior is actually shaped, though unknowingly, to conform to a label. A teacher or a parent may either consciously or unconsciously expect a child to behave in accordance with the diagnosis the child has been given, and the child eventually behaves that way consistently. In effect, the expectations (either correct or incorrect) held by a teacher or parent actually shape the anticipated behaviors of a child. For example, parents may be particularly alert to deviant or antisocial behavior if a child is labeled "predelinquent." Consequently, the parents may lecture and scold the child, and may attend particularly to his undesirable behavior and ignore his positive behavior. As a result, the child may behave even more antisocially than before he was labeled (Rosenthal & Jacobson, 1968). Despite the intuitive appeal of the expectancy or "Pygmalion" explanation, there is little formal evidence for its effect in the

A boy who has been labeled as the worst kid in class is seldom expected to behave well or do good work.

classroom (Rosenthal, 1987; Wineburg, 1987). The research suggesting the existence of self-fulfilling prophecy in teachers' perceptions of students was severely flawed and unreplicable, so the everyday effects of labels on teachers' expectations of children are uncertain (Merton, 1987).

Nevertheless, labeling can have negative consequences. Individuals who have been diagnosed and labeled as mentally ill may have particular problems in social acceptance and employment, and may lose some legal rights such as child custody (Caplan, 1995). Labels generally emphasize behavioral deficits and negative behaviors; rarely do they highlight positive behavior or accomplishments. This negative focus affects the teacher's expectation of handicapped children's capabilities (Foster

et al, 1975; Ysseldyke & Foster, 1978). It also undoubtedly affects the child's view of herself. Some labels such as mental retardation are particularly damaging to the child's self-esteem, since no one is proud of being dull (Guskin, Bartel, & MacMillan, 1975). Children may try to appear normal even when the handicap is obvious, such as severe reading disability (Guskin et al., 1975; Jones, 1972). Parents may want their children to appear less handicapped and so may shop among clinicians to find one who will provide more socially acceptable labels, for example, learning disabilities rather than mental retardation or emotional disturbance.

Individual information about the child is either lost or ignored through the labeling and classification process. So why label? As mentioned previously, labeling is

---

BOX 12-6 PYGMALION IN THE CLASSROOM

Eliza: . . . "You see, really and truly, apart from the things anyone can pick up (the dressing and the proper way of speaking, and so on), the difference between a lady and a flower girl is not how she behaves, but how she's treated. I shall always be a flower girl to Professor Higgins, because he always treats me as a flower girl, and always will; but I know I can be a lady to you, because you always treat me as a lady, and always will."

G. B. Shaw, Pygmalion

Eliza Doolittle, as the quote indicates, was a simple flower girl in a George Bernard Shaw play whom Professor Higgins transformed into a lady by training her to dress and speak properly. However, she was destined to be just a flower girl to Professor Higgins because he expected her to be so, no matter how ladylike she behaved.

Teachers can have similar expectations about their students, depending on the students' labels, as suggested in a study by Rosenthal and Jacobson (1968). In this experiment, children in the first through the sixth grades from the Oak School were tested by teachers using a nonverbal IQ test (Test of General Ability, or TOGA) at the beginning of the school year. Half of the children were randomly selected (the experimental group), and the teachers were told that the test scores indicated that these children would show unusual academic gains during the coming school year. The other half of the children who were tested (the control group) started the school year without a prediction of unusual academic gains. Actually, the experimental group did not differ significantly from the control group in IQ test scores; what was being tested was the effect of the teachers' expectations on the children's progress.

At the end of the year, all the children were again tested with the TOGA IQ test, and the scores between the experimental and control groups were compared. The results showed that the experimental-group children in the first and second grades made large gains in IQ points (15 more points for the first-graders and 9 more points for the second-graders) than the control group. Since the experimental group had not differed from the control group at the beginning of the school year, the difference in IQ points seemed to be a result of the teachers' expectation that the children in the experimental group would do better academically. The effect was not found for the older children in third through sixth grades in the experimental group. The older children may have had well-established academic reputations, their school assignments were more frequent and demanding, and their teachers' expectations could not be easily changed.

No one knows exactly why the younger children made such large IQ gains. It might have been that since the teachers expected higher academic performance from this group, they gave these students more attention or encouragement, which resulted in better test scores. This experiment teaches us two lessons: Be alert to expectancy effects so you can guard against them, and don't take the results of any single experiment as definitive.

SOURCE: Rosenthal, R. L., & Jacobson, L. (1968). *Pygmalion in the classroom: Teacher expectation and pupils' intellectual development*. New York: Holt, Rinehart and Winston. Copyright 1968 by Holt, Rinehart and Winston, Inc. Reprinted by permission of the publisher.

---

necessary to gain services for handicapped children and funds to support these services. With very few exceptions, funding for services is dependent on labeling (Gallagher et al., 1975). Labeling children's problems focuses society's attention on their needs, permitting interest groups such as those formed by affected families of autistic or hyperactive children to press for prevention and treatment programs (Kolstoe, 1972). Without a recognized diagnostic label, a child probably will not receive services. As an illustration, let us consider the case of *Doe v. San Francisco Unified School District* (Martin, 1977). In this case, an 18-year-old high school student graduated from school but was functionally illiterate. The boy and his parents brought suit against the school district on grounds of negligence in failing to provide instruction in

basic skills. Ultimately, the court could not decide on an acceptable standard of basic education for a normal (unlabeled) student, so the case was dismissed. Doe had never been labeled as educationally handicapped.

If Doe had been classified as handicapped, he would have received far different treatment. For example, in a similar case in New Hampshire, a National Honor Society student's parents sued the school district for not providing appropriate special education services for their daughter, Karen. Karen had difficulty reading and had to resort to cheating in order to progress to the ninth grade: "I did a lot of taking other kids' papers, erasing their names. Just cheating mostly. I really didn't think about it. It was a question of survival" (1986). Despite her reading disability, Karen became an honors student, student council president, and captain of the soccer team. She was also labeled learning-disabled in the ninth grade. The school authorities, however, "did little more than assure her she wasn't stupid" and provided little remedial work. Karen's parents placed her in a private remedial school, and she progressed to college. The important point is that because Karen was labeled as handicapped, she had grounds to sue for recovery of the special education costs in the private school. Doe had never been labeled as handicapped, and his case was dismissed. Research on the power of labels is described in Box 12-6.

Labels are necessary and they are here to stay in the treatment of children with behavior disorders. Clinicians must develop classification procedures to minimize the bad effects of labeling and to maximize accuracy and access to appropriate services. New approaches to classification are being developed for children that go beyond human memory capabilities and judgment. In future, computers may be used routinely to identify and classify children's disorders.

ARTIFICIAL INTELLIGENCE, COMPUTERS, AND CLASSIFICATION

Modern computer technology can provide a promising new computer-based technique for classification. Important new developments are being made in classification via artificial intelligence—that is, computer-based classification with *expert systems.* These systems are called "expert" because a computer is programmed to make decisions like a human expert. For example, in a pioneering effort, A. Hoffmeister and J. Ferraro (personal communication, 1986) programmed an IBM personal computer, using an artificial intelligence system called the MI-Inference Engine, to make classification decisions concerning handicapped children. Originally, the MI-Inference Engine system was developed at Stanford University to make difficult medical diagnoses. Hoffmeister and Ferraro (personal communication, 1986) adapted the system to diagnose learning-disabled and behaviorally handicapped children. The system holds in its memory the state educational system's classification rules, the federal classification rules, and 600 research findings concerning the accurate classification of learning-disabled children. The system repeatedly asks for in-

formation about a child, consults the rules and research findings held in its memory, and then gives a probability statement that a child is actually learning-disabled. The probability statement provides information on accuracy beyond that provided by the diagnostician in the traditional assessment situation. Usually, the diagnostician simply offers an opinion on the classification of the disorder the client exhibits, but does not quantify the degree of certainty with which the diagnosis is given.

The accuracy of a diagnosis using this computerized system is dependent on the quality and extensiveness of the information that is fed into it. Surprisingly, when compared to human judgment using the same information, the computer was 50 percent more accurate in diagnosing learning disabilities. In a similar project (Geist, 1990), a computer program made DSM diagnoses very accurately for all diagnostic categories, including those for children, but the psychiatric residents resisted using it. A computer-assisted diagnostic process will not replace the judgment of human clinicians, but can be used as a second opinion with difficult cases. In the future, computer programs may also be used to recommend appropriate research-based intervention strategies for behaviorally handicapped children.

SUMMARY

Classification systems vary in purpose (funding, placement, treatment, and/or research) and theoretical and professional foundations (medical, behavioral, or educational). Table 12-5 lists and evaluates the various classification systems reviewed in this chapter. As Table 12-5 indicates, expecting too much from a classification system and including a category for every possible disorder yields a system with overly extensive coverage and low reliability. This often happens when funding for children's educational and treatment services is dependent on children's diagnostic labels. Classification systems that are more limited in number of categories and are linked to specific treatments typically have better reliability and validity. Box 12-7 describes a disturbed child and then classifies the child's behavior according to several of the systems reviewed.

It is important to remember that all classification systems are imperfect, with the imperfections being dependent on several factors including the primary uses of the system, its theoretical assumptions about the nature of

TABLE 12-5 Evaluation of Classification Systems

System	Reliability	Validity	Coverage	Parsimony	Mutually Exclusive Definitions	Usage
DSM-IV	Fair	Good	Broad	Questionable	Fair	Frequent
GAP	Fair	Fair	Broad	Questionable	Questionable	Rare
ICD	Fair	Fair	Moderate	Questionable	Questionable	Frequent (internationally)
Behavioral classification	Excellent	Good	Moderate	Good	Good	Rare to moderate
Educational classification	Unknown	Unknown	Broad	Questionable	Questionable	Frequent

NOTE: Ratings are based on the highest performance level achieved by each system.

BOX 12-7 Marty, a Boy with Multiple Problems and Problem Classifications

Marty is an 8-year-old boy who has had a great deal of difficulty during the past year getting along with his family, teachers, and classmates. His problem is aggressive behavior—he just does not get along with anyone. When someone asks him to do something, instead of complying, Marty often explodes, breaks things, and hurts people. He is the least popular boy in his third-grade class and is always last one chosen when they form teams or study groups. Recently Marty's behavior problem came to a head when his mother caught him doing what she long suspected, stealing money from her purse. His mother locked his bicycle up for a week because of the stealing incident. To get even, he opened up a trap door in the bathroom which led to the basement and covered the opening with a rug. He then filled the bathtub full of water, got in, and started to scream to his mother for help. When she ran into the bathroom, she fell through the trap door and broke both her ankles. Marty laughed.

Clearly, Marty has a behavior disorder in which aggression and the inability to take directions from adults are key problems. What follows is how a number of classification systems would diagnose his behavior.

A. GAP: *Personality disorder: tension discharge disorder.* Children in this category exhibit chronic patterns of emotional expression of aggressive and sexual impulses that conflict with society's norms. They directly act out their feelings or impulses toward people or society in antisocial or destructive fashion, rather than inhibiting or repressing these responses and developing other modes of psychological defense or symptomatology. Note that this system assumes that aggressive actions stem from underlying, unconscious feelings of anxiety and hostility.

B. DSM-IV: *Conduct disorder, childhood-onset type.* The essential features are a failure to establish a normal degree of affection, empathy, or bonding with others; a pattern of aggressive antisocial behavior to people and animals, destruction of property, theft or deceitfulness, and serious violations of rules. Had Marty's behavior been less serious, it might have been diagnosed oppositional defiant disorder.

Axis I: Clinical psychiatric syndrome: conduct disorder, childhood-onset type (occurs before age 10)
Axis II: Mental retardation or personality disorder: none
Axis III: Physical disorder: none
Axis IV: Psychosocial stressors: Problems with primary support group and problems related to the social environment, educational problems
Axis V: Current global assessment functioning (GAF) = 50, serious symptoms or impairment in functioning

C. Behavioral classification: High rates of aggressive behavior (verbal and physical).

Antecedents: Requests or commands from adults, conflict
Behavior: Excessive rates of hitting, temper tantrums, destruction of property, injuring others
Consequences: Escape from or avoidance of negative consequences such as complying to requests or punishment

D. Educational classification (Utah State Board of Education): Behaviorally handicapped. A behaviorally handicapped child is distinguished by inability or difficulty in handling problems, or by ineffective methods of adjusting or coping. Behaviorally handicapped children tend to resort to immature, unrealistic, aggressive, acting-out, withdrawal, or avoidance behaviors in trying to find solutions.

psychopathology, and technical considerations of reliability and validity. Even though people commonly speak about the autistic, hyperactive, or retarded child, in actuality no *child* is classified; only the child's possibly transitory, *current behavior* is classified. If we classify a child and speak of her or him only as having the disorder, then we may stigmatize the child, thus exacerbating the problem. If a child's problem behavior alone is classified, we assume that the child may have many strengths aside from the problem and that the problem behavior can be changed with appropriate treatment or may be overcome spontaneously.

ASSESSMENT OF CHILDHOOD

BEHAVIOR DISORDERS

Key Terms

Assessment. An information gathering process that leads to decisions concerning classification, placement, treatment, and program evaluation.

Behavior observation. An assessment technique in which data are collected by observing a subject and then recording the occurrence of behaviors using an observation code.

Criterion referenced test. Tests that emphasize a child's absolute mastery of a specific skill area or behavior.

Cross informant analysis. Use of multiple, parallel test forms by several evaluators to obtain an accurate and complete portrayal of the person being assessed.

False positive. An error in which an assessment process has been used and has positively identified a problem when one does not exist.

Norm referenced test. Tests that emphasize a child's relative standing in comparison to a group of children.

Psychological test. A psychological test is an objective and standardized measure of a sample of behavior.

Structured interview. A structured interview involves directly asking a subject a set of predetermined questions concerning a problem or situation.

Utility. The utility of an assessment process is the extent to which the assessment information gathered is used to make a cost-effective decision.

What does it take to accurately assess children with behavioral disabilities? Are complicated psychological measures needed to identify children with psychological problems and disabilities? Or, can parents and teachers easily and accurately identify children with behavior disorders? What are the advantages and limitations of psychological assessment? Can psychological assessment by itself cause possible harm?

In this chapter, we answer these questions and discuss several assessment methods that are used to make decisions concerning children's behavior problems. We review specific assessment techniques such as psychological testing, structured interviewing, behavioral observation, and new computer aided assessment. In addition, we discuss criteria for judging the adequacy of assessment procedures and offer recommendations for judging adequate assessment practices.

ASSESSMENT: A DEFINITION

Assessment can be as controversial as religion, politics, or the newest approaches to treatment. It is difficult to get a consensus from the majority of professionals about a well accepted definition for assessment. Table 13-1 lists several definitions of assessment from a number of leading textbooks on assessment. The issue that stands out from this list is the diversity of the characteristics of assessment. However, most of these definitions do emphasize some common features. First, precise *measurement* is stressed in most of these definitions. Second, comprehensive *information* gathering is essential to good assessment practices.

Assessment methods used to gather information can vary from systematic procedures such as structured behavioral observation to relatively unstructured procedures such as informal interviews. Table 13-2 depicts the various types of information that can be gathered and the procedures used to collect this information. However, good assessment should go beyond merely collecting information; it involves making relevant decisions about classification, diagnosis, placement, treatment, and evaluation of children (Anastasi, 1988; Cole, 1978; Cronbach, 1960, 1990).

Classification and Diagnostic Decisions. Most classification systems (medical, educational, and behavioral) base a diagnosis on some type of gathered assessment information. For example, psychological tests and psychiatric interviews are commonly used to arrive at a diagnosis. Similarly, federal legislation mandates that the classification of a student with disabilities be based on measures that are designed specifically to validly assess that disorder. Some *assessment systems* use several types of related assessment measures (i.e., behavior checklists, interviews, and observations) and several informants (i.e., teachers, parents, and the child) to reduce error (Achenbach, 1991).

Placement. Few children are placed in special education or treatment settings without a decision that was at least partially based on assessment information. For example, before a child can be placed in most special education settings, a battery of academic, intellectual, and behavioral assessment measures are given to see if a legitimate need exists for such a placement.

A battery of measures are required because courts have seriously questioned the practice of using the sole judgment of one professional or primarily one measure, such as an IQ test, as a criterion for placement (Martin,

TABLE 13-1   COMMON DEFINITIONS OF ASSESSMENT AND TESTING

1. A *test* is a systematic procedure for observing behavior and describing it with the aid of numerical scales or fixed categories. (Cronbach, 1990)
2. The term *assessment* implies that there are many ways of evaluating individual differences. Testing is one way, but there is also interviewing, observations of behavior in the natural or structured settings, and recording of various physiological functions. (Goldstein & Hersen, 1990)
3. Assessment is the process of collecting data for the purpose of (a) specifying and verifying problems and (b) making decisions about students. (Salvia & Ysseldyke, 1991)
4. Traditionally, the function of psychological tests has been to measure differences between individuals or between the reactions of the same individual on different occasions. (Anastasi, 1988)
5. Although treatment and care have changed radically during the past two decades, the goals of psychological assessment have not changed very much at all. They remain diagnosis, measurement of the process of change, and evaluation of outcome. (Katz & Wetzler, 1989)

TABLE 13-2   TYPES OF INFORMATION AND COLLECTION PROCEDURES USED IN ASSESSMENT

Tests	Standardized intelligence and achievement tests
	Projective personality tests
	Objective personality tests
	Criterion-referenced tests
Observations	Objective behavior observations by an independent observer
	Self-monitoring
	Behavior ratings by teachers or parents
Interviews	Behavioral interviews
	Social history interviews
	Child psychiatric examinations

time. These tests are generally administered in the fall and then again in the spring to assess individual gains. Finer-grained evaluations for academic programs are yielded by curriculum-based probes that are taken frequently during the week and used to make judgments about a program's effectiveness (Shapiro, 1987; Shinn, 1989).

In summary, assessment is a two-part process. First, measurements are taken and information is gathered. Second, decisions are made from the information regarding classification, diagnosis, placement, treatment, and evaluation of a child. The information gathering phase of assessment substantially affects the appropriateness of the decisions made concerning the child. If the information is in error or inadequate, then accurate decisions will be affected. It is critical to understand how the quality of assessment information is judged.

Standards for Assessment

Any type of assessment method is subject to error. No method is perfect. For instance, if we are trying to measure the motor activity of children in a classroom and several of these children are ill, then our activity measurements will probably be lower than if the children were in good health. In a sense, the information gathered by an assessment method is only an approximation of the real phenomena that are being measured because of error. In our example, the random event that the children were sick would result in an underestimate of motor activity. The type of error that happens by chance has been

1979). Too many abuses have occurred. This has been particularly a problem in the assessment of culturally diverse children. Students from diverse cultural backgrounds have been overly identified in the past and misplaced in special education classrooms. The sentiment against the cultural bias of certain assessment measures, such as intelligence tests, has resulted in bans or severe restrictions in some states on their use in identifying students with disabilities (*Larry P. v. Riles*) (as reviewed by Salvia & Ysseldyke, 1991).

Treatment and Program Planning. Good assessment procedures lead to specific treatment recommendations. For instance, some types of prescriptive measures pinpoint a child's deficiencies and prescribe treatment programs and interventions (Cummings, 1988).

Evaluation. Assessment procedures such as psychological tests are frequently used to evaluate both an individual child's progress in a treatment program and the treatment program as a whole (Salvia & Ysseldyke, 1991). For example, academic achievement tests can be used to assess a child's academic achievement gains over one year's termed *random error* (Althauser & Herberlein, 1970; Carmines & Zeller, 1979; Nunnaly, 1962; Wert & Linn, 1979). Another type of error that also affects assessment is *systematic error*. With systematic errors, the assessment procedure or person using it is *always* off by a certain degree. With our example, a systematic error in measurement might occur because the pedometer (a device that measures motor activity) malfunctions and always records too low a record of motor activity. Both random and systematic errors are important because they are at the root of difficulty with assessment reliability and validity. Using assessment measures that have poor reliability and validity can lead to large consequences in selecting psychological treatments (Dahlstrom, 1993).

RELIABILITY

The reliability of an assessment procedure is a measure of the consistency of the procedure (Anastasi, 1988). For example, if a measure is repeatedly given, it would be considered reliable if the same or similar scores are yielded each time. Conceptually, we can assume that the information given by an assessment device contains the true score (Swanson & Watson, 1982). However, on each administration of the assessment procedure random error is always present, which affects the true score. If the assessment procedure is unreliable, then large amounts of random error are present causing the assessment score to greatly vary. If only a small amount of random error is present, then the scores are similar and cluster around the true score. For example, if an intelligence test is repeatedly given to a child who has a true IQ score of 100, and the test results are 50, 107, 36, 129, then the measure would be unreliable. However, if the test scores were 105, 99, 103, 101 (which are close to the true score of 100), then the test would be reliable. Factors that reduce the degree of consistency of information and result in significant random error include:

1. Ambiguous assessment procedures that leave a great deal of interpretation up to the evaluator;
2. Poorly trained evaluators who are not familiar with the assessment procedures;
3. Widely changing or varying behavior of the children being evaluated (as in our example of motor activity and ill children);
4. Growth and development, which cause differences in children's ability and behavior (common when

significant periods of time elapse between assessments);
5. Varying assessment conditions such as a loud or distracting environment.

There are two basic types of reliability, that are important in judging assessment procedures for children. Our example of repeated IQ testing is an example of *test-retest* reliability, which is obtained by using an assessment measure, waiting, and then re-administering the procedure. If the results are similar on the occasions when the assessment procedure is repeated, then the procedure has good test-retest reliability.

Interrater reliability is different from test-retest reliability in that two evaluators use the same assessment procedure at the same time on the same subject. For example, a behavioral observation code might be used by two observers simultaneously watching a child in a classroom. If both observers record similar scores for the child, the coding system would be considered to have good reliability.

If the information that is gathered by an assessment measure is not reliable, then a child is at risk. If the measure has poor test-retest reliability, then it becomes difficult to use the measure to judge treatment effectiveness. Is the difference between the assessment measures taken before and after treatment a function of the treatment's effectiveness or an artifact of random error? Similarly, interrater reliability is important in identifying behaviorally disordered children. If one observer judges the child's behavior to be problematic and another judges it to be normal, then the disagreement may result in the child not getting help.

VALIDITY

Although reliability is a measure of random error, it is not a measure of systematic error, which also affects assessment information. Validity is a much better measure of systematic error. As stated in Chapter 12, validity is a reality check on the meaning of an assessment measure or how accurately a procedure measures what it purports to measure (Anastasi, 1988; Messick, 1995). For instance, if a new test purports to diagnose children's behavior disorders accurately, we might compare the results of the new test given to several children with the diagnostic judgment of a group of experienced clinical psychologists. If the test's results closely match the results from the psychologists, we would assume that it has good va-lidity. However, if the results are not similar, we would question the test's validity. It is important to point out in this example that if the test has poor validity, it would always (or systematically) be in disagreement with the psychologist's judgment. If the test had poor reliability, it would sometimes agree and sometimes disagree (ran-domly) with the psychologist's results.

It is also important to point out that the criterion in this example, the psychologist's diagnostic judgment, which is used to judge the new test must be valid to make this procedure useful. If neither assessment procedure (the criterion measure or the new test) has high validity, one cannot be used as a criterion against which to judge the other. This type of validity is called *concurrent validity* because the new assessment procedure is administered at the same time (concurrently) as the valid criterion (the psychologist's judgments). Good concurrent validity is necessary if a new assessment measure is going to be ac-cepted and used by practitioners in the field.

A similar validity to concurrent validity is *predictive validity* in which predictions about the future are made. For predictive validity, the criterion variable that is used in judging an assessment procedure is some type of future outcome. For example, if an autistic child has an intel-ligence score of 50 or lower and has no language, then the future outcome for the child will likely be poor (i.e., institutionalization, unemployment, dependence). In this example, the IQ score and language ability overshadow all other variables in predicting the future. They would have good predictive validity in forecasting the future of autistic children if indeed autistic children had poor out-comes that exhibited these characteristics. Unfortunately they do.

Other types of validity used to judge the adequacy of assessment procedures include content, construct, and face validity. *Content validity* is the extent to which an assessment device actually contains or represents items found in the content area that it is designed to measure. The sampling of assessment items should be sufficient to give an adequate representation of the area being assessed (Messick, 1980; Salvia & Ysseldyke, 1991; Swanson & Watson, 1982). For example, a social skills behavior checklist used to assess a child's peer relations should contain enough items to adequately represent the essen-tial skills needed to interact with peers. An example, of such a checklist is given in Table 13-3 (Gresham & Elliott, 1990).

Similarly, academic achievement tests are another ex-ample where content validity is important. If an achieve-ment test purports to measure the arithmetic skills of third-graders, then the test should have some arithmetic problems from the third-grade curriculum. Sattler (1990, p. 30) has listed three basic questions that are central in establishing the content validity of an assessment measure:

1. Are the questions appropriate test questions and does the test measure the domain of interest?
2. Does the test contain enough information to cover appropriately what it is supposed to measure?
3. What is the level of mastery at which the content is being assessed?

Construct validity indicates how well an assessment pro-cedure score represents a *theoretical construct* such as a trait, ability, or characteristic and the meaning of the score (Anastasi, 1988; Messick, 1995). Such theoretical constructs include extroversion, dependency (traits), in-telligence, creativity (abilities), or depression, anxiety, or honesty (characteristics). Construct validity is measured in an indirect way, by using test scores to predict some other features of these test-taker's behavior. For instance, if a test actually measures anxiety, then children who score high on anxiety should behave differently than chil-dren who score low. Anxiety often interferes with per-formance on demanding tasks such as solving difficult mathematics problems. If children who score high on the anxiety test also perform more poorly on demanding tasks than do children with low anxiety, then one might conclude that the test has measured the construct anxiety. Of course, the high- and low-scoring children would have to be matched on other variables such as intelligence and quantitative ability, which could also affect performance on the difficult mathematical problems. Construct valid-ity is very important for personality inventories and be-havior checklists that rely upon factor analysis (a statis-tical procedure used to identify which behaviors or traits cluster together or are related to each other) to diagnose behavior disorders.

Face validity means "what a test appears to measure, not what it actually measures" (Sattler, 1990). Generally, items are first selected by a test developer because she feels they represent a content area. This initial item se-lection is based on personal judgment and experience of the test developer. It can never be a substitute for the more rigorous forms of validity that have already been

TABLE 13-3 SAMPLE OF THE SOCIAL SKILLS RATING SCALES

FOR OFFICE USE ONLY How Often?			Social Skills	How Often?			How Important?		
C	A	S		Never	Sometimes	Very Often	Not Important	Important	Critical
			1. Controls temper in conflict situations with peers.	0	1	2	0	1	2
			2. Introduces herself or himself to new people without being told.	0	1	2	0	1	2
			3. Appropriately questions rules that may be unfair.	0	1	2	0	1	2
			4. Compromises in conflict situations by changing own ideas to reach agreement.	0	1	2	0	1	2
			5. Responds appropriately to peer pressure.	0	1	2	0	1	2
			6. Says nice things about himself or herself when appropriate.	0	1	2	0	1	2
			7. Invites others to join in activities.	0	1	2	0	1	2
			8. Uses free time in an acceptable way.	0	1	2	0	1	2
			9. Finishes class assignments within time limits.	0	1	2	0	1	2
			10. Makes friends easily.	0	1	2	0	1	2
			11. Responds appropriately to teasing by peers.	0	1	2	0	1	2
			12. Controls temper in conflict situations with adults.	0	1	2	0	1	2
			13. Receives criticism well.	0	1	2	0	1	2
			14. Initiates conversations with peers.	0	1	2	0	1	2
			15. Uses time appropriately while waiting for help.	0	1	2	0	1	2
			16. Produces correct schoolwork.	0	1	2	0	1	2
			17. Appropriately tells you when he or she thinks you have treated him or her unfairly.	0	1	2	0	1	2
			18. Accepts peers' ideas for group activities.	0	1	2	0	1	2
			19. Gives compliments to peers.	0	1	2	0	1	2
			20. Follows your directions.	0	1	2	0	1	2
			21. Puts work materials or school property away.	0	1	2	0	1	2
			22. Cooperates with peers without prompting.	0	1	2	0	1	2
			23. Volunteers to help peers with classroom tasks.	0	1	2	0	1	2
			24. Joins ongoing activity or group without being told to do so.	0	1	2	0	1	2
			25. Responds appropriately when pushed or hit by other children.	0	1	2	0	1	2
			26. Ignores peer distractions when doing class work.	0	1	2	0	1	2
			27. Keeps desk clean and neat without being reminded.	0	1	2	0	1	2
			28. Attends to your instructions.	0	1	2	0	1	2
			29. Easily makes transition from one classroom activity to another.	0	1	2	0	1	2
			30. Gets along with other people who are different.	0	1	2	0	1	2
C	A	S	SUMS OF How Often? COLUMNS						

SOURCE: Gresham, F. M., & Elliott, S. N. (1990). *Social skills rating system manual* (p. 22). Circle Pines, MN: American Guidance Service.

discussed. Many first selected items have to be discarded when they are found to be inadequate after other validity measures are implemented.

Other factors that affect the adequacy of assessment of children include the reactivity of the assessment procedure and the ability of the procedure to handle substantial developmental changes in children. *Reactivity* is the extent to which an assessment procedure itself alters the behavior of the subject who is being assessed (Foster, & Cone, 1986; Goldfried & Linehan, 1977; Harris & Lahey, 1982; Sattler, 1990). If an observer goes to a classroom to collect data on a child and her presence makes the child behave atypically, then we get an invalid estimate of the child's behavior. In this case, the observer may be a stranger who stands out in the class and makes the child feel uncomfortable. Similarly, if giving him a test booklet causes the child to become so anxious that he cannot perform at his best, then the information gathered by the test is an inaccurate estimate of the child's true potential. In these examples, the observer's obtrusive presence or the test booklet's intimidating presentation have altered the actual behavior of the children being assessed.

The child's developmental level can also affect the validity of an assessment measure. If a child is too young or developmentally incapable of responding to the assessment procedure (e.g., one requiring writing) then the procedure is not valid for use with the child. An example of the child's developmental level interfering with a test's construct and predictive validity is encountered in the use of some intelligence tests with very young children. Intelligence tests given to children younger than age 5 do not correlate well with measures taken when the child is older, such as re-administered intelligence tests or academic performance. This issue will be discussed more fully when intelligence tests are reviewed.

In summary, validity is a measure of systematic error in assessment which can affect a procedure's usefulness. Factors that can limit the validity of a measure include:

1. Sampling the wrong or irrelevant content area;
2. The measure's reactivity, which affects the behavior of the child being assessed;
3. The child's developmental level, which is inadequate to meet the demands of the procedure;
4. The measure's low reliability, which sets an upper limit on validity.

UTILITY

Assessment information is only valuable if it is used to make decisions concerning a behaviorally disordered child's placement and treatment. Without these decisions, the assessment process is only half accomplished. Yet, many behaviorally disordered children are extensively assessed with little thought about treatment. The last method used to judge the adequacy of an assessment technique addresses the utility of making practical decisions. The *utility* of an assessment procedure is the extent to which the assessment information is used to make a cost-effective decision (Cronbach, 1990; Hartmann, Roper, & Bradford, 1979).

In judging the practical utility of an assessment procedure, three general questions have to be answered (Wiggins, 1973):

1. What is the percentage of correct and incorrect decisions made using the assessment measure?
2. What are the values or costs associated with making a correct or incorrect decision?
3. What are the costs involved in getting the assessment information?

The importance of questions one and two are fundamental to any assessment technique. No practitioner, teacher, or parent wants to use an assessment technique that can lead to incorrect decisions. However, many assessment techniques lead to dubious decisions if they are used incorrectly or with the wrong population. The cost of an incorrect decision also varies with the type of behavior disorder. For example, making a wrong decision and not identifying an autistic child for treatment may later have dramatic implications for the child. When a condition truly exists and it is missed, then this type of error is called a *false negative*. In this example, valuable time is wasted that could have been used for early intervention.

In the opposite type of situation, an assessment technique might incorrectly identify a child has having a behavior disorder. This type of error might not be costly if the behavior disorder is a relatively minor condition such as an adjustment reaction. However, the costs can be quite dear if the behavior disorder is stigmatizing. For example, identifying culturally or racially different children as mentally retarded because they score poorly on an intelligence test can have damaging results. This type of error is called a *false positive*. The word *positive* may be a bit confusing here. It means that the assessment process has positively identified a problem when one does not exist.

The last question concerning utility is important and often overlooked. The cost of collecting the information is important for parents, insurance companies, and taxpayers that have to pay bills of assessment. If information is expensively collected and does not address treatment issues, then by definition the assessment procedure has poor utility. Accuracy in decisions and cost effectiveness are central to good utility. Inexpensive, but erroneous information is no bargain. Correct information that is extremely expensive to gather also has limited utility. Good utility is balanced on correctness of the information, its cost, and the decisions based on the information.

Methods to Reduce Assessment Error

All assessment procedures have both random and systematic error associated with each method. There are no perfect assessment measures; even assessment procedures that have excellent reliability and validity are subject to some error. A single assessment technique can lead to serious errors in assessment information. It is important to reduce this error when evaluating children with psychological disabilities because effective treatments can be delayed or mis-prescribed. There are several approaches that reduce assessment error and are best practiced with assessment techniques (Jenson & Morgan, 1990; Rhode, Jenson, Reavis, 1992). These approaches use *multiple* sources of information from several different assessment methods. When multiple sources of assessment information are used, then the error associated with any one type of measure tends to cancel or average out. In a sense, one measure helps cancel out another measure's error.

The first error reduction method uses *multiple assessment measures* or different types of assessment methods. For example, using a behavior checklist, behavioral observation, and an interviewing method averages out the error associated with any single type of measure. Like single assessment measures, single evaluators can also lead to significant error. *Multiple evaluators* using the same type of assessment instrument, are more likely to yield accurate information. One evaluator may be non-objective or biased in his or her judgments when using

an instrument. For instance, if two teachers and the child's parents have essentially the same results using the same assessment method (i.e., behavior checklist), then we can be more confident the results are real and valid. If one teacher had a very different rating from the other teacher and the parents, then that rating would be suspect. Similarly, measures across *multiple settings* (home, school, and unstructured social setting like recess) are far less prone to error than a measure taken in one setting. A classic example of an error prone measure is to have an attention-deficit disordered child (hyperactive) assessed only in the doctor's office. The child can be well behaved and sit still for a short period of time in the doctor's office, but is extremely difficult in almost all other settings.

Assessment should lead to decisions for a child, so it should be continuous and dynamic since children are constantly evolving and changing. *Multiple times* or *instances* lead to the best assessment decisions for children. Pre- and post-assessments are static assessments that tend to freeze a child in time and do not lead to flexible decision-making. A child can waste a whole year in an unproductive program if testing is only done in the fall (pre) and again in the spring (post). Good assessment procedures are employed across multiple times (hours, days, or weeks) to fine tune therapeutic interventions. Months or years is much too long of an assessment period for a fast developing child that may need many midcourse treatment corrections.

Multiple approaches substantially reduce errors associated with the assessment of children's behavior. Multiple measures, evaluators, settings, and times greatly reduce the chances of making incorrect treatment choices for children or leaving them in nonproductive therapeutic settings. However, there is a base level for extreme assessment error. If the assessment methods selected are extremely error prone and poorly designed, then multiple methods can not make up this difference and make them appropriate. In addition, multiple approaches require assessment approaches that have good utility. Each method must be cost effective and lead to practical treatment information.

PSYCHOLOGICAL TESTS

Generally when people think of assessment they think of psychological tests. These tests are used to assess characteristics ranging from a child's academic abilities to his fantasy life. In general, "a psychological test is essentially an objective and standardized measure of a sample of behavior" (Anastasi, 1988). An important aspect of this definition is the term *standardized measure*, because it indicates that explicitly defined procedures are to be employed in administering the test. Intelligence tests, academic achievement tests, and personality tests for children are all standardized so that comparisons can be made between the child not taking the test and the group of children on whom the test was first developed.

The standardization of a test can be viewed as a psychological experiment in which the conditions (procedures) are held constant so that an accurate result can be obtained. Holding the testing conditions constant generally means that:

1. The same items or test questions are given in the same order to all subjects;
2. The same test instructions are given to all subjects in an identical fashion;
3. All subjects have the same amount of time to finish the test;
4. The testing environment is held relatively constant and free from noise and distraction for all subjects. (Korchin, 1976)

If these conditions are met, then the results obtained from the standardization group define what is normal for other children, and these results are commonly referred to as testing "norms" (see Box 13-1). The distribution of test scores are generally across a bell-shaped "normal curve" with the average score in the middle of the curve and the two tails or ends representing extreme scores. The simplicity of the normal curve concept has led to considerable controversy when intelligence and class structure are compared on the curve, as in the book, *The Bell Curve* (Frisby, 1995; Herrnstein & Murry, 1994).

To make valid comparisons, groups of children included in the standardization sample should generally resemble those who will be tested later. The sample should reflect the characteristics of the population of children with whom the test will be used routinely. For example, the standardization group should be of the appropriate age, developmental level, ethnic background, socioeconomic level, and geographical distribution (Anastasi, 1988).

What Tests Measure

Our definition of a psychological test includes the idea that a person's behavior is sampled. This definition emphasizes the fact that some type of behavior, whether it is academic performance, intellectual ability, or abnormal behavior, is directly sampled or observed in a specific situation. Once the sample has been collected or the observation has been made in a situation, then comparisons to standardized norms can be made to determine the child's abilities and deficiencies.

There are alternative views to the "sample-situation approach," which proposes that psychological tests measure *traits* and *states* (this view is described but not advocated by Mischel, 1993). The trait view holds that test scores are signs of underlying traits that govern behavior. These traits are assumed to be stable across time and situations. In a sense, a trait is a shorthand method of describing a child's personality or behavior. Trait words are ingrained in our everyday language and are used to describe a child's behavior irrespective of his immediate surroundings or history. For example, a child might be labeled lazy, outgoing (extroversion), shy (introversion), or dependent.

There is no simple answer to the trait versus sample-situation approach to psychological assessment (Ozer, 1986). Some theorists believe that behavioral stability varies across situations according to the individual assessed (Bem & Allen, 1974). Others feel that if averages from several people are used to determine a trait, then important sources of individual differences are lost (Mischel, 1993). Single test measures of a trait have generally had poor reliability and validity across situations (Mischel, 1968). However, multiple measures of a trait over several situations and times improve the reliability and validity of a trait measure (Epstein, 1979). For example, a single test that reports a child as being an "aggressive type" would probably have poor reliability. However, several confirming measures that include the test score, a teacher interview, and an observation of the child in school would be far more reliable and valid. This approach is similar to the reasons given above for multiple measures in assessment.

Possibly the best approach to a trait versus situation-sample controversy is the compromise position of the *interactionalists* (Bowers, 1973; Ekenhammer, 1974) who believe that behavior is a product of both the person

---

BOX 13-1 THE NORMAL CURVE AND ASSESSMENT

The *normal curve* is a mathematical concept that allows meaningful comparisons of different assessment scores. An example of the normal or "bell"-shaped curve is given in Figure 13-1. Actually, this curve is a representation of many scores; some are high, some are low, but most of them are average. The *average* or *mean score* is represented on the curve by the X. The hump at the average indicates that most scores are average or near-average. As we get to the extreme scores (at the ends of the curve), the curve gets flatter, indicating that there are fewer scores in these ranges. The SDs on the curve are *standard deviation markers*. A standard deviation is a statistical measure of variability on the curve. It is also an indicator of the percentage of scores that fall within the standard deviation markers. For example, approximately 68 percent of all the scores are within 1 standard deviation up and 1 standard deviation down from the mean. Also, standard deviations can be measured from the ends of the curve. For example, 97.7 percent of all the scores fall on or below the +2 SD mark on the curve.

FIGURE 13-1 Normal curve with T and Z scores

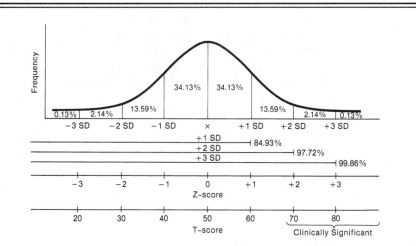

The normal curve is important for assessment because it allows a psychologist to make meaningful judgments about how average or different a particular score might be. If a score is average, we know that approximately 50 percent of all the other scores are above and 50 percent are below the average score. In a sense, the average score is right in the middle of the distribution. Also, if a score is +2 SD from the mean, it is in the range that many psychological tests and checklists describe as "clinically different." For instance, if a score on the hyperactivity factor of the Achenbach Child Behavior Profile is +2 SD from the mean, then the score is considered clinically significant. This is because 98 percent of all the other children in the standardization group fell on or below this mark. Only 2 percent (a very small number) of the children in this group were above the +2 SD mark. This 2 percent would have been the very hyperactive children.

There are also several different types of standard scores that are used in assessment. A T-score has a mean of 50 and a standard deviation of 10. A Z-score has a mean of 0 and a standard deviation of 1. These scores are important because such tests as the Personality Inventory for Children (PIC) and the Achenbach Child Behavior Profile use T-scores in measuring a child's performance on the normal curve. These tests are discussed in detail later in this chapter.

(traits) and the situation. According to this view, people do have traits that govern their behavior; however, situations are always exerting strong effects that can influence and affect traits. For assessment purposes, the interac-

tionalists value multiple measures of traits and the recognition of the powerful effects of environmental situations on behavior. One important factor particularly in the assessment is the interaction or relationship between the tester (evaluator) and the testee (child) (Miller, 1994). An impersonal, demanding evaluator may get dramatically different results in comparison to a caring evaluator who is willing to take the time and establish a relationship with the child. Even though both evaluators follow the same standardization procedures, the testing relationship can powerfully affect the assessment outcome (Dahlstrom, 1993).

Intelligence Tests

When the term "psychological test" is mentioned, many individuals think of intelligence tests with their accompanying complex tasks, questions, and puzzles. These tests were originally designed as a series of complex problems to screen children for academic readiness. In 1905, Alfred Binet was appointed by the French Ministry of Public Instruction to design an intelligence test consisting of 30 subtests containing problems of increasing difficulty, which were designed to measure children's judgment, reasoning, and comprehension (Anastasi, 1988; Sattler, 1990). The original 1905 version of Binet's test was developed by administering the test problems to normal children as well as to mentally retarded children and adults. What made Binet's work unique was the development of norms so that comparisons could be made between disabled and nondisabled children (Sattler, 1990).

Shortly after Binet's original work, L. M. Terman in 1916 helped refine and standardize the test on American children. Terman and others (Stern, 1914) developed the idea of the IQ or intelligence quotient for use in comparing the relative intelligence of children at different ages. To calculate an IQ, a child's mental age (as determined by how well he does on the test) is divided by his chronological age and multiplied by 100 (IQ = MA/CA × 100). For example, if a child scores on the test at the 76 month level (mental age) and is 8 years old (chronological age is thus 96 months), then his IQ would be 80 = 76/96 × 100. The average child has a mental age approximately equal to his chronological age, and so has an IQ of approximately 100 (i.e., IQ 100 = 96 months mental age/96 months chronological age × 100).

Since the Binet intelligence test was first devised, many types of intelligence tests for children have been developed (see Table 13-4). One of the most frequently used children's intelligence tests is the Wechsler Intelligence

---

TABLE 13-4 TYPES OF CHILDREN'S INTELLIGENCE TESTS

Wechsler Intelligence Scale for Children-III (WISC-III): This is one of the best intelligence tests for children through adolescence (6–16 years). It contains both a verbal and nonverbal performance component and yields a Verbal IQ, a Performance IQ, and a Full Scale IQ. Excellent reliability and validity characteristics.

Wechsler Preschool and Primary Scale of Intelligence-Revised (WPPSI-R): This test is similar to the WISC-III except that it is used with younger children (3–7). It also yields a Verbal IQ, Performance IQ, and a Full Scale IQ. Excellent reliability and validity characteristics. The WPPSI is currently under revision.

Stanford Binet Intelligence Test-Fourth Edition (SB-4th): This test is an outgrowth of Binet's early work with intelligence. It has been revised several times with the newest revision done in 1986. It yields a global measure of intelligence and can be used with children from ages 2–12. Excellent reliability and validity.

Leiter International Performance Scale (LIPS): This is a nonverbal intelligence test that is useful for individuals that cannot talk. The test is a series of puzzles based on small blocks. The test can be used with 2-year-old children up to adults. This test has been criticized because the norms are outdated and the standardization is inadequate. This test should be used with children only when other verbally based intelligence tests cannot be used.

Kaufman Assessment Battery for Children (K-ABC): This intelligence test is designed for children ages 2–12. It assesses two types of intellectual processing, simultaneous processing and successive processing. This test has excellent reliability and validity characteristics but more research is needed to determine if it adds any useful information that the WISC-III or Binet miss.

Scale for Children-Revised (WISC-III). A basic advantage of the WISC-III is that it combines both verbal subscales and performance or motor subscales in assessing a child's intellectual ability (see Table 13-5). The WISC-III thus yields an overall intelligence score, plus separate verbal and performance IQ scores that can be useful in assessing children who are more proficient in one area than the other.

Both the Stanford-Binet Fourth Edition and WISC-III are popular intelligence tests for children and both have good reliability characteristics. However, there is a great deal of controversy over the construct validity of intelligence tests. Or, exactly what is intelligence.

Binet (Binet & Simon, 1905), the originator of the intelligence test, considered intelligence to be a set of abil-

TABLE 13-5 DESCRIPTIONS OF THE WISC-III SUBTESTS

Subtest	Description
Picture completion	A set of colorful pictures of common objects and scenes each of which is missing an important part which the child identifies.
Information	A series of orally presented questions that tap the child's knowledge about common events, objects, places, and people.
Coding	A series of simple shapes (Coding A) or numbers (Coding B), each paired with a simple symbol. The child draws the symbol in its corresponding shape (Coding A) or under its corresponding number (Coding B), according to a key. Coding A and B are included on a single perforated sheet in the Record Form.
Similarities	A series of orally presented pairs of words for which the child explains the similarity of the common objects or concepts they represent.
Picture arrangement	A set of colorful pictures, presented in mixed-up order, which the child rearranges into a logical story sequence.
Arithmetic	A series of arithmetic problems which the child solves mentally and responds to orally.
Block design	A set of modeled or printed two-dimensional geometric patterns that the child replicates using two-color cubes.
Vocabulary	A series of orally presented words that the child orally defines.
Object assembly	A set of puzzles of common objects, each presented in a standardized configuration, which the child assembles to form a meaningful whole.
Comprehension	A series of orally presented questions that require the child's solving of everyday problems or understanding of social rules and concepts.
Symbol search	A series of paired groups of symbols, each pair consisting of a target group and a search group. The child scans the two groups and indicates whether or not a target symbol appears in the search group. Both levels of the subtest are included in a single response booklet.
Digit span	A series of orally presented number sequences that the child repeats verbatim for Digits Forward and in reverse order for Digits Backwards.
Mazes	A set of increasingly difficult mazes, printed in a response booklet, which the child solves with a pencil.

SOURCE: Wechsler, D. (1991). *WISC-III manual.* San Antonio, TX: Harcourt, Brace, Jovanovich.

ities which include comprehension, reasoning, judgment, and the ability to adapt. Wechsler (1958) has similarly defined intelligence to be a set of abilities which include the capacity "to act purposefully, to think rationally, and to deal effectively with the environment." Frequently, this ability has been described as the "g" factor or general ability factor, which has its origins in John Galton's (1869) pioneering work in measuring individual sensory and motor differences. Spearman (1927) refined the concept of the "g" factor to mean basic mental energy with complex mental tasks as containing the greatest amount of "g".

However, there may be a problem in assuming intelligence is an entity that exists inside a child. All of the above definitions and the concept of the "g" intelligence factor rely on indirect measures of intelligence by sampling selected behaviors under controlled conditions. In essence, intelligence is inferred from behaviors sampled under strict environmental stimulus conditions:

No one, however, has seen a thing called intelligence. Rather, we observe differences in the ways people behave—either difference in everyday behavior in a variety of situations or differences in responses to standard stimuli or sets of stimuli; then we infer a construct called intelligence. In this sense, intelligence is an inferred entity, a term or construct we use to explain differences in present behavior and to predict differences in future behavior. (Salvia & Ysseldyke, 1991, p. 161)

The "predicted differences" depend upon what intelligence tests sample and measure, and these tests primarily measure (1) *verbal ability*, which is associated with general information and language acquired at home, and a general factor of (2) *perceptual* and *performance* ability associated with reasoning, problem-solving, and comprehension. Other factors that may be measured by intelligence tests include the ability to attend to a task, numerical reasoning, recall, and memory. Since all of these

Even with an adult examiner of the same ethnic group, individual IQ testing can be intimidating for children.

abilities are particularly important in school settings, intelligence tests are good at predicting success in schools (Aiken 1979; Anastasi, 1988; Hallahan & Kaufmann, 1986). Jensen (1980) believes that two basic components are measures by intelligence tests. First, is an *associative ability* that involves rote memory and short-term memory. The second, *cognitive ability*, involves reasoning, problem-solving, and the ability to successfully grapple with complexity.

The standardized intelligence tests for school-age children are not always applicable to preschool children. The reason is that assessment of infants and preschoolers differs from the assessment of older children in several ways. The younger children tend to be less motivated, more distractible, and have less sophisticated verbal skills than older children. Most infant and preschool-based intelligence tests measure motor ability and developing social behavior. The results from intelligence tests for very young children and infants correlate poorly with the children's later intellectual ability at school age (Bayley, 1970; Lewis, 1973; McCall, Hogarty, & Hurlburt, 1972; Thomas, 1970). Infant intelligence tests such as the Cattell Infant Intelligence Scale or the Bayley Infant Scales

best predict conditions associated with neurological abnormalities or developmental disorders. Infant and preschool tests are limited, however, in predicting later school performance or behavior disorders.

While intelligence scores are fairly good predictors of school achievement for older children, the exact relationship between intelligence test results and childhood behavior disorders is less clear. There appears to be a direct link between later adjustment (prognosis) and a child's IQ score for the conditions of mental retardation (Ando & Yoshimura, 1970) and infantile autism (DeMyer, Hingtgen, & Jackson, 1981; Rutter, 1978). The lower the IQ score, the poorer the prognosis for these conditions. For conduct disordered and attention-deficit disordered children, the relationship with intelligence is less clear. Kaufmann (1985) in his review of behaviorally disordered children, found that these children tended to score in the dull to normal range. Sattler (1990) has reported that on average, delinquents have higher scores on the performance IQ than on the verbal IQ for the Weschler Intelligence Tests. However, this difference is not consistent enough to be a diagnostic sign for delinquency (Sattler, 1990). Weiss and Hechtman (1993) have reviewed a series of studies and reported that IQ can be an important variable in predicting academic success and adult outcome for attention-deficit disordered children, particularly when combined with other factors such as socioeconomic status, presence of learning disabilities, and family conditions. However, intelligence tests or specific subtests such as the "freedom from distractibility factor" from the WISC-R or WISC-III should not be used to make a diagnosis of attention-deficit disorder.

> *"I do not recommend that this factor be used in assessing attention or in establishing evidence for or against the diagnosis of ADHD." (Barkley, 1990, p. 331)*

The links between IQ and other childhood disorders such as suicide (Pfeffer, 1986) or anxiety disorders (Gittelman, 1986) are less robust.

Possibly the greatest failure and controversy surrounding the use of intelligence tests have been their use with children from diverse cultures. This is particularly true of children who use English as their second language in their homes. Sattler (1990) suggests, "I believe that standardized intelligence and special abilities tests should be used but only with recognition of their shortcomings and difficulties when applied to the evaluation of children from ethnic minority groups" (p. 592). These shortcomings include the inability of many intelligence tests to accommodate different response styles of culturally diverse children, the use of standardized norms that are based primarily on Caucasian children, bilingualism that may affect the verbal scores, poverty, and the distrust of many subcultures of the dominant culture. When these issues are ignored, abuses occur which result in the disproportionate diagnosis and placement of Hispanic, Native American, African-American, and Asian children as disabled when they are not (Chinn & Hughes, 1987; Dunn, 1968; Mercer, 1973; Reid, 1995).

In summary, standardized intelligence tests have good test-retest reliability and interrater reliability. For construct validity, there are some disagreements; however, for predictive validity, intelligence tests have value in forecasting for school-age children later academic achievement and adjustment. The diagnostic utility of intelligence tests is also limited, particularly by cultural differences. Clearly, intellectual assessment is important in diagnosing mental retardation and infantile autism, both in defining the severity of the condition and in estimating the child's prognosis and future outcome. For other types of behavior disorders, intelligence tests are less useful. For very young children, intelligence tests are best at uncovering developmental delays and have limited predictive validity for school performance or the development of behavior disorders. Intelligence tests have virtually *no* utility by themselves in identifying behaviorally disordered children. Characteristics such as subtest patterning (specific patterns of subtests) or the difference between verbal and performance IQ scores are not reliable or valid in identifying behaviorally disordered children (Mark, 1986; Sattler, 1990). Similarly, using a single intelligence measure to establish the diagnosis of intellectual disability or mental retardation is too error prone. Intelligence tests should only be used in conjunction with other assessment measures that are culturally sensitive in making the determination of intellectual disability (Sattler, 1990).

Projective Tests

Projective techniques are very different from standardized intelligence tests. The latter are based on standardized groups and permit users to make comparisons among children. Most projective tests are not based on rigorous standardization procedures, but stem from the *projective hypothesis* (Anastasi, 1988; Sundberg, 1977). The projective hypothesis contains the assumption that a child is driven by underlying psychological forces such as sexual and aggressive urges. These urges emerge early in a child's development and are affected by family interactions. For some children, these underlying forces can be so disturbing that they are blocked from consciousness by repression and denial. To attempt to reveal the unconscious urges, projective techniques employ ambiguous or open-ended stimuli on which the child has to project meaning and structure and thus, in an indirect way, reveal unconscious conflicts.

> *A major distinguishing feature of projective techniques is to be found in their assignment of a relatively unstructured task, i.e., a task that permits an almost unlimited variety of responses. In order to allow free play to the individual's fantasy, only brief general instructions are provided. For the same reason, the test stimuli are usually vague or ambiguous. The underlying hypothesis is that the way in which the individual perceives and interprets material, or "structures" the situation, will reflect fundamental aspects of her or his psychological functioning. In other words, it is expected that the test materials will serve*

FIGURE 13-2 An inkblot used in the Rorschach Test

SOURCE: Rorschach, H. (1948). *Psychodiagnostics: A diagnostic test based on perception* (4th ed.). New York: Grune & Stratton. Reprinted by permission.

as a sort of screen on which respondents "project" their characteristic thought processes, needs, anxieties, and conflicts. (Anastasi, 1988, pp 594–595)

The projective testing hypothesis is based primarily on psychoanalytic assumptions regarding children's behavior (Knoff, Batsche, & Carlyon, 1993). Pathological trait and underlying emotional forces are supposedly revealed by deviant responses to the ambiguous projective stimuli. The assessment of direct samples of behavior collected under standardized testing conditions is de-emphasized as revealing only shallow surface symptoms.

Projective techniques can be categorized into five basic groups (Lindzey, 1959, 1961):

1. *Association techniques*: A child is asked to tell what he sees in a set of materials (such as inkblots) or to give the first word that comes into his mind after the therapist says a word (word association).
2. *Construction techniques*: In this approach a child is asked to create a product such as a story after she has seen some test materials (e.g., in the Thematic Apperception Test the child makes up a story to accompany a set of pictures).
3. *Completion techniques*: A child is asked to complete a statement or brief story (sentence completion test).
4. *Choice of ordering technique*: A child is asked to rank a set of materials in order of preference (e.g., to indicate which of a set of picture activities would be most enjoyable).
5. *Expressive techniques*: A child is asked to create a product of his own choice (e.g., play in sand or finger painting).

The association and construction techniques are the most frequently used with children, such as the Rorschach Ink-

TABLE 13-6 INTERPRETATION OF DATA FROM THE RORSCHACH TEST FOR CHILDREN AND ADULTS

Response to Cards	Interpretation
Blood content followed by evasion:	Hostile impulses defended against by avoidance, resentful passive compliance or withdrawal
Color naming, cool colors:	Depressive trend which is defended against
Color denial and avoidance:	Withdrawal tendency
Body mutilation:	Fantasies or fears
Smoke:	Children with average or above average intelligence; apprehension, depression, social maladjustment
Gums and teeth:	Aggressive response to frustrated dependency needs; more common in adolescents and children; resentfulness
Completely unmodified, unqualified terse responses:	Children; organics; people in trouble with the law; persons resistant to social pressure

SOURCE: Gilbert, J. (1978). *Interpreting psychological test data.* New York: Van Nostrand Reinhold. Reprinted by permission of publisher. Copyright © 1975 by Van Nostrand Reinhold.

blot Test (1921) (see Figure 13-2) and the Thematic Apperception Test (Murray, 1943). The Rorschach Inkblot Test was first developed in Germany for use primarily with adults, but it also has been widely used with children (Halpren, 1953). The test consists of 10 cards with symmetrical inkblots, half are black and white and half are colored. The cards are shown to the child one at a time in a set order and the child is asked what each inkblot represents (free association stage). Later, more detailed information is gathered by asking the child to justify his responses and to describe them in more detail (inquiry stage). There are several ways to score Rorschach responses (Exner, 1969, 1974) and Table 13-6 lists a number of interpretations based on responses to the cards.

The Thematic Apperception Test (TAT) is second only to the Rorschach both in clinical usage and published studies (Korchin, 1976; O'Leary & Johnson, 1979). The TAT is a constructive projective technique in which 20 to 30 cards (such as the one depicted in Figure 13-3) are shown to a child; each card consists of a drawing or

FIGURE 13-3   A sample picture from the Thematic Apperception Test

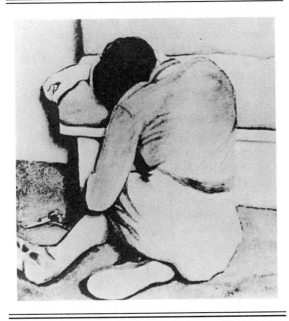

SOURCE: Murray, H. A. (1943). *Thematic Apperception Test manual.* Cambridge, MA: Harvard University Press. Reprinted by permission.

fantasy scene. After a card is shown, the child is then asked to make up a story about the picture. The child's stories are tape-recorded or written. After a sufficient number of cards have been shown (the number may vary from clinician to clinician) the results are interpreted. The interpretation generally includes major elements of the story such as the choice of a hero, the needs and qualities of the hero, the basic themes of the story, the emotional tone, and the general outcome of the story. In clinical practice, there is no universally accepted method for scoring the TAT cards.

A similar technique to the TAT is the Children's Apperception Test (Bellak, 1954) or the CAT. This technique is used with younger children (ages 3 to 10) and is based on the pictures of animals instead of adults. The pictures depict scenes that are designed to elicit response on sibling rivalry, attitudes toward parents, aggression, feeding problems, toileting behavior, acceptance, and loneliness. It is assumed that young children relate more easily to animals than to adults.

One of the most popular projective techniques for use with children is the Draw a Person or Human Figure

FIGURE 13-4   Koppitz's Example of Human Figure Drawing

SOURCE: Koppitz, E. M. (1968). *Psychological evaluation of children's Human Figure Drawings.* New York: Grune & Stratton.

Drawing technique (Goh & Fuller, 1983; Prout, 1983; Wilson & Reschly, 1996). With this test, a child is asked to draw a human figure and, through the drawing, reveals emotional difficulties. Figure 13-4 gives a Human Figure Drawing example from a 9-year-old boy who was having emotional difficulties with anger, poor school achievement, and hostility towards his father. It is assumed that the picture is a representation of Juan's father who was authoritarian and punitive. The emotional indicators from the picture were "crossed eyes and teeth reveal hostile and aggressive attitudes, while the arms show rigid self-control and difficulty in making contact with others" (Koppitz, 1968). The basic appeal of drawing human figures is that drawing is generally a nonthreatening and enjoyable task for a child. From this test, inferences have been drawn concerning emotional problems, indicators of intelligence, and predictions concerning academic achievement (Bardos, 1993; Holtzman, 1993; Naglieri, 1993).

BOX 13-2   PERSONALITY INVENTORY FOR CHILDREN (PIC) ANALYSIS OF A HYPERACTIVE CHILD

FIGURE 13-5   Profile study: Hyperactivity

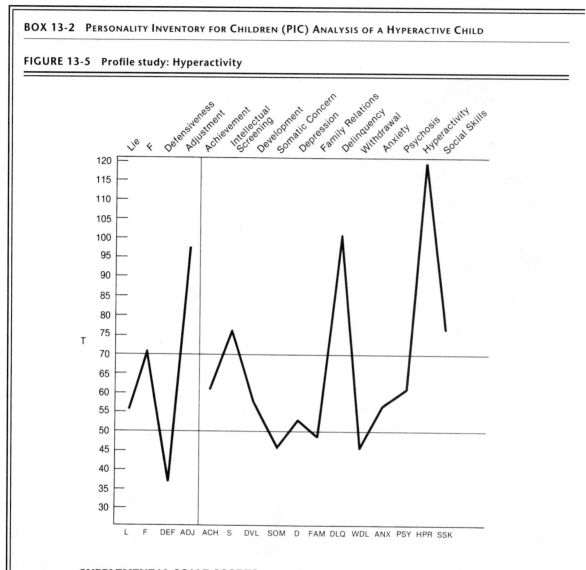

SUPPLEMENTAL SCALE SCORES

	AGM	AGN	ASO	CDY	DP	EGO	EXC	EXT	INT
Raw Score	29	12	21	22	26	30	10	27	9
T-score	79	88	91	41	101	28	69	88	58
	INF	I-E	K	LDP	RDS	SR	SD	SM	
Raw Score	1	35	11	29	8	19	14	9	
T-score	61	72	23	60	69	40	20	51	

PRESENTING CLINICAL PROBLEM

This 9-year-old boy was referred to the clinic by his pediatrician because he was very overactive and a serious behavior problem at school.

Box 13-2 *(continued)*

PROFILE ANALYSIS

1. *Profile interpretability*

   The validity scales indicate the profile [see Figure 13-5] to be interpretable, though the very high ADJ suggests the respondent sees the child to be quite disturbed.

2. *Response styles tendencies*

   The mother is expressing a moderate degree of distress surrounding the clinical problem (F, ADJ) and the somewhat elevated F may indicate that she selectively perceives and reacts to the negative aspect of the child's behavior, thereby supporting its reoccurrence. At the same time, this mother would appear to be open and verbally accessible, suggesting a favorable response to clinical intervention (DEF).

3. *Emotional disturbances*

   The elevated Adjustment Scale (ADJ) clearly indicates the presence of emotional disturbance.

4. *Linear scanning*

   The Achievement Scale (ACH) is elevated above its cutting score and the poor Development Scale (DVL) is borderline, suggesting mild academic problems. However, the profile peaks on the Delinquency (DLQ) and Hyperactivity (HPR) scales, indicating disruptive hyperactivity and conduct problems, both of which stand out clearly in the clinical picture.

   There are moderate elevations on Development (DVL) and the Supplemental Scales, Reality Distortion (RDS) and Excitement (EXC), and considerable elevation on Social Skills (SSK) and the Supplemental Scales of Aggression (AGN) and Asocial Behavior (ASO). These data suggest that both further pediatric neurological and neuropsychological studies be conducted.

   The boy's mother was involved in a car accident while she was still pregnant. The boy was born three weeks premature. Apparently, the boy was hard to manage since early childhood. Following the death of his mother from cancer when he was five years old, his maternal grandmother cared for him, making little effort to manage him. He was described by the clinic psychologist as having temper tantrums, sleeping problems, and bad dreams, and as showing a very high activity level "even when watching television and doing other favored activities." The PIC was administered at this time.

   The pediatrician had been treating the child with Ritalin for five months after the PIC was administered, at which time the staff psychiatrist reported that the medicine had "been helping him to remain calmer and perform better in school." School staff and the psychiatrist thought the medicine had reduced the boy's activity level to within normal limits. He could sit still in a chair for about ten minutes. However, he took money from his parents three times, and chewing gum from a store during the five-month period. The behavior problem had not been reduced. The father had remarried during the past year, and both parents were seen as sincerely desiring to work together with their child on these problems.

5. *Group profile comparison*

   The profile configuration of this study is similar in topography to that of the group profile for hyperactive boys. The DLQ and HPR scales are much more elevated than in the group profile. The similarity suggests that this boy will appear behaviorally similar to that of boys diagnosed as hyperactive.

6. *Supplemental scale/critical item inspection*

   The supplemental scales do not add to this profile interpretation. The critical items convey the volatile nature of the boy's behavior.

   Sample critical items:

   My child has had to have drugs to relax. (T)

   My child seems to enjoy destroying things. (T)

   The school says my child needs help in getting along with other children. (T)

   At times, my child scratches his (her) face until it bleeds. (T)

   My child has been in trouble for attacking others. (T)

   My child smashes things when angry. (T)

   The child's mother frequently has crying spells. (T)

   School teachers complain that my child can't sit still. (T)

   My child was a premature or overdue baby. (T)

   Neither parent has ever been mentally ill. (F)

SOURCE: Wirt, R. D., Lachar, D., Klinedinst, J. K., & Seat, P. D. (1977). *Multidimensional description of child personality: Manual for the personality inventory for children* (pp. 56–57). Los Angeles: Western Psychological Services. Reprinted by permission.

Although projective techniques have been extremely popular, their usefulness with behaviorally disordered children has been repeatedly criticized. Since by definition (projective hypothesis) the stimuli associated with these tests have to be ambiguous, their reliability is generally low. Even the validity of the projective hypothesis itself has been criticized (Anastasi, 1988; Epstein, 1966). Anastasi (1988) regards projective techniques as "clinical tools" and not psychological tests because they do not measure up to acceptable psychometric standards of basic reliability and validity. Similarly, research reviews of projective techniques and their use with behaviorally disordered children have questioned their utility (French, Graves, & Levitt, 1983; Gittelman-Klein, 1978). One leading researcher (Gittelman-Klein, 1978, 1980) has stated concerning projective techniques: "Sometimes they tell us poorly something we already know." The Human Figure Drawing (HFD) has come under particular criticism recently. It has been criticized for having little if any predictive, construct, or concurrent validity and yet it continues to be popularly used (Motta, Little, & Tobin, 1993). In an even stronger statement, Gresham (1993) has stated;

> "The HFD represents an assessment technique whose time has passed. It has questionable psychometric properties and the potential for more abuse than appropriate use in making decisions for children." p. 185

However, even with these criticisms, projective techniques remain some of the most popular methods for assessing children, particularly in the schools (Wilson & Reschly, 1996).

Child Personality Tests

Personality inventory tests are trait measures that consist of hundreds of questions. Several questions correlated or cluster with one another and thus form an indication of a trait. For example, 50 questions from a 600-question personality inventory may statistically interrelate with each other forming a description of a trait such as hyperactivity. All personality inventories are given under standardized conditions with a normed comparison group. In a sense, they are the opposite of projective techniques in their standardization and normative properties. The most frequently used personality tests are the Cali-

TABLE 13-7 THE SCALES OF THE PERSONALITY INVENTORY FOR CHILDREN

Scale Name	Abbreviation
Validity and screening scales	
Lie	L
F	F
Defensiveness	DEF
Adjustment	ADJ
Clinical scales	
Achievement	ACH
Intellectual Screening	IS
Development	DVL
Somatic Concern	SOM
Depression	D
Family Relations	FAM
Delinquency	DLQ
Withdrawal	WDL
Anxiety	ANX
Psychosis	PSY
Hyperactivity	HPR
Social Skills	SSK

SOURCE: Wirt, R. D., Lachar, D., Klinedinst, J. K., & Seat, P. D. (1977). *Multidimensional description of child personality: Manual for the Personality Inventory for Children* (p. 9). Los Angeles: Western Psychological Services. Reprinted by permission.

fornia Psychological Inventory, and the Minnesota Multiphasic Personality Inventory (MMPI-II), the Jessness Personality Inventory, and the Personality Inventory for Children (PIC).

One of the most comprehensive personality inventories for children is the PIC (Lachar, 1982; Wirt, Lachar, Klinedinst, & Seat, 1977). This test consists of 600 Yes and No questions that a parent fills out in relation to their child. The test is then scored and the individual scores are transposed to a profile sheet (see example Box 13-2). The profile sheet consists of several factors or traits (i.e., hyperactivity, social skills, social withdrawal; see Table 13-7) and allows comparison to the standardization group of nondisabled children. For example, the average score for a nondisabled child on any factor of the PIC profile sheet is T-50, and a clinically significant score for most factors is T-70 (two standard deviations from the mean, see Box 13-1 on Normal Curve). This test is also unique in that it gives a series of validity scales describing the informant's (parent's) response characteristics (DEF = defensive, L = lying, F = symptom exaggeration). In addition, there are overall adjustment (ADJ), achieve-

FIGURE 13-6 Woodcock-Johnson Profile

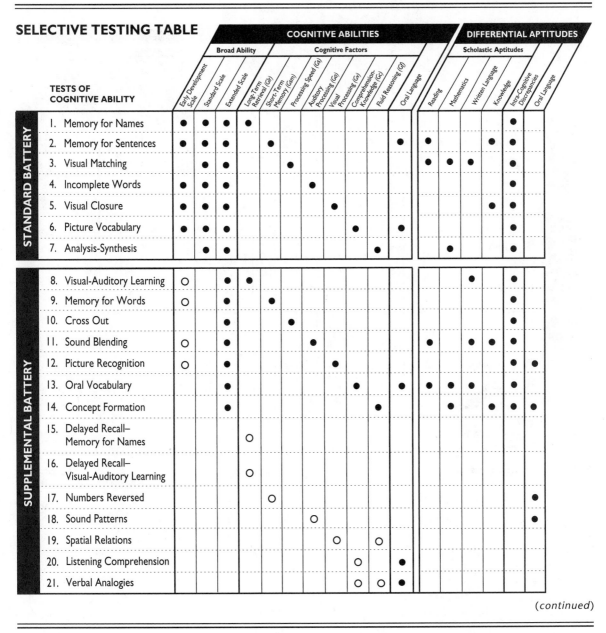

(continued)

ment (ACH), intellectual screening (IS), developmental (DVL), and family stability (FAM) scales. An example of how a PIC profile is interpreted for a hyperactive boy is given in Box 13-2.

The reliability of subscales within most personality inventories ranges from adequate for some subscales to poor for others. The reliabilities for the subscales of the PIC are good with the test-retest reliability scores for the 16 profile scales averaging a correlation of .86 (Wirt, Lachar, Klinedinst, & Seat, 1977). Although, some scales such as the defensiveness scales had marginal reliabilities. Similarly, concurrent validity for the clinical factors when

FIGURE 13-6 (*continued*)

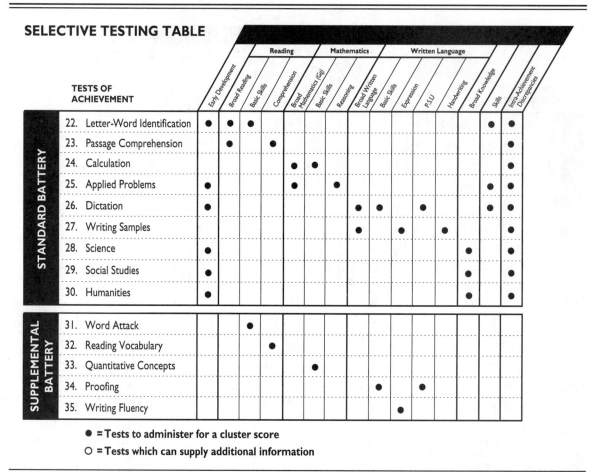

SELECTIVE TESTING TABLE

● = Tests to administer for a cluster score
○ = Tests which can supply additional information

SOURCE: Reprinted from the *Woodcock-Johnson Tests of Cognitive Ability—Standard and Supplemental Batteries Examiner's Manual.* (Woodcock & Mather, 1989a, p. 12). Used with permission of DLM.

compared to independent ratings of parents, teachers, and clinicians was good. However, trait-based personality assessments of children that rely on a single measure predict poorly across different situations and times. To demonstrate good predictive validity, multiple measurements of a trait (Epstein, 1979) should be taken and the effects of situational variables in the environment should be taken in account (Mischel, 1993). Very few personality inventories for children currently meet these two requirements.

Educational Tests

Most of the prestige and publicity of testing goes to psychological testing, however, most of the actual testing

done with children is academic or educational. The importance of educational ability and its relationship to successfully treating behaviorally disordered children is critical. Researchers have found high correlations with academic deficiencies and conduct disorders (Hinshaw, 1992; Rutter & Yule, 1978) and hyperactivity (Barkley, 1990; Weiss & Hechtman, 1993). If academic deficits are ignored and not assessed for behaviorally disordered children, then most long-term therapeutic gains often will fail.

The most frequently administered educational tests are standardized achievement tests. Basic achievement tests such as the Peabody Individual Achievement Test-Revised (PIAT-R), Stanford Achievement Tests (SAT), California Achievement Test (CAT), Metropolitan

Achievement Test (MAT), the Wide Range Achievement Test-Revised (WRAT-R) and the Woodcock-Johnson Psychoeducational Battery-Revised assess basic academic skills such as reading, mathematics, spelling, and general information (see Figure 13-6). Standardized achievement tests in effect, "... estimate the extent to which an individual has acquired the skills and concepts that other students of the same age have acquired" (Salvia & Ysseldyke, 1991, p. 337). The tests are *norm referenced* because they compare an individual child to the standardized comparison norms of a group (Glaser, 1963). Norm referenced achievement tests emphasize an individual's relative standing compared to the group on which the test was standardized. For example, a norm referenced achievement test might indicate that an individual third-grade child is below average (as determined by the standardization group) in reading and spelling but on grade level for mathematics.

A different type of educational test, *criterion referenced*, provides a great deal of information about individual deficiencies. Criterion referenced tests measure the absolute mastery a child has over a specific skill area or behavior (Glaser, 1963). A child is compared to a specific standard or criterion, not a comparison group. This objectively defined standard is called a domain which consists of subskills that increase in difficulty from simple to complex (Gronlund, 1993). Table 13-8 presents an example of social speech objectives (a set of reference criteria) from the Brigance Diagnostic Inventory of Early Development (Brigance, 1978). In this example, the first step in social language is to point, gesture, or indicate needs verbally. The most complex step to be measured is taking a message from the phone and delivering it to the right person. The child's score is determined by the number of speech skills she can demonstrate.

Both standardized achievement tests and criterion referenced tests have been praised and criticized for a variety of reasons. The content validity of standardized achievement tests have been criticized because of the poor overlap between the items on the test and what is actually taught in the classroom (Good & Salvia, 1988; Jenkins & Pany, 1978). In addition, standardized achievement tests have been criticized because they yield a composite or average score and do not give information about specific deficiencies that need remediation (Shapiro, 1989).

Similarly, criterion referenced tests have been criticized because it is difficult to get agreement from educators about essential educational objectives and which

TABLE 13-8	SOCIAL SPEECH OBJECTIVES FROM THE BRIGANCE INVENTORY OF EARLY DEVELOPMENT

OBJECTIVES: By (*date*), when in the appropriate situation, (*child's name*) will . . . (add as appropriate)

1. point, gesture, or verbalize wants and needs.	10. make verbal greeting (e.g., "Hi").
2. respond appropriately when asked a simple "yes" or "no" question.	11. acknowledge compliments or thanks.
3. call at least ____ persons by name.	12. say "Excuse me" when disturbing or interrupting.
4. ask for food by name at the table.	13. participate in a conversation without monopolizing it.
5. verbalize toilet needs.	14. answer the phone and summon the person requested.
6. respond appropriately when asked a question involving two or more choices.	15. deliver a two-part oral message.
7. say "thank you" and "please" appropriately and without being reminded.	16. answer the phone, take a simple message, and deliver the message to the right person.
8. deliver a simple message.	
9. show an interest in the conversation of others.	

SOURCE: Brigance, A. H. (1978). *Brigance Diagnostic Inventory of Early Development* (p. 130). North Billerica, MA: Curriculum Associates. Copyright 1978 by Curriculum Associates, Inc. Reprinted by permission.

are necessary for complete mastery (Ebel, 1971; Lidz, 1979). "They (criterion referenced tests) require a degree of detail in the specification of objectives or outcomes that is quite unrealistic to expect and impractical to use, except at the most elementary level of education" (Ebel, 1971). As the complexity of the academic skill area increases, the content sampling which ensures good content validity becomes more difficult. In addition, the reliability measures for criterion reference test items are limited for specific items and subtests (Salvia & Ysseldyke, 1991; Shapiro & Lentz, 1986).

However, even with their difficulties, standardized achievement tests and criterion based tests are necessary in assessing most behaviorally disordered children. Again, the combination or use of multiple academic measures is the best in compensating for the drawbacks of individual tests. One of the finest grained assessments for academic ability involves using the child's performance in the classroom curriculum using assessment probes. This technique, called *curriculum based assessment*, shows

TABLE 13-9 OBSERVATION METHODS

Frequency Recording

Frequency recording has also been called *tallying* or *event recording*. With this method, an observer simply counts the number of times a behavior occurs within a predetermined amount of time (for example, the number of head bangs in a 10-minute period). A restriction of the frequency method is that it should be used with discrete behaviors—that is, behaviors that have a clear onset or offset, such as head bangs. Behaviors that do not have a clear start or ending, such as a conversation between two people, are difficult to measure with the frequency method. The types of behaviors with which the frequency method has been used include eye contact, self-stimulation, and self-injurious behavior.

Interval Recording

Interval recording is the most popular method of recording behavior, because it can be used with both discrete and nondiscrete behaviors. With interval recording, a block of time is divided into small equal units. For example, a 10-minute period of observation time may be broken into ten 1-minute intervals of time. If the target behavior occurs during a 1-minute interval, it is scored. Generally, only one behavior is scored per interval even if more than one behavior occurs. This type of system does not depend on the starting or stopping of a behavior. The only requirement is that the behavior must be scored if it occurs during the 1-minute interval. The types of target behaviors that interval recording has been used with include play activity, aggressive behaviors, and eating and drinking.

Duration Recording

Duration recording must also be used with discrete behaviors that have a clear onset and offset. The duration of a behavior is generally timed from the onset to the offset of the behavior. This type of method is useful when the amount of time a subject engages in a behavior is important. Duration methods have been used to assess time spent doing homework, watching television, engaging in an exercise program, and thumbsucking.

Latency Recording

With *latency recording*, the amount of time from some stimulus to the start of a behavior is timed. Again, this requires a discrete response with a clear onset. The latency method is useful when the lapse in time from a stimulus to the starting of a behavior is important. For example, latency recording has been used to measure how long it takes a child to start to comply after a request has been given by an adult.

---

particular promise because this method uses the actual curriculum materials used in the child's classroom (Shapiro, 1989; Shinn, 1989). Probes for accuracy and rate are constructed using the exact curriculum materials utilized for instruction in the classroom. The basic advantage of this system is that the derived probes ensure content overlap with the specific curriculum that is used with the student (good content validity).

BEHAVIORAL OBSERVATION METHODS

Behavioral observation is the most direct form of assessment. A basic assumption of behavioral assessment is that public events, rather than private or assumed underlying traits, are the important target for measurement (Haynes, 1978). Another assumption of behavioral observation is that the environment in which the behavior occurs is critically important to the learning and maintenance of that behavior. Unlike other tests in which the child comes to the evaluator's office to be assessed, with behavioral observation the evaluator goes to the child's environment to collect the data. Gathering information in the child's natural environment in which the problem behavior occurs may be a more informative method in that events which precede the behavior (antecedents), the behavior itself, and the events which follow the behavior (consequences) can be directly observed and measured. This type of observation leads to a "functional analysis" of under what conditions and why a behavior occurs (Umbreit, 1995; Vollmer & Northrup, 1996).

To be scored as correct in-seat behavior, the child must be sitting in her chair, not slouching, have both feet on the floor, and her hands on the desk.

There are several methods for collecting observational data (see Table 13-9) each of which has advantages and disadvantages depending on the type of behavior being observed. Each of these methods, however, requires the precise definition of *target behaviors*, which leaves little guesswork or interpretations to the observer. For example, an adequate definition of in-seat behavior for a hyperactive child may read: The child must be sitting in the chair with both feet on the floor, both buttocks touching the seat, with his hands on the desk. Target behaviors are generally defined as: (1) the duration or time involved in responding, (2) the intensity or amplitude of the response, or (3) the topography of the response. In addition, target behaviors can be classed as discrete responses that have a clear beginning and ending, such as biting or hitting, or nondiscrete responses that have no clear beginning or ending, such as a long conversation between two people.

A set of explicitly defined target behaviors that are designed for observation in one environmental setting such as a classroom, playground, or home is called an *observation code*. An observational code has the advantage of describing several different behaviors that can occur in one setting, giving a global picture of the child's behavior in that setting. This observational global picture has been likened to a photograph of a behavior (Foster

TABLE 13-10 BEHAVIORAL OBSERVATION CODE USED WITH FAMILIES

AP	Approval
AT	Attention
CM	Command
CN	Command negative
CO	Compliance
CR	Cry
DI	Disapproval
DP	Dependency
DS	Destructiveness
HR	High rate (occurring at a high frequency and over time so that the behavior is aversive)
HU	Humiliate
IG	Ignore
IN	Indulgence (doing something helpful for another individual who is capable of doing it for himself without being asked)
LA	Laugh
NC	Noncompliance
NE	Negativism
NO	Normative (routine behavior which fits no other code)
NR	No Response
PL	Play
PN	Physical negative
PP	Physical positive
RC	Receive (when a person receives an object from another person and shows no response)
SS	Self-stimulation (a child bounces, rocks body, or sucks thumb)
TA	Talk
TE	Tease
TH	Touch
WH	Whine
WK	Work
YE	Yell

SOURCE: Reid, J. B. (1978). *A social learning approach to family intervention: Vol. 2. Observation in the home setting* (p. 35). Eugene, OR: Castalia. Reprinted by permission of the author and the publisher.

& Cone, 1986; Kent & Foster, 1977). If the camera's settings are incorrectly adjusted or the camera is improperly used, then the picture will be inaccurate and fuzzy. The settings and use of an observational system depend on an accurate observational code and proper selection of an observation system (see Table 13-10).

A good example of an observational code that is used with an interval data collection system is given in Table 13-10. This code includes 29 behaviors that are used to

FIGURE 13-7   Behavior observation form

BEHAVIOR OBSERVATION FORM

Target Student_____ M/F_____ Grade_____ Date_____

School_____ Teacher_____

Observer_____

Class Activity_____

Position   ❑ Teacher directed whole class   ❑ Teacher directed small group   ❑ Independent work session

DIRECTIONS: Ten-second interval. Observe each student once; then record data. This is a partial interval recording. If possible, collect full 15 minutes under teacher directed or independent condition. If not, put a slash when classroom condition changes. **Classmates observed must be the same sex as the target student.**

	1	2	3

Target
Student*

*Classmates of same sex.

	4	5	6

Target
Student*

*Classmates of same sex.

	7	8	9

Target
Student*

*Classmates of same sex.

	10	11	12

Target
Student*

*Classmates of same sex.

	13	14	15

Target
Student*

*Classmates of same sex.

NOTE: To observe class–begin with the first same sex student in row 1. Record each subsequent same sex student in following intervals. Data reflect an average of classroom behavior. **Skip unobservable students.**

ON-TASK CODES: Eye contact with teacher or task and performing the requested task.

OFF-TASK CODES:

   T = **Talking Out/Noise:** Inappropriate verbalization or making sounds with object, mouth, or body.

   O = **Out of Seat:** Student fully or partially out of assigned seat without teacher permission.

   I   = **Inactive:** Student not engaged with assigned task and passively waiting, sitting, etc.

   N = **Noncompliance:** Breaking a classroom rule or not following teacher directions within 15 seconds.

   P = **Playing With Object:** Manipulating objects without teacher permission.

   + = **Positive Teacher Interaction:** One-on-one positive comment, smiling, touching, or gesture.

   -   = **Negative Teacher Interaction:** One-on-one reprimand, implementing negative consequence, or negative gesture.

SOURCE: Rhode, G., Jenson, W. R., & Reavis, K. (1992). *The Tough Kid Book: Practical classroom management strategies.* Longmont, CO: Sopris West.

describe the interactions between a child and his family (Reid, 1978). These behaviors range from positive behaviors such as "approve" and "play" to very negative behaviors such as "humiliate," "tease," and "destroy property."

Response Discrepancy Observation

One problem with observational techniques is that they do not generally allow comparison to standardized norms. In most instances, children are compared to themselves. For example, a child may be observed prior to an intervention and after the interventions with the comparison of interest being the difference between the pre- and post-intervention observations. However, such a comparison does not tell an observer what is average, below average, or exceptional performance for that particular setting. For instance, how are other children behaving in the classroom, at recess, or in the home? A variation of standard observational techniques, *response discrepancy observation*, has been developed to allow meaningful normative comparisons (Alessi, 1980; Deno, 1980).

The term *response discrepancy* means that a discrepancy or difference between the observed behavior of a target child (referred child) and an index child (nonreferred child) is assessed. Data are collected simultaneously on the target and index children across several intervals for direct comparison. The major advantage of this system is that it allows normative comparisons across children, and yet, it still allows the pre- and post-comparisons for individual children. An example of an application of a response discrepancy system is given in Figure 13-7 (Rhode, Jenson, & Reavis, 1992).

The behaviors observed in a classroom with this system included on- and off-task (talking, out-of-seat, noncompliance and others). This system is designed for 15-minute observations of a student across 10-second intervals. The observer waits until the end of each 10-second interval and then observes the student (time sampling). If the student is on-task, the whole interval is scored as such. If the student is off-task (with any of the behaviors listed in Figure 13-7), the whole interval is scored as off-task. While the referred child is being observed for each 10-second interval, a same-sex peer is randomly selected and observed simultaneously. At the

FIGURE 13-8 Picture of bar code recording device

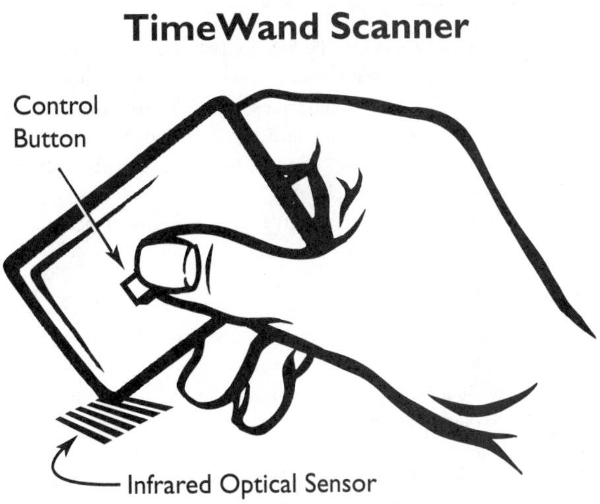

TimeWand Scanner

Control Button

Infrared Optical Sensor

Source: Saunders, M. D., Saunders, J. L., & Saunders, R. (1990). *Classroom data collection with bar codes* (Working Paper No. 348). Parsons, KS: Parsons Research Center.

end of the 15-minute observation interval, this system yields a micro-norm for the classroom for the same-sex peers (for comparisons) and the specific on-task percentage for the referred child.

Both standard and response discrepancy observation techniques present several methodological problems that affect reliability, validity, and cost (Foster & Cone, 1986; Wildman & Erickson, 1977). First, behavioral observation requires a considerable time investment in training observers to use the various codes and collect the data. Lack of familiarity with target behavior definitions can significantly reduce the reliability of recorded data. Continual training and recalibration with behavior definitions decrease observer disagreements and increase interrater reliability. Observer *drift* is another factor that affects observer reliability (Johnson & Bolstad, 1973; O'Leary & Kent, 1973). Drift usually occurs when two observers in an observation team agree closely but both have drifted away from using the original definitions of the target behaviors (Foster & Cone, 1986). In effect, the observers have unintentionally changed the original definitions of the target behaviors by frequently discussing them. Drift can usually be detected if a third, unfamiliar observer randomly checks the observer teams. Closely

---

BOX 13-3   SELF-RECORDING AND STUDY BEHAVIOR

An experiment conducted by Broden, Hall, and Mitts (1971) investigated the effects of self-recording behavior on increasing a child's study behavior in the classroom. The subject was an eighth-grade junior high school student named Liza who had been failing her history course. Weekly counseling sessions in which her poor academic performance was discussed had failed to change Liza's study behavior. Observation in the classroom indicated that Liza studied only a small percentage of the time even when she told the counselor that she would "really try" to do better. Her talking about the problem with the counselor and her actually doing something about it in class were not highly related.

Self-recording was implemented by asking Liza to record her study behavior on a slip of paper "when she thought of it." Study and non-study behavior were defined as follows:

> "Study" was defined as attending to the teacher-assigned tasks and meant that when it was appropriate Liza should be facing the teacher, writing down lecture notes, facing a child who was responding to a teacher question, or reciting when called upon by the teacher. "Non-study" behavior meant that Liza was out of her seat without permission, talking out without being recognized by the teacher, facing the window, fingering non-academic objects such as her make-up, comb, or purse, or working on an assignment for another class. (Broden, Hall, & Mitts, 1971, p. 192)

Figure 13-9 presents the results of the self-recording on Liza's study behavior. During the baseline conditions (Baseline$_1$ and Baseline$_2$) when no self-recording was occurring, Liza studied only 30 percent of the time. However, when she started to self-record (Self-Recording$_1$ and Self-Recording$_2$), her study behavior jumped to approximately 80 percent of the class time. When the teacher was asked to pay attention and praise Liza for study behavior and Liza was self-recording (Self-Recording Plus Praise condition), her studying increased further to 88 percent of the time. At this point Liza was asked not to record her own behavior, and the teacher continued to give her special attention for studying (Praise Only condition); the study behavior stayed at 77 percent. Prior to the experiment, the teacher had not been able to motivate Liza to study. The last condition was a return to baseline (Baseline$_3$) in which self-recording and teacher praise were stopped. It can be seen in Figure 13-5 that Liza's studying behavior continued. She had begun studying in her history class without special help. In Liza's next report card, she had improved her history grade from a D− to a passing C.

It should be remembered that the main intervention in this experiment was self-recording, an observation technique. No rewards were promised to Liza, nor is it likely that teacher praise by itself would have changed Liza's study behavior so dramatically. Broden and associates suggested that requiring her to observe and record her studying probably became a cue to start studying, thus increasing the time Liza spent on schoolwork.

---

related to observer drift is observer *bias* in which the observer has an expectation about the kind of behavior that child should exhibit (Kass & O'Leary, 1970; Skindrud, 1973). For example, if an observer is told to take activity data on a "hyperactive child," he may score the behavior in the direction of overactivity even when the child's behavior is normal. Also, when observers know a treatment attempt is under way, they may see improvement in the treated child's behavior when none actually exists. Keeping the observer as naive as possible about the child's background is one way of partially controlling bias. Unfortunately, this solution is generally not practical in most clinical and educational settings.

Observer bias and drift affect the reliability of using observational techniques. *Reactivity* affects the validity of observational techniques. "A reactive measure is one which affects the object it is designed to measure" (Haynes, 1978). In a sense, reactivity is a comparison of obtrusive (stands out) as opposed to unobtrusive observational measures (Harris & Lahey, 1982). For instance, an obtrusive observer might stare at a child in a classroom while taking data. Such an observer probably would make the child feel uneasy and thus effect the natural way the child behaves in the classroom. A less obtrusive observer might observe from a partially hidden vantage point (i.e., one-way mirror or a partition) and make himself as inconspicuous as possible.

One new technological solution to the high cost and to some of the recording problems associated with observation is infra-red bar code readers (see Figure 13-8). These small cards work on the same principle as the lasers in grocery store check-out lines except they are pro-

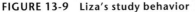

Box 13-3 (continued)

FIGURE 13-9   Liza's study behavior

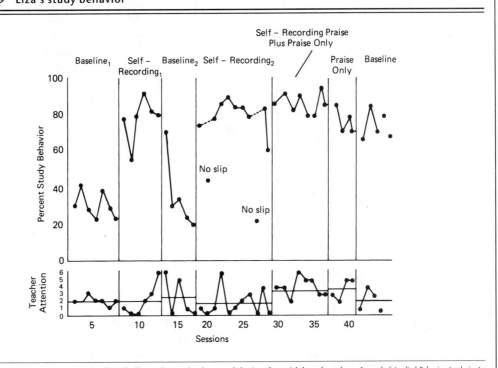

grammed with observation codes. The observer simply sweeps the card across the appropriate bar code lines when behaviors occur, thus never having to write down the collected data. The individual behavioral occurrences and the time of their occurrences are recorded in the card's memory. The system can record for many hours on several subjects and the data are analyzed using a desktop computer.

Self-Monitoring

Behavioral observation does not necessarily require independent observers who are trained to collect data on someone else. A child can be taught to collect data on herself, which saves money, training time, and produces an unexpected benefit. The benefit is that by simply re-

cording data on oneself, the observed behavior changes. In a sense, the person reacts to collecting data on a target behavior which produces positive results (as reviewed by Mace & Kratochwill, 1988). For example, Herbert and Baer (1972) found that having mothers self-monitor positive statements they made to their children increased the frequency of such positive statements. It has been used to increase social skills and reduce disruptive behavior in autistic children (Koegel, Koegel, Hurley, & Frea, 1992). Self-monitoring has also been used extensively to improve on-task behavior and academic performance of attention-deficit disordered and learning disabled students (Carr & Punzo, 1993; Lam, Cole, Shapiro, & Bambara, 1994) Box 13-3 describes a classic situation in which the studying behavior of an eighth-grade girl was improved by self-monitoring.

These behavior changes are due to reactivity, which frequently increases appropriate behavior and decreases inappropriate behaviors. However, these effects are generally temporary unless they are specifically rewarded (Bornstein, Hamilton, & Bornstein, 1986).

Rhodes, Morgan, and Young (1981) used a self-monitoring procedure with behaviorally disordered students who rated their own appropriate behavior in a special education classroom and awarded themselves reward points. The teachers would randomly match their ratings with the student's ratings. If there was a 100 percent match, the student earned a bonus point; if the match was only 90 percent correct, the student was allowed to keep their awarded points; if the match was below 90 percent, the student lost all of his points. The effects of this study were dramatic with students behaving appropriately and accurately assessing their behaviors. Eventually, the self-monitoring with random matches was used to successfully integrate the student back into regular education classes. This procedure also taught the students to be accurately sensitive to adult's perceptions about their behaviors.

Behavior Checklists

When behavior checklists are used, raters who are familiar with a child are asked to score the child's behavior along several predetermined dimensions. Unlike behavioral observation, which utilizes systematic recording techniques, behavior checklists seldom use a tally, duration, or interval scoring method. Instead, an adult (parent, teacher, or ward attendant) is asked to rate a child's behavior in comparison to a standard or to the behaviors of other children. For example, the checklist shown in Table 13-11 requires a parent to rate a behavior as 2 = Very True, 1 = Often True, or 0 = Not True if they have observed the child engaging in the behavior in the past six months.

Factor analysis techniques are commonly used to identify behavioral dimensions included in checklists. Specific checklists such as the Child Depression Inventory (Kovacs 1992), Reynolds Suicide Ideation Scales (Reynolds, 1987), and the Social Skills Checklists (Demaray, Rffalo, Carlson, Busse, McManus, Leventhal, & Swanson, 1995; Gresham & Elliot, 1990) are used to identify distinct behavior problems in children. Other general problem behavior checklists such as the Behavior Checklist (Quay, 1977; Quay & Petersen, 1975), Walker Problem Behavior Identification Checklist-Revised (Walker, 1970, 1983), and Child Behavior Checklist (Achenbach, 1991) identify many problematic behaviors and are used for screening. Generally, behaviors in these checklists are grouped into *broad spectrum behavior problems* such as internalizing behaviors (problems direct inward toward the self) and externalizing behaviors (problems directed towards others and the environment). The broad spectrum factors are then further subdivided into *narrow band factors* such as aggression, hyperactivity, depression, and social withdrawal.

Figure 13-10 gives an example of a profile sheet from the Child Behavior Checklist (Achenbach, 1991, 1992) which shows the broad and narrow factors. A parent fills out the checklist in Table 13-11, and then the scores are transposed onto a profile sheet. In this example, both the father (dotted line) and mother (solid line) rated the child's behavior with their individual scores of 0, 1, or 2 for each item from the checklist listed below the factors on the profile sheet (i.e., "argues" rated a 1 by the father and a 2 by the mother under the aggressive factor). The profile sheet also allows a normative comparison to a standardization group. For example, if the scores of the individual factors are above T-70 (dotted line across the profile), then 98 percent of the standardization population fell on or below this line. The T-70 scores, which are two standard deviations from the mean, are considered clinically significant for most of the factors. In this particular case, the mother rated the aggressive factor as significant (T-75) while the father rated it as nonsignificant (T-62), indicating disagreement between the parents about the severity of the child's aggressive problems.

The advantage to most behavior checklists is that they have good validity, particularly if they are derived using multivariate statistics. In addition, most behavior checklists have good reliability characteristics. For instance, the test-retest reliability for the total score from the Child Behavior Checklist (Achenbach, 1991) is over .90. Some of the more advanced behavior checklists such as the Child Behavior Checklists are really assessment systems in that there are multiple forms for several evaluators, the parent (CBCL), the teacher (TRF), and the youth (YRF). This allows input from multiple evaluators and has been termed a *cross-informant* analysis, which yields one of the most complete pictures of children with psychological problems (McConaughy, 1993).

TABLE 13-11 SAMPLE ITEMS FROM THE NEW CBCL

CHILD BEHAVIOR CHECKLIST

Below is a list of items that describe children and youth. For each item that describes your child now or within the past 6 months, please circle the 2 if the item is very true or often true of your child. Circle the 1 if the item is somewhat or sometimes true of your child. If the item is not true of your child, circle the 0. Please answer all items as well as you can, even if some do not seem to apply to your child.

0=Not True (as far as you know)   1=Somewhat or Sometimes True   2=Very True or Often True

0 1 2   1. Acts too young for his/her age

0 1 2   2. Allergy (describe):_____

0 1 2   3. Argues a lot

0 1 2   4. Asthma

0 1 2   5. Behaves like opposite sex

0 1 2   6. Bowel movements outside toilet

0 1 2   7. Bragging, boasting

0 1 2   8. Can't concentrate, can't pay attention for long

0 1 2   9. Can't get his/her mind off certain thoughts; obsessions (describe):

0 1 2   10. Can't sit still, restless, or hyperactive

0 1 2   11. Clings to adults or too dependent

0 1 2   12. Complains of loneliness

0 1 2   13. Confused or seems to be in a fog

0 1 2   14. Cries a lot

0 1 2   15. Cruel to animals

0 1 2   16. Cruelty, bullying, or meanness to others

0 1 2   17. Day-dreams or gets lost in his/her thoughts

0 1 2   18. Deliberately harms self or attempts suicide

0 1 2   19. Demands a lot of attention

0 1 2   20. Destroys his/her own things

0 1 2   21. Destroys things belonging to his/her family or others

0 1 2   22. Disobedient at home

0 1 2   23. Disobedient at school

0 1 2   24. Doesn't eat well

0 1 2   25. Doesn't get along with other kids

0 1 2   26. Doesn't seem to feel guilty after misbehaving

0 1 2   27. Easily jealous

0 1 2   28. Eats or drinks things that are not food—*don't* include sweets (describe):

0 1 2   29. Fears certain animals, situations, or places, other than school (describe):

0 1 2   30. Fears going to school

0 1 2   31. Fears he/she might think or do something bad

0 1 2   32. Feels he/she has to be perfect

0 1 2   33. Feels or complains that no one loves him/her

0 1 2   34. Feels others are out to get him/her

0 1 2   35. Feels worthless or inferior

0 1 2   36. Gets hurt a lot, accident-prone

0 1 2   37. Gets in many fights

0 1 2   38. Gets teased a lot

0 1 2   39. Hangs around with others who get in trouble

0 1 2   40. Hears sounds or voices that aren't there (describe): _____

0 1 2   41. Impulsive or acts without thinking

0 1 2   42. Would rather be alone than with others

0 1 2   43. Lying or cheating

0 1 2   44. Bites fingernails

0 1 2   45. Nervous, highstrung, or tense

0 1 2   46. Nervous movements or twitching (describe): _____

0 1 2   47. Nightmares

0 1 2   48. Not liked by other kids

0 1 2   49. Constipated, doesn't move bowels

0 1 2   50. Too fearful or anxious

0 1 2   51. Feels dizzy

0 1 2   52. Feels too guilty

0 1 2   53. Overeating

0 1 2   54. Overtired

0 1 2   55. Overweight

56. Physical problems without known medical cause:

0 1 2   a. Aches or pains (*not* headaches)

0 1 2   b. Headaches

0 1 2   c. Nausea, feels sick

0 1 2   d. Problems with eyes (describe): _____

0 1 2   e. Rashes or other skin problems

0 1 2   f. Stomachaches or cramps

0 1 2   g. Vomiting, throwing up

0 1 2   h. Other (describe): _____

SOURCE: Achenbach, T. M. (1991). *Manual for the Child Behavior Checklist/4–18 and 1991 Profile* (p. 11). Department of Psychiatry, University of Vermont: Burlington.

FIGURE 13-10 Sample of the Achenbach CBCL profile

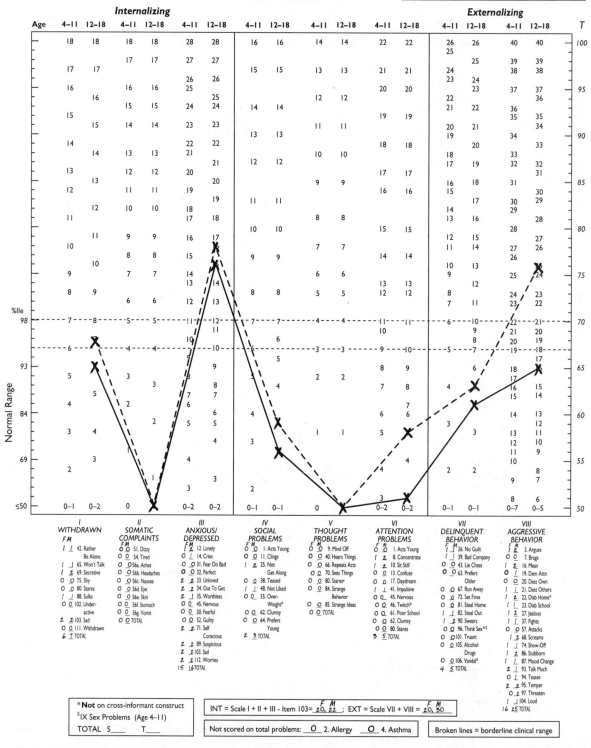

Interviewing is the most popular type of assessment procedure used with children and their parents. The interview format allows a clinician to develop a relationship with the child and explore interesting points that might not be included in other assessment techniques.

There are also several disadvantages in using behavior checklists with behaviorally disordered children. First, most behavior checklists do not have validity scales to determine if the informant filling out the checklist is over- or underreporting problem behaviors. The only check is to use another validity check such as a behavioral observation or several raters. Second, most checklists are only *descriptive* in assessing a behavior. Once the behavior is identified and described, they tell us little about what to do. However, behavior checklists can go beyond a description and function in a *prescriptive* manner suggesting some interventions (Cummings, 1988; McCarney, 1993). Third, as with intelligence tests, behavior checklists are prone to cultural differences (Reid, 1995). What is behaviorally acceptable for a minority culture may be quite different from what is acceptable in the culture on which the behavior checklist was standardized.

INTERVIEWING

Interviewing has been called the "clinician's basic technique" (Korchin, 1979), the "universal method" of data collection (O'Leary & Johnson, 1979), and the "corner stone of child clinical assessment" (Edelbrock & Costello, 1990). Interviewing with a child and his parents is generally used to start an assessment process that may involve other techniques after basic information has been gathered (Hughes & Baker, 1990). Interviewing includes such widely used techniques as a social history (a history of a client's social development), an intake interview (a method used to decide whether an agency's facilities meets the client's needs), a child psychiatric interview (a health and psychiatric history), a diagnostic interview, a behavioral interview, a research interview, and many more.

There are several reasons why interviewing is such a popular assessment technique (Evans & Nelson, 1986; Hughes, 1989; Hughes & Baker, 1990). First, interviewing generally utilizes open-ended questions that allow a child or parent to explain or elaborate answers instead of being forced to choose an answer from a predetermined list. Second, interviewing helps to establish a relationship between a clinician and a client, which facilitates the assessment process. Unlike formal psychological testing in which the interaction between the evaluator and client is kept to a minimum, interviewing involves a less structured exchange of information. Interviewing both the child and parents together (conjoint interview) also gives the clinician a picture of the family's interaction. For example, the following questions can be answered:

1. Does the parent set rules for the child during the interview and consistently enforce them?
2. Are the rules overly harsh or are they lax and easily broken with no consequence?
3. Is the child highly dependent and does she cling to the parent or is she independent and explores the office while the parent talks?
4. Do the parent and child disagree in answering questions that the interviewer asks and how are these disputes handled?
5. Does the parent have exceptionally high or low expectations for the child that are observed during the interview?

One of the most frequently used interview techniques used in mental health facilities is the child *psychiatric interview*. The psychiatric interview is performed by a medical doctor with the intent of providing a diagnostic formulation and recommendations for treatment. Generally, the psychiatric interview consists of a mental status exam and a basic content section. The mental status exam has been defined as "a description of the child's appearance and behavior during two or three hours of psychiatric interviewing" (Simmons, 1974). The content section includes the child's direct answers to the psychiatrist's questions such as "If you could have three wishes what would they be?" Of particular interest to most child psychiatrists is the genetic and developmental history of the child. Many child psychiatric evaluations also include projective techniques, a brief neurological screening, and an observation of the child at play. A good example of a child psychiatric evaluation is that of Kestenbaum and Bird, which is outlined in Table 13-12. This outline has not changed substantially over many years and covers all aspects of the mental status exam from physical appearance to language and thinking. The interviewer's questions cover the child's feelings, dreams, moral judgments, and the ability to deal with anxiety. Only a topic outline is provided and the psychiatrist is free to phrase questions as she chooses.

Several structured *diagnostic* interviews have been developed that are used primarily to diagnose and classify children (Bierman & Schwartz, 1986; Edelbrock & Costello, 1990). Most of these interviews contain open-ended questions for both the child and the parent such as the Kiddie-SADS (Puig-Antich & Chambers, 1978) or the Diagnostic Interview for Children and Adolescents (Herjanic & Reich, 1982). Other interviews such as the Children's Assessment Schedule (CAS) (Hodges, Kline, Stern, Cytryn, & McKnew, 1982) or the Diagnostic Interview Schedule for Children (DISC-R) (Shaffer, Schwab-Stone, Fisher, & Cohen, 1993) contain a series of questions that parallel the major childhood disorders listed in the *Diagnostic and Statistical Manual of the American Psychiatric Association*. By answering a set of questions, the child provides the information that is essential in making a formal diagnosis. When these structured interviews are combined with other assessment techniques such as behavior checklists from parents and teachers, they provide some of the most accurate diagnostic assessments for clinical and research use (McConaughy & Achenbach, 1996).

Behavioral interviewing is fundamentally different from diagnostic and psychiatric interviews primarily because the emphasis is not placed on a diagnostic classification. Instead, in a behavioral interview stress is placed on assessing the child's environment and particularly a functional analysis of that environment (Gelfand & Hartmann, 1985; Mash & Terdal, 1988). A functional analysis classification (see Chapter 12) involves pinpointing target behaviors and assessing antecedents (events that precede a behavior) and consequences (events that follow a behavior). Antecedents and consequences are important because they can maintain or reinforce the occurrence of a problem behavior.

An example of an outline for behaviorally interviewing parents, suggested by Gelfand and Hartmann (1985), is given in Table 13-13. The interviewer first attempts to specify problem target behaviors that can be measured. The rate or frequency (last incident, rate, changes in rate) is determined to see if the behavior is unusually high or low in frequency. The setting (antecedent and consequences) is also assessed to determine how the environment maintains the problem behaviors. This method also allows interviewers to inquire about attempts which parents may have made in the past (but unsuccessfully) to modify the problem behavior.

TABLE 13-12 OUTLINE OF THE MENTAL HEALTH ASSESSMENT FORM FOR SCHOOL-AGED CHILDREN

Part I—Mental Status	Part II—Content of the Interview
I. Physical Appearance	VI. Feeling States
A. General attractiveness	A. Depression
B. Physical characteristics	B. Elation
C. Physical maturation	C. Mixed disturbances (other)
D. Observable deviations in physical characteristics	D. Anger
E. Grooming and dress	E. Anxiety
F. Gender differential (clearly looks male or female)	VII. Interpersonal Relations
II. Motoric Behavior and Speech	A. The child's relationship to his family
A. Motor activity	B. The child's relationship with other adult authority figures
B. Motor coordination	C. Relations with peers
C. Presence of unusual motoric patterns, habit patterns, and mannerisms	D. Relationships to pets
D. Speech	E. Modes of interaction with others
III. Relatedness during Interview	F. Aggressive behavior
A. Quality of relatedness as judged by nonverbal behavior	G. Sexual behavior
B. Quality of relatedness as judged by verbal behavior	VIII. Symbolic Representation (Dreams and Fantasies)
IV. A. Inappropriate Affect	A. Fantasy
B. Constriction of affect	B. Dreams
C. Elated affect	IX. Self-Concept
D. Depressive affect	A. Dissatisfaction with self
E. Labile (changing, unstable) affect	B. Comparison of self to peers
F. Over-anxious affect	C. Comparison between self and ideal self
G. Angry affect	X. Conscience—Moral Judgment
H. Histrionic (exaggerated mannerisms, theatrical) affect	A. Deficit in development of conscience
V. Language and Thinking	B. Antisocial behavior
A. Overall intelligence	XI. General Level of Adaptation
B. Cognitive functions (e.g., memory, ability to reason, use of vocabulary)	A. Personality characteristics
C. External reality testing (e.g., absence of hallucinations, illusions, and perceptual distortions)	B. Defense mechanisms
D. Use of language	C. Maladaptive solutions in dealing with anxiety
E. Thought processes	
F. Attention span	

SOURCE: C. J. Kestenbaum & H. R. A. Bird. (1978). A reliability study of the Mental Health Assessment Form for School-Aged Children. *Journal of the American Academy of Child Psychiatry, 17,* 338–347. Reprinted by permission of the authors and Yale University Press.

It is difficult to judge the soundness of most interviewing techniques because of the lack of objective research and the diversity of interviewing techniques. However, some guidelines do exist. Generally, the more structured interviews tend to have better psychometric properties. For example, the highly structured DISC-R and CAS have good to moderate reliability and validity (Hodges, Cools, & McKnew, 1989; Shaffer et al., 1993). Parents are likely to report data that are distorted to conform with cultural stereotypes (McCord & McCord, 1961); they may report exceptionally fast development (precocity) for their children (Hetherington & Martin, 1979), and they are least reliable about events with high emotional content (Wenar & Coulter, 1962). The reliability of interview information varies with the child's age, with younger children tending to be less reliable reporters (Edelbrock, Costello, Dulcan, Kalas, & Conover, 1985).

Finally, a caution must also be applied in the case of children's reports of information about themselves, their current adjustment, their families, and especially their

TABLE 13-13   INITIAL CARETAKER INTERVIEW

These are the basic questions to ask caretakers concerning the child's problem behavior:

1. Specific description

   "Can you tell me what (child's name)'s problem seems to be?" (If caretaker responds in generalities such as, "He is always grouchy," or that the child is rebellious, uncooperative, or overly shy, ask him to describe the behavior more explicitly.)

   "What, exactly, does (he or she) do when (he or she) is acting this way? What kinds of things will (he or she) say?"

2. Last incident

   "Could you tell me just what happened the last time you saw (the child) acting like this? What did you do?"

3. Rate

   "How often does this behavior occur? About how many times a day (or hour or week) does it occur?"

4. Changes in rate

   "Would you say this behavior is starting to happen more often, less often, or staying about the same?"

5. Setting

   "In what situations does it occur? At home? At school? In public places or when (the child) is alone?" (If in public places) "Who is usually with him? How do they respond?"

   "At what times of day does this happen?"

   "What else is (the child) likely to be doing at the time?"

6. Antecedents

   "What usually has happened right before (he or she) does this? Does anything in particular seem to start this behavior?"

7. Consequent events

   "What usually happens right afterwards?"

8. Modification attempts

   "What things have you tried to stop (him or her) from behaving this way?"

   "How long did you try that?"

   "How well did it work?"

   "Have you ever tried anything else?"

SOURCE: D. M. Gelfand & D. P. Hartmann. (1984). *Child behavior analysis and therapy* (2nd ed.) (New York: Pergamon Press), pp. 230–232. Reprinted by permission.

---

emotional status. Research and developmental theory both suggest that children are not particularly reliable in reporting information about themselves, either over time or in relation to the reports of others about them. (Barkley, 1990, p.249)

SUMMARY

Assessment methods are information gathering procedures that should lead to sound decisions concerning the diagnosis and treatment of behaviorally disordered children. The individual assessment procedures differ in their information collection methods and the theoretical assumptions about what they are measuring. Some assessment procedures use extremely structured and standardized collection methods such as intelligence tests, and others use relatively unstructured collection methods such as projective techniques and interviews. The theoretical assumptions about the types of information gath-

ering also differ widely. Observations, checklists, and curriculum based measurement generally sample behavior directly. Personality inventories, projective tests, and some intelligence tests are assumed to measure underlying traits or construct which control behavior across different situations and time. The direct sample techniques value observable behavior, and the trait techniques value underlying traits and consider observable behavior as only a reflection of these underlying traits.

Without exception, no assessment procedure is perfect and all procedures are subject to measurement error. Each procedure can be judged by its ability to meet a basic set of reliability and validity criteria. Assessment procedures that are not reliable are not consistent in their information gathering capabilities. An unreliable procedure cannot have good validity; reliability sets an upper limit on validity.

Since any single assessment procedure is subject to error and since none has perfect reliability or validity, it is good clinical practice to use *multiple measures, settings, evaluators, and times* in assessing a child. If one procedure is weak in an area, then a second or third procedure may cover this area. For example, an IQ test can be used in diagnosing an intellectual disability. However, an IQ test used by itself is subject to significant error such as cultural bias. Other measures, such as checklists to assess how well a child adapts at home and school, behavioral observa-tion of the child, interviewing of parents and caretakers, and academic testing, are needed to make an adequate diagnosis of intellectual disability. It should be remem-bered, however, that using assessment, even multiple measure assessment, merely to label a child is an expen-sive mistake. To be useful, assessment should guide the clinician both in the classification and *treatment* of the child.

CHAPTER I4

TREATMENT METHODS

Key Terms

Antipsychotic drugs. Also called neuroleptic drugs. These drugs reduce psychotic thinking and behavior in adults and may control aggressive, disoriented, hyperactive, or confused thinking in children.

Insight. Achieving an understanding about the actual basis or significance of one's own disturbed behavior. Whether or not a client succeeds in achieving insight is decided by the psychotherapist.

Psychoactive drugs. Pharmacological agents that affect the central nervous system and functions including alertness, attention, mood, motivation, and impulse control.

Psychotherapist. One who treats disordered behavior or mental disorders. Can be a professionally trained psychiatrist, psychologist, social worker or an allied profession, or a nonprofessional therapist, such as a teacher or parent, who is instructed and supervised by a therapist.

Side effects. Undesirable effects of certain drugs, such as appetite suppression, gastric upset, tremors, agitation, etc. Drugs differ in their probability of producing undesirable side effects, and individuals differ in their susceptibility to these effects.

CHAPTER OVERVIEW

This chapter examines the psychosocial and pharmacological or drug treatments for the major types of child disorders. Descriptions are offered of the insight-oriented therapies for children, including psychodynamic play therapy and client-centered therapy, in addition to behavioral therapy and cognitive-behavioral therapy. The systems, behavioral, and eclectic types of family therapy are also reviewed. When children and adolescents must be removed from their families in order to improve, they may be sent for foster family care or institutional group care, both of which are described. Finally, the effectiveness of various prescription drugs and their side effects are discussed.

INTRODUCTION

Child psychological treatment clients are very different from adults. Although their independent interests and rights as mental health treatment clients are increasingly recognized, children have less autonomy than adults in decisions regarding the type, timing, and duration of intervention they receive. Typically, parents are the ones who choose to have their children professionally assessed and then treated, if that is advisable. Children, particularly younger ones, may have very little part in determining whether or not they will receive psychological treatment.

The first professional treatment interventions for children were developed around the beginning of the 20th century. Since then, many treatments have been developed, with some treating the child alone, others focusing mostly or exclusively on the parents' problems, and some requiring the participation of the whole family. There is no general agreement on whether the therapy should focus on the child's psychological inner dynamics or on the control of deviant behavior and learning positive behaviors. As discussed later in this chapter, research has revealed that, on the whole, troubled children profit from some types of psychotherapy, medication, and residential treatment (Weisz, Weiss, Han, Granger, & Morton, 1995). Nevertheless, there is a wide array of possible treatments for children's problems, and it is not easy to

prescribe the best type of intervention for an individual child.

Psychosocial therapies and medications are designed to help the child become a better-functioning, happier member of the family, school, peer group, and community, but different treatments prescribe different routes to these goals. In this chapter we review the most frequently used individual and group approaches to the treatment of children's abnormal behavior. The treatment types described include behavioral and cognitive-behavioral therapy, social skills training, parenting training, nondirective therapy, psychodynamic therapy, residential treatment, and psychoactive medications. These interventions are compared in Table 14-1.

Many children and their families participate in several different types of therapy, either concurrently or at different times. Multiple interventions may prove helpful when people experience several different types of problems, such as child aggressive behavior coupled with parental marital conflict and maternal depression, but a single form of intervention often proves to be as effective as combined interventions (Kazdin, 1996). Many children and teens require treatment for more than one serious adjustment problem, for example, a child may suffer from both depression and conduct disorder, or anxiety and hyperactivity (Nottelmann & Jensen, 1995). Further, the child is not always the only or primary family member who is troubled. Even when the child initially is "the

TABLE 14-1   WHO IS TREATED IN MAJOR FORMS OF THERAPY

Primary Recipient	Treatment Type
The child alone	Psychodynamic play therapy, nondirective play therapy, individual behavioral or cognitive behavioral therapy, drug therapy, institutionalization
The parents alone	Group therapy for parents, support groups for parents, parent education
Parents and child	Parent training combined with child therapy
All immediate family	Systems, behavioral, or eclectic family therapy
The classroom or play group	Group play therapy, group token reinforcement programs

TABLE 14-2   MATCHING PSYCHOSOCIAL TREATMENTS WITH CHILDREN'S DEVELOPMENTAL LEVELS

Child Age Range	Common Treatment Methods
Infants and Toddlers	Training mother in more sensitive, responsive parenting; therapeutic group care for infants
Preschool children	Parent training in behavior management, play therapy, therapeutic preschool programs
Elementary school	Insight-oriented psychodynamic or client-centered therapy; individual or group behavioral therapy; systems, behavioral, or eclectic family therapy; foster or institutional care
Preadolescents and adolescents	Group psychotherapy of various types, family therapy, individual psychotherapy, foster or institutional care

identified client," closer acquaintance with the family often reveals that other relatives also have problems in living that require professional attention. It is necessary to understand the child's adjustment difficulties in the context of family relationships, demands of the school, the functioning of the peer group, and the child's developmental status and challenges. In the next section, we examine the role of developmental considerations in matching treatment types to children's needs. Interventions must accommodate child clients' developmental levels.

DEVELOPMENTAL CONSIDERATIONS

Most therapies for children have their roots in techniques first developed for adults. This observation is as true for drug or pharmacological treatments as it is for psychotherapy. Children have often received "hand-me-downs" from adult psychology and psychiatry. Like all hand-me-downs, some did not fit their juvenile recipients too well and had to be cut-to-size. How much modification of adult techniques is required depends in part upon the child's cognitive maturity. Developmental psychology theory and research indicate that young children and adults may differ more widely in thinking and problem-solving than do adults from dissimilar cultures, such as New Guinea hunters and gatherers, Inuit tribes people in

the Arctic, and European-American city dwellers. To avoid selecting a developmentally inappropriate, and hence ineffective, form of therapy for a child, one must have some acquaintance with the course of normal psychological development and the important differences in skill and thinking associated with age.

In order to determine the most appropriate type of treatment for a child client, a therapist must consider several factors including the nature, severity and number of problems, the child's age and developmental status, and the family composition. Often the child's developmental level is related to the child's present problem. The characteristics and adjustment problems typical of children of different ages are a major consideration in the choice of treatment, as shown in Table 14-2. The youngest children may have difficulty in forming secure attachments with their primary caretakers, and so parent training may be necessary, or the children may need help in achieving developmental milestones such as toilet training, expressive speech, or social skills with peers. In the middle childhood years, peer interaction skills become very important, and children must learn to control their aggression, hyperactivity, and impulsivity, be kind to others, and act appropriately in school. Still later, in the teen years, adult forms of mood disorders appear, notably depression, and youngsters who have had difficulty with school achievement may become alienated and isolated from the mainstream. Thus, each age period has its own particular features and challenges (as described in Chapter 1), which must be considered in diagnosis and treatment.

Attitude and Motivation

Whereas troubled adult clients typically request mental health services, children seldom seek such professional help and may seem to lack motivation to make personal changes (Chess & Hassibi, 1978). More typically, children and adolescents ascribe their difficulties to undesirable situations or a teacher, classmates, or family members with whom they do not get along. A child with this external construction of an interpersonal problem makes an uncooperative, resistant recipient of treatment of any type. A desire to change is a prerequisite for therapeutic effectiveness.

Use of Play

Therapists who work with children must all first win the child's interest and trust (A. Freud, 1945). Play activities and games are familiar and interesting to children, so therapists who treat children frequently use free play or structured play activities as a vehicle of communication with young children. Children communicate more freely through play than through formal verbal interviews, and play also allows them to express and receive the therapist's help in dealing with problems. Guided play activities are the most common type of intervention for children (Koocher & D'Angelo, 1992) and are particularly useful in the treatment of children's fears and anxieties (Russ, 1995).

Common Features of Psychotherapies for Children

Most psychotherapies for children share several characteristics. Many interventions feature free (undirected) or structured play, which is a familiar, nonthreatening activity for children. Therapies must also take into account developmental differences, so more interviewing is used with adolescents and older children, and more nonverbal and play interaction is used to communicate with younger ones. Many, but not all forms of therapy for

Unlike adult psychotherapy, child psychotherapy often involves play to establish a relationship and to provide a vehicle for communication.

children include skill instruction, such as how to initiate interactions with other children or how to inhibit impulsive responding, in addition to attention to the child's emotions. Formal instruction in developmental psychology is helpful to therapists of all persuasions so they can better understand and help their child clients. In addition to these features, which many child psychotherapy approaches share, each type of therapy has some distinctive features, which are discussed next.

MAJOR APPROACHES TO TREATMENT
Insight-Oriented Therapies

The goals of *insight-oriented therapies* are to resolve internal conflict and to help the child adjust to challenges such as mastering developmental crises (adjusting to the birth of a sibling, parental divorce, or moving to a new school and neighborhood) or advancing to a new, more mature psychosocial stage (described in Chapter 2). The insight-oriented therapies discussed in this section include *psychoanalysis* or *psychoanalytically oriented therapy* and *client-centered* or *nondirective counseling*. Many additional therapy approaches combine features of these insight-oriented and other types of counseling or psychotherapy; they are termed *eclectic psychotherapy*. Psychoanalysis is distinguished from psychoanalytically oriented therapy chiefly by its greater length and intensity. Child psychoanalysis may require 45 to 50 minute sessions three to five times a week, while psychoanalytically oriented therapy is less demanding, with sessions one to two times a week. Both forms of psychodynamic therapy may require as much as two years of treatment (Tuma & Russ, 1993). Insight-oriented interventions assume that unconscious inner emotional turmoil, particularly anxiety, lies at the heart of the child's problems. The child's disturbed behavior and emotional distress presumably result from underlying mental conflict of which the child is unaware, much as a high fever is caused by infection in medical explanations of physical illness (see Chapter 2). As one example in the client-centered approach, the child's problem is traced to real or imagined parental and social demands that the child behave perfectly. In contrast, the psychoanalytic view attributes psychopathology to abnormalities occurring at one of the early psychosexual stages such as the anal or oral stage. Resulting conflict and negative emotions and symptoms may persist until the child receives adequate treatment.

The child psychoanalyst attempts to reduce the child's unconscious emotional disturbance by attempting to remove the presumed underlying emotional cause. This type of therapy is termed insight-oriented because enlightenment about one's feelings is expected to remove the need to protect oneself by repressing or denying them. Then the psychopathology should disappear. Thus, this approach attempts a redirection of the child's development into more mature and healthy channels. The insight-oriented psychotherapist may use play as a natural medium of communication (Kovacs & Paulauskas, 1986), and label and offer interpretations of the child's play themes, dreams, and fantasies. Many repetitions and elaborations of key play themes and associated therapist interpretations may be required in the process of *working through* problematic material. In the process of analytic play therapy, children may develop powerful *negative*

transference reactions toward the analyst. *Transference* consists of the repetition with the therapist of emotional reactions that originated in response to significant childhood figures. Feelings are transferred from significant past relationships (particularly with parents) to new ones, for which they may be inappropriate. When negative transference takes place, the child may feel antagonism toward the previously liked therapist, sometimes attacking the therapist verbally and physically (Tuma & Russ, 1993). The analyst's role is to help the child interpret his feelings accurately as being based on past rather than present relationships, which is a higher level of understanding. The primary goal of the insight-oriented interventions is to help children accept themselves and others as they are, rather than to instruct children in new problem-solving techniques, as the behavioral therapies do. The two major approaches discussed here—the psychoanalytic and the client-centered—aim to help children clarify their understanding of their problems.

CRITIQUE OF PSYCHODYNAMIC PLAY THERAPY

About 25 percent of today's clinical child psychologists utilize a psychodynamic approach to child therapy (Tuma & Russ, 1993), although there is remarkably little rigorous research evaluation of this intervention's effectiveness as compared with behavioral interventions (Kovacs & Paulauskas, 1986). A review of a small number of nonbehavioral individual psychotherapy outcome studies by Tuma (1988; reported in Heinicke, 1989) indicated that these approaches, which include psychoanalytically oriented child therapy, produced significantly better outcomes for children than did no therapy. However, Weisz et al. (1995) found that therapy effects were reliably more positive for behavioral than for nonbehavioral treatments. It appears unlikely that children can truly understand complex psychodynamic explanations of their thoughts and feelings, even from a warm, sensitive therapist. Nevertheless, some psychotherapists continue their allegiance to psychodynamically oriented therapies, and many use at least some techniques, such as interpretation of play themes, that were originally developed by psychodynamically oriented therapists.

CLIENT-CENTERED OR NONDIRECTIVE PLAY THERAPY

Client-centered treatment also was first developed for adults and proved an appealing approach to use with troubled children. Based on the work of Carl Rogers (1951), client-centered (humanistic) psychotherapy respects clients' abilities to think for themselves and direct themselves rather than relying on experts such as the therapist. Rogers maintained that each person possesses a strong tendency toward psychological growth and self-actualization. These healthy tendencies to overcome anxiety, depression, and hostility and to fulfill one's talents and abilities can be blocked by harmful experiences such as rejection, which reduces self-esteem. Client-centered therapy aims to combat the effects of such threatening experiences by unobtrusively helping the client develop and accept more realistic expectations.

Virginia Axline (1974, 1976) developed play therapy methods based on the principles of client-centered psychotherapy for adults. The guiding principle in this approach is trust in the self-directing ability of the therapy client, whether adult or child. Treatment is typically much briefer than in psychoanalytic therapy. Axline stressed establishing a warm relationship with the child, within which the therapist accepts the child exactly as she is, and encourages the child to express her feelings, whatever they may be. The therapist recognizes the child's feelings by *reflecting or expressing those feelings back to the child*, who thereby gains insight into her behavior. For example, the therapist might echo back the child's expressions of disgust about a doll's nastiness so the child can begin to accept these emotions as her own. It is presumed that the child's behavior problems are caused by a profound lack of self-acceptance, probably because of criticism and rejection from parents and other important people in the child's life. The therapist's *unconditional positive regard* for the child helps the child begin to accept herself, lower her guard, and direct her energies to positive developmental goals.

CRITIQUE OF CLIENT-CENTERED THERAPY

Recent years have seen very few published evaluations of the effectiveness of client-centered psychotherapy with children, despite the method's continued popularity in clinical use. The client-centered approach is particularly well-suited for children's internalizing problems such as anxiety, fear, and depression (Ellinwood & Raskin, 1993). However, many children need to build new social and cognitive skills as well as recognize and accept their negative emotions. More active treatments may be required for children with marked skills deficits such as those who need remedial teaching programs for academic skills, basic social skills training and control of aggression, and language instruction.

Behavioral Therapy

Many behavioral interventions work directly to modify children's maladaptive behavior, rather than attempting to change the child's attitudes first and hoping for later behavioral improvement, as is typical of insight-oriented psychotherapy. In behavioral therapy, fearful children are taught to relax or to approach the feared situation in small successful steps after watching a model demonstrate how to do so. Children with specific learning disabilities are administered carefully developed instructional materials emphasizing skill building, given practice in carefully graded tasks, and earn reinforcement for their efforts. Or timid, withdrawn children are given coaching and rehearsal in the social skills necessary to make friends in the classroom. All such behavioral programs teach children specific skills and motivate them to practice new skills until their abilities have noticeably improved. Behavioral therapists believe that most child adjustment problems result from faulty or inadequate learning experiences (rather than from internal psychological conflict), and current environmental factors (rather than childhood conflicts) are thought to maintain the maladaptive behavior. Thus current situations can be managed in order to advance the children's skill levels. Often the parents or teachers rather than the child are the ones who are taught new skills, and sometimes the therapist has little direct contact with the child after the initial assessment. In the behavioral view, environmentally produced child behavioral improvements will also improve the youngster's attitudes and self-concept, because success builds self-esteem. In contrast, the insight-oriented therapies assume that emotional change must *precede* any significant, enduring behavioral improvement.

SKINNERIAN THERAPY TECHNIQUES

This approach is known alternately as the applied analysis of behavior. Many of today's behavioral treatment methods originated in the laboratory research and theories of B. F. Skinner (Skinner & Ferster, 1957). Skinner illustrated the power of positive reinforcement in producing behavioral change in humans as well as in animals. His principle of positive reinforcement has since been applied in modification of many types of voluntary behavior in adults and children (see Chapter 2). A *positive reinforcer* is any stimulus or event that makes an immediately preceding voluntary behavior more likely to occur again. Common positive reinforcers include praise, tokens that can be exchanged for toys or treats, and any sign of attention or recognition. However, children may also escalate the behaviors that are followed by warnings, threats, and even corporal punishment, in which case these consequences must also be considered to be positive reinforcers for that particular child. The power of Skinner's analysis lies in the recognition that positive reinforcers are individually defined by observation of a child's actual behavior and are not logically determined in advance. Once identified, reinforcers can be used to modify children's behavior in developmentally desirable directions. Precision is a hallmark of the behavioral approach, and behavior analysts have insisted on precise behavioral definitions of clients' problems. Thus, an applied behavior therapist will wish to determine and record exactly how many times per day a child defies his mother, issues commands, or complies with a teacher's requests. Then a realistic goal is set for the child to meet in order to earn reinforcement, and gradually an increasingly normal or standard frequency of performance is required of the child. The child's actual behavior is recorded faithfully throughout the therapy in order to chart the course of the treatment and evaluate the outcome.

Increasing Rates of Desirable Behavior

Behavioral techniques for promoting desirable child behavior include modeling, verbal instructions, and shaping or reinforcing closer, and closer approximations to the desired behavior. In teaching a new behavior, the therapist might first model or demonstrate the action, and then use verbal or physical *prompts* to assist the child in performing the response. For example, the therapist may wish to teach a new speech sound to a developmentally delayed little girl. To begin, the therapist demonstrates the required sound ("Mm") and then instructs the child to imitate it ("Mary, say 'mm' "). At first, any sound the child makes is reinforced with a hug, praise, or a bit of food in order to encourage her vocalization. To help the child approximate the correct sound more closely, the therapist may use a *prompt* to direct the child's at-

tention to important information—for example, holding a bit of food beside his own mouth while uttering the sound. As a further aid, the therapist may gently squeeze the child's lips together as the child makes a sound. The therapist's physical assistance is removed or *faded* as soon as possible, lest the child's performance become dependent on it. As the child progresses, more is required for a reward, perhaps several words or an entire sentence.

The therapist's goal is to achieve spontaneous speech, so the artificial reinforcement for speech is gradually decreased and finally entirely removed as the child receives normal reinforcement for speaking. Similar approaches have been used to teach children a wide variety of developmentally appropriate skills.

Reducing Rates of Undesirable Behavior

Most attempts to reduce inappropriate behavior do not occur in isolation, but are accompanied by programs to encourage desirable behavior and teach new skills. The techniques most commonly employed to control deviant behavior include *extinction*, which is accompanied by reinforcement of alternative, desired responses: *time out from positive reinforcement*; *response cost*; *token reinforcement programs*; and *overcorrection*. Some of these techniques are used with many types of child problems, while others, such as overcorrection, are confined to use with only the most serious problems. These techniques are described in the following passages. Each method has its advantages and problems, and is appropriate for use under particular circumstances. A careful analysis of the child's behavior, and in some cases a thorough scrutiny of the treatment plan by a review board, are required in order to select the safest, least restrictive, and most effective treatment program.

EXTINCTION

In an *extinction* procedure, reinforcement previously given for a particular behavior is discontinued. The child is neither threatened nor prevented from performing the response, but receives no reinforcement when she does so. The complete witholding of the rewarding consequence *eventually* results in a reduction of the previously reinforced behavior. In many settings, withdrawal of teachers' or parents' attention has decreased young children's inappropriate behavior. Nursery school teachers have reduced shy children's clinging and exclusive inter-action with adults by ignoring it and instead praising them when they approach other children, and kinder-garten children's quarreling and fighting have also di-minished when the classroom teacher has placed such behavior on an extinction schedule by ignoring it—a procedure unlikely to succeed with the more seriously aggressive actions of older students.

It is often difficult to correctly identify and be able to control children's reinforcers in order to use extinction procedures effectively. Consequently, extinction is used most often with closely supervised young children in tightly controlled educational and treatment programs.

TIME OUT FROM POSITIVE REINFORCEMENT

A useful alternative to extinction is *time out from positive reinforcement*, in which reinforcing events are withheld briefly when the child has misbehaved. Often this tech-nique involves briefly isolating the child in an unoccupied room or other uninteresting location. Each time-out pe-riod is short, ranging from a minute or less for very young or highly disturbed children to a maximum of about 10 minutes of continuous appropriate behavior for older ones (Gelfand & Hartmann, 1984). When the specified time period has elapsed and the child is behaving appro-priately, the time-out period is terminated. However, misbehavior extends the time-out period until the child regains self-control and will clean up any mess she has made. In most cases, the child's angry, destructive be-havior diminishes rapidly.

When correctly and consistently administered, time out is an effective and humane way of controlling young children's moderately severely disruptive, antisocial, or aggressive actions. The time-out method is nearly always used in combination with a program of reinforcement for the child's desirable behavior.

RESPONSE COST

Response cost is a punishment procedure that results in the loss of previously earned rewards. This technique is commonly used in homes and treatment programs, and it essentially fines children for misbehavior. Many edu-cational and therapeutic programs for children are run on *points systems* or *token economies*, which utilize points or tokens as reinforcers and fines for breaking the rules. When employed correctly and fairly, response cost is a mild and useful deterrent to misbehavior, especially if it

is combined with positive reinforcement for appropriate conduct, a system described next. Angry adults may act immoderately when issuing fines. We know of one mother who once achieved a record: She withdrew her daughter's privileges for 99 years (but later relented). Such empty threats soon lose their power to influence children's behavior.

TOKEN REINFORCEMENT PROGRAMS

Sometimes informal or limited intervention tactics fail to bring about improvement. The *token economy* or *token reinforcement programs* consist of a set of rules specifying the manner in which, over time, children may earn points or tokens toward desired activities. Most token programs also include fines for certain types of misbehavior (re-sponse cost). These programs encourage children to be-have as well as possible in order to earn various types of privileges. A sample token reinforcement program for an individual child is described in Box 14-1. Token economy programs are often used to treat classes of schoolchildren in special education, in residential treatment programs with delinquents, and in helping parents deal with their own children at home.

OVERCORRECTION

The unusual technique of *overcorrection* is used with se-verely retarded or psychotic children who do not respond to other corrective measures. Some of these children en-gage in repetitive, self-stimulatory activities, which pre-occupy them for long periods of time and prevent them from learning more appropriate behaviors. They may re-peatedly clap or flap their hands, stamp their feet, weave their heads from side to side, or mouth their bodies or other objects. Their bizarre routines have resisted treat-ment and isolated them from normal instructional activi-ties. Foxx and Azrin (1973) developed the technique of overcorrection, which has proved to be remarkably ef-fective in reducing self-stimulation. Immediately after the occurrence of self-stimulation, the therapist (1) firmly tells the child "No," and restrains the child if necessary to stop the inappropriate movements; (2) tells the child to perform a simple exercise (e.g., raising and lowering her arms) for a required brief time period, usually about 15 seconds; (3) physically guides the child in the exer-cise; and (4) instructs the child to engage in sev-eral different exercises for 2 to 5 minutes. This mild, but time-consuming routine can effectively dissuade

---

BOX 14-1   HOW MUCH DOES IT COST TO HIT YOUR BROTHER?

The following contract was arranged by a behavioral therapist to help a family deal with their 9-year-old son, Shawn, who was hyperactive and inattentive at school, in trouble much of the time for starting fights with classmates at school and his younger brother at home, and highly defiant and oppositional with his parents. He hit, spat, tantrummed, and ran away from home when disciplined, one time for an entire day. His parents finally sought professional help when Shawn sneaked out and drove the family car to a neighboring town, which his parents discovered when he was apprehended for running through a red stoplight. Shawn seemed to be getting more uncontrollable with each passing year.

One central part of the treatment program for Shawn consisted of a token economy system at home in which he earned rewards for specific good behaviors and lost points and privileges for aggressive, noncompliant behaviors, as shown in Table 14-3. The therapist guided Shawn and his parents in agreeing on a contingency contract to control some of his most objectionable behaviors and increase the rate of appropriate behaviors. Shawn could turn in the points he earned each day for a later bedtime, viewing his most highly preferred TV programs, play time with his friends, and attending ball games with his father and brother. Fines for misbehavior deprived him of these highly desirable activities. Contingency contracting helped the entire family become more consistent, less hostile toward each other, and improved Shawn's behavior to an impressive degree. The next step is to extend the contracting system to include Shawn's teacher at school so Shawn will become a better and more popular student.

TABLE 14-3   A TOKEN ECONOMY SYSTEM (BEHAVIORAL CONTRACT) FOR SHAWN AND HIS PARENTS

Shawn's Behavior	Points for Good Behavior	Fines for Bad Behavior	Other Negative Consequences for Misbehavior
Undesirable behaviors			
Hitting, kicking, biting, scratching	2 for not misbehaving	5 points	Time out in his room
Not complying, defying	1 for not misbehaving	2 points	Time out in his room
Stealing, property destruction	2 for not misbehaving	5 points	Restitution, such as repaying owner, or restoring defaced objects
Desirable behaviors			
Helping with house cleaning	2 points	None	None
Walking the dog	1 point	None	None
Helping brother with homework	1 point	None	None

SOURCE: The case of Shawn represents a composite picture of token economy programs devised for home use. Each program is developed through a family's discussions with a therapist, who guides the negotiations between parents and child to produce a realistic, achievable goal and help the family to adjust the program as necessary to produce success.

---

children from engaging in stereotyped, repetitive, or self-mutilating behaviors.

However, overcorrection interrupts other instructional programs for extended periods and is usually an intervention of last choice. Typically, overcorrection is used sparingly with very disturbed children and only in combination with positive reinforcement programs.

CRITIQUE OF SKINNERIAN BEHAVIORAL INTERVENTIONS

Is it right to pay, bribe, reward, or reinforce children for being good, for doing what they are supposed to do? Many critics who object to reinforcing children for increasing their desirable behaviors do not themselves object to receiving pay for their work or awards for their exemplary job-related, athletic, community-service, or other performances. Nor do they object to fines imposed on wrongdoers by the criminal justice system. In fact, our social system, including families, schools, and government are all based on reward and punishment. Therefore, it seems both inconsistent and unwise to expect that children should not be rewarded for their efforts to improve.

Reinforcement contingency management and related interventions have been demonstrated to control specific forms of misbehavior and teach children new, adaptive behaviors in many thousands of cases (Weisz et al., 1995). A limitation of this behavioral approach and, indeed, of any therapy is that the effects can prove transitory and may not generalize outside the treatment setting, whether it is the schoolroom, clinic, or home, unless extensive, aggressive programming for generalization is provided (Stokes & Osnes, 1989). This may require an unceasing effort on the part of parents, teachers, and other caretakers to continue to manage the child's daily reinforcement contingencies over a period of years. That is, in the more troublesome cases, treatment may have to continue indefinitely, as is true of children with severe autistic disorders discussed in Chapter 11. When the contingency management effort is withdrawn, the child's behavior tends to deteriorate, because the reinforcement contingencies in the child's natural everyday environment are insufficient to sustain treatment-based behavioral improvements. This criticism can be applied to all treatment types. Unfortunately, few or no alternative treatments are more successful in producing lasting improvements in many children over a wide variety of environmental settings. However, the social learning and cognitive-behavioral approaches, which are discussed next, specifically attempt to provide the child with techniques for resisting harmful environmental pressures.

COGNITIVE-BEHAVIORAL THERAPIES

As the name implies, cognitive-behavioral therapies incorporate both behavioral techniques and the client's cognitions in the treatment effort (Kendall, 1991). Cognitive-behavioral therapists believe that behavior has roots both in the constraints and opportunities of the external environment and in a client's own thoughts, moods, and feelings. Therapeutic changes in the client's thinking, feeling, and behavior are brought about through modeling, training, and rehearsal of desired new behavioral routines. Appropriate response consequences are provided at first by the therapist, and ultimately by the client to enhance his or her own performance. The cognitive-behavioral approach integrates cognitive, behavioral, emotional, and social strategies for therapeutic change (Kendall, 1991). This approach is firmly rooted in research, and assumes that thoughts or cognitions guide behavior and that emotional reactions to a situation depend on the person's expectancies, assumptions, and evaluations. Further, particular patterns of maladaptive cognitions are thought to characterize specific psychological disorders, so intervention should aim to modify these faulty thought patterns.

Cognitive-behavioral approaches take many different forms. Some concentrate on the modification of deviant perceptions of self and others, while other cognitive-behavioral therapies focus more on altering the child's environment. The first techniques considered here are the cognitive social approaches, which feature modeling and guided participation to alter self-evaluation as well as to teach new behavioral skills.

The *cognitive social approach* (also called *social learning*) stresses that children can be noncoercively instructed in desired behavior patterns, even without many special incentives, through providing them with interesting and appropriate models. Such models are particularly useful when the behaviors to be acquired are subtle, complex, and unlikely to be learned in the child's normal setting. For example, an aggressive child may fail to observe prosocial, peaceful models, and instead watch violent TV programs, play violent video games, and have antisocial friends and family members. For such a child, treatment may consist, in part, of exposing the child to less aggressive and more positive models, and reinforcing the child systematically for emulating them. Socially appropriate peer models are frequently employed with some success in the treatment of children with social skills deficits (see the section in this chapter on Social Skills Training). If children rarely see constructive interactions, they are unlikely to engage in them spontaneously. For nearly all children, social development consists largely of learning to delay gratification, inhibit aggressive behavior, and be kind to others. These behaviors are not easily learned, and children who are delayed or deficient in prosocial behavior require careful nurturing in order to become well socialized, constructive adults.

MODELING AND GUIDED PARTICIPATION

Child and family psychotherapists are increasingly using *modeling*, or the client's observation of another's (the model's) behavior and its consequences (Bandura, 1969). The systematic presentation of live or filmed persons modeling desired patterns of behavior is seeing increased use in the treatment of fearful, anxious children, as well as aggressive youngsters with conduct disorders, and their families (Powers & Rickard, 1992). Children naturally learn patterns of social behavior from observing and imitating others, including family members and models of various types and ages. Behavioral models may be presented symbolically on television and in reading material as well as in live interactions. Given the proper circumstances and inducements, children will imitate behaviors of prosocial as well as deviant models.

There are several ingredients to successful imitation of models. Bandura (1977) separates the modeling process into the following steps. Successful modeling is based on: (1) the child's attention to the model, which depends on both the child's and the model's characteristics, (2) the child's ability to encode and remember the model's actions, (3) the child's physical ability to perform the behaviors, and (4) the child's motivation to imitate the model, which can be enhanced through reinforcement for imitation. Only when all of the preceding components are in place can successful imitation take place.

In addition to the frequent use of modeling procedures in social skills training and parent training programs, which is described elsewhere in this chapter, modeling procedures have often been used to reduce children's fears and anxieties (Barrios & Hartmann, 1988; Kendall & Panichelli-Mindel, 1995). In *guided participation treatment*, which is a particularly effective intervention (Rosenthal & Bandura, 1978), the fearful child first observes fearless models coping successfully with the feared situation. Next the child is physically assisted, if necessary, to approach the feared stimulus. In the case of a fear of dogs, the child might wear padded gloves and might be helped by the model to slowly approach a small, friendly dog who is restrained in a playpen. The child's approach might start from a distance of 20 feet or whatever the child can tolerate, and proceed in 5-foot steps or stages until the child holds the model's arm while the model pets the dog. A next step might be for the child to pet the dog, but with the gloves on; then to remove the gloves to pet the dog; and ultimately to pet and play with the animal freely.

CRITIQUE OF THE COGNITIVE SOCIAL (SOCIAL LEARNING) APPROACH

Modeling is most often combined with other therapeutic interventions such as verbal instructions to the child regarding how to behave, rehearsal of desired behavior with immediate feedback on the child's performance, and systematic positive reinforcement for performance improvements. Some of the most dramatic improvements resulting from modeling interventions have been obtained in treating the fears of children who are to undergo painful medical or dental procedures. In such an intervention, child medical patients are acquainted with the medical setting, personnel, and equipment by visiting the hospital, and seeing another child or a video of a child model experience the scheduled treatment. This modeling treatment has been highly successful and has become routine practice in many pediatric treatment settings (Ollendick & Francis, 1988). Benefits to the child include reduced fear, fewer behavior problems, greater compliance with medical instructions, fewer medical complications, and significantly shorter hospital stays (Hughes, 1993). Modeling procedures are also used extensively in parent training therapy and social skills training therapy, which are discussed next.

Social Skills Training and Self-Regulation Therapy

The aim of self-regulation training is to provide the client with the tools for self-control in everyday life. Children as well as adults can profit from self-regulation training, although disturbed children who are particularly poor at controlling themselves require specially designed training procedures somewhat different from those used with adults (Meichenbaum, 1979). In self-regulation training, children are systematically taught to observe their own behavior in selected problem situations. Then they are instructed in how to evaluate their own performance and provide themselves with appropriate consequences for their success or failure at the specific behavior they are attempting to perform. This means that with only minimal adult guidance, the children learn to bring their behavior under the control of consequences such as self-praise and perhaps self-administered privileges or treats as reinforcers for improved behavior.

One type of self-regulation is the *operant* method developed by Karoly and Kanfer (1982). The operant method consists of four steps: (1) deciding to modify a certain behavior, such as increasing quantity and quality of homework; (2) selecting a specific behavioral goal (for example, at first completing one page of arithmetic homework at 80 percent accuracy, and later increasing amount and percentage of correct answers); (3) monitoring and evaluating one's own behavior in comparison to the goal (completing the page and comparing the answers with those given in the back of the book); and (4) selecting and delivering the specified reward, but only if the goal was reached (self-praise, pointing out the completed homework to parents, watching a favorite television program). The operant approach stresses the child's self-management of reinforcement contingencies as the major effective ingredient of the treatment.

A second and somewhat more widely used form of self-regulation training is the *cognitive self-instructional training* technique developed by Meichenbaum (1979) and Kendall and his colleagues (Kendall & Finch, 1979; Kendall & Hollon, 1979). In self-instructional training, self-directed speech and verbal instructions are used to control behavior. Training in self-instruction was first used with highly impulsive children who were careless in their work and failed at difficult projects because they abandoned them too readily in the face of obstacles. Meichenbaum (1977) developed procedures in which impulsive children were trained to monitor and control their own problem-solving activities. In the first step of Meichenbaum's cognitive self-instruction training, the therapist demonstrates deliberate and effective problem-solving procedures to the child. Then the child imitates the therapist, saying the instructions to herself first aloud and then silently, which will be more appropriate in the classroom. Here is how Meichenbaum and Goodman (1971) transfer control of the child's behavior from the therapist to the child:

1. The adult therapist performs the task while providing self-instructions aloud (modeling).
2. The adult gives the child instructions on how to perform the task (external guidance).
3. The child performs the task while instructing herself aloud (overt self-instruction).
4. The child whispers the instructions to herself while performing the task (gradual removal of overt self-guidance).
5. The child rehearses the instructions to herself silently while performing the task (covert self-guidance).
6. If the child's efforts have failed, she is provided with statements to help her cope with frustration (e.g., "No one succeeds all the time. Take it easy and go back over it again. I can do it.") (Kendall & Braswell, 1985).

Ideally, after a period of training and practice, the correct problem-solving approach becomes so familiar and useful to the child that no specific overt or covert self-instructions are necessary. The child simply performs the task appropriately. Cognitive self-instructional training teaches impulsive children to pause and reflect in order to understand the problem and to consider several possible solutions rather than plunging ahead impulsively with no apparent plan or a doomed plan (see Table 14-4). Moreover, the child is shown how to detect and correct errors in a controlled, matter-of-fact manner, rather than exploding in frustration and giving up. In the final step of the procedure, the child evaluates her own efforts and rewards herself for success, but withholds self-rewards for failure and then tries again.

EVALUATION OF SELF-INSTRUCTIONAL TRAINING FOR IMPULSIVITY

The promise of self-instructional training has not yet been realized. Practical limitations in the lives of troubled children and their families reduce children's abilities to control their own thoughts and behaviors. Self-monitoring and self-reinforcement often do not succeed unless therapists, teachers, or parents also reward the students for accurate recording of their own behavior (Lloyd & Hilliard, 1989). In the treatment of impulsive, hyperactive children, cognitive-behavioral training has reduced one feature of attention-deficit with hyperactivity disorder, namely impulsivity, but it has not always rectified other features of this disorder (Kendall, 1993). Only a few studies have assessed long-term improvement from cognitive-behavioral treatment, and those studies produced mixed results (Horn, Ialongo, Greenberg, Packard, & Smith-Winberry, 1990; Kendall & Braswell, 1993). Hughes (1990) concluded that the effectiveness of

TABLE 14-4 COMPONENTS OF COGNITIVE SELF-INSTRUCTION

Step in Self-Instruction

1. Pausing to define the problem
2. Considering several alternative solutions
3. Giving self-instructions on how to perform the task
4. Checking one's work and correcting errors calmly
5. Reinforcing oneself for a correct solution

Examples of Self-Instruction

"What does the teacher want me to do?" "I must stop and think before I begin."

"What plans could I try?" "How well would that work?" "What else might work?"

"I have to go slowly and carefully." "Okay, draw the line down, down, good; then to the right . . . Remember, go slowly."

"Have I got it right so far? That's a mistake. I'll just erase it." "That's OK . . . Even if I make an error, I can go on slowly and carefully."

"Good, I'm doing fine." "I've done a pretty good job." "Good for me!"

SOURCES: Meichenbaum, D., & Goodman, J. (1971). Training impulsive children to talk to themselves: A means of developing self-control. *Journal of Abnormal Psychology, 77,* 115–126.

self-control training with impulsive and hyperactive children has not been established despite more than 20 years of research. Operant techniques (contingency management) in which the therapist monitors and reinforces the child's behavior have proved at least equally successful at less cost. Although children do appear to benefit from cognitive-behavioral treatment, other therapies, particularly behavioral therapies, may be equally effective (Hart & Morgan, 1993).

OTHER DISORDERS TREATED WITH SELF-REGULATION TRAINING

In addition to treating impulsive children, self-regulation training has been administered to those with various problems that are resistant to more traditional forms of intervention. Self-regulation training has been at least partially successful in treating difficult problems such as aggression, delinquency, fears and phobias, and social

withdrawal (Hughes, 1993). Depression is a mental condition (described in Chapter 7) that is intimately linked with negative thoughts and unrealistically severe self-criticism. Depressed children dwell on negative events, and criticize and punish themselves for poor performance more than do other children (Kaslow, Stark, Printz, Livingston, & Tsai, 1992). These features of depression led investigators to some success in applying self-instructional techniques to the treatment of children's depression. Depressed children were helped to set more realistic standards for judging their own performance, set attainable immediate goals, and reinforce themselves more and punish themselves less. The depressed children were also trained to view themselves more positively, much as nondepressed children do. They were helped to attribute their task success to their stable, desirable characteristics such as their high intelligence, and their task failure to temporary factors such as bad luck, insufficient effort, or an extremely difficult task, much as nondepressed individuals do (Stark, Reynolds, & Kaslow, 1987). In cases in which the depressed child's problem is not exclusively attitudinal, but instead represents a skill deficit, the child may also receive training in appropriate academic, social, or athletic skills. This multifaceted therapeutic approach using self-instructional, coping training techniques holds considerable promise in the treatment of childhood depression (Stark et al., 1987; Stark, Rouse, & Livingston, 1991).

CRITIQUE OF COGNITIVE-BEHAVIORAL THERAPIES

Overall, the cognitive-behavioral therapies for children appear promising, but they generally have not proven to be more effective than reinforcement contingency management programs, which train children directly in social and academic skills (Van Hasselt & Hersen, 1993). Treatment techniques such as modeling and guided participation have been demonstrated to be effective in treating specific phobias and apprehension about painful medical treatment, but in general little is known about the long-term efficacy of cognitive-behavioral treatments used with children (Mash, 1989). An intensive research effort is required to establish the relative effectiveness of cognitive-behavioral treatment and other therapeutic approaches. Unfortunately, most of the available research support and effort have been directed to adults' needs, with children being relatively neglected.

SOCIAL SKILLS TRAINING

Treatment for children and families increasingly consists of combining various specific training programs in a general "package" geared to the needs of the participants (Hackmann, 1993). Many intervention programs for children feature *social skills training (SST)*, which provides rejected or neglected children with improved methods of making new acquaintances and getting along with others. Children who have a number of different types of adjustment problems all experience difficulty in social relations. Examples are children who are inappropriately aggressive or hyperactive, and whose antagonistic behavior drives away peers and adults; children who are timid and suffer from social phobia and fearfully avoid others; and those who are mildly handicapped with learning disabilities or mild retardation. Social skills training programs are based on the assumption that social skills are acquired primarily through social learning and can be improved through teaching children specific social behaviors to make them more responsive, effective, and appropriate in their interactions with others (Michelson, Sugai, Wood, & Kazdin, 1985). In turn, the children's improved behavior should make them more acceptable companions for their peers, teachers, and family. Others with whom they interact will increasingly reinforce the children for their improved behavior.

Specific techniques used in SST include a general focus on positive behaviors and positive change methods including modeling more appropriate comments and behaviors, coaching the child in what to do and when to do it in the course of a social interaction, and providing generous praise for improvements (Elliott & Gresham, 1993). SST can be individual or can take place in a treatment group, and socially skilled peers can be trained to act as coaches in protective situations devised to make it easy for the unskilled child to succeed. The approach requires some modification for use with adolescents. Peer coaches are useful for children and are particularly attractive to unskilled adolescents, since they are much better informed about the teen culture than are adults, even therapists. The adolescent peer group may have unique teenage speech and behavior patterns and may reject more formal modes of social interaction that character-

ize adult social groups (Christopher, Nagle, & Hansen, 1993).

CRITIQUE OF SOCIAL SKILLS TRAINING

Although early SST programs produced mixed effects, more recent efforts, which have concentrated on training for aggressive, unpopular boys, have been more effective (Bierman & Montminy, 1993). During SST, the rejected boys gradually improved their conversational skills with peers, which produced greater acceptance by other children. SST was more effective if the children also learned what *not* to do through receiving prohibitions about engaging in inappropriate behavior (e.g., "Remember not to grab anyone's toys.") (Bierman, 1989). If the SST is successful and they do not continue to experience the pain of rejection, aggressive boys may well develop more normally and avoid future problems they otherwise would encounter. SST provides a promising intervention for children with very difficult psychological problems.

Family Therapies

The preceding treatment approaches typically treat individual children and their problems, yet most professionals realize that psychological problems develop and are maintained within families. Family therapy originated out of the recognition of the role played by close relatives, sometimes including the grandparents, in the disturbances of individuals (Everett & Volgy, 1993). *Systems-oriented family therapy* rejects the traditional psychotherapy focus on the individual's symptomatology and instead portrays the entire family unit or system as malfunctioning and causing its members to engage in problematic behavior. According to this family systems view, families target particular members as deviant (*the identified patient*) when, in fact, it is the family interactional system that is creating problems. For instance, Patterson (1975) found that children referred by their parents for treatment for aggression were actually no more aggressive than their supposedly normal siblings. However, the other family members all felt it was a particular child who was the antisocial one. In such situations, it would do no good to treat the identified patient alone, since the parents' perceptions and treatment of each other and the children all require modification. Thus, the entire family

A skilled psychotherapist engages the child as well as the parents during a family therapy session. It is the family interaction, rather than the child, who is the focus of family therapy.

as a unit or dynamic system is the focus of assessment and treatment, rather than the individual members.

FAMILY SYSTEMS THERAPY

There are many different types of family therapy ranging from psychoanalytic to family systems and behavioral approaches. Among the most popular at this time are the systems approach and the behavioral approach. The *systems approach* to conjoint family therapy (Haley, 1963; Jackson & Weakland, 1961; Satir, 1967) stresses understanding the roles played by every family member. The identified patient's problem is viewed as attributable to the family's atypical interactions. Systems therapists view a child's deviant behavior as serving some function for the family, which explains the problem's intensity and persistence. For example, a child's hostile attacks on siblings and classmates may distract attention from the parents' unhappy marriage and constant bickering. This useful function of the child's problematic behavior may cause the others to unknowingly encourage and maintain the child's aggression, and thus conceal the unhealthy marriage. Therefore, the family maintains its balance or homeostasis and remains together to fulfill at least some

of its members' needs for security, affection, and support. The dysfunctional family may resist any form of change, including improvements in order to maintain the shaky balance. Because the source of the problem lies in the interactions of the family, the treatment should include the entire family, even the younger children.

Therapists with a systems or communications orientation analyze the verbal and nonverbal messages exchanged in family interactions. Satir (1967) stressed the importance of *covert family rules*, or unverbalized expectations governing each member's responding. The therapist attempts to uncover these dysfunctional rules in order to allow the family to change them. As an example, a family rule might allow the daughter to subtly point out what others are doing wrong, which gets them into trouble, while she appears to be a caring, perfect child. Another covert rule might allow the mother to dominate the others and prevent them from leading lives of their own by means of frequent psychologically based physical complaints of migraine headaches, asthma attacks, or fainting. In *enmeshed families*, the members continuously intrude into each other's affairs, often demanding to be informed on the whereabouts and activities of family members, dictating their actions, and even their emotions. In *disengaged families*, the isolated members offer each other little emotional support, affection, or assistance. In each case, the family rules are dysfunctional, resulting in frustrated and unhappy family members. The therapist identifies and points out these family rules and so provides the family the opportunity to make positive changes toward healthier relationships. Communications therapists might relabel individual's behaviors in more positive terms to help family members view them differently. The child who has been viewed as stubborn or selfish in the family might be described as becoming more grown-up and independent. The therapist might also "prescribe the symptom" and direct family members to caricature their customary maladaptive behavior, such as by using exaggerated terms to criticize each other's eating habits, dress, speech, and cleanliness in ridiculously strong terms, which may help them attain a sense of proportion, humor, and greater tolerance for each other.

CRITIQUE OF FAMILY SYSTEMS THERAPY

This type of intervention cannot be attempted when one or more of the central members of the family refuse to participate. Fathers very often are unavailable or unwilling to participate, which rules out treating the family system directly. Further, children who are too young or oppositional might decline to take part. In addition, recognizing troublesome interaction patterns might not suffice to improve the situation, and family members might need instruction and guided rehearsal in more functional behaviors. Thus, the eclectic or combined types of family therapies (as described later) might be preferable.

BEHAVIORAL FAMILY THERAPY

The aim of many behavioral family therapies is to reduce family members' reliance on coercion and increase the exchange of positive reinforcement in order to promote improved family relationships (Patterson et al., 1975). In troubled families, positive events are infrequent, and members notice and respond to the negative and disruptive actions of the others. Punitive, coercive exchanges are common, and children's aggressive, coercive behaviors are shaped when the others give in to them rather than continuing to fight. The behavioral family therapist attempts to train the members to detect both positive and coercive exchanges and systematically increase the rate

of positive interactions. *Contingency contracting* is frequently used to ensure that the child's desirable behaviors are noted and reinforced by his parents and that the child understands exactly what behaviors are required of him. *Modeling and role playing or rehearsal* (discussed later) may be used to teach family members how to respond to each other more positively. Therapy sessions may be held in the family's home to allow the therapist to observe their behavior and implement treatment programs in their usual environment. A related form of intervention, parent training therapy, is discussed later in this chapter.

CRITIQUE OF BEHAVIORAL FAMILY THERAPY

Some parents find this approach uninviting because it requires so much sustained and systematic effort on their part. For example, contingency contracting requires parents to make daily observations of their child's behavior, record the behavior, calculate reinforcers and perhaps fines, and give the child the earnings for behavioral improvements. Parents must have the motivation, energy, and dedication to do this over a period of weeks, months, and sometimes years. A complicating factor is that parental discouragement and depression leads to failure to cooperate with therapists in the treatment plan and premature withdrawal from treatment. Nevertheless, although all types of family therapy are beneficial, behavioral family therapy has tended to outperform nonbehavioral family therapies in comparisons of results of many studies (Shadish, Montgomery, Wilson, Wilson, Bright, & Okwumabua, 1993). If the family has broken up or its members become so dysfunctional that they will not or cannot participate, behaviorally oriented foster family care (Patterson, Dishion, & Chamberlain, 1993) may be provided for the child, as discussed later in this chapter.

ECLECTIC FAMILY THERAPY

Practicing psychotherapists are likely to adopt any treatment technique that holds promise, regardless of its theoretical origin. Consequently, it is often difficult to characterize a particular therapist's approach as behavioral, client-centered, or other, since they use a mixture of interventions. Some combined approaches to family therapy explicitly employ techniques adapted from various theoretical orientations. Alexander's *functional family therapy* (Alexander & Malouf, 1983) employs a systems perspective on the family, but also uses behavioral methods such as modeling and contingency contracting to modify specific problem behaviors. Families of adolescent delinquents are trained to communicate with each other more clearly and accurately, to increase reciprocity in their exchanges as opposed to having one person dominate. Families are also helped to break out of dysfunctional practices and explore alternative solutions for problems that resemble those of well-functioning families.

Critique of Eclectic Family Therapy

Although there has been little well-controlled study of functional family therapy (Patterson et al., 1993), earlier outcome reports were positive, and both adolescent delinquents and their siblings appeared to benefit from the treatment (Klein, Alexander, & Parsons, 1977).

EFFECTS OF PSYCHOTHERAPY

To the general, perhaps oversimplified question of whether psychotherapy is effective with children and adolescents, the answer is *yes*. Analyses of the results of many studies of psychotherapy outcomes indicate that various types of psychotherapy produced results that were better than those observed in two-thirds to three-quarters of untreated children. When compared to no treatment or a nonspecific (placebo) intervention consisting only of extra attention, psychotherapy was superior regardless of the type of psychotherapy administered (Casey & Berman, 1985; Kazdin, 1991; Weisz, Weiss, & Donenberg, 1992; Weisz et al., 1995). The next question to be answered is whether any particular type of psychotherapy is superior to any other. Here again a simple answer might be yes: Research studies indicate that *behavioral therapy* produces larger treatment effects on average than other methods (Casey & Berman, 1985; Kazdin, 1991; Weisz et al., 1995). However, here the picture becomes less clear, because the outcomes or measures of success used in behavioral therapies tend to be more specific and shorter term than those adopted in other therapy approaches such as psychodynamic therapies (Weisz & Weiss, 1993). The measure of success in behavioral therapy might be a decrease in a child's observed oppositional behavior toward parents and teachers. In contrast, the goal of a psychodynamic psychotherapist may

be the child's more balanced use of various ego defenses. The behavioral therapist's aim of reducing oppositional behavior appears more modest and more readily obtainable than the psychodynamic therapist's re-working of the child's anxiety management tactics. The outcome goal of the psychodynamic approach is much more global, long-range, and difficult to measure than the specific behavioral goal of reinforcement contingency management interventions. Consequently, it is difficult to judge comparative efficacy fairly. However, a recent review (Weisz et al., 1995) found behavioral approaches to be more effective than nonbehavioral ones, even when outcome measures were restricted to behaviors not directly treated. Box 14-2 describes the difficult process of evaluating treatment effectiveness.

Therapy Outcome and Child Gender

Child psychotherapy clients differ on many dimensions, some of which could affect their receptivity to psychosocial interventions. It is not known conclusively whether psychotherapy works equally well with younger children and older teenagers, girls and boys, or children of various ethnic and social groups. Over a large number of outcome studies, better results are reported with girls than boys, particularly with adolescent girls (Weisz et al., 1995). This greater success with girls may be associated with their greater interest in exploring psychological topics related to their lives or it may be due to sex differences in rates of difficult-to-treat antisocial conduct disorders. Many more boys develop conduct disorder and problems in aggression control than do girls, and such externalizing problems are among the most resistant to treatment of any type of juvenile psychiatric disorder (see Chapter 5). Thus, boys could appear to be less responsive to psychotherapy than girls simply because more boys are conduct disordered. A fairer question is whether boys and girls respond significantly differently to treatment when the boys and girls have exactly the same types of behavior problems. Unfortunately, the answer to this more specific and fairer question is not yet completely known, because too few therapy outcome studies exist at this level of specificity (comparing girls and boys with the same types and severity of disorders at the same ages).

With at least one exception, studies indicate that the client's age does not seem to make an important differ-

---

BOX 14-2 TOUGH TESTS OF TREATMENT EFFECTIVENESS

Dr. Linda Jessup is a child clinical psychologist who works in the outpatient child and family services of a private hospital for children. Parents who consult with her often ask: "Will psychotherapy with you really help us and our child?" How can she answer this very reasonable question?

Precise and carefully controlled treatment evaluation research is required to assess treatment effects, usually in tests with large groups of children or families. Extreme care must be taken to minimize bias in selecting the experimental groups and judging clients' outcomes. In acceptable therapy evaluation experiments, clients are carefully selected and extensively tested so their *baseline level of performance* is identified. Thus, in the case of children who are truant, defiant, and shoplift, the target groups might be composed of children between the ages of 10 and 12 years who have been rated as highly aggressive by parents and teachers, and who were apprehended shoplifting at least three times and appeared in juvenile court. This is the baseline for their antisocial behavior. Each child also would be comprehensively psychologically tested for IQ level, personality attributes, attitudes, and psychological disorders.

The children would then be randomly assigned to at least two different groups: (1) a treatment group to receive the therapy being evaluated, and (2) a comparison or control group. The comparison subjects might receive no special treatment at first, but then participate in the experimental therapy at a later time (as a wait-list control group). Alternatively, comparison group members might receive a treatment of known effectiveness as a basis of comparison with the treatment being studied. Sometimes a particular form of psychotherapy and a drug treatment are compared.

Experimenters have a stake in identifying effective treatments, so they must be experimentally "blind," and be completely unaware of which children receive the experimental treatment and which children do not. Only the experiment director knows which group receives the treatment.

Therapy researchers place credence in reports of the effectiveness of a particular form of therapy only when: (1) a large group of children is studied who are very similar to those who eventually receive the treatment; (2) assignment to the experimental groups is determined *randomly*, so the more seriously disturbed children are not systematically assigned to either group; and (3) appropriate treatment outcome measures are administered. In the case of the children who shoplift, it is important to assess long-term effects, such as whether the treatment reduces their shoplifting as much as a year or two later.

Treatment outcome research is expensive and time-consuming, but the results support the use of psychosocial therapy with children. Thus, Dr. Jessup can tell the concerned parents that many others have been helped by child or family psychotherapy, although there is no guarantee of therapy effectiveness in an individual case. In the future, we will be even better able to judge the relative effectiveness of various therapy alternatives, thanks to the dedicated efforts of many research investigators.

---

ence in psychotherapy success. The exception occurred in one review of outcome studies of cognitive-behavioral therapy, which found that older children between the ages of 11 and 13 years had better outcomes from psychotherapy than younger children 5–7 years of age (Durlak, Fuhrman, & Lampman, 1991). However, most reviewers have concluded that the effects reported for child and adolescent psychotherapy are generally comparable to the success levels reported for psychotherapy with adults (Weisz, Weiss, & Donenberg, 1992). Psychotherapy tends to be as effective for younger clients as for adults.

Therapy Research Limitations

There are several problems with therapy outcome research. First, child clients of both sexes and very diverse ages, from preschoolers to adolescents, are often grouped together, when a treatment may be much more appropriate for girls or boys or for children of a certain age and developmental status (Kazdin, 1993). Further, the site where the treatment trial takes place seems to be related to its success. The greatest success rates are found in *controlled experimental studies* that take place in research units and are not representative of psychotherapy as it is usually delivered to children in treatment agencies, clinics, and hospitals. In fact, conditions may be optimal in special experimental studies in which therapists are usually better trained and supervised in the administration of the therapy techniques under study, the child clients are carefully selected to have limited rather than pervasive problems, and the child clients may be less seriously disturbed than children who are usually seen in clinics. In a better-controlled experimental comparison, therapeutic interventions may appear to be more effective than they are in actual clinical practice with more seriously disturbed youngsters and families, where therapy is conducted by rushed, overworked, less adequately trained and supervised therapists. It is, however, of limited practical use to determine that child psychotherapy is effective under the best-controlled conditions when cost is not a consideration. Those ideal conditions cannot be approximated in community practice where most children and families are actually treated.

Knowing that psychotherapy is more effective than no psychotherapy provides parents and therapists with little practical guidance in selecting the type of treatment to be offered to a particular child or teenager. Instead, the child's cultural context and individual needs and characteristics must be taken into account in devising a treatment plan. The child's progress in treatment must be evaluated carefully, and the plan must be adjusted accordingly. Even though some form of intervention, such as behavior therapy, is more effective on average than other interventions, this generalization may not hold true for any particular child. To best decide how to treat an individual client requires expert assessment and diagnosis of the child's and family's problems, and a review of the research literature to determine each treatment alternative's likelihood of success with a child of similar age, ethnicity, and family situation. Ultimately, practical limitations such as cost to the family, insurer, or government agency and the local availability of different types of care may weigh most heavily in decisions regarding the child's treatment plan.

CHILDREN IN CONTEXT: TREATMENT IN THE FAMILY, COMMUNITY, AND CULTURE

Cultural factors should also be considered in examining the outcome of conventional psychotherapies and in identifying new, more culturally appropriate interventions. Traditional clinical interventions that may be quite effective with the white, middle-class population for which they are developed could prove ineffective or even counterproductive with clients from other social and cultural backgrounds. Too many impoverished minority children are growing up in chronically dangerous situations where violence is a fact of life (Vraniak & Pickett,

1993). For these children, traditional interventions may be insufficient and ineffective, and such treatments have little relationship to the problems they face in their daily lives. Moreover, simply receiving any type of conventional mental health service is stigmatizing in some ethnic minority and immigrant communities in the United States, such as Mexican-American and Japanese-American, so members of those communities avoid seeking professional help (Marsella, 1993).

Individual or group psychotherapy may be less appropriate and consequently less effective for members of many ethnic groups than culturally familiar, group- or family-based interventions. More familiar and culturally compatible treatments may include employing a consultant who is not a mental health professional—perhaps a neighbor or teacher—who is knowledgeable about the referred family's culture and values. The consultant can help clients and their neighbors organize for mutual assistance. Such contextual interventions ultimately benefit the development of the community, particularly the referred children and families (Tharp, 1991). As an example of how such community intervention could take place, one school-based program for Hispanic families established ties among the residents and their extended families, their friends (compadres), church workers, existing community support systems, and the school in order to provide an extensive, caring network of support for children and families. Where individualized treatment could lead to further isolation and demoralization of children from Hispanic families, community organization appears more appropriate and more likely to succeed.

Treatment modalities such as psychotherapy, which were devised by and for European-Americans, are not equally appropriate for use with groups with very different cultural characteristics. In fact, cultural differences can lead to profound misunderstandings between psychotherapists and their clients. As an example, psychotherapists often look directly at a client to indicate feelings of interest, involvement, and empathy. However, the direct gaze that indicates intense interest in Western European culture could unintentionally convey hostile intrusion to a traditional Japanese-American client, which is the opposite of the psychotherapist's intent (Marsella, 1993). Such miscommunication arising from basic cultural differences in communication styles would probably significantly decrease the psychotherapist's ability to

---

BOX 14-3 CULTURALLY APPROPRIATE TREATMENTS: PERHAPS OUR GRANDPARENTS DID KNOW BEST

By the year 2000, approximately 30 percent of school-age children will belong to a minority group of some type, including black, Hispanic, Asian, American Indian, or Pacific Islander, or some combination of ethnic groups (Gibbs & Huang, 1991). How well are their mental health needs being served? So few minority children are receiving mental health services that little is known about the effectiveness of traditional assessment and treatment services for them (Kazdin, 1993).

However, psychologists are accepting the challenge to develop culturally sensitive, relevant, and acceptable treatments for minority youth. One group of investigators (Malgady, Rogler, & Costantino, 1990) devised and tested treatments specifically for Puerto Rican children and adolescents. Within a cognitive social treatment model, children were informed about appropriate behavior in a number of different situations. Since storytelling and presentation of famous people as examples were culturally familiar activities, stories were used preventively to boost self-efficacy beliefs, increase ethnic identity, and provide young people with models of desirable behavior. Young children and preschoolers were told folktales (*cuentos*) in either English or Spanish featuring characters learning socially appropriate behavior such as cooperating and helping others. Small groups of adolescents took turns reading aloud and discussing carefully prepared stories featuring outstanding adult role models from Puerto Rican history. The aim was to inspire prosocial behavior, foster ethnic pride, and provide children with examples of coping with commonly encountered stresses common to the Puerto Rican community, for example, how to deal with poverty, illness, or racially prejudiced taunts from other children.

It may not be necessary or possible to develop separate treatment programs for each of the many distinct ethnic groups. However, it is necessary that mental health interventions be seen as inviting and accessible by potential clients, or they will not be used. Making the process culturally sensitive and appropriate is an important first step to providing needed services to all sectors of the community.

SOURCES: Gibbs, J. T., & Huang, L. N. (Eds.). (1991). *Children of color: Psychological interventions with minority youth.* San Francisco: Jossey-Bass; Kazdin, A. E. (1993). Psychotherapy for children and adolescents: Current progress and future research directions. *American Psychologist, 48,* 644–657; Malgady, R. G., Rogler, L. H., & Costantino, G. (1990). Culturally sensitive psychotherapy for Puerto Rican children and adolescents: A program of treatment. *Journal of Consulting and Clinical Psychology, 58,* 704–712.

---

aid the client. Box 14-3 describes an intervention that may be more culturally acceptable to Puerto Rican families than traditional psychosocial therapies.

The situation in the United States is complicated by patterns of immigration, residential segregation, and the increasing numbers and diversity of cultural groups. Each cultural group may have particular needs and values that determine the most effective type of treatment. In today's multicultural schools and neighborhoods, the challenge is to deliver educational and mental health services in a form that each child and family will welcome, can understand, and will accept (Tharp, 1993).

Nonprofessional Family Support

One form of helping that may be acceptable to most groups is the *family support movement* (Zigler & Black, 1989), which was first developed as a preventive intervention of the Head Start program. A family support movement has developed because of the expense and unavailability of educational programs for young children and professional mental health care. Moreover, some families find the use of mental health services to be lo-

gistically difficult because of time and transportation problems, or they may consider mental health services stigmatizing and uninviting. Parents have formed family support programs to strengthen informal systems by enhancing parents' feelings of empowerment so they become better able to help themselves and their children. Community volunteers, with or without the help of professionals, establish support groups, drop-in centers for child care, information and referral programs, parent education groups, parent and child activities, and other family services. The family support movement is definitely optimistic, assuming that all parents have coping strengths that can be used to develop their abilities to cope with difficult situations and increase their family's ability to adapt to the community.

CRITIQUE OF FAMILY SUPPORT PROGRAMS

Although the family support movement is gaining momentum, there are serious obstacles. Many needed services are not inexpensive and some, such as child care, require appropriate housing and trained personnel if the services are to be of good quality and meet city and state requirements. All-volunteer activities often lack stability and cease to exist once their enthusiastic and energetic originators leave. There is also the question about the effectiveness of family support programs. Much further research will be needed before it is known whether family support programs actually confer the hoped-for benefits on their participants or whether they, like some attractive sounding fads of the past, will prove ineffective and be replaced with other types of assistance.

Long-Term Residential Treatment

Long-term residential care is a treatment alternative of last choice for children who, for various reasons, cannot be treated in the less restrictive, more natural surroundings of their homes and neighborhoods. Our society is notably reluctant to deprive children or adults of their liberty. We are particularly reluctant to separate children from their homes and families and confine them in an institution for 24 hours a day, sometimes for periods of months or years. Most residential treatment programs for children and youth offer regular or special education, psychosocial treatment and medication, and recreation to small groups of children of similar ages. Visits from family members are usually permitted under controlled circumstances, and as the child's condition improves, progressively longer home stays are scheduled. Sometimes parenting training is offered so parents can sustain the child's improvements. Residential treatment has been variously criticized as intrusive, overused, potentially neglectful or abusive, possibly ineffective, and prohibitively costly (Wells, 1991). Many people who experienced residential treatment as children and teenagers look back on their hospitalization as punishment rather than a helpful treatment (Curry, 1991). Because of these criticisms, residential treatment is officially discouraged, and recent legislation has limited federal third-party payments to residential treatment centers to no more than 150 days per year per child (1990, Department of Defense Authorization Bill). Yet there is no alternative to long-term residential care for some damaged or dangerous children.

Sometimes there is no acceptable alternative to institutionalization for children who have been severely and repeatedly abused and cannot be placed in foster homes, have committed serious criminal offenses, require prolonged psychiatric hospitalization, or seriously and persistently attempt suicide. Wells (1991) recounts the case of two brothers who were so inadequately cared for and

abused by their parents that they were in residential placement. The neglected and unsupervised 8-year-old was hit by a car while riding his bicycle on a freeway. His 6-year-old brother tried to leap from a second-floor window after his father was jailed for throwing the boys' 2-year-old brother out of the window in a fit of rage. The 6-year-old was not safe from his father or himself, no relatives could or would take the boys, and thus there was no choice but to place both in residential care.

Residential treatment can take many forms. There are large, well-established residential treatment centers, small group homes, and community residences throughout the United States. The quality of care offered to the residents is largely dependent on the funding of the institution and professionalism of the staff, so the programs range from superior to inadequate. Because children in residential care are among the most disturbed and difficult group to care for, institutions find it a challenge to recruit, train, and retain highly qualified workers. Residential staff members find society's disapproval of their work demoralizing. They observe: ". . . we in the field have been reporting, usually to each other, a worsening struggle to work with a much more damaged group of children and families, and a scramble to adjust our practice methods to meet both client needs and policy directives that may or may not have anything to do with client needs" (Small, Kennedy, & Bender, 1991, p. 331).

Good residential care aims not only to treat and train the children themselves, but to improve the family's functioning as well. Treatment should consist of group therapy for the children (possibly individual therapy as well) and training in parenting practices (possibly also in anger control and social skills). In many cases, institutional care for children must be accompanied by family therapy, alcohol or drug abuse treatment, and specific skills training for the parents.

Although residential treatment is officially discouraged in favor of less restrictive alternatives, increasing numbers of children are referred for institutionalization. In 1986, 25,334 children were in nonprofit residential treatment centers, which was a 32 percent increase in only three years (Select Committee on Children, Youth, and Families, 1990). The Select Committee on Children, Youth, and Families projected that 30,000 children would be in nonprofit residential treatment centers in 1995, and that the number would rise in the foreseeable future. Since the trend is toward increasing use of residential treatment for children, it is important to evaluate the effectiveness of this type of care.

CRITIQUE OF RESIDENTIAL TREATMENT

The few controlled research studies reported showed that between 27 percent and 63 percent of the ex-residents remained improved after their discharge. However, there were poor outcomes in 27 percent to 31 percent of the cases, and 50 percent of one discharged group were re-hospitalized in the decade following their release. As might be expected, better outcomes were obtained for children who had (1) more supportive peer and family relationships, (2) less serious diagnoses, (3) at least average intelligence, and (4) problem behaviors in reaction to stressful situations. Children who stayed at least three months and continued to receive therapy after discharge also had better outcomes than children and teens who were institutionalized more briefly and were not given follow-up treatment. These same positive circumstances benefit children receiving any form of educational or psychological treatment.

Parent Training

Parent training therapy offers a popular and often effective means of helping younger antisocial, aggressive children and their parents. The development of parent training therapy is a substantial contribution to the well-being of thousands of families, especially those with out-of-control, aggressive youngsters. Without effective treatment, the outlook is not favorable for many children with serious aggressive, externalizing disorders. Conduct disorder persists in approximately 45 percent of children who develop this problem by ages 4–12, and it is even more resistant to treatment in adolescence, persisting for at least four years in nearly 60 percent of the cases (Offord, Boyle, Racine, Fleming, Cadman, Blum et al., 1992). The seriousness and marked persistence of conduct disorder lend high priority to the development of effective treatment interventions.

Parent training programs aim to improve parenting practices and relationships within the family under the assumption that improved family functioning will promote normal child development. Within a supportive, caring treatment environment, parents are instructed to use various behavioral techniques adapted to the age of the child. With young children, appropriate management techniques include distraction, selective attention to positive behaviors, and ignoring mildly inappropriate behavior (Forehand & McMahon, 1981; Patterson, Reid, Jones, & Conger, 1975; Webster-Stratton, 1990). Time-out from on-going positive reinforcement such as parental attention, playing with toys, or watching television is carefully scheduled to control problems such as physically attacking others or throwing temper tantrums. Therapists also work to change parents' attitudes so they become more warm, approving, and closer to their children.

Parents learn to apply programs of positive reinforcement and discipline that are strictly dependent on the child's behavior, and not on the parent's mood, energy level, or whim. Parents may set up written contracts and token economies with their child and administer points for appropriate behavior, followed by larger delayed reinforcers administered as the child earns them. Fines, privilege removal, and time-out may be made contingent on inappropriate behavior. Because the family may have multiple problems, additional therapeutic interventions may be employed, such as drug or alcohol abuse treatment groups, anger control groups, special education classes, social skills training, and group or individual therapy for the parents or child (Patterson et al., 1993).

Parents improve their management of their children more if they receive support and facilitation in therapy groups, rather than instructions alone (Goldfried & Castonguary, 1993; Patterson & Forgatch, 1985). Their whole approach to childrearing, their attitudes, and much of their behavior toward their children must be changed if the situation is to improve. The task for parents and therapists is described in Box 14-4.

PARENT TRAINING EFFECTIVENESS

Reviews of research evaluations of the treatment of child conduct disorder indicate that parent training therapy is the most effective intervention currently available (Dumas, 1989; McMahon & Wells, 1989; Patterson et al., 1993). Parent training is more effective among those with children between the ages of 3 years and 8 years than it is among parents of older children. Generally, the younger the child, the more successful is parent training (Dishion, 1984). Older children and their parents find change more difficult. Patterson and Stoolmiller (1991) found that parent training produces less improvement in parental discipline practices when children are older than

---

BOX 14-4　DON'T JUST TELL THEM WHAT TO DO: THE ART AND SCIENCE OF PARENT TRAINING THERAPY

Parent training involves much more than simply providing information on how parents should interact with their children. Parent training experts Carolyn Webster-Stratton and Martin Herbert (1993) advise therapists to begin by establishing a supportive, nonjudgmental relationship with the parents, reinforcing and validating parents' observations, and encouraging them to explore various solutions to the family's problems rather than seeking a "quick fix." Parents of children with conduct disorders frequently feel inadequate as parents and hopeless about their children. Such parents might be taught that they need not be incapacitated by their excessive worry about their situation and instructed to think of reassuring self-statements, for example, that all parents face problems with their children and become discouraged at times, but that the situation will improve if they persevere.

Parents meet in groups with a therapist, are taught general problem-solving skills, and are encouraged to focus on long-term goals of improved child behavior rather than giving in to the insistent demands of a coercive child for the sake of achieving temporary peace in the family. At the same time, they are encouraged to accept the child's limitations and recognize that the child also feels miserable. Webster-Stratton and Herbert (1993) have the following excellent advice for parents who may be inclined to accept defeat too readily:

"Your child needs hundreds of chances to try to learn from his mistakes. His learning more appropriate social skills is just like when he was a baby and was learning how to walk. Do you remember how often he tried to get up and fell down? . . . Well this is just the same. It takes lots of small steps and experiments for a child to learn appropriate social skills. And just as you must constantly support the baby who is stumbling, . . . so must you the child who is developing his social skills" (p. 449).

Therapists teach parents in a nondirective fashion through modeling and gently persuading, suggesting, and explaining (e.g., "It is frustrating, but you know it looks like you're doing a nice job of beginning to help him understand the perspective of others in a situation," p. 427). Groups may also view and discuss videotapes of other parent models performing adaptively or incorrectly as they deal with children in various common situations, such as handling child disobedience.

Finally, parents in parent training groups are encouraged to continue to meet with each other informally for support after the therapy is concluded. They are encouraged to babysit for each other to provide one another with recreation and some time away from their children.

This program is sensitive to the parents' needs and frustrations as well as to their children's problems. Through a combination of clinical training and experience, plus knowledge derived from therapy research, therapists are offering help to many troubled families.

SOURCES: Webster-Stratton, C., & Herbert, M. (1993). "What really happens in parent training?" *Behavior Modification*, 17, 407–456.
Also see:
Webster-Stratton, C., & Herbert, M. (1994). *Troubled families–problem children: A collaborative approach to working with families.* Chichester, England: Wiley.

---

approximately 9 years. Older children and adolescents with conduct problems typically have had trouble with their parents for a number of years, and the conflict may become more intense as the pre-adolescent or adolescent seeks independence from the family. Although older children and adolescents appear to improve and become less antisocial in their behavior during treatment, many resume their aggressive, deviant behavior after the treatment is concluded. Thus, it is important to engage the family in therapy while the child is young and the benefits can extend over a period of years (Patterson et al., 1993).

Therapeutic Foster Family Treatment for Adolescents

At present, the only promising treatment intervention for severely conduct disordered or delinquent adolescents is removal from the family of origin and placement in

family foster home care with psychologically trained, carefully supervised foster parents (Chamberlain, 1996; Chamberlain & Reid, 1991). Such teenagers may engage in chronic truancy, angry defiance of their parents, theft, drug use, alcoholism, and serious criminal behavior. In foster care, chronic juvenile offenders are individually placed in foster families where they receive individual therapy, an individualized home management program conducted by the foster parents, and a school program monitored by teachers in close cooperation with the foster parents. The foster parents might be graduate students or have college degrees and special training in the helping professions and they provide the youth with a structured behavioral management program based on social learning principles (Chamberlain, 1996). The foster parents and the adolescent agree on a set of daily responsibilities, with appropriate reinforcement for completion, such as points for outings, movies and other recreational time, or inviting friends to the house. The youth's contacts are closely monitored and supervised to minimize antisocial influences. That is, each adolescent is shielded from gang members and other antisocial influences while in the foster care program. Simultaneously, the actual parents receive training to improve the home situation to which the youth will return. It is too soon to judge the comparative effectiveness of foster home treatment for adolescent delinquents over long time periods, but the immediate results appear promising (Patterson et al., 1993). Controlling antisocial behavior is one of the greatest challenges facing our society, and interventions to prevent and control seriously aggressive conduct should have very high priority with local and national governments.

Treatment with Psychoactive Drugs

Psychoactive drugs (those that affect mood, activity level, or thinking) can provide relief from some of the troublesome behaviors associated with children's psychological disturbances. Psychoactive drugs (sometimes called psychotropic drugs) may be prescribed for a number of reasons: (1) to suppress dangerous behaviors such as self-injurious, suicidal, or physically aggressive behaviors; (2) to suppress behaviors that interfere with a child's education, such as the hyperactive, inattentive, and aggressive behavior of children with ADHD; (3) to suppress bizarre, socially unacceptable behavior of children with developmental disabilities (e.g., stereotyped, repetitive routines, vocal outbursts, disruptive behaviors); and (4) to enhance adaptive, prosocial behavior, such as attentiveness and social relatedness (Gadow & Pomeroy, 1993). Despite the increasing use of a wide variety of medications in the management of psychologically disturbed children, there have been surprisingly few controlled experiments on the effectiveness or even the safety of most of the frequently prescribed psychoactive pediatric medications. Even when a pediatric drug's effectiveness and safety have been established, long-range effects in adolescence and adulthood are largely unexplored. In this section, we present information regarding the best-known, most often prescribed psychoactive drugs for children, the disorders for which they are administered, their unintended side effects, and research findings concerning their effectiveness. Also discussed are guidelines for safe and appropriate use of psychoactive medications with children. As will be seen, some clinicians' enthusiasm for prescribing psychiatric medications for children has far outstripped available research findings on these agents' effectiveness and specific effects.

PSYCHOSTIMULANTS

Psychostimulants are perhaps the most often prescribed drugs for the treatment of childhood psychological disorders. Over the past 40 years, most psychopharmacological research has evaluated the use of psychostimulants (central nervous system stimulants), particularly Ritalin or methylphenidate, for children with attention-deficit/hyperactivity disorder (ADHD) (Biederman, 1991). As discussed in Chapter 5, research evidence suggests that ADHD may result from an alteration in brain neurochemistry, particularly in the monoamine neurotransmitter system (Zametkin & Rapoport, 1987). The presence and precise nature of the neurochemical problem have not been identified, and much of the evidence cited comes from animal research and inferences from observations that children with ADHD respond positively to psychostimulants (Murphy, Greenstein, & Pelham, 1993). Other psychostimulants frequently prescribed for hyperactive children include *d*-amphetamine (Dexedrine) and magnesium pemoline (Cylert).

All three types of stimulants have alerting, antifatiguing effects on adults and appear to affect children similarly by helping impulsive children attend to and persist in tasks better, particularly in school. When receiving psychostimulants, children with ADHD often are more attentive, work faster, and their rates of errors decrease (Murphy et al., 1993). In addition, stimulant medication can reduce ADHD-related disruptive and antisocial behavior in the classroom such as destruction of property, disturbance of classmates, noncompliance, and aggressive verbal attacks on others (Kaplan & Hussain, 1995). Nevertheless, the long-term effectiveness and safety of the use of psychostimulants in childhood remain unknown. This is a disturbing situation, given the thousands of children currently receiving stimulant medication of hyperactivity.

In fact, the popularity of Ritalin has grown so great that it is being taken by children and adults who do not have attention-deficit disorders, but are impulsive, have difficulty paying attention to tasks, or feel they are easily distracted (Kolata, 1996). In response, the production of Ritalin has increased by nearly 500 percent in the five years from 1991 to 1995, according to the Drug Enforcement Administration (Kolata, 1996). It appears that some

TABLE 14-5   SELECTED DRUGS USED TO TREAT CHILDREN'S PSYCHOLOGICAL DISORDERS

Generic and Trade Name	Primary Use and Common Side Effects

I. Psychostimulants
   Methylphenidate (Ritalin)
   Dextroamphetamine (Dexedrine)
	For Attention-Deficit/Hyperactivity Disorder, ADHD.
	Control impulsivity, attention problems, hyperactivity.
	(Side Effects: Growth, weight suppression, temporary sleep, gastric, and mood problems, increased heart rate and blood pressure, jaw clenching, biting or chewing, tongue thrusts. Drug can be abused by other family members.)

II. Tricyclic Antidepressants
   Imipramine (Tofranil)
   Amitriptyline (Elavil)
   Desipramine (Pertofrane, Norpranin)
	Control enuresis, treat mood disorders (depression).
	(Side Effects: Heart beat irregularities, possibly life threatening; ineffective with childhood depression.)

III. Major Tranquilizers (Antipsychotics)
   Chlorpromazine (Thorazine)
   Thioridazine (Mellaril)
   Trifluoperazine (Stelazine)
	For Autistic and other Pervasive Developmental Disorders, Schizophrenia with Childhood Onset.
	Control excitability, aggression, self-injury in children with serious disorders. Trifluoperazine used for Tourette's and other movement disorders.
	(Side Effects: Reduced alertness, impaired problem-solving, involuntary movements, grimacing, drooling, tongue protrusion, which can be treated with other medication, headache, gastric upset, seizures.)

adults are taking Ritalin themselves or getting it for their children simply to improve their mental or school performance.

Critique of Psychostimulants

No psychoactive drug is entirely without side effects, and the side effects of psychostimulants have been well-studied. Side effects sometimes associated with stimulant use include stomachaches and nausea, loss of appetite and weight loss, dizziness, drowsiness, insomnia, irregular heart beat (tachycardia), and peculiar movements of the mouth, jaw, and tongue (see Table 14-5). A major concern with the use of stimulants is their ability to suppress children's growth in terms of weight or height. This effect may be reduced by limiting the daily and weekly administration of psychostimulants to school hours only. However, some investigators have reported a small decrease in growth in height and weight during the first year of stimulant treatment, with larger dosages of stimulants being related to greater growth retardation (Mattes & Gittelman, 1983). Such findings dictate caution in the administration of stimulants to children, even though the growth limitation effects have been slight. Alternative interventions such as behavior therapy are sometimes pre-

ferred by adolescents with attention-deficit disorder (Gadow & Pomeroy, 1993).

ANTIPSYCHOTIC DRUGS

The antipsychotic or neuroleptic drugs such as the phenothiazines, thiaoxanthenes, and haloperidol were originally developed and administered in order to control the bizarre, hallucinatory, and occasionally violent behavior of adult psychotic patients. These drugs are sometimes prescribed to children chiefly to control the violent or agitated behavior of profoundly retarded, brain-injured, or psychotic children and adolescents. In particular, antipsychotic drugs have been found to reduce severely mentally retarded children's assaultiveness, destructiveness, self-injury, and extreme restlessness.

Critique of Antipsychotic Drugs

Antipsychotics have several unfortunate side effects, since they can act as sedatives, reducing children's alertness and impairing their thinking and problem-solving skills at least temporarily (Wiener, 1984; Winsberg & Yepes, 1978). Thus, although antipsychotic drugs make children with mental retardation more tractable, these drugs do nothing to improve their retardation. Even more worrisome side effects of neuroleptics include muscle rigidity and *tardive dyskinesia* (involuntary tongue protrusion, grimacing, drooling, tremor, and stereotyped movements of the head, limbs, and trunk). These undesirable effects also limit the use of antipsychotics with adult psychotic patients and can be controlled by other medication. However, long-term use of this class of psychoactive drugs is inadvisable, and, although they make children more manageable, they do not reduce thought disturbances or aid their learning. It may be safe to say that, "This drug effect results in a much more manageable child, but one who is seriously ill, nevertheless" (Gittelman & Kanner, 1986, p. 460). Moreover, so little sound, controlled research has been conducted on the use of antipsychotic pharmaceuticals with children and adolescents that their administration is exploratory at best.

ANTIDEPRESSANT DRUGS

Drugs that have been identified as having antidepressant properties with adults are used with children to treat enuresis, severe eating disorders such as anorexia nervosa and bulimia (see Chapter 10 for a discussion of these uses), or mood disorders, particularly depression. Two major types of antidepressants used with adult patients are the *tricyclic antidepressants* such as imipramine (Tofranil) and amitryptiline (Elavil), and the *monoamine oxidase inhibitors (MAO inhibitors)* such as phenelzine or Nardil (Gittelman & Kanner, 1986).

Critique of Antidepressant Drugs

Little is known about the safety and efficacy of the MAO inhibitors with children, but the tricyclic agents commonly produce dry mouth, sweating, and constipation, as well as tension, tremor, tearfulness, and slight weight loss (Gittelman & Kanner, 1986). In high dosages, tricyclic antidepressants have been found to have complex effects on cardiac function and could be dangerous. The MAO inhibitors can raise blood pressure if combined with a compound found in fermented foodstuffs such as cheese. Because of its effectiveness in alleviating adult major depression, imipramine (Tofranil) has been most often used in research on the treatment of juvenile depression and also for separation anxiety, ADHD, and enuresis. The results have proven to be disappointing thus far. In controlled double-blind studies where neither doctor nor patient knew which drug was being administered, imipramine proved no better than an inactive drug in treating children's major depressive disorders (Campbell, Godfrey, & Magee, 1992). Therefore, tricyclic antidepressants and MAO inhibitors have not yet proved effective in the treatment of childhood depression (Kaplan & Hussain, 1995). Tricyclic antidepressants are also dangerous because they are among the drugs that adolescents prefer for suicide attempts (Fazen, Lovejoy, & Crone, 1986), so parents must be extremely careful with the storage and administration of these drugs.

DEVELOPMENTAL DIFFERENCES IN DRUG EFFECTS

Drugs that have been developed for adult psychiatric conditions do not always work with children, and virtually no drugs have been developed specifically for children's use. In the few existing studies of the effects of antidepressant drugs with mood disordered children, common antidepressants such as imipramine proved no more effective than inactive placebo tablets in the relief of juvenile depression (Biederman, 1991). Moreover, pharmacological research is unpromising or nonexistent on the treatment of children's anxiety disorders, conduct disorders, and many other childhood disorders. The field of childhood psychopharmacology is a neglected one despite the demonstrated utility of psychoactive medication for adults' disorders. Perhaps the question about their safety is one reason why children's medications have been neglected. If a drug is of unknown safety and may have adverse long-range effects on development, it is clearly better to use a psychosocial rather than a pharmacological treatment. In the next section, we consider how clinicians may safely prescribe psychoactive drugs for children.

Guidelines for Drug Therapy

Moderate to severe negative side effects may occur in any drug that is potent enough to affect psychological functioning. Therefore, the administration of psychoactive drugs should be considered a moderately restrictive, potentially dangerous treatment that should be used with caution. Teachers and parents should be aware of the following guidelines for the safe and conservative use of drug therapy (Murphy, Greenstein, & Pelham, 1993; Wiener, 1977):

1. Drug therapy should nearly always be an additional treatment and *not* the sole or main treatment for a child psychiatric disorder.

2. Drug therapy should *not* be the first treatment tried, but in most cases should follow psychological and educational interventions (Gadow & Pomeroy, 1993).

3. Before any administration of psychoactive drugs, the child should receive a thorough physical and psychological evaluation.

4. The child's parents or guardian should give informed consent for drug therapy. To avoid coercion, the child should also be asked to assent to the treatment. To give informed consent, the parents and, if age-appropriate, the child should be given an understandable explanation of the reason to use medication, a review of less invasive treatment options, such as psychotherapy, and a treatment prognosis if medication or an alternative treatment is used. It is important for the physician to describe the drug action, dosage schedule, common and possibly dangerous side effects, and necessary precautions to avoid harmful effects. The family also needs to know how long the drug must be taken and when it can be discontinued (Murphy, Greenstein, & Pelham, 1993).

5. There should be a formal treatment plan for the child, with specific, well-defined goals, regular monitoring for side effects, and periodic follow-up evaluations by qualified professionals.

   Treatment for children and families increasingly consists of combining various specific training programs in a general "package" geared to the needs of the participants (Hackman, 1993). Many intervention programs for children feature social skills training (SST), which provides rejected or neglected children with improved methods of making new acquaintances and getting along with others. Children who have a number of different types of problems have a common difficulty in social relations. Examples are children who are inappropriately aggressive or hyperactive, and whose externalizing problems drive away peers and adults;

children who are timid and suffer from social phobia and fearfully avoid others; and those who are mildly handicapped with learning disabilities or are mildly retarded.

6. Drug therapy should always begin with the minimum therapeutic dose of an adequately tested drug. The dose should be increased until either improvement is evident or unwanted side effects occur.

7. Drug-free periods should be scheduled to establish the earliest time when drug therapy can be discontinued. Continual monitoring is required, since drug administration should cease as quickly as possible. The child's physician should be trained and qualified to administer psychoactive medication to children.

Psychopharmacologists are very cautious about recommending prescribing drugs for children, especially when the drugs have not been carefully and thoroughly tested in the exact dosages to be used over a lengthy period with children of the same age as the patient. Safer methods such as psychotherapy should be tried first, and medication should never be considered the sole answer to the child's problems. Children need to learn and develop, so educational and psychological interventions are usually more appropriate for them than drugs. To protect children's health, they should receive the smallest dosage possible and for the briefest possible period. Pharmacotherapy has a demonstrated place in the treatment of childhood disorders, but only when used wisely and conservatively by expertly trained medical specialists. Regrettably, commercial marketing practices of the pharmaceutical industry may be encouraging both consumers and physicians to turn first to chemical treatments for the ills of children, pregnant women, and nursing mothers, despite various dangerous side effects. In an editorial in the *American Journal of Orthopsychiatry*, Dumont (1990) urged physicians who treat children to resist pharmaceutical industry advertisements, gifts averaging $2,500 per physician per year (Lexchin, 1988), and research grants from drug manufacturers that promote the use of drugs. Although the psychopharmacology literature stresses thorough assessment and first-line use of nonchemical treatments for disturbed children, the lucrative drug industry makes it easy and profitable to ad-

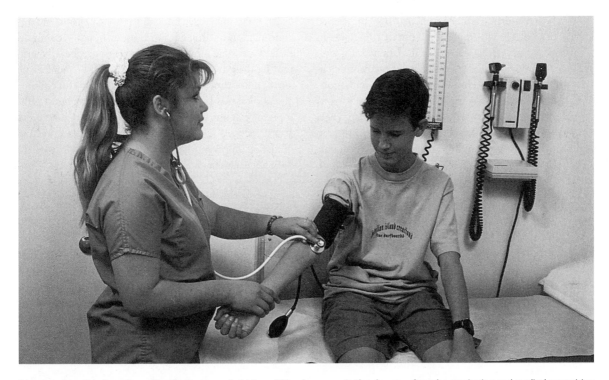

Many psychoactive drugs have side effects, some of which could be dangerous in the absence of regular monitoring and medical supervision by a specialist. Pharmacology is considered a coercive form of treatment since the child cannot choose to refuse it and cannot resist the drug's effects.

minister drug therapy instead. An industry that cannot police itself invites government regulation if the health of the nation's children is at stake.

SUMMARY

A child's age, problem type and severity, family situation, and treatment resources in the community must all be considered in selecting an appropriate treatment. In general, younger, less cognitively advanced children are likely to be best served through training programs for their parents, direct behavioral training to remedy the children's skill deficits or developmental delays, and play therapy of some type. Older children may also benefit from parent training, behavioral skill training, play therapy, participation in family therapy, and self-regulation training therapy. Insight-oriented psychotherapies such as psychoanalytic or client-centered therapy aims to help the

child understand her own emotions and accept herself, thereby reducing the emotional conflict that is presumed to underlie the problem. Behavioral and educational approaches attempt to remedy the child's skill deficits directly and teach new skills through modeling and management of positive reinforcement contingencies. Conjoint family therapy is used when the child's problems stem from faulty family communications and family-wide maladaptive patterns of interaction. Children who do not profit from these outpatient interventions and who have severe retardation or are dangerously unmanageable, cannot be placed with foster families and may be institutionalized in restrictive 24-hour residential programs.

Psychosocial treatments do benefit children. There is a positive effect of moderate size for all major types of child psychotherapy, with the behavioral treatments appearing to have the best outcomes. Long-term outcomes are unstudied in most cases.

Psychoactive drugs are being increasingly prescribed for children. Research supports the use of stimulants in the treatment of ADHD, especially in combination with behavior therapy, but the effectiveness of medications in treating most other childhood conditions is undemonstrated in controlled drug trials. Side effects may be minimal, bothersome, or dangerous, depending on child age, drug type, and dosage. Authorities strongly recommend a thorough assessment and use of non-drug treatments first before recourse to pharmacotherapy for children. Drugs should be administered in minimum dosages and be carefully supervised and adjusted; suspension and discontinuation of drug administration should occur at the earliest possible time. Manufacturers are heavily promoting drug treatment for children's adjustment problems. At this time, effective pharmacotherapy for children and adolescents is limited to a few disorders, but it is the topic of intense interest by consumers, manufacturers, and physicians. Developing effective, safe, and practical modes of intervention should be a first priority of the nation's health agenda.

ABUSE, NEGLECT, AND
CHILDREN'S RIGHTS

Key Terms

Child neglect. Parent or legal guardian provides grossly inadequate supervision, health care, protection from emotional trauma or risk of delinquency, or fails to oversee child's education.

Confirmed abuse. Case in which the abuse was confessed to by the perpetrator.

Due process. Constitutional guarantee of legal procedures designed to protect individuals' rights and liberties, e.g., the right to confront one's accuser in court.

Least restrictive treatment. The most widely used and voluntary educational or mental health intervention, both socially or psychologically. An inescapable treatment is restrictive, but an intervention accepted willingly is less restrictive. Drug treatments are restrictive if the child has no choice whether to take the drug.

Physical abuse. Physical assault on a child intense enough to cause physical harm. Goes beyond socially acceptable corporal punishment and qualifies as cruel and antisocial.

Posttraumatic Stress Disorder in childhood. A reaction to experiencing or witnessing extremely traumatic events, or developmentally inappropriate sexual experiences resulting in disorganized or agitated behavior, distressing dreams, repetitive play themes centering on the traumatic event, and physical symptoms such as stomachaches and headaches (American Psychiatric Association, 1994).

Sexual abuse. Developmentally inappropriate sexual contact with a child, ranging from physical penetration to exhibitionism, fondling, pornographic filming, or exposing the child to pornography.

Status offenders. Children who engage in activities that are criminal only for juveniles such as drinking alcohol, smoking, and truancy from school or home.

This chapter reveals the extent of neglect and physical and sexual abuse of children and the consequences of maltreatment in children's lives. Long an avoided and denied topic, the mistreatment of children is now a major social concern, and is recognized as a threat to their physical and mental health. In this chapter, we review a range of measures that could be used to reduce child neglect and abuse. Further, we examine children's moral and legal rights to humane treatment and why children's rights are sometimes restricted for the benefit of their families and their own future welfare. The impact of reduced public spending on children's welfare is also considered, and we conclude that governmental spending to improve children's education and mental and physical health constitutes an enlightened investment in the future.

ABUSE AND NEGLECT OF CHILDREN

Children are helpless and trusting, and are dependent on their parents to provide for them for many years before they are capable of functioning on their own. Most adults recognize young children's vulnerability and try to protect them from harm. But some people do not truly understand that children are vulnerable and must be protected, while others become enraged when young children inconvenience them by acting immaturely, crying for long periods, and wetting or soiling themselves. *Child abuse* occurs when these caretakers lash out and physically injure the child, sometimes to the point of death. Whether combined with physical attacks or occurring alone, *child neglect* consists of caretakers failing to feed, clothe, or clean children or not providing for their health care. Box 15-1 describes an all-too-typical case of child abuse and neglect that one might encounter in the files of a child protection agency anywhere in the United States.

We seek to understand the roots and nature of child neglect and abuse, and how such maltreatment affects children's lives. Important efforts to prevent child abuse will be featured and we review what is known about prevention and treatment for abused and neglected children.

How does abuse affect a child's emotional stability, trust of adults, school performance, sexual adjustment, and later adjustment and ability to be a good parent? A review of the best available social science research studies provides clues for understanding why adults may strike out at, torture, or sexually exploit young children, and how their cruelty affects the children.

Prevalence of Abuse and Neglect

The statistics are overwhelming. Homicide is one of the five leading causes of child mortality in the United States, and these statistics fail to count many additional child abuse and neglect fatalities (Ewigman, Kivlahan, & Land, 1993). During a recent national study, nearly 5 children per 1,000 were reported to be physically abused and over 2 per 1,000 were sexually abused, with abuse rates being substantially higher among 3- to 17-year-olds than among infants and toddlers (Cappelleri, Eckenrode, & Powers, 1993). Physical neglect is the most common form of maltreatment of children, with an incidence rate of 9.1 per 1,000. Educational neglect is estimated at 4.6 per 1,000, and emotional (nonphysical) neglect at 3.5 children per 1,000 (U.S. Department of Health and Human Services, DHHS, 1988). Many more boys than girls suffer physical abuse and become homicide victims, and

---

BOX 15-1 SHAWNA'S STORY

Perhaps even more terrifying than being hit herself was 6-year-old Shawna's watching her father beat her mother, Toni, during his violent, alcoholic rages. Alex, her father, was a frequently unemployed construction worker who became increasingly unable to work and stayed at home watching TV and drinking. Irascible, paranoid, and assaultive, Alex took his rage and frustration out on his wife, two elementary school aged sons, and Shawna. Following a bout of heavy drinking, Alex would lash out at his wife for imaginary offenses, punch her in the face and stomach with his fist, drag her by the hair, and throw her out of the house, locking the door behind her. When she tried to take the children and escape, Alex would follow them, insist on their return, and loudly threaten to "Kill the bitch," all in front of the children. The children were not safe from his attacks either, and he recently hit Shawna, cutting her lip which required stitches, and blackening her eye when she failed to get him more beer from an empty refrigerator.

Once a bright, inquisitive child, Shawna has become extremely shy and insecure, avoiding eye contact with people, mumbling rather than speaking clearly, and avoiding social contacts. She has no friends, suffers from terrifying nightmares, and shows little interest in or affection for family members. At school, her teacher says that Shawna doesn't seem to pay attention or concentrate on her work, but spends much of her time sitting quietly by herself and staring vacantly out the window. Shawna's family is being investigated by the state child protective services division for possible child abuse, but there are so many cases to investigate and so few staff available that much time and pain will pass before the family can be helped. The mother has been counseled about the availability of a community shelter for abused women and children, but at this point she is insisting that Alex is a good husband and father except for his drinking. Once again, Alex has vowed that he loves Toni and promises to reform.

The prognosis for this family, including Shawna, depends on the control of the father's alcoholism and rage, and the family's and society's ability to protect the mother and children from physical and psychological harm. Too often, a parent's alcoholism or drug abuse goes untreated and the wife is too helpless to leave the relationship or attempts to do so but cannot escape pursuit and victimization by the violent husband continues, so the abuse and its evil effects on the family continue for many years. What is needed are adequate prevention programs featuring parenting skills, skills for independent living for single parents, anger management training, better alcohol and drug abuse treatments, and effective law enforcement to protect battered spouses and children.

---

more girls are sexually abused, particularly among low-income white families (Cappelleri et al., 1993). It is shocking to realize that almost 1 child in 100 is so badly treated as to meet the criteria for physical neglect, and nearly 1 child in 200 is physically abused. It is important to determine the effects of such ill treatment on children's development.

Physical Abuse

It is not true that parents are the most frequent abusers of children. In fact, siblings and other schoolchildren are many times more likely to physically attack children than are parents (Finkelhor & Dziuba-Leatherman, 1994). Indeed, sibling violence seems to be the most prevalent type of physical assault of young children. The attacks on children by other children occur in part because they spend relatively more time with each other than with adults, and in part because of juveniles' incomplete or inadequate social training in the control of aggressive impulses. Thus, many children who are not physically punished or abused at home are justifiably terrified at possibly becoming a child bully's or teenage gangster's next victim. As a result, children are more victimized than adults (Finkelhor & Dziuba-Leatherman, 1994). The rates of assault, rape, and robbery are two to three times higher for 12- to 19-year-olds than for the adult population (National Crime Survey, Bureau of Justice Statistics, 1990). The only violent crime category for which teens are less often victimized than adults is homicide, and that difference is negligible (0.09 homicides per 1,000 teens and 0.10 homicides per 1,000 adults, Finkelhor & Dziuba-Leatherman, 1994). That youth is considered a time of innocence and protection from harm seems ironic given the terrible experiences of the many youthful assault victims.

DEFINITION OF PHYSICAL ABUSE

In a society that sanctions parents' slapping and spanking children, what constitutes physical abuse? **Physical abuse clearly goes beyond minor physical reprimands, such as slapping, pushing, or spanking a child, to the point of seriously assaulting the child.** Physical abuse could include attacking a child with a weapon such as a knife

Children more often are the victims of violence than are adults, and often at the hands of other children. Through being victimized, many learn to attack others and never become adequately socialized. Parents, teachers, and other adults can help by providing supervision of their play.

or firearm, knocking him to the ground and repeatedly kicking him, choking, seriously biting, burning, or otherwise seriously injuring a child. Some authorities (Straus, Gelles, & Steinmetz, 1980) estimate that as many as one-third of all American children are seriously assaulted each year, with perhaps two-thirds being seriously assaulted by a parent sometime during their childhood. This estimate may be too high, however, since it includes an estimate of unreported as well as the reported cases, and may define as incidents of abuse acts which others view as legitimate physical punishment.

There are also national differences in definitions of punishment as contrasted with abuse. In some European countries such as Sweden, even parents are legally barred from physically punishing children, a practice that has been deemed morally and ethically impermissible in that country. Thus, there is a social judgment element in the

definition of physical abuse, and there are borderline cases on which people disagree. For practical purposes, we will limit our discussion to clear cases in which the assault threatens the physical health and may threaten the mental health of the child as well.

ROOTS OF CHILD ABUSE

Many people are deeply shocked to learn of the full extent of violence toward children, especially parental violence. We wonder why parents should so pitilessly attack their own children. There are various roots of child abuse, some of them societal, others reside in patterns of family life, and yet others are individual, representing the psychopathology of individual perpetrators.

Among the *social factors* are cultural beliefs and practices that can either promote or inhibit use of physical force with children. Gil (1970) argues that cultural approval of the use of force against children encourages physical abuse, since abuse is unknown in cultures that prohibit physical punishment of children. In contrast, the overriding majority of U.S. parents state that they use physical punishment with their children, including some parents' hitting their children with objects, kicking, biting, hitting with their fists, and even threatening their children with knives and guns (Gelles, 1979). The violence estimates would undoubtedly increase by including the parents who underreported their use of corporal punishment because they were embarrassed or ashamed about their actions. Physical punishment of children is widely approved as an effective way to teach them obedience and discipline, and many people want to allow teachers to use physical discipline with disobedient children. "Spare the whip and spoil the child" is an adage that continues to have adherents today. However, if this widespread approval of using force against disobedient children is carried too far, it can encourage injurious, potentially lethal attacks. Feelings of irritability, anger, and hostility can interfere with adults' ability to restrain themselves when correcting children and lead to physical child abuse.

FAMILY FACTORS

Only rarely do abusing parents meet diagnostic criteria for mental disorders (Oliver, 1993). Child abusers often complain of stress, particularly stress resulting from being a parent, but they are generally not mentally ill nor do they share particular personality attributes. Lower income, less well-educated people are more likely to be identified as child abusers, but it is unclear whether they actually are more abusive or whether they are less shielded from abuse charges because their poverty brings welfare case workers, police officers, and public health staff members into their homes. Perhaps white upper-class parents who abuse their children are not as likely to be reported to authorities as are poorer, less influential parents. This potential reporting bias makes it difficult to determine whether the poor are actually more likely to be abusers or whether their rates appear higher because their abusive treatment of their children is more likely to be detected.

It is generally believed that most abusing caretakers hurt children because they were abused themselves as children, but this belief may be untrue. The problem is that we cannot separate the adverse effects of poverty,

extreme stress, poor parenting skills, and social isolation from the effects of having been abused as a child. All are closely linked, and each factor alone weakly predicts engaging in child abuse. Child abuse rates are higher where parents are poor, ill-educated, stressed, and have a history of abuse themselves (Peterson & Brown, 1994). However, the experience of having been abused as a child does not by itself predict abusiveness toward others (Kaufman & Zigler, 1986). Few abused children later abuse their own children, particularly if they had at least one supportive parent, presently experience little stress, and enjoy a good relationship with a spouse or partner (Egeland, Jacobvitz, & Papatola, 1987). In the absence of these protective factors though, stress may lead parents to fall back on their own family's parenting practices, imitating the harshness of their families (Kendziora & O'Leary, 1993).

Abusing families frequently are socially isolated. Factors such as stressful transitions such as separation or divorce, job loss, financial problems, or simply moving to a new neighborhood can lead to loss of friends and decreased contacts with one's extended family. Added to the stressful transition is the loss of emotional support, advice, and help from friends and relatives. The family is left with few resources, they begin to irritate each other, and violence is more likely to break out.

Families with characteristically abnormal high levels of arguing, fighting, and physical roughness produce more abuse than do calmer families. Although they also share good moments, these battling parents are unusually hostile and irritable toward each other and toward their children. Parents' coercive and explosive behavior usually extends to their treatment of their nonabused children, as well as to their most frequently victimized children, but they treat certain victimized children the worst (Reid, 1984).

CHILD CHARACTERISTICS

Children are not equally vulnerable to parental abuse. Those whose appearance or behavior irritates or displeases their parents are at greater risk for abuse than are other children. Children who remind a parent of a hated relative or ex-spouse; those who are physically unattractive, irritable, inconsolable infants with piercing, high-pitched cries; ones who taunt and tease, but rarely cooperate; children who are developmentally delayed or of below-average intelligence—all of them may be at heightened risk of becoming abuse victims. A child's chronic, frequent misbehavior and hyperactivity can serve as an irritant, precipitating parental abuse. Ironically, abusive parents are often poor teachers and disciplinarians, which inadvertently stimulates the very type of defiant child behavior that irritates the parent the most (Kendziora & O'Leary, 1993). Punitive parenting promotes conduct problems and aggression, and mothers who rely on physical punishment tend to have children who are noncompliant and display poor impulse control. Inept, punitive parenting and child aggression and defiance tend to reinforce and maintain each other, sometimes resulting in child abuse.

The research link between certain child characteristics and abuse is only correlational, and does not tell us whether the child characteristics preceded and caused or followed and were stimulated by the abuse. In a few cases, it is clear which factor came first; for example, it is likely that, being genetically based, the child's physical similarity to someone the abusing parent hates precipitated the mistreatment. Other early conditions including prematurity, low birthweight, and early mother-baby separation are associated with higher risk of child abuse, especially among low-SES families (Daly & Wilson, 1980). However, these factors in themselves are not sufficient to produce abuse, and most difficult babies and unattractive children are loved and tenderly cared for by their parents. It is likely that child characteristics, family factors, and social beliefs and customs dynamically interact to affect and be affected by child maltreatment. The causes and effects of child abuse are multiple, so it would be misguided to seek a single cause.

Neglect

> "*Physical neglect includes refusal of or delay in seeking health care, abandonment, expulsion from home or not allowing a runaway to return home, and inadequate supervision. Educational neglect includes permission of chronic truancy, failure to enroll a child of mandatory school age, and inattention to a special educational need. Emotional neglect includes such actions as chronic or extreme spouse abuse in the child's presence, permission of drug or alcohol use by the child, and refusal of or failure to provide needed psychological care.*" (U.S. Department of Health and Human Services, DHHS, 1989, p. 6)

Roughly twice as many children are neglected as are abused, but many suffer both types of maltreatment (Cappelleri, Eckenrode, & Powers, 1993; U.S. Department of Health and Human Services, DHHS, 1988). Physical neglect is the most common type of neglect, affecting 9.1 children per 1,000, followed by educational and emotional neglect, affecting 4.6 and 3.5 children per 1,000 respectively. One must be active in some way in order to be an abuser, while neglect is more an act of omission, or failing to meet the basic, essential needs of the child. In *physical neglect*, the caretaker may fail to provide food of the proper type and amount, not clothe the child appropriately for the weather, as in sending the child to school without shoes or a sweater in sub-freezing weather, or leave the child's illnesses untreated. *Emotional neglect* is somewhat more difficult to identify, but occurs when the child's psychological needs and care are obviously neglected, as when the child is not protected from hostile scenes or family violence, substance abuse, or other criminal activity which might encourage antisocial conduct or terrify the child. It is difficult to imagine the occurrence of physical abuse or neglect without accompanying emotional neglect, but emotional neglect can occur alone. *Educational neglect* is defined by state laws concerning mandatory school attendance. Caretakers who defy those laws and fail to send their children to school or otherwise educate them or who encourage their children in truancy are considered to be educationally neglectful.

NEGLECTFUL PARENTS AND FAMILIES

Neglect does not victimize either girls or boys more nor any particular ethnic group more frequently than others. However, risk factors for child neglect include parents' lower incomes and less formal education and large families, with the rate of neglect for larger families being nearly double that for families with three or fewer children (Paget, Philp, & Abramczyk, 1993). Neglectful mothers of infants are likely to appear less sensitive and responsive to their children, and more withdrawn and uninvolved with them than normal mothers (Crittenden, 1988). More neglect is found in deteriorating neighborhoods with low-income, single-family dwellings, many vacant houses, and high family mobility (Zuravin, 1989). Fatalities stemming from neglect are most likely to occur for male children, younger than 3, living in a single-parent household headed by a mother and having two or

Depressed mothers who are beset by marital conflict and financial problems are often distracted and unresponsive to their children. Research shows that such children have abnormally high rates of adjustment problems.

three siblings (Margolin, 1990). Presumably, these families experience extremely high stress levels because of poverty and inadequate resources and mothers lack both the knowledge and means to care for their children properly.

Child Sexual Abuse

Only in recent years have people begun to realize the full extent of sexual abuse of children. Child protection agencies, hospital and clinic staffs, and law enforcement agencies have always been aware that child sexual abuse occurs, but few others knew how many children are sexually exploited. Even today, much child sexual abuse goes undetected. Many sexual violations of children remain hidden because family members who know or suspect that the abuse is taking place fail to report it, and child victims are afraid or unable to complain about their molesters

because they are too young, unprotected, and might not be believed. However, new, tougher reporting laws in the United States and other countries require health professionals to report abuse. Also, people who suspect that a child is being abused are legally protected from recriminations if they alert child protection authorities. Official estimates of sexual abuse prevalence continue to rise, in part because of growing public awareness of the threat and because the laws have been changed to encourage reports of abuse and protect those who report possible cases. The problem cannot be ignored when so many children are victimized. *As many as three million U.S. children may suffer some form of physical or sexual abuse each year* (National Center for Child Abuse and Neglect, 1993).

As might be expected, the estimated prevalence of child sexual abuse depends largely on the exact definition of sexual abuse used, and whether all reported cases or only the substantiated cases are included. Even using the most restrictive definition of sexual abuse (which should provide a minimal estimate of prevalence) yields a shockingly high rate of assaults on children. For the year 1991, the National Center for Child Abuse and Neglect (1993) reported nearly 130,000 indicated or substantiated cases of child sexual abuse. *Indicated cases* are those about which a complaint is filed, while *substantiated* ones have some officially accepted confirmation of the validity of the complaint. This number yields an annual incidence rate for childhood sexual abuse of somewhat less than 1 percent of children abused each year. This estimate may be too low, since unsubstantiated and many unreported cases are not included in the official report. Higher prevalence rates are reported in national surveys of random samples of adults who were asked whether they were sexually abused as children. In these surveys, between 2.1 and 6.3 persons per 1,000 reported being sexually abused before they reached the age of 18. Moreover, national samples of teenagers have reported astounding lifetime prevalence rates of up to 118 rapes per 1,000 teens (Finkelhor & Dziuba-Leatherman, 1994). Legal and educational measures are needed to prevent such victimization of the young.

WHAT IS SEXUAL ABUSE?

Some types of sexual abuse are more easily identified than others, and it is sometimes difficult to define sexual abuse. For example, having sexual relations, including penetration, with a child below the legal age of consent clearly constitutes sexual abuse. Other cases involving the child's observing others engaged in sexual behavior or being fondled are less clear. Fears of litigation and being charged with a sexual offense are running high as a result of a number of well-publicized cases, especially among spouses engaged in bitter divorces. Stepfathers, biological fathers, teachers, and childcare workers of both sexes are so wary of being charged with sexual abuse that many report being unwilling to perform simple caretaking tasks such as changing diapers or picking up or hugging a child who is crying. In general, **sexual abuse consists of the age-inappropriate sexual exploitation of a child.** The abuse can be direct, as in engaging the child in sexual contact of any type, or indirect, as in exhibitionism or exposing the child to pornography.

WHO ARE THE VICTIMS, WHO THE PERPETRATORS?

Victims of sexual abuse tend to be young. According to adult victims' recollections, nearly two-thirds of sexual victimizations (64 percent) occur before age 12 (Finkelhor, Hotaling, Lewis, & Smith, 1990). In New York, nearly 40 percent of the official sexual abuse cases involved children younger than 7 (Doris, 1993). Perpetrators may target younger children in order to protect themselves from detection and punishment. Younger children cannot report the abuse or retaliate against the abuser, especially when the abuser is a parent, legal guardian, babysitter, or other adult caretaker. Younger children are less likely to understand what is happening to them and less able to provide a coherent description of the experience. Consequently, younger children are less likely to be understood and believed than are older victims. The limited credibility of young informants presents major social and legal issues about their own and others' protection and will be considered more fully later.

More Victims Are Female

The majority of victims are girls. According to national crime statistics, girls are eight times more likely to be raped than are boys (Finkelhor & Dziuba-Leatherman, 1994). In recalling their own childhood experiences, women report twice as many incidents of sexual abuse as men (Ceci & Bruck, 1993). So few boys have been legally identified as sexually abused that their psychological characteristics and the circumstances of their abuse are largely unknown. It is unlikely that this imbalance in the sex of the identified victims means that boys are only very rarely sexually victimized. There is reason to suspect that sexual abuse of boys is grossly underreported. Masculine role prescriptions may make boys less likely than girls to report being molested or raped. Being victimized in this fashion is particularly socially unacceptable for males, who are expected to be able to appear masculine and defend themselves. Consequently, the prevalence rates for boys may be much higher than the government statistics indicate.

EFFECTS OF SEXUAL ABUSE

The effects of sexual abuse on children are still incompletely known, particularly the long-term consequences, but some abuse patterns are related to serious child adjustment and health problems. The child is more likely to be harmed in the following circumstances:

- The sexual abuse is repeated over a period of time.
- Sexual abuse is coerced by physical threats.
- The attack involves penetration rather than being limited to fondling or exhibitionism.
- The perpetrator is a close family member such as a father or stepfather (Kendall-Tackett, Williams, & Finkelhor, 1993).

Child victims may also contract sexually transmitted diseases, including HIV and AIDS. Parents report that their sexually abused children have more adjustment problems, and the children themselves report experiencing more depression, anxiety, anger, and low self-esteem. Overall, *mental health problems are reported for between 50 percent and 80 percent of sex abuse victims* (Spaccarelli, 1994). Children subjected to sexual abuse also may have posttraumatic stress disorder symptoms, such as reexperiencing the trauma, avoidance to stimuli related to the traumatic abuse, withdrawal and preoccupation, and hyperarousal, with difficulty in concentrating and sleeping, and irritability (Wolfe & Birt, 1995). Young children, in particular, had physical complaints about headaches, stomachaches, appetite loss, nausea, and vomiting. The posttraumatic stress symptoms may increase with time, and become common and strong one year after disclosure of the abuse (Wolfe & Birt, 1995). Thus, the research findings are mixed. Some victims seem to experience no lasting disturbance, while others may develop debilitating adjustment problems.

The varying findings may be due to limitations in the research studies as well as the unavailability of good records and sufficient cases for adequate study. Most studies have been short term, assessing the child only at the time of the detection of the attack and failing to evaluate the child either before or long after the crime. Also, studies have been based on the very small samples of children who are available to participate at a single time and place, which has necessitated combining the data for girls and boys and for children of widely varying ages in order to achieve a sufficiently large sample for statistical analysis. However, combining the sexes and ages has obscured differences in reactions of different groups of children. Adequate sample size is necessary to produce the statistical power required to detect small to moderate differences

between abused and nonabused children. Despite these limitations, the research evidence suggests the following conclusions:

- Preschool children who have been sexually abused tend to develop internalizing problems including fear and depressed mood. Sexual abuse victims are especially likely to display strong anxiety (Finkelhor, 1990; Trickett & McBride-Chang, 1995).
- Preschool and kindergarten-age children may exhibit inappropriate sexual behavior such as excessive, public masturbation or make socially inappropriate overt sexual advances to others. Inappropriate sexual behavior may be more detectable in young sexually abused children than in older ones because of social constraints. By the time they reach school age, most girls have learned to comply with social norms prohibiting overt sexual displays in public (Friedrich, Beilke, & Urquiza, 1987).
- Sexually abused elementary school girls may withdraw socially and become isolated from peers and adults. Alternatively, a small number may become aggressive and angry. Teachers report that sexually abused children tend to have learning problems, but their actual academic performance resembles that of their classmates (Trickett, 1993).
- In adolescence, both internalizing and externalizing problems are typical, and relationships with peers tend to be poor. Some sexually abused adolescent girls develop antisocial, delinquent behavior (Friedrich et al., 1987). They also show earlier onset of adult sexual activity than most teens (Trickett & McBride-Chang, 1995). Higher rates of depression, self-injurious behavior and suicidal gestures or attempts have been reported (Bemporad & Romano, 1992). Long-term adjustment problems include greater risk of substance abuse, binge eating, physical symptoms, and suicidal behaviors (Polusny & Follette, 1995).
- Some child problems are characteristic of *posttraumatic stress disorder (PTSD)*, a constellation of symptoms that can follow serious injury, threatened death, or a comparably devastating psychological experience. These symptoms include persistently reexperiencing the traumatic event or avoiding things associated with the event, anxiety, or numbing of responsiveness, and amnesia for an important aspect of the event. Children

may become disorganized and distracted, and experience headaches, stomachaches, or other physical reactions. This syndrome is rare.

In sum, research studies reveal that, as a group, sexually abused children experience above average rates of adjustment problems of both internalizing and externalizing or aggressive types. Some children show behavior similar to posttraumatic stress disorder. Most victims' academic work may not suffer detectably, but their teachers judge them to be less capable than average. Some sexual abuse victims display distinctive, socially inappropriate sexual behavior such as excessive, public masturbation or indiscriminate, openly sexually provocative behavior toward their teachers, doctors, case workers, or other adults.

> *"Perhaps the riskiest coping strategy for a victim is to make a conscious effort to deny or avoid the reality of what has happened." (Spaccarelli, 1994, p. 351)*

Long-Term Consequences

As yet, there are virtually no longitudinal studies following the adjustment of sexually victimized children over a significant period of years. However, child victims tend to believe that sexual abuse is rampant and that adults are likely to exploit children. Many female victims report difficulty in trusting men, and become socially isolated in order to protect themselves from additional harm (Wyatt & Newcomb, 1990). Wariness and loss of trust are understandable reactions to early sexual exploitation. Information about long-range psychiatric consequences is scant and tends to come from the recollections of adult psychotherapy patients who complain during the course of their treatment about childhood sexual abuse. In the absence of independent supporting data corroborating the abuse, such recollections are unconvincing as evidence because of possible distortion arising from faulty memory of events that happened years ago during childhood. Adult psychiatric patients' accounts are also potentially biased by their current adjustment disorders. For example, adults with depressive disorders often report experiencing neglect and mistreatment as children, but their reports may be colored by their current depressive mood disorder. Similarly, persons with borderline personality disorder are likely to recount a personal history of parental neglect, loss, conflict, and physical and sexual abuse (American Psychiatric Association, 1994).

The diagnostic features of borderline personality disorder include dramatic swings between idealizing and condemning the people who are close to them in addition to marked impulsivity. Such people may suddenly, unaccountably change from "a needy supplicant for help to a righteous avenger of past mistakes" (American Psychiatric Association, 1994, p. 651). A research informant who is this changeable could impulsively report either past sexual abuse or an ideal childhood, and perhaps later offer a contrasting version. Research findings based on the retrospective accounts of adults, and particularly those with serious mental and personality disorders, must be confirmed by other types of more trustworthy evidence, such as corroboration by others who know the facts. It is often impossible to establish what actually happened many years ago.

Nevertheless, the available research evidence suggests that sexual abuse has malignant effects on the victim's long-term mental health. Childhood sexual assaults are estimated by some authorities to have been suffered by 8 percent of all adults who are psychiatrically disturbed (Scott, 1992). Some authors have suggested that child sexual abuse produces a 400 percent increase in lifetime risk for psychiatric disorder of any type, and a 300 percent increase in risk for substance abuse (Saunders, Villeponteaux, Lipovsky, Kilpatrick, & Veronen, 1992). A note of caution is necessary in interpreting these estimates. They are based very heavily on retrospective, unverified accounts of childhood abuse offered by adult psychiatric patients, and so are vulnerable to the types of overestimation bias discussed previously.

Assessment of Child Sexual Abuse

The question of how to assess sexual abuse of children is one of the most hotly debated issues in the field of child mental health and jurisprudence. With society's sudden realization that sexual abuse of children is a serious community problem come insistent demands for immediate steps to protect children, weed out the abuse, and punish perpetrators harshly. All of these measures require accurate assessment of sexual abuse, which presents a difficult diagnostic problem for several reasons.

1. Sexual abuse tends to be covert, occurring secretly, often within the family home.

2. Because the abuse is concealed, usually only the abuser and the child know about it with certainty.

3. There is a power disparity between perpetrators and victims. Abusers usually are older than their victims and are more physically and socially powerful. They may be parents or other blood relatives (in which case the abuse constitutes incest), stepparents, caretakers in some official or unofficial capacity (as in babysitters), or friends or acquaintances of the family.

Less frequently, they are the dangerous strangers that parents so often warn their children about. Abusers' parental, supervisory, or caretaking responsibility over their victims discourages others' suspicions about their abuse and confuses their young victims. The youngsters may interpret sexual approaches by adults they know well as being appropriate and condoned by other adults. Thus, assessment of childhood sexual abuse is impeded by the covert nature of the act, the lack of witnesses, and some abusers' parental or caretaking authority over the child victim.

CHILD INTERVIEWS

Obtaining accurate, reliable information from young children about suspected abuse is a challenging endeavor. Very few standardized tests or interviews are available, so clinicians often rely on informal interviews and play observations. Unfortunately, in most instances, these interview and observation techniques are either of unknown accuracy or have been studied and found to be susceptible to examiner bias. That is, the assessment results may too often reflect the examiner's initial expectations regarding whether or not some type of abuse occurred.

The most frequently used assessment device is the *anatomically correct or accurate doll*, which, unlike children's usual dolls, has detailed genitalia (see Box 15-2). The purpose in presenting the anatomical doll to the suspected child victim of sexual abuse is to allow young children, who are unskilled in verbal expression, with a means to show the examiner what the perpetrator did to them. At the beginning of the interview, the clinician might use an anatomical doll to provide the child with an opportunity to discuss sexual issues ("Does this doll look like a girl or a boy?"). Also, the child can be asked to name the parts of the doll to reveal precocious or developmentally advanced knowledge of sexuality and sexual anatomy. Anatomical dolls have been used to aid children's recall of events, and to allow the child to demonstrate what happened (Boat & Everson, 1993). It is this last use that is the most controversial. Critics claim that examiners grossly influence the child's statements by insistently demanding that the child state that she has been abused by a certain suspect. Box 15-3 presents some suggestive, accusatory child interview techniques used in actual cases of alleged sexual abuse (Ceci & Bruck, 1993). Note that many of these tactics would be unethical or even illegal if used with adult witnesses.

In reply, clinicians who use the dolls assert that children are unable to report their experiences in adult-style interviews, so the dolls are necessary to help the children make accurate statements. For example, Boat and Everson (1993) advocate the use of anatomical dolls to focus the interview, assess the child's knowledge of sexuality, stimulate memories of sexual experiences, and enable the child to show what happened. However, Boat and Everson caution that simple observation of the child's behavior with the doll does not prove abuse. A professionally skilled interview is also necessary.

Some defenders of the diagnostic use of anatomical dolls have claimed that children simply do not lie when asked about their abuse experiences, so any child testimony yielded by such interviews must be trusted. A more moderate version of this claim is that children are suggestible, but not about events that involve their own bodies and experiences. The consensus from research on children's memories contradicts even this more moderate view. In fact, children's accuracy varies widely, and they may be especially inaccurate about personal bodily experiences such as genital examinations administered during medical physical examinations. Young girls who received genital exams incorrectly demonstrated on anatomical dolls that the doctor had inserted fingers into anal or genital cavities, which did not occur. An amazing 75 percent of the girls who did *not* receive genital exams demonstrated with the dolls how the doctor supposedly had touched their genitals or buttocks (Bruck, Ceci, Francoeur, & Barr, 1995). If these results apply to the assessment of sexual abuse in interviews employing anatomical dolls, there is serious question about the validity of such interviews. Much more research is needed, and the important question remains of whether young children can be credible witnesses in sex abuse cases. If so, how must their accounts of their experiences be obtained? That is, what examiner training is necessary and what tests, interviews, or observations must be used?

BOX 15-2   SHOULD ANATOMICALLY CORRECT DOLLS BE USED IN CHILD INTERVIEWS?
ARGUMENTS PRO AND CON

Individuals differ in their opinions regarding the appropriateness of using anatomically detailed dolls in interviews with children who may have been sexually abused. In general, social workers, juvenile justice workers, and prosecutors are more likely to favor using the dolls, while opponents include many research psychologists, defense attorneys, and civil libertarians, who favor strict adherence to defendants' legal rights. Both sides vigorously argue their positions, and both are strongly committed to justice and the protection of children.

THE CASE FOR USING ANATOMICAL DOLLS

- Doll play is the natural language of children, putting them at ease. Anatomically correct dolls reveal whether the child has overly mature knowledge of genitalia and sexual practices.
- Children with limited verbal expression skills can point to parts of the doll to show how they were sexually abused. The child's shame and embarrassment in recounting the crime can be reduced through use of dolls.
- The dolls prompt children's memories of abuse, serving as a trigger for the child's memory about traumatic experiences.
- Sexually abused children may play with the dolls in a distinctive manner, so doll play serves as a diagnostic test of sexual victimization. They may show anger or fear toward the perpetrator or enact their own fear or arousal, or show other distinctive play features.

THE CASE AGAINST USING ANATOMICAL DOLLS

- Examiners lacking education and training in child development or clinical service provision are using anatomically correct dolls in interviews and reaching unjustified conclusions about child sexual abuse.
- Even if trained in child interviewing, some clinicians are overly zealous in attempting to protect the children, insist that children use the dolls to "show how he hurt you," and do not question the guilt of the accused perpetrator.
- The dolls excite and confuse children. Research shows that it is not unusual for children who have never been abused to nevertheless enact abuse themes in play with anatomically correct dolls. The unusual appearance of the dolls alone stimulates children to play out sexual encounters.
- In cases of suspected child sexual abuse, children are subjected to repeated interviews using the dolls over a period of time, in which different interviewers insistently suggest that the children were abused by certain people. This scenario is particularly likely to lead to children's accusations against selected alleged perpetrators, according to research by Ceci and his colleagues (1995).
- There are no standard doll play procedures and no child age and sex norms indicating which play features are normal and which deviant, indicating probable abuse.

SUMMATION

Although anatomical dolls are widely used in questioning children about suspected sexual abuse, a growing body of research evidence dictates caution. Children must be protected. However, examiners must be sophisticated about children's cognitive development and suggestibility, and must have relevant training in order to use child interviews using the dolls properly. Examiners and prosecutors must maintain professional objectivity despite heightened family, community, and media indignation about alleged sexual abuse. A number of highly publicized court cases in recent years have resulted either in hung juries or verdicts of innocence.

SOURCES: Ceci, S. J., & Bruck, M. (1995). *Jeopardy in the courtroom: A scientific analysis of children's testimony*. Washington, DC: American Psychological Association; Goodman, G. S., & Bottoms, B. L. (Eds.). (1993). *Child victims, child witnesses: Understanding and improving testimony*. New York: Guilford; Murray, K., & Gough, D. A. (1991). *Intervening in child sexual abuse*. Edinburgh: Scottish Academic Press.

STANDARDS OF ACCURATE TESTING

Adequate psychological testing of children must take into account their cognitive and social immaturity, characteristics which make them poor informants. Even if accurate, their accounts of happenings tend to be extremely brief and unelaborated. For example, when asked where he went with his father, a young boy might simply say, "To the zoo" or "To McDonald's," without any further description. Much questioning and reminding might be required in order to obtain a fuller description. Unfortunately, the questioning itself might play a major role in determining the account given by the child. Recall that

---

BOX 15-3   QUESTIONABLE INTERVIEW PRACTICES IN CASES OF SUSPECTED CHILD SEXUAL ABUSE

The following interview tactics are highly controversial because they may lead children to give the answers the interviewer expects rather than what the child actually thinks and remembers:

- Children are interviewed repeatedly, many times under emotionally charged circumstances, often in the presence of parents who are accusing someone of molesting the children.
- Bribes and threats are used to lead the children's testimony. The interviewer calls them "smart" for agreeing with the interviewer, but coldly calls them "dumb" if they disagree.
- Children are told that other children have already told about the abuse. The other children are pointed to as models for imitation.
- The interviewer may ask the children about events of several years ago when they were preschool age or younger and unlikely to have clear memories.
- The clinician may name a doll after the defendant and scold the doll for abusing the child, "You are naughty for hurting Allison."
- The interviewer may simply appear more enthusiastic, approving, and supportive when the child says something that confirms the interviewer's expectations. These behavior patterns may suffice to lead children to tell the interviewers what they apparently want to hear.

SOURCE: Ceci, S. J., & Bruck, M. (1995). *Jeopardy in the courtroom: A scientific analysis of children's testimony.* Washington, DC: American Psychological Association.

---

adults are much more powerful in all senses than children and that children are especially wary of adults who might become displeased with them or hurt them. Interviewers are especially threatening to children because they are strangers, work in an imposing office building, are authority figures, perhaps police or child protection agency employees, and they are experts to whom others defer. Even adults might be intimidated and eager to please such powerful and intimidating persons. Because child protection agency and police interviewers are dedicated to defending children, they are eager to help punish adults who prey upon children, and may underestimate their own power to influence what the children claim.

How can the accuracy of child sexual abuse assessments be improved? Several steps can be taken:

1. *Improving interviewer skill* is an essential ingredient. Interviewers require special formal training in interviewing and observing children who may have been abused, so the clinicians will be appropriately sensitive but objective and fair to all parties in the case. A number of forensic psychology, psychiatry, and social work programs offer graduate training in the specialty, and in-service workshops are offered to interviewers in many juvenile justice agencies. There is a strong consensus that child sexual abuse investigators require special, advanced train-

ing, and that such assignments should not be given to people lacking professional credentials and expertise in assessing children.

2. *Developing special interviews, observations, and tests* is highly desirable as a reform measure, but this goal is difficult to achieve. Since the behavioral results of sexual abuse are highly diverse, and adjustment problems may even be absent in up to 50 percent of sexually abused children (Spaccarelli, 1994), symptoms of abuse are difficult to test for. Clinicians are left to rely on widely used symptoms checklists such as the Achenbach and Edelbrock Child Behavior Checklist, which are sensitive to a broad range of psychopathology.

3. *Using multiple information sources.* At present, the best course seems to be to obtain information about the abused child from *multiple informants* (child, parents, siblings, teacher, others) using *multiple assessment techniques* (interviews, psychological tests, observations) in diverse settings (O'Donohue & Elliott, 1991). This tactic is expensive and time-consuming, but necessary, since child sexual abuse has few if any direct behavioral consequences.

"There are remarkably few treatment outcome studies with this population ... at this time insufficient evidence exists to claim that effective interventions

*with the sexually abused child exist." O'Donohue &
Elliott, 1991, p. 218*

Treatment of Sexually Abused Children

FOSTER HOME PLACEMENT

Children whose families have severely abused or neglected them may be placed in foster homes in order to protect them. Such placements are avoided except when the maltreatment is so severe as to endanger the child's physical safety or be life-threatening. Child welfare and protection services in many states focus on the preservation of families, and have kept families together even in the face of evidence of nonaccidental broken limbs, suffocation, near drowning, and other terrible injuries. News stories of small children being fatally assaulted by family members in Connecticut in 1995, and later in New York in 1996 (Stoesz & Karger, 1996), led to greater official alertness to possible murderous attacks on children and quicker placement of endangered children in foster care (McLarin, 1995). Unfortunately, foster care itself can also endanger children, who may stay in the system for years and are sent from home to home with little regard for their wishes or feelings. One New York boy was placed in 37 different homes during a two-month period, while another had lived with 17 families in less than a month (Stoesz & Karger, 1996). It is difficult to see how such treatment would help a child, except a child whose very life was in danger. The seriously underfunded child welfare system simply fails to protect too many children.

MENTAL HEALTH TREATMENT

Many sexually abused children receive psychotherapy to help them deal with their experiences. Unfortunately, too few adequate studies have been conducted to provide evidence for the effectiveness of any type of psychotherapy for children with this history of abuse. Cognitive-behavioral therapy may help teenagers and adults who experienced forcible rape and who are suffering from posttraumatic stress disorder (PTSD; see Chapter 7 and the earlier discussion of this condition in this chapter). This therapeutic approach features the client's repeated emotional reliving of the trauma under therapeutic guidance so the fear can be reexperienced and modified (Foa

& Riggs, 1995). Information that is incompatible with the fear (e.g., that the threat is now absent and the woman is resilient and can handle it) is introduced repeatedly in several sessions. Evaluations of the effectiveness of the cognitive-behavioral therapy have yielded encouraging results (Foa & Riggs, 1995). Less is known about treatment of sexual victimization that does not involve trauma and extreme fear and anxiety. The absence of adequate research-based evidence concerning effective therapies for sex abuse victims is particularly ironic since some of Freud's earliest patients complained about this type of victimization. Yet well over a century later, the victims still await understanding and adequate care.

Effects of Maltreatment

Children are recognized to be capable of great physical and psychological recovery, yet many suffer long-term consequences of victimization. In a developing child, effects vary depending on the child's age and circumstances. The type of maltreatment also makes a difference. Since abuse and neglect effects can be varied, it is helpful to review them according to the developmental status of the victim.

EFFECTS DURING INFANCY AND EARLY CHILDHOOD

Children who have been neglected or physically abused early in life are more likely to suffer insecure attachment, especially of a disorganized and disoriented nature, than other children (Crittenden, 1988). They may display delays in cognitive development. Girls are more likely to become withdrawn and wary, and all children are more likely to become aggressive and noncompliant. Sexual abuse is related to internalizing problems including anxiety, social withdrawal, and enuresis, particularly in girls, and somatic/physical complaints in boys (Kendall-Tackett et al., 1993; Trickett & McBride-Chang, 1995).

EFFECTS DURING MIDDLE CHILDHOOD

Physically abused children have low self-esteem and high rates of adjustment problems of all types, and tend to be rejected by their peers. Neglected children in particular produce low school grades, academic deficiencies, especially in reading, and low tested intelligence, possibly as a result of lack of cognitive stimulation and emotional support from their neglectful parents. Children who are sexually abused may show inappropriate, premature sexual behavior such as public masturbation and sexual activity. Sexually abused children have higher than average rates of adjustment problems of all types and poor peer relations (Wolfe & Birt, 1995). They may become confused about the norms of appropriate sexual behavior because of the abuse, and so display developmentally precocious and disapproved sexuality, which leads them to be shunned by their peers.

EFFECTS DURING ADOLESCENCE AND ADULTHOOD

Abused and neglected adolescents show heightened psychopathology of all types, low self-esteem, low social competence, and poor school and peer adjustment. The neglected group has the lowest school grades, standardized test scores, and is most likely to have to repeat a grade (Eckenrode, Laird, & Doris, 1993). Early onset of sexual activity and promiscuity are more likely among sexually abused teenagers. Serious adjustment problems may develop, including self-injurious and suicidal behavior (Kendall-Tackett et al., 1993). Academic problems may continue, as well as lower IQ (Eckenrode et al., 1993). Retrospective studies of adults with major or unipolar depression show a significantly greater history of childhood maltreatment than in the general population or among people with other types of psychiatric disorder (Bemporad & Romano, 1992). That is, early maltreatment, especially parental coldness, hostility, rejection, and intrusiveness, is more likely to lead to adult depression than is the early loss of a parent.

As this survey of problems suggests, it is impossible to say without qualification that one type of maltreatment is any more dangerous to children's adjustment than another. Rather, maltreatment can be said to be associated with many different difficulties in social, emotional, and cognitive development. In addition, victimization rarely occurs in untroubled families, so most of these abused and neglected young people also bear the burden of parental marital conflict, family social isolation, economic and interpersonal stress, and other problems. Sometimes they require a great deal of professional care and social services to help them.

PREVENTION AND TREATMENT

"The attitudes that tolerate and ignore violence in the society as a whole also tolerate the violence acted out in individual communities and homes throughout the country." (Violence Study Group, National Center for Clinical Infant Programs, 1994, p. 40)

Prevention of Abuse

Most social scientists agree that violence toward children is part of a national climate encouraging and tolerating violence as a solution to personal and social problems. Violence and fear of becoming a victim of violence fuel each other, raising the level and intensity of assaults. If many people are armed with weapons, then children will be shot accidentally or in anger. If television and movie productions feature high rates of high intensity violence, then children will copy and improvise on violent solutions to interpersonal conflicts, and as adults, they may imitate the disciplinary tactics they experienced as children (Bandura, 1969). Juvenile gangs occupy the streets of large U.S. cities and even the small towns, and violent attacks are provoked by use of illicit drugs and alcohol. Adults feel unprotected from assault themselves and helpless to protect their children. Guns are commonly found in schools, even elementary schools, and, in response, the schools themselves begin to resemble correctional facilities, with weapons detection systems, heavy, windowless walls, and police surveillance. More and more of our national resources are being poured into law enforcement and prisons, yet people do not feel safer and the situation does not improve. Is this situation inevitable, or can something be done?

SEPARATE CHILDREN AND WEAPONS

The National Center for Clinical Infant Programs (Osofsky & Fenichel, 1994) convened a Study Group on Violence to examine the roots of violence against children. The study group concluded that there should be a national agenda to combat our society's apparent complacency and tolerance of growing trends in violence. They noted that neighboring Canada is a much less violent society. During 1990, 222 U.S. children under age 10 were killed with guns, but in striking contrast, only 68 Canadians *of all ages* were killed with handguns (Osofsky & Fenichel, 1994). So long as guns are readily obtainable, violence is inevitable. Individuals and civic groups must make serious attempts to change laws that now encourage violence and place guns in children's hands. The high level of present violence severely limits our ability to protect children from attacks.

IMPROVE PARENTING QUALITY

Children are more likely to suffer injury or abuse if their parents are emotionally disturbed, were abused as children, are risk-taking, substance abusing, young, single, hold unrealistic expectations of their children, and have poor parenting skills (Peterson & Brown, 1994). Thus, child protection programs have targeted mothers with these types of problems. One program (Olds, Hendersen, Chamberlin, & Tatelbaum, 1986) successfully reduced the rate of child abuse in a group of high-risk families by sending nurse home visitors to teach them improved parenting practices and help them form supportive social networks. During pregnancy and the child's first two years of life, mothers also received free transportation to prenatal and well-child health appointments. Abuse and neglect rates were 19 percent in comparable families studied, but only 4 percent in the families who received the prevention program. This study indicates that home-visit and well-baby medical services can reduce the incidence of child abuse.

SELF-CONTROL TRAINING FOR OLDER CHILDREN

Other abuse prevention services can focus on teaching the potential child victim skills that help them avoid abuse. Abused children tend to be more difficult, hyperactive, distractible, and provocative, for example, disobeying and engaging in "back talk" to caregivers (Peterson & Brown, 1994). These children's chances of goading their parents into physically abusing them might be reduced if the children learned self-control techniques (described in Chapter 14). Walker, Bonner, and Kaufman (1988) recommend interventions to teach children to obey adults' instructions, avoid talking back and other provocative behavior, and to recognize and avoid interactions at high-risk times. They also suggested teaching relaxation skills and problem-solving techniques the children could use to protect themselves.

STATE SOCIAL SERVICES

Some states are providing social services that might help prevent child neglect and abuse. Since abuse can have many different causes, many different prevention measures must be used. Hawaii's Healthy Start Program offers families of newborns a wide array of services designed to promote physical and mental health and educate parents and reduce their stress (Osofsky & Fenichel, 1994). Prevention services, emotional support, family crisis resolution strategies, and mental health services are provided to at-risk families in the belief that this is a good investment. It is much cheaper in state tax resources and individual suffering to prevent conflict and maltreatment of children than it is to incarcerate them later, after they have become criminals. In addition, in most of the nation's major cities, university-affiliated projects coordinate law enforcement and human services to intervene in cases in which a child witnesses or is the victim of a violent crime.

Prevention of Neglect

A number of effective parent training programs have been developed to teach neglectful mothers to care for their youngsters. Behavior therapy procedures including training in self-observation, self-reinforcement for good performance, and problem-solving strategies have been shown to be effective. Mothers with mental retardation have been taught to provide adequate diets for their children; abusive and neglectful mothers were successfully prompted to remove hazardous conditions in the home; and parents were helped to improve their children's personal hygiene through the application of behavioral treatments (Lutzker, 1990). This research suggests that child neglect may stem largely from mothers' deficits in relevant parenting skills or motivation, both of which can be effectively treated (Paget et al., 1993). A limitation in the behavioral approach is that, as yet, only small numbers of cases have been intensively treated and observed. Because so many neglectful families need help, a less labor-intensive, less costly intervention approach is needed.

Neglected children have many needs, both psychological and educational. They are the most likely of the maltreated children to perform poorly on intelligence tests and on schoolwork, suggesting that they would profit from special education services. In addition, they may need social skills training to enable them to make and keep friends. Younger neglected children need a parent or surrogate to provide them with verbal stimulation, emotional responsiveness, warmth, and security. Parent training is the most effective intervention for neglected infants, toddlers, and preschoolers. These various treatment alternatives are presented in more detail in Chapter 14.

CHILDREN'S MORAL AND LEGAL RIGHTS

The consideration of neglect and abuse raises the question about the moral and legal rights children have and should receive. Children's rights and status are changing. This section considers new developments in the field of child law and definitions of children's legal and human rights. Some basic legal questions will be considered. Are children considered *persons* as adults are or are they the *property* of their parents? Are their rights and prerogatives much more restricted than those of adults? When their parents separate, do children have the right to live with the parent they prefer? Do children have a right to appropriate mental health treatment, and must parents obtain appropriate treatment for their disturbed children? Can parents institutionalize their children against their wills? These searching questions address the core of our beliefs about the capacities of children and the nature of childhood. The quest for answers opens many different areas of study including law, ethics, social science, education, and government, illustrating the interdisciplinary nature of the field of childhood psychopathology.

It is important to distinguish between legal rights and human or moral rights. *Legal rights* are guaranteed by the Constitution or by statute and are enforced by the police and the courts. *Human rights* are more broadly and less precisely defined and pertain to the conditions necessary for children to become healthy, well-adjusted, competent, and productive citizens. Many people believe that children have a right to be loved, and that they are harmed by parents who do not want or love them. Yet no legal right to loving care exists in law so long as children's physical health and safety are assured.

Global Rights for Children

The world's nations attempt to guard children's welfare by agreeing to certain standards and attempting to persuade other nations to share these standards. Reflecting this concern, the United Nations General Assembly held a convention on the rights of the child, and in 1989 adopted a declaration that children are persons who are entitled to both protection and respect. After 20 nations ratified the document (not including the United States), this treaty went into force (Limber & Flekkoy, 1995; Wilcox & Naimark, 1991). The treaty states that certain rights should apply to all children:

1. The best interests of the *child*, not of parents, teachers, or others, should be the most important consideration in legislation to protect children.
2. All children should have adequate prenatal and postnatal care, nutrition and housing, free, compulsory primary education, and recreation opportunities.
3. They should be protected from economic exploitation as laborers, and their government should financially assist parents who cannot provide an adequate standard of living for their children.
4. The UN convention found it necessary to state that children have a right to live, children under the age of 15 should not be recruited into armed conflict, and that they should be protected from illegal narcotic and psychotropic drugs, sexual exploitation, and abuse.
5. Children should be raised in an atmosphere of affection and emotional security. Ideally they should be cared for by their parents, but if separated from their parents, they should receive society's protection.
6. Children should be spared all forms of cruelty, neglect, and exploitation for commercial gain. They should be among the first to receive relief in times of natural disaster, famine, or war.
7. To ensure peaceful relations among the peoples of the world, children should be protected from discrimination and prejudice, whether racial, religious, political, or any other type.

Protecting children is a challenging task in a world in which millions of children are unnecessarily injured

---

BOX 15-4   EQUAL RIGHTS FOR CHILDREN

Philosopher Howard Cohen (1985) has said that "Children, in my view, should be entitled to all of the rights adults are entitled to in law and in custom" (p. 150). This view contrasts sharply with the prevalent law and opinion that children should be protected above all, even when such protection deprives them of their liberty. For example, children's custody may be awarded to the parent they dislike; they may be unwillingly removed from the home of legally defined "unfit" parents or caretakers; they are legally compelled to attend school; and their lives may be otherwise controlled to further their ultimate welfare. In Cohen's view, one should treat people equally unless and until there is a justification for unequal treatment (Feinberg, 1973). This implies that the burden of proof is on those who would treat adults and children differently. If the argument is offered that children lack adult mental capacities, then this must be scientifically demonstrated. In fact, it is sometimes difficult to establish group differences in such abilities between adults and children. Both adults and children can be enticed into supporting unscrupulous politicians who treat them and others unjustly while appearing to be respectable and fair. Both age groups can act impulsively and contrary to their own long-term financial and occupational interests, and can otherwise reason and behave irrationally. And because individual children develop their full reasoning capacities at different ages (and some older people may lose their mental acuity), it is impossible to maintain fairly that 21 years or some other arbitrarily selected age represents the age of reason.

   Even proponents of equal legal rights for children recognize gross age differences in capacity, however, and would not choose to extend all liberties to inexperienced and cognitively limited preschoolers or to children who cannot understand their situation because of mental retardation or other cognitive handicaps (Cohen, 1985). To make wise decisions, children may require educational and financial advisors, but then so do most adults. With such assistance, children would not harm themselves nor be harmed by others; they would be free to live with whom they choose, seek the type of medical treatment they might prefer, and manage their own financial affairs with the assistance of objective adult counselors. Cohen (1980, 1985) acknowledges that this goal would be difficult to attain because of numerous practical and theoretical difficulties. However, he believes that under the present system, children are systematically and unjustly being denied their legitimate rights.

SOURCES: Cohen, H. (1980). *Equal rights for children.* Totowa, NJ: Littlefield, Adams; Cohen, H. (1985). Ending the double standard: Equal rights for children. In A. Cafagna, R. T. Peterson, & C. Staudenbaur (Eds.), *Child nurturance: Philosophy, children, and the family* (Vol. 1). New York: Plenum; Feinberg, J. (1973). *Social philosophy.* Englewood Cliffs, NJ: Prentice-Hall.

---

or killed each year, even in economically advantaged nations. Any day's news accounts demonstrate just how far we are from achieving these humane goals (see Box 15-4).

"Increases in rights have been associated with increases in the degree to which children are considered to be persons." (Hart, 1991, p. 55)

Children's Legal Rights

This section reviews some of children's legal rights, many of which have been only recently enacted into law. Three *fundamental principles* guide legal and ethical codes affecting children: autonomy, beneficence, and justice (Levine, Anderson, Ferretti, & Steinberg, 1993).

1. The principle of *autonomy* refers to the ability to make personal decisions based on an adequate understanding of the circumstances. Previously, chil-

dren were regarded as their parents' property and were almost completely subjected to their parents' decisions, however ill-advised or cruel. Today, children and adolescents are granted greater autonomy from parents.

2. The principle of *beneficence* advocates protecting children by removing or preventing harm, working to benefit them, and not intentionally harming them.

3. The *justice* principle asserts that children and adults should have equal rights, and juveniles' rights should be limited only by their still-maturing judgment and intelligence. Children should be treated justly so they will not be goaded into alienation and rebellion (Levine et al., 1993).

BASES FOR RESTRICTION OF CHILDREN'S LIBERTY

Although children have some legal rights as persons, they also require special protection. Teitelbaum and Ellis

Courts of law are not designed for children who may be intimidated by unfamiliar adult interviewers and may unintentionally give them misinformation. Methods of obtaining more accurate testimony from children are described in the text.

(1978) offer three principal reasons for legal restrictions on children's liberty:

1. *Vulnerability to harm.* Children require greater protection because they are more vulnerable than adults. Thus, they are prohibited from harmful activities such as smoking, drinking alcohol, using drugs, and engaging in dangerous and taxing work that might endanger their health.
2. *Immature judgment.* Children cannot make informed decisions about important matters because they are uninformed and unable to foresee the long-range consequences of their decisions.
3. *Maintenance of family strength.* The family is the best and most appropriate agent for the socialization and protection of the child. The child is legally prohibited from leaving the family and from defying the parents' wishes so that family strength, cohesion, and discipline can be maintained.

Many decisions pit the child's personal liberty and due process considerations against the authority of parents and the state (Cohen, 1985; Koocher & Keith-Spiegel, 1990). In the process, parental rights may be limited. For this reason, conservative religious and political groups sometimes seek to restrict children's rights. However, there is a growing consensus that children's legal rights should be safeguarded and possibly expanded if their welfare is endangered.

CHILD CUSTODY DECISIONS

When parents separate or divorce, they have the option of joint custody or one of them may gain sole custody of the children while the other receives visitation privileges. When neither parent is competent, motivated, or available, the children are placed in foster care. Custody decisions are important for children and parents alike. Parents knowingly or unwittingly may encourage their children to take sides in their marital disputes, and children develop strong preferences regarding their custodial parent. Acrimonious family arguments and civil suits may follow. Some states require consideration of children's wishes in custody decisions if the children are at least preadolescents. Children's desires are given more weight if they are strongly held, and less weight if: (1) the court decides that the child has insufficient mental capacity to make a wise choice, (2) one parent has exerted undue influence on the child, or (3) the child's preference is based on a desire to escape from one parent's reasonable and desirable but firm discipline (Siegel & Hurley, 1977). The judge may require the child to state a preference for a custodial parent at a hearing, which is an upsetting public rejection of the other parent (Emery, Hetherington, & DiLalla, 1984). Judges attempt to base custody decisions on the *best interests of the child* (*Finlay v. Finlay*, 1925, p. 626), but it is extremely difficult to identify what is best for a child. The Uniform Marriage and Divorce Act defines the child's best interests as based on the wishes of the parent(s) and the child, the quality of interactions among family members, the child's adjustment status, and the mental and physical health of all individuals involved (Charlow, 1994). Very young children are usually assigned to their mother's custody. It is widely believed that there is a special bond between mother and infant, that mothers are more likely than fathers to stay at home and care for their infants personally, and that women are better caregivers than men. One possible solution is joint custody by mother and father, but available research reveals no clear benefit to children from joint as opposed to one-parent custody (Charlow, 1994). Rather, the intensity and persistence of conflict between the parents seems to be the principal determinant of children's adjustment.

While older children may be placed with either parent, the vast majority reside with their mothers (Emery et al., 1984), even though many mother-headed families are forced into poverty following a divorce. Single mothers usually hold lower-paying jobs and are less able to provide for the children economically than are their former husbands. Mother-headed families mostly experience a lowered standard of living, reduced educational opportunities for the children, and increased conflicts about financial and other family life issues. The use of professional mediators by divorcing couples has somewhat reduced the intensity of custody and child support battles, to the benefit of all concerned (Ackerman, 1995).

"As society has moved into the 1990s, mothers still receive placement of children 90% of the time in all divorce actions and 60% of the time in contested divorce actions." (Ackerman, 1995)

CHILDREN'S RIGHTS IN THE SCHOOLS

In the past, few parents challenged the authority and wisdom of teachers and principals to instruct, supervise, and discipline their children. Parents with little formal education felt unqualified to judge the quality of their children's educational services. School discipline was strict, and disobedient and troublesome pupils could be physically punished for even minor rule infractions, sent to sit in a corner, forced to wear a "dunce cap," or expelled from school for misbehavior. The groundbreaking federal Education for All Handicapped Children Act of 1975 (PL 94-142) specified that public schools must adequately serve emotionally, mentally, and physically handicapped children and their families. Families formerly had to bear nearly the entire financial and personal burden of training or educating their handicapped youngsters, but henceforth the public schools were required to do so. Unfortunately, Congress appropriated no additional money for this praiseworthy endeavor, so school districts were compelled to assume enormous additional costs without federal assistance. Federal laws providing appropriate educational services for all children are costly because they require free and appropriate education for every individual child, no matter how unusual or disabled. Schools are prohibited from excluding any children simply because they are difficult, defiant, or expensive to educate. Nor can children be excluded because the school cannot afford to provide the necessary physical accommodations or trained instructors, such as teachers versed in American Sign Language or Braille. Further, teachers are no longer automatically assumed to be in the right in disputes involving children who are difficult to manage or violent, and these children cannot be expelled from school without an impartial, due process hearing. A more restrictive, special education classroom placement can be used only if convincing evidence is presented to show that a student has found it impossible to adjust to the regular classroom situation.

The current emphasis is on *mainstreaming* or integrating atypical students with their normal classmates as much as possible. The law requires that the child be educated in the least restrictive environment possible, consistent with the child's abilities. Judges and legislators assume that contact with normal classmates is highly advantageous, or even necessary for normal socialization, but there may be risks as well (Zigler & Muenchow, 1992). Normal children can be cruel to those who are different in appearance or behavior in any way and can make their lives miserable both during and after school. Children who are visibly different from the others are often avoided by the majority. Social barriers in a mainstream environment can isolate children with disabilities just as powerfully as the physical barriers of separate classrooms, and can add rejection to their burdens. There is no objective research evidence that students can learn better academically when mainstreamed than when segregated (Quinn, 1985). Special efforts are needed to include them in social as well as academic activities.

Parents also enjoy expanded rights regarding their child's education under recent legislation. They must be consulted regarding their child's classroom placement and special services, which they need not pay for privately, and they must be informed about their child's progress. If properly implemented, the legislation aimed to benefit handicapped students would achieve these laudable aims, but governments have failed to provide the funds to do so, and as a result, a few children with disabilities whose parents assertively seek services from the schools, receive the bulk of the special services the schools can provide.

RIGHTS OF JUVENILES ACCUSED OF ILLEGAL ACTS

The 1967 Supreme Court decision *In Re Gault* held that minors who might be deprived of their freedom and sent to correctional institutions have certain rights. Under the due process clause of the Fourteenth Amendment, they must be given notice that a hearing will be held, they have a right to be represented by counsel, and they cannot be forced to give self-incriminating testimony. Through their attorneys, minors may also confront their accusers and cross-examine witnesses. The court later ruled that juveniles cannot be sent to correctional institutions on mere suspicion of guilt, but had to be proven guilty by the same exacting standard as that used with adults, that is, beyond a reasonable doubt. Unlike adults, children have no right to a jury trial, although they cannot be sentenced to a correctional facility without a hearing.

The legal protection for a status offender is somewhat less clear than for an accused criminal delinquent. *Status offenders* are children and adolescents who run away from home, refuse to attend school, drink, smoke and take drugs, congregate with criminals, steal from and defy their families, and generally prove ungovernable. These status offenses fall short of criminal delinquency, but are matters of serious concern. Some parents ultimately ask the juvenile court to declare their recalcitrant children to be incorrigible "persons in need of supervision."

INDEPENDENT LIVING FOR EMANCIPATED TEENS

Several states have enacted laws to permit some teenagers to be declared legally independent of their parents and to be considered adults for most legal purposes. These are not typically status offenders, but may have markedly inadequate homes or serious, persistent conflict with their parents. Their parents must consent to or at least fail to oppose their teenagers' emancipation in order for the young people to live independently. However, they must be able to find jobs, support themselves, and manage their own lives. This seems a sad but constructive solution to impossible family situations when adolescents are capable of independent living. Many young people are affected. In 1993, 10 percent of males and 14 percent of the females ages 15 to 19 were living alone rather than with a spouse or relatives (U.S. Bureau of the Census, 1994).

Children's Rights to Mental Health Treatment

It is widely assumed that parents know best regarding their children's psychological and medical treatment. Yet the child's interests may differ from those of the parents and "It is the child who will suffer if the gamble is lost" (Keniston, 1977, p. 202). The 1989 United Nations Convention on the Rights of Children requires that child mental health service clients be active participants in their own treatment planning and decision-making and that they be provided with understandable information relevant to those decisions (Melton, 1991). Actual U.S. case law permits parents to institutionalize their children regardless of the child's wishes and authorize other treatments for the children against their will. Because children have no choice, practitioners have a special obligation to protect children's moral or human rights in treatment decisions. Table 15-1 describes some of the human rights that have been recommended to protect children in treatment.

The question of children's rights becomes acute when unpleasant, confining, or coercive treatment methods are used. For example, a child's treatment plan might employ

TABLE 15-1   A "BILL OF RIGHTS" FOR CHILDREN IN PSYCHOTHERAPY

1. *The Right to Be Told the Truth:* Children should be informed of events that affect them and should never be lied to by the therapist. As Ross (1980) has stated, "When children are old enough to be talked to, they are old enough to be told the truth" (p. 68).

2. *The Right to Be Treated as a Person:* This implies that the child's right to privacy and confidentiality should be respected and that the therapist should not divulge information shared by the child in treatment sessions nor should sessions be recorded or observed without the child's knowledge or permission.

3. *The Right to Be Taken Seriously:* The therapist, in particular, should listen carefully to the child and neither dismiss nor make light of the child's observations, opinions, or feelings.

4. *The Right to Participate in Decision-Making:* Like adults, children should be allowed to express their opinions in matters involving their lives, and their opinions should carry some weight. Too often, adults make the important decisions involving children and only later inform the children. Therapists, in particular, should not behave in this cavalier fashion toward children.

SOURCE: Koocher, G. P. (1976). A bill of rights for children in psychotherapy. In G. Koocher (Ed.), *Children's rights and the mental health professions.* New York: Wiley.

both positive reinforcement for appropriate behavior and some form of punishment such as brief periods of time-out from enjoyable activities. Many treatment agencies and schools now require a mandatory *independent* evaluation of each proposed treatment plan by people who are not personally involved in the child's treatment. Any extreme therapy such as electric shock, psychosurgery, or aversive methods is typically reviewed by a peer review board or ethics committee acting independently of the therapist, hospital or clinic, and the child's parents. Such autonomy is important because some therapists or institutions could be uncritical proponents of aversive methods and could unduly influence anxious and insecure parents to agree. Consequently, an unbiased independent evaluation is necessary in order to protect the children's interests. Nearly all clinics and hospitals require such reviews.

CHILDREN'S RIGHTS AND RESTRICTIVE TREATMENTS

Most intellectually normal adolescents are capable of making competent treatment decisions (Weithorn,

1985), and young elementary school children may participate in such choices (Lewis, Lewis, & Lefkwunigue, 1978). Treatments can be ranked according to how innocuous or drastic they are. Most forms of child psychotherapy resemble the child's everyday activities and require no special safeguards, whereas the more restrictive treatments deprive children of their freedom in some way. For example, physically restrictive treatments constrain children's freedom of movement or confine them to institutions. For these reasons, the use of physically restrictive treatment is legally controlled.

Intermediate in restrictiveness between psychological therapies and physical restraint are most psychoactive medications or prescribed drugs. Psychoactive medications are considered to be restrictive for the following reasons:

1. Drug effects cannot be resisted. The child has more choice when psychotherapy is used because they can choose whether to participate (Shapiro, 1974).

2. Drugs may make children more manageable, but don't require them or their parents to learn new and better ways to cope with problems (Grinspoon & Singer, 1973).

3. Most drugs that are strong enough to affect mood and behavior also produce unwanted side effects, some of which can prove dangerous.

4. Drugs can be obtained and misused by the child or family members (Weithorn, 1979), sometimes with dangerous consequences.

5. Drugs can be used punitively. In the case of *Morales v. Turman* (1974) the U.S. District Court in Texas ruled that juveniles held in correctional institutions must be protected from "indiscriminate, unsupervised, unnecessary, or excessive psychotropic medication" if used as an alternative to psychotherapy. In this case, institutional staff members employed painful intramuscular injections of tranquilizers as punishment. In another case, (*Nelson v. Heyne*) the court ruled that such injections represented cruel and unusual punishment when given by inadequately trained and medically unqualified personnel. Even in outpatient settings, drugs may be given too readily and mainly because parents and teachers complain about a child's behavior. Chapter 14 offers further guidelines concerning the use of medications with children.

INVOLUNTARY INSTITUTION OF CHILDREN

Although judicial decisions in the past 20 years have increasingly recognized minors' constitutional rights, significant limitations remain. Parents may institutionalize their children for treatment, and the children have no right to independent legal counsel or a due process hearing (*Parham v. J.R.* No. 75-1690, June 20, 1979). In *Parham*, a formalized, fact-finding hearing was barred, because it could have dangerously intruded into the parent-child relationship, pitting parents against child as adversaries (*Parham*, 442, U.S. at 609). In this view, parental authority and autonomy are the primary considerations, and parents and mental health specialists can be relied on to act in the best interests of the child. To prevent abuses, the court also required that public institutions meet high professional standards and that children initially be admitted only as outpatients and then evaluated. Decisions regarding institutionalization must be made by an interdisciplinary team, and periodic reviews are mandated to determine whether the child is ready to return home. Unfortunately, relatively few institutions can afford to meet the court's high standards (Plotkin, 1979), so the checks and quality guarantees specified by the court are absent. In fact, the questionable quality of care in many institutions is a matter of considerable public and professional concern.

Institutionalizing children is a drastic measure, and the price for the child is high if institutionalization is actually not necessary. There have been widely publicized cases of children falsely diagnosed with mental disorders by hospitals that have a financial interest in admitting as many patients as possible. A few unscrupulous providers have persuaded parents to institutionalize their well children for long periods while the staff and institutions derive many millions of dollars from the family's health insurance benefits. Thus, there is growing public and professional sentiment to reform child psychiatric treatment systems and revisit the issue of children's due process rights regarding their institutionalization.

Most ethical and legal codes now insist that the *least restrictive treatment* criterion be applied when choosing a course of mental health treatment or educational placement. Children should be given the safest, least confining treatment that could be expected to prove effective. Only when the milder techniques prove unhelpful are more radical solutions considered. Treatment and educational plans are implemented only with parents' informed approval and increasingly with the consent of the children who are old enough to participate.

In this volume, we have described an historic movement toward more humane treatment of disturbed children, which mirrors better treatment of adults with psychological disorders. Children are now given free public education, even if they have major disabilities, but their mental health and prevention treatments still lag. Maladjustment problems are no longer attributed to children's character flaws or the problems of their parents, but are recognized to stem from a wide array of conditions including poverty, poor living conditions, inadequate diets, environmental toxins, drug abuse, inadequate education, crime, violence and the ready availability of deadly weapons, neglect, and sexual and physical abuse. A war on these crippling conditions would be a much worthier social cause than many of the other national priorities that consume so much time, effort, and national wealth.

SUMMARY

Social sanctions for the use of corporal punishment of children seem to encourage physical abuse, especially when the caretaker is angry or under the influence of alcohol or drugs. Physical abuse is more prevalent for boys and sexual abuse is more likely for girls. Sexual abuse is more frequently covert and difficult to identify and prevent, especially abuse of younger children whose complaints may be unconvincing. Physical neglect is the most common of the various types of child abuse and neglect, and seems to be based largely on parents' lack of skills and motivation. On a small scale, physical neglect is readily treated with behavioral techniques. Emotional neglect is more difficult to define, but includes exposing children to harmful environments as in marital violence and illegal drug usage. Educational neglect consists of the parent's failing to see that the child obtains legally decreed schooling. Neglect can produce educational failure, adjustment problems, and precocious sexuality. Abuse produces internalizing and externalizing adjustment problems, and peer and school problems. Society-wide focus on prevention is needed, including reduction in the general level of violence, reduced availability of weapons, and training in nonviolent conflict resolution. Services to new parents, with training in parenting skills, should be widely available in order to prevent child neglect, abuse, and later antisocial aggression.

International child protection groups suggest that children have moral or human rights to health, safety, freedom, including freedom of expression and belief, and education. Actually, children's legal rights are much more limited, and their medical and mental health treatment, including institutionalization, is determined by their parents, acting on the advice of treatment professionals. Children's liberty is restricted because they are presumed to lack mature judgment and are more vulnerable to harm than are adults. Restrictions on children are also imposed in order to maintain family strength and avoid parent-child conflict. By law, children with disabilities are entitled to appropriate individualized education at public expense. All children must be educated and treated in the least restrictive manner possible. Inadequate funding prevents many schools and treatment agencies from achieving this high standard. A major national effort will be required to prevent and treat children's emotional and behavioral disorders.

REFERENCES

CHAPTER 1

Achenbach, T. M., & Edelbrock, C. S. (1978). The classification of child psychopathology: A review and analysis of empirical effects. *Psychological Bulletin, 78,* 1275–1301.

Achenbach, T. M., & Howell, C. T. (1993). Are American children's problems getting worse? A 13-year comparison. *Journal of the American Academy of Child and Adolescent Psychiatry, 32,* 1145–1154.

Al-Issa, I. (1982a). Gender and adult psychopathology. In I. Al-Issa (Ed.), *Gender and psychopathology.* New York: Academic Press.

Al-Issa, I. (1982b). Gender and child psychopathology. In I. Al-Issa (Ed.), *Gender and psychopathology.* New York: Academic Press.

American Psychiatric Association. (1994). *Diagnostic and statistical manual of mental disorders* (4th ed., DSM-IV). Washington, DC: Author.

American Psychologist. (1991). UN Convention on the Rights of the Child: Unofficial summary of articles. *46,* 50–52.

Andersson, B. (1992). Effects of day-care on cognitive and socio-emotional competence of thirteen-year-old Swedish schoolchildren. *Child Development, 63,* 20–36.

Angier, N. (July 24, 1994). The debilitating malady called boyhood. *New York Times,* (Section 4; 1, 16).

Aries, P. (1962). *Centuries of childhood: A social history of family life* (R. Baldick, Trans.). London: Gape.

Arnett, J. (1995). The young and the reckless: Adolescent reckless behavior. *Current Directions in Psychological Science, 4,* 67–70.

Asians in college. (1986, August 5). *New York Times,* p. 26y

Bachman, J. G. (1970). *Youth in transition: The impact of family background and intelligence on tenth-grade boys* (Vol. 2). Ann Arbor: Institute for Social Research, University of Michigan.

Bailey, J. M., & Zucker, K. J. (1995). Childhood sex-typed behavior and sexual orientation: A conceptual analysis and quantitative review. *Developmental Psychology, 31,* 43–55.

Bartak, L., & Rutter, M. L. (1975). A three-and-one-half- to four-year follow-up study of special educational treatment of autistic children. In R. Wirt, G. Winokur, & M. Roff (Eds.), *Life history research in psychopathology* (Vol. 4). Minneapolis: University of Minnesota Press.

Beckman, D. (1977). *The mechanical baby: A popular history of the theory and practice of child raising.* Westport, CT: Lawrence Hill.

Belsky, J., & Cassidy, J. (1994). Attachment: Theory and evidence. In M. Rutter & D. Hay (Eds.), *Development through life: A handbook for clinicians* (pp. 373–402). Oxford, England: Blackwell.

Berg, I. (1970). A follow-up study of school phobic adolescents admitted to an inpatient unit. *Journal of Child Psychology and Psychiatry and Allied Disciplines, 11,* 37–47.

Borstelmann, L. J. (1983). Children before psychology: Ideas about children from antiquity to the late 1800s. In W. Kessen (Ed.), *Handbook of child psychology* (4th ed., vol. 1). New York: Wiley.

Bremner, R. H. (Ed.). (1971). *Children and youth in America: A documentary history, Vol. 2., 1866–1932.* Cambridge, MA: Harvard University Press.

Bruch, H. (1982). Anorexia nervosa: Therapy and theory. *American Journal of Psychiatry, 139,* 1531–1538.

Brumberg, J. J. (1986). "Fasting girls": Reflections on writing the history of anorexia nervosa. In A. B. Smuts & J. W. Hagen (Eds.), History and research in child development. *Monographs of the Society for Research in Child Development, 50* (4–5, Serial No. 211).

Bukowski, W. M., & Newcomb, A. F. (1984). Stability and determinants of sociometric status and friendship choice: A longitudinal perspective. *Developmental Psychology, 20,* 941–952.

Cairns, R. B., & Cairns, B. D. (1994). *Lifelines and risks: Pathways of youth in our time.* Cambridge, England: Cambridge University Press.

Cicchetti, D., Toth, S. L., & Lynch, M. (1995). Bowlby's dream comes full circle: The application of attachment theory to risk and psychopathology. In T. Ollendick & R. Prinz (Eds.), *Advances in Clinical Child Psychology, Vol. 17,* pp. 1–75. New York: Plenum.

Clifford, A. (1923). *The diary of the Lady Anne Clifford* (V. Sackville-West, Ed.). London: Heinemann.

Coie, J. D., & Dodge, K. A. (1983). Continuities and change in children's social status: A five-year longitudinal study. *Merrill-Palmer Quarterly, 29,* 261–281.

Coleman, J. C., Butcher, J. N., & Carson, R. C. (1980). *Abnormal psychology and modern life* (6th ed.). Glenview, IL: Scott, Foresman.

Crisp, A. H. (1976). How common is anorexia nervosa? A prevalence study. *British Journal of Psychiatry, 128,* 349–354.

Crowther, J., Bond, L., & Rolf, J. (1981). The incidence, prevalence, and severity of internalizing and externalizing behavior problems among preschool children in day care. *Journal of Abnormal Child Psychology, 9,* 23–42.

deMause, L. (1974). The evolution of childhood. In L. deMause (Ed.), *The history of childhood.* New York: Psychohistory Press.

Douvan, E., & Adelson, J. (1966). *The adolescent experience.* New York: Wiley.

Drew, C. J., Hardman, M. L., & Logan, D. R. (1996). *Mental retardation: A life cycle approach* (6th ed.). Englewood Cliffs, NJ: Prentice Hall.

Dunn, J., Kendrick, C., & MacNamee, R. (1981). The reaction of first-born children to the birth of a sibling: Mothers' reports. *Journal of Child Psychology and Psychiatry, 22,* 1–18.

Erikson, E. H. (1956). The problems of ego identity. *Journal of the American Psychoanalytic Association, 4,* 56–121.

Fagot, B. I. (1977). Consequences of moderate crossgender behavior in preschool children. *Child Development, 48,* 902–907.

Fagot, B. I. (1985). Changes in thinking about early sex role development. *Developmental Review, 5,* 83–98.

Fergusson, D. M., Horwood, L. J., & Lynskey, M. T. (1994). The comorbidities of adolescent problem behaviors: A latent class model. *Journal of Abnormal Child Psychology, 22*, 339–372.

Gelfand, D. M., & Peterson, L. (1985). *Child development and psychopathology*. Beverly Hills, CA: Sage.

Goodenough, F. L. (1931). *Anger in young children*. Minneapolis: University of Minnesota Press.

Gordon, M. (1978). *The American family in socialhistorical perspective* (2nd ed.). New York: St. Martin's Press.

Greenfeld, J. (1978). *A place for Noah*. New York: Holt, Rinehart & Winston.

Greenfeld, J. (1986). *A client called Noah: A family journey continued*. New York: Henry Holt.

Hershberger, S. L., & D'Augelli, R. D. (1995). The impact of victimization on the mental health and suicidality of lesbian, gay, and bisexual youths. *Developmental Psychology, 31*, 65–74.

Huston, A. C. (1983). Sex-typing. In P. H. Mussen (General Ed.), *Handbook of child psychology* (4th ed.): Vol. 4. *Socialization, personality, and social development* (E. M. Hetherington, Vol. Ed.). New York: Wiley.

Institute of Medicine, National Academy of Sciences. (1989). *Research on children and adolescents with mental, behavioral, and developmental disorders: Mobilizing a national initiative*. Washington, DC: National Academy Press.

Jessor, R., & Jessor, S. L. (1977). *Problem behavior and psychosocial development: A longitudinal study of youth*. New York: Academic Press.

Jordan, C., & Tharp, R. G. (1979). Culture and education. In A. Marsella, R. Tharp, & T. Ciborowski (Eds.), *Perspectives on cross-cultural psychology*. New York: Academic Press.

Kagan, J. (1978). The child in the family. In A. Rossi, J. Kagan, & T. Hareven (Eds.), *The family*. New York: Norton.

Kelly, T. J., Bullock, L. M., & Dykes, M. K. (1978). Behavioral disorders: Teachers' perceptions. *Exceptional Children, 43*, 316–318.

Kessen, W. (1965). *The child*. New York: Wiley.

Kessler, R. C., McGonagle, K. A., Zhao, S., Nelson, C., Highes, M., Eshleman, S., Wittchen, H., & Kendler, K. (1994). Lifetime and 12-month prevalence of DSM-III-R psychiatric disorders in the United States. *Archives of General Psychiatry, 51*, 8–19.

King, N. (1993). Simple and social phobias. In T. Ollendick & R. Prinz (Eds.), *Advances in clinical child psychology*, Vol. 15, pp. 305–341. New York: Plenum.

Kohlberg, L., LaCrosse, J., & Ricks, D. (1972). The predictability of adult mental health from childhood behavior. In B. Wolman (Ed.), *Manual of child psychopathology*. New York: McGraw-Hill.

Kramer, M. (1977). *Psychiatric services and the changing institutional scene, 1950–1985* (DHEW Publication No. ADM 77–77–433). Washington, DC: U.S. Government Printing Office.

Lamb, M. E., & Roopnarine, J. F. (1979). Peer influences on sex-role development in preschoolers. *Child Development, 50*, 1219–1222.

Levine, M., & Levine, A. (1970). *A social history of helping services*. New York: Appleton-Century-Crofts.

Lewinsohn, P. M., & Rohde, P. (1993). The cognitive-behavioral treatment of depression in adolescents: Research and suggestions. *The Clinical Psychologist, 46*, 177–183.

Lewis, W. W. (1965). Continuity and intervention in emotional disturbance: A review. *Exceptional Children, 31*, 465–475.

Loeber, R. (1990). Development and risk factors of juvenile antisocial behavior and delinquency. *Clinical Psychology Review, 10*, 1–41.

Lykken, D. T. (1993). Predicting violence in the violent society. *Applied and Preventive Psychology, 2*, 13–20.

Macfarlane, J. W. (1963). From infancy to adulthood. *Childhood Education, 39*, 336–342.

Macfarlane, J. W. (1964). Perspectives on personality consistency and change from The Guidance Study. *Vita Humana, 7*, 115–126.

Macfarlane, J. W., Allen, L., & Honzik, M. (1954). *A developmental study of the behavior problems of normal children between twenty-one months and fourteen years*. Berkeley: University of California Press.

Marsella, A. J. (1979). Cross-cultural studies of mental disorders. In A. Marsella, R. Tharp, & T. Ciborowski (Eds.), *Perspectives on cross-cultural psychology*. New York: Academic Press.

Maziade, M., Capera, M., Laplante, B., Boudreault, B., Thivierge, J., Cote, R., & Boutin, P. (1985). The value of difficult temperament among 7-year-olds in the general population for predicting psychiatric diagnosis at age 12. *American Journal of Pediatrics, 142*, 943–946.

McCall, R. B., Appelbaum, M. I., & Hogarty, P. S. (1973). Developmental changes in mental performance. *Monographs of the Society for Research in Child Development, 38* (Serial No. 150).

Meissner, W. W. (1965). Parental interaction of the adolescent boy. *Journal of Genetic Psychology, 107*, 225–233.

Murphy, J. M. (1976). Psychiatric labeling in cross-cultural perspective. *Science, 191*, 1019–1028.

Nash, S. E., & Feldman, S. S. (1981). Sex role and sex-related attributions: Constancy and change across the family life cycle. In M. E. Lamb & A. L. Brown (Eds.), *Advances in developmental psychology* (Vol. 1). Hillsdale, NJ: Erlbaum.

Offer, D., & Offer, J. B. (1975). *From teenage to young manhood: A psychological study*. New York: Basic Books.

Peters, R. D., McMahon, R. J., & Quincy, V. L. (Eds.). (1992). *Aggression and violence throughout the life span*. Newbury Park, CA: Sage.

Pollock, L. A. (1983). *Forgotten children: Parent-child relations from 1500 to 1900*. Cambridge, England: Cambridge University Press.

Quay, H. D. (1986). Classification. In H. D. Quay & J. S. Werry (Eds.), *Psychopathological disorders of childhood* (4th ed., pp. 1–34). New York: Wiley.

Rie, H. E. (1971). Historical perspectives on concepts of child psychopathology. In H. Rie (Ed.), *Perspectives in child psychopathology*. Chicago: Aldine-Atherton.

Robins, L. N. (1966). *A sociological and psychiatric study of sociopathic personality*. Baltimore: Williams & Wilkins.

Rolf, J., Hakola, J., Klemchuk, H., & Hasazi, J. (1976). *The incidence, prevalence and severity of behavior disorders among preschool aged children*. Paper presented at the meeting of the Eastern Psychological Association, New York.

Rosenfeld, G. (1971). *"Shut those thick lips!" A study of slum school failure*. New York: Holt, Rinehart & Winston.

Rubin, R. A., & Balow, B. (1971). Learning and behavior disorders: A longitudinal study. *Exceptional Children, 38*, 293–299.

Rubin, R. A., & Balow, B. (1978). Prevalence of teacher identified behavior problems: A longitudinal study. *Exceptional Children, 45*, 102–111.

Rutter, M., & Garmezy, N. (1983). Developmental psychopathology. In P. H. Mussen (General Ed.), *Handbook of child psychology* (4th ed.): Vol. 4, *Socialization, personality, and social development* (E. M. Hetherington, Vol. Ed.). New York: Wiley.

Shepherd, M., Oppenheim, B., & Mitchell, S. (Eds.). (1971). *Childhood behaviour and mental health.* London: University of London Press.

Shorter, E. (1975). *The making of the modern family.* New York: Basic Books.

Snapper, K. J., & Ohms, J. S. (1977). *The status of children 1977.* Washington, DC: U.S. Government Printing Office.

Sparks, J. L., & Younie, W. J. (1969). Adult adjustment of the mentally retarded: Implications for teacher education. *Exceptional Children, 36,* 13–18.

Spitzka, E. C. (1890). Insanity. In J. Keating (Ed.), *Cyclopaedia of the diseases of children, medical and surgical.* Philadelphia: J. B. Lippincott.

Strauss, J. S. (1979). Social and cultural influences on psychopathology. *Annual Review of Psychology, 30,* 397–415.

Swedo, S. E., Lenanare, M., Rettew, D., Hamburger, S., Bartko, J., & Rapoport, J. L. (1993). A 2- to 7-year follow-up study of 54 obsessive-compulsive children and adolescents. *Archives of General Psychiatry, 50,* 429–440.

Tarnowski, K. J., & Rorhrbeck, C. A. (1993). Disadvantaged children and families. In T. Ollendick & R. Prinz (Eds.), *Advances in clinical child psychology* (Vol. 15, pp. 41–79). New York: Plenum.

Tharp, R. G., & Gallimore, R. (1988). *Rousing minds to life: Teaching, learning, and schooling in social context.* New York: Cambridge University Press.

Tuchman, B. (1978). *A distant mirror: The calamitous 14th century.* New York: Knopf.

U.S. Bureau of the Census. (1994). *Statistical Abstract of the United States. 1994.* Washington, DC: U.S. Government Printing Office.

U.S. Office of Education, Bureau of Education for the Handicapped. (1975, May 16). *State education agency estimates unserved by type of handicap.* Washington, DC: Author, Aid to State Branch.

Watson-Gegeo, K. A., & Boggs, S. T. (1977). From verbal play to talk-story: The role of routines in speech events among Hawaiian children. In S. Ervin-Tripp & C. Mitchell-Kernan (Eds.), *Child discourse.* New York: Academic Press.

Watt, N. F. (1986). Prevention of schizophrenic disorders. In B. Edelstein & L. Michelson (Eds.), *Handbook of prevention.* New York: Plenum.

Weiner, I. B. (1982). Child and adolescent psychopathology. New York: Wiley.

Werner, E. E. (1995). Resilience in development. *Current Directions in Psychological Science, 4,* 81–85.

Werner, E. E., Bierman, J. M., & French, F. E. (1971). *The children of Kauai.* Honolulu: University of Hawaii Press.

Werner, E. E., & Smith, R. S. (1977). *Kauai's children come of age.* Honolulu: University of Hawaii Press.

Werner, E. E., & Smith, R. W. (1992). *Overcoming the odds: High risk children from birth to adulthood.* Ithaca, NY: Cornell University Press.

Zax, M., & Cowen, E. L. (1967). Early identification and prevention of emotional disturbance in a public school. In E. L. Cowen, E. Gardner, & M. Zax (Eds.), *Emergent approaches to mental health problems.* New York: Appleton-Century-Crofts.

CHAPTER 2

Abramson, L. Y., Seligman, M. E. P., & Teasdale, J. D. (1978). Learned helplessness in humans: Critique and reformation. *Journal of Abnormal Psychology, 87,* 49–74.

Achenbach, T. M. (1991). The derivation of taxonomic constructs: A necessary stage in the development of developmental psychopathology. In D. Cicchetti & S. L. Toth (Eds.), *Rochester Symposium on Developmental Psychopathology* (Vol. 3, pp. 43–74). Rochester, NY: University of Rochester Press.

Ainsworth, M. D. S., Blehar, M. C., Waters, E., & Wall, S. (1978). *Patterns of attachment.* Hillsdale, NJ: Lawrence Erlbaum.

Audi, R. (1976). B. F. Skinner on freedom, dignity, and the explanation of behavior. *Behaviorism, 4,* 163–186.

Bandura, A. (1968). A social learning interpretation of psychological dysfunctions. In P. London & D. Rosenhan (Eds.), *Foundations of abnormal psychology.* New York: Holt, Rinehart and Winston.

Bandura, A. (1969). *Principles of behavior modification.* New York: Holt, Rinehart and Winston.

Bandura, A. (1977). *Social learning theory.* Englewood Cliffs, NJ: Prentice-Hall.

Bandura, A. (1981). Self-referent thought: The development of self-efficacy. In J. Flavell & L. Ross (Eds.), *Social cognitive development.* New York: Cambridge University Press.

Bandura, A. (1995). Exercise of personal and collective efficacy in changing societies. In A. Bandura (Ed.), *Self-efficacy in changing societies* (pp. 1–45). Cambridge, England: Cambridge University Press.

Bandura, A., & Walters, R. J. (1963). *Social and personality development.* New York: Holt, Rinehart and Winston.

Benjamin, L. S. (1974). Structural analysis of social behavior (SASB). *Psychological Review, 81,* 392–425.

Benjamin, L. S. (1994). *Interpersonal diagnosis and treatment of personality disorders.* New York: Guilford.

Biglan, A., & Kass, D. J. (1977). The empirical nature of behavior therapies. *Behaviorism, 5,* 1–15.

Borkowski, J., & Day, J. (1987). *Cognition in special children: Comparative approaches to retardation, learning disabilities, and giftedness.* Norwood, NJ: Ablex.

Bouchard, T. J. (1993). Genetic and environmental influences on adult personality: Evaluating the evidence. In J. Hettema & I. J. Deary (Eds.), *Foundations of personality* (pp. 15–44). Dordrecht, Netherlands: Kluwer Academic.

Bouchard, T. J., Lykken, D. T., McGue, M., Segal, N. L., & Tellegen, A. (1990). Sources of human psychological differences: The Minnesota study of twins reared apart. *Science, 250,* 223–228.

Bowlby, J. (1969). *Attachment and loss: Vol. 1. Attachment.* New York: Basic Books.

Buhler, C., & Allen, C. (1972). *Introduction of humanistic psychology.* Monterey, CA.: Brooks/Cole.

Buss, A. H., & Plomin, R. (1984). *Temperament: Early developing personality traits.* Hillsdale, NJ: Erlbaum.

Cairns, R. B., & Cairns, B. D. (1994). *Lifelines and risks: Pathways of youth in our time.* Cambridge, England: Cambridge University Press.

Capute, A. J., Neidermayer, E. F. L., & Richardson, F. (1968). The electroencephalogram in children with minimal cerebral dysfunction. *Pediatrics, 41,* 1104.

Cashdan, S. (1988). *Object relations theory: Using the relationship.* New York: Norton and Co.

Chaplin, J. P., & Krawiec, T. (1979). *Systems and theories of psychology* (4th ed.). New York: Holt, Rinehart and Winston.

Chomsky, N. (1959). Review of Verbal Behavior by B. F. Skinner. *Language, 35,* 26–58.

Cicchetti, D. (1984). The emergence of developmental psychopathology. *Child Development, 55,* 1–7.

Cicchetti, D., Toth, S. L., & Lynch, M. (1995). Bowlby's dream comes full circle: The application of attachment theory to risk and psychopathology. In T. Ollendick & R. Prinz (Eds.), *Advances in clinical child psychology* (Vol. 17, pp. 1–75). New York: Plenum.

Crews, F. (1996). The verdict on Freud. *Psychological Science, 7,* 63–68.

Elkind, D. (1976). *Child development and education.* New York: Norton.

Epstein, S. (1973). The self-concept revisited: Or a theory of a theory. *American Psychologist, 28,* 404–416.

Erikson, E. H. (1963). *Childhood and society* (2nd ed.). New York: Norton.

Erikson, E. H. (1968). *Identity: Youth and crisis.* New York: Norton.

Ferster, C. B., & Skinner, B. F. (1957) *Schedules of reinforcement.* New York: Appleton.

Flavell, J. H. (1963). *The developmental psychology of Jean Piaget.* New York: Van Nostrand Reinhold.

Freud, A. (1946). *The ego and the mechanisms of defence.* New York: International Universities.

Freud, S. (1965). *New introductory lecture on psychoanalysis* (Trans. J. Strachey). New York: Norton.

Gelfand, D. M., & Peterson, L. (1985). *Child development and psychopathology.* Beverly Hills, CA: Sage.

Gelman, R., & Baillargeon, R. (1983). A review of some Piagetian concepts. In P. Mussen (Ed.), *Handbook of child psychology* (Vol. III). New York: Wiley.

Hagerman, R. J. (1996). Biomedical advances in developmental psychology: The case of fragile X syndrome. *Developmental Psychology, 32,* 416–424.

Hall, C. S. (1954). *A primer of Freudian psychology.* Cleveland: World Publishing.

Hall, C. S., & Lindzey, G. (1978). *Theories of personality* (3rd ed.). New York: Wiley.

Hanson, N. R. (1958). *Patterns of discovery.* London: Cambridge University Press.

Hartmann, H., Kris, E., & Loewenstein, R. M. (1947). Comments on the formation of psychic structure. In A. Freud et al. (Eds.), *The psychoanalytic study of the child* (Vol. 2). New York: International Universities.

Henry, W., Schacht, T., & Strupp, H. H. (1986). Structural analysis of social behavior: Application to a study of interpersonal process in differential psychotherapeutic outcome. *Journal of Consulting and Clinical Psychology, 54,* 27–31.

Hilgard, E. R., & Bower, G. H. (1975) *Theories of learning* (4th ed.). Englewood Cliffs, NJ: Prentice-Hall.

Holland, J. G. (1992). B. F. Skinner (1904–1990). *American Psychologist, 47,* 665–667.

Kagan, J. (1995). *Galen's prophecy: Temperament in human nature.* New York: Basic Books.

Karmiloff-Smith, A. (1993, Spring). NeoPiagetians: A theoretical misnomer? *SRCD (Society for Research in Child Development) Newsletter, 3,* 6–7.

Kelsoe, J. R. (1992). The search for genes for psychiatric illness. *Neuropsychopharmacology, 6,* 215–217.

Kernberg, O. (1984). *Severe personality disorders.* New Haven, CT: Yale University Press.

Kringlen, E. (1976). Twins—still our best method. *Schizophrenia Bulletin, 2,* 429–433.

Kuhn, T. S. (1977). *The essential tension.* Chicago: University of Chicago Press.

Macmillan, M. (1991). *Freud evaluated: The completed arc. Advances in psychology.* Amsterdam: North-Holland.

Medina, J. (1996, April). Genetic study of human behavior: Its progress and limitations. *Harvard Mental Health Letter, 12,* 4–5.

Meltzer, H. Y., & Stahl, S. (1976). The dopamine hypothesis of schizophrenia: A review. *Schizophrenia Bulletin, 2,* 19–96.

Miller, N. E., & Dollard, J. (1941). *Social learning and imitation.* New Haven, CT: Yale University Press.

Mischel, W. (1968). *Personality and assessment.* New York: Wiley.

Mischel, W. (1973). Toward a cognitive social learning reconceptualization of personality. *Psychological Review, 80,* 252–283.

Mischel, W. (1993). *Introduction to personality* (5th ed.). New York: Holt, Rinehart and Winston.

Moffitt, T. E., Caspi, A., Harkness, A. R., & Silva, P. A. (1993). The natural history of change in intellectual performance. Who changes? How much? Is it meaningful? *Journal of Child Psychology and Psychiatry, 34,* 455–506.

Overton, W. F., & Horowitz, H. A. (1991). Developmental psychopathology: Integrations and differentiations. In D. Cicchetti & S. L. Toth (Eds.), *Rochester symposium on developmental psychopathology. Models and integrations* (Vol. 3, pp. 1–42). Rochester, NY: University of Rochester Press.

Pederson, N. L., Plomin, R., McClearn, G. E., & Friberg, L. (1988). Neuroticism, extraversion and related traits in adult twins reared apart and reared together. *Journal of Personality and Social Psychology, 55,* 950–957.

Phillips, J. L. (1975). *The origins of intellect: Piaget's theory.* San Francisco: W. H. Freeman.

Reed, E. (1975). Genetic anomalies in development. In F. Horowitz (Ed.), *Review of child development research* (Vol. 4). Chicago: University of Chicago Press.

Rende, R., & Plomin, R. (1992). Diathesis-stress models of psychopathology: A quantitative genetic perspective. *Applied & Preventive Psychology, 1,* 177–182.

Rescorla, R. A. (1988). Pavlovian conditioning: It's not what you think it is. *American Psychologist, 43,* 151–160.

Rogers, C. R., (1961). *On becoming a person.* Boston: Houghton Mifflin.

Rotter, J. B. (1954). *Social learning and clinical psychology.* Englewood Cliffs, NJ: Prentice-Hall.

Schlinger, H. D. (1992). Theory in behavior analysis: An application to child development. *American Psychologist, 47,* 1396–1410.

Selye, H. (1980). The stress concept today. In I. L. Kutash, L. B. Schlesinger, & Associates (Eds.), *Handbook on stress and anxiety.* San Francisco: Jossey-Bass.

Selye, H. (1982). History and present status of the stress concept. In L. Goldberger & S. Breznitz (Eds.), *Handbook of stress: Theoretical and clinical aspects.* New York: Free Press.

Shoda, Y., Mischel, W., & Peake, P. K. (1990). Predicting adolescent cognitive and self-regulatory competencies from preschool delay of gratification: Identifying diagnostic conditions. *Developmental Psychology, 26,* 978–986.

Simonoff, E., Rutter, M., & Bolton, P. (1996). Mental retardation: Genetic findings, clinical implications and research agenda. *Journal of Child Psychology and Psychiatry, 37,* 259–280.

Skinner, B. F. (1953). *Science and human behavior.* New York: Macmillan.

Sroufe, L. A., & Rutter, M. (1984). The domain of developmental psychopathology. *Child Development, 55,* 17–29.

St. George-Hyslop, P. H., Haines, J. L., Farrer, L. A., Polinsky, R., Van Broeckhoven, C., Goate, A., McLachlan, D. R., Orr, H., Bruni, A., & Sorbi, S. (1990). Genetic linkage studies suggest that Alzheimer's disease is not a single homogeneous disorder. *Nature, 347,* 194–197.

Stevenson, H. (1983). How children learn—The quest for a theory. In W. Kessen (Ed.), *Handbook of child psychology* (Vol. 1, 4th ed.). New York: Wiley.

Tellegen, A., Lykken, D., Bouchard, T., Wilcox, K., Segal, N., & Rich, S. (1988). Personality similarities in twins reared apart. *Journal of Personality and Social Psychology, 54,* 1031–1039.

Teti, D. M., Heaton, N., Benjamin, L. S., & Gelfand, D. M. (1995, May). Quality of attachment and caregiving among depressed mother-child dyads: Strange Situation classifications and the SASB coding system. In S. Petrovich (Chair), *Patterns of early socialization: Behavioral ecology of attachment.* Symposium conducted at the meeting of the Society of Applied Behavior Analysis, Washington, DC.

Thomas, R. M. (1979). *Comparing theories of child development.* Belmont, CA: Wadsworth.

Todd, J. T., & Morris, E. K. (1992). Case histories in the great power of steady misrepresentation. *American Psychologist, 47,* 1441–1453.

Witschi, E. (1971). Overripeness of the egg as a possible cause in mental and physical disorders. In I. Gottesman & L. Erlenmeyer-Kimling (Eds.), *Differential reproduction in individuals with mental and physical disorder. Social Biology Supplement, 18,* S9–S15.

Yablonsky, L. (1962) *The violent gang.* New York: Crowell-Collier and Macmillan.

Zuckerman, M. (1995). Good and bad humors: Biochemical bases of personality and its disorders. *Psychological Science, 6,* 325–332.

CHAPTER 3

American Psychological Association Ethics Committee, (1992). Ethical principles of psychologists and code of conduct. *American Psychologist, 47,* 1597–1611.

Bailey, K. D. (1994). *Methods of social research* (4th ed.). New York: Free Press.

Baumrind, D. (1985). Research on using intentional deception: Ethical issues revisited. *American Psychologist, 40,* 165–174.

Baumrind, D. (1990). Doing good well. In C. B. Fisher & W. W. Tryon (Eds.). *Ethics in applied developmental psychology: Emerging issues in an emerging field. Annual advances in applied developmental psychology* (Vol. 4, pp. 17–28). Norwood, NJ: Ablex.

Blanco, R. F., & Rosenfeld, J. G. (1978). *Case studies in clinical and school psychology.* Springfield, IL: Charles C. Thomas.

Borg, W. R., Gall, J. P., & Gall, M. D. (1993). *Applying educational research: A practical guide* (3rd ed.). New York: Longman.

Campbell, D. T. (1957). Factors relevant to the validity of experiments in social settings. *Psychological Bulletin, 54,* 297–312.

Campbell, D. T., & Stanley, J. C. (1963). Experimental and quasi-experimental designs for research on teaching. In N. L. Gage (Ed.), *Handbook of research on teaching* (pp. 171–246). Chicago: Rand McNally.

Cochran, W. G. (1977). *Sampling techniques* (3rd ed.). New York: Wiley.

Cook, T. D., & Campbell, D. T. (1990). Quasi experimentation. In M. D. Dunnette & L. M. Hough (Eds.), *Handbook of industrial and organizational psychology* (Vol. 1, 2nd ed., pp. 491–576). Palo Alto, CA: Consulting Psychologists Press.

Drew, C. J., Hardman, M. L., & Hart, A. W. (1996). *Designing and conducting research: Inquiry in education and social science.* Boston: Allyn & Bacon.

Drew, C. J., Hardman, M. L., & Logan, D. R. (1996). *Mental retardation: A life cycle approach* (6th ed.). New York: Macmillan.

Eaves, R. C. (1992). Autism. In P. J. McLaughlin & P. Wehman (Eds.), *Developmental disabilities: A handbook for best practices* (pp. 68–81). Boston: Andover Medical Publishers.

Fisher, C. B., & Tryon, W. W. (Eds.). (1990). *Ethics in applied developmental psychology: Emerging issues in an emerging field. Annual advances in applied developmental psychology* (Vol. 4). Norwood, NJ: Ablex.

Fraenkel, J. R., & Wallen, N. E. (1993). *How to design and evaluate research in education* (2nd ed.). New York: McGraw-Hill.

Gelfand, D. M., & Hartmann, D. P. (1984). *Child behavior analysis and therapy* (2nd ed.). New York: Pergamon Press.

Hartmann, D. P. (Ed.). (1982). *Using observers to study behavior: New directions for methodology of social and behavioral science.* San Francisco: Jossey-Bass.

Kazdin, A. E. (1992). *Research design in clinical psychology* (2nd ed.). Boston: Allyn & Bacon.

Kimmel, A. J. (1988). *Ethics and values in applied social research.* Newbury Park, CA: Sage.

Kratochwill, T. R., & Levin, J. R. (Eds.). (1992). *Single-case research design and analysis: New directions for psychology and education.* Hillsdale, NJ: Lawrence Erlbaum.

Lancy, D. F. (1993). *Qualitative research in education: An introduction to the major traditions.* New York: Longman.

Li, H., Rosenthal, R., & Rubin, D. B. (1996). Reliability of measurement in psychology: From Spearman-Brown to maximal reliability. *Psychological Methods, 1,* 98–107.

Love, S. R., Matson, J. L., & West, D. (1990). Mothers as effective therapists for autistic children's phobias. *Journal of Applied Behavior Analysis, 23,* 379–385.

Ogloff, J. R., & Otto, R. K. (1991). Are research participants truly informed? Readability of informed consent forms used in research. *Ethics and Behavior*, 1, 239–252.

Parker, T. B., Freston, C. W., & Drew, C. J. (1975). Comparison of verbal performance of normal and learning disabled children as a function of input organization. *Journal of Learning Disabilities*, 8, 386–393.

Patton, M. Q. (1990). *Qualitative evaluation and research methods* (2nd ed.). Newbury Park, CA: Sage.

Russell, A., Russell, G., & Midwinter, D. (1992). Observer influences on mothers and fathers: Self-reported influence during a home observation. *Merrill Palmer Quarterly*, 38, 263–283.

Sheridan, S. M., Dee, C. C., Morgan, J., McCormick, M., & Walker, D. (1996). A multimethod intervention for social skills deficits in children with ADHD and their parents. *School Psychology Review*, 25, 57–76.

Sieber, J. E. (1992). *Planning ethically responsible research: A guide for students and internal review boards*. Newbury Park, CA: Sage.

Siegel, P. S., & Ellis, N. R. (1985). Note on the recruitment of subjects for mental retardation research. *American Journal of Mental Deficiency*, 89, 431–433.

Sudman, S. (1976). *Applied sampling*. New York: Academic Press.

Turnbull, H. R., III. (Ed.). (1977). *Consent handbook*. Washington, DC: American Association on Mental Deficiency.

Welch, R. F., & Drew, C. J. (1972). Effects of reward anticipation and performance expectancy on the learning rate of EMR adolescents. *American Journal of Mental Deficiency*, 77, 291–295.

Wermuth, B. M., Davis, K. L., Hollister, L. E., & Stunkard, A. J. (1977). Phenytoin treatment of the binge-eating syndrome. *American Journal of Psychiatry*, 134, 1249–1253.

CHAPTER 4

Aber, J. L., Brooks-Gunn, J., & Maynard, R. A. (1995). Effects of welfare reform on teenage parents and their children. *The Future of Children*, 5, No. 3, 53–71.

Amato, P. R., & Keith, B. (1991). Parental divorce and the well-being of children: A meta-analysis. *Psychological Bulletin*, 110, 26–46.

Arendell, T. (1986). *Mothers and divorce: Legal, economic, and social dilemmas*. Berkeley, CA: University of California Press.

Barber, B. L., & Eccles, J. S. (1992). Influence of divorce and single parenting on adolescent family- and work-related values, behaviors, and aspirations. *Psychological Bulletin*, 111, 108–126.

Bauerfeld, S. L., & Lachenmeyer, J. R. (1992). Prenatal nutritional status and intellectual development: Critical review and evaluation. In B. Lahey & A. E. Kazdin (Eds.), *Advances in clinical child psychology*, (Vol. 14, pp. 191–222). New York: Plenum.

Birch, H. G., & Gussow, J. D. (1970). *Disadvantaged children: Health nutrition, and school failure*. New York: Harcourt Brace Jovanovich.

Bradley, R. H., & Caldwell, B. (1976). The relation of infants' home environments to mental test performance at fifty-four months. *Child Development*, 47, 1172–1174.

Bradley, R. H., & Caldwell, B. M. (1978). Screening the environment. *American Journal of Orthopsychiatry*, 48, 114–130.

Centers for Disease Control and Prevention (CDC). (1991a). *Preventing lead poisoning in young children: A statement by the Centers for Disease Control*. Atlanta, GA: U.S. Department of Health and Human Services.

Centers for Disease Control and Prevention. (1991b). Weapon-carrying among high school students—United States, 1990. In R. A. Goodman (Ed.), *Chronic disease and health promotion: 1990–1991: Youth risk behavior surveillance system* (pp. 17–19). Atlanta: Author.

Cohn, J. F., & Campbell, S. B. (1992). Influence of maternal depression on infant affect regulation. In D. Cicchetti & S. Toth (Eds.), *Rochester Symposium on Developmental Psychopathology: Vol. 2. Developmental perspectives on depression* (pp. 103–130). Rochester, NY: University of Rochester Press.

Collins, R. C. (1983, Summer). Head Start: An update on program effects. *Newsletter of the Society for Research in Child Development*, pp. 1–2.

Coverman, S. (1989). Role overload, role conflict, and stress: Addressing consequences of multiple role demands. *Social Forces*, 67, 965–982.

Davies, P. T., & Cummings, E. M. (1994). Marital conflict and child adjustment: An emotional security hypothesis. *Psychological Bulletin*, 116, 387–411.

Duncan, G. J. (1991). The economic environment of childhood. In A. C. Huston (Ed.), *Children in poverty: Child development and public policy* (pp. 23–50). New York: Cambridge University Press.

Elder, G. H., Jr. (1995). Life trajectories in changing societies. In A. Bandura (Ed.), *Self-efficacy in changing societies* (pp. 46–68). Cambridge, England: Cambridge University Press.

Fergusson, D. M., & Lynskey, M. T. (1996). Adolescent resiliency to family adversity. *Journal of Child Psychology & Psychiatry*, 37, 281–292.

Field, T., Widmayer, S. M., Stringer, S., & Ignatoff, E. (1980). Teen-age, lower class black mothers and their preterm infants: An intervention and developmental follow-up. *Child Development*, 51, 426–436.

Foster, S. L., Martinez, C. R., & Kulberg, A. M. (1996). Race, ethnicity, and children's peer relations. In T. Ollendick & R. Prinz (Eds.), *Advances in clinical child psychology* (Vol. 18, pp. 133–172). New York: Plenum.

Frick, P. J. (1994). Family dysfunction and the disruptive behavior disorders: A review of recent empirical findings. In T. H. Ollendick & R. J. Prinz (Eds.), *Advances in clinical child psychology* (Vol. 16, pp. 203–226). New York: Plenum Press.

Garbarino, J. (1992). The meaning of poverty in the world of children. *American Behavioral Scientist*, 35, 220–237.

Garmezy, N., & Streitman, S. (1974). Children at risk: The search for the antecedents of schizophrenia. *Schizophrenia Bulletin*, 8, 14–90.

Gelfand, D. M., & Teti, D. M. (1990). The effects of maternal depression on children. *Clinical Psychology Review*, 10, 329–345.

Glick, P. C. (1979). Children of divorced parents in demographic perspective. *Journal of Social Issues*, 35, 112–125.

Gould, S. J. (1981). *The mismeasure of man*. New York: W. W. Norton.

Greenwood, C. R., Carta, J. J., Hart, B., Kamps, D., Terry, B., Arreaga-Mayer, C., Atwater, J., Walker, D., Risley, T., & Delquadri, J. (1992). Out of the laboratory and into the community: 26 years of applied behavior analysis at the Juniper Gardens Children's Project. *American Psychologist*, 47, 1464–1474.

Hernandez, D. J. (1994). Children's changing access to resources: A historical perspective. *Social Policy Report. Society for Research in Child Development*, 8, No. 1.

Herrnstein, R., & Murray, C. (1994). *The bell curve*. New York: Free Press.

Hetheringon, E. M., Cox, M., & Cox, R. (1978). The aftermath of divorce. In J. Stevens & M. Matthews (Eds.), *Mother-child and father-child relations*. Washington, DC: National Association for the Education of Young Children.

Hetherington, E. M., Cox, M., & Cox, R. (1982). Effects of divorce on parents and children. In M. Lamb (Ed.), *Nontraditional families*. Hillsdale, NJ: Erlbaum.

Hetherinton, E. M., & Parke, R. D. (1979). *Child psychology: A contemporary viewpoint* (2nd ed.). New York: McGraw-Hill.

Hilts, P. J. (1995, July 26). Maternal-health ranking puts U.S. in 18th place. *New York Times*, p. B13.

Hood, J. (1992, December). *Caveat emptor: The Head Start scam* (Policy Analysis No. 187), Washington, DC: Cato Institute.

Huston, A. C. (1994). Children in poverty: Designing research to affect policy. *Social Policy Report. Society for Research in Child Development, 8*, No. 2.

Institute of Medicine, National Academy of Sciences. (1988). *Homelessness, health, and human needs*. Washington, DC: National Academy Press.

Institute of Medicine Committee to Study Outreach for Prenatal Care, National Academy of Sciences. (1988). *Prenatal care: Reaching mothers, reaching infants.* Washington, DC: National Academy Press.

Jacobson, J. L., & Jacobson, S. W. (1996). Methodological considerations in behavioral toxicology in infants and children. *Developmental Psychology, 32*, 390–403.

Katz, L. F., & Gottman, J. M. (1993). Patterns of marital conflict predict children's internalizing and externalizing behaviors. *Developmental Psychology, 29*, 940–950.

Kendziora, K. T., & O'Leary, S. G. (1993). Dysfunctional parenting as a focus for prevention and treatment of child behavior problems. In T. H. Ollendick & R. J. Prinz (Eds.), *Advances in clinical child psychology* (Vol. 15, pp. 175–206). New York: Plenum Press.

Keniston, K. (1977). *All our children: The American family under-pressure*. New York: Harcourt Brace Jovanovich.

Kimbrough, R. D., LeVois, M., & Webb, D. R. (1994). Management of children with slightly elevated blood lead levels. *Pediatrics, 93*, 188–191.

Klerman, L. V. (1991). *Alive and well? A research and policy review of health programs for poor young children*. New York: National Center for Children in Poverty, Columbia University School of Public Health.

Lazar, I., & Darlington, R. (1982). Lasting effects of early education: A report from the Consortium for Longitudinal Studies. *Monographs of the Society for Research in Child Development, 47*, (2–3, Serial No. 195).

Lewis, M., & Freedle, R. The mother and infant communication system: The effects of poverty. In H. McGurk (Ed.), *Ecological factors in human development*. Amsterdam: North-Holland.

Lin-Fu, J. (1992). Modern history of lead poisoning: A century of discovery and rediscovery. In H. L. Needleman (Ed.), *Human lead exposure* (pp. 23–43). Boca Raton: CRC Press.

Link, B., Phelan, J., Bresnahan, M., Stueve, A., Moore, R., & Susser, E. (1995). Lifetime and five-year prevalence of homelessness in the United States: New evidence on an old debate. *American Journal of Orthopsychiatry, 65*, 347–354.

Luthor, S. S., & Zigler, E. (1991). Vulnerability and competence: A review of research on resilience in childhood. *American Journal of Orthopsychiatry, 61*, 6–22.

Magrab, P. R., Sostek, A. M., & Powell, B. Z. (1984). Prevention in the prenatal period. In M. C. Roberts & L. Peterson (Eds.), *Prevention of problems in childhood: Psychological research and applications*. New York: Wiley-Interscience.

McLoyd, V. C. (1990). The impact of economic hardship on black families and children: Psychological distress, parenting, and socioemotional development. *Child Development, 61*, 311–346.

McLoyd, V. C., & Wilson, L. (1991). The strain of living poor: Parenting, social support, and child mental health. In A. C. Huston (Ed.), *Children in poverty: Child development and public policy* (pp. 105–135). New York: Cambridge University Press.

Masten, A. S., Miliotis, D., Graham-Bermann, S. A., Ramirez, M., & Neemann, J. (1993). Children in homeless families: Risks to mental health and development. *Journal of Consulting and Clinical Psychology, 61*, 355–343.

Mifflin, L. (1995, May 31). Study finds educational TV lends preschoolers even greater advantages. *New York Times*, p. A18.

Minuchin, P. P., & Shapiro, E. K. (1983). The school as a context for social development. In P. Mussen (Ed., E. M. Hetherington (Vol. Ed.). *Handbook of child psychology, Vol. 4*. New York: Wiley.

Needleman, H. L. (Ed.). (1992). *Human lead exposure* (pp. 45–64). Boca Raton: CRC Press.

Needleman, H. L., Riess, J. A., Tobin, M. J., Biesecher, G. E., & Greenbouse, J. B. (1996). Bone lead levels and delinquent behavior. *Journal of the American Medical Association, 275*, 363–369.

Nolen-Hoeksema, S. (1992). Children coping with uncontrollable stressors. *Applied and Preventive Psychology, 1*, 183–189.

O'Donnell, C. R. (1995). Firearm deaths among children and youth. *American Psychologist, 50*, 771–776.

Patterson, C. (1992). Children of lesbian and gay parents. *Child Development, 63*, 1025–1034.

Pedro-Carroll, J. L., Alpert-Gillis, L. J., & Cowen, E. L. (1992). An evaluation of the efficacy of a preventive intervention of 4th–6th grade urban children of divorce. *Journal of Primary Prevention, 13*, 115–130.

Phares, V., & Compas, B. E. (1992). The role of fathers in child and adolescent psychopathology: Make room for daddy. *Psychological Bulletin, 111*, 387–412.

Phinney, J. S. (1990). Ethnic identity in adolescents and adults: Review of research. *Psychological Bulletin, 108*, 499–514.

Pollitt, E., Gorman, K., Engle, P., Martorell, R., & Rivera, J. (1993). Early supplementary feeding and cognition: Effects over two decades. *Monographs of the Society for Research in Child Development, 58* (6, Serial No. 235).

Public Health Service. (1994). Health risk behaviors among adolescents who do and do not attend school—United States, 1992. *Morbidity and Mortality Weekly Report, 43*, 129–132.

Reynolds, A. J. (1994). Effects of a preschool plus follow-on intervention for children at risk. *Developmental Psychology, 30*, 787–804.

Ricciuti, H. N. (1993). Nutrition and mental development. *Current Directions in Psychological Science, 2*, 43–46.

Rutter, M. (1978). Family, area and school influences in the genesis of conduct disorders. In L. Hersov, M. Berger, & D. Shaffer (Eds.), *Aggression and anti-social behavior in childhood and adolescence*. Oxford: Pergamon Press.

Rutter, M., Yule, B., Quinton, D., Rowlands, O., Yule, W., & Berger, M. (1975). Attainment and adjustment in two geographical areas. *British Journal of Psychiatry, 126*, 520–533.

Scanlan, C. (1993, July 20). New poll finds youths have easy access to guns. *The (Columbia, SC) State*, p. 1a.

Scarr, S. (1981). *Race, social class, and individual differences.* Hillsdale, NJ: Erlbaum.

Scheper-Hughes, N. (1985). The 1985 Stirling Award Essay. Culture, scarcity, and maternal thinking: Maternal detachment and infant survival in a Brazilian shantytown. *Ethos, 13*, 291–317.

Sigman, M. (1995). Nutrition and child development: More food for thought. *Current Directions in Psychological Science, 4*, 52–55.

Sigman, M., Neumann, E., Carter, D. J., Cattle, S., D'Souza, & Bwibo, N. (1988). Home interactions and the development of Embu toddlers in Kenya. *Child Development, 59*, 1251–1261.

Steinberg, L., Dornbusch, S. M., & Brown, B. B. (1992). Ethnic differences in adolescent achievement: An ecological perspective. *American Psychologist, 47*, 723–729.

Sternberg, R. J. (1995). For whom the bell curve tolls: A review of *the bell curve. Psychological Science, 6*, 257–261.

Stevenson, H. W., Chen, C., & Uttal, D. H. (1990). Beliefs and achievement: A study of black, white, and Hispanic children. *Child Development, 61*, 508–523.

Strawn, J. (1992). The states and the poor: Child poverty rises as the safety net shrinks. *Social Policy Report. Society for Research in Child Development, 7*, No. 3.

Super, C. M., Herrera, M. G., & Mora, J. O. (1990). Long-term effects of food supplementation and psychosocial intervention on the physical growth of Colombian infants at risk of malnutrition. *Child Development, 61*, 29–49.

Tarnowski, K. J., & Rohrbeck, C. A. (1993). Disadvantaged children and families. In T. H. Ollendick & R. J. Prinz (Eds.), *Advances in clinical child psychology* (Vol. 15, pp. 41–80). New York: Plenum Press.

Tesman, J. R., & Hills, A. (1994). Developmental effects of lead exposure in children. *Social Policy Report. Society for Research in Child Development, 8*, No. 3.

Thomson, G. O. B., Raab, G. M., Hepburn, W. S., Hunter, R., Fulton, M., & Laxen, D. P. (1989). Blood-lead levels and children's behavior: Results from the Edinburgh lead study. *Journal of Child Psychology and Psychiatry, 30*, 515–528.

U.S. Bureau of the Census. (1991). *Marital Status and Living Arrangements. Current Population Reports.* Series P–20, No. 450. Washington, DC: U.S. Department of Commerce.

U.S. Bureau of the Census. (1992). *Poverty in the U.S.: 1991.* Washington, DC: U.S. Department of Commerce.

U.S. Bureau of the Census. (1994). *Statistical abstract of the United States, 1994.* Washington, DC: U.S. Department of Commerce.

U.S. Conference of Mayors. (1989). *A status report on hunger and homelessness in America's cities: A 27-city survey.* Washington, DC: Author.

U.S. Department of Housing and Urban Development. (1990). *Comprehensive and workable plan for the abatement of lead-based paint in privately owned housing: Report to Congress.* Washington, DC: Author.

Usdansky, M. L. (1966, February 11). Single motherhood: Stereotypes vs. statistics. *New York Times*, p. E4.

Wagner, H. (1972). Attitudes toward and of disadvantaged students. *Adolescence, 7*, 435–446.

Werner, E. E. (1989). High risk children in young adulthood: A longitudinal study from birth to 32 years. *American Journal of Orthopsychiatry, 59*, 72–81.

Werner, E. E., & Smith, R. W. (1992). *Overcoming the odds: High risk children from birth to adulthood.* Ithaca, NY: Cornell University Press.

Wilson, M. N., & Tolson, F. J. (1990). Familial support in the black community. *Journal of Clinical Child Psychology, 19*, 347–355.

Zigler, E., & Muenchow, S. (1992). *Head Start: The inside story of America's most successful educational experiment.* New York: Basic Books.

Zigler, E., & Styfco, S. J. (1993). Using research and theory to justify and inform Head Start expansion. *Social Policy Report. Society for Research in Child Development, 8*, No. 2.

Zigler, E., & Styfco, S. J. (1994). Head Start: Criticisms in a constructive context. *American Psychologist, 49*, 127–132.

Zill, N. (1983). *Happy, healthy and insecure.* Garden City, NJ: Doubleday/Anchor.

CHAPTER 5

Abikoff, H., & Gittelman, R. (1985). The normalizing effects of methylphenidate on the classroom behavior of ADDH children. *Journal of Abnormal Child Psychology, 13*, 33–44.

Abramowitz, A., & O'Leary, S. G. (1991). Behavioral interventions for the classroom: Implications for students with ADHD. *School Psychology Review, 20*, 220–234.

Achenbach, T. M. (1982). *Developmental psychopathology* (2nd ed.), New York: Wiley.

Achenbach, T. M. (1991). *Manual for the child behavior checklist and 1991 profile.* Burlington, VT: University of Vermont, Department of Psychiatry.

Aichhorn, A. (1964). *Delinquency and child guidance: Selected papers.* O. Fleischman, P. Kramer, & H. Ross (Eds.). International Universities Press.

Amato, P. R., & Keith, B. (1991). Parental divorce and the well-being of children: A meta analysis. *Psychological Bulletin, 110*, 26–46.

American Pediatric Association. (1990). Policy statement: Children, adolescents, and television. *Pediatrics, 85*, 1119–1120.

American Psychiatric Association. (1994). *Diagnostic and statistical manual of mental disorders* (DSM IV). Washington DC: American Psychiatric Association.

American Psychological Association. (1993). *Violence and youth: Psychology's response* (Vol. 1): Summary Report of the American Psychological Association Commission on Violence and Youth. Washington DC: American Psychological Association.

American Psychiatric Association-Work Group to Revise. (1985). *Diagnostic and statistical manual of mental disorders* (DSM III-R). Washington DC: American Psychiatric Association.

Andreasen, M. S. (1990). Evolution in the family's use of television: Normative data from the industry and academe. In J. Bryant (Ed.), *Television and the American family* (pp. 3–55). Hillside, NJ: Lawrence Erlbaum.

Archer, A., & Gleason, M. (1992). *Skills for school success: School behaviors and organization skills.* Billerica, MA: Curriculum Associates.

Associated Press. (1996). Scientists pinpoint "excitable gene", *Salt Lake City Tribune.*

Ayllon, T., & Rosenbaum, M. S. (1977). The behavioral treatment of disruption and hyperactivity in school settings. In B. B. Lahey & A. E.

Kazdin (Eds.), *Advances in clinical child psychology* (Vol. 1). New York: Plenum.

Bandura, A. (1973). *Aggression: A social learning analysis.* Englewood Cliffs, NJ: Prentice-Hall.

Bandura, A., Ross, D., & Ross, S. A. (1963). Imitation of filmed mediated aggressive models. *Journal of Abnormal and Social Psychology, 66,* 3–11.

Bandura, A., & Walters, R. H. (1959). *Adolescent aggression.* New York: Ronald Press.

Barkley, R. A. (1977). A review of stimulant drug research with hyperactive children. *Journal of Psychology and Psychiatry, 18,* 137–165.

Barkley, R. A. (1985). Attention deficit disorders. In P. H. Bornstein and A. E. Kazdin (Eds.), *Handbook of clinical behavior therapy with children.* Homewood, IL: Dorsey Press.

Barkley, R. A. (1990). *Attention-deficit hyperactivity disorder: A handbook for the diagnosis and treatment.* New York: Guilford.

Barkley, R. A. (1995). *Taking charge of ADHD: The complete, authoritative guide for parents.* New York: Guilford.

Barkley, R. A., & Cunningham, C. E. (1978). Do stimulant drugs improve the academic performance of hyperkinetic children? *Clinical Pediatrics, 17,* 85–92.

Barkley, R. A., & Cunningham, C. E. (1979). The effects of methylphenidate on the mother-child interactions of hyperactive children. *Archives of General Psychiatry, 36,* 201–208.

Barkley, R. A., & Jackson, T. (1976). The effects of methylphenidate on autonomic arousal and its relationship to improvement in activity and attention in hyperactive children. Unpublished manuscript, Bowling Green State University, OH.

Barkley, R. A., Karlsson, J., & Pollard, S. (1985). Effects of age on the mother-child interactions of ADD-H and normal boys. *Journal of Abnormal Child Psychology, 13,* 631–637.

Barkley, R. A., & Ullmann, D. G. (1975). A comparison of objective measures of activity and distractibility in hyperactive and nonhyperactive children. *Journal of Abnormal Child Psychology, 3,* 231–244.

Baron, R. A., & Richardson, D. R. (1994). *Human aggression,* 2nd ed. New York: Plenum

Bartollos, C., Miller, S. J., & Dinitz, S. (1976). *Juvenile victimization: The institutional paradox.* New York: Wiley.

Battle, E. S., & Lacey, B. (1972). A context for hyperactivity in children, over time. *Child Development, 43,* 757–773.

Bernal, M. E. (1969). Behavioral feedback in the modification of the brat behaviors. *Journal of Nervous and Mental Disease, 148,* 375–385.

Bradely, C. (1937). The behavior of children receiving benzedrine. *American Journal of Psychiatry, 94,* 577–585.

Brendtro, L. K., & College, A. (1993). Furious kids and treatment myths. *Rage and Aggression, 2,* 8–13.

Bugental, D. B., Whalen, C. K., & Henker, B. (1977). Causal attributions of hyperactive children and motivational assumptions of two behavior-change approaches: Evidence for an interactionist position. *Child Development, 48,* 874–884.

Cairns, R. B., Cairns, B. D., Neckerman, H. J., Gest, S. D., & Gariepy, J. L. (1988). Social networks and aggressive behavior—peer support or peer rejection. *Developmental Psychology, 24,* 815–823.

Campbell, S. B., Breaux, A. M., Ewing, L. J., & Szumowski, E. K. (1986). Correlates and predictors of hyperactivity and aggression: A longitudinal study of parent-referred problem preschoolers. *Journal of Abnormal Child Psychology, 14,* 217–234.

Campbell, S. B., & Paulauskas, S. (1979). Peer relations in hyperactive children. *Journal of Child Psychology and Psychiatry, 20,* 233–246.

Cantwell, D. P. (1975). Epidemiology: clinical picture and classification of the hyperactive child syndrome. In D. P. Cantwell (Ed.), *The hyperactive child.* New York: Spectrum.

Carter, K. (1987). *School psychologists' perceptions of childhood psychopathology.* Unpublished doctoral dissertation, University of Utah, Salt Lake City.

Charles, L., & Schain, R. (1981). A four-year follow-up study of the effects of methylphenidate on the behavior of academic achievement of hyperactive children. *Journal of Abnormal Child Psychology, 9,* 495–505.

Chess, S., & Thomas, A. (1983). *Evolution of behavior disorders: From infancy to early adult life.* New York: Brunner/Mazel.

Cline, V. B., Croft, R. G., & Courrier, S. (1973). Desensitization of children to television violence. *Journal of Personality and Social Psychology, 27,* 360–365.

Cloninger, C. R., & Gottsman, I. I. (1987). Genetic and environmental factors in antisocial behavior disorders. In S. A. Mednick, T. E. Moffit, & S. A. Stack (Eds.), *The causes of crime: New biological approaches* (pp. 92–109). New York: Cambridge University Press.

Comstock, G. A., & Rubinstein, E. A. (Eds.). (1972). *Television and social behavior,* Washington, DC: U.S. Government Printing Office.

Comstock, G. A., & Strasburger, V. C. (1990). Deceptive appearances: Television violence and aggressive behavior. *Journal of Adolescent Health Care, 11,* 31–44.

Conduct Problems Prevention Research Group. (1992). A developmental and clinical model for the prevention of conduct disorder: The FAST Track program. *Development and Psychopathology, 4,* 509–527.

Condry, J. C. (1989). *The psychology of television.* Hillsdale, NJ: Lawrence Erlbaum.

Conners, C. K. (1969). A teacher rating scale for use in drug studies with children. *American Journal of Psychiatry, 126,* 884–888.

Conners, C. K. (1975). Rating scales for use in drug studies with children. *Pharmacology Bulletin, 8,* 24–29.

Conners, C. K. (1980). Artificial colors and the diet of disruptive behavior: Current status of research. In R. M. Knights & D. J. Bakker (Eds.), *Treatment of hyperactive and learning disabled children.* Baltimore, MD: University Park Press.

Connors, C. K. (1986). Medical Grand Rounds, Medical School, University of Utah, Salt Lake City.

Cruickshank, W. M., Bentzen, F. A., Razeburg, F. H., & Tannhauser, M. T. (1961). *A teaching method for brain injured and hyperactive children.* New York: Syracuse University Press.

Cunningham, C. E., & Barkley, R. A. (1978). The effects of methylphenidate on the mother-child interactions of hyperactive identical twins. *Developmental Medical Child Neurology, 20,* 634–642.

Cunningham, C. E., & Barkley, R. A. (1979) The role of academic failure in hyperactive behavior. *Journal of Learning Disabilities, 11,* 15–21.

Cunningham, C. E., Siegel, L., & Offord, D. (1980). *Peer relations among hyperactive children.* Paper presented at the meeting of the American Psychological Association, Montreal.

David, O. J., Clark, J., & Voeller, K. (1972). Lead and hyperactivity. *Lancet, 2,* 900–903.

deHass, P. A., & Young, D. R. (1984). Attention styles of hyperactive and normal girls. *Journal of Abnormal Child Psychology, 12,* 531–546.

Denckla, M. B., LeMay, M., & Chapman, C. A. (1985). Few CT scan abnormalities found even in neurologically impaired learning disabled children. *Journal of Learning Disabilities, 18,* 132–135.

Dishion, T. J., & Loeber, R. (1985). Adolescent marijuana and alcohol use: The role of parents and peers revisited. *American Journal of Drug and Alcohol Abuse, 11,* 11–25.

Dishion, T. J., Loeber, R., Stouthamer-Loeber, M., & Patterson, G. R. (1984). Skills deficits and male adolescent delinquency. *Journal of Abnormal Child Psychology, 12,* 37–54.

Dishion, T. J., Patterson, G. R., & Griesler, P. C. (1994). Peer adaptations in the development of antisocial behavior: A confluence model. In L. R. Huesman (Ed.), *Aggressive behavior: Current perspectives* (pp. 61–90). New York: Plenum.

DuPaul, G. J., & Barkley, R. A. (1990). Medication therapy. In R. A. Barkley, *Attention-Deficit Hyperactivity Disorder: A handbook for diagnosis and treatment* (pp. 573–612). New York: Guilford Press.

DuPaul, G., Barkley, R. A., & McMurray, M. B. (1991). Therapeutic effects of medication on ADHD: Implications for school psychologists, *School Psychology Review, 20,* 203–219.

DuPaul, G. J., & Stoner, G. (1994). *ADHD in the schools: Assessment and intervention strategies.* New York: Guilford.

Ebaugh, L. D. (1923). Neuropsychiatric sequelae of acute epidemic encephalitis in children. *American Journal of Diseases of Children, 67,* 89–97.

Eron, L. D. (1963). Relationship of TV viewing habits and aggressive behavior in children. *Journal of Abnormal and Social Psychology, 67,* 193–196.

Eron, L. D., & Huesman, L. R. (1984). The control of aggressive behavior by changes in attitudes, values, and the conditions of learning. In R. J. Blanchard & D. C. Blanchard (Eds.), *Advances in the study of aggression* (Vol. 1). Orlando, FL: Academic Press.

Fagan, J. A., & Hartstone, E. (1984). Strategic planning in juvenile justice: Defining the toughest kids. In R. A. Mathias, P. DeMuro, & R. S. Albinson (Eds.), *Violent juvenile offenders.* San Francisco: National Council on Crime and Delinquency.

Feingold, B. F. (1975a). *Why is your child hyperactive.* New York: Random House.

Feingold, B. F. (1975b). Hyperkinesis and learning disabilities linked to artificial food flavors and colors. *American Journal of Nursing, 75,* 797–803.

Ferguson, H. B., & Rapoport, J. L. (1983). Nosological issues and biological variation. In M. Rutter (Ed.), *Developmental neuropsychiatry* (pp. 369–384). New York: Guilford Press.

Feshbach, S. (1956). The catharsis hypothesis and some consequences of interaction with aggressive and neutral play objects. *Journal of Personality, 24,* 449–462.

Fowles, D. C., & Furuseth, A. M. (1994). Electrodermal hyperactivity and antisocial behavior. In D. K. Routh (Ed.), *Disruptive behavior disorders in childhood* (pp. 181–206). New York: Plenum.

Forehand, R. (1977). Child compliance to parental requests: Behavioral analysis. In M. Hersen, R. Eisler, & P. Miller (Eds.), *Progress in behavior modification* (Vol 5). New York: Academic Press.

Forehand, R., King, H. E., Peeds, S., & Yoder, P. (1975). Mother-child interactions: Comparison of a noncompliant clinic group and a non-clinic group. *Behaviour in Research and Therapy, 113,* 79–84.

Forehand, R., & McMahon, R. J. (1981). *Helping the noncompliant child: A clinician's guide to parent training.* New York: Guilford Press.

Freeman, E. (1962). *Effects of aggressive expression after frustration on performance: A test of the catharsis hypothesis.* Unpublished doctoral dissertation, Stanford University.

Freud, S. (1933). *Introductory lectures on psychoanalysis.* New York: Norton.

Frick, P. J. (1993). Childhood conduct problems in a family context, *School Psychology Review, 22,* 376–385.

Gadow, K. D., & Sprafkin, J. (1993). Televison "violence" and children with emotional and behavior disorders. *Journal of Emotional and Behavioral Disorders, 1,* 54–63.

Gerber, G., Gross, L., & Signorielli, N. (1980). The "mainstreaming" of America: Violence profile no. 11. *Journal of Communication, 30,* 10–29.

Gerbner, G., Morgan, M., & Signorielli, N. (1993). *Televison violence profile: The turning point.* Maunscript, University of Pennsylvania, Annenberg School of Communications.

Gerbner, G., & Signorielli, N. (1990). *Violence profile, 1967 through 1988–89: Enduring patterns.* Manuscript, University of Pennsylvania, Annenberg School of Communications.

Gittleman-Klein, R., Klein, D. F., Abikoff, S., Katz, A., Gloisten, C., & Kates, W. (1976). Relative efficacy of methylphenidate and behavior modification in hyperkinetic children: An interim report. *Journal of Abnormal Child Psychology, 4,* 361–379.

Goldstein, K. (1942). *After-effects of brain injury in war.* New York: Grune & Stratton.

Goldstein, A. P., Glick, B., Reiner, S., Zimmerman, D., & Coultry, T. M. (1987). *Aggression replacement training: A comprehensive intervention for aggressive youth.* Champaign, IL: Research Press.

Goldstein, A. P., Sprakin, R. P., Gershaw, N. J., & Klein, P. (1980). *Skillstreaming the adolescent: A structured learning approach to teaching prosocial skills.* Champaign, IL: Research Press.

Goldstein, S. (1995). *Understanding and managing children's classroom behavior.* New York: Wiley.

Goldstein, S., & Ingersoll, B. (1992). Controversial treatments for children with attention deficit hyperactivity disorder. *Chadder,* 19–22.

Goodman, J. R., & Stevenson, J. (1989). A twin study of hyperactivity: II. The aetiological role of genes, family relationships, and perinatal adversity. *Journal of Child Psychology and Psychiatry, 30,* 691–709.

Gordon, M. (1979). The assessment of impulsivity and mediating behaviors in hyperactive and nonhyperactive boys. *Journal of Abnormal Child Psychology, 7,* 317–326.

Graham, P., Rutter, M., & George, S. (1973). Temperamental characteristics as predictors of behavior disorders in children. *Journal of Orthopsychiatry, 43,* 328–339.

Gray, J. A. (1987). *The psychology of fear and stress,* Cambridge: Cambridge Press.

Griest, D. L., & Wells, K. C. (1983). Behavior family therapy with conduct disorders in children. *Behavior Therapy, 14,* 37–53.

Griffin, B. S., & Griffin, C. T. (1978). *Juvenile delinquency in perspective.* New York: Harper & Row.

Halperin, J. M., Gittelman, R., Klein, D., & Rudel, R. (1984). Reading-disabled hyperactive children: A distinct subgroup of attention deficit disordered with hyperactivity. *Journal of Abnormal Child Psychology, 12,* 1–14.

Harley, J. P., & Matthews, C. G. (1980). Food additives and hyperactive children: Experimental investigations. In R. M. Knights & D. J.

Bakker (Eds.), *Treatment of hyperactive and learning disabled children.* Baltimore, MD: University Park Press.

Hechtman, L., Weiss, G., Perlman, T., & Amsel, R. (1984). Hyperactives as young adults: Initial predictors of adult outcome. *Journal of the American Academy of Child Psychiatry, 23,* 250–260.

Hendersen, H. S., Jenson, W. R., & Erken, N. (1986). Focus article: Variable interval reinforcement for increasing on task behavior in classrooms. *Education and Treatment of Children, 9,* 250–263.

Herbert, M. (1978). *Conduct disorders of childhood and adolescence: A behavioural approach to assessment and treatment.* New York: Wiley.

Hetherington, E. M. (1979). Divorce: A child's perspective. *American Psychologist, 34,* 851–858.

Hetherington, E. M., Cox, M., & Cox, R. (1977a). *The development of children in mother-headed families.* Papers presented at Conference on Families in Contemporary America at George Washington University.

Hetherington, E. M., Cox, M., & Cox, R. (1977b). The aftermath of divorce. In J. H. Stevens, Jr., & M. Mattews (Eds.), *Mother-child, father-child behaviors.* Washington, DC: N.A.F.Y.C.

Hetherington, E. M., & Martin, B. (1979). Family interaction. In H. C. Quay & J. S. Werry (Eds.), *Psychopathological disorders of childhood.* New York: Wiley.

Hinshaw, S. P. (1992). Externalizing behavior problems and academic under-achievement in childhood and adolescence: Causal relationships and underlying mechanisms. *Psychological Bulletin, 111,* 127–155.

Hinshaw, S. P., Henker, B., & Whalen, C. K. (1984). Cognitive-behavioral and pharmacological interventions for hyperactive boys: Comparative and combined effects. *Journal of Consulting and Clinical Psychology, 52,* 739–749.

Hohman, L. B. (1922). Post-encephalitic behavior disorders in children. *Johns Hopkins Hospital Bulletin, 33,* 372–375.

Hollander, H. E., & Turner, F. D. (1985). Characteristics of incarcerated delinquents: Relationship between developmental disorders, environmental and family factors, and patterns of offense and recidivism. *Journal of the American Academy of Child Psychiatry, 24,* 221–226.

Horn, W. F., Ialongo, N., Greenberg, G., Packard, T., & Smith-Winberry, C. (1990). Additive effects of behavioral parent training and self-control therapy with attention deficit hyperactivity disordered children. *Journal of Clinical Child Psychology, 19,* 98–110.

Huesman, L. R., & Miller, L. S. (1994). Long-term effects of repeated exposure to media violence in childhood. In L. R. Huesman (Ed.). *Aggressive behavior: Current perspectives* (pp. 153–180). New York: Plenum.

Jacob, R. G., O'Leary, K. D., & Rosenbald, C. (1978). Formal and informal classroom settings: Effects on hyperactivity. *Journal of Abnormal Child Psychology, 6,* 47–60.

Jenson, W. R. (1978). Behavior modification in secondary schools: A review. *Journal of Research and Development in Education, 11,* 53–63.

Jenson, W. R., Reavis, K., & Rhode, G. (1987). A conceptual analysis of childhood behavior disorders: A practical educational approach. In B. Scott & J. Gilliam (Eds.), *Topics in behavior disorders.* Austin, TX: Behavioral Learning Center.

Jurkovic, G. J., & Prentice, N. M. (1977). Relation of moral and cognitive development to dimensions of juvenile delinquency. *Journal of Abnormal Psychology, 86,* 414–420.

Kagan, J. (1966). Reflection-impulsivity: The generality and dynamics of conceptual tempo. *Journal of Abnormal Psychology, 71,* 17–24.

Kagan, J. (1994). *Galen's prophecy.* New York: Basic Books.

Kazdin, A. E. (1985). *Treatment of antisocial behavior in children and adolescents.* Homewood, IL: Dorsey Press.

Kazdin, A. E. (1987). Treatment of antisocial behavior in children: Current status and future directions. *Psychological Bulletin, 102,* 187–203.

Kazdin, A. E. (1989). Conduct disorder. *Psychiatric Hospital, 20,* 153–158.

Kazdin, A. E. (1993). Treatment of conduct disorder: Progress and directions in psychotherapy research. Special issue: Toward a developmental perspective on conduct disorder. *Development and Psychopathology, 5,* 277–310.

Kazdin, A. E., Esveldt-Dawson, K., French, N. H., & Unis, A. S. (1987). Problem-solving skills training and relationship therapy in the treatment of antisocial behavior. *Journal of Clinical and Consulting Psychology, 55,* 76–85.

Kazdin, A. E., Siegel, T. C., & Bass, D. (1992). Cognitive problem-solving skills training and parent management training in the treatment of antisocial behavior in children. *Journal of Clinical and Consulting Psychology, 60,* 733–747.

Kendall, P. C., & Braswell, L. (1985). *Cognitive behavioral therapy for impulsive children.* New York: Guilford.

Kenny, D. J. (1952). *An experimental test of the catharsis theory of aggression.* Unpublished doctoral dissertation, University of Washington.

Kesler, J. (1987). *Corrective reading: A method for changing the learning rate of behavior disordered children.* Unpublished master's thesis, University of Utah, Salt Lake City.

Kirigin, K., Braukmann, C. J., Atwater, J. D., & Wolf, M. M. (1982). An evaluation of teaching-family (Achievement Place) group homes for juvenile offenders. *Journal of Applied Behavior Analysis, 15,* 1–16.

Kirigin, K. A., Wolf, M. M., Braukmann, C. J., Fixen, D. L., & Philips, E. L. (1979). Achievement place: A preliminary outcome evaluation. In J. S. Stumphauzer (Ed.), *Progress in behavior therapy with delinquents.* Springfield, IL: Charles C. Thomas.

Kirkland, K. D., & Thelen, M. H. (1977). Uses of modeling in child treatment. In B. B. Lahey & A. E. Kazdin (Eds.), *Advances in clinical child psychology* (Vol. 1). New York: Plenum.

Koles, M., & Jenson, W. R. (1985). A comprehensive treatment approach for chronic firesetting in a boy. *Journal of Behavior Therapy and Experimental Psychiatry, 16,* 81–86.

Kolobye, A. (Chair). (1976). *First report of the preliminary findings and recommendations of the Interagency Collaboration Group on Hyperkinesis.* Submitted to the Assistant Secretary of Health, HEW, Washington, DC.

Lahey, B., Hobbs, S. A., Kupfer, D. L., & Delamater, A. (1979). Current perspectives on hyperactivity and learning disabilities. In B. Lahey (Ed.), *Behavior therapy with hyperactive and learning disabled children.* New York: Oxford University Press.

Lahey, B., Piacentini, J. C., McBurnett, K., Stone, P., Hartdagen, S., & Hynd, G. (1988). Psychopathology in the parents of children with conduct disorder and hyperactivity. *Journal of the American Academy of Child and Adolescent Psychiatry, 27,* 163–170.

Lambert, N. M., & Sandoval, J. (1980). The prevalence of learning disabilities in a sample of children considered hyperactive. *Journal of Abnormal Child Psychology, 8,* 33–50.

Langhorne, J. E., Loney, J., Paternite, C. E., & Bechtoldt, H. P. (1976). Childhood hyperkinesis: A return to the source. *Journal of Abnormal Psychology, 85,* 201–209.

Leyens, J. P., Camino, R., Parke, D., & Berkowitz, L. (1975). Effects of movie violence on aggression in a field setting. *Journal of Personality and Social Psychology, 32,* 346–360.

Liebert, R. M., & Baron, R. A. (1972). Some immediate effects of televised violence on children's behavior. *Developmental Psychology, 6,* 469–475.

Liebert, R. M., Sprafkin, J. N., & Davidson, E. S. (1982). *The early window: Effects of television on children and youth.* New York: Pergamon Press.

Loeber, R., & Patterson, G. R. (1981). The aggressive child: A concomitant of a coercive system. *Advances in Family Intervention, Assessment and Theory, 2,* 47–87.

Loeber, R., & Schmaling, K. B. (1985a). The utility of differentiating between mixed and pure forms of antisocial child behavior. *Journal of Abnormal Child Psychology, 13,* 315–336.

Loeber, R., & Schmaling, K. B. (1985b). Empirical evidence for overt and covert patterns of antisocial conduct problems: A metaanalysis. *Journal of Abnormal Child Psychology, 13,* 337–352.

Loeber, R., & Stouthamer-Loeber, M. (1986). Family factors as correlates and predictors of juvenile conduct problems and delinquency. In M. Tonry & N. Morris (Eds.), *Crime and justice* (Vol. 17, pp. 29–149). Chicago: University of Chicago Press.

Loeber, R., Weissman, W., & Reid, J. B. (1983). Family interactions of assaultive adolescents, stealers, and nondelinquents. *Journal of Abnormal Child Psychology, 11,* 1–14.

Loney, J., Whaley-Klahn, M. A., Koiser, T., & Conboy, J. (1981). *Hyperactive boys and their brothers at 21: Predictors of aggression and antisocial outcomes.* Paper presented at a meeting of the Society for Lie History Research, Monterey, CA.

Mace, F. C., Hock, M. L., Lalli, J. S., West, B. J., Belfiore, P., Pinter, E., & Brown, D. K. (1988). Behavioral momentum in the treatment of noncompliance. *Journal of Applied Behavior Analysis, 21,* 123–141.

Maynard, R. (1970, June 29). Omaha pupils given "behavior" drugs. *Washington Post.*

McMahon, R. C. (1980). Genetic etiology in the hyperactive child syndrome: A critical review. *American Journal of Orthopsychiatry, 50,* 145–150.

Mallick, S. K., & McCandless, B. R. (1966). A study of catharsis of aggression. *Journal of Personality and Social Psychology, 4,* 591–596.

Marlowe, M., Cossairt, A., Moon, C., Errera, J., MacNeel, A., Peak, R., Ray, J., & Schroeder, C. (1985). Main and interaction effect of metallic toxins on classroom behavior. *Journal of Abnormal Child Psychology, 13,* 185–198.

Mash, E. J., & Dalby, J. T. (1979). Behavioral interventions for hyperactivity. In R. L. Trites (Ed.), *Hyperactivity in children: etiology, measurement, and treatment implications.* Baltimore, MD: University Park Press.

Mash, E. J., & Johnston, C. (1983). Parental perceptions of child behavior problems, parenting self-esteem, and mother's reported stress in younger and older hyperactive and normal children. *Journal of Consulting and Clinical Psychology, 51,* 86–99.

McBurnett, K. (1992). Psychobiological approaches to personality and their appllication to child psychopathology, In B. B. Lahey & A. E. Kazdin (Eds.), *Advances in clinical child psychology* (pp. 107–164). New York: Plenum.

McConaughy, S. H., & Skiba, R. J. (1993). Comorbidity of externalizing and internalizing problems, *School Psychology Review, 22,* 421–436.

McCord, W., McCord, J., & Zola, I. K. (1959). *Origins or crime.* New York: Columbia University Press.

McGee, R., Williams, S., & Silva, P. A. (1984). Behavioral and developmental characteristics of aggressive, hyperactive and aggressive-hyperactive boys. *Journal of the American Academy of Child Psychiatry, 23,* 270–279.

Mendelson, W., Johnson, N., & Stewart, M. A. (1971). Hyperactive children as teenagers: A follow-up study. *Journal of Nervous and Mental Disease, 153,* 273–279.

Menkes, M. M., Rowe, J. S., & Menkes, J. H. (1967). A twenty year follow-up study on the hyperkinetic child with minimal brain dysfunction. *Pediatrics, 39,* 393–399.

Messer, S. B. (1976). Reflection-impulsivity: A review. *Psychological Bulletin, 83,* 1026–1052.

Montgomery, R. W. (1993). The collateral effect of compliance training on aggression. *Behavioral Residential Treatment, 8,* 9–20.

Morgan, D., & Jenson, W. R. (1988). *Teaching behaviorally disordered children: Preferred practices.* Columbus, OH: Merrill.

Morris, H. H., Escoll, P. J., & Wexler, R. (1956). Aggressive behavior disorders of childhood: A follow-up study. *American Journal of Psychiatry, 112,* 991–997.

Morrison, J. R. (1980). Adult psychiatric disorders in parents of hyperactive children. *American Journal of Psychiatry, 137,* 955–958.

Morrison, J. R., & Stewart, M. A. (1971). A family study of the hyperactive child syndrome. *Biological Psychiatry, 3,* 189–195.

Murray, J. P. (1995). Children and television violence. *Kansas Journal of Law and Public Policy, 4,* 7–14.

Murray, J. P., & Lonnborg, B. (1995). *Children and television: Using TV sensibly.* Manhattan, KS: Cooperative Extension Service.

National Institute of Mental Health. (1982). *Television and behavior: Ten years of scientific progress and implications for the eighties* (Vol. 1). Summary Report, Washington, DC: U.S. Goverment Printing Office.

Newby, R. F., Fischer, M., & Roman, M. A. (1991). Parent training for families of children with ADHD. *School Psychology Review, 20,* 252–265.

Nelsen, E. A. (1969). Social reinforcement for expression vs. suppression of aggression. *Merrill-Palmer Quarterly, 15,* 259–278.

O'Leary, K. D. (1980). Pills or skills for hyperactive children. *Journal of Applied Behavior Analysis, 13,* 191–204.

O'Leary, D. K., Pelham, W. E., Rosenbaum, A., & Price, G. H. (1976). Behavioral treatment of hyperkinetic children. *Clinical Pediatrics, 15,* 510–515.

Olweus, D. (1984). Development of stable aggression reaction patterns in males. In R. J. Blanchard & D. C. Blanchard (Eds.), *Advances in the study of aggression* (Vol. 1). Orlando, FL: Academic Press.

Orris, J. B. (1969). Visual monitoring performance in three subgroups of male delinquents. *Journal of Abnormal Psychology, 74,* 227–229.

Paik, H., & Comstock, G. (1994). The effects of television violence on antisocial behavior: A meta-analysis. *Communications Research, 21,* 516–546.

Parke R. D., & Slaby, R. G. (1982). The development of aggression. In P. H. Mussen & E. M. Hetherington (Eds.), *Handbook of child psychology: Socialization, personality, and social development* (Vol. IV). New York: Wiley.

Patterson, G. R. (1964a). An application of conditioning techniques to the control of a hyperactive child. In L. P. Ulmann & L. Krasner (Eds.), *Case studies in behavior modification*. New York: Holt, Rhinehart and Winston.

Patterson, G. R. (1974). Interventions for boys with conduct problems: Multiple settings, treatments, and criteria. *Journal of Consulting and Clinical Psychology, 42,* 471–481.

Patterson, G. R. (1976a). The aggressive child: Victim and architect of a coercive system. In E. J. Mash, L. A. Hamerlynck, & L. C. Handy (Eds.), *Behavior modification and families*. New York: Brunner/Mazel.

Patterson, G. R. (1976b). Follow-up analysis of behavioral treatment program for boys with conduct problems: A reply to Kent. *Journal of Consulting and Clinical Psychology, 44,* 299–301.

Patterson, G. R. (1982). *Coercive family process*. Eugene, OR: Castalia.

Patterson, G. R. (1984). Siblings: Fellow travelers in the coercive process. In R. J. Blanchard & D. C. Blanchard (Eds.), *Advances in the study of aggression* (Vol. 1). Orlando, FL: Academic Press.

Patterson, G. R. (1986). Performance models for antisocial boys. *American Psychologist, 41,* 432–444.

Patterson, G. R., & Fleischman, M. J. (1979). Maintenance of treatment effects: Some considerations concerning family systems and follow-up data. *Behavior Therapy, 10,* 168–185.

Patterson, G. R., Ray, R. S., Shaw, D. A., & Cobb, J. A. (1969). *Manual for coding of family interactions*. Document # 01234, Microfiche, 440 Park Avenue, New York, NY.

Patterson, G. R., & Reid, J. B. (1970). Reciprocity and coercion: Two facets of social systems. In C. Neuringer & J. D. Michael (Eds.), *Behavior modification in clinical psychology*. New York: Appleton-Century-Crofts.

Patterson, G. R., Reid, J. B., & Dishion, T. J. (1993). *Antisocial boys*. Eugene, OR: Castalia.

Patterson, G. R., Reid, J. B., Jones, J., & Conger, R. E. (1975). *A social learning approach to family intervention: Families with aggressive children* (Vol. 1). Eugene, OR: Castalia.

Pelham, W. E., Bender, M. E., Caddell, J., Booth, S., & Moore, S. H. (1985). Methylphenidate and children with attention deficit disorder. *Archives of General Psychiatry, 42,* 948–952.

Pfiffner, L. J., & Barkley, R. A. (1990). Educational placement and classroom management. In R. A. Barkley (Ed.), *Attention-Deficit hyperactivity disorder: A handbook for diagnosis and treatment* (pp. 498–539). New York: Guilford.

Philips, E. L. (1968). Achievement place: Token reinforcement procedure in a home style rehabilitation setting for predelinquent boys. *Journal of Applied Behavior Analysis, 1,* 213–223.

Pollock, V., Mednick, S. A., & Gabrielli, W. F. (1983). Crime causation: Biological theories. In S. Kadish (Ed.), *Encyclopedia of crime and delinquency* (pp. 308–316). New York: Free Press.

Prinz, R. J., Connor, P. A., & Wilson, C. C. (1981). Hyperactive and aggressive behaviors in childhood: Intertwined dimensions. *Journal of Abnormal Psychology, 9,* 191–202.

Prinz, R. J., Roberts, W. A., & Hantman, E. (1980). Dietary correlates of hyperactive behavior in children. *Journal of Consulting and Clinical Psychology, 48,* 760–769.

Quay, H. C. (1972). Patterns of aggression, withdrawal, and immaturity. In H. C. Quay & J. S. Werry (Eds.), *Psychopathological disorders of childhood*. New York: Wiley.

Quay, H. C. (1977). Psychopathic behavior: Reflections on the nature, origins, and temperament. In F. Weizman & I. Uzgiris (Eds.), *Structuring of experience*. New York: Plenum.

Quay, H. C. (1988). The behavioral reward and inhibition systems in childhood behavior disorders. In L. M. Bloomingdale (Ed.), *Attention deficit disorder* (Vol. 3, pp. 176–186). Oxford: Pergamon.

Quay, H. C. (1993). The psychobiology of undersocialized aggressive conduct disorder: A theoretical perspective. *Development and Psychopathology, 5,* 165–180.

Reid, R., Maag, J. W., & Vasa, S. F. (1993). Attention deficit hyperactivity as a disability catagory: A critique. *Exceptional Children, 60,* 198–214.

Rhode, G., Jenson, W. R., & Reavis, K. (1993). *Tough kid book*. Longmont, CO: Sopris West.

Rie, H. E. (1980). Definitional problems. In H. E. Rie & E. D. Rie (Eds.), *Handbook of minimal brain dysfunction: A critical review*. New York: Wiley.

Rie, H. E., & Rie, E. D. (1980). *Handbook of minimal brain dysfunctions: A critical review*. New York: Wiley.

Rie, H. E., Rie, E. D., Stewart, S., & Ambuel, J. P. (1976a). Effects of methylphenidate on underachieving students. *Journal of Consulting and Clinical Psychology, 44,* 250–269.

Rie, H. E., Rie, E. D., Stewart, S., & Ambuel, J. P. (1976b). Effects of Ritalin on underachieving children: A replication. *American Journal of Orthopsychiatry, 46,* 313–322.

Robins, L. N. (1966). *Deviant children grown up*. Baltimore: Williams and Wilkins.

Robins, L. N. (1974). *Deviant children grown up*. Huntington, NY: Robert E. E. Krieger.

Robins, L. N. (1979). Follow-up studies. In H. C. Quay & J. S. Werry (Eds.), *Psychopathological disorders of childhood* (3rd ed.). New York: Wiley.

Rosen, L. A., O'Leary, S. G., & Conway, G. (1985). The withdrawal of stimulant medication for hyperactivity: Overcoming detrimental attributions. *Behavior Therapy, 16,* 538–544.

Ross, D. M., & Ross, S. A. (1976). *Hyperactivity: Research, theory, and action*. New York: Wiley.

Ross, D. M., & Ross, S. A. (1982). *Hyperactivity: Current issues, research, and theory*. New York: Wiley.

Routh, D. K. (1980). Developmental and social aspects of hyperactivity. In C. K. Whalen & Y B. Henker (Eds.), *Hyperactive children: The social ecology of identification and treatment*. New York: Academic Press.

Routh, D. K., & Schroeder, C. S. (1976). Standardized playroom measures as indices of hyperactivity. *Journal of Abnormal Child Psychology, 4,* 199–207.

Russo, D. C., Cataldo, M. F., & Cushing, P. J. (1981). Compliance training and behavioral contracting in the treatment of multiple behavior problems. *Journal of Applied Behavior Analysis, 14,* 209–222.

Rutter, M. (1977). Brain damage syndromes in childhood: Concepts and findings. *Journal of Child Psychology and Psychiatry, 18,* 1–21.

Rutter, M. (1979). Maternal deprivation, 1972–1978: New findings, new concepts, new approaches. *Child Development, 50,* 283–305.

Rutter, M. (1982). Syndromes attributed to minimal brain dysfunction in childhood. *American Journal of Psychiatry, 139,* 21–33.

Rutter, M. (1983). Stress, coping, and development. In N. Garmezy & M. Rutter (Eds.), *Stress, coping, and development in children.* New York: McGraw-Hill.

Rutter, M., Tizard, J., Yule, W., Graham, P., & Whitmore, K. (1976). Research report Isle of Wight studies (1964–1974). *Psychological Medicine, 6,* 313–332.

Rutter, M., & Yule, W. (1973). Specific reading retardation. In L. Mann & D. Sabatino (Eds.), *The first review of special education.* Philadelphia: Buttonwood Farms.

Rutter M., & Yule, W. (1978). Reading difficulties. In M. Rutter & L. Hersov (Eds.), *Child psychiatry: Modern perspectives.* London: Blackwell Scientific Publications.

Safer, D. J., & Allen, R. P. (1976). *Hyperactive children: Diagnosis and management.* Baltimore: University Park Press.

Safer, D., Allen, R., & Barr, E. (1972). Depression of growth in hyperactive children on stimulants. *New England Journal of Medicine, 287,* 217–220.

Sarason, S. B. (1949). *Psychological problems in mental deficiency.* New York: Harper.

Satterfield, J. H., Cantwell, D. P., & Satterfield, B. T. (1979). Multimodal treatment: A one year follow-up of 87 hyperactive boys. *Archives of General Psychiatry, 36,* 965–974.

Schwarz, J. C. (1979). Childhood origins of psychopathology. *American Psychologist, 34,* 879–885.

Seeberg, E. (1943). Analysis of aggression in a five-year-old girl. *American Journal of Orthorpsychiatry, 13,* 53–62.

Semier, I., Eron, J., Myerson, L. D., & Williams, J. (1967). Relationship of aggression in third grade children to certain pupil characteristics. *Psychology in the Schools, 4,* 85–88.

Shapiro, S. K., & Hynd, G. W. (1993). Psychobiological basis of conduct disorder. *School Psychology Review, 22,* 386–402.

Sheridan, S. (1995). *Tough kid social skills training book.* Longmont, CO: Sopris West.

Short, R. J., & Shapiro, S. K. (1993). Conduct disorders: A framework for understanding and intervention in schools and communities. *School Psychology Review, 22,* 362–375.

Skinner, B. F. (1954). *Science and human behavior.* New York: Macmillan.

Spitzer, A., Webster-Stratton, C., & Hollinsworth, T. (1991). Coping with conduct-problem children: Parents gaining knowledge and control. *Journal of Clinical Child Psychology, 20,* 413–427.

Stewart, M. A., & Olds, S. W. (1973). *Raising a hyperactive child.* New York: Harper & Row.

Strauss, A. A., & Kephart, N. C. (1955). *Psychopathology and education of the brain-injured child: Progress in theory and clinic* (Vol. 2). New York: Grune & Stratton.

Strauss, A. A., & L. E. Lehtinen (1947). *Psychopathology and education of the brain-injured child.* New York: Grune and Stratton.

Strecker, E. (1929). Behavior problems in encephalitis. *Archives of Neurology and Psychiatry, 21,* 137–144.

Strecker, E., & Ebaugh, F. (1924). Neuropsychiatric sequelae of cerebral trauma in children. *Archives of Neurology and Psychiatry, 12,* 443–453.

Stumphauzer, J. S. (1979). *Progress in behavior therapy.* Springfield, IL: Charles C. Thomas.

Swanson, J. M., & Kinsbourne, M. (1980). Artificial color and hyperactive behavior. In R. M. Knights & D. J. Bakker (Eds.), *Treatment of hyperactive and learning disabled children.* Baltimore: University Park Press.

Szatmari, P., Offord, D. R., & Boyle, M. H. (1989). Correlates, associated impairments, and patterns of service utilization of children with attention deficit disorders: Findings from the Ontario Child Health Study. *Journal of Child Psychology and Psychiatry, 30,* 205–217.

Taylor, H. G., & Fletcher, J. M. (1983). Biological foundations of "specific developmental disorders": Methods, findings, and future directions. *Journal of Clinical Child Psychology, 12,* 46–65.

Thomas, A., & Chess, S. (1977). *Temperament and development.* New York: Brunner/Mazel.

Thomas, A., Chess, S., & Birch, H. G. (1969). *Temperament and behavior disorders in children.* New York: New York University Press.

Thomas, M. H., Horton, R. W., Lippincott, E. C., & Drabman, S. (1977). Desensitization to portrayals of real-life aggression as a function of exposure to television violence. *Journal of Personality and Social Psychology, 23.* 222–231.

Torgerson, A. M. (1976). *Temperamental differences in infants: Their cause as shown through twin studies.* Unpublished doctoral dissertation, University of Oslo, Norway.

Tremblay, R. E., Masse, B., Perron, D., Leblanc, M., Schwartzman, A. E., & Ledingham, J. E. (1992). Early disruptive behavior, poor school achievement, delinquent, and delinquent personality: Longitudinal analyses. *Journal of Consulting and Clinical Psychology, 60,* 1–10.

Trites, R. L., Tryphonas, H., & Ferguson, H. B. (1980). Diet treatment for hyperactive children with food additives. In R. M. Knights & D. J. Bakker (Eds.), *Treatment of hyperactive and learning disabled children.* Baltimore: University Park Press.

Uniform Crime Reports in the United States (1970–1984). Federal Bureau of Investigation. Washington DC: U.S. Government Printing Office.

Varley, C. K. (1984). Diet and the behavior of children with attention deficit disorder. *Journal of the American Academy of Child Psychiatry, 23,* 182–185.

Wahl, G., Johnson, S. M., Johansson, S., & Martin, S. (1974). An operant analysis of child-family interaction. *Behavior Therapy, 5,* 64–78.

Walker, H. M. (1991). Where is school along the path to prison? *Educational Leadership,* 14–16.

Walker, H. M. (1995). *The acting out child: Coping with classroom disruption.* Longmont, CO: Sopris West.

Walker, H. M., O'Neill, R., Shinn, M., Ramsey, B., Patterson, G. R., Reid, J., & Capaldi, D. (1986). *Longitudinal assessment and long term follow-up of antisocial behavior in fourth grade boys: Rationale, methodology, measures, and results.* Unpublished paper, University of Oregon.

Wallander, J. L., & Hubert, N. C. (1985). Long-term prognosis for children with attention deficit disorder with hyperactivity (ADD/H). In B. B. Lahey & A. E. Kazdin (Eds.), *Advances in clinical child psychology* (Vol. 8). New York: Plenum Press.

Washington State University. (1994). *Research review: Television violence.* Pullman, WA: Washington State University Cooperative Extension Research Reviews.

Webster-Stratton, C. (1983, May). Intervention approaches to conduct disorders in the young. *Nurse Practitioner,* 2334.

Weiss, G., & Hechtman, L. T. (1986). *Hyperactive children grown up: Empirical findings and theoretical considerations.* New York: Guilford.

Weiss, G., & Hechtman, L. T. (1993). *Hyperactive children grown up* (2nd ed.). New York: Guilford.

Weiss, G., Minde, K., Werry, J. S., Douglas, V. I., & Nemeth, E. (1971). Studies on the hyperactive child: VII. Five year follow-up. *Archives of General Psychiatry, 24,* 409–414.

Wells, K. C., & Forehand, R. (1981). Childhood behavior problems in the home. In S. M. Turner, K. S. Calhoun, & H. E. Adams (Eds.), *Handbook of clinical behavior therapy.* New York: Wiley.

Wells, K. C., & Forehand, R. (1985). Conduct and oppositional disorders. In P. H. Bornstein & A. E. Kazdin (Eds.), *Handbook of clinical behavior therapy with children.* Homewood, IL: Dorsey Press.

Wender, P. J. (1971). *Minimal brain dysfunction in children.* New York: Wiley.

Wender, P. J. (1972). The minimal brain dysfunction syndrome in children. *Journal of Nervous and Mental Disease, 155,* 55–71.

Whalen, C. K., & Henker, B. (1976). Psychostimulants and children: A review and analysis. *Psychological Bulletin, 83,* 1113–1130.

Whalen, C. K., Henker, B., Buhrmester, D., Hinshaw, S. P., Huber, A., & Laski, K. (1989). Does stimulant medication improve the peer status of hyperactive children? *Jounral of Consulting and Clinical Psychology, 57,* 5435–5449.

Whalen, C. K., Henker, B., Collins, B. E., Fink, D., & Dotemoto, S. (1979). A social ecology of hyperactive boys: Medication effects in systematically structured classroom environments. *Journal of Applied Behavior Analysis, 12,* 65–81.

Whalen, C. K., Henker, B., & Hinshaw, S. P. (1985). Cognitive-behavioral therapies for hyperactive children: Premises, problems, and prospects. *Journal of Abnormal Child Psychology, 13,* 391–410.

Willerman, L. (1973). Activity level and hyperactivity in twins. *Child Development, 44,* 288–293.

Wiltz, N. A., & Patterson, G. R. (1974). An evolution of parent training procedures designed to alter inappropriate aggressive behavior in boys. *Behavior Therapy, 5,* 215–221.

Witkin, H. A., Mednick, S. A., Schulsinger, F., Bakkestrom, E., Christiansen, K. O., Goodenough, D. R., Hirschhorn, K., Lundsteen, C., Owen, D. R., Philip, J., Rubin, D. B., & Stocking, M. (1976). Criminality in XYY and XXY men. *Science, 196,* 547–555.

Wolf, S. (1971). Dimensions and clusters of symptoms in disturbed children. *British Journal of Psychiatry, 118,* 421.

Wolraich, M., Drummond, T., Salomon, M. K., O'Brian, M. L., Sivage, C. (1978). Effects of methylphenidate alone and in combination with behavior modification procedures on the behavior and academic performance of hyperactive children. *Journal of Abnormal Child Psychology, 6,* 149–161.

Wolraich, M. L., Wilson, D. B., & White, W. (1995). The effect of sugar on behavior or cognition in children: A meta-analysis. *Journal of the American Medical Association, 274,* 1617–1621.

Zametkin, A. J., Nordahl, T. E., Gross, M., King, A. C., Semple, W. E., Rumsey, J., Hamburger, S., & Cohen, R. (1990). Cerebral glucose metabolism in adults with hyperactivity of childhood onset. *New England Journal of Medicine, 323,* 1361–1366.

CHAPTER 6

American Psychiatric Association. (1994). *Diagnostic and statistical manual of mental disorders* (4th ed.) (DSM-IV). Washington, DC: American Psychiatric Association.

Arnett, J. (1992). Reckless behavior in adolescence: A developmental perspective. *Developmental Review, 12,* 339–373.

Baer, J. S., Marlatt, G. A., Kivlahan, D. R., Fromme, K., Larimer, M. E., & Williams, E. (1992). An experimental test of three methods of alcohol risk reduction with young adults. *Journal of Consulting and Clinical Psychology, 60,* 974–979.

Bandura, A. (1977). *Social learning theory.* Englewood Cliffs, NJ: Prentice-Hall.

Bass, M. (1970). Sudden sniffing death. *Journal of the American Medical Association, 212,* 2075.

Barry, H., III. (1977). Alcohol. In S. Pradhan & S. Dutta (Eds.), *Drug abuse: Clinical and basic aspects.* St. Louis: C. V. Mosby.

Biase, D. V. (1973). Some approaches to the treatment of adolescent drug addicts and abusers. In E. Harms (Ed.), *Drugs and youth: The challenge of today.* New York: Pergamon Press.

Botvin, B. J., Baker, E., Dusenbury, L., Tortu, S., & Botvin, E. M. (1990). Preventing adolescent drug abuse through a multimodal cognitive-behavioral approach: Results of a 3-year study. *Journal of Consulting and Clinical Psychology, 58,* 437–446.

Botvin, G. J., & Botvin, E. M. (1992). Adolescent tobacco, alcohol, and drug abuse: Prevention strategies, empirical findings, and assessment issues.

Botvin, G. J., Schinke, S., & Orlandi, M. A. (1995). School-based health promotion: Substance abuse and sexual behavior. *Applied & Preventive Psychology, 4,* 167–184.

Brecher, E. M., & the Editors of Consumer Reports. (Eds.). (1972). *Licit and illicit drugs.* Boston: Little, Brown.

Cadoret, R. (1987). Genetic and environmental factors in alcohol abuse and antisocial personality. *Journal of Studies of Alcohol, 48,* 1–8.

Calhoun, B. C., & Watson, P. T. (1991). The cost of maternal cocaine use: I. Perinatal cost. *Obstetrics and Gynecology, 78,* 731–734.

Catalano, R. F., Hawkins, J. D., Krenz, C., Gillmore, M., Morrison, D., Wells, E., & Abbott, R. (1993). Using research to guide culturally appropriate drug abuse prevention. *Journal of Consulting and Clinical Psychology, 61,* 804–811.

Chassin, L., Pillow, D. R., Curran, P. J., Molina, B. S., & Barrera, M. (1993). Relation of parental alcoholism to early adolescent substance use: A test of three mediating mechanisms. *Journal of Abnormal Psychology, 102,* 3–19.

Cohen, S. (1977). Abuse of inhalants. In S. Pradhan & S. Dutta (Eds.), *Drug abuse: Clinical and basic aspects.* St. Louis: C. V. Mosby.

Comstock, E., & Comstock, B. S. (1977). Medical evaluation of inhalant abusers. In C. Sharp & M. Brehm (Eds.), *Review of inhalants: Euphoria to dysfunction* (NIDA Research Monograph 15). Washington, DC: U.S. Government Printing Office.

Cooper, J. R. (Ed.). (1977). *Sedative-hypnotic drugs: Risks and benefits.* National Institute on Drug Abuse, Rockville, MD: Department of Health, Education, and Welfare.

De Leon, P. (1984). Changing drinking patterns of adolescents since the 1960s. In M. Greenblatt & M. Schuckit (Eds.), *Alcoholism problems in women and children.* New York: Grune & Stratton.

DiClemente, C. C. (1993). Changing addictive behaviors: A process perspective. *Current Directions in Psychological Science, 2,* 101–105.

Dobkin, P. L., Tremblay, R. E., Masse, L. C., & Vitaro, F. (1995). Individual and peer characteristics in predicting boys' early onset of substance abuse: A seven-year longitudinal study. *Child Development*, 66, 1198–1214.

Donaldson, S. I. (1995). Peer influence on adolescent drug use: A perspective from the trenches of experimental evaluation research. In *American Psychologist*, 50, 801–802.

Farrell, M., & Danish, S. J. (1993). Peer drug associations and emotional restraint: Causes or consequences of adolescents' drug use? *Journal of Consulting and Clinical Psychology*, 61, 327–334.

Galanter, M., & Kleber, H. D. (1994). *Textbook of substance abuse treatment*. Washington, DC: American Psychiatric Association Press.

Greenspan, S. I. (1977). Substance abuse: An understanding from psychoanalytic, developmental, and learning perspectives. In J. Blaine & D. Julius (Eds.), *Psychodynamics of drug dependence* (NIDA Research Monograph 12). Washington, DC: U.S. Government Printing Office.

Hamilton-Russell, M. A. (1971). Cigarette smoking: Natural history of a dependence disorder. *British Journal of Medical Psychology*, 44, 1–15.

Hawley, T. L., & Disney, E. R. (1992). Crack's children: The consequences of maternal cocaine abuse. *Social Policy Report, Society for Research in Child Development*, 7, No. 4, whole issue.

Hickey, P. (1994). Behavior therapy and traditional chemical dependency treatment. *The Behavior Therapist*, 17, 79–84.

Huba, G. J., Wingard, J. A., & Bentler, P.M. (1979). Beginning adolescent drug use and peer and adult interaction patterns. *Journal of Consulting and Clinical Psychology*, 47, 265–276.

Jessor, R. (1992). Risk behavior in adolescence: A psychosocial framework for understanding and action. *Developmental Review*, 12, 374–390.

Jessor, R., & Jessor, S. L. (1977). *Problem behavior and psychosocial development*. New York: Academic Press.

Johnson, C. A., Pentz, M. A., Weber, M. D., Dwyer, J. H., Baer, N., MacKinnon, D., Hansen, W., & Flay, B. R. (1990). Relative effectiveness of comprehensive community programming for drug abuse prevention with high-risk and low-risk adolescents. *Journal of Consulting and Clinical Psychology*, 58, 447–457.

Johnston, L. D., O'Malley, P. M., & Bachman, J. G. (1993). *High school senior survey: Monitoring the future study*. Washington, DC: U.S. Government Printing Office.

Johnston, L. D., et al. (1995). *High school senior survey: Monitoring the future study*. Washington, DC: U.S. Government Printing Office.

Kalichman, S. C., Russell, R. L., Hunter, T. L., & Sarwer, D. B. (1993). Earvin "Magic" Johnson's HIV Serostatus disclosure: Effects on men's perceptions of AIDS. *Journal of Consulting and Clinical Psychology*, 61, 887–891.

Kandel, D. B., Davies, M., Karus, D., & Yamaguchi, K. (1986). The consequences in young adulthood of adolescent drug involvement. *Archives of General Psychiatry*, 43, 746–754.

Kandel, D. B., & Faust, R. (1975). Sequence and stages in patterns of adolescent drug use. *Archives of General Psychiatry*, 4, 281–292.

Lichtenstein, E. (1982). The smoking problem: A behavioral perspective. *Journal of Consulting and Clinical Psychology*, 50, 804–819.

Louria, D. (1977). The epidemiology of drug abuse rehabilitation. In M. Glatt (Ed.), *Drug dependence: Current problems and issues*. Baltimore: University Park Press.

MacCoun, R. J. (1993). Drugs and the law: A psychological analysis of drug prohibition. *Psychological Bulletin*, 113, 497–512.

Maisto. S. A., Galizio, M., & Connors, G. J. (1991). *Drug use and misuse*. Fort Worth, TX: Harcourt Brace.

Marijuana and health. Eighth Annual Report to the U.S. Congress from the Secretary of Health, Education, and Welfare. (1980). DHEW Publication No. (ADM) 80-945. Washington, DC: U.S. Government Printing Office, 1980.

Nadelmann, E. A. (1989). Drug prohibition in the United States: Costs, consequences, and alternatives. *Science*, 245, 239–245.

National Institute on Drug Abuse. (1992). *NIDA Capsules*, No. C–83–4, Revised August, 1992. Washington, DC: U. S. Government Printing Office.

National Institute on Drug Abuse. (1993). *NIDA Capsules*, No. C–83–07, Revised April, 1993. Washington, DC: U. S. Government Printing Office.

National Institute on Drug Abuse. (1993). *National survey results on drug use from the monitoring the future study, 1975–1992. Vol. I: Secondary school students*. National Institute on Drug Abuse, Washington, DC: U.S. Government Printing Office.

Newcomb, M. D., & Bentler, P. M. (1988). *Consequences of adolescent drug use: Impact on the lives of young adults*. New York: Sage.

Nye, C. L., Zucker, R. A., & Fitzgerald, H. E. (1995). Early intervention in the path to alcohol problems through conduct problems: Treatment involvement and child behavior change. *Journal of Consulting and Clinical Psychology*, 63, 831–840.

Ostrea, E. M., Brady, M., Gause, S., Raymundo, A. L., & Stevens, M. (1992). Drug screening of newborns by meconium analysis: A large-scale, prospective epidemiological study. *Pediatrics*, 89, 107–113.

Peterson, R. C. (1984). Marijuana overview. In M. D. Glantz (Ed.), *Correlates and consequences of marijuana use* (NIDA Research Monograph No. ADM 84-1276). Washington, DC: U.S. Government Printing Office.

Petraitis, J., Flay, B. R., & Miller, T. Q. (1995). Reviewing theories of adolescent substance use: Organizing pieces in the puzzle. *Psychological Bulletin*, 117, 67–86.

Robins, L., & McEvoy, L. (1990). Conduct problems and substance abuse. In L. N. Robins & M. Rutter (Eds.), *Straight and devious pathways from childhood to adulthood*. Cambridge: Cambridge University Press.

Salmon, R., & Salmon, S. (1977). The causes of heroin addiction: A review of the literature, Part I. *International Journal of the Addictions*, 12, 679–696.

Schilling, R. F., & McAlister, A. L. (1990). Preventing drug use in adolescents through media interventions. *Journal of Consulting and Clinical Psychology*, 58, 416–424.

Sells, S. B. (1979, September). Treatment effectiveness. In R. Dupont, A. Goldstin, & J. O'Donnell (Eds.), *Handbook on drug abuse*. National Institute on Drug Abuse, Washington, DC: U.S. Government Printing Office.

Shedler, J., & Block, J. (1990). Adolescent drug use and psychological health. *American Psychologist*, 45, 612–630.

Shenk, J. W. (1995, October). Why you can hate drugs and still want to legalize them. *The Washington Monthly*, pp. 32–40.

Sher, K. J., Walitzer, K. S., Wood, P., & Brent, E. E. (1991). Characteristics of children of alcoholics: Putative risk factors, substance use and abuse, and psychopathology. *Journal of Abnormal Psychology*, 100, 427–448.

Shiffman, S. (1993). Smoking cessation treatment: Any progress? *Journal of Consulting and Clinical Psychology*, 61, 718–722.

Shiffman, S., Paty, J. A., Kassel, J. D., Gnys, M., & Zettler-Segal, M. (1944). Smoking behavior and smoking history of tobacco chippers. *Experimental and Clinical Psychopharmacology, 2*, 126–142.

Smotherman, W. P., & Robinson, S. R. (1996). The development of behavior before birth. *Developmental Psychology, 32*, 425–434.

Statistical abstract of the United States: 1994. Department of Commerce, Economics and Statistics Administration, Bureau of the Census. Washington, DC: Author.

Streissguth, A. P., Martin, D. C., Martin, J. C., & Barr, H. M. (1981). The Seattle longitudinal prospective study on alcohol and pregnancy. *Neurobehavioral Toxicology and Teratology, 3*, 223–233.

Tinklenberg, J. R. (1977). Abuse of marijuana. In S. Pradhan & S. Dutta (Eds.), *Drug abuse: Clinical and basic aspects.* St. Louis: C. V. Mosby.

Treatment of drug abuse and addiction: Part I. (1995, August). *The Harvard Mental Health Letter, 12*, 1–4.

U.S. Department of Health and Human Services, Office of the Inspector General. (1992). *Youth and alcohol: A national survey. Drinking habits, access, attitudes, and knowledge* (DHHS Publication No. OEI-09-91-00652). Washington, DC: U.S. Government Printing Office.

U.S. Department of Health and Human Services, Office of Inspector General. (1993). *Youth and alcohol: Dangerous and deadly consequences* (DHHS Publication No. OEI-09-00261). Washington, DC: U.S. Government Printing Office.

U.S. Department of Health, Education, and Welfare. (1979). *Smoking and health: A report of the Surgeon General* (DHEW Publication No. [PHS] 79-50066). Washington, DC: U.S. Government Printing Office.

Wills, T. A., & Filer, M. (1996). Stress-coping model of adolescent substance use. In T. Ollendick & R. Prinz (Eds.), *Advances in clinical child psychology* (Vol. 18, pp. 91–132). New York: Plenum.

Zucker, R. A. (1976). Parental influences on the drinking patterns of their children. In M. Greenblatt & M. Schuckit (Eds.), *Alcoholism problems in women and children.* New York: Grune & Stratton.

CHAPTER 7

Abramson, L. Y., Seligman, M. E. P., & Teasdale, J. D. (1978). Learned helplessness in humans. *Journal of Abnormal Psychology, 87*, 49–73.

Achenbach, T. M., & Edelbrock, C. S. (1978). The classification of child psychopathology: A review and analysis of empirical efforts. *Psychological Bulletin, 85*, 1275–1301.

Agras, W. S., Chapin, H. N., & Oliveau, D. C. (1972). The natural history of phobia. *Archives of General Psychiatry, 26*, 315–317.

Ambrosini, P. J., Bianchi, M. D., Rabinovich, H., & Elia, J. (1993). Antidepressant treatments in children and adolescents I: Affective disorders. *Journal of the American Academy of Child & Adolescent Psychiatry, 32*, 1–6.

American Psychiatric Association. (1994). *Diagnostic and statistical manual of mental disorders* (4th ed.). Washington, DC: Author.

Anderson, J. C. (1994). Epidemiological issues. In T. Ollendick, N. King, & W. Yule (Eds.), *International handbook of phobic and anxiety disorders in children and adolescents* (pp. 43–66). New York: Plenum.

Andrews, J. A., & Lewinsohn, P. M. (1992). Suicidal attempts among older adolescents: Prevalence and co-occurrence with psychiatric dis-

orders. *Journal of the American Academy of Child and Adolescent Psychiatry, 31*, 655–662.

Bandura, A. (1969). *Principles of behavior modification.* New York: Holt, Rinehart and Winston.

Bandura, A., Blanchard, E. B., & Ritter, B. (1969). Relative efficacy of desensitization and modeling approaches for inducing behavioral, affective, and attitudinal changes. *Journal of Personality and Social Psychology, 13*, 173–199.

Bandura, A., & Menlove, F. L. (1968). Factors determining vicarious extinction of avoidance behavior through symbolic modeling. *Journal of Personality and Social Psychology, 8*, 99–108.

Baron, M., Klotz, J., Mendlewica, J., & Rainer, J. (1981). Multiple-threshold transmission of affective disorders. *Archives of General Psychiatry, 38*, 79–84.

Bauer, D. H. (1976). An exploratory study of developmental changes in children's fears. *Journal of Child Psychology and Psychiatry, 17*, 69–74.

Bauer, D. H. (1980). Childhood fears in developmental perspective. In L. A. Hersov & I. Berg (Eds.), *Out of school: Modern perspectives in truancy and school refusal.* Chichester, England: Wiley.

Beidel, D. C., Christ, M. G., & Long, P. J. (1991). Somatic complaints in anxious children. *Journal of Abnormal Child Psychology, 19*, 659–670.

Berg, I. (1970). A follow-up study of school phobic adolescents admitted to an in-patient unit. *Journal of Child Psychology and Psychiatry, 11*, 37–47.

Berg, I. (1981). When truants and school refusers grow up. *British Journal of Psychiatry, 141*, 208–210.

Berger, J. (1988, October 5). Facing up to school phobia and dealing with it. *New York Times*, B9.

Berlin, I. N. (1986). Psychopathology and its antecedents among American Indian adolescents. In B. B. Lahey & A. E. Kazdin (Eds.), *Advances in clinical child psychology* (Vol. 9). New York: Plenum Press.

Bowlby, J. (1969/1982). *Attachment and loss, Vol. 1: Attachment.* New York: Basic Books.

Breuer, J., & Freud, S. (1955). Studies on hysteria. (J. Strachey, Ed. and Trans.). *Standard edition of the complete psychological works of Sigmund Freud* (Vol. 2). London: Hogarth Press. (Original work published 1895.)

Burke, J. D., Borus, J. F., & Burns, B. J. (1982). Changes in children's behavior after a natural disaster. *American Journal of Psychiatry, 139*, 725–730.

Childers, P., & Wimmer, M. (1971). The concept of death in early childhood. *Child Development, 42*, 1299–1301.

Cicchetti, D., Toth, S. L., & Lynch, M. (1995). Bowlby's dream comes full circle: The application of attachment theory to risk and psychopathology. In T. Ollendick & R. Prinz (Eds.), *Advances in clinical child psychology* (Vol. 17, pp. 1–76). New York: Plenum.

Clarizio, H. F. (1991). Obsessive-compulsive disorder: The secretive syndrome. *Psychology in the Schools, 28*, 106–115.

Clarke, D. C. (1993). Suicidal behavior in childhood and adolescence: Recent studies and clinical implications. *Psychiatric Annals, 23*, 271–283.

Clarke, G., Hops, H., Lewinsohn, P. M., Andrews, J., Seeley, J. R., & Williams, J. (1992). Cognitive-behavioral group treatment of adolescent depression: Prediction of outcome. *Behavior Therapy, 23*, 341–354.

Cole, D. A., & Carpentieri, S. (1990). Social status and the comorbidity of child depression and conduct disorder. *Journal of Consulting and Clinical Psychology, 58*, 748–757.

Collins, P. F., & Depue, R. A. (1992). A neurobehavioral systems approach to developmental psychopathology: Implications for disorders of affect. In D. Cicchetti & S. Toth (Eds.), *Developmental perspectives on depression. Rochester Symposium on Developmental Psychopathology* (Vol. 4, pp. 29–103). Rochester, NY: University of Rochester Press.

Cytryn, L., & McKnew, D. H. (1974). Factors influencing the changing clinical expression of the depressive process in children. *American Journal of Psychiatry, 131,* 879–881.

Dweck, C. S. (1977). Learned helplessness: A developmental approach. In J. Schulferbrandt & A. Baskin (Eds.), Depression in childhood: Diagnosis, treatment, and conceptual models (pp. 135–140). New York: Raven Press.

Endicott, J., & Spitzer, R. L. (1978). A diagnostic interview: The schedule for affective disorders and schizophrenia. *Archives of General Psychiatry, 35,* 837–844.

Ferster, C. B. (1974). Behavioral approaches to depression. In R. Friedman & M. Katz (Eds.), *The psychology of depression: Contemporary theory and research.* New York: Wiley.

Ficula, T., Gelfand, D. M., Richards, G., & Ulloa, A. (1983, August). *Factors associated with school refusal in adolescents.* Paper presented at the meeting of the American Psychological Association, Anaheim, CA.

Fischer, M., Rolf, J., Hasazi, J. E., & Cummings, L. (1984). Follow-up of a preschool epidemiological sample: Cross-age continuities and predictions of later adjustment with internalizing and externalizing dimensions of behavior. *Child Development, 55,* 137–150.

Foa, E. B., Steketee, G., & Milby, J. B. (1980). Differential effects of exposure and response prevention in obsessive-compulsive washers. *Journal of Consulting and Clinical Psychology, 48,* 71–79.

Freud, A. (1977). Fears, anxieties, and phobic phenomena. *The Psychoanalytic Study of the Child, 32,* 85–90.

Freud, S. (1950). *Collected papers* (Vol. 3). London: Hogarth Press. (Originally published in 1909.)

Freud, S. (1965). *Mourning and melancholia* (standard ed.). London: Hogarth Press. (Originally published in 1917.)

Gadow, K. D. (1991). Clinical issues in child and adolescent psychopharmacology. *Journal of Consulting and Clinical Psychology, 59,* 842–852.

Gelfand, D. M. (1978). Social withdrawal and negative emotional states: Behavioral treatment. In B. Wolman, J. Egan, & A. Ross (Eds.), *Handbook of treatment of mental disorders in childhood and adolescence.* Englewood Cliffs, NJ: Prentice-Hall.

Gillham, J. E., Reivich, K. J., Jaycos, L. H., & Seligman, M. E. P. (1995). Prevention of depressive symptoms in school children: Two-year follow-up. *Psychological Science, 6,* 343–351.

Heinecke, C. M. (1989). Psychodynamic psychotherapy with children: Current status and guidelines for future research. In B. Lahey & A. Kazdin (Eds.), *Advances in clinical child psychology* (Vol. 12, pp. 1–26). New York: Plenum.

Herzog, D. B., & Rathbun, J. M. (1982). Childhood depression: Developmental considerations. *American Journal of Diseases in Children, 136,* 115–120.

Ialongo, N., Edelsohn, G., Werthamer-Larsson, L., Crockett, L., & Kellam, S. (1994). The significance of self-reported anxious symptoms in first-grade children. *Journal of Abnormal Child Psychology, 22,* 411–455.

Jackimow-Venulet, B. (1981). Hereditary factors in the pathogenesis of affective illness. *British Journal of Psychiatry, 139,* 450–456.

Jensen, P. S., Ryan, N. D., & Prien, R. (1992). Psychopharmacology of child and adolescent major depression: Present status and future directions. *Journal of Child and Adolescent Psychopharmacology, 2,* 31–45.

Kaplan, C. A., & Hussain, S. (1995). Use of drugs in child and adolescent psychiatry. *British Journal of Psychiatry, 166,* 291–298.

Kaufman, R. L. (1994). Wanted: One rat runner. Excellent opportunity for the right person. *The Behavior Therapist, 17,* 107–109.

Keller, M. B., Lavori, P. W., Wunder, J., Beardslee, W. R., Schwartz, C. E., & Roth, J. (1992). Chronic course of anxiety disorders in children and adolescents. *Journal of the American Academy of Child and Adolescent Psychiatry, 31,* 595–599.

Kendall, P. C. (1993). Cognitive-behavioral therapies with youth: Guiding theory, current status, and emerging developments. *Journal of Consulting and Clinical Psychology, 61,* 235–247.

Kendall, P. C. (1995). Issues in the transportability of treatment: The case of anxiety disorders in youths. *Journal of Consulting and Clinical Psychology, 63,* 702–708.

Kendall, P. C., Chansky, T. E., Kane, M. T., Kim, R., Kortlander, E., Ronan, K., Sessa, F., & Siqueland, L. (1992). *Anxiety disorders in youth: Cognitive-behavioral interventions.* Needham Heights, MA: Allyn & Bacon.

Kendall, P. C., & Ronan, K. D. (1990). Assessment of children's anxieties, fears, and phobias: Cognitive-behavioral models and methods. In C. Reynolds & R. Kamphaus (Eds.), *Handbook of psychological and educational assessment of children: Vol. 2. Personality, behavior, and context* (pp. 223–244). New York: Guilford Press.

Kendall, P. C., & Southam-Gerow, M. A. (1995). Issues in the transportability of treatment: The case of anxiety disorders in youths. *Journal of Consulting and Clinical Psychology, 63,* 702–708.

Kennedy, W. A. (1965). School phobia: Rapid treatment of fifty cases. *Journal of Abnormal Behavior, 70,* 285–289.

King, N. J. (1993). Simple and social phobias. In T. Ollendick & R. Prinz (Eds.), *Advances in clinical child psychology* (Vol 15, pp. 305–341). New York: Plenum.

King, R. A., Pfeffer, C., Gammon, G. D., & Cohen, D. J. (1992). Suicidality of childhood and adolescence. In B. Lahey & A. Kazdin (Eds.), *Advances in clinical child psychology* (Vol. 14, pp. 297–325). New York: Plenum.

Kovacs, M., & Beck, A. T. (1977). An empirical clinical approach toward a definition of childhood depression. In J. Schulterbrandt & A. Raskin (Eds.), *Depression in childhood: Diagnosis, treatment, and conceptual models* (pp. 1–25). New York: Raven Press.

Kovacs, M., Feinberg, T. L., & Crouse-Novak, M. (1984). Depressive disorders in childhood, II: A longitudinal study of the risk for a subsequent major depression. *Archives of General Psychiatry, 41,* 643–649.

Last, C. G., & Strauss, C. C. (1990). School refusal in anxiety-disordered children and adolescents. *Journal of the American Academy of Child and Adolescent Psychiatry, 29,* 31–35.

Levy, J. E., & Kunitz, S. J. (1987). A suicide prevention program for Hopi youth. *Social Science and Medicine, 25,* 931–940.

Lewinsohn, P. M. (1974). A behavioral approach to depression. In R. Friedman & M. Katz (Eds.), *The psychology of depression: Contemporary theory and research.* Washington DC: V. H. Winston.

Lewinsohn, P. M., & Amenson, C. S. (1981). An investigation into the observed sex difference in prevalence of unipolar depression. *Journal of Abnormal Psychology, 90,* 1–13.

Lewinsohn, P. M., Clarke, G. N., Hops, H., & Andrews, J. (1990). Cognitive-behavioral treatment for depressed adolescents. *Behavior Therapy, 21*, 385–401.

Lewinsohn, P. M., & Rohde, P. (1993). The cognitive-behavioral treatment of depression in adolescents: Research and suggestions. *The Clinical Psychologist, 46*, 177–183.

Lewinsohn, P. M., Rohde, P., & Seeley, J. R. (1993). Psychosocial characteristics of adolescents with a history of suicide attempts. *Journal of the American Academy of Child and Adolescent Psychiatry, 32*, 600–668.

Lumsden, W. W. (1980). Intentional self-injury in school age children. *Journal of Adolescence, 3*, 217–228.

Macfarlane, J. W., Allen, L., & Honzik, M. P. (1954). *A developmental study of the behavior problems of normal children between 21 months and 14 years.* Berkeley: University of California Press.

Mahler, M. (1952). On child psychosis and schizophrenia: Autistic and symbiotic infantile psychosis. In A. Freud, H. Hartmann, & E. Kris (Eds.), *Psychoanalytic study of the child* (Vol. 7). New York: International Universities Press.

Malmquist, C. P. (1977). Childhood depression: A clinical and behavioral perspective. In J. Schulterbrandt & A. Raskin (Eds.), *Depression in childhood: Diagnosis, treatment, and conceptual models.* Rockville, MD: U. S. Department of Health, Education and Welfare.

McCarthy, P. R., & Foa, E. B. (1988). Obsessive-compulsive disorder. In M. Hersen & C. Last (Eds.), *Child behavior therapy casebook* (pp. 55–69). New York: Plenum.

McGee, R., Feehan, M., Williams, S., Partridge, F., Silva, P. A., & Kelly, J. (1990). DSM-III disorders in a large sample of adolescents. *Journal of the American Academy of Child and Adolescent Psychiatry, 29*, 611–619.

McGough, J. J., Speier, P. L., & Cantwell, D. P. (1993). Obsessive-compulsive disorder in childhood and adolescence. *School Psychology Review, 22*, 243–251.

McNeal, E. T., & Cimbolic, P. (1986). Antidepressants and biochemical theories of depression. *Psychological Bulletin, 99*, 361–374.

Menzies, R. G., & Clarke, J. C. (1993). A comparison of in vivo and vicarious exposure in the treatment of childhood water phobia. *Behaviour Research and Therapy, 31*, 9–15.

Mills, H. L., Agras, W. S., Barlow, D. H., & Mills, J. R. (1975). Compulsive rituals treated by response prevention. *Archives of General Psychiatry, 32*, 933–936.

Morris, R. J., & Kratochwill, T. R. (1983). *Treating children's fears and phobias.* New York: Pergamon.

Nurcombe, B. (1992). The evolution and validity of the diagnosis of major depression in childhood and adolescence. In D. Cicchetti & S. Toth (Eds.), *Developmental perspectives on depression. Rochester symposium on developmental psychopathology* (Vol. 4, pp. 1–28). Rochester, NY: University of Rochester Press.

Pelham, W. E. (1993). Recent developments in pharmacological treatment for child and adolescent mental health disorders. *School Psychology Review, 22*, 158–161.

Pfeffer, C. R. (1981). Suicidal behavior of children: A review with implications for research and practice. *American Journal of Psychiatry, 138*, 154–159.

Popper, C. W. (1992). Are clinicians ahead of researchers in finding a treatment for adolescent depression? *Journal of Child and Adolescent Psychopharmacology, 2*, 1–3.

Popper, C. W. (1993). Psychopharmacologic treatment of anxiety disorders in adolescents and children. *Journal of Clinical Psychiatry, 54*, 52–63.

Post-traumatic stress disorder: Part I. (1966, June). *The Harvard Mental Health Letter, 12*, 1–4.

Puig-Antich, J., Goetz, D., Davies, M., Kaplan, T., Davies, S., Ostrow, L., Asnis, L., Toomey, J., Iyengar, S., & Ryan, N. (1989). A controlled family history study of prepubertal major depressive disorder. *Archives of General Psychiatry, 46*, 406–418.

Rachman, S., & Hodgson, R. (1980). Obsessions and compulsion. Englewood Cliffs, NJ: Prentice-Hall.

Rapoport, J. L., Swedo, S. E., & Leonard, H. L. (1992). Childhood obsessive compulsive disorder. *Journal of Clinical Psychiatry, 53*, 11–16.

Reiser, M. F. (1994). Does psychoanalysis have a future? Yes. *The Harvard Mental Health Letter, 11*(5), 4–5.

Reynolds, W. J., & Graves, A. (1989). Reliability of children's reports of depressive symptomatology. *Journal of Abnormal Child Psychology, 17*, 647–655.

Reynolds, W. M. (1994). Depression in adolescents. In T. Ollendick & R. Prinz (Eds.), *Advances in clinical child psychology* (Vol. 16, pp. 261–316).

Rincover, A., Newsom, D. C., & Carr, E. G. (1979). Using sensory extinction procedures in the treatment of compulsivelike behavior of developmentally disabled children. *Journal of Consulting and Clinical Psychology, 47*, 695–701.

Ritter, B . (1968). The group desensitization of children's snake phobias using vicarious and contact desensitization procedures. *Behaviour Research and Therapy, 6*, 1–6.

Roberts, M. C., & Peterson, L. (Eds.). (1984). *Prevention of problems in childhood.* New York: Wiley.

Romano, B. A., & Nelson, R. O. (1988). Discriminant and concurrent validity of measures of children's depression. *Journal of Clinical Child Psychology, 17*, 255–259.

Rosenthal, T. L., & Bandura, A. (1978). Psychological modeling: Theory and practice. In S. Garfield & A. Bergin (Eds.), *Handbook of psychotherapy and behavior change.* (Vol. 2, pp. 132–151). New York: Wiley.

Russ, S. W. (1995). Play psychotherapy research: State of the science. In T. Ollendick & R. Prinz (Eds.), *Advances in clinical child psychology* (Vol. 17, pp. 365–391). New York: Plenum.

Rutter, M., & Garmezy, N. (1983). Developmental psychopathology. In E. M. Hetherington (Ed.), *Handbook of child psychology* (Vol. IV). New York: Wiley.

Rutter, M., Tizard, J., & Whitmore, K. (Eds.). (1981). *Education, health and Behaviour.* Huntington, NY: Krieger.

Ryan, N. D., Williamson, D. E., Iyengar, S., Orvaschel, H., Reich, T., Dahl, R. E., & Puig-Antich, J. (1992). A secular increase in child and adolescent onset affective disorder. *Journal of the American Academy of Child and Adolescent Psychiatry, 31*, 600–605.

Seligman, M. E. P. (1975). *Helplessness: On depression, development, and death.* San Francisco: W. H. Freeman.

Shafi, M., Carrigan, S., Wittinghill, J. R., & Derrick, A. (1985). Characteristics of suicidal children and adolescents. *American Journal of Psychiatry, 142*, 1061–1064.

Silverman, W. K. (1992). Taxonomy of anxiety disorders in children. In G. Burrows, M. Roth, & R. Noyes (Eds.), *Handbook of anxiety* (Vol. 5, pp. 1–27). New York: Elsevier.

Social phobia, Part II. (1994, November). *The Harvard Mental Health Letter, 11*, 1–3.

Sterba, E. (1959). Child analysis. In M. Levitt (Ed.), *Readings in psychoanalytic psychology*. New York: Appleton.

Stark, K. D., Humphrey, L., Laurent, J., Livingston, R., & Christopher, J. (1993). Cognitive, behavioral, and family factors in the differentiation of depressive and anxiety disorders during childhood. *Journal of Consulting and Clinical Psychology, 61*, 878–886.

Stark, K. D., Napolitano, S., Swearer, S., Schmidt, K., Jaramillo, D., & Hoyle, J. (1996). Issues in the treatment of depressed children. *Applied & Preventive Psychology, 5*, 59–83.

Swedo, S. E., Lenanare, M., Rettew, D., Hamburger, S., Bartko, J., & Rapoport, J. (1993). A 2- to 7-year follow-up study of 54 obsessive-compulsive children and adolescents. *Archives of General Psychiatry, 50*, 429–440.

Thyer, B. A. (1991). Diagnosis and treatment of child and adolescent anxiety disorders. *Behavior Modification, 15*, 310–325.

Vasey, M. W. (1993). Development and cognition in childhood anxiety: The example of worry. In T. Ollendick & R. Prinz (Eds.), *Advances in clinical child psychology* (Vol. 15, pp. 1–40). New York: Plenum.

Vernberg, E. M., La Greca, A. M., Silverman, W. K., & Prinstein, M. J. (1996). Prediction of posttraumatic stress symptoms in children after Hurricane Andrew. *Journal of Abnormal Psychology, 105*, 237–248.

Vernberg, E. M., & Vogel, J. M. (1993). Interventions with children after disasters. *Journal of Clinical Child Psychology, 22*, 485–498.

Vogel, J. M., & Vernberg, E. M. (1993). Children's psychological responses to disasters. *Journal of Clinical Child Psychology, 22*, 464–484.

Walton, D., & Mather, M. D. (1963). The application of learning principles to the treatment of obsessive-compulsive states in the acute and chronic phases of illness. *Behaviour Research and Therapy, 1*, 163–174.

Weisenberg, M., Schwarzwald, J., Waysman, M., Solomon, Z., & Klingman, A. (1993). Coping of school-age children in the sealed room during Scud missile bombardments and postwar stress reactions. *Journal of Consulting and Clinical Psychology, 61*, 462–467.

Welner, A., Welner, Z., & Fishman, R. (1979). Psychiatric adolescent inpatients: Eight- to ten-years follow-up. *Archives of General Psychiatry, 36*, 698–700.

Wilson, G. L. (1991). Comment: Suicidal behavior—Clinical considerations and risk factors. *Journal of Consulting and Clinical Psychology, 59*, 869–873.

Wolpe, J. (1958). *Reciprocal inhibition therapy*. Stanford, CA: Stanford University Press.

CHAPTER 8

Abrams, J. C. (1991). The affective component: Emotional needs of individuals with reading and related learning disorders. *Journal of Reading, Writing, and Learning Disabilities International, 7*(3), 171–182.

American Psychiatric Association. (1994). *Diagnostic and statistical manual of mental disorders* (4th ed.). Washington, DC: Author.

Anderman, E. M., & Maehr, M. L. (1994). Motivation and schooling in the middle grades. *Review of Educational Research, 64*, 287–309.

Bender, W. N. (1995). *Learning disabilities: Characteristics, identification, and teaching strategies* (2nd ed.). Boston: Allyn & Bacon.

Bender, W. N., & Golden, L. B. (1990). Subtypes of students with learning disabilities as derived from cognitive, academic, behavioral, and self-concept measures. *Learning Disability Quarterly, 13*(3), 183–194.

Berk, L. E., & Landau, S. (1993). Private speech of learning disabled and normally achieving children in classroom and laboratory contexts. *Child Development, 64*, 556–571.

Bigler, E. D. (1992). The neurobiology and neuropsychology of adult learning disorders. *Journal of Learning Disabilities, 25*, 488–506.

Billingsley, B. S., & Ferro-Almeida, S. C. (1993). Strategies to facilitate reading comprehension in students with learning disabilities. *Reading and Writing Quarterly Overcoming Learning Difficulties, 9*(3), 263–278.

Binney, V. (1992). Staff training to run activity groups with people with profound learning disabilities: Evaluation of attitude, knowledge and skill changes. *Behavioural Psychotherapy, 20*, 267–278.

Bonnet, K. A. (1989). Learning disabilities: A neurobiological perspective in humans. *Journal of Remedial and Special Education, 10*, 8–19.

Bowers, T. G., Risser, M. G., Suchanec, J. F., & Tinker, D. E. (1992). A developmental index using the Wechsler Intelligence scale for children: Implications for the diagnosis and nature of ADHD. *Journal of Learning Disabilities, 25*, 179–185, 195.

Bryan, T. H., & Bryan, J. H. (1991). Positive mood and math performance. *Journal of Learning Disabilities, 24*(8), 490–494.

Cameron, J., & Pierce, W. D. (1994). Reinforcement, reward, and intrinsic motivation: A meta-analysis. *Review of Educational Research, 64*, 363–423.

Carlson, C. L., & Bunner, M. R. (1993). Effects of methylphenidate on the academic performance of children with attention-deficit hyperactivity disorder and learning disabilities. *School Psychology Review, 22*, 184–198.

Chittooran, M. M., D'Amato, R. C., Lassiter, K. S., & Dean, R. S. (1993). Factor structure of psychoeducational and neuropsychological measures of learning disabled children. *Psychology in the Schools, 30*(2), 109–118.

Choate, J. S., & Rakes, T. A. (1989). *Reading: Detection and correcting special needs*. Boston: Allyn & Bacon.

Conte, R., & Andrews, J. (1993). Social skills in the context of learning disability definitions: A reply to Greshamm and Elliott in directions for the future. *Journal of Learning Disabilities, 26*, 146–153.

Dalley, M. B., Bolocofsky, D. N., Alcorn, M. B., & Baker, C. (1992). Depressive symptomatology, attributional style, dysfunctional attitude, and social competency in adolescents with and without learning disabilities. *School Psychology Review, 21*, 444–458.

Deci, E. L., Hodges, R., Pierson, L. H., & Tomassone, J. (1992). Autonomy and competence as motivational factors in students with learning disabilities and emotional handicaps. *Journal of Learning Disabilities, 25*, 457–471.

Denckla, M. B. (1993). The child with developmental disabilities grown up: Adult residua of childhood disorders. *Neurologic Clinics, 11*, 105–125.

Dickey, K. D., & Satcher, J. (1994). The selection of postsecondary placement options by school counselors for students with learning disabilities. *School Counselor, 41*, 347–351.

Drew, C. J., Hardman, M. L., & Hart, A. W. (1996). *Designing and conducting research: Inquiry in education and social science*. Boston: Allyn & Bacon.

Eme, R. F. (1992). Selective female affliction in the developmental disorders of childhood: A literature review. *Journal of Clinical Child Psychology*, 21, 354–364.

Englert, C. A., & Palincsar, A. S. (1988). The reading process. In D. K. Reid (Ed.). *Teaching the learning disabled: A cognitive developmental approach* (pp. 162–189). Boston: Allyn & Bacon.

Enright, B. E. (1989). *Basic mathematics: Detecting and correcting special needs*. Boston: Allyn & Bacon.

Faigel, H. C., Doak, E., Howard, S. D., & Sigel, M. L. (1992). Emotional disorders in learning disabled adolescents. *Child Psychiatry and Human Development*, 23, 31–40.

Faraone, S. V., Biederman, J., Lehmman, B. K., & Keenan, K. (1993). Evidence for the independent familial transmission of attention deficit hyperactivity disorder and learning disabilities: Results from a family genetic study. *American Journal of Psychiatry*, 150, 891–895.

Fuchs, L. S., Fuchs, D., & Bishop, N. (1992). Instructional adaptation for students at risk. *Journal of Educational Research*, 86(2), 70–84.

Garnett, K. (1992). Developing fluency with basic number facts: Intervention for students with learning disabilities. *Learning Disabilities Research and Practice*, 7(4), 210–216.

Gartner, A., & Lipsky, D. K. (1989, June 7–8). *Equity and excellence for all students. The education of students with disabilities: Where do we stand?* Briefing paper for testimony given at hearings conducted by the National Council on the Handicapped, Washington, DC.

Goldstein, K. (1936). The modifications of behavior consequent to cerebral lesions. *Psychiatric Quarterly*, 10, 586–610.

Goldstein, K. (1939). *The organism*. New York: American Book.

Grace, J., & Malloy, P. (1992). Neuropsychiatric aspects of right hemisphere learning disability. *Neuropsychiatry, Neuropsychology, and Behavioral Neurology*, 5(3), 194–204.

Gresham, F. M. (1992). Social skills and learning disabilities: Causal, concomitant, or correlational? *School Psychology Review*, 21, 348–360.

Grinnell, P. C. (1988). Teaching handwriting and spelling. In D. K. Reid (Ed.), *Teaching the learning disabled: A cognitive developmental approach* (pp. 245–278). Boston: Allyn & Bacon.

Hammill, D. D. (1990). On defining learning disabilities: An emerging consensus. *Journal of Learning Disabilities*, 23, 74–84.

Hardman, M. L., Drew, C. J., & Egan, M. W. (1996). *Human exceptionality: Society, school, and family* (5th ed.). Newton, MA: Allyn & Bacon.

Hildreth, B. L., Dixon, M. E., Frerichs, D. K., & Heflin, L. J. (1994). College readiness for students with learning disabilities: The role of the school counselor. *School Counselor*, 41, 343–346.

Huntington, D. D., & Bender, W. N. (1993). Adolescents with learning disabilities at risk? Emotional well-being, depression, suicide. *Journal of Learning Disabilities*, 26, 159–166.

Jones, K. H., Bender, W. N., & McLaughlin, P. (1992). Implementation of project RIDE: Responding to individual differences in education. *Journal of Instructional Psychology*, 19, 107–112.

Kamann, M. P., & Wong, B. Y. L. (1993). Inducing adaptive coping self-statements in children with learning disabilities through self-instruction training. *Journal of Learning Disabilities* 26, 630–638.

Kirk, S. A. (1963). Behavioral diagnosis and remediation of learning disabilities. *Proceedings, Conference on Exploration into the Problems of the Perceptually Handicapped Child. First Annual Meeting* (Vol. 1). Chicago.

Kraker, M. J. (1993). Learning to write: Children's use of notation. *Reading Research and Instruction*, 32(2), 55–75.

Larsen-Miller, L. (1994). *An investigation to determine the effects of a video-mediated metacognitive reading comprehension strategy in a complimentary environment*. Unpublished Master's Thesis, University of Utah.

Lefrancois, G. R. (1995). *Of children: An introduction to child development* (8th ed.). Belmont, CA: Wadsworth.

Leviton, A., Bellinger, D., & Allred, E. (1993). The Boston teacher questionnaire, III: A reassessment. *Journal of Child Neurology*, 8, 64–72.

Levy, F. (1989). CNS stimulant controversies. *Australian and New Zealand Journal of Psychiatry*, 23, 497–502.

Light, J. G., & DeFries, J. C. (1995). Comorbidity of reading and mathematics disabilities: Genetic and environmental etiologies. *Journal of Learning Disabilities*, 28, 96–106.

Lorsbach, T. C., Sodoro, J., & Brown, J. S. (1992). The dissociation of repetition priming and recognition memory in language/learning disabled children. *Journal of Experimental Child Psychology*, 54, 121–146.

McCusker, C. G., Clare, I. C., Cullen, C., & Reep, J. (1993). Alcohol-related knowledge and attitudes in people with a mild learning disability: The effects of a "sensible drinking" group. *Journal of Community and Applied Social Psychology*, 3, 29–40.

McIntosh, D. E., & Gridley, B. E. (1993). Differential ability scales: Profiles of learning-disabled subtypes. *Psychology in the Schools*, 30, 11–24.

McKinney, J. D., Montague, M., & Hocutt, A. M. (1993). Educational assessment of students with attention deficit disorder. *Exceptional Children*, 60, 125–131.

Miller, J. L. (1990). Apocalypse or Renaissance or something in between? Toward a realistic appraisal of The Learning Mystique. *Journal of Learning Disabilities*, 23, 86–91.

Morgane, P. J., Austin-LaFrance, R., Bronzino, J. D., & Tonkiss, J. (1993). Prenatal malnutrition and development of the brain. *Neuroscience and Biobehavioral Reviews*, 17, 91–128.

Nass, R., & Baker, S. (1991). Androgen effects on cognition: Congenital adrenal hyperplasia. *Psychoneuroendocrinology*, 16, 189–201.

Nelson, J. R., Smith, D. J., & Dodd, J. M. (1992). The effects of teaching a summary skills strategy to students identified as learning disabled on their comprehension of science text. *Education and Treatment of Children*, 15(3), 228–243.

Nester, M. A. (1993). Psychometric testing and reasonable accommodations for persons with disabilities. *Rehabilitation Psychology*, 38(2), 75–85.

Nestor, P. G. (1992). Neuropsychological and clinical correlates of murder and other forms of extreme violence in a forensic psychiatric population. *Journal of Nervous and Mental Disease*, 180(7), 418–423.

Ohtsuka, A. (1993). Current and future issues in the definition of learning disabilities. *Japanese Journal of Special Education*, 30(5), 29–40.

Pearl, R., & Bryan, T. (1992). Students' expectations about peer pressure to engage in misconduct. *Journal of Learning Disabilities*, 25, 582–585, 597.

Rakes, T. A., & Choate, J. S. (1989). *Language arts: Detecting and correcting special needs*. Boston: Allyn & Bacon.

Raviv, D., & Stone, C. A. (1991). Individual differences in the self-image of adolescents with learning disabilities: The roles of severity, time of diagnosis, and parental perceptions. *Journal of Learning Disabilities, 24*, 602–611, 629.

Reid, D. K. (1988). Learning disabilities and the cognitive developmental approach. In D. K. Reid (Ed.), *Teaching the learning disabled: A cognitive developmental approach* (pp. 29–46). Boston: Allyn & Bacon.

Reiff, H. B., Gerber, P. J., & Ginsberg, R. (1993). Definitions of learning disabilities: The insiders' perspectives. *Learning Disability Quarterly, 16*, 114–125.

Richards, C. M., Symons, D. K., Greene, C. A., & Szuszkiewicz, T. (1995). The bidirectional relationship between achievement and externalizing behavior problems of students with learning disabilities. *Journal of Learning Disabilities, 28*, 8–17.

Richards, G. P., Samuels, S. J., Tumure, J. E., & Ysseldyke, J. E. (1990). Sustained and selective attention in children with learning disabilities. *Journal of Learning Disabilities, 23*, 129–136.

Roffman, A. J., Herzog, J. E., & Gershba-Gerson, P. M. (1994). Helping young adults understand their learning disabilities. *Journal of Learning Disabilities, 27*, 413–419.

Ross, G., Lipper, E., & Auld, P. A. (1992). Hand preference, prematurity and developmental outcome at school age. *Neuropsychologia, 30*(5), 483–494.

Ruhl, K. L., & Suritsky, S. (1995). The pause procedure and/or an outline: Effect on immediate free recall and lecture notes taken by college students with learning disabilities. *Learning Disability Quarterly, 18*, 2–11.

Ryan, A. G. (1994). Life adjustments of college freshmen with and without learning disabilities. *Annals of Dyslexia, 44*, 227–249.

Salyer, K. M., Holmstrom, R. W., & Noshpitz, J. D. (1991). Learning disabilities as a childhood manifestation of severe psychopathology. *American Journal of Orthopsychiatry, 61*, 230–240.

Sandler, A. D., Hooper, S. R., Watson, T. E., & Coleman, W. L. (1993). Talkative children: Verbal fluency as a marker for problematic peer relationships in clinic-referred children with attention deficits. *Perceptual and Motor Skills, 76*, 943–951.

Schonemann, P. H., & Schonemann, R. D. (1994). Environmental versus genetic models for Osborne's personality data on identical and fraternal twins. *Current Psychology of Cognition, 13*(2), 141–167.

Scott, S. S. (1994). Determining reasonable academic adjustments for college students with learning disabilities. *Journal of Learning Disabilities, 27*, 403–412.

Scruggs, T. E., & Mastropieri, M. A. (1993). Special education for the twenty-first century: Integrating learning strategies and thinking skills. *Journal of Learning Disabilities, 26*, 392–398.

Seidenberg, P. L. (1989). Relating text-processing research to reading and writing instruction for learning disabled students. *Learning Disabilities Focus, 5*, 4–12.

Seidenberg, P. L. (1993). Understanding learning disabilities. In D. K. Bernstein & E. Tiegerman (Eds.). *Language and communication disorders in children* (3rd ed., pp. 326–365). New York: Merrill/Macmillan.

Semrud-Clikeman, M., Biederman, J., Sprich-Buckminster, S., & Lehman, B. K. (1992). Comorbidity between ADDH and learning disability: A review and report in a clinically referred sample. *Journal of the American Academy of Child and Adolescent Psychiatry, 31*, 439–448.

Shafrir, U., & Siegel, L. S. (1994). Preference for visual scanning strategies versus phonological rehearsal in university students with reading disabilities. *Journal of Learning Disabilities, 27*, 583–588.

Shea, C. (1994). "Invisible" maladies: Students who say they have learning disabilities encounter skepticism. *The Chronicle of Higher Education, XLI*(2), 53, 55.

Short, E. J. (1992). Cognitive, metacognitive, motivational, and affective differences among normally achieving, learning-disabled, and developmentally handicapped students: How much do they affect school achievement? *Journal of Clinical Child Psychology, 21*, 229–239.

Sigler, G., & Mackelprang, R. W. (1993). Cognitive impairments: Psychosocial and sexual implications and strategies for social work intervention. *Journal of Social Work and Human Sexuality, 8*(2), 89–106.

Smith, C. R. (1994). *Learning disabilities: The interaction of learner, task, and setting* (3rd ed.). Boston: Allyn & Bacon.

Smith, S. M. (1989). Congenital syndromes and mildly handicapped students: Implications for special educators. *Journal of Remedial and Special Education, 10*, 20–30.

Snow, J. H., English, R., & Lange, B. (1992). *Journal of Psychoeducational Assessment, 10*(2), 153–160.

Sonksen, P. M., Petrie, A., & Drew, K. J. (1991). Promotion of visual development of severely visually impaired babies: Evaluation of a developmentally based programme. *Developmental Medicine and Child Neurology, 33*(4), 320–335.

Sorrel, A. L. (1990). Three reading comprehension strategies: TELLS, story mapping, and QARS. *Academic Therapy, 25*, 359–368.

Spekman, N. J., Goldberg, R. J., & Herman, K. L. (1992). Learning disabled children grow up: A search for factors related to success in the young adult years. *Learning Disabilities Research and Practice, 7*(3), 161–170.

Swanson, H. L. (1991). Operational definitions and learning disabilities: An overview. *Learning Disability Quarterly, 14*(4), 242–254.

Swanson, H. L. (1992). Operational definitions and learning disabilities: An overview: Erratum. *Learning Disability Quarterly, 15*(1), 19.

Swanson, H. L. (1993). Working memory in learning disability subgroups. *Journal of Experimental Child Psychology, 56*, 87–114.

Swanson, J. M., McBurnett, K., Wigal, T., Pfiffner, L. J., Lerner, M. A., Williams, L., Christian, D. L., Tamm, L., Wilcutt, E., Crowley, K., Clevenger, W., Khouzam, N., Woo, C., Crinella, F. M., & Fisher, T. D. (1993). Effect of stimulant medication on children with attention deficit disorder: A "review of reviews." *Exceptional Children, 60*, 154–162.

Tallal, P. (1991). Hormonal influences in developmental learning disabilities. *Psychoneuroendocrinology, 16*, 203–211.

U.S. Department of Education, Office of Special Education Programs. (1994). *Sixteenth Annual Report to Congress on the Implementation of the Individuals with Disabilities Education Act*. Washington, DC: Author.

Vauras, M., Lehtinen, E., Olkinuora, E., & Salonen, P. (1993). Devices and desires: Integrative strategy instruction from a motivational perspective. *Journal of Learning Disabilities, 26*, 384–391.

Weinberg, W. A., & Harper, C. R. (1993). Vigilance and its disorders. *Neurologic Clinics, 11*, 59–78.

Welch, M., & Sheridan, S. M. (1995). *Educational partnerships: An ecological approach to serving students at risk.* San Francisco: Harcourt Brace Jovanovich.

Werner, H., & Strauss, A. A. (1939). Types of visuo-motor activity in their relation to low and high performance ages. *Proceedings of the American Association on Mental Deficiency, 44,* 163–168.

Werner, H., & Strauss, A. A. (1941). Pathology of figure-background relation in the child. *Journal of Abnormal and Social Psychology, 36,* 236–248.

Wilczenski, F. L. (1993). Comparison of academic performances, graduation rates, and timing of drop out for LD and nonLD college students. *College Student Journal, 27*(2), 184–194.

Wong, B. Y. (1993). Pursuing an elusive goal: Molding strategic teachers and learners. *Journal of Learning Disabilities, 26,* 354–357.

Yanok, J. (1993). College students with learning disabilities enrolled in developmental education programs. *College Student Journal, 27*(2), 166–174.

Zentall, S. S., & Ferkis, M. A. (1993). Mathematical problem solving for youth with ADHD, with and without learning disabilities. *Learning Disability Quarterly, 16,* 6–18.

CHAPTER 9

American Association on Mental Retardation. (1992). *Mental retardation: Definition, classification, and systems of supports* (9th ed.). Washington, DC: Author.

American Psychiatric Association. (1994). *Diagnostic and statistical manual of mental disorders* (4th ed.)(DSM-IV). Washington, DC: Author.

Bailey, D. B., & Wolery, M. (1989). *Assessing infants and preschoolers with handicaps.* Columbus, OH: Merrill.

Birch, H. G., Richardson, S. A., Baird, D., Horobin, G., & Illsley, R. (1970). *Mental subnormality in the community: A clinical and epidemiological study.* Baltimore: Williams & Wilkins.

Borthwick-Duffy, S. (1994). Review of *Mental retardation: Definition, classification, and systems of support. American Journal on Mental Retardation, 98,* 541–544.

Brendt, R. L., & Beckman, D. A. (1990). Teratology. In R. D. Eden & F. H. Boehm (Eds.), *Assessment and care of the fetus: Physiological, clinical, and medicolegal principles* (pp. 223–244). Norwalk, CT: Appleton & Lange.

Cahalane, S. F. (1989). Screening for genetic disease. In G. B. Reed, A. E. Claireaux, & A. D. Bain (Eds.), *Diseases of the fetus and newborn: Pathology, radiology and genetics* (pp. 599–614). St. Louis: C.V. Mosby.

Chen, T., Bruininks, R. H., Lakin, K. C., & Haden, M. (1993). Personal competencies and community participation in small community residential programs: A multiple discriminant analysis. *American Journal on Mental Retardation, 98,* 390–399.

Chez, R. A., & Chervenak, J. L. (1990). Nutrition in pregnancy. In R. D. Eden & F. H. Boehm (Eds.), *Assessment and care of the fetus: Physiological, clinical, and medicolegal principles* (pp. 215–222). Norwalk, CT: Appleton & Lange.

Chiarenza, G. A. (1993). Movement-related brain macropotentials of persons with Down syndrome during skilled performance. *American Journal on Mental Retardation, 97,* 449–467.

Claireaux, A. E., & Reed, G. B. (1989). The pancreas. In G. B. Reed, A. E. Claireaux, & A. D. Bain (Eds.), *Diseases of the fetus and newborn: Pathology, radiology and genetics* (pp. 291–298). St. Louis: C.V. Mosby.

Creasy, R. K. (1990). Preterm labor. In R. D. Eden & F. H. Boehm (Eds.), *Assessment and care of the fetus: Physiological, clinical, and medicolegal principles* (pp. 617–630). Norwalk, CT: Appleton & Lange.

Criscione, T., Kastner, T. A., O'Brien, D., & Nathanson, R. (1994). Replication of a managed health care initiative for people with mental retardation living in the community. *Mental Retardation, 32,* 43–52.

Cuskelly, M., & Gunn, P. (1993). Maternal reports of behavior of siblings of children with Down Syndrome. *American Journal on Mental Retardation, 97,* 521–529.

Drew, C. J., Logan, D. R., & Hardman, M. L. (1992). *Mental retardation: A life cycle approach* (5th ed.). New York: Macmillan.

Drew, C. J., Hardman, M. L., & Logan, D. R. (1996). *Mental retardation: A life cycle approach* (6th ed.). New York: Macmillan.

Dykens, E. M., Hodapp, R. M., & Evans, D. W. (1994). Profiles and development of adaptive behavior in children with Down syndrome. *American Journal on Mental Retardation, 98,* 580–587.

Eden, R. D., & Boehm, F. H. (Eds.). (1990). *Assessment and care of the fetus: Physiological, clinical, and medicolegal principles.* Norwalk, CT: Appleton & Lange.

Edgerton, R. B. (1990). Quality of life from a longitudinal research perspective. In R. L. Schalock (Ed.), *Quality of life: Perspectives and issues* (pp. 149–160). Washington, DC: American Association on Mental Retardation.

Frankenberger, W., & Harper, J. (1988). States' definitions and procedures for identifying children with mental retardation: Comparison of 1981–1982 and 1985–1986 guidelines. *Mental Retardation, 26,* 133–136.

Grand, T. I. (1992). Altricial and precocial mammals: A model of neural and muscular development. *Zoo Biology, 11,* 3–15.

Haddow, J. E., Palomaki, G. E., Knight, G. J., & Williams, J. (1992). Prenatal screening for Down syndrome with use of maternal serum markers. *New England Journal of Medicine, 327,* 588–593.

Hardman, M. L. (1994). *Inclusion: Issues of educating students with disabilities in regular settings.* Boston: Allyn & Bacon.

Hardman, M. L., Drew, C. J., Egan, M. W. (1996). *Human exceptionality: Society, school, and family* (5th ed.). Boston: Allyn & Bacon.

Heller, T., & Factor, A. (1993). Aging family caregivers: Support resources and changes in burden and placement desire. *American Journal on Mental Retardation, 98,* 417–426.

Jack, B. W., & Culpepper, L. (1991). Preconception care. *Journal of Family Practice, 32,* 306–315.

Jackson v. Indiana. (1972). 406 U.S. 715.

Jacobson, J. W. (1994). Review of *Mental retardation: Definition, classification, and systems of support. American Journal on Mental Retardation, 98,* 539–541.

Jacobson, J. W., & Mulick, J. A. (1992). A new definition of mentally retarded or a new definition of practice. *Psychology in Mental Retardation and Developmental Disabilities, 18*(2), 9–14.

Johnson, K. E. (1988). *Human developmental anatomy.* New York: Wiley.

Kauffman, J. M. (1993). *Characteristics of emotional and behavioral disorders of children and youth* (5th ed.). New York: Macmillan/Merrill.

Kastner, T., Nathanson, R., & Friedman, D. L. (1993). Mortality among individuals with mental retardation living in the community. *American Journal on Mental Retardation, 98,* 285–292.

Kerby, D. S., & Dawson, B. L. (1994). Autistic features, personality, and adaptive behaviors in males with the fragile X syndrome and no autism. *American Journal on Mental Retardation, 98,* 455–462.

Lachiewicz, A. M., Spiridigliozzi, G. A., Gullion, C. M., Ransford, S. N., & Rao, K. (1994). Aberrant behaviors of young boys with fragile X syndrome. *American Journal on Mental Retardation, 98,* 567–579.

LeClair, D. A., Pollock, B. J., & Elliott, D. (1993). Movement preparation in adults with and without Down syndrome. *American Journal on Mental Retardation, 97,* 628–633.

Lemkau, P. V., & Imre, P. D. (1969). Results of a field epidemiologic study. *American Journal of Mental Deficiency, 73,* 858–863.

Little, G. A. (1990). Fetal growth and development. In R. D. Eden & F. H. Boehm (Eds.), *Assessment and care of the fetus: Physiological, clinical, and medicolegal principles* (pp. 3–15). Norwalk, CT: Appleton & Lange.

Lowitzer, A. C. (1987). Maternal phenylketonuria: Cause for concern among women with PKU. *Research in Developmental Disabilities, 8,* 1–14.

MacMillan, D. L., Gresham, F. M., & Siperstein, G. N. (1993). Conceptual and psychometric concerns about the 1992 AAMR definition of mental retardation. *American Journal on Mental Retardation, 98,* 325–335.

Mahnovski, V., & Pavlova, Z. (1989). Blood disorders. In G. B. Reed, A. E. Claireaux, & A. D. Bain (Eds.), *Diseases of the fetus and newborn: Pathology, radiology and genetics* (pp. 417–440). St. Louis: C.V. Mosby.

McDonnell, J., Wilcox, B., & Hardman, M. L. (1991). *Secondary programs for students with developmental disabilities.* Boston: Allyn & Bacon.

Menkes, J. H., Hurst, P. L., & Craig, J. M. (1954). A new syndrome: Progressive familial infantile cerebral dysfunction associated with an unusual urinary substance. *Pediatrics, 14,* 462–467.

Mercer, J. R. (1973). *Labelling the mentally retarded.* Berkeley: University of California Press.

Meyer, L. H., Peck, C. A., & Brown, L. (Eds.). (1991). *Critical issues in the lives of people with severe disabilities.* Baltimore: Paul H. Brookes.

Nielsen, J. B., Lou, H. C., & Guttler, F. (1988). Effects of diet discontinuation and dietary tryptophan supplementation on neurotransmitter metabolism in phenylketonuria. *Brain Dysfunction, 1*(1), 51–56.

Ramey, C. T., & Ramey, S. L. (1992). At risk does not mean doomed. *National Health/Education Consortium Occasional Paper #4.* Washington, DC: National Commission to Prevent Infant Mortality.

Reed, G. B., Claireaux, A. E., & Bain, A. D. (Eds.). (1989). *Diseases of the fetus and newborn: Pathology, radiology and genetics.* St. Louis: C.V. Mosby.

Ricciuti, H. N. (1993). Nutrition and mental development. *Current Directions in Psychological Science, 2*(2), 43–46.

Ruskin, E. M., Mundy, P., Kasari, C., & Sigman, M. (1994). Object mastery motivation of children with Down syndrome. *American Journal on Mental Retardation, 98,* 499–509.

Schalock, R. L., & Genung, L. T. (1993). Placement from a community-based mental retardation program: A 15-year follow-up. *American Journal on Mental Retardation, 98,* 400–407.

Scheerenberger, R. C. (1983). *A history of mental retardation.* Baltimore: Brookes.

Seltzer, M. M., Krauss, M. W., & Tsunematsu, N. (1993). Adults with Down syndrome and their aging mothers: Diagnostic group differences. *American Journal on Mental Retardation, 97,* 496–508.

Short, R. H., & Hess, G. C. (1995). Fetal alcohol syndrome: Characteristics and remedial implications. *Developmental Disabilities Bulletin, 23,* 12–29.

Simensen, R. J. (1993). Review of *Fragile X syndrome: Diagnosis, treatment, and research.* R. J. Hagerman & A. C. Silverman (Eds.), Baltimore: Johns Hopkins University Press. *American Journal on Mental Retardation, 97,* 477–479.

Stainback, W., & Stainback, S. (1990). *Support networks for inclusive schooling.* Baltimore: Paul H. Brookes.

Steele, S. (1989). Phenylketonuria: Counseling and teaching functions of the nurse on an interdisciplinary team. *Issues in Comprehensive Pediatric Nursing, 12,* 395–409.

U.S. Department of Education. (1993). To assure the free appropriate public education of all children with disabilities. *Fifteenth Annual Report to Congress on the Implementation of the Individuals with Disabilities Education Act.* Washington, DC: U.S. Government Printing Office.

Williams, B. F., Howard, V. F., & McLaughlin, T. F. (1994). Fetal alcohol syndrome: Developmental characteristics and directions for further research. *Education and Treatment of Children, 17,* 86–97.

CHAPTER 10

Abraham, S., & Llewellyn-Jones, D. (1992). *Eating disorders: The facts* (3rd ed.). Oxford: Oxford University Press.

Adams, M. R. (1990). The demands and capacities model: I. Theoretical elaborations. *Journal of Fluency Disorders, 15*(3), 135–141.

Advokat, C., & Kutlesic, V. (1995). Pharmacotherapy of the eating disorders: A commentary. *Neuroscience and Biobehavioral Reviews, 19,* 59–66.

Agras, W. S. (1995). The big picture. In D. B. Allison (Ed.), *Handbook of assessment methods for eating behaviors and weight-related problems: Measures, theory, and research* (pp. 561–579). Thousand Oaks, CA: Sage.

Agras, W. S., Telch, C. F., Arnow, B., & Eldredge, K. (1995). Does interpersonal therapy help patients with binge eating disorder who fail to respond to cognitive-behavioral therapy? *Journal of Consulting and Clinical Psychology, 63,* 356–360.

Aldrich, M. S. (1990). Narcolepsy. *New England Journal of Medicine, 323,* 389–394.

Aldrich, M. S. (1992). Narcolepsy. *Neurology, 42*(7, Suppl. 6), 34–43.

Alexander-Mott, L. A. (1994). Anorexia nervosa: Definition, diagnostic criteria, and associated psychological problems. In L. A. Alexander-Mott & D. B. Lumsden (Eds.), *Understanding eating disorders: Anorexia nervosa, bulimia nervosa, and obesity* (pp. 101–122). Washington, DC: Taylor & Francis.

Alfonso, V. C. (1995). Measures of quality of life, subjective well-being, and satisfaction with life. In D. B. Allison (Ed.), *Handbook of assessment methods for eating behaviors and weight-related problems: Measures, theory, and research* (pp. 23–80). Thousand Oaks, CA: Sage.

Alger, S. A. (1992). The "obesities": Causes and management. In R. Lemberg (Ed.), *Controlling eating disorders with facts, advice, and resources* (pp. 49–53). Phoenix, AZ: Oryx Press.

Allison, D. B. (1995). Introduction. In D. B. Allison (Ed.), *Handbook of assessment methods for eating behaviors and weight-related problems: Measures, theory, and research* (pp. ix–xx). Thousand Oaks, CA: Sage.

Alpert, J. E., Maddocks, A., Rosenbaum, J. F., & Fava, M. (1994). Childhood psychopathology retrospectively assessed among adults with early onset major depression. *Journal of Affective Disorders, 31*(3), 165–171.

American Psychiatric Association. (1994). *Diagnostic and statistical manual of mental disorders (DSM-IV)* (4th ed.). Washington, DC: Author.

Andrews, B., Valentine, E. R., & Valentine, J. D. (1995). Depression and eating disorders following abuse in childhood in two generations of women. *British Journal of Clinical Psychology, 34*, 37–52.

Appelberg, B., Rimon, R., Nikkila, H., & Ahlroth, J. (1989). Neuroleptic-induced somnambulism as a cause of nocturnal confusion in a psychotic patient: A case description. *Nordisk Psykiatrisk Tidsskrift, 43*(5), 473–474.

Aronson, A. E. (1990). *Clinical voice disorders: An interdisciplinary approach* (3rd ed.). New York: Thieme.

Bastiani, A. M., Rao, R., Weltzin, T., & Kaye, W. H. (1995). Perfectionism in anorexia nervosa. *International Journal of Eating Disorders, 17*, 147–152.

Bernard-Bonnin, A. C., Haley, N., Belanger, S., & Nadeau, D. (1993). Parental and patient perceptions about encopresis and its treatment. *Journal of Developmental and Behavioral Pediatrics, 14*, 397–400.

Binnie, C. D., & Prior, P. F. (1994). Electroencephalography. *Journal of Neurology, Neurosurgery and Psychiatry, 57*, 1308–1319.

Blanes, T., Burgess, M., Marks, I. M., & Gill, M. (1993). Dream anxiety disorders (nightmares): A review. *Behavioural Psychotherapy, 21*, 37–43.

Brabbins, C. J., Dewey, M. E., Copeland, J. R., & Davidson, I. A. (1993). Insomnia in the elderly: Prevalence, gender differences and relationships with morbidity and mortality. *International Journal of Geriatric Psychiatry, 8*(6), 473–480.

Braet, C., & Verhofstadt, D. L. (1994). Different types of eating behavior in obese and nonobese children. *Kind en Adolescent, 15*(3), 154–159.

Braun, C. M., & Chouinard, M. J. (1992). Is anorexia nervosa a neuropsychological disease? *Neuropsychology Review, 2*(2), 171–212.

Brody, J. E. (1996, January 17). Personal health. *New York Times,* p. B8.

Brooks-Gunn, J., Graber, J. A., & Paikoff, R. L. (1994). Studying links between hormones and negative affect: Models and measures. *Journal of Research on Adolescence, 4*, 469–486.

Broughton, R., & Mullington, J. (1994). Chronobiological aspects of narcolepsy. *Sleep, 17*(8, Suppl.), S35–S44.

Broughton, W. A., & Broughton, R. J. (1994). Psychosocial impact of narcolepsy. *Sleep, 17*(8, Suppl.), S45–S49.

Brown, P. J. (1991). Culture and the evolution of obesity. *Human Nature, 2*(1), 31–57.

Brownell, K. D., & Wadden, T. A. (1991). The heterogeneity of obesity: Fitting treatments to individuals. *Behavior Therapy, 22*, 153–177.

Brownell, K. D., & Wadden, T. A. (1992). Etiology and treatment of obesity: Understanding a serious, prevalent, and refractory disorder. *Journal of Consulting and Clinical Psychology, 60*, 505–517.

Bucci, S., Chiarelli, R., & Spagnolo, R. (1994). Sleep-somnambulism-dream: A possible train. *Giornale de Neuropsichiatria dell'Eta Evolutiva, 14*(2), 117–130.

Buchanan, A., & Clayden, G. (1992). *Children who soil: Assessment and treatment.* Chichester, England: John Wiley & Sons.

Bull, R. H., & Legorreta, G. (1991). Outcome of gastric surgery for morbid obesity: Weight changes and personality traits. *Psychotherapy and Psychosomatics, 56*, 146–156.

Case, J. L. (1991). *Clinical management of voice disorders* (2nd ed.). Austin, TX: Pro-Ed.

Chambers, M. J. (1992). Therapeutic issues in the behavioral treatment of insomnia. *Professional Psychology Research and Practice, 23*(2), 131–138.

Christophersen, E. R., & Edwards, K. J. (1992). Treatment of elimination disorders: State of the art 1991. *Applied and Preventive Psychology, 1*(1), 15–22.

Christophersen, E. R., & Rapoff, M. A. (1992). Toileting problems in children. In C. E. Walker & M. C. Roberts (Eds.). *Handbook of clinical child psychology* (2nd ed.), (pp. 399–411). New York: Wiley.

Cohen, F. L., Ferrans, C. E., & Eshler, B. (1992). Reported accidents in narcolepsy. *Loss, Grief and Care, 5*(3–4), 71–80.

Cohen, N. J., Davine, M., Horodezky, N., & Lipsett, L. (1993). Unsuspected language impairment in psychiatrically disturbed children: Prevalence and language and behavioral characteristics. *Journal of the American Academy of Child and Adolescent Psychiatry, 32*, 595–603.

Cooper, E. B., & Cooper, C. S. (1992). A fluency disorders prevention program for preschoolers and children in the primary grades. *American Journal of Speech-Language Pathology, 1*(1), 28–31.

Coren, S. (1994). The prevalence of self-reported sleep disturbances in young adults. *International Journal of Neuroscience, 79*(1–2), 67–73.

Cox, D. J., Sutphen, J., Borowitz, S., & Dickens, M. N. (1994). Simple electromyographic biofeedback treatment for chronic pediatric constipation/encopresis: Preliminary report. *Biofeedback and Self Regulation, 19*(1), 41–50.

Crow, S. J., & Mitchell, J. E. (1994). Bulimia nervosa: Methods of treatment. In L. A. Alexander-Mott & D. B. Lumsden (Eds.), *Understanding eating disorders: Anorexia nervosa, bulimia nervosa, and obesity* (pp. 203–219). Washington, DC: Taylor & Francis.

Cuisinier, M., & Hoogduin, K. (1991). Success and relapse in the treatment of a man with pavor nocturnus and sleepwalking. *Gedragstherapie, 24*, 41–54.

Dahl, R. E. (1992). The pharmacologic treatment of sleep disorders. *Psychiatric Clinics of North America, 15*, 161–178.

Dare, C., Eisler, I., Colahan, M., & Crowther, C. (1995). The listening heart and the chi square: Clinical and empirical perceptions in the family therapy of anorexia nervosa. *Journal of Family Therapy, 17*, 31–57.

Dare, C., LeGrange, D., Eisler, I., & Rutherford, J. (1994). Redefining the psychosomatic family: Family process of 26 eating disorder families. *International Journal of Eating Disorders, 16*(3), 211–226.

Davis, E., Fennoy, I., Laraque, D., & Kanem, N. (1992). Autism and developmental abnormalities in children with perinatal cocaine exposure. *Journal of the National Medical Association, 84*, 315–319.

Denny, A. D., Marks, S. M., & Olif-Carneol, S. (1993). Correction of velopharyngeal insufficiency by pharyngeal augmentation using autologous cartilage: A preliminary report. *Cleft Palate-Craniofacial Journal, 30*, 46–54.

De Peuter, R., Withers, R. T., Brinkman, M., Tomas, F. M., & Clark, D. G. (1992). No differences in rates of energy expenditure between post-obese women and their matched, lean controls. *International Journal of Obesity*, 801–808.

DiNicola, V. F. (1993, May). Family interventions and eating disorders. Paper presented at 4th Eating Disorders Symposium, Vancouver, Canada.

Dodge, E., Hodes, M., Eisler, I., & Dare, C. (1995). Family therapy for bulimia nervosa in adolescents: An exploratory study. *Journal of Family Therapy*, 17, 59–77.

Drew, C. J., Hardman, M. L., & Hart, A. W. (1996). *Designing and conducting research: Inquiry in education and social science* (2nd ed.). Boston: Allyn & Bacon.

Dufour, M., & Fuller, R. K. (1995). Alcohol in the elderly. *Annual Review of Medicine*, 46, 123–132.

Dwivedi, K. N., & Bell, S. (1993). Encopresis. In K. N. Dwivedi (Ed.), *Group work with children and adolescents.* London: Jessica Kingsley Publishers, Ltd.

Edwards, M., Cape, J., & Brown, D. (1989). Patterns of referral for children with speech disorders. *Child Care, Health and Development*, 15, 417–424.

Elbert, M., Powell, T. W., & Swartzlander, P. (1991). Toward a technology of generalization: How many exemplars are sufficient? *Journal of Speech and Hearing Research*, 34, 81–87.

Ettorre, E., Klaukka, T., & Riska, E. (1994). Psychotropic drugs: Long-term use, dependency and the gender factor. *Social Science and Medicine*, 39, 1667–1673.

Fabrega, H., & Miller, B. D. (1995). A cultural analysis of adolescent psychopathology. *Journal of Adolescent Research*, 10, 197–226.

Fairburn, C. G., Norman, P. A., & Welch, S. L. (1995). A prospective study of outcome in bulimia and the long-term effects of three psychological treatments. *Archives of General Psychiatry*, 52, 304–312.

Felsenfeld, S., Broen, P. A., & McGue, M. (1992). A 28-year follow-up of adults with a history of moderate phonological disorder: Linguistic and personality results. *Journal of Speech and Hearing Resarch*, 35, 1114–1125.

Foreyt, J. P., & Goodrick, G. K. (1994). Attributes of successful approaches to weight loss and control. *Applied and Preventive Psychology*, 3(4), 209–215.

Foreyt, J. P., & Goodrick, G. K. (1995). Obesity. In R. T. Ammerman & M. Hersen (Eds.), *Handbook of child behavior therapy in the psychiatric setting* (pp. 409–425). New York: Wiley.

Friman, P. C., & Vollmer, D. (1995). Successful use of the nocturnal urine alarm for diurnal enuresis. *Journal of Applied Behavior Analysis*, 28, 89–90.

Friman, P. C., & Warzak, W. J. (1990). Nocturnal enuresis: A prevalent, persistent, yet curable parasomnia. *Pediatrician*, 17, 38–45.

Gardner, H. (1989). An investigation of maternal interaction with phonologically disordered children as compared to two groups of normally developing children. *British Journal of Disorders of Communication*, 24, 41–59.

Gagnon, M., & Ladouceur, R. (1992). Behavioral treatment of child stutterers: Replication and extension. *Behavior Therapy*, 23, 113–129.

Garland, E. J., & Smith, D. H. (1991). Simultaneous prepubertal onset of panic disorder, night terrors, and somnambulism. *Journal of the American Academy of Child and Adolescent Psychiatry*, 30, 553–555.

Garma, L., & Marchand, F. (1994). Non-pharmacological approaches to the treatment of narcolepsy. *Sleep*, 17(8, Suppl.), S97–S102.

Gillberg, I. C., Rastam, M., & Gillberg, C. (1995). Anorexia nervosa 6 years after onset: I. Personality disorders. *Comprehensive Psychiatry*, 36, 61–69.

Goldner, E. M., & Birmingham, C. L. (1994). Anorexia nervosa: Methods of treatment. In L. A. Alexander-Mott & D. B. Lumsden (Eds.), *Understanding eating disorders: Anorexia nervosa, bulimia nervosa, and obesity* (pp. 135–157). Washington, DC: Taylor & Francis.

Graber, J. A., Brooks-Gunn, J., Paikoff, R. L., & Warren, M. P. (1994). Prediction of eating problems: An 8-year study of adolescent girls. *Developmental Psychology*, 30, 823–834.

Gray, S. I., & Shelton, R. L. (1992). Self-monitoring effects on articulation carryover in school-age children. *Language, Speech, and Hearing Services in the Schools*, 23, 334–342.

Greeno, C. G., & Wing, R. R. (1994). Stress-induced eating. *Psychological Bulletin*, 115, 444–464.

Hackett, L., & Hackett, R. (1994). Child-rearing practices and psychiatric disorder in Gujarati and British children. *British Journal of Social Work*, 24(2), 191–202.

Hardman, M. L., Drew, C. J., & Egan, M. W. (1996). *Human exceptionality: Society, school, and family* (5th ed.). Boston: Allyn & Bacon.

Harris, Y., Gorelick, P. B., Cohen, D., & Dollear, W. (1994). Psychiatric symptoms in dementia associated with stroke: A case-control analysis among predominantly African-American patients. *Journal of the National Medical Association*, 86, 697–702.

Hart, K. E. (1991). Obsessive-compulsiveness in obese weight-loss patients and normal weight adults. *Journal of Clinical Psychology*, 47, 358–361.

Heebink, D. M., Sunday, S. R., & Halmi, K. A. (1995). Anorexia nervosa and bulimia nervosa in adolescence: Effects of age and menstrual status on psychological variables. *Journal of the American Academy of Child and Adolescent Psychiatry*, 34, 378–382.

Hinsberger, A., Sharma, V., & Mazmanian, D. (1994). Cognitive deterioration from long-term abuse of dextromethorphan: A case report. *Journal of Psychiatry and Neuroscience*, 19(5), 375–377.

Hobson, J. A., & Stickgold, R. (1994). Dreaming: A neurocognitive approach. *Consciousness and Cognition An International Journal*, 3(1), 1–15.

Hohagen, F., Kappler, C., Schramm, E., & Rink, K. (1994). Prevalence of insomnia in elderly general practice attenders and the current treatment modalities. *Acta Psychiatrica Scandinavica*, 90(2), 102–108.

Hohagen, F., Montero, R. F., Weiss, E., & Lis, S. (1994). Treatment of primary insomnia with trimipramine: An alternative to benzodiazepine hypnotics? *European Archives of Psychiatry and Clinical Neuroscience*, 244(2), 65–72.

Holderness, C. C., Brooks-Gunn, J., & Warren, M. P. (1994). Comorbidity of eating disorders and substance abuse review of the literature. *International Journal of Eating Disorders*, 16, 1–34.

Horne, J. A. (1992). Sleep and its disorders in children. *Journal of Child Psychology and Psychiatry and Allied Disciplines*, 33, 473–487.

Houts, A. C. (1991). Nocturnal enuresis as a biobehavioral problem. *Behavior Therapy*, 22(2), 133–151.

Houts, A. C., & Abramson, H. (1990). Assessment ant treatment for functional childhood enuresis and encopresis: Toward a partnership between health psychologists and physicians. In S. B. Morgan & T. M.

Okwumabua (Eds.), *Child and adolescent disorders: Developmental and health psychology perspectives* (pp. 47–103). Hillsdale, NJ: Lawrence Erlbaum.

Houts, A. C., Berman, J. S., & Abramson, H. (1994). Effectiveness of psychological and pharmacological treatments for nocturnal enuresis. *Journal of Consulting and Clinical Psychology, 62*, 737–745.

International Society of Sport Psychology. (1993). The use of anabolic-androgenic steroids (AAS) in sport and physical activity: A position statement. *International Journal of Sport Psychology, 24*, 74–78.

Irwin, E. G. (1993). A focused overview of anorexia nervosa and bulimia: I. Etiological issues. *Archives of Psychiatric Nursing, 7*(6), 342–346.

Ivanova, G. A., Lapa, A. Z., Lokhov, M. I., & Movsisyants, S. A. (1991). Features of stuttering preschool children. *Neuroscience and Behavioral Physiology, 21*, 284–287.

Johnson, D. W. (1994). Hypertension: Psychological factors in aetiology and management. *Irish Journal of Psychology, 15*, 27–42.

Kaplan, C. A., & Hussain, S. (1995). Use of drugs in child and adolescent psychiatry. *British Journal of Psychiatry, 166*, 291–298.

Kavey, N. B., & Whyte, J. (1993). Somnambulism associated with hallucinations. *Psychosomatics, 34*, 86–90.

Keilbach, H. (1976). Treatment of an 8-year-old boy with encopresis acquisita as main symptom. *Praxis der Kinderpsychologie un Kinderpsychiatrie, 25*(3), 81–91.

Kenny, D., & Adams, R. (1994). The relationship between eating attitudes, body mass index, age, and gender in Australian university students. *Australian Psychologist, 29*, 128–134.

Kingsbury, S. J. (1993). Brief hypnotic treatment of repetitive nightmares. *American Journal of Clinical Hypnosis, 35*(3), 161–169.

Kinoy, B. P., & Holman, A. M. (1992). What is anorexia nervosa? What is bulimia nervosa? In R. Lemberg (Ed.), *Controlling eating disorders with facts, advice, and resources* (pp. 3–9). Phoenix, AZ: Oryx Press.

Kinzie, J. D., Sack, R. L., & Riley, C. M. (1994). The polysomnographic effects of clonidine on sleep disorders in posttraumatic stress disorder: A pilot study with Cambodian patients. *Journal of Nervous and Mental Disease, 182*(10), 585–587.

Kirsch, I., Montgomery, G., & Sapirstein, G. (1995). Hypnosis as an adjunct to cognitive-behavioral psychotherapy: A meta-analysis. *Journal of Consulting and Clinical Psychology, 63*, 214–220.

Kirschenbaum, D. S., & Fitzgibbon, M. L. (1995). Controversy about the treatment of obesity: Criticisms or challenges? *Behavior Therapy, 26*, 43–68.

Koenig, H. G., O'Connor, C. M., Guarisco, S. A., & Zabel, K. M. (1993). Depressive disorder in older medical inpatients on general medicine and cardiology services at a university teaching hospital. *American Journal of Geriatric Psychiatry, 1*(3), 197–210.

Kraemer, H. C., Berkowitz, R. I., & Hammer, D. L. (1990). Methodologic difficulties in studies of obesity: I. Measurement issues. *Annals of Behavioral Medicine, 12*, 112–118.

Lepkifker, E., Dannon, P. N., Iancu, I., & Ziv, R. (1995). Nightmares related to fluoxetine treatment. *Clinical Neuropharmacology, 18*, 90–94.

Lepola, U., Koponen, H., & Lienonen, E. (1994). Sleep in panic disorders. *Journal of Psychosomatic Research, 38* (1, Suppl.), 105–111.

Leung, A. K., & Robson, W. L. (1993). Nightmares. *Journal of the National Medical Association, 85*(3), 233–235.

Lewis, B. A., & Thompson, L. A. (1992). A study of developmental speech and language disorders in twins. *Journal of Speech and Hearing Research, 35*, 1086–1094.

Lichstein, K. L., & Fanning, J. (1990). Cognitive anxiety in insomnia: An analogue test. *Stress Medicine, 6*(1), 47–51.

Lichstein, K. L., Riedel, B. W. (1994). Behavioral assessment and treatment of insomnia: A review with an emphasis on clinical application. *Behavior Therapy, 25*, 659–688.

Lillywhite, A. R., Wilson, S. J., & Nutt, D. J. (1994). Successful treatment of night terrors and somnambulism with paroxetine. *British Journal of Psychiatry, 164*, 551–554.

Lonigan, C. J., Fischel, J. E., Whitehurst, G. J., & Arnold, D. S. (1992). The role of otitis media in the development of expressive language disorder. *Developmental Psychology, 28*, 430–440.

Love, R. J. (1992). *Childhood motor speech disability.* New York: Macmillan.

Lowe, M. R. (1993). The effects of dieting on eating behavior: A three-factor model. *Psychological Bulletin, 114*, 100–121.

Luxem, M., & Christophersen, E. (1994). Behavioral toilet training in early childhood: Research, practice, and implications. *Journal of Developmental and Behavioral Pediatrics, 15*(5), 370–378.

Manley, R. S., & Needham, L. (1995). An anti-bulimia group for adolescent girls. *Journal of Child and Adolescent Group Therapy, 5*, 19–33.

Marx, R. D. (1994). Anorexia nervosa: Theories of etiology. In L. A. Alexander-Mott & D. B. Lumsden (Eds.), *Understanding eating disorders: Anorexia nervosa, bulimia nervosa, and obesity* (pp. 123–134). Washington, DC: Taylor & Francis.

Mellon, M. W., & Houts, A. C. (1995). Elimination disorders. In R. T. Ammerman & M. Hersen (Eds.), *Handbook of child behavior therapy in the psychiatric setting* (pp. 341–366). New York: Wiley.

Mindell, J. A. (1993). Sleep disorders in children. *Health Psychology, 12*(2), 151–162.

Mishne, J. M. (1993). Primary nocturnal enuresis: A psychodynamic clinical perspective. *Child and Adolescent Social Work Journal, 10*, 469–495.

Mitler, M. M. (1994). Evaluation of treatment with stimulants in narcolepsy. *Sleep, 17*(8, Suppl.), S103–S106.

Mitrani, J. L. (1993). "Unmentalized" experience in the etiology and treatment of psychosomatic asthma. *Contemporary Psychoanalysis, 29*(2), 314–342.

Moreno, A. B., & Thelen, M. H. (1995). Eating behavior in junior high school females. *Adolescence, 30*(117), 171–174.

Morley, J. E., Flood, J. F., & Silver, A. J. (1992). Effects of peripheral hormones on memory and ingestive behaviors. *Psychoneuroendocrinology, 17*, 391–399.

Mutzell, S. (1994). Alcoholism in women. *Early Child Development and Care, 101*, 71–80.

Myers, P. N., & Biocca, F. A. (1992). The elastic body image: The effect of television advertising and programming on body image distortions in young women. *Journal of Communication, 42*(3), 108–133.

Nakra, B. R., Gfeller, J. D., & Hassan, R. (1992). A double-blind comparison of the effects of temazepam and triazolam on residual daytime performance in elderly insomniacs. *International Psychogeriatrics, 4*(1), 45–53.

Nelson, N. W. (1993a). *Childhood language disorders in context: Infancy through adolescence.* New York: Macmillan.

Nelson, N. W. (1993b). Language intervention in school settings. In D. K. Bernstein & E. Tiegerman (Eds.), *Language and communication disorders in children* (3rd ed., pp. 273–324). Columbus, OH: Merrill.

Norgaard, J. P., & Djurhuus, J. C. (1993, July). The pathophysiology of enuresis in children and young adults. *Clinical Pediatrics,* 5–9.

Ojha, H., & Pramanick, M. (1992). Religio-cultural variation in childrearing practices. *Psychological Studies, 37*(1), 65–72.

Onslow, M. (1992). Choosing a treatment procedure for early stuttering: Issues and future directions. *Journal of Speech and Hearing Research, 35,* 983–993.

Owens, R. E., Jr. (1995). *Language disorders: A functional approach to assessment and intervention* (2nd ed.). Needham Heights, MA: Allyn & Bacon.

Park, R. J., Lawrie, S. M., & Freeman, C. P. (1995). Post-viral onset of anorexia nervosa. *British Journal of Psychiatry, 166,* 386–389.

Parks, D. (1994). Introduction to the mechanism of action of different treatments of narcolepsy. *Sleep, 17*(8, Suppl.), S93–S96.

Parrino, L., Spaggiari, M. C., Boselli, M., & DiGiovanni, G. (1994). Clinical and polysomnographic effects of trazodone CR in chronic insomnia associated with dysthymia. *Psychopharmacology, 116*(4), 389–395.

Parry-Jones, B. (1994). Merycism or rumination disorder: A historical investigation and current assessment. *British Journal of Psychiatry, 165,* 303–314.

Partinen, M. (1994). Sleep disorders and stress. *Journal of Psychosomatic Research, 38* (1, Suppl.), 89–91.

Pathania, R., & Chaudhary, N. (1993). Toilet training practices among mothers of Chandigarh City. *Indian Journal of Behaviour, 17*(3), 1–4.

Patton, J. R., Kauffman, J. M., Blackbourn, J. M., & Brown, G. B. (1991). *Exceptional children in focus* (5th ed.). New York: Macmillan.

Peltzer, K., & Taiwo, O. (1993). Enuresis in a population of Nigerian children. *Journal of Psychology in Africa, 1*(5), 136–150.

Perkins, W. H., Kent, R. D., & Curlee, R. F. (1991). A theory of neuropsycholinguistic function in stuttering. *Journal of Speech and Hearing Research, 34,* 734–752.

Pike, K. M., Loeb, K., & Walsh, B. T. (1995). Binge eating and purging. In D. B. Allison (Ed.), *Handbook of assessment methods for eating behaviors and weight-related problems: Measures, theory, and research* (pp. 303–346). Thousand Oaks, CA: Sage.

Ponton, L. E. (1995). A review of eating disorders in adolescents. In R. C. Marohn & S. C. Feinstein (Eds.). *Adolescent psychiatry: Developmental and clinical studies* (Vol. 20, pp. 267–285). Hillsdale, NJ: Analytic Press, Inc.

Pope, H. G., Mangweth, B., Negrao, A. B., & Hudson, J. I. (1994). Childhood sexual abuse and bulimia nervosa: A comparison of American, Austrian, and Brazilian women. *American Journal of Psychiatry, 151,* 732–737.

Popper, C. W., & Steingard, R. J. (1994). Disorders usually first diagnosed in infancy, childhood, or adolescence. In R. E. Hales, S. C. Yudofsky, & J. A. Talbott (Eds.), *The American Psychiatric Press textbook of psychiatry* (2nd ed., pp. 729–832). Washington, DC: American Psychiatric Press, Inc.

Poulos, M. G., & Webster, W. G. (1991). Family history as a basis for subgrouping people who stutter. *Journal of Speech and Hearing Research, 34,* 5–10.

Radziewicz, C., & Antonellis, S. (1993). Considerations and implications for habilitation of hearing impaired children. In D. K. Bernstein & E. Tiegerman (Eds.), *Language and communication disorders in children* (3rd ed., pp. 482–514). Columbus, OH: Merrill.

Rastam, M., Gillberg, I., & Gillberg, C. (1995). Anorexia nervosa 6 years after onset: II. Comorbid psychiatric problems. *Comprehensive Psychiatry, 36,* 70–76.

Rastatter, M. P., & Loren, C. A. (1988). Visual coding dominance in stuttering: Some evidence from central tachistoscopic stimulation (tachistoscopic viewing and stuttering). *Journal of Fluency Disorders, 13,* 89–95.

Ratokalau, N. B., & Robb, M. P. (1993). Early communication assessment and intervention: An interactive process. In D. K. Bernstein & E. Tiegerman (Eds.), *Language and communication disorders in children* (3rd ed., pp. 148–184). Columbus, OH: Merrill.

Regestein, Q. R., & Monk, T. H. (1995). Delayed sleep phase syndrome: A review of its clinical aspects. *American Journal of Psychiatry, 152,* 602–608.

Riedel, B. W., Lichstein, K. L., & Dwyer, W. O. (1995). Sleep compression and sleep education for older insomniacs: Self-help versus therapist guidance. *Psychology and Aging, 10,* 54–63.

Robinson, D. (1994). In the galley of a whaling ship: The continuing search for the initial sensitizing event. *Medical Hypnoanalysis Journal, 9*(3), 113–118.

Rockwell, K. (1992). Eating disorder treatment: The importance of research. In R. Lemberg (Ed.), *Controlling eating disorders with facts, advice, and resources* (pp. 76–82). Phoenix, AZ: Oryx Press.

Rosen, J. C., Orosan, P., & Reiter, J. (1995). Cognitive behavior therapy for negative body image in obese women. *Behavior Therapy, 26,* 25–42.

Sansone, R. A., & Sansone, L. A. (1994). Bulimia nervosa: Medical complications. In L. A. Alexander-Mott & D. B. Lumsden (Eds.), *Understanding eating disorders: Anorexia nervosa, bulimia nervosa, and obesity* (pp. 181–201). Washington, DC: Taylor & Francis.

Schulze, H., & Johannsen, H. S. (1991). Importance of parent-child interaction in the genesis of stuttering. *Folia Phoniatrica, 43*(3), 133–134.

Schwartz, M. B., & Brownell, K. D. (1995). Matching individuals to weight loss treatments: A survey of obesity experts. *Journal of Consulting and Clinical Psychology, 63,* 149–153.

Shafer, C., & Garner, D. M. (1995). Eating disorders. In R. T. Ammerman & M. Hersen (Eds.), *Handbook of child behavior therapy in the psychiatric setting* (pp. 301–321). New York: Wiley.

Shisslak, C. M., & Crago, M. (1992). Eating disorders among athletes. In R. Lemberg (Ed.), *Controlling eating disorders with facts, advice, and resources* (pp. 29–36). Phoenix, AZ: Oryx Press.

Silverman, F. H. (1992). *Stuttering and other fluency disorders.* Englewood Cliffs, NJ: Prentice-Hall.

Silverman, F. H. (1995). *Speech, language, and hearing disorders.* Boston: Allyn & Bacon.

Sitton, S. C. (1994). Obesity: Methods of treatment. In L. A. Alexander-Mott & D. B. Lumsden (Eds.), *Understanding eating disorders: Anorexia nervosa, bulimia nervosa, and obesity* (pp. 271–287). Washington, DC: Taylor & Francis.

Sitton, S. C., & Miller, H. G. (1991). The effect of pretreatment eating patterns on the completion of a very low calorie diet. *International Journal of Eating Disorders, 10,* 369–372.

Sloan E. P., & Shapiro, C. M. (1995). Obstructive sleep apnea in a consecutive series of obese women. *International Journal of Eating Disorders, 17*(2), 167–173.

Smith, L. J. (1994). A behavioral approach to the treatment of non-retentive nocturnal encopresis in an adult with severe learning disabilities. *Journal of Behavior Therapy and Experimental Psychiatry, 25*, 81–86.

Sohlberg, S., & Strober, M. (1994). Personality in anorexia nervosa: An update and a theoretical integration. *Acta Psychiatrica Scandinavica, 89*(378, Suppl.), 1–16.

Soldatos, C. R. (1994). Insomnia in relation to depression and anxiety: Epidemiologic considerations. *Journal of Psychomatic Research, 38*(1, Suppl.), 3–8.

Srinivasagam, N. M., Kaye, W. H., Plotnicov, K. H., Greeno, C., Weltzin, T. E., & Rao, R. (1995). Persistent perfectionism, symmetry, and exactness after long-term recovery from anorexia nervosa. *American Journal of Psychiatry, 152*, 1630–1635.

Steiger, H. (1993). Anorexia nervosa: Is it tie syndrome or the theorist that is culture- and gender-bound. *Transcultural Psychiatric Research Review, 30*, 347–358.

Stepanski, E., Glinn, M., Zorick, F., & Roehrs, T. (1994). Heart rate changes in chronic insomnia. *Stress Medicine, 10*(4), 261–266.

Stice, E. (1994). Review of the evidence for a sociocultural model of bulimia nervosa and an exploration of the mechanisms of action. *Clinical Psychology Review, 14*(7), 633–661.

Stickgold, R., Pace-Schott, E., & Hobson, J. A. (1994). A new paradigm for dream research: Mentation reports following spontaneous arousal for REM and NREM sleep recorded in a home setting. *Consciousness and Cognition An International Journal, 3*(1), 16–29.

Stoohs, R. A., Guilleminault, C., & Dement, W. C. (1993). Sleep apnea and hypertension in commercial truck drivers. *Sleep, 16*(8, Suppl.), S11–S14.

Sundgot-Borgen, J. (1994). Risk and trigger factors for the development of eating disorders in female elite athletes. *Medicine and Science in Sports and Exercise, 26*, 414–419.

Thapar, A., Davies, G., Jones, T., & Revett, M. (1992). Treatment of childhood encopresis: A review. *Child Care, Health and Development, 18*(6), 343–353.

Thiel, A., Broocks, A., Ohlmeier, M., & Jacoby, G. E. (1995). Obsessive-compulsive disorder among patients with anorexia nervosa and bulimia nervosa. *American Journal of Psychiatry, 152*, 72–75.

Thompson, R. A., & Sherman, R. T. (1993). *Helping athletes with eating disorders.* Champaign, IL: Human Kinetics Publishers.

Thompson, S., & Rey, J. M. (1995). Functional enuresis: Is desmopressin the answer? *Journal of the American Academy of Child and Adolescent Psychiatry, 34*, 266–271.

Thyer, B. A. (1995). Effective psychosocial treatment for children. *Early Child Development and Care, 106*, 137–147.

Tiegerman, E. (1993a). The social bases of language. In D. K. Bernstein & E. Tiegerman (Eds.), *Language and communication disorders in children* (3rd ed., pp. 24–43). Columbus, OH: Merrill.

Tiegerman, E. (1993b). Early language development. In D. K. Bernstein & E. Tiegerman (Eds.), *Language and communication disorders in children* (3rd ed., pp. 24–43). Columbus, OH: Merrill.

Tordjman, S., Zittoun, C., Anderson, G. M., & Flament, M. (1994). Preliminary study of eating disorders among French female adolescents and young adults. *International Journal of Eating Disorders, 16*, 301–305.

Travis, F. (1994). The junction point model: A field model of waking, sleeping, and dreaming, relating dream witnessing, the waking/sleeping transition, and transcendental meditation in terms of a common psychophysiologic state. *Dreaming Journal of the Association for the Study of Dreams, 4*(2), 91–104.

Tso, R. D. (1992). Statistics about eating disorders. In R. Lemberg (Ed.), *Controlling eating disorders with facts, advice, and resources* (pp. xii–xvi). Phoenix, AZ: Oryx Press.

U.S. Bureau of the Census. (1993). *Current population reports* (Series P–60, No. 181). Education Statistics on Disk. Washington, DC: U.S. Department of Education, Office of Educational Research and Improvement, National Center for Education Statistics.

U.S. Department of Education, Office of Special Education Programs. (1994). *Sixteenth Annual Report to Congress on the Implementation of the Individuals with Disabilities Education Act.* Washington, DC: Author.

Van Riper, C., & Emerick, L. (1990). *Speech correction: An introduction to speech pathology and audiology* (8th ed.). Engelwood Cliffs, NJ: Prentice-Hall.

Van Tassel, E. B. (1985). The relative influence of child and environmental characteristics on sleep disturbances in the first and second years of life. *Journal of Developmental and Behavioral Pediatrics, 6*, 81–85.

Vaz-Leal, F. J., & Salcedo-Salcedo, M. S. (1995). Using the Milan approach in the inpatient management of anorexia nervosa (varying the "invariant prescription"). *Journal of Family Therapy, 17*, 97–113.

Wagner, S. (1992). Eating disorder treatment stories: Four cases. In R. Lemberg (Ed.), *Controlling eating disorders with facts, advice, and resources* (pp. 58–64). Phoenix, AZ: Oryx Press.

Walters, E. E., & Kendler, K. S. (1995). Anorexia nervosa and anorexic-like syndromes in a population-based female twin sample. *American Journal of Psychiatry, 152*, 64–71.

Wardle, J. (1995). The assessment of obesity: Theoretical background and practical advice. *Behaviour Research and Therapy, 33*, 107–117.

Warzak, W. J., & Friman, P. C. (1994). Current concepts in pediatric primary nocturnal enuresis. *Child and Adolescent Social Work Journal, 11*, 507–523.

Webster, W. G. (1988). Neural mechanisms underlying stuttering: Evidence from bimanual handwriting performance. *Brain and Language, 33*, 226–244.

Weintraub, M. (1992). Long-term weight control study: Conclusion. *Clinical Pharmacology and Therapeutics, 52*, 642–646.

Weiss, A. L. (1993). Planning language intervention for young children. In D. K. Bernstein & E. Tiegerman (Eds.), *Language and communication disorders in children* (3rd ed., pp. 229–272). Columbus, OH: Merrill.

Weiss, L., Katzman, M., & Wolchik, S. (1994). Bulimia nervosa: Definition, diagnostic criteria, and associated psychological problems. In L. A. Alexander-Mott & D. B. Lumsden (Eds.), *Understanding eating disorders: Anorexia nervosa, bulimia nervosa, and obesity* (pp. 161–180). Washington, DC: Taylor & Francis.

Wilson, G. T. (1994). Behavioral treatment of obesity: Thirty years and counting. *Advances in Behaviour Research and Therapy, 16*, 31–75.

Wilson, G. T., & Fairburn, C. G. (1993). Cognitive treatments for eating disorders. *Journal of Consulting and Clinical Psychology, 61,* 261–269.

Wing, R. R. (1993). Obesity and related eating and exercise behaviors in women. *Annals of Behavioral Medicine, 15*(2–3), 124–134.

Wing, R. R., Shiffman, S., Drapkin, R. G., & Grilo, C. M. (1995). Moderate versus restrictive diets: Implications for relapse. *Behavior Therapy, 26,* 5–24.

Yairi, E., & Ambrose, N. (1992). Onset of stuttering in preschool children: Selected factors. *Journal of Speech and Hearing Research, 35,* 782–788.

Yairi, E., Ambrose, N., & Niermann, R. (1993). The early months of stuttering: A developmental study. *Journal of Speech and Hearing Research, 36,* 521–528.

Yairi, E., & Carrico, D. M. (1992). Early childhood stuttering: Pediatricians' attitudes and practices. *American Journal of Speech-Language Pathology, 1*(3), 54–62.

Yoshida, H., Michi, K., Yamashita, Y., & Ohno, K. (1993). A comparison of surgical and prosthetic treatment for speech disorders attributable to surgically acquired soft palate defects. *Journal of Oral and Maxillofacial Surgery, 17*(3), 287–295.

Zebrowski, P. M., & Schum, R. L. (1993). Counseling parents of children who stutter. *American Journal of Speech-Language Pathology, 2*(2), 65–73.

CHAPTER 11

Abraham, K. (1955). *Selected papers on psychoanalysis.* New York: Basic Books.

American Psychiatric Association. (1994). *Diagnostic and statistical manual of mental disorders (DSM-IV)* (4th ed.). Washington, DC: Author.

Asarnow, J. R., Tompson, M. C., & Goldstein, M. J. (1994). Childhood-onset schizophrenia: A followup study. *Schizophrenia Bulletin, 20,* 599–617.

Asarnow, R. F., Asamen, J., Granholm, E., & Sherman, T. (1994). Cognitive/neuropsychological studies of children with a schizophrenic disorder. *Schizophrenia Bulletin, 20,* 647–669.

Bagenholm, A., & Gillberg, C. (1991). Psychosocial effects on siblings of children with autism and mental retardation: A population-based study. *Journal of Mental Deficiency Research, 35,* 291–307.

Bailey, A. J. (1993). The biology of autism. *Psychological Medicine, 23,* 7–11.

Bailey, A. J., Bolton, P., Butler, L., & le Couteur, A. (1993). Prevalence of the fragile X anomaly amongst autistic twins and singletons. *Journal of Child Psychology and Psychiatry and Allied Disciplines, 34,* 673–688.

Bettelheim, B. (1967). *The empty fortress.* New York: Free Press.

Biklen, D. (1990). Communication unbound: Autism and praxis. *Harvard Educational Review, 60,* 291–314.

Biklen, D. (1992). Typing to talk: Facilitated communication. *American Journal of Speech-Language Pathology, 1*(2), 15–17.

Bleuler, E. (1950). *Dementia praecox or the group of schizophrenics* (Joseph Zinkin, Trans.). New York: International University Press. (Originally published, Leipzig: Beutiche, 1911)

Bodfish, J. W., Crawford, T. W., Powell, S. B., Parker, D. E., Golden, R. N., & Lewis, M. H. (1995). Compulsions in adults with mental retardation: Prevalence, phenomenology, and comorbidity with stereotypy and self-injury. *American Journal on Mental Retardation, 100,* 183–192.

Bolton, P., Pickles, A., Butler, L., & Summers, D. (1992). Fragile X in families multiplex for autism and related phenotypes: Prevalence and criteria for cytogenic diagnosis. *Psychiatric Genetics, 2*(4), 277–300.

Brady, J. V. (1993). Behavior analysis applications and interdisciplinary research strategies. *American Psychologist, 48,* 435–440.

Bristol, M. M., Gallagher, J. J., & Holt, K. D. (1993). Maternal depressive symptoms in autism: Response to psychoeducational intervention. *Rehabilitation Psychology, 38,* 3–10.

Brook, I. (1995). Anaerobic infections in children with neurological impairments. *American Journal on Mental Retardation, 99,* 579–594.

Bryson, S. E., Clark, B. S., & Smith, I. M. (1988). First report of a Canadian epidemiological study of autistic syndromes. *Journal of Child Psychology and Psychiatry and Allied Disciplines, 29,* 433–445.

Cammisa, K. M., & Hobbs, S. H. (1993). Etiology of autism: A review of recent biogenic theories and research. *Occupational Therapy in Mental Health, 12*(2), 39–67,

Caplan, R. (1994). Thought disorder in childhood. *Journal of the American Academy of Child and Adolescent Psychiatry, 33,* 605–615.

Capps, L., Kasari, C., Yirmiya, N., & Sigman, M. (1993). Parental perception of emotional expressiveness in children with autism. *Journal of Consulting and Clinical Psychology, 61,* 475–484.

Carr, E. G., & Carlson, J. I. (1993). Reduction of severe behavior problems in the community using a multicomponent treatment approach. *Journal of Applied Behavior Analysis, 26,* 157–172.

Chapman, S., Fisher, W., Piazza, C. C., & Kurtz, P. F. (1993). Functional assessment and treatment of life-threatening drug ingestion in a dually diagnosed youth. *Journal of Applied Behavior Analysis, 26,* 255–256.

Ciadella, P., & Mamebe, N. (1989). An epidemiological study of infantile autism in a French department (Rhone): A research note. *Journal of Child Psychology and Psychiatry and Allied Disciplines, 30,* 165–175.

Cohen, D. J., Volmar, F., Anderson, G. M., & Klin, A. (1993). Integrating biological and behavioral perspectives in the study and care of autistic individuals: The future. *Israel Journal of Psychiatry and Related Sciences, 30,* 15–32.

Coleman, M., & Gillberg, C. (1985). *The biology of autistic syndromes,* New York: Praeger.

Cook, W. L., Asarnow, J. R., Goldstein, M. J., & Marshall, V. G. (1990). Mother-child dynamics in early-onset depression and childhood schizophrenia spectrum disorders. *Development and Psychopathology, 2*(1), 71–84.

Cuccaro, M. L., Wright, H. H., Abramson, R. K., & Marstellar, F. A. (1993). Whole-blood serotonin and cognitive functioning in autistic individuals and their first-degree relatives. *Journal of Neuropsychiatry and Clinical Neurosciences, 5*(1), 94–101.

Cummins, R. A., & Prior, M. P. (1992). Autism and assisted communication: A response to Biklen. *Harvard Educational Review, 62,* 228–241.

Dalrymple, N. (1989). *Developing a functional and longitudinal individual plan.* Functional programming for people with autism: A series. Bloomington: Indiana Resource Center for Autism, Institute for the Study of Developmental Disabilities, Indiana University.

David, A. S., Wacharasindhu, A., & Lishman, W. A., (1993). Severe psychiatric disturbance and abnormalities of the corpus callosum: Review and case series. *Journal of Neurology, Neurosurgery and Psychiatry, 56*, 85–93.

Davis, C. A., Brady, M. P., Williams, R. E., & Hamilton, R. (1992). Effects of high-probability requests on the acquisition and generalization of responses to requests in young children with behavior disorders. *Journal of Applied Behavior Analysis, 25*, 905–916.

Davis, E., Fennoy, I., Laraque, D., & Kanem, N. (1992). Autism and developmental abnormalities in children with perinatal cocaine exposure. *Journal of the National Medical Association, 84*, 315–319.

Dawson, G., Finley, C., Phillips, S., & Lewy, A. (1989). A comparison of hemispheric asymmetries in speech-related brain potentials of autistic and dysphasic children. *Brain and Language, 37*, 26–41.

deBenedetti-Gaddini, R. (1993). On autism. *Psychoanalytic Inquiry, 13*, 134–143.

Donenberg, G., & Baker, B. L. (1993). The impact of young children with externalizing behaviors on their families. *Journal of Abnormal Child Psychology, 21*, 179–198.

Drew, C. J., Hardman, M. L., & Logan, D. R. (1996). *Mental retardation: A life cycle approach* (6th ed.). Columbus, OH: Merrill.

Durand, V. M., & Carr, E. G. (1992). An analysis of maintenance following functional communication training. *Journal of Applied Behavior Analysis, 25*, 777–794.

Ekman, G., Miranda-Linne, F., Gillberg, C., Garle, M., & Wetterberg, L. (1989). Fenfluramine treatment of twenty children with autism. *Journal of Autism and Developmental Disorders, 19*, 511–532.

Elia, M., Musumeci, S. A., Ferri, R., & Bergonzi, P. (1995). Clinical and neurophysiological aspects of epilepsy in subjects with autism and mental retardation. *American Journal on Mental Retardation, 100*, 6–16.

Fotheringham, J. B. (1991). Autism: Its primary psychological and neurological deficit. *Canadian Journal of Psychiatry, 36*, 686–692.

Fombonne, E., & du Mazaubrun, C. (1992). Prevalence of infantile autism in four French regions. *Social Psychiatry and Psychiatric Epidemiology, 27*(4) 203–210.

Ghaziuddin, M., Butler, E., Tsai, L., & Ghaziuddin, N. (1994). Is clumsiness a marker for Asperger syndrome? *Journal of Intellectual Disability Research, 38*, 519–527.

Gillberg, C. (1990a). Autism and pervasive developmental disorders. *Journal of Child Psychology and Psychiatry and Allied Disciplines, 31*, 99–119.

Gillberg, C. (1990b). Infantile autism: Diagnosis and treatment. *Acta Psychiatrica Scandinavia, 81*, 209–215.

Gillberg, C., Gillberg, I. C., & Steffenburg, S. (1992). Siblings and parents of children with autism: A controlled population-based study. *Developmental Medicine and Child Neurology, 34*(5), 389–398.

Gold, N. (1993). Depression and social adjustment in siblings of boys with autism. *Journal of Autism and Developmental Disorders, 23*, 147–163.

Gorbachevskaya, N. L., Yakupova, L. P., Kozhushko, L. F., & Bashina, V. M. (1992). Topographic EEG mapping in child psychiatry. *Human Physiology, 18*, 404–410.

Gordon, C. T., Frazier, J. A., McKenna, K., Giedd, J. (1994). Childhood-onset schizophrenia: An NIMH study in progress. *Schizophrenia Bulletin, 20*, 697–712.

Gordon, C. T., State, R. C., Nelson, J. E., & Hamburger, S. D. (1993). A double-blind comparison of clomipramine, desipramine, and placebo in the treatment of autistic disorder. *Archives of General Psychiatry, 50*, 441–447.

Gorwood, P., Leboyer, M., Jay, M., & Payan, C. (1995). Gender and age at onset in schizophrenia: Impact of family history. *American Journal of Psychiatry, 152*, 208–212.

Gray, D. E. (1993). Negotiating autism: Relations between parents and treatment staff. *Social Science and Medicine, 36*, 1037–1046.

Gross, J. (1994). Asperger syndrome: A label worth having? *Educational Psychology in Practice, 10*, 104–110.

Gualtieri, C. T. (1992). New developments in the psychopharmacology of autism. IV. *Italian Journal of Intellective Impairment, 5*(2), 127–136.

Haag, G. (1993). Fear of fusion and projective identification in autistic children. *Psychoanalytic Inquiry, 13*, 63–68.

Hall, D. M. (1992). Child health promotion, screening and surveillance. *Journal of Child Psychology and Psychiatry and Allied Disciplines, 33*, 649–657.

Handlan, S., & Bloom, L. A. (1993). The effect of educational curricula and modeling/coaching on the interactions of kindergarten children with their peers with autism. *Focus on Autistic Behavior, 8*(2), 1–11.

Hardman, M. L., Drew, C. J., & Egan, M. W. (1996). *Human exceptionality: Society, school, and family* (5th ed.). Boston: Allyn & Bacon.

Harty, J. R. (1990). Pharmacology in infantile autism. *Focus on Autistic Behavior, 5*(2), 1–15.

Hasimoto, O., Shimizu, Y., & Kawasaki, Y. (1993). Brief report: Low frequency of the fragile X syndrome among Japanese autistic subjects. *Journal of Autism and Developmental Disorders, 23*, 201–209.

Hiroshi, K. (1989). Heller's syndrome as a type of pervasive developmental disorder. *Journal of Mental Health, 35*, 71–81.

Hiroshi, K., Michiko, K., & Miyake, Y. (1992). A comparative study of development and symptoms among disintegrative psychosis and infantile autism with and without speech loss. *Journal of Autism and Developmental Disorders, 22*, 175–188.

Joseph, A. B. (1994). Observations on the epidemiology of the delusional misidentification syndromes in the Boston metropolitan area: April 1983–June 1984. *Psychopathology, 27*, 150–153.

Kanner, L. (1943). Autistic disturbances of affective contact. *Nervous Child, 2*, 217–250.

Kanner, L. (1992). Follow-up study of 11 autistic children originally reported in 1943. *Focus on Autistic Behavior, 7*(5), 1–11.

Kauffman, J. M. (1993). *Characteristics of emotional and behavioral disorders of children and youth* (5th ed.). New York: Macmillan.

Konstantareas, M. M., & Homatidis, S. (1989). Assessing child symptom severity and stress in parents of autistic children. *Journal of Child Psychology and Psychiatry and Allied Disciplines, 30*, 459–470.

Kraepelin, E. (1896). *Psychiatrie.* Adulf. Leipzig: Meiner.

Krantz, P. J., MacDuff, M. T., & McClannahan, L. E. (1993). Programming participation in family activities for children with autism: Parents' use of photographic activity schedules. *Journal of Applied Behavior Analysis, 26*, 137–138.

Leboyer, M., Bouvard, M. P., Recasens, C., & Philippe, A. (1994). Differences between plasma N- and C-terminally directed b-endorphin immunoreactivity in infantile autism. *American Journal of Psychiatry, 151*, 1797–1801.

Lemanek, K. L., Stone, W. L., & Fishel, P. T. (1993). Parent-child interactions in handicapped preschoolers: The relation between parent behaviors and compliance. *Journal of Clinical Child Psychology, 22,* 68–77.

Levinson, L. L., & Reid, G. (1993). The effects of exercise intensity on the stereotypic behaviors of individuals with autism. *Adapted Physical Activity Quarterly, 10,* 255–268.

Loveland, K. A., McEvoy, R. E., & Tunali, B. (1990). Narrative story telling in autism and Down syndrome. *British Journal of Developmental Psychology, 8,* 9–23.

Mahler, M. (1952). On child psychosis and schizophrenia: Autistic and symbiotic infantile psychosis. *Psychoanalytic Study of the Child, 7,* 286–305.

Malhotra, S., & Singh, S. P. (1993). Disintegrative psychosis of childhood: An appraisal and case study. *Acta Paedopsychiatrica International Journal of Child and Adolescent Psychiatry, 56,* 37–40.

McClellan, J. M., & Werry, J. S. (1992). Schizophrenia. *Psychiatric Clinics of North America, 15*(1), 131–148.

McClellan, J., & Werry, J. (1994). Practice parameters for the assessment and treatment of children and adolescents with schizophrenia. *Journal of the American Academy of Child and Adolescent Psychiatry, 33,* 616–635.

McKenna, K., Gordon, C. T., & Rapoport, J. L. (1994). Childhood-onset schizophrenia: Timely neurobiological research. *Journal of the American Academy of Child and Adolescent Psychiatry, 33,* 771–781.

Menage, P., Thibault, G., Berthelemy, C., & Lelord, G. (1992). CD4 + CD45RA + T lymphocyte deficiency in autistic children: Effect of a pyridoxine-magnesium treatment. *Brain Dysfunction, 5,* 326–333.

Mesibov, G. B., & Stephens, J. (1990). Perceptions of popularity among a group of high-functioning adults with autism. *Journal of Autism and Developmental Disorders, 20,* 33–43.

Moreno, S. J., & Donellan, A. M. (1991). *High-functioning individuals with autism: Advice and information for parents and others who care.* Crown Point, IN: Maap Services.

Moss, H. A., Brouwers, P., Wolters, P. L., & Wiener, L. (1994). The development of a Q-sort behavioral rating procedure for pediatric HIV patients. *Journal of Pediatric Psychology, 19,* 27–46.

Museti, L., Albizzati, A., Grioni, A., & Rossetti, M. (1993). Autistic disorder associated with congenital HIV infection. *European Child and Adolescent Psychiatry, 2*(4), 221–225.

Myer, E. C., Tripathi, H. L., Brase, D. A., & Dewey, W. L. (1992). Elevated CSF beta-endorphin immunoreactivity in Rett's syndrome: Report of 158 cases and comparison with leukemic children. *Neurology, 42,* 357–360.

Myles, B. S., Anderson, J., Constant, J. A., & Simpson, R. L. (1989). Educational assessment of students with higher-functioning autistic disorder. *Focus on Autistic Behavior, 4*(1), 1–14.

Nelson, E. C., & Pribor, E. F. (1993). A calendar savant with autism and Tourette syndrome: Response to treatment and thoughts on the interrelationships of these conditions. *Annals of Clinical Psychiatry, 5,* 135–140.

Nientimp, E. G., & Cole, C. L. (1992). Teaching socially valid social interaction responses to students with severe disabilities in an integrated school setting. *Journal of School Psychology, 30,* 343–354.

Nigg, J. T., & Goldsmith, H. H. (1994). Genetics of personality disorders: Perspectives from personality and psychopathology research. *Psychological Bulletin, 115,* 346–380.

Norton, P., & Drew, C. J. (1994). Autism and potential family stressors. *American Journal of Family Therapy, 22,* 68–77.

Oades, R. D., Stern, L. M., Walker, M. K., & Clark, C. R. (1990). Event-related potentials and monoamines in autistic children on a clinical trial of fenfluramine. *International Journal of Psychophysiology, 8,* 197–212.

Ohtaki, E., Kawano, Y., Urabe, F., & Komori, H. (1992). The prevalence of Rett syndrome and infantile autism in Chikugo district, the southwestern area of Fukuoka prefecture, Japan. *Journal of Autism and Developmental Disorders, 22,* 452–454.

Osman, O. T., & Loschen, E. L. (1992). Self-injurious behavior in the developmentally disabled: Pharmacologic treatment. *Psychopharmacology Bulletin, 28,* 439–449.

Panksepp, J., & Lensing, P. (1991). A synopsis of an open-trial of naltrexone treatment of autism with four children. *Journal of Autism and Developmental Disorders, 21,* 243–249.

Plioplys, A. V., Greaves, A., Kazemi, K., & Silverman, E. (1994). Immunoglobin reactivity in autism and Rett's syndrome. *Developmental Brain Dysfunction, 7,* 12–16.

Potter, H. (1933). Schizophrenia in children. *American Journal of Psychiatry, 12,* 1253–1268.

Powers, S., Thibadeau, S., & Rose, K. (1992). Antecedent exercise and its effects on self-stimulation. *Behavioral Residential Treatment, 7,* 15–22.

Prior, M. (1989). Biological factors in childhood autism. *NIMHANS Journal, 7,* 91–101.

Ramm, S. (1990). The use of the duvet (quilt) for treatment of autistic, violent behaviors (an experiential account). *Journal of Autism and Developmental Disorders, 20,* 279–280.

Rapoport, J. L. (1994). Clozapine and child psychiatry. *Journal of Child and Adolescent Psychopharmacology, 4*(1), 1–3.

Reichelt, K. L., Knivsberg, A. M., Lind, G., & Nodland, M. (1991). Probable etiology and possible treatment of childhood autism. *Brain Dysfunction, 4*(6), 308–319.

Remschmidt, H. E., Schulz, E., Martin, M., & Warnke, A. (1994). Childhood-onset schizophrenia: History of the concept and recent studies. *Schizophrenia Bulletin, 20,* 727–745.

Ricks, D. (1989). Child autism: II. Differential diagnosis. *NIMHANS Journal, 7,* 71–75.

Ritvo, E. R., Freeman, B. J., Pingree, C., Mason-Brothers, A., Jorde, L., Jenson, W. R., McMahon, W. M., Petersen, P. B., Mo, A., & Ritvo, A. (1989). The UCLA-University of Utah epidemiologic survey of autism: Prevalence. *American Journal of Psychiatry, 146,* 194–199.

Rutter, M. (1991). Autism: Pathways from syndrome definition to pathogenesis. *Comprehensive Mental Health Care, 1*(1), 5–26.

Ryan, R. M. (1992). Treatment-resistant chronic mental illness: Is it Asperger's syndrome? *Hospital and Community Psychiatry, 43,* 807–811.

Sacks, O. (1993). A neurologist's notebook: An anthropologist on Mars. *The New Yorker,* December 27, 1993/January 3, 1994, pp. 106–125.

Sherman, J., Factor, D. C., Swinson, R., & Darjes, R. W. (1989). The effects of fenfluramine (hydrochloride) on the behaviors of fifteen autistic children. *Journal of Autism and Developmental Disorders, 19,* 533–543.

Siegel, B. V., Asarnow, R., Tanguay, P., & Call, J. D. (1992). Regional cerebral glucose metabolism and attention in adults with a history of childhood autism. *Journal of Neuropsychiatry and Clinical Neurosciences, 4*(4), 406–414.

Simpson, R. L. (1993). What about this facilitated communication? Or, to paraphrase George Bush and Bill Clinton, Is this another matter of trust? *Focus on Autistic Behavior, 8*(2), 12–15.

Smith, I. M., & Bryson, S. E. (1994). Imitation and action in autism: A critical review. *Psychological Bulletin, 116,* 259–273.

Spencer, E. K., & Campbell, M. (1994). Children with schizophrenia: Diagnosis, phenomenology, and pharmacotherapy. *Schizophrenia Bulletin, 20,* 713–725.

Stahmer, A. C., & Schreibman, L. (1992). Teaching children with autism appropriate play in unsupervised environments using a self-management treatment package. *Journal of Applied Behavior Analysis, 25,* 447–459.

Sue, D., & Sue, S. (1990). *Understanding abnormal behavior* (3rd ed.). Boston: Houghton Mifflin.

Szatmari, P. (1991). Asperger's syndrome: Diagnosis, treatment, and outcome. *Psychiatric Clinics of North America, 14,* 81–93.

Szatmari, P., Archer, L., Fisman, S., & Steiner, D. L. (1994). Parent and teacher agreement in the assessment of pervasive developmental disorders. *Journal of Autism and Developmental Disorders, 24,* 703–717.

Szatmari, P., Bartolucci, G., & Bremner, R. (1989). Asperger's syndrome and autism: Comparison of early history and outcome. *Developmental Medicine and Child Neurology, 31,* 709–720.

Szempruch, J., & Jacobson, J. W. (1993). Evaluating facilitated communications of people with developmental disabilities. *Research in Developmental Disabilities, 14*(4), 253–264.

Taiminen, T. (1994). Asperger's syndrome or schizophrenia: Is differential diagnosis necessary for adult patients? *Nordic Journal of Psychiatry, 48,* 325–328.

Thompson, T. (1993, January). A reign of error. Facilitated communication. *Vanderbilt University Kennedy Center News,* No. 22, 3–5.

Tirosh, E., & Canby, J. (1993). Autism with hyperlexia: A distinct syndrome? *American Journal on Mental Retardation, 98,* 84–92.

Tridon, P., Schweitzer, F., & Six, V. (1989). About Rett's syndrome. *Annales Medico Psychologiques, 147,* 245–250.

U.S. Department of Education. (1991, August 19). Notice of proposed rulemaking. *Federal Register, 56*(160), 41271.

Van-Lancker, D., Cornelius, C., & Needleman, R. (1991). Comprehension of verbal terms for emotions in normal, autistic, and schizophrenic children. *Developmental Neuropsychology, 7,* 1–18.

Volkmar, F. R. (1992). Childhood disintegrative disorder: Issues for DSM-IV. *Journal of Autism and Developmental Disorders, 22,* 625–642.

Volkmar, F. R., Klin, A., Siegel, B., & Szatmari, P., (1994). *American Journal of Psychiatry, 151,* 1361–1367.

Volkmar, F. R., Szatmari, P., & Sparrow, S. S. (1993). Sex differences in pervasive developmental disorders. *Journal of Autism and Developmental Disorders, 23,* 579–591.

Weininger, O. (1993). Attachment, affective contact, and autism. *Psychoanalytic Inquiry, 13,* 49–62.

Wenk, G. L., Naidu, S., Casanova, M. F., & Kitt, C. A. (1991). Altered neurochemical markers in Rett's syndrome. *Neurology, 41,* 1753–1756.

Wheeler, D. L., Jacobson, J. W., Paglieri, R. A., & Schwartz, A. A. (1993). An experimental assessment of facilitated communication. *Mental Retardation, 31,* 49–60.

Williams, D. (1992). *Nobody nowhere: The extraordinary autobiography of an autistic.* New York: Avon Books.

Zimmerman, D. P. (1994). Bruno Bettelheim: The mysterious other: Historical reflections on the treatment of childhood psychosis. *Psychoanalytic Review, 81,* 411–450.

Zissermann, L. (1992). The effects of deep pressure on self-stimulating behaviors in a child with autism and other disabilities. *American Journal of Occupational Therapy, 46,* 547–551.

CHAPTER 12

Achenbach, T. M. (1966). The classification of children's psychiatric symptoms: A factor analytic study. *Psychological Monographs: General and Applied, 615,* 1–37.

Achenbach, T. M. (1974). *Developmental psychopathology.* New York: Ronald Press.

Achenbach, T. M. (1978). The Child Behavior Profile: 1. Boys aged 6–11. *Journal of Clinical and Consulting Psychology, 46,* 478–488.

Achenbach, T. M. (1980). The DSM III classification of psychiatric disorders in infancy, childhood, and adolescence. *Journal of the American Academy of Child Psychiatry, 19,* 395–412.

Achenbach, T. M. (1982). *Developmental psychopathology* (2nd ed.). New York: Wiley.

Achenbach, T. M. (1985). *Assessment and taxonomy of child and adolescent psychopathology.* Beverly Hills, CA: Sage.

Achenbach, T. M., & Edelbrock, C. S. (1978). The classification of child psychopathology: A review and analysis of empirical efforts. *Journal of Consulting and Clinical Psychology, 78,* 1275–1301.

Achenbach, T. M., & Edelbrock, C. S. (1979). The Child Behavior Profile: 11. Boys aged 12–16 and girls 6–11 and 12–16. *Journal of Consulting and Clinical Psychology, 47,* 223–233.

American Psychiatric Association. (1952). *Diagnostic and statistical manual of mental disorders.* Washington, DC: Author.

American Psychiatric Association. (1968). *Diagnostic and statistical manual of mental disorders* (2nd ed.). Washington, DC: Author.

American Psychiatric Association. (1980). *Diagnostic and statistical manual of mental disorders* (3rd ed.). Washington, DC: Author.

American Psychiatric Association. (1987). *Diagnostic and statistical manual of mental disorders,* (3rd ed., rev.). Washington, DC: Author.

American Psychiatric Association. (1994). *Diagnostic and statistical manual of mental disorders* (4th ed.). Washington, DC: Author.

Bellack, A. S., Hersen, M., & Kazdin, A. E. (1982). *International handbook of behavior modification and therapy.* New York: Plenum.

Bijou, S. W., & Peterson, R. F. (1971). Functional analysis in the assessment of children. In P. McReynolds (Ed.), *Advances in psychological assessment.* Palo Alto, CA: Science and Behavior Books.

Blashfield, R. K. (1984). *The classification of psychopathology: Neo-Kraepelinian and quantitative approaches.* New York: Plenum.

Blashfield, R. K., & Draguns, J. G. (1976a). Evaluation criteria for psychiatric classification. *Journal of Abnormal Psychology, 85,* 1940–1950.

Blashfield, R. K., & Draguns, J. G. (1976b). Toward a taxonomy of psychopathology: The purpose of psychiatric classification. *British Journal of Psychiatry, 129,* 1574–1583.

Bridgman, P. W. (1927). *The logic of modern physics.* New York: Macmillan.

Brunner, J. S. (1963). *On knowing: Essays for the left hand.* Cambridge, MA: Harvard University Press.

Brunner, J. S., Goodnow, J. J., & Austin, G. A. (1956). *Study of thinking.* New York: Wiley.

Cantwell, D. P., & Baker, L. (1989). Stability and natural history of DSM-III childhood diagnoses. *Journal of the American Academy of Child and Adolescent Psychiatry, 28,* 691–700.

Cantwell, D. P., Russell, A. T., Mattison, R., & Will, L. (1979). A comparison of the DSM-II and DSM-III in the diagnosis of childhood psychiatric diagnosis. 1. Agreement with expected diagnosis. *Archives of General Psychiatry, 36,* 1208–1213.

Caplan, P. J. (1995). *They say you're crazy: How the world's most powerful psychiatrists decide who is normal.* Reading, MA: Addison-Wesley.

Carey, G., & Gottesman, I. I. (1978). Reliability and validity in binary ratings. *Archives of General Psychiatry, 35,* 1454–1459.

Carson, R. C. (1991). Dilemmas in the pathway of the DSM-IV. *Journal of Abnormal Psychology, 100,* 302–307.

Carter, C. (1987). *School psychologists' perceptions of internalizing and externalizing behaviorally disordered children.* Unpublished doctoral dissertation, University of Utah.

Cerreto, M. C., & Tuma, J. M. (1977). Distribution of DSM II diagnoses in a child psychiatric setting. *Journal of Abnormal Child Psychology, 5,* 147–155.

Chess, S., & Hassibi, K. (1978). *Principles of child psychiatry.* New York: Plenum.

Cromwell, R. L., Blashfield, R. K., & Strauss, J. S. (1975). Criteria for classification systems. In N. Hobbs (Ed.), *Issues in the classification of children* (Vol. 1). San Francisco: Jossey-Bass.

Cullinan, D., Epstein, M. H., & McLinden, D. (1986). Status and change in state administrative definitions of behavior disorder. *School Psychology Review, 15,* 383–392.

DeMyer, M. K., Barton, S., DeMyer, W. E., Norton, J. A., Allen, J., & Steele, R. (1973). Prognosis in autism: A follow-up study. *Journal of Autism and Childhood Schizophrenia, 3,* 199–246.

Draguns, J. G., & Phillips, L. (1971). *Psychiatric classification and diagnosis: An overview and critique.* Morristown, NJ: General Learning Press.

Dreger, R. M. (1982). The classification of children and their emotional problems. *Clinical Psychology Review, 2,* 349–385.

Drew, C. J., Hardman, M. L., & Logan, D. R. (1996). *Mental retardation: A life cycle approach* (6th ed.). Englewood Cliffs, NJ: Prentice Hall.

Education for All Handicapped Children Act of 1975 (P. L. 94–142).

Faust, D., & Miner, R. A. (1986). The empiricist and his new clothes: DSM-III in perspective. *American Journal of Psychiatry, 143,* 962–967.

Fernando, T., Mellsop, G., Nelson, K., Peace, K., & Wilson, J. (1986). The reliability of Axis V of the DSM-III. *American Journal of Psychiatry, 143,* 752–755.

Fish, B. (1969). Limitation of the new nomenclature for children's disorders. *International Journal of Psychiatry, 7,* 393–398.

Foa, E. B., & Kozak, M. J. (1995). DSM-IV field trial: Obsessive-compulsive disorder. *American Journal of Psychiatry, 152,* 90–96.

Foster, G. G., Ysseldyke, J. E., & Reese, J. (1975). I never would have seen it if I hadn't believed it. *Exceptional Children, 41,* 469–474.

Gallagher, J. J. (1972). The special education contract for mildly handicapped children. *Exceptional Children, 38,* 527–535.

Gallagher, J. J., Forsythe, P., Ringelheim, D., & Weintraub, F. J. (1975). Funding patterns and labeling. In N. Hobbs (Ed.), *Issues in the classification of children* (Vol. 1). San Francisco: Jossey-Bass.

Geist, J. H. (1990). Computers and psychiatric diagnosis. In D. Baskin (Ed.), *Computer applications in psychiatry and psychology* (pp. 21–42). New York: Brunner/Mazel

Gelfand, D. M., & Hartmann, D. P. (1984). *Child behavior analysis and therapy* (2nd ed.). New York: Pergamon Press.

Goldfried, M. R., & Kent, R. N. (1972). Traditional versus behavioral assessment: A comparison of methodological and theoretical assumption. *Psychological Bulletin, 77,* 409–420.

Group for the Advancement of Psychiatry (GAP). (1974). *Psychopathological disorders in childhood: Theoretical considerations and a proposed classification.* New York: Jason Aronson.

Guskin, S. L., Bartel, N. R., & MacMillan, D. L. (1975). Perspectives of the labeled child. In N. Hobbs (Ed.), *Issues in the classification of children* (Vol. 1). San Francisco: Jossey-Bass.

Hallahan, D. P., & Kauffman, J. M. (1986). *Exceptional children* (3rd ed.). Englewood Cliffs, NJ: Prentice-Hall.

Hartmann, D. P., Roper, B. L., & Bradford, D. C. (1979). Some relationships between behavioral and traditional assessment. *Journal of Behavioral Assessment, 1,* 3–21.

Helzer, J. E., Robins, L. N., Taibleson, M., Woodruff, R. A., Reich, T., & Wish, E. D. (1977). Reliability of psychiatric diagnosis. *Archives of General Psychiatry, 34,* 129–132.

Hempel, C. G. (1965). *Aspects of scientific explanation and other essays in the philosophy of science.* New York: Free Press.

Hobbs, N. (1975a). *The future of children.* San Francisco: Jossey-Bass.

Hobbs, N. (Ed.). (1975b). *Issues in the classification of children* (Vols. 1 and 2). San Francisco: Jossey-Bass.

Howell, K. W., Kaplan, J. S., & O'Connell, Y. O. (1979). *Evaluating exceptional children: A task analysis approach.* Columbus, OH: Merrill.

Jampala, V. C., Sierles, F. S., & Taylor, M. A. (1986). Consumers' views of DSM-III: Attitudes and practices of U.S. psychiatrists and 1984 graduating residents. *American Journal of Psychiatry, 143,* 148–153.

Jensen, P. S., Koretz, D., Locke, B., Schneider, S., Radke-Yarrow, M., Richters, J., & Rumsey, J. (1993). Child and adolescent psychopathology research: Problems and prospects for the 1990s. *Journal of Abnormal Child Psychology, 21,* 551–580.

Jenson, W. R. (1985). *Severely emotionally disturbed vs. behavior disorders: Consideration of a label change* (Field Report #2, University of Utah Graduate School of Education Report Series). Salt Lake City: University of Utah.

Jones, R. L. (1972). Labels and the stigma in special education. *Exceptional Children, 38,* 553–564.

Kanfer, F. H. (1985). Target selection for clinical change programs. *Behavioral Assessment, 7,* 7–20.

Kanfer, F. H., & Saslow, G. (1965). Behavioral analysis: An alternative to diagnostic classification. *Archives of General Psychiatry, 12,* 848–853.

Kauffman, J. M. (1982). Social policy issues in special education and related services for emotionally disturbed children and youth. In M. M. Noel & N. G. Haring (Eds.), *Issues in educating the emotionally disturbed: Identification and program planning* (Vol. 1). Seattle: University of Washington Press.

Kazdin, A. E. (1985). Selection of target behaviors: The relationship of the treatment focus to clinical dysfunction. *Behavioral Assessment, 7,* 33–47.

Keller, M. B., Klein, D. N., Hirshfeld, R. M., Kocsis, J. H., McCullough, M., et al. (1995). Results of the DSM-IV mood disorders field trial. *American Journal of Psychiatry, 152,* 843–849.

Kendall, P. C., & Urbain, E. S. (1981). Cognitive-behavioral intervention with a hyperactive girl: Evaluation via behavioral observation and cognitive performance. *Behavioral Assessment, 3,* 345–357.

Kendall, R. E. (1975). *The role of diagnosis in psychiatry.* Oxford: Blackwell.

Kraeplin, E. (1899). *Psychiatrie.* Leipzig: Barth.

Kolstoe, O. (1972). Programs for the retarded: A reply to the critics. *Exceptional Children, 39,* 51–56.

Krasner, W. (1976). *Labeling the children.* Washington, DC: U.S. Department of Health, Education and Welfare.

Kratochwill, T. R. (1985). Selection of target behaviors in behavioral consultation. *Behavioral Assessment, 7,* 49–61.

La Bruzza, A. L., & Mendez-Villarnubia, J. M. (1994). *Using DSM-IV: A clinician's guide to psychiatric diagnosis.* Northvale, NJ: J. Aronson.

Levitas, A., Haggerman, R. J., Braden, M., Rimiand B., McBogg, P., & Matus, I. (1983). Autism and the fragile X syndrome. *Journal of Developmental and Behavioral Pediatrics, 4,* 151–158.

Liebert, R. M., Poulos, R. W., & Strauss, G. D. (1974). *Developmental psychology.* Englewood Cliffs, NJ: Prentice-Hall.

Macmillan, D. L., & Kavale, K. A. (1986). Educational intervention. In H. C. Quay & J. S. Werry (Eds.), *Psychopathological disorders of childhood* (3rd ed., pp. 583–621). New York: Wiley.

Mahoney, M. (1974). *Cognition and behavior modification.* Cambridge, MA: Ballinger.

Martin, R. (1977). Minimum level of education. *Law and Behavior, 2,* 2.

Maser, J. D., Kaelber, C., & Weise, R. (1991). International use and attitudes toward DSM-III and DSM-III-R: Growing consensus in psychiatric classification. *Journal of Abnormal Psychology, 100,* 271–179.

Mash, E. J. (1985). Some comments on target selection in behavior therapy. *Behavioral Assessment, 7,* 63–78.

Mattison, R., Cantwell, D. P., Russell, A. T., & Will, L. A. (1979). A comparison of DSM-II and DSM-III in the diagnosis of childhood psychiatric disorders: II. Interrater agreement. *Archives of General Psychiatry, 36,* 1217–1222.

Meichenbaum, D. (1977). *Cognitive-behavior modification: An integrated approach.* New York: Plenum .

Mercer, J. R. (1975). Psychological assessment and the rights of children. In N. Hobbs (Ed.), *Issues in the classification of children* (Vol. 1). San Francisco: Jossey-Bass.

Morey, L. C. (1991). Classification of mental disorder as a collection of hypothetical constructs. *Journal of Abnormal Psychology, 100,* 289–293.

Morris, D. P., Soroker, E., & Burruss, G. (1954). Follow-up studies of shy, withdrawn children. *American Journal of Orthopsychiatry, 24,* 743–754.

Morris, H. H., Escoll, P. J., & Wexler, R. (1956). Aggressive behavior disorders of childhood: A follow-up study. *American Journal of Psychiatry, 112,* 991–997.

Morris, R. J., & Kratochwill, R. T. (1983). *The practice of child therapy.* New York: Pergamon Press.

Mutimer, D., & Rosemier, R. A. (1967). Behavior problems of children viewed by teachers and children themselves. *Journal of Consulting Psychology, 31,* 583–587.

Nelson, R. O. (1983). Behavior assessment: Past, present, and future. *Behavioral Assessment, 5,* 195–206.

Patterson, G. R. (1964). An empirical approach to the classification of disturbed children. *Journal of Clinical Psychology, 20,* 326–337.

Patterson, G. R. (1983). *Longitudinal assessment of fourth grade boys.* (National Institute of Mental Health Research Grant). Eugene: Oregon Social Learning Center.

Peterson, D. R. (1961). Behavior problems of middle childhood. *Journal of Consulting Psychology, 25,* 205–209.

Quay, H. C. (1964). Dimensions of personality in delinquent boys as inferred from the factor analysis of case history data. *Child Development, 35,* 477–484.

Quay, H. C. (1979). Classification. In H. C. Quay & J. S. Werry (Eds.), *Psychopathological disorders of childhood* (2nd ed.). New York: Wiley.

Quay, H. C., & Peterson, D. R. (1975). *Manual for the problem behavior checklist.* Unpublished manuscript.

Quay, H. C., & Quay, L. C. (1965). Behavior problems in early adolescence. *Child Development, 36,* 215–220.

Rapoport, J. L. (1996). *DSM-IV training guide for diagnosis of childhood disorders.* New York: Brunner/Mazel.

Ritvo, E. R., Freeman, B. J., Mason-Brothers, A., Mo, A., & Ritvo, A. (1985). Concordance for the syndrome of autism in 40 pairs of afflicted twins. *American Journal of Psychiatry, 142,* 74–77.

Robins, L. N. (1966). *Deviant children grown up.* Baltimore: Williams & Wilkins.

Robins, L. N. (1979). Follow-up studies. In H. C. Quay & J. S. Werry (Eds.), *Psychopathological disorders of childhood* (2nd ed.). New York: Wiley.

Rosenthal, R. (1987). Pygmalion effects: Existence, magnitude, and social importance. *Educational Research, 16,* 37–41.

Rosenthal, R. L., & Jacobson, L. (1968). *Pygmalion in the classroom: Teacher expectation and pupils' intellectual development.* New York: Holt, Rinehart & Winston.

Ross, D. M., & Ross, S. A. (1982). *Hyperactivity: Current issues, research, and theory.* New York: Wiley.

Rutter, M. (1965). Classification and categorization in child psychiatry. *Journal of Child Psychology and Psychiatry, 6,* 71–83.

Rutter, M., & Shaffer, D. (1980). DSM III: A step forward or back in terms of the classification of child psychiatric disorders. *Journal of the American Academy of Child Psychiatry, 19,* 371–394.

Shoben, E. J. (1966). Personal worth in educational counseling. In J. D. Krumboltz (Ed.), *Revolutions in counseling.* Boston: Houghton Mifflin.

Sokal, R. R. (1974). Classification: Purposes, principles, progress, prospects. *Science, 185,* 1115–1123.

Spitzer, R. L., & Endicott, J. (1978). Medical and mental disorders: Proposed definition and criteria. In R. L. Spitzer & D. F. Klein (Eds.), *Critical issues in psychiatric diagnosis.* New York: Raven Press.

Spitzer, R. L., & Fleiss, J. L. (1974). A re-analysis of the reliability of psychiatric diagnosis. *British Journal of Psychiatry, 125,* 341–347.

Spitzer, R. L., Sheehy, M., & Endicott, J. (1977). DSM III: Guided principles. In V. Rakoff, H. Stancer, & H. B. Kewards (Eds.), *Psychiatric diagnosis*. New York: Brunner/Mazel.

Stouffer, G. A. (1952). Behavior problems of children as viewed by teachers and mental hygienists. *Mental Hygiene, 36,* 271–285.

Strober, M., Green, J., & Carlson, G. (1981). The reliability of psychiatric diagnosis in hospitalized adolescents: Interrater agreement using the DSM III. *Archives of General Psychiatry, 38,* 141–145.

Sundberg, N. D. (1977). *Assessment of persons*. Englewood Cliffs, NJ: Prentice-Hall.

Taylor, C. B. (1983). DSM-III and behavioral assessment. *Behavioral Assessment, 5,* 5–14.

Tryon, W. (1976). A system of behavioral diagnosis. *Professional Psychology, 4,* 495–506.

Ullmann, L. P., & Krasner, L. (1965). *Case studies in behavior modification*. New York: Holt, Rinehart & Winston.

Ullmann, L. P., & Krasner, L. (1969). *A psychological approach to abnormal behavior*. Englewood Cliffs, NJ: Prentice-Hall.

U.S. Department of Education. (1985). *Special study on terminology: Comprehensive review and evaluation report*. Washington, DC: U.S. Government Printing Office.

U.S. Department of Education. (1991). *Digest of education statistics: 1991*. Washington, DC: Government Printing Office.

Volkman, F. R., Kline, A., Siegil, B., Szatmori, P., Lord, C., Campbell, Freeman, B. J., et al. (1994). Field trial for autistic disorder in DSM-IV. *American Journal of Psychiatry, 151,* 1361–1367.

Walker, H. M. (1970). *Walker Problem Behavior Identification Checklist*. Los Angeles: Western Psychological Services.

Walker, H. M. (1982). *Walker Problem Behavior Identification Checklist—revised*. Los Angeles: Western Psychological Services.

Walker, H. M., O'Neill, R., Shinn, M., Ramsey, B., Patterson, G. R., Reid, J., & Capaldi, D. (1986). *Longitudinal assessment and long term follow up of antisocial behavior in fourth grade boys: Rationale, methodology, measures, and results*. Unpublished manuscript, Oregon Social Learning Center, Eugene.

Walker, H. M., Reavis, H. K., Rhode, G., & Jenson, W. R. (1985). A conceptual model for delivery of behavioral services to behavior disordered children in a continuum of educational settings. In A. Kazdin & P. Bornstein (Eds.), *Handbook of clinical behavior therapy with children*. Homewood, IL: Dorsey Press.

Ward, C. H., Beck, A. T., Mendelson, M., Mock, J. E., & Erbaugh, J. K. (1962). The psychiatric nomenclature. *Archives of General Psychiatry, 7,* 198–205.

Weiss, G., & Hechtman, L. T. (1986). *Hyperactive children grown up: Empirical findings and theoretical considerations*. New York: Guilford Press.

Werner, E. E., & Smith, R. W. (1992). *Overcoming the odds: High risk children from birth to adulthood*. Ithaca, NY: Cornell University Press.

Werry, J. S., Methven, R. J., Fitzpatrick, J., & Dixon, H. (1983). The interrater reliability of DSM-III in children. *Journal of Abnormal and Child Psychology, 11,* 341–354.

Wickman, E. K. (1928). *Children's behavior and teachers' attitudes*. New York: Commonwealth Fund.

Wilson, F. E., & Evans, I. M. (1983). The reliability of target-behavior selection in behavioral assessment. *Behavioral Assessment, 5,* 15–32.

Wing, J. K. (1978). *Reasoning about madness*. London: Oxford University Press.

Wirt, R. D., Lachar, D., Klinedinst, J. K., & Seat, P. D. (1977). *Multidimensional description of child personality: A manual for the Personality Inventory for Children*. Los Angeles: Western Psychological Services.

World Health Organization (WHO). (1977). *International classification of diseases* (9th ed.). Geneva: Author.

World Health Organization (1992). *The ICD–10 classification of mental and behavioural disorders: Clinical descriptions and diagnostic guidelines*. Geneva: Author.

World Health Organization (1993). *The ICD–10 classification of mental and behavioural disorders: Diagnostic criteria for research*. Geneva: Author.

Yates, A. J. (1970). *Behavior therapy*. New York: Wiley.

Ysseldyke, J. E., & Foster, G. C. (1978). Bias in teacher's observation of emotionally disturbed and learning disabled children. *Exceptional Children, 44,* 613–615.

Zigler, E., & Phillips, L. (1960). Social effectiveness and symptomatic behaviors. *Journal of Abnormal and Social Psychology, 62,* 231–238.

Zigler, E., & Phillips, L. (1961). Psychiatric diagnosis: A critique. *Journal of Abnormal and Social Psychology, 63,* 607–618.

Zubin, J. (1967). Classification of the behavior disorders. *Annual Review of Psychology, 18,* 373–406.

CHAPTER 13

Achenbach, T. M. (1991). *Manual for the Child Behavior Checklist and Revised Child Behavior Profile*. Burlington: University of Vermont, Department of Psychiatry.

Achenbach, T. M. (1992). *Manual for the Child Behavior Checklist/2–3 and the 1992 Profile*. Burlington: University of Vermont, Department of Psychiatry.

Aiken, L. R. (1979). *Psychological testing and assessment*. Boston: Allyn & Bacon.

Alessi, G. F. (1980). Behavioral observation for the school psychologist: Response-discrepancy model. *School Psychology Review, 9,* 31–45.

Althauser, R. P., & Herberlein, T. A. (1970). Validity and the multitrait multimethod matrix. In E. F. Borgatta & G. W. Bohrnstedt (Eds.), *Sociological Methodology*. San Francisco: Jossey-Bass.

Anastasi, A. (1988). *Psychological testing* (6th ed.). New York, Macmillan.

Ando, H., & Yoshimura, I. (1970). Prevalence of maladaptive behavior in retarded children as a function of IQ and age. *Journal of Abnormal Child Psychology* (3d ed.). New York: Wiley.

Bardos, A. N. (1993). Human Figure Drawings: Abusing the abused. *School Psychology Quarterly, 8,* 177–181.

Barkley, R. A. (1990). *Attention-deficit hyperactivity disorder: A handbook for diagnosis and treatment*. New York: Guilford Press.

Bayley, N. (1970). Development of mental abilities. In P. H. Mussen (Ed.), *Carmichael's manual of child psychology* (3rd ed.). New York: Wiley.

Bellak, L. (1954). *The Thematic Apperception Test and the Children's Apperception Test in clinical use*. New York: Grune & Stratton.

Bem, D. J., & Allen, A. (1974). On predicting some of the people some of the time: The search for cross-situational consistencies in behavior. *Psychological Review, 81,* 506–520.

Bierman, K. L., & Schwartz, L. A. (1986). Clinical child interviews: Approaches and developmental considerations. *Journal of Child and Adolescent Psychotherapy, 3,* 267–278.

Binet, A., & Simon, T. (1905). Methodes nouvelles pour le diagnostic du niveau intellectuel des anormaux. *L'Annee Psychologique, 11,* 191–244.

Bornstein, P. H., Hamilton, S. C., & Bornstein, M. T. (1986). Self-monitoring procedures. In A. R. Ciminero, K. S. Calhoun, & H. E. Adams (Eds.), *Handbook of behavioral assessment* (2nd ed.). New York: Wiley.

Bowers, K.S. (1973). Situationalism in psychology: An analysis and a critique. *Psychological Review, 80,* 307–336.

Brigance, A. H. (1978). *Brigance Diagnostic Inventory of Early Development.* Woburn, MA: Curriculum Associates.

Broden, M., Hall, R. V., & Mitts, B. (1971). The effect of self-recording on the classroom behavior of two eighth grade students. *Journal of Applied Behavior Analysis, 4,* 191–200.

Brown, L. J., Black, D. D., & Downs, J. C. (1984). *School social skills.* East Aurora, NY: Slosson Educational Publications.

Carmines, E. G., & Zeller, R. A. (1979). Reliability and validity assessment. In J. L. Sullivan (Ed.), *Series: Quantitative applications in social sciences.* Beverly Hills, CA: Sage.

Carr, S. C., & Punzo, R. P. (1993). The effects of self-monitoring of academic accuracy and productivity on the performance of students with behavioral disorders. *Behavior Disorders, 18,* 241–250.

Chinn, P. C., & Hughes, S. E. (1987). Representation of minority students in special education classes. *Remedial and Special Education, 8,* 195–202.

Cole, P. (1978). Personal communication.

Conners, C. K. (1969). A teacher rating scale for use in drug studies with children. *American Journal of Psychiatry, 126,* 884–888.

Cronbach, L. J. (1960). *Essentials of psychological testing* (2nd ed.). New York: Harper & Row.

Cronbach, L. J. (1990). *Essentials of psychological testing* (3rd ed.). New York: Harper & Row.

Cummings, K. K. (1988). *Teachers' guide to behavioral interventions.* Columbia, MO: Hawthorne Educationals Services.

Dahlstrom, W. G. (1993). Tests: Small samples, large consequences. *American Psychologist, 48,* 393–399.

Demaray, M. K., Ruffalo, S. L., Carlson, J., Olson, A. E., McManus, S. M., & Leventhal, A. (1995). Social skills assessment: A comparative evaluation of six published rating scales. *School Psychology Review, 24,* 648–671.

DeMyer, M. K., Hingtgen, J. N., & Jackson, R. K. (1981). Infantile autism reviewed: A decade of research. *Schizophrenia Bulletin, 7,* 388–451.

Deno, S. L. (1980). Direct observation approach to measuring classroom behavior. *Exceptional Children, 46,* 396–399.

Dunn, L. M. (1968). Special education for the mildly retarded: Is much of it justified? *Exceptional Children, 35,* 5–22.

Dunn, L. M., & Markwardt, F. C. (1970). *Peabody individual achievement test.* Circle Pines, MN: American Guidance Service.

Ebel, R. L. (1971). Criterion-referenced measurements: Limitations. *School Review, 79,* 282–288.

Edelbrock, C., & Costello, A. J. (1990). Structured interviews for children and adolescents. In G. Goldstein & M. Hersen (Eds.), *Handbook of psychological assessment* (pp. 308–323). New York: Pergamon Press.

Edelbrock, C., Costello, A. J., Dulcan, M. K., Kalas, R., & Conover, N. C. (1985). Age differences in the reliability of the psychiatric interview of the child. *Child Development, 56,* 265–275.

Ekenhammer, B. (1974). Interactionism in personality from a historical perspective. *Psychological Bulletin, 81,* 1026–1048.

Epstein, S. (1966). Some theoretical considerations on the nature of ambiguity and the use of stimulus dimensions in projective techniques. *Journal of Consulting Psychology, 30,* 183–192.

Epstein, S. (1979). The stability of behavior: I. On predicting most of the people much of the time. *Journal of Personality and Social Psychology, 37,* 1097–1126.

Evans, I. M., & Nelson, R. O. (1977). Assessment of child behavior problems. In A. R. Ciminero, K. S. Calhoun, & H. E. Adams (Eds.), *Handbook of behavior assessment.* New York: Wiley.

Evans, I. M., & Nelson, R. O. (1986). Assessment of children. In A. R. Ciminero, K. S. Calhoun, & H. E. Adams (Eds.), *Handbook of behavioral assessment.* New York: Wiley.

Exner, J. E., Jr. (1969). *The Rorschach systems.* New York: Grune & Stratton.

Exner, J. E., Jr. (1974). *The Rorschach: A comprehensive system.* New York: Wiley.

Foster, S. L., & Cone, J. D. (1986). Design and use of direct observation. In A. R. Ciminero, K. S. Calhoun, & H. E. Adams (Eds.), *Handbook of behavioral assessment* (2nd ed.). New York: Wiley.

Gelfand, D. M., & Hartmann, D. P. (1985). *Child behavior analysis and therapy* (2nd ed.). New York: Pergamon Press.

Gittelman, R. (1986). *Anxiety disorders of childhood.* New York: Guilford Press.

Gittelman-Klein, R. (1978). Validity of projective tests for psychodiagnosis for children. In R. L. Spitzer & D. F. Klein (Eds.), *Critical issues in psychiatric diagnosis.* New York: Raven Press.

Gittelman-Klein, R. (1980). The role of tests for differential diagnosis in child psychiatry. *Journal of the American Academy of Child Psychiatry, 19,* 413–438.

Glaser, R. (1963). Instructional technology and the measurement of learning outcome: Some questions. *American Psychologist, 18,* 519–522.

Goh, D. S., & Fuller, G. B. (1983). Current practices in the assessment of personality and behavior by school psychologists. *School Psychology Review, 12,* 240–243.

Goldfried, M. R., & Linehan, M. M. (1977). Basic issues in behavioral assessment. In A. R. Ciminero, K. S. Calhoun, & H. E. Adams (Eds.), *Handbook of behavioral assessment.* New York: Wiley-Interscience.

Goldstein, G., & Hersen, M. (1990). Historial perspectives. In G. Goldstein & M. Hersen (Eds.), *Handbook of psychological assessment* (2nd ed., pp. 3–17). New York: Pergamon.

Good, R. H., & Salvia, J. (1988). Curriculum bias in published, norm referenced reading tests: Demonstrable effects. *School Psychology Review, 17,* 51–60.

Graham, J. R., & Lilly, R. S. (1984). *Psychological testing*. Engelwood Cliffs, NJ: Prentice-Hall.

Gresham, F. M. (1993). "What's wrong with this picture? Response to Motta et al.'s review of human figure drawing. *School Psychology Quarterly*, 8, 182–186.

Gresham, F. M., & Ellott, S. N. (1990). *Social skills rating system manual*. Circle Pines, MN: American Guidance Service.

Gronlund, N. E. (1993). *How to make achievement tests and assessments* (5th ed.). Boston: Allyn & Bacon.

Hallahan, D. P., & Kaufmann, J. M. (1986). *Exceptional children* (3rd. ed.). Englewood Cliffs, NJ: Prentice-Hall.

Halpren, F. (1953). *A clinical approach to children's Rorschachs*. New York: Grune & Stratton.

Harris, F. C., & Lahey, B. B. (1982). Subject reactivity in direct observation assessment: A review and critical analysis. *Clinical Psychology Review*, 2, 523–538.

Hartmann, D. P., Roper, B. L., & Bradford, D. C. (1979). Some relationships between behavioral and traditional assessment. *Journal of Behavioral Assessment*, 1, 3–21.

Haynes, S. N. (1978). *Principles of behavioral assessment*. New York: Gardner Press.

Haynes, S. N., & Jensen, B. J. (1979). The interview as a behavioral assessment instrument. *Behavioral Assessment*, 1, 97–106.

Herbert, E. W., & Baer, D. M. (1972). Training parents as behavior modifiers: Self-recording of contingent attention. *Journal of Applied Behavior Analysis*, 5, 139–149.

Herjanic, B., & Reich, W. (1982). Development of a structured psychiatric interview for children: Agreement between child and parent on individual symptoms. *Journal of Abnormal Child Psychology*, 10, 307–324.

Hetherington, E. M., & Martin, B. (1979). Family interaction. In H. C. Quay & J. S. Werry (Eds.), *Psychopathological disorders of childhood*. New York: Wiley.

Hinshaw, S. P. (1992). Externalizing behavior problems and academic under-achievement in childhood and adolescence: Causal relationships and underlying mechanisms. *Psychological Bulletin*, 111, 127–155.

Hodges, K., Kline, J., Kashani, D., Cytyrn, L., Stern, L., & McKnew, D. (1982). *Child assessment survey*. Unpublished manuscript, University of Missouri.

Hodges, K., Kline, J., Stern, L., Cytryn, L., & McKnew, D. (1982). The development of a child assessment interview for research and clinical use. *Journal of Abnormal Child Psychology*, 10, 173–189.

Holtzman, W. H. (1993). An unjustified, sweeping indictment by Motta et al. of Human Figure Drawings for assessing psychological functioning. *School Psychology Quarterly*, 8, 189–190.

Hughes, J. N., & Baker, D. (1990). *The clinical child interview*. New York: Guilford Press.

Jenkins, J. R., & Pany, D. (1978). Standardized achievement tests: How useful for special education? *Exceptional Children*, 7, 448–453.

Jensen, A. R. (1980). *Bias in mental testing*. New York: Free Press.

Jenson, W. R., & Morgan, D. (1990). *Handbook for assessing behaviorally disordered students*. Salt Lake City: Utah State Office of Education.

Johnson, S. M., & Bolstad, O. D. (1973). Methodological issues in naturalistic observation: Some problems and solutions for field research.

In L. A. Hamerlynck, L. C. Handy, & E. J. Mash (Eds.), *Behavioral change: Methodology, concepts, and practice*. Champaign, IL: Research Press.

Kass, R. E., & O'Leary, K. D. (1970). *The effects of observer bias in field-experimental settings*. Paper presented at the Behavior Analysis in Education Symposium, University of Kansas.

Kaufmann, J. M. (1985). *Characteristics of children's behavior disorders* (3rd. ed.). Columbus, OH: Merrill.

Kent, R. A., & Foster, S. L. (1977). Direct observation procedures: Methodological issues in applied settings. In A. R. Ciminero, K. S. Calhoun, & H. E. Adams (Eds.), *Handbook of behavioral assessment*. New York: Wiley.

Kesternbaum, C. J., & Bird, H. R. (1978). A reliability study of the mental health assessment form for school-aged children. *Journal of the American Academy of Child Psychiatry*, 17, 338–347.

Knoff, H. M., Batsche, G. M., & Carlyon, W. (1993). Projective techniques. In T. R. Kratochwill & R. J. Morris (Eds.), *Handbook of psychotherapy with children and adolescents* (pp. 9–37). Boston: Allyn & Bacon.

Koegel, L. K., Koegel, R. L., Hurley, C., & Frea, W. D. (1992). Improving social skills and disruptive behavior in children with autism through self-management. *Journal of Applied Behavior Analysis*, 25, 341–354.

Koppitz, E. M. (1968). *Psychological evaluation of Children's Human Figure Drawings*. New York: Grune & Stratton.

Korchin, S. J. (1976). *Modern clinical psychology*. New York: Basic Books.

Kovas, M. (1992). *Children's depression inventory*. North Tonawanda, NY: Multi-Health Systems.

Lachar, D. (1982). *Personality inventory for children (PIC) revised format manual supplement*. Los Angeles: Western Psychological Services.

Lam, S. L, Cole, C. L., Shapiro, E. S., & Bambara, L. M. (1994). Relative effects of self-monitoring on-task behavior, academic accuracy, and disruptive behavior in students with behavior disorders. *School Psychology Review*, 23, 44–58.

Lewis, M. (1973). Infant intelligence tests: Their use and misuse. *Human Development*, 16, 108–118.

Lidz, C. S. (1981). Criterion referenced assessment: The new bandwagon? *Exceptional Children*, 46, 131–132.

Lindzey, G. (1959). On the classification of projective techniques. *Psychological Bulletin*, 56, 158–168.

Lindzey, G. (1961). *Projective techniques and cross cultural research*. New York: Appleton.

Mace, C., & Kratochwill, T. R. (1988). Self-monitoring. In J. C. Witt, S. N. Elliot, & F. M. Gresham (Eds.), *Handbook of behavior therapy in education* (pp. 834–854). New York: Plenum.

Mark, S. J. (1986). *WISC-R profile analysis for conduct disordered inpatients*. Unpublished masters thesis, University of Utah, Salt Lake City.

Martin, R. (1979). *Educating handicapped children: The legal mandate*. Champaign, IL: Research Park.

Mash, E. J., & Terdal, L. G. (1988). Behavioral assessment of child and family disturbance. In E. J. Mash & L. G. Terdal (Eds.), *Behavioral assessment of child disorders* (2nd ed., pp. 3–65). New York: Guilford Press.

McCall, R. B., Hogarty, P. S., & Hurlburt, N. (1972). Transitions in infant sensorimotor development and the prediction of childhood IQ. *American Psychologist, 27,* 728–748.

McCarney, S. (1993). *The pre-referral intervention manual.* Columbia, MO: Hawthorne Educational Services.

McConaughy, S. H. (1993). Evaluating behavioral and emotional disorders with CBCL, TRF, and YRS cross-informant scales. *Journal of Emotional and Behavioral Disorders, 1,* 40–53.

McCord, J., & McCord, W. (1961). Cultural stereotypes and the validity of interviews for research in child development. *Child Development, 32,* 171–185.

Mercer, J. (1973). *Labeling the mentally retarded.* Berkeley: University of California Press.

Messick, S. (1980). Test validity and the ethics of assessment. *American Psychologist, 35,* 1012–1027.

Messick, S. (1995). Validity of psychological assessment: Validation of inferences from persons' responses and performances as scientific inquiry into meaning, *American Psychologist, 50,* 741–749.

Miller, M. J. (1994). "Testing" a relationship. *American Psychologist, 49,* 758.

Mischel, W. (1968). *Personality assessment.* New York: Wiley.

Mischel, W. (1993). *Introduction to personality* (5th ed.). New York: Harcourt, Brace, Jovanovich.

Morganstern, K. P. (1976). Behavioral interviewing: The initial stages of assessment. In M. Hersen & A. S. Bellack (Eds.), *Behavioral assessment: A practical handbook.* New York: Pergamon.

Motta, R. W., Little, S. G., & Tobin, M. I. (1993). The use and abuse of Human Figure Drawings. *School Psychology Quarterly, 8,* 162–169.

Murray, H. A. (1943). *Thematic Appreception Test Manual.* Cambridge, MA: Harvard University Press.

Naglieri, J. A. (1993). Human figure drawings in perspective. *School Psychology Quarterly, 8,* 170–176.

Nunnaly, J. (1962). *Psychometric theory.* New York: McGraw-Hill.

O'Leary, K. D., & Johnson, S. B. (1979). Psychological assessment. In H. C. Quay & J. S. Werry (Eds.), *Psychopathological disorders of children.* New York: Wiley.

O'Leary, K. D., & Kent, R. (1973). Behavior modification for social action: Research tactics and problems. In L. A. Hamerlynck, L. C. Handy, & E. J. Mash (Eds.), *Behavior change: Methodology, concepts, and practice.* Champaign, IL: Research Park.

Ozer, D. J. (1986). *Consistency in personality: A methodological framework.* Berlin: Springer-Verlag.

Popovich, D. (1977). *Prescriptive behavioral checklist for the profoundly retarded.* Baltimore: University Park Press.

Prout, H. (1983). School psychologists and social-emotional assessment techniques. *School Psychology Review, 12,* 377–383.

Puig-Antich, J. (1978). *The schedule for affective disorders and schizophrenia for school age children (Kiddie-SADS).* New York: New York State Psychiatric Association.

Quay, H. C. (1977). Measuring dimensions of deviant behavior: The behavior problem checklist. *Journal of Abnormal Child Psychology, 5,* 277–289.

Quay, H. C., & Patterson, D. R. (1987). *Manual for the revised problem behavior checklist.* Unpublished paper.

Reid, J. B. (1978). *A social learning approach to family intervention: Observation in the home setting* (Vol. 2). Eugene, OR: Castalia Publishing.

Reid, R. (1995). Assessment of ADHD with culturally different groups: The use of behavioral rating scales. *School Psychology Review, 24,* 537–560.

Reid, R., & Harris, K. R. (1993). Self-monitoring of attention versus self-monitoring of performance: Effects on attention and academic performance. *Exceptional Children, 60,* 29–40.

Reynolds, W. M. (1987). *Suicide ideation scale.* Odessa, FL: Psychological Assessment Resources.

Rhode, G., Jenson, W. R., & Reavis, K. (1992). *The tough kid book.* Longmont, CO: Sopris West Publishing.

Rhode, G., Morgan, D. P., & Young, K. R. (1981). Generalization and maintenance of treatment gains of behaviorally handicapped students from resource rooms to regular classrooms using self-evaluation procedures. *Journal of Applied Behavior Analysis, 16,* 171–188.

Rorschach, H. (1948). *Psychodiagnostics: A diagnostic test based on perception* (4th ed.). New York: Grune & Stratton. (Originally published in 1921)

Rutter, M. (1978). Developmental issues and prognosis. In M. Rutter & E. Schopler (Eds.), *Autism: A reappraisal of concepts and treatment.* New York: Plenum Press.

Rutter, M., & Yule, W. (1973). Specific reading retardation. In L. Mann & D. Sabatino (Eds.), *The first review of special education.* Philadelphia: Buttonwood Farms.

Salvia, J., & Ysseldyke, J. E. (1991). *Assessment in special education and remedial education.* Boston: Houghton Mifflin.

Sattler, J. M. (1990). *Assessment of children's intelligence and special abilities* (3rd ed.). San Diego: Sattler Publisher.

Sattler, J. M. (1992). *Assessment of children: WISC-III and WPPSI-R.* San Diego: Sattler Publisher.

Shaffer, D., Schwab-Stone, M., Fisher, P., & Cohen, P. (1993). The Diagnostic Interview Schedule for Children-Revised (DISC-R): I Preparation, field testing, interrater reliability, and acceptability. *Journal of the American Academy of Child and Adolescent Psychiatry, 32,* 643–650.

Shapiro, E. S. (1987). *Behavioral assessment in school psychology.* Hillsdale, NJ: Lawrence Erlbaum.

Shapiro, E. S. (1989). *Academic skills problems: Direct assessment and intervention.* New York: Guilford Press.

Shapiro, E. S., & Lentz, F. E. (1985). Assessing academic behavior: A behavioral approach. *School Psychology Review, 14,* 325–338.

Shapiro, E. S., & Lentz, F. E. (1986). Behavioral assessment of academic skills. In T. R. Kratochwill (Ed.), *Advances in school psychology* (Vol. V). Hillsdale, NJ: Lawrence Erlbaum.

Shinn, M. R. (1989). *Curriculum-based measurement: Assessing special children.* New York: Guilford Press.

Simmons, J. E. (1974). *Psychiatric examination of children.* Philadelphia: Lea & Febiger.

Skindrud, K. (1973). Field evaluation of observer bias under overt and covert monitoring. In L. A. Hammerlynck, L. S. Handy, & E. J. Mash (Eds.), *Behavior change: Methodology, concepts and practice.* Champaign, IL: Research Press.

Spearman, C. E. (1927). *The abilities of man.* New York: Macmillan.

Stern, W. (1914). *The psychological methods of testing intelligence.* Baltimore, MD: Warwick & York.

Sundberg N. D. (1977). *Assessment of persons.* Englewood Cliffs, NJ: Prentice-Hall.

Swanson, H. L., & Watson, B. L. (1982). *Educational and psychological assessment of exceptional children: Theories, strategies, and applications.* St. Louis: Mosby.

Terman, L. M. (1916). *The measurement of intelligence.* Boston: Houghton Mifflin.

Thomas, H. (1970). Psychological assessment instruments for use with human infants. *Merrill-Palmer Quarterly, 16,* 179–223.

Turkat, I. D. (1986). The behavioral interview. In A. R. Ciminero, K. S. Calhoun, & H. E. Adams (Eds.), *Handbook of behavioral assessment* (2nd ed.). New York: Wiley.

Walker, H. M. (1970). *Walker Problem Behavior Identification Checklist.* Los Angeles: Western Psychological Services.

Walker, H. M. (1983). *Walker Problem Behavior Identification Checklist-Revised.* Los Angeles: Western Psychological Services.

Wechsler, D. (1958). *The measurement and appraisal of adult intelligence* (4th ed.). Baltimore: Williams & Wilkins.

Weiner, E. A., & Stewart, B. J. (1983). *Assessing individuals: Psychological and educational tests and measurements.* Boston: Little, Brown and Company.

Weiss, G., & Hechtman, L. T. (1993). *Hyperactive children grown up: Empirical findings and theoretical considerations* (2nd ed.). New York: Guilford Press.

Wenar, C., & Coulter J. B. (1962). A reliability study of developmental histories. *Child Development, 33,* 453–462.

Wert, C. E., & Linn, R. N. (1970). Cautions in applying various procedures for determining the reliability and validity of multiple item scales. *American Sociological Review, 35,* 757–759.

Wetzler, S., & Katz, M. (1989). Preface. In S. Wetzler & M. M. Katz (Eds), *Contemporary approaches to psychological assessment* (p. 16). New York: Brunner Mazel.

Wiggins, J. S. (1973). *Personality and prediction: Principles of personality assessment.* Reading, MA: Addison-Wesley.

Wildman, B.G., & Erickson, M. T. (1977). Methodological problems in behavioral observation. In J.D. Cone & R. P. Hawkins (Eds.), *Behavioral assessment: New directions in clinical psychology.* New York: Brunner/Mazel.

Wirt, R. D., Lachar, D., Klinedinst, J. K., & Seat, P. D. (1977). *Multidimensional description of child personality: A manual for the personality inventory for children.* Los Angeles: Western Psychological Services.

CHAPTER 14

Alexander, J. F., & Malouf, R. E. (1983). Intervention with children experiencing problems in personality and social development. In P. Mussen (General Ed.), *Handbook of child psychology* (4th ed.): *Vol. 4. Socialization, personality, and social development* (E. M. Hetherington, Vol. Ed.). New York: Wiley.

Axline, V. M. (1974). *Play therapy.* Boston: Houghton Mifflin.

Axline, V. M. (1976). Play therapy procedures and results. In C. Schaefer (Ed.), *The therapeutic use of child's play.* New York: Jason Aronson.

Bandura, A. (1969). *Principles of behavior modification.* New York: Holt, Rinehart & Winston.

Bandura, A. (1977). *Social learning theory.* Englewood Cliffs, NJ: Prentice-Hall.

Barrios, B. A., & Hartmann, D. P. (1988). Fear and anxieties. In E. Mash & L. Terdal (Eds.), *Behavioral assessment of childhood disorders* (2nd ed., pp. 196–264). New York: Guilford Press.

Biederman, J. (1991). Psychopharmacology. In J. Wiener (Ed.), *Textbook of child and adolescent psychiatry* (pp. 545–570). Washington, DC: American Psychiatric Press.

Bierman, K. L. (1989). Improving the peer relationships of rejected children. In B. Lahey & A. Kazdin (Eds.), *Advances in clinical child psychology* (Vol. 12, pp. 53–84). New York: Plenum.

Bierman, K. L., & Montminy, H. P. (1993). Developmental issues in social-skills assessment and intervention with children and adolescents. *Behavior Modification, 17,* 229–254.

Campbell, M., Godfrey, K. A., & Magee, H. J. (1992). Pharmacotherapy. In C. Walker & M. Roberts (Eds.), *Handbook of clinical child psychology* (2nd ed., pp. 873–898). New York: Wiley.

Casey, R. J., & Berman, J. S. (1985). The outcome of psychotherapy with children. *Psychological Bulletin, 98,* 388–408.

Chamberlain, P. (1996). Community-based residential treatment for adolescents with conduct disorder. In T. Ollendick & R. Prinz (Eds.), *Advances in clinical child psychology* (Vol. 18, pp. 63–90). New York: Plenum.

Chamberlain, P., & Reid, J. B. (1991). Using a specialized foster care treatment model for children and adolescents leaving the state mental hospital. *Journal of Community Psychology, 19,* 266–276.

Chess, S., & Hassibi, M. (1978). *Principles and practice of child psychiatry.* New York: Plenum.

Christopher, J. S., Nagle, D. W., & Hansen, D. J. (1993). Social-skills interventions with adolescents. *Behavior Modification, 17,* 314–338.

Curry, J. F. (1991). Outcome research on residential treatment: Implications and suggested directions. *American Journal of Orthopsychiatry, 61,* 348–357.

Dishion, T. J. (1984). *Changing child social aggression within the context of the family: Factors producing improvement in parent training.* Unpublished manuscript. (Available from the Oregon Social Learning Center, 207 E. 5th Ave., Suite 202, Eugene.)

Douglas, V., Parry P., Marton, P., & Garson, C. (1976). Assessment of a cognitive training program for hyperactive children. *Journal of Abnormal Child Psychology, 4,* 389–410.

Dumas, J. E. (1989). Effectiveness of psychotherapy with children and adolescents. *Journal of Consulting and Clinical Psychology, 59,* 785–798.

Dumont, M. P. (1990). Editorial. In bed together at the market: Psychiatry and the pharmaceutical industry. *American Journal of Orthopsychiatry, 60,* 484–485.

Durlak, J. A., Fuhrman, T., & Lampman, C. (1991). Effectiveness of cognitive-behavioral therapy for maladapting children: A meta-analysis. *Psychological Bulletin, 110,* 204–214.

Ellinwood, C., & Raskin, N. J. (1993). Client-centered/humanistic psychotherapy. In T. R. Kratochwill & R. J. Morris (Eds.), *Handbook of psychotherapy with children and adolescents* (pp. 258–287). Boston: Allyn & Bacon.

Elliott, S. N., & Gresham, F. M. (1993). Social skills interventions for children. *Behavior Modification, 17,* 287–313.

Everett, C. A., & Volgy, S. S. (1993). Treating the child in systemic family therapy. In T. Kratochwill & R. Morris (Eds.), *Handbook of psychotherapy with children and adolescents* (pp. 247–257). Boston: Allyn & Bacon.

Fazen, L. E., Lovejoy, F. H., & Crone, R. K. (1986). Acute poisoning in a children's hospital: A 2-year experience. *Pediatrics, 77,* 144–151.

Forehand, R., & McMahon, R. (1981). *Helping the noncompliant child: A clinician's guide to parent training.* New York: Guilford.

Foxx, R. M., & Azrin, N. H. (1973). The elimination of autistic self-stimulatory behavior by overcorrection. *Journal of Applied Behavior Analysis, 6,* 1–14.

Freud, A. (1945). *The psychoanalytic study of the child: Vol. 1. Indications for child analysis.* New York: International Universities Press.

Gadow, K. D., & Pomeroy, J. C. (1993). Pediatric psychopharmacotherapy: A clinical perspective. In T. Kratochwill & R. Morris (Eds.), *Handbook of psychotherapy with children and adolescents* (pp. 356–402). Boston: Allyn & Bacon.

Gelfand, D. M., & Hartmann, D. P. (1984). *Child behavior analysis and therapy* (2nd ed.). New York: Pergamon Press.

Gibbs, J. T., & Huang, L. N. (Eds.). (1991). *Children of color: Psychological interventions with minority youth.* San Francisco: Jossey-Bass.

Gittelman, R., & Kanner, A. (1986). Psychopharmacotherapy. In H. Quay & J. Werry (Eds.), *Psychopathological disorders of childhood* (pp. 455–495). New York: Wiley.

Goldfried, M. R., & Castonguary, L. G. (1993). Behavior therapy: Redefining strengths and limitations. *Behavior Therapy, 24,* 505–526.

Hackmann, A. (1993). Behavioral and cognitive psychotherapies: Past history, current applications and future registration issues. *Behavioural and Cognitive Psychotherapy,* Supplement 1, 1–75.

Haley, J. (1963). Marriage therapy. *Archives of General Psychiatry, 8,* 213–224.

Hart, K. J., & Morgan, J. R. (1993). Cognitive-behavioral procedures with children. In A. Finch, Jr., W. Nelson III, & E. Ott (Eds.), *Cognitive-behavioral procedures with children and adolescents* (pp. 1–24). Boston: Allyn & Bacon.

Heinicke, C. M. (1989). Psychodynamic psychotherapy with children: Current status and guidelines for future research. In B. Lahey & A. Kazdin (Eds.), *Advances in clinical child psychology* (Vol. 12, pp. 1–26). New York: Plenum Press.

Horn, W. F., Ialongo, N., Greenberg, G., Packard, T., & Smith-Winberry, C. (1990). Additive effects of behavioral parent training and self-control therapy with attention deficit hyperactivity disordered children. *Journal of Clinical Child Psychology, 19,* 98–110.

Hughes, J. (1993). Behavior therapy. In T. R. Kratochwill & R. J. Morris (Eds.), *Handbook of psychotherapy with children and adolescents* (pp. 185–220). Boston: Allyn & Bacon.

Jackson, D. D., & Weakland, J. H. (1961). Conjoint family therapy: Some considerations on theory, technique and results. *Psychiatry, 24,* 30–45.

Kaplan, C. A., & Hussain, S. (1995). Use of drugs in child and adolescent psychiatry. *British Journal of Psychiatry, 166,* 291–298.

Karoly, P., & Kanfer, F. H. (1982). *Self-management and behavior change: From theory to practice.* New York: Pergamon Press.

Kaslow, N. J., Stark, K. D., Printz, B., Livingston, R., & Tsai, Y. (1992). Cognitive Triad Inventory for Children: Development and relationship to depression and anxiety. *Journal of Clinical Child Psychology, 21,* 339–347.

Kazdin, A. E. (1991). Behavior modification. In J. M. Wiener (Ed.), *Textbook of child and adolescent psychiatry* (pp. 576–593). Washington, DC: American Psychiatric Press.

Kazdin, A. E. (1993). Psychotherapy for children and adolescents: Current progress and future research directions. *American Psychologist, 48,* 644–657.

Kazdin, A. E. (1996). Combined and multimodal treatments in child and adolescent psychotherapy: Issues, challenges, and research directions. *Clinical Psychology Science and Practice, 3,* 69–100.

Kendall, P. C. (1991). *Child and adolescent therapy: Cognitive-behavioral procedures.* New York: Guilford Press.

Kendall, P. C. (1993). Cognitive-behavioral therapies with youth: Guiding theory, current status, and emerging developments. *Journal of Consulting and Clinical Psychology, 61,* 235–247.

Kendall, P. C., & Braswell, L. (1985). *Cognitive-behavioral therapy for impulsive children.* New York: Guilford Press.

Kendall, P. C., & Braswell, L. (1993). *Cognitive-behavioral therapy for impulsive children* (2nd ed.). New York: Guilford Press.

Kendall, P. C., & Finch, A. J. (1979). Developing non-impulsive behavior in children's cognitive-behavioral strategies on self-control. In P. Kendall & S. Hollon (Eds.), *Cognitive-behavioral interventions: Theory, research, and procedures.* New York: Academic Press.

Kendall, P. C., & Hollon, D. S. (1979). *Cognitive-behavioral interventions: Theory, research, and procedures.* New York: Academic Press.

Kendall, P. C., & Panichelli-Mindel, S. M. (1995). Cognitive-behavioral treatment. *Journal of Abnormal Child Psychology, 23,* 107–124.

Klein, N. C., Alexander, J. F., & Parsons, B. V. (1977). Impact of family systems intervention on recidivism and sibling delinquency: A model of primary prevention and program evaluation. *Journal of Consulting and Clinical Psychology, 45,* 469–474.

Kolata, G. (1996, May 15). Boom in Ritalin sales raises ethical issues. *New York Times,* B8.

Koocher, G., & D'Angelo, E. J. (1992). Evolution of practice in child psychotherapy. In I. Freedheim (Ed.), *History of psychotherapy* (pp. 457–492). Washington, DC: American Psychological Association.

Kovacs, M., & Paulauskas, S. (1986). The traditional psychotherapies. In H. Quay & J. Werry (Eds.), *Psychopathological disorders of childhood* (3rd ed., pp. 496–522). New York: Wiley.

Lexchin, J. (1988). The medical profession and the pharmaceutical industry: An unhealthy alliance. *International Journal of Health Services, 18,* 603.

Malgady, R. G., Rogler, L. H., & Costantino, G. (1990). Culturally sensitive psychotherapy for Puerto Rican children and adolescents: A program of treatment. *Journal of Consulting and Clinical Psychology, 58,* 704–712.

Marsella, A. J. (1993). Counseling and psychotherapy with Japanese Americans: Cross-cultural considerations. *American Journal of Orthopsychiatry, 63,* 200–208.

Mash, E. J. (1989). Treatment of child and family disturbance: A behavioral-systems perspective. In E. Mash & R. Barkley (Eds.), *Treatment of childhood disorders* (pp. 205–237). New York: Guilford Press.

Mattes, J. A., & Gittelman, R. (1983). Growth of hyperactive children on maintenance regimen of methylphenidate. *Archives of General Psychiatry, 40,* 317–321.

McMahon, R. J., & Wells, K. C. (1989). Conduct disorders. In E. Mash & R. Barkley (Eds.), *Treatment of childhood disorders* (pp. 73–132). New York: Guilford.

Meichenbaum, D. (1977). *Cognitive-behavior modification: An integrative approach.* New York: Plenum.

Meichenbaum, D. (1979). Teaching children self-control. In B. Lahey & A. Kazdin (Ed.), *Advances in clinical child psychology* (Vol. 2). New York: Plenum.

Meichenbaum, D., & Goodman, J. (1971). Training impulsive children to talk to themselves: A means of developing self-control. *Journal of Abnormal Psychology, 77,* 115–126.

Michelson, L., Sugai, D. P., Wood, R. P., & Kazdin, A. E. (1985). *Social skills assessment and training with children: An empirically based approach.* New York: Plenum.

Murphy, D. A., Greenstein, J. J., & Pelham, W. E. (1993). Pharmacological treatment. In V. B. Van Hasselt & M. Hersen (Eds.), *Handbook of behavior therapy and pharmacotherapy for children* (pp. 333–378). Boston: Allyn & Bacon.

Nottelmann, E. D., & Jensen, P. S. (1995). Comorbidity of disorders in children and adolescents: Developmental perspectives. In T. Ollendick & R. Prinz (Eds.), *Advances in clinical child psychology* (Vol. 17, pp. 109–156). New York: Plenum Press.

Offord, D. R., Boyle, M., Racine, Y., Fleming, J., Cadman, D., Blum, H., Byrne, C., Links, P., Lipman, E., McMillan, H., Grant, N., Sanford, M., Szatmari, P., Thomas, H., & Woodward, C. (1992). Outcome, prognosis, and risk in a longitudinal follow-up study. *Journal of the American Academy of Child and Adolescent Psychiatry, 31,* 916–923.

Ollendick, T. H., & Francis, G. (1988). Behavioral assessment and treatment of childhood phobias. *Behavior Modification, 12,* 165–204.

Patterson, G. R. (1975). The aggressive child: Victim or architect of a coercive system. In L. A. Hamerlynck, L. C. Handy, & E. J. Mash (Eds.), *Behavior modification and families: Vol. 1. Theory and research.* New York: Brunner/Mazel.

Patterson, G. R., Dishion, T. J., & Chamberlain, P. (1993). Outcomes and methodological issues relating to treatment of antisocial children. In T. R. Giles (Ed.), *Handbook of effective psychotherapy* (pp. 43–88). New York: Plenum.

Patterson, G. R., & Forgatch, M. S. (1985). Therapist behavior as a determinant for client noncompliance: A paradox for the behavior modifier. *Journal of Clinical and Counseling Psychology, 53,* 846–851.

Patterson, G. R., Reid, J. B., & Dishion, T. J. (1992). *Antisocial boys.* Eugene, OR: Castalia.

Patterson, G. R., Reid, J. B., Jones, R. R., & Conger, R. E. (1975). *A social learning approach: I. Families with aggressive children.* Eugene, OR: Castalia.

Patterson, G. R., & Stoolmiller, M. (1991). Replications of a dual failure model for boys' depressed mood. *Journal of Consulting and Clinical Psychology, 59,* 491–498.

Powers, S. W., & Rickard, H. C. (1992). Behavior therapy with children. In C. E. Walker & M. C. Roberts (Eds.), *Handbook of clinical child psychology* (2nd ed., pp. 749–764). New York: Wiley.

Rogers, C. T. (1951). *Client-centered therapy: Its current practice, implications, and therory.* Boston: Houghton Mifflin.

Rosenthal, T. L., & Bandura, A. (1978). Psychological modeling: Theory and Practice. In S. Garfield & A. E. Bergin (Eds.), *Handbook of psychotherapy and behavior change: An empirical analysis* (2nd ed.). New York: Wiley.

Russ, S. W. (1995). Play psychotherapy research: State of the science. In T. Ollendick & R. Prinz (Eds.), *Advances in clinical child psychology* (Vol. 17, pp. 365–392). New York: Plenum Press.

Satir, V. (1967). *Conjoint family therapy: A guide.* Palo Alto, CA: Science and Behavior Books.

Select Committee on Children, Youth, and Families, U.S. House of Representatives. (1990). *No place to call home: Discarded children in America.* Washington, DC: U.S. Government Printing Office.

Shadish, W. R., Montgomery, L. M., Wilson, P., Wilson, M. R., Bright, I., & Okwumabua, T. (1993). Effects of family and marital psychotherapies: A meta-analysis. *Journal of Consulting and Clinical Psychology, 61,* 992–1002.

Skinner, B. F., & Ferster, C. B. (1957). *Schedules of reinforcement.* New York: Appleton-Century-Crofts.

Small, R., Kennedy, K., & Bender, B. (1991). Critical issues for practice in residential treatment: The view from within. *American Journal of Orthopsychiatry, 61,* 327–338.

Stark, K. D., Reynolds, W. M., & Kaslow, N. J. (1987). A comparison of the relative efficacy of self-control therapy and a behavioral problem-solving therapy for depression in children. *Journal of Abnormal Child Psychology, 15,* 91–113.

Stark, K. D., Rouse, L. W., & Livingston, R. (1991). Treatment of depression during childhood and adolescence: Cognitive-behavioral procedures for the individual and family. In P. C. Kendall (Ed.), *Child and adolescent therapy: Cognitive-behavioral procedures* (pp. 165–206). New York: Guilford Press.

Stokes, T. F., & Osnes, P. G. (1989). An operant pursuit of generalization. *Behavior Therapy, 20,* 337–355.

Tharp, R. G. (1991). Cultural diversity and treatment of children. *Journal of Consulting and Clinical Psychology, 59,* 799–812.

Tuma, J. M. (1988). *Current status of insight oriented therapy with children.* Unpublished manuscript. Louisiana State University, Department of Psychology.

Tuma, J., & Russ, S. W. (1993). Psychoanalytic psychotherapy with children. In T. Kratochwill & R. Morris (Eds.), *Handbook of psychotherapy with children and adolescents* (pp. 131–161). Boston: Allyn & Bacon.

Van Hasselt, V. B., & Hersen, M. (1993). Overview of behaviortherapy. In B. Van Hasselt & M. Hersen (Eds.), *Handbook of behavior therapy and pharmacotherapy for children* (pp. 1–12). Boston: Allyn & Bacon.

Vraniak, D. A., & Pickett, S. A. (1993). Improving interventions with American ethnic minority children: Recurrent and recalcitrant challenges. In T. Kratochwill & R. Morris (Eds.), *Handbook of psychotherapy with children and adolescents* (pp. 502–540). Boston: Allyn & Bacon.

Webster-Stratton, C. (1990). Long-term follow-up of families with young conduct problem children: From preschool to grade school. *Journal of Clinical Child Psychology, 19,* 144–149.

Webster-Stratton, C., & Herbert, M. (1994). *Troubled families-problem children: A collaborative approach to working with families.* Chichester, England: Wiley.

Webster-Stratton, C., & Herbert, M. (1993). What really happens in parent training. *Behavior Modification, 17,* 407–456.

Weisz, J. R., & Weiss, B. (1993). *Effects of psychotherapy with children and adolescents.* Newbury Park, CA: Sage.

Weisz, J. R., Weiss, B., & Donenberg, G. R. (1992). The lab versus the clinic: Effects of child and adolescent psychotherapy. *American Psychologist, 47,* 1578–1585.

Weisz, J. R., Weiss, B., Han, S. S., Granger, D. A., & Morton, T. (1995). Effects of psychotherapy with children and adolescents revisited: A meta-analysis of treatment outcome studies. *Psychological Bulletin, 117,* 450–468.

Wells, K. (1991). Long-term residential treatment for children: Introduction. *American Journal of Orthopsychiatry, 61,* 323–326.

Wiener, J. M. (1977). Summary. In J. Wiener (Ed.), *Psychopharmacology in childhood and adolescence.* New York: Basic Books.

Wiener, J. M. (1984). Psychopharmacology in childhood disorders. In C. R. Lake (Ed.), *Psychiatric clinics of North America* (Vol. 7). Philadelphia: W. B. Saunders.

Winsberg, B. G., & Yepes, L. E. (1978). Antipsychotics (major tranquilizers, neuroleptics). In J. S. Werry (Ed.), *Pediatric psychopharmacology.* New York: Brunner/Mazel.

Zametkin, A. J., & Rapoport, J. L. (1987). Neurobiology of attention deficit disorder with hyperactivity: Where have we come in 50 years? *Journal of the American Academy of Child Psychiatry, 26,* 676–686.

Zigler, E., & Black, K. B. (1989). America's family support movement: Strengths and limitations. *American Journal of Orthopsychiatry, 59,* 6–19.

CHAPTER 15

Ackerman, M. J. (1995). *Clinician's guide to child custody evaluations.* New York: Wiley.

Al-Issa, I. (1982a). Gender and adult psychopathology. In I. Al-Issa (Ed.), *Gender and psychopathology.* New York: Academic Press.

Al-Issa, I. (1982b). Gender and child psychopathology. In I. Al-Issa (Ed.), *Gender and psychopathology.* New York: Academic Press.

American Psychiatric Association. (1994). *Diagnostic and statistical manual of mental disorders (DSM-IV)* (4th ed.). Washington, DC: Author.

American Psychologist. (1991). UN Convention on the Rights of the Child: Unofficial summary of articles. *46,* 50–52.

Bandura, A. (1969). *Principles of behavior modification.* New York: Holt, Rinehart & Winston.

Bemporad, J. W., & Romano, S. J. (1992). Childhood maltreatment and adult depression: A review of research. In D. Cicchetti & S. L. Toth (Eds.), *Developmental perspectives on depression* (Vol. 4, pp. 351–376). Rochester, NY: University of Rochester Press.

Boat, B. W., & Everson, M. D. (1993). The use of anatomical dolls in sexual abuse evaluations: Current research and practice. In G. S. Goodman & B. L. Bottoms (Eds.), *Child victims, child witnesses: Understanding and improving testimony* (pp. 47–70). New York: Guilford Press.

Bruck, M., Ceci, S. J., Francoeur, E., & Barr, R. (1995). "I hardly cried when I got my shot": Influencing children's reports about a visit to their pediatrician. *Child Development, 66,* 193–208.

Cappelleri, J. C., Eckenrode, J., & Powers, J. L. (1993). The epidemiology of child abuse: Findings from the Second National Incidence and Prevalence Study of Child Abuse and Neglect. *American Journal of Public Health, 83,* 1622–1624.

Ceci, S. J., & Bruck, M. (1993, Fall). Child witnesses: Translating research into policy. *Social Policy Report. Society for Research in Child Development, 7,* Whole No. 3.

Ceci, S. J., & Bruck, M. (1995). *Jeopardy in the courtroom: A scientific analysis of children's testimony.* Washington, DC: American Psychological Association.

Charlow, A. (1994). Awarding custody: The best interests of the child and other fictions. In S. R. Humm (Ed.), *Child, parent, and state: Law and policy reader* (pp. 3–26). Philadelphia: Temple University Press.

Cohen, H. (1980). *Equal rights for children.* Totowa, NJ: Littlefield, Adams.

Cohen, H. (1985). Ending the double standard: Equal rights for children. In A. Cafagna, R. T. Peterson, & C. Staudenbaur (Eds.), *Child nurturance: Philosophy, children, and the family* (Vol. 1). New York: Plenum.

Crittenden, P. M. (1988). Maltreated infants: Vulnerability and resilience. *Journal of Child Psychology and Psychiatry, 26,* 85–96.

Daly, M., & Wilson, M. I. (1980). Abuse and neglect of children in evolutionary perspective. In R. D. Alexander & D. W. Tinkle (Eds.), *Natural selection and social behavior.* New York: Chiron.

Doris, J. (1993). *Child witness conference.* Supplemental RFP Children's Justice and Assistance Act funds. Submitted by the Family Life Development Center, Cornell University. (Cited in Ceci & Bruck, 1993.)

Eckenrode, J., Laird, M., & Doris, J. (1993). School performance and disciplinary problems among abused and neglected children. *Developmental Psychology, 29,* 53–62.

Egeland, B., Jacobvitz, D., & Papatola, K. (1987). Intergenerational continuity of abuse. In R. J. Gelles & J. B. Lancaster (Eds.), *Child abuse and neglect: Biosocial dimensions* (pp. 255–276). New York: Aldine de Gruyter.

Emery, R. E., Hetherington, E. M., & DiLalla, L. F. (1984). Divorce, children, and social policy. In H. Stevenson & A. Siegel (Eds.), *Child development research and social policy* (Vol. 1). Chicago: University of Chicago Press.

Ewigman, B., Kivlahan, C., & Land, G. (1993). The Missouri Child Fatality Study: Underreporting of maltreatment fatalities among children younger than five years of age: 1983 through 1966. *Pediatrics, 91,* 330–337.

Feinberg, J. (1973). *Social philosophy.* Englewood Cliffs, NJ: Prentice-Hall.

Finkelhor, D. (1990). Early and long-term effects of child sexual abuse: An update. *Professional Psychology: Research and Practice, 21,* 325–330.

Finkelhor, D., & Dziuba-Leatherman, J. (1994). Victimization of children. *American Psychologist, 49,* 173–183.

Finkelhor, D., Hotaling, G. T., Lewis, I. A., & Smith, C. (1990). Sexual abuse in a national survey of adult men and women: Prevalence, characteristics, and risk factors. *Child Abuse and Neglect, 14,* 19–28.

Finlay v. Finlay, 148 N.E. 624 (N.Y.) 1925.

Foa, E. B., & Riggs, D. S. (1995). Posttraumatic Stress Disorder following assault: Theoretical considerations and empirical findings. *Current Directions in Psychological Science, 4,* 61–65.

Friedrich, W. N., Beilke, R. L., & Urquiza, A. J. (1987). Children from sexually abusive families: A behavioral comparison. *Journal of Interpersonal Violence, 2,* 391–402.

Gelles, R. J. (1979). *Family violence.* Beverly Hills, CA: Sage.

Gil, D. G. (1970). *Violence against children: Physical child abuse in the United States.* Cambridge, MA: Harvard University Press.

Goodman, G. S., & Bottoms, B. L. (Eds.). (1993). *Child victims, child witnesses: Understanding and improving testimony.* New York: Guilford.

Goodman, G. S., Taub, E. P., Jones, D. P., England, P., Port, L. K., Rudy, L., & Prado, L. (1992). Testifying in criminal court: Emotional effects on child sexual assault victims. *Monographs of the Society for Research in Child Development, 57,* (5, Serial No. 229).

Grinspoon, L., & Singer, S. B. (1973). Amphetamines in the treatment of hyperkinetic children. *Harvard Educational Review, 43,* 515–555.

Hart, S. N. (1991). From property to person status: Historical perspective on children's rights. *American Psychologist, 46,* 53–59.

Kaufman, J., & Zigler, E. (1986). *Do abused children become abusive parents?* Unpublished manuscript, Yale University.

Kendall-Tackett, K. A., Williams, L. M., & Finkelhor, D. (1993). Impact of sexual abuse on children: A review and synthesis of recent empirical studies. *Psychological Bulletin, 113,* 164–180.

Kendziora, K. T., & O'Leary, S. G. (1993). Dysfunctional parenting as a focus for prevention and treatment of child behavior problems. In T. H. Ollendick & R. J. Prinz (Eds.), *Advances in clinical child psychology* (Vol. 15, pp. 175–206). New York: Plenum Press.

Keniston, K. (1977). *All our children: The American family under pressure.* New York: Harcourt Brace Jovanovich.

Koocher, G. P. (1976). A bill of rights for children in psychotherapy. In G. Koocher (Ed.), *Children's rights and the mental health professions.* New York: Wiley.

Koocher, G. P., & Keith-Spiegel, P. C. (1990). *Children, ethics, and the law.* Lincoln: University of Nebraska Press.

Levine, M., Anderson, E., Ferretti, L., & Steinberg, K. (1993). Legal and ethical issues affecting clinical child psychology. In T. Ollendick & R. Prinz (Eds.), *Advances in clinical child psychology* (Vol. 15, pp. 81–120). New York: Plenum Press.

Lewis, C. E., Lewis, M. A., & Lefkwunigue, M. (1978). Informed consent by children & participation in an influenza vaccine trial. *American Journal of Public Health, 68,* 1079–1082.

Limber, S. P., & Flekkoy, M. G. (1995). The U.N. Convention on the Rights of the Child: Its relevance for social scientists. *Social Policy Report. Society for Research in Child Development, 9,* No. 2.

Lutzker, J. R. (1990). Behavioral treatment of child neglect. *Behavior Modification, 14,* 301–315.

Margolin, L. (1990). Fatal child neglect. *Child Welfare, 69,* 309–319.

McGough, L. S. (1994). *Child witnesses: Fragile voices in the American legal system.* New Haven, CT: Yale University Press.

McLarin, K. J. (1995, July 30). Slaying of Connecticut infant shifts policy on child abuse. *New York Times,* p. A1.

Melton, G. B. (1991). Socialization in the global community: Respect for the dignity of children. *American Psychologist, 46,* 66–71.

Murray, K., & Gough, D. A. (1991). *Intervening in child sexual abuse.* Edinburgh: Scottish Academic Press.

National Center for Child Abuse and Neglect. (1993). *National Child Abuse and Neglect Data System, 1991: Summary data component.* Gaithersburg, MD: U.S. Department of Health and Human Services.

National Crime Survey, 1990. (1992). Bureau of Justice Statistics. Washington, DC: Author.

O'Donohue, W. O., & Elliott, A. N. (1991). A model for the clinical assessment of the sexually abused child. *Behavioral Assessment, 13,* 325–340.

Olds, D. L., Hendersen, C. R., Chamberlin, R., & Tatelbaum, R. (1986). Preventing child abuse and neglect: A randomized trial of nurse home visitation. *Pediatrics, 78,* 65–78.

Oliver, J. E. (1993). Intergenerational transmission of child abuse: Rates, research, and clinical implications. *American Journal of Psychiatry, 150,* 1315–1324.

Osofsky, J. D., & Fenichel, E. (Eds.). (1993, December–1994, January). Caring for infants and toddlers in violent environments: Hurt, healing, and hope. *Zero to Three* (Vol. 14). National Center for Clinical Infant Programs. Arlington, VA: Author.

Paget, K. D., Philp, J. D., & Abramczyk, L. W. (1993). Recent developments in child neglect. In T. H. Ollendick & R. J. Prinz (Eds.), *Advances in clinical child psychology* (Vol. 15, pp. 121–174). New York: Plenum.

Peterson, L., & Brown, D. (1994). Integrating child injury and abuse-neglect research: Common histories, etiologies, and solutions. *Psychological Bulletin, 116,* 293–315.

Plotkin, R. (1979). In the balance: *Parham v. J. R. APA Monitor, 10*(9–10), 27.

Polusny, M. A., & Follette, V. M. (1995). Long-term correlates of child sexual abuse: Theory and review of the empirical literature. *Applied and Preventive Psychology, 4,* 143–166.

Quinn, K. M. (1985). Legal issues and the schools. In D. Schetky & E. Benedek (Eds.), *Emerging issues in child psychiatry and the law.* New York: Brunner/Mazel.

Reid, J. B. (1984). Social-interactional patterns in families of abused and nonabused children. In C. Zahn-Waxler, M. Cummings, & M. Radke-Yarrow (Eds.), *Social and biological origins of altruism and aggression.* Cambridge, England: Cambridge University Press.

Saunders, B. E., Villeponteaux, L. A., Lipovsky, J. A., Kilpatrick, D. G., & Veronen, L. J. (1992). Child sexual assault as a risk factor for mental disorders among women: A community survey. *Journal of Interpersonal Violence, 7,* 189–204.

Scott, K. D. (1992). Childhood sexual abuse: Impact on a community's mental health status. *Child Abuse and Neglect, 16,* 285–295.

Shapiro, M. H. (1974). Legislating the control of behavior control: Autonomy and the coercive use of organic therapies. *Southern California Law Review, 47,* 327–356.

Siegel, D. M., & Hurley, S. (1977). The role of the child's preference in custody proceedings. *Family Law Quarterly, 11,* 1–58.

Spaccarelli, S. (1994). Stress, appraisal, and coping in child sexual abuse: A theoretical and empirical review. *Psychological Bulletin, 116,* 340–362.

Stoesz, D., & Karger, H. J. (1996, June). Suffer the children: How government fails its most vulnerable citizens—abused and neglected kids. *The Washington Monthly,* 20–25.

Straus, M. A., Gelles, R. J., & Steinmetz, S. K. (1980). *Behind closed doors: Violence in the American family.* Garden City, NJ: Doubleday/Anchor.

Teitelbaum, L. E., & Ellis, J. W. (1978). The liberty interest of children: Due process rights and their application. *Family Law Quarterly, 12,* 153–202.

Trickett, P. K. (1993). Maladaptive development of school-aged, physically abused children: Relations with the child rearing context. *Journal of Family Psychology, 7,* 148–158.

Trickett, P. K., & McBride-Chang, C. (1995). The developmental impact of different forms of child abuse and neglect. *Developmental Review, 15,* 311–337.

U.S. Bureau of the Census. (1994). *Statistical Abstract of the United States, 1994.* Washington, DC: U.S. Government Printing Office.

U.S. Department of Health and Human Services (DHHS, 1988). *Study findings: Study of national incidence and prevalence of child abuse and neglect.* Washington, DC: Author.

U.S. Department of Health and Human Services (DHHS, 1989). *Child abuse and neglect: A shared community concern.* Washington, DC: Author.

Walker, C. E., Bonner, B., & Kaufman, K. (1988). *The physically and sexually abused child.* Elmsford, NY: Pergamon Press.

Weithorn, L. A. (1979). Drug therapy and children's rights. In M. J. Cohen (Ed.), *Drugs and the special child.* New York: Gardner Press.

Weithorn, L. A. (1985). Children's capacities for participation in treatment decision-making. In D. Schetky & E. P. Benedek (Eds.), *Emerging issues in child psychiatry and the law.* New York: Brunner/Mazel.

Wilcox, B. L., & Naimark, H. (1991). The rights of the child: Progress toward human dignity. *American Psychologist, 46,* 49.

Wodarski, J. S., Kurtz, P. D., Gaudin, J. M., & Howing, P. T. (1990). Maltreatment and the school-age child: Major academic, socioemotional, and adaptive outcomes. *Social Work, 35,* 506–513.

Wolfe, V., & Birt, J. (1995). The psychological sequel of child sexual abuse. In T. H. Ollendick & R. J. Prinz (Eds.), *Advances in clinical child psychology* (Vol. 17, pp. 233–263). New York: Plenum.

Wyatt, G. E., & Newcomb, M. (1990). Internal and external mediators of women's sexual abuse in childhood. *Journal of Consulting and Clinical Psychology, 58,* 758–767.

Zigler, E. F., & Muenchow, S. (1992). *Head Start: The inside story of America's most successful educational experiment.* New York: Basic Books.

Zuravin, S. J. (1989). The ecology of child abuse and neglect: Review of the literature and presentation of data. *Violence and Victims, 4,* 101–120.

NAME INDEX

SUBJECT INDEX

Photo Credits